T0258935

THE ROUTLEDGE HANDBOOK OF EMBODIED COGNITION

Embodied cognition is one of the foremost areas of study and research in philosophy of mind, philosophy of psychology, and cognitive science. *The Routledge Handbook of Embodied Cognition* is an outstanding guide and reference source to the key topics and debates in this exciting subject and essential reading for any student and scholar of philosophy of mind and cognitive science.

Extensively revised and enlarged for this second edition, the Handbook comprises 42 chapters by an international team of expert contributors and is divided into ten parts:

- Historical Underpinnings
- Perspectives on Embodied Cognition
- Embodied Cognition and Predictive Processing
- Perception
- Language
- Reasoning and Education
- Virtual Reality
- Social and Moral Cognition and Emotion
- Action and Memory
- Reflections on Embodied Cognition.

The early chapters of the Handbook cover empirical and philosophical foundations of embodied cognition, focusing on Gibsonian and phenomenological approaches. Subsequent chapters cover additional, important themes common to work in embodied cognition, including embedded, extended, and enactive cognition as well as chapters on empirical research in perception, language, reasoning, social and moral cognition, emotion, consciousness, memory, and learning and development.

For the second edition many existing chapters have been revised and seven new chapters added on: AI and robotics, predictive processing, second-language learning, animal cognition, sport psychology, sense of self, and critiques of embodied cognition, bringing the Handbook fully up to date with current research and debate.

Lawrence Shapiro is the Berent Enç Professor of Philosophy at the University of Wisconsin–Madison, USA. The American Philosophical Association awarded his book *Embodied Cognition* the Gittler Award for outstanding contribution in the field of philosophy of the social sciences (second edition 2019, Routledge).

Shannon Spaulding is Professor of Philosophy at Oklahoma State University, USA. Her research focuses on social cognition, imagination, and embodied cognition. She is the author of the book *How We Understand Others: Philosophy and Social Cognition* (Routledge 2018).

ROUTLEDGE HANDBOOKS IN PHILOSOPHY

Routledge Handbooks in Philosophy are state-of-the-art surveys of emerging, newly refreshed, and important fields in philosophy, providing accessible yet thorough assessments of key problems, themes, thinkers, and recent developments in research.

All chapters for each volume are specially commissioned, and written by leading scholars in the field. Carefully edited and organized, *Routledge Handbooks in Philosophy* provide indispensable reference tools for students and researchers seeking a comprehensive overview of new and exciting topics in philosophy. They are also valuable teaching resources as accompaniments to textbooks, anthologies, and research-orientated publications.

ALSO AVAILABLE:

THE ROUTLEDGE HANDBOOK OF PHENOMENOLOGY OF MINDFULNESS
Edited by Susi Ferrarello and Christos Hadjioannou

THE ROUTLEDGE HANDBOOK OF CONTEMPORARY EXISTENTIALISM
Edited by Kevin Aho, Megan Altman, and Hans Pedersen

THE ROUTLEDGE HANDBOOK OF ESSENCE IN PHILOSOPHY
Edited by Kathrin Koslicki and Michael J. Raven

THE ROUTLEDGE HANDBOOK OF POLITICAL PHENOMENOLOGY
Edited by Nils Baratella, Steffen Herrmann, Sophie Loidolt, Tobias Matzner, and Gerhard Thonhauser

THE ROUTLEDGE HANDBOOK OF EMBODIED COGNITION, SECOND **EDITION**
Edited by Lawrence Shapiro and Shannon Spaulding

For more information about this series, please visit: https://www.routledge.com/Routledge-Handbooks-in-Philosophy/book-series/RHP

THE ROUTLEDGE HANDBOOK OF EMBODIED COGNITION

Second Edition

Edited by Lawrence Shapiro and Shannon Spaulding

LONDON AND NEW YORK

Cover image: © Getty Images

Second edition published 2024
by Routledge
4 Park Square, Milton Park, Abingdon, Oxon OX14 4RN

and by Routledge
605 Third Avenue, New York, NY 10158

*Routledge is an imprint of the Taylor & Francis Group, an informa
business*

© 2024 selection and editorial matter Lawrence Shapiro and Shannon
Spaulding; individual chapters, the contributors

First edition published 2014 by Routledge.

British Library Cataloguing-in-Publication Data
A catalogue record for this book is available from the British Library

Library of Congress Cataloging-in-Publication Data
Names: Shapiro, Lawrence A., editor. | Spaulding, Shannon, editor.
Title: The Routledge handbook of embodied cognition / edited by
Lawrence Shapiro and Shannon Spaulding.
Description: Second edition. | Abingdon, Oxon ; New York, NY :
Routledge, 2024. | Series: Routledge handbooks in philosophy | Includes
bibliographical references and index.
Identifiers: LCCN 2023056990 (print) | LCCN 2023056991 (ebook) |
ISBN 9781032345123 (hardback) | ISBN 9781032345147 (paperback) |
ISBN 9781003322511 (ebook)
Subjects: LCSH: Philosophy of mind. | Cognition. | Cognitive science.
Classification: LCC BD418.3 .R77 2024 (print) | LCC BD418.3 (ebook) |
DDC 128/.2--dc23/eng/20240318
LC record available at https://lccn.loc.gov/2023056990
LC ebook record available at https://lccn.loc.gov/2023056991

ISBN: 978-1-032-34512-3 (hbk)
ISBN: 978-1-032-34514-7 (pbk)
ISBN: 978-1-003-32251-1 (ebk)

DOI: 10.4324/9781003322511

Typeset in Sabon
by SPi Technologies India Pvt Ltd (Straive)

CONTENTS

Acknowledgments   *xii*
Contributors   *xiii*

Introduction   1
Lawrence Shapiro and Shannon Spaulding

PART 1
Historical Underpinnings   **11**

1 Phenomenology and Embodied Cognition   13
  Shaun Gallagher

2 A Ten Commandments for Ecological Psychology   23
  Claire F. Michaels and Zsolt Palatinus

PART 2
Perspectives on Embodied Cognition   **35**

3 First-order Embodiment, Second-order Embodiment,
  Third-order Embodiment   37
  Thomas Metzinger

4 Extended Cognition   54
  Ken Aizawa

5 Complex Dynamical Systems and Embodiment   63
Michael J. Richardson and Anthony Chemero

6 Embedded and Situated Cognition   76
Michael R. W. Dawson

7 The Enactive Approach   85
Ezequiel A. Di Paolo and Evan Thompson

PART 3
Embodied Cognition and Predictive Processing   **99**

8 Integrating Embodied Cognition and Predictive Processing   101
Elmarie Venter

9 Predicting the Body or Embodied Prediction? New
Directions in Embodied Predictive Processing   110
Luke Kersten

10 Predictive Processing and Embodiment in Emotion   120
*Fiorella Del Popolo Cristaldi, Suzanne Oosterwijk,
and Lisa Feldman Barrett*

11 Visual Experience   130
Michael Madary

PART 4
Perception   **141**

12 Extended Reality (XR) in Embodied Musical Art
and Science   143
*Pieter-Jan Maes, Bavo van Kerrebroeck, Mattia Rosso,
Ioulia Marouda, and Marc Leman*

13 Enactive Vision   156
Erik Myin and Farid Zahnoun

14 Perception and/for/with/as Action   169
Cedar Riener and Jeanine Stefanucci

Contents

PART 5
Language   179

15 Bodily Relativity   181
    Daniel Casasanto

16 Embodied Approaches to Language Comprehension   191
    Michael P. Kaschak, Michael Long, and Julie Madden

17 The Grounding of Concrete and Abstract Language:
    Consolidated Evidence, Open Issues, and New Challenges   200
    Claudia Scorolli and Claudia Mazzuca

18 Linking Words to World: An Embodiment Perspective   219
    Chen Yu

PART 6
Reasoning and Education   231

19 Gesture in Reasoning: An Embodied Perspective   233
    Martha W. Alibali, Rebecca Boncoddo, and Autumn B. Hostetter

20 The Embodied Dynamics of Problem Solving: New Structure
    from Multiscale Interactions   246
    *James A. Dixon, Damian G. Kelty-Stephen, Benjamin De Bari,
    and Jason Anastas*

21 Advances in Grounded and Embodied Mathematical Reasoning:
    Theory, Technology, and Research Methods   260
    Mitchell J. Nathan

22 Embodiment in Education   279
    Virginia J. Flood

23 Embodied Learning: Translating Embodied Cognition Research   291
    Sheila L. Macrine and Jennifer M.B. Fugate

PART 7
Virtual Reality   303

24 Embodied Experiences in Game Play   305
    Tarja Susi and Niklas Torstensson

25 Minds in the Matrix: Embodied Cognition and Virtual Reality   313
    Paul Smart

26 Embodied Cognition and Movement-Driven Practices   322
    Zuzanna Rucińska and Susanne Ravn

27 Human Augmentation: Re-inventing Embodiment   334
    Frédérique de Vignemont

PART 8
Social and Moral Cognition and Emotion   **345**

28 Embodied Cognition and Theory of Mind   347
    Shannon Spaulding

29 Mindshaping and Embodied Habits   357
    Michelle Maiese

30 The Embodiment of Culture   367
    Tamer Soliman and Arthur M. Glenberg

31 The Constitution of Group Cognition   381
    Gerry Stahl

32 Varieties of Group Cognition   394
    Georg Theiner

33 Morality in the Body   406
    Brendan Strejcek and Chen-Bo Zhong

34 Embodied Emotion Concepts   417
    *Paula M. Niedenthal, Adrienne Wood, Magdalena
    Rychlowska, and Anna Orlowska*

PART 9
Action and Memory   **429**

35 Memory and Action   431
    Katinka Dijkstra

Contents

36 Motor Resonance: Neurophysiological Origin, Functional
Role, and Contribution of the Motivational, Moral, and
Social Aspects of Action   442
   Laila Craighero

37 The Embodiment of Attention in the Perception-Action Loop   452
   Michael J. Spivey and Stephanie Huette

38 Embodied Remembering   461
   John Sutton and Kellie Williamson

PART 10
Reflections on Embodied Cognition   **473**

39 The Replication Crisis in Embodied Cognition Research   475
   Edouard Machery

40 Embodied Cognition Needs an Upgrade   485
   Guy Dove

41 Cognition   495
   Gary Hatfield

42 Revolution, Reform or Business as Usual? The Future
Prospects for Embodied Cognition   509
   Michael Wheeler

Index   *520*

ACKNOWLEDGMENTS

We thank the team at Routledge for suggesting and supporting this second edition of the Handbook. Deserving special thanks are Tony Bruce and Adam Johnson for their editorial work, and Lindsey Esplin, Keith Povey, and Divya Muthu for work on production.

CONTRIBUTORS

Ken Aizawa received his PhD in history and philosophy of science from the University of Pittsburgh in 1989. He works primarily in the history and philosophy of psychology. He is the author of *The Systematicity Arguments* and, with Fred Adams, *The Bounds of Cognition*. *Compositional Abduction and Scientific Interpretation: A Granular Approach* should be published in 2025. He has been Professor of Philosophy at Rutgers University, Newark, since fall 2013.

Martha W. Alibali is Vilas Distinguished Achievement Professor of Psychology at the University of Wisconsin–Madison. Her research investigates processes of change in cognitive development and mathematics learning. A central focus of her work is the role of gestures in thinking, learning, and communicating.

Jason Anastas received his PhD in psychology from the University of Connecticut in 2013. His research is about the self-organizing processes which underlie cognition in general, and executive function in particular.

Lisa Feldman Barrett is a University Distinguished Professor of Psychology at Northeastern University with appointments at the Massachusetts General Hospital and Harvard Medical School. She studies how the brain and body in context create the mind.

Rebecca Boncoddo is Associate Professor of Psychological Science at Central Connecticut State University. Her research focuses on the role of action and gesture in children's mathematical thinking and reasoning.

Daniel Casasanto is the director of the Experience and Cognition Lab at Cornell University in Ithaca, New York (USA), where he is an Associate Professor of Psychology. He studies how language, culture, and bodily experiences shape our brains and minds.

Anthony Chemero is Distinguished Research Professor of Philosophy and Psychology at the University of Cincinnati. He is the author of *Radical Embodied Cognitive Science* (2011) and, with Stephan Käufer, *Phenomenology: An Introduction* (2021).

Laila Craighero is Professor of Psychobiology and Psychophysiology at the University of Ferrara, Italy. Her research investigates the origin and development of sensorimotor representations and their role in cognitive functions.

Fiorella Del Popolo Cristaldi is currently a postdoctoral researcher at the Department of General Psychology, University of Padova, Italy, where she received her PhD in psychological sciences in 2022. Her research focuses on affective neuroscience and psychophysiology.

Michael R. W. Dawson is a Professor of Psychology at the University of Alberta. He is the author of numerous scientific papers and books including *Minds and Machines* (2004), *From Bricks to Brains: The Embodied Cognitive Science of LEGO Robots* (2010), *Mind, Body, World: Foundations of Cognitive Science* (2013), *Connectionist Representations of Tonal Music* (2018) and *What Is Cognitive Psychology?* (2022).

Benjamin De Bari is Visiting Assistant Professor of Psychology at Lehigh University. He studies perception-action-cognition from the perspective of complexity sciences and self-organization.

Frédérique de Vignemont is a CNRS senior researcher at the Jean-Nicod Institute (Paris). She works in philosophy of mind. Her interests include self-consciousness, bodily awareness, embodied social cognition, and empathy.

Ezequiel A. Di Paolo is Research Professor at Ikerbasque, the Basque Foundation for Science in Spain and Visiting Professor at the Department of Informatics, University of Sussex, UK. He is the (co)author of over 180 publications on embodied cognition, enaction, philosophy of mind, robotics, and theoretical biology including the books *Sensorimotor Life* (2017, OUP) and *Linguistic Bodies* (2018, MIT Press).

Katinka Dijkstra is a Professor in Psychology at the Erasmus University Rotterdam, the Netherlands. Her research focuses on embodied cognition, episodic memory, and cognitive aging.

James A. Dixon is Professor of Psychological Sciences and Director of the Center for the Ecological Study of Perception and Action at the University of Connecticut. His research concerns the thermodynamic bases of perception, action, and cognition.

Guy Dove is a Professor in the Philosophy Department of the University of Louisville. His work addresses the grounded nature of concepts, the role of language in thought, and the place of consciousness in the physical world. He is the author of *Abstract Concepts and the Embodied Mind* (2022) and, with Andreas Elpidorou, *Consciousness and Physicalism* (2018).

Virginia J. Flood is an Assistant Professor of Learning Sciences at the University at Buffalo, The State University of New York. Her research investigates embodiment and gesture in the teaching and learning of mathematics, science, and computer science.

Jennifer M.B. Fugate, Ph.D., Associate Professor of Health Service Psychology, Kansas City University, Kansas City, MO.

Shaun Gallagher is the Lillian and Morrie Moss Professor of Excellence in Philosophy at the University of Memphis, and Professorial Fellow at the University of Wollongong in Australia. Recent books include *Enactivist Interventions* (Oxford 2017), *Action and Interaction* (2020), and *Embodied and Enactive Approaches to Cognition* (Cambridge 2023).

Arthur M. Glenberg is an Emeritus Professor in the Department of Psychology at Arizona State University and Emeritus Professor of Psychology at the University of Wisconsin–Madison.

Gary Hatfield teaches philosophy and visual studies at the University of Pennsylvania, where he is the Adam Seybert Professor in Moral and Intellectual Philosophy. His books include *The Natural and the Normative: Theories of Spatial Perception from Kant to Helmholtz* (1990), *Perception and Cognition: Essays in the Philosophy of Psychology* (2009), and, co-edited with Sarah Allred, *Visual Experience: Sensation, Cognition, and Constancy* (2012).

Autumn B. Hostetter received her PhD in psychology from the University of Wisconsin–Madison, and is now Kurt D. Kaufman Professor of Psychology at Kalamazoo College, Michigan.

Stephanie Huette received her PhD in cognitive and information sciences at the University of California, Merced. She is currently an Associate Professor of Psychology at the University of Memphis. Her research focuses on the dynamics of language and visual processing.

Michael P. Kaschak received his PhD from the University of Wisconsin–Madison. He is currently a Professor of Psychology at Florida State University.

Damian G. Kelty-Stephen received his PhD in psychology from the University of Connecticut-Storrs and continued his work as a postdoctoral fellow at Harvard University's Wyss Institute for Biologically Inspired Engineering. He has been an Assistant Professor in Psychology at Grinnell College for eight years and then at SUNY New Paltz since fall 2021.

Luke Kersten is a Killam Postdoctoral Fellow in the Department of Philosophy at the University of Alberta. His research focuses primarily on issues in philosophy of mind and cognition, with additional interests in philosophy of science. He received his PhD in philosophy from the University of Edinburgh

Marc Leman is Methusalem Research Professor in Systematic Musicology and the Director of IPEM at Ghent University, Belgium. He has published about 300 papers on topics related to (embodied) music cognition. Recent books are *Embodied Music Cognition and Mediation Technology* (2008), *Musical Gestures* (co-editor, 2010), and *The Power of Music* (co-editor, 2013).

Michael Long received his MS from Nova Southeastern University. He is currently pursuing his PhD at Florida State University.

Edouard Machery is Distinguished Professor in the Department of History and Philosophy of Science at the University of Pittsburgh and the Director of the Center for Philosophy of Science. He is the author of *Doing Without Concepts* (OUP, 2009) and *Philosophy Within Its Proper Bounds* (OUP, 2017).

Sheila L. Macrine, PhD, is a professor and cognitive psychologist at the University of Massachusetts Dartmouth where she directs the Special Education Program. Her research interests focus on embodied cognition, cognitive development, alternative assessments, and the learning sciences. She has published numerous articles on embodied cognition with Jennifer Fugate, including their recent Open Access edited volume, *Movement Matters: How Embodied Cognition Informs Teaching and Learning* with MIT Press.

Michael Madary is an Associate Professor of Philosophy at University of the Pacific. He is the author of *Visual Phenomenology* (2017) and is currently researching the role of technology in human cognition.

Julie Madden received her PhD from Florida State University. She is currently a lecturer at University of Tennessee–Chattanooga.

Pieter-Jan Maes is a research Professor in Systematic Musicology at IPEM and co-director of the Art and Science Interaction Lab (ASIL) at Ghent University. His research delves into the fundaments of human bodily coordination in music through experimental research augmented with extended reality technologies and data analysis.

Michelle Maiese is Professor of Philosophy at Emmanuel College. Her research focuses on philosophy of mind, the emotions, and philosophy of psychiatry. She is the author of *Embodiment, Emotion, and Cognition* (2011), *Embodied Selves and Divided Minds* (2015), and *Autonomy, Enactivism, and Mental Disorder* (2022), and the co-author of *Embodied Minds in Action* (2009) and *The Mind-Body Politic* (2019).

Ioulia Marouda is a doctoral fellow in Art Science at IPEM (Institute for Psychoacoustics and Electronic Music) at Ghent University. Her interests lie in exploring the connections between science, artistic practices, and human tradition using immersive and interactive technologies.

Claudia Mazzuca is a postdoctoral researcher in the Department of Dynamic, Clinical Psychology and Health at Sapienza University of Rome. Her research focuses on the interplay between language(s), culture, body, and cognition, and their impact on conceptual representations.

Thomas Metzinger is Emeritus Professor of Theoretical Philosophy, Johannes Gutenberg-Universität Mainz, and a member of the German National Academy of Sciences, Leopoldina.

Claire F. Michaels is a long-standing advocate of and researcher in the ecological approach to perception and action. She received her PhD with Michael Turvey and held positions at Lake Forest College and VU University before returning to the University of Connecticut where she is a Research Professor.

Erik Myin is Professor at the Department of Philosophy at the University of Antwerp, Belgium. He has published papers on philosophical psychology and on the philosophy of cognitive science, and is co-author (with Daniel Hutto) of *Radicalizing Enactivism: Basic Minds without Content* (2013) and *Evolving Enactivism: Basic Minds Meet Content* (2017).

Mitchell J. Nathan, PhD, BSEE, is the Vilas Distinguished Achievement Professor of Educational Psychology (Learning Sciences), Curriculum & Instruction, and Psychology at the University of Wisconsin–Madison, and Director of the MAGIC Lab, which engineers designs and conducts scientific investigations of the nature of cognitive, embodied, and social processes for teaching and learning mathematics and integrated STEM (science, technology, engineering, and mathematics) in controlled and authentic learning environments.

Paula M. Niedenthal was a member of the National Centre for Scientific Research in France for more than a decade and is now Professor of Psychology at the University of Wisconsin–Madison and Invited Professor at the Université de Genève. Her areas of research include emotion-cognition interaction, representational models of emotion, and the processing of facial expression. Dr Niedenthal is a fellow of the Society for Personality and Social Psychology.

Suzanne Oosterwijk is an Associate Professor at the University of Amsterdam. She studies how emotions are produced by the brain and how people understand the emotions of other people. Recently, her research has focused on curiosity for emotionally evocative content.

Anna Orlowska earned her PhD from the Institute of Psychology, Polish Academy of Sciences. Her research interests center around emotion perception in the general population and clinical groups. As a certified psychotherapist and lecturer in postgraduate training, she aims to integrate research knowledge and expertise into practical applications.

Zsolt Palatinus is an Assistant Professor in the Institute of Psychology at the University of Szeged. His research focus is finding multiscale correlates of perception, action, and cognition phenomena in movement data.

Susanne Ravn is Professor and Head of the Research Unit *Movement, Culture, and Society* at the Department of Sports Science and Clinical Biomechanics, University of Southern Denmark. Her research focuses on bodily self-awareness, interaction, skills, and improvisation in sports, dance, and martial arts practices.

Michael J. Richardson is a Professor in the School of Psychological Sciences at Macquarie University and the Director of the Centre for Elite Performance Expertise and Training (CEPET) in Sydney, Australia. His research is directed towards modeling the dynamics of human perception, action, and cognition for the development of human–machine systems.

Cedar Riener is Professor and Chair of the Department of Psychology and Neuroscience at Randolph-Macon College. He is the co-author, with Daniel Willingham, of *Cognition: The*

Thinking Animal, 4th edition (2019) and upcoming 5the edition (2024). His research focuses on perception of the natural world and how our body influences that perception. His second area of research interest is applying cognitive science to education.

Mattia Rosso is a postdoctoral researcher collaborating with IPEM at Ghent University (BE) and the Center for Music in the Brain at Aarhus University (DK). His research investigates the behavioral and neural dynamics of human interactions, with a primary focus on rhythmic coordination.

Zuzanna Rucińska is a senior postdoctoral fellow of the Research Foundation Flanders (FWO) at the Centre for Philosophical Psychology, University of Antwerp, Belgium. She recently edited the special issue "Pretense and imagination from the perspective of 4E cognitive science" for *Phenomenology and the Cognitive Sciences* (2022). Her research focuses on pretense, imagination, embodied cognition, affordances, sport psychology, and virtual reality.

Magdalena Rychlowska is an Assistant Professor in the School of Psychology at Queen's University Belfast.

Claudia Scorolli is a senior research fellow at the University of Bologna (Italy). Her work focuses on the grounding of language in sensorimotor processes, as well as on language as a social tool that modifies the way humans interact with the world.

Lawrence Shapiro is the Berent Enç Professor of Philosophy at the University of Wisconsin–Madison. His many articles and books range widely over philosophy of mind and cognitive science, with special interest in topics such as multiple realization and reduction, as well as embodied cognition. The American Philosophical Association awarded his book *Embodied Cognition* the Gittler Award for outstanding contribution in the field of philosophy of the social sciences.

Paul Smart is a senior research fellow at the University of Southampton in the UK. His current research activities seek to understand the effect of network structures on collective problem solving using computer simulations. He is also exploring some of the philosophical issues related to cognitive extension in contemporary and near-future network environments.

Tamer Soliman is a graduate student in the Cognitive Science area of Arizona State University. His research exploits the theory of embodied cognition to reach a uniform understanding of human cognitive, social, and cultural behavior.

Shannon Spaulding is Professor of Philosophy at Oklahoma State University. Her research focuses on social cognition, imagination, and embodied cognition. She is the author of the book *How We Understand Others: Philosophy and Social Cognition*.

Michael J. Spivey received his PhD in brain and cognitive sciences from the University of Rochester. He is currently Professor of Cognitive and Information Sciences at the University of California, Merced. His research examines the real-time interaction of vision and language.

Gerry Stahl is Professor Emeritus at the School of Information Science and Technology, Drexel University, Philadelphia, USA. He directs the Virtual Math Teams Project at the Math Forum and is founding editor of the *International Journal of Computer-Supported Collaborative Learning*.

Jeanine Stefanucci is a Professor of Psychology at the University of Utah. She received her PhD from the University of Virginia. She takes an embodied approach to understanding perception, including a focus on how emotional states modulate space perception and spatial cognition.

Brendan Strejcek is an Associate Professor in the OB & Marketing Areas teaching stream at Rotman School of Management in Toronto.

Tarja Susi is Professor in the Department of Philosophy at the University of Antwerp, Belgium. He has published papers on philosophical psychology and on the philosophy of cognitive science, and is co-author (with Daniel Hutto) of *Radicalizing Enactivism: Basic Minds without Content* (2013) and *Evolving Enactivism: Basic Minds Meet Content* (2017).

John Sutton is Emeritus Professor of Philosophy and Cognitive Science at Macquarie University, Sydney. He has recently held visiting fellowships at Durham and Stirling in the UK, and at the Paris Institute for Advanced Study. He is co-editor of *Collaborative Remembering: theories, research, and applications* (2018), and *Collaborative Embodied Performance: ecologies of skill* (2022). His recent research addresses memory, place, and skill, and includes case studies on expertise in dance, film, music, and sport.

Georg Theiner is Associate Professor at Villanova University, USA. He received his PhD in philosophy, with a joint PhD in cognitive science, at Indiana University. Before joining Villanova, he was a Killam Postdoctoral Fellow at the University of Alberta. His main areas of research are theories of embodied cognition, group cognition, and the "extended mind" thesis.

Evan Thompson is Professor of Philosophy at the University of British Columbia and a Fellow of the Royal Society of Canada. He is the author of *Waking, Dreaming, Being: New Light on the Self and Consciousness from Neuroscience, Meditation, and Philosophy* (forthcoming), *Mind in Life: Biology, Phenomenology, and the Sciences of Mind* (2007), *Colour Vision: A Study in Cognitive Science and the Philosophy of Perception* (1995), and co-author of *The Embodied Mind: Cognitive Science and Human Experience* (1991).

Niklas Torstensson is a senior lecturer at University of Skövde in Sweden. He has a background in computational linguistics and cognitive science. His research is now focused on various aspects of user experience design, computer games, and gameplay.

Bavo van Kerrebroeck is a postdoctoral researcher in the Sequence Production and Input Devices and Music Interaction Labs at McGill University, Montreal. He works with computational models of synchrony and extended reality to investigate interpersonal musical coordination.

Elmarie Venter is a postdoctoral fellow at Ruhr Universität Bochum. In previous work, she explored debates in philosophy of perception, including intentionality and accuracy conditions, and how this relates to the role and nature of the perceiver. Her current work places a focus on the integration of embodied cognition and predictive processing.

Michael Wheeler is Professor of Philosophy at the University of Stirling. His research interests are in philosophy of cognitive science, philosophy of biology, and Heidegger. He is the author of *Reconstructing the Cognitive World: The Next Step* (2005).

Kellie Williamson has a PhD in cognitive science and philosophy from Macquarie University, Sydney. She is the co-author of papers appearing in *Educational Philosophy and Theory*, and in the volume *Brain Theory* edited by Charles Wolfe (2012).

Adrienne Wood is an Assistant Professor in the Department of Psychology at the University of Virginia. She studies social connection, social networks, and laughter.

Chen Yu is Charles and Sarah Seay Regents Professor in the Department of Psychology and Center for Perceptual Systems at the University of Texas at Austin. His research focuses on embodied cognition, development and learning, and perception, action, and cognition.

Farid Zahnoun is a postdoctoral researcher in philosophical psychology and cognitive science with an expertise in the topics of mental representation, perception, and the notion of information within theoretical neuroscience. He is currently affiliated to the University of Antwerp (UA) and the Catholic University of Louvain (UCL). Previously, he held research positions at the Federal University of Santa Maria and the Free University of Berlin. He is the author of the book *The Embodiment of Meaning: Why Matter matters for Cognition and Experience* (Routledge, 2023).

Chen-Bo Zhong is Professor of Organizational Behavior and Human Resource Management at Rotman School of Management. His research focuses on ethics, moral psychology, decision making, and unconscious processes. He currently serves on the editorial board of *Journal of Experimental Social Psychology* and *Journal of Experimental Psychology: General*.

INTRODUCTION

Lawrence Shapiro and Shannon Spaulding

The Introduction to the first edition of this handbook described its contents as aiming to "situate, motivate, illuminate, illustrate, and critically evaluate embodied cognition in all its facets." This second edition shares that goal. It remains true, we believe, that "Whether seeking to understand the historical roots of embodied cognition, gain perspective on the variety of distinct approaches that practitioners of embodied cognition employ, witness the array of cognitive functions to which ideas of embodiment have been applied, or consider the nature of cognition and the extent to which a focus on embodiment marks a shift from the methods and mores of conventional cognitive science, this book answers the call."

In the years since publication of the first edition, embodied cognition shows no sign of slowing down. Indeed, given the increasing number of topics that embodied cognition researchers seek to investigate and the expanding literature on issues that have long been at its center, it made sense to bring another editor on board for the project. This second edition marks a joint and equal effort from Shapiro *and* Spaulding. Included in this volume are chapters from new authors (Chapters 8, 9, 22, 23, 26, 39, 40), substantially revised or new chapters from original authors (Chapters 10, 11, 12, 16, 20, 21, 24, 25, 27, 29, 36), and, in other cases, chapters that authors elected to revise lightly, update, or leave unchanged (Chapters 1, 2, 3, 4, 5, 6, 7, 13, 14, 15, 17, 18, 19, 28, 30, 31, 32, 33, 34, 35, 37, 38, 41, 42). In total, the collection now includes seven more chapters than the original. In addition to the areas of investigation covered in the earlier anthology, we've added chapters on predictive processing, education, and virtual reality. Naturally, as embodied cognition wins more converts, it also finds itself a target of more criticism. Reflecting this heightened scrutiny, the volume's final section now contains two critical chapters: one that questions a common embodied conception of the nature of concepts, and another that raises concerns about the replicability of the psychological findings often cited in defense of embodied theories of cognition.

In organizing the sections of this second edition, we elected to group the chapters into ten sections rather than the six in the first edition. In part this reflects the addition of new topics, but we also found that revisions to chapters brought some closer to each other in content while others moved farther apart. In the end, the joints we carved between chapters landed us with four more sections than appeared in the original edition.

DOI: 10.4324/9781003322511-1

The first two chapters set the scene for current research in embodied cognition, tracing its ancestry back to quite distinct lineages. Shaun Gallagher, in his revised chapter, describes a cluster of ideas arising from within the phenomenological tradition that have influenced contemporary thinking on the body's role in cognition, from Husserl's notion of the "I can" that characterizes the objects of perception in terms of what our bodies can do with them, to the Merleau-Pontean appreciation of the motor processes involved in perception. Phenomenology, Gallagher argues, remains crucial as well in neuroscientific investigations of experience, insofar as it provides the tools for describing those aspects of experience that correlate with neural activity. Among the new features of this chapter is a discussion of the role of bias and prejudice, as well as sexism, in affecting one's own body schema.

Coming from an entirely different tradition, Claire Michaels and Zsolt Palatinus offer a biblically inspired recounting of ecological psychology, in which the axioms of the Gibsonian approach are crystalized in ten commandments. Their case study of the famous outfielder problem illustrates a number of principles that, while not universally adopted, have attained prominence in embodied cognition, such as the role of action in creating opportunities for perception, and an antagonism toward representationalist and computationalist accounts of information processing. Their claim that the ten commandments of ecological psychology must be accepted as a complete package might best be evaluated in the context of the many chapters in this book that seem not to obey this precept. Similarly, the chapters to follow provide ample material with which to assess the importance of phenomenological thinking in a contemporary science of cognition.

Following this section on the historical antecedents of embodied cognition is a collection of chapters dedicated to presenting a variety of perspectives on what it means to describe cognition as embodied, or on what embodiment brings to the study of cognition. These chapters develop themes that recur in the chapters of the next, applied, section, thus situating them in a theoretical context.

Thomas Metzinger's studies of out-of-body experiences comprise some of the most intriguing work in embodied theories of awareness. His pursuit of an explanation of the phenomenology of selfhood – of the feeling of being an embodied self – has led to a series of experiments that induce out-of-body experiences in his subjects. In this chapter he describes three orders of embodiment that he believes to be critical components in a full account of self-awareness.

Ken Aizawa examines arguments for the claim that embodiment, in some cases, suffices to extend cognitive processes beyond their traditionally conceived boundaries within the skull. Focusing on two such arguments – one involving the idea of cognitive equivalence and the other on special forms of connection between the brain and the world – Aizawa carefully considers the burdens such arguments face as well as the distinctions, such as those between derived and non-derived content, and between causal influence and constituency, that matter to their assessment.

Michael Richardson and Anthony Chemero's presentation of dynamical systems approaches to cognition and neuroscience delivers an accessible guide to a related group of concepts, such as self-organization, soft assembly, and non-linearity, that promises to revolutionize the study of cognition. Dynamical approaches are rewriting the rulebook for investigating cognitive capacities such as problem solving, and posing challenges to entrenched conceptions of mind such as the view that cognition is significantly modular.

Michael Dawson grapples with the distinctions between embodied, embedded, and situated cognition, drawing contrasts to standard cognitive science. He illustrates these distinct versions of embodied cognition through an examination of echolocation in bats. Conceiving of the bat as embedded, or situated, in its environment is necessary for understanding its use of informational feedback in capturing prey, and appeal to features of the bat's body, such as the shape of its ears, is necessary to understand how it solves the underdetermination problem of perception that vexes traditional cognitive theories.

The idea of embeddedness develops even further in Di Paolo and Thompson's chapter on enactive theories of cognition. The authors explain the centrality of the concept of autonomy in enactivist psychology. Autonomy refers to the capacity of organisms to maintain their distinctness from their environments while at the same time constantly exchanging matter and energy with their environments *in order* to retain their distinctness. Di Paolo and Thompson develop the idea of a *precarious operationally closed system* and show how such a system, in the course of adapting to its environment, creates norms that dictate a kind of relevance for action. Cognition, for the enactivist, involves regulating the body so that it adapts to the world for the sake of its own preservation.

With historical groundwork set, and perspectives on embodiment clarified, the handbook turns next to a new section dedicated to understanding the relationship and application of predictive processing to embodied cognition. Central to predictive-processing accounts of cognition is the idea that the brain is constantly generating predictions about how the world will be in the next instant, seeking to minimize the error between this prediction and the incoming stimulation that reveals how the world actually is. Alternatively, rather than changing its expectations about the world in the face of contrary stimulation, the brain might cause the body to act on the world, thereby altering the world so that it conforms more closely with its expectations. With interest in predictive processing surging, embodied cognition researchers have sought to clarify whether the predictive-processing approach is compatible with the main tenets of embodied cognition. Some prominent proponents of predictive processing, including Jakob Hohwy (2016), have expressed skepticism that predictive processing can be easily integrated with the embodied cognition research program while others, such as Andy Clark (2017), see the approaches as complementary.

Elmarie Venter, in her chapter, jumps into this fray, defending Clark's optimism for a happy marriage between predictive processing and embodied cognition. Crucial to her case is a novel thesis about how the error minimization that drives predictive processing is to proceed. Venter offers a single process for doing so: sensorimotor inference. Because sensorimotor inference produces predictions involving embodied action, these predictions have built into them information about how bodies of particular sorts are likely to respond to or change the environments in which they are situated, revealing how predictive processing and embodied cognition can together explain cognitive activity.

In the following chapter, Luke Kersten identifies two issues that complicate decisions about the compatibility of predictive processing with embodied cognition. The first concerns how to conceive of these paradigms. Are they theories, research programs, hypotheses? Because these categories differ in terms of abstractness and other features, judgments about their potential for interaction requires clarification of their status. Secondly, we need a clearer sense of the ontological and methodological commitments of each to determine the extent to which they might be integrated. Kersten hopes that attention to philosophy of science, which is especially well equipped to investigate the questions on which he sees the compatibility of predictive processing and embodied cognition resting, can lead us toward a resolution.

Fiorella Del Popolo Cristaldi, Suzanne Oosterwijk, and Lisa Feldman Barrett show how our emotion concepts arise from the sorts of predictive processes canvassed in the previous two chapters. Their idea is that our brain is constantly generating predictions about the future visceromotor states of our bodies, which in turn ground emotional experience. These predictions, as well as others concerning future perceptual inputs and future bodily motions, will, if confirmed, produce the emotional experiences on which the predictions are based. The authors speculate that such predictive processes may be crucial to social cognition – our understanding of others – as our brains rely on models of our own internal states to predict the emotional lives of those around us.

In the final chapter of this section, Michael Madary has updated his original chapter on visual experience to address the suitability of the predictive-processing framework for shedding light on this topic. His primary interest remains visual consciousness. He describes the distinct contributions that enactive, embedded, and extended theories of vision make to an overall understanding of the sense of visual presence, and provides a state-of-the-art survey of objections and responses to these approaches, clarifying the role of action in visual perception. However, he asks, would a predictive-processing theory of visual experience require that the contents of these experiences contain a predictive element? Similarly, given that predictive processes are probabilistic, Madary wonders whether the character of visual experience must likewise be probabilistic.

In the revised perception section, Pieter-Jan Maes, Bavo van Kerrebroeck, Mattia Rosso, Ioulia Marouda, and Marc Leman present their ideas about how to incorporate digital technologies, including virtual reality domains, into the study of music perception and cognition. These technologies, they argue, provide individuals with a capacity to extend action-perception processes directly into computer-generated worlds. In turn, subjects' feelings of presence in these worlds offer insights into how to design varieties of musical spaces, such as concert halls.

Erik Myin and Farid Zahoun explain the basics of an enactive approach to vision, defending a theory that seeks to replace cognitivist conceptions of vision, which depend on a framework of rules and representations, with one that emphasizes an organism's sensorimotor interactions with the environment. Critics have charged enactivist views with being unable to explain perceptual events that appear not to depend on environmental interactions, such as dreams or hallucinations. But these experiences, Myin and Zahoun argue, differ importantly from ordinary visual experiences, or depend asymmetrically on ordinary visual experiences, thus blunting the critics' concerns.

Finally, Cedar Riener and Jeanine Stefanucci discuss space representation, using it as an example to illustrate the tight connections between perception and action. Perception, they claim, functions to plan for action, but also constitutes a kind of action in virtue of sharing a representational code. The chapter is cleverly organized around the different words one might use to describe the link between perception and action: perception *and* action, but also perception *for*, *with*, or *as* action.

The section on language begins with Daniel Casasanto's provocative defense of the body-specificity thesis, according to which an organism's body determines how it conceptualizes the world. In a number of studies involving subjects that differ in handedness (left- or right-dominant), Casasanto reveals how handedness influences perception and judgment, and how simply wearing a ski-glove on one's dominant hand can induce changes in perception and judgment.

Michael Kaschak, Michael Long, and Julie Madden present their work on language comprehension, arguing that comprehension depends on the construction of internal sensorimotor simulations. New to this chapter are responses to recent criticisms that have targeted embodied theories of language. Mahon and Caramazza (2008), for instance, draw on neuroscientific evidence to challenge the idea that motor simulations play a constitutive role in language comprehension. Kaschak et al. suggest, in response, a broader conception of the meaning of embodiment that remains consistent with Mahon and Caramazza's findings.

Claudia Scorolli together with Claudia Mazzuca investigates more precisely which features of sensorimotor simulations participate in language comprehension and explores the effect of grammar on simulations. Of particular interest is their account of how bodily simulations might contribute to the comprehension of abstract nouns and verbs. Also intriguing is the finding that the use of some words can affect how a person experiences peripersonal space, just as the use of tools might do.

Finally, Chen Yu looks to embodiment to resolve issues concerning the indeterminacy of reference. Relying on machine learning techniques, Yu focuses on interactions between the child's body, the body of the language teacher (usually the parent), and the environment in order to explain how the task of reference fixing becomes tractable.

The next topic, reasoning and education, begins with Martha Alibali, Rebecca Boncoddo, and Autumn Hostetter's research on gesture. Gesture, they show, contributes significantly to reasoning, and often arises as a result of mentally simulating bodily actions. Gestures are, in effect, the body's response to the brain's inability to suppress all the activation it generates when simulating action. Their data show that subjects gesture more frequently when describing information they've learned through physical actions than, e.g., through vision; and gesture facilitates even abstract reasoning with numbers.

James Dixon, Damian Kelty-Stephen, Benjamin De Bari, and Jason Anastas are interested in instances of problem solving that call for innovative solutions. They argue that traditional computational approaches to problem solving appear poorly suited to explain innovation because, presumably, computations rely on fixed symbols and rules. Departing radically from computationalism, they reconceptualize how to understand problem solving in terms of the behavior of "dissipative structures," the analyses of which require tools from the science of thermodynamics.

Mitchell Nathan, in a wholly revised chapter, elaborates his GEL framework (grounded and embodied learning), explaining how from this perspective we should understand the human capacity for mathematical reasoning. The GEL framework describes four types of embodiment. Nathan's aim is to show how these four types of embodiment, when interacting with learning processes, explain the development of mathematical reasoning. Also in this chapter, Nathan reviews how an embodied approach to mathematical reasoning can inform instructional practices.

Virginia Flood surveys a variety of different forms that embodied theories of cognition have taken, explaining the implications of each for the design of learning spaces as well as for classroom pedagogy. Drawing on Lakoff and Johnson's theory of conceptual metaphor, for instance, she explains how students rely on body-based metaphors to ease comprehension of abstract ideas. Similarly, the embodied theories of concepts, which assume that a concept's content depends on the body's re-enactment of sensorimotor processes, inspire styles of learning that ask students to move in ways that facilitate concept learning. The several ways to understand how cognition is embodied lead to different yet effective teaching methods.

The final entry in this section is Sheila Macrine and Jennifer Fugate's discussion of embodied learning. Their goal is to address a troubling puzzle: despite advances in embodied cognition and clear evidence of the positive contributions it can offer educators, why has it not had a bigger impact on educational theory and policy? They offer their "translational framework" as a tool for introducing to a wider population of educators the benefits that embodied approaches to pedagogy can offer, with the hope that this increased attention will narrow the "research-to-practice" gap in education.

Increasing interest in virtual reality and its connections to embodied cognition prompted us to include a new section on this topic. In the opening chapter, Tarja Susi and Niklas Torstensson describe a game they created, the design of which took inspiration from embodied cognition. Geared toward 8–10-year-old children, the game's hidden purpose is to teach children not to send photographs to online predators. The game was built using principles from the Tangible Learning Design Framework, which emphasizes learning through interaction with physical and digital objects. The objects' design requires that children act on them in specific ways – ways that facilitate learning those concepts that prepare children to recognize potential manipulators.

Paul Smart draws connections between virtual reality and embodied cognition even more directly, explaining how a close examination of virtual reality can inform our understanding of embodied cognition. Especially important in this context is the use of virtual reality to construct virtual agents whose precisely controlled interactions with virtual environments provide us with insights into topics that remain controversial in discussions of "real-world" embodied cognition. For instance, Smart argues that reflection on virtual worlds might help us to resolve the dispute regarding whether extra-neural resources ought to be conceived as causal contributors to cognition or, much more provocatively, actual constituents of a cognitive process.

Zuzanna Rucinska and Susanne Ravn's fascinating discussion of embodied cognition as it relates to sports and esports asks intriguing questions about how embodied processes might be involved in virtual actions that seem to involve the actual body only minimally. However, they argue, the integration of the body with the technology used in esports extends the actual into the virtual world. Thus, the same kinds of sensorimotor processes that are central in embodied accounts of perception and action in the real world remain crucial for understanding the activities of esports participants in virtual worlds.

We close this section on virtual reality with Frédérique de Vignemont's entirely new chapter on human augmentation. De Vignemont asks whether augmentations to the body, such as artificial limbs, might be experienced as proper parts of the body or, weaker, be merely incorporated into a representation of the body that suffices to guide the motor system in guiding action. Still other questions concern how augmentations to the body differ, if they do, from ordinary tool use. De Vignemont argues that, in the end, we should be less focused on whether augmentations provide us with new bodies and more on how they endow us with new skills.

Social and moral cognition has been an especially active research area within embodied cognition. Shannon Spaulding explains the subject matter of social cognition and then distinguishes embodied theories from the two prevailing theories: *theory theory* and the competing *simulation theory*. Spaulding presents embodied accounts of social cognition as a deflationary alternative, in the sense that they eschew mentalistic and representational resources, instead explaining social interactions by appeal to the direct perception of others' intentions through their expressions and bodily movements.

In her chapter, Michelle Maiese introduces the idea of *mindshaping*, a process by which an individual unknowingly internalizes sociocultural rules and expectations, sometimes to their detriment. She turns to the concept of *embodied habits* as a tool for understanding how mindshaping comes about and how it might be promoted or attenuated. The core of her account of embodied habits rests on the idea of bodily coordination between agents which results in the sharing of social norms.

Tamer Soliman and Art Glenberg, in perhaps the most speculative chapter of the book, outline an account of how culture might emerge from a web of motor programs, perceptual schemata, and emotional reactions that arises as bodies act in response to each other and their environments. Joint action, they argue, provides opportunities for sensorimotor bonds that create a distinction between in- and out-groups, the basis for culture.

Gerry Stahl studies the interactions between members of online math teams as they interact to solve mathematical problems. He argues that the teams exhibit group cognition only when meeting three pre-conditions. They must demonstrate an extended sequential approach to the problem they examine, display persistent co-attention, and work with a shared understanding of the problem.

Group cognition remains the central topic in Georg Theiner's chapter. Theiner is especially interested in the varieties of group cognition. In an effort to operationalize the idea of group cognition, Theiner offers a taxonomy of distinct dimensions along which group tasks can be distinguished from each other. He pays special attention to the phenomena of group memory and group problem solving, comparing group performance to the performance of individuals and explaining the variables that seem to improve or degrade group performance.

In their chapter, Brendan Strejcek and Chen-Bo Zhong survey embodied theories of morality. They reveal connections between moral judgments and emotions, such as disgust, that in turn reflect facts of embodiment. The work they describe shows a deep overlap between physical and moral domains, as when purity becomes associated with cleanliness, the color black with immorality, or fishy smells with suspicious behavior.

Wrapping up this section is Paula Niedenthal, Adrienne Wood, Magdalena Rychlowska, and Anna Orlowska's discussion of emotion concepts. How do people represent emotion concepts, and how do people identify facial expressions as having particular emotional content? On their view, emotion concepts refer to forms of behavior, including facial expressions and gestures. Among the interesting evidence they cite are associations between the activation of particular facial muscles and the processing of nouns that suggest emotional content, as well as a degradation in the ability to process emotion words when activity in facial muscles is suppressed.

Memory and attention are next on the list of cognitive functions that embodied cognition researchers have targeted. Katinka Dijkstra describes research that reveals a number of interesting connections between memory and action. Memory, she argues, draws on the same neural resources that were activated in the original experience of which the memory is a trace. Thus, the neuroscience of memory shows the crucial role of simulating (or re-enacting) the actions and perceptions of the experience that constitutes the content of the memory. From this perspective, it's perhaps not surprising that memories are easier to recall when assuming the bodily positions and postures that were present during the remembered experience. Also in this chapter is a discussion of work in clinical psychology that suggests links between body posture and depressive symptoms.

The concept of motor resonance is at the center of Laila Craighero's chapter. When a person (or monkey) watches another performing an action, their motor system *resonates* with this action: the observer's sensorimotor system encodes not just the kinematics of the other, but also the goal of the other's action. Craighero walks us through the neurophysiological basis of motor resonance, explaining the function of mirror neurons, and offers thoughts on the purpose of motor resonance in learning new actions as well as in predicting the actions of others.

Next in this section, Michael Spivey and Stephanie Huette defend a conception of attention as an extended process, involving a perception-action loop that involves actions which redirect perception to unnoticed or new parts of the environment, which changes the nature of the stimulus reaching the perceptual organ, which leads to new actions, redirecting perception yet again, and so on. All parts of this loop, including the environment, are in their view constituents of attention. They contrast this model of attention to earlier ones that conceived attention as a simple filtering mechanism.

Finally, John Sutton and Kellie Williamson close this section with a discussion of embodied memory. They provide a useful survey of historical and current studies of various memory-related phenomena and explain the sense in which memory is an embodied skill. On their view, memory incorporates bodily experiences, and movements of the body contribute significantly to the triggering or particular memories, showing the body to be a vehicle of memory.

The final section of the handbook offers critical reflection on not just particular research within embodied cognition but also on the nature of cognition generally and the relationship embodied cognition bears toward the traditional computational theory of cognition that it often claims to replace. First in this section is Edouard Machery's account of the replication crisis that has afflicted many of those studies on which depend some of embodied cognition's more prominent theses. After a careful analysis of the meaning and importance of replication, Machery reviews replication failures in two important areas of embodied cognition: mind-body coupling and the role of perceptual and motor representations in cognition and language comprehension. He urges greater caution, if not outright skepticism, toward the empirical work that many of the authors of this volume cite (or, in some cases, have produced).

Guy Dove's chapter takes aim at what he calls the grounded cognition model, which emphasizes the concept of motor resonance we saw Craighero discussing in her chapter. According to this model, concepts are built from re-activation of the sensorimotor areas of the brain that had been activated in response to whatever stimuli caused sensorimotor activation originally. Dove considers research suggesting that concepts instead involve multisensory representation – so that activation of visual concepts, for instance, might arise through auditory stimulation. Similarly, there is evidence suggesting that abstract concepts rely on parts of the brain not associated with sensorimotor activity. Dove concludes that the grounded cognition model cannot be the whole story behind concept acquisition and use.

Gary Hatfield's chapter begins with a question that has probably occurred to any reflective follower of recent trends in cognitive science: What is cognition? Is there a shared conception of cognition that unites the diversity of research programs represented in this book? If so, is it an understanding of cognition that members of the "standard" cognitive science community would recognize? Hatfield's answer to these questions begins with an examination of some prominent early work in cognitive science, especially Ulric Neisser's, before moving on to more contemporary literature including Jerry Fodor's influential defense of a language of thought and David Marr's theory of vision. Interestingly, Hatfield finds room for Gibson's ecological psychology within a computational and representational framework (but, significantly, one that is non-symbolic), challenging Michaels and Palatinus's claim that the ten commandments of ecological psychology (Chapter 2) must be endorsed, all or none. In another surprising turn, Hatfield presents Descartes, a punchbag for many in the field of embodied cognition, as an early advocate of embodied cognition, especially of embodied memory. In the end, Hatfield settles on a description of cognition as that which produces intelligent behavior. Accordingly, he urges that cognitive scientists attend more closely to varieties of intelligent behavior, and suggests that investigations of the evolution of mind might provide a rich source of material for identifying and classifying intelligent behavior.

Closing the volume is Michael Wheeler's chapter on the relationship between embodied cognition and traditional, or computational, cognitive science. His more particular focus is extended cognition, which he examines in part to determine whether, *qua* paradigm of embodied cognition, it demands a departure from the conventional commitments of cognitive science. As Wheeler sees matters, extended cognition remains consistent with the functionalist theory of mind that grounds traditional cognitive science, requiring for its investigation nothing in addition to the computational, representational resources that traditional cognitive science delivers. Rejection of traditional cognitive science, he contends, was motivated in large part by a perception among many researchers that computational theories of cognition found an insuperable obstacle in the so-called frame problem. However, he responds, the theoretical apparatus deployed by members of the embodiment community in an effort to overcome the frame problem fares no better. In cases of a draw, such as this one, the deciding factor ought to be conservativism. The methods and ontological commitments of standard cognitive science win out because of their proven track record. Notice, however, that this is not a denunciation of embodied cognition, but rather an effort to trim its more radical expressions so that it might fit into the more familiar clothing of traditional cognitive science.

References

Clark, A. (2017) "Busting out: Predictive brains, embodied minds, and the puzzle of the evidentiary veil," *Nous*, *51*(4), 727–753.

Hohwy, J. (2016) "The self-evidencing brain," *Nous*, *50*(2), 259–285.

Mahon, B. Z., and Caramazza, A. (2008) "A critical look at the embodied cognition hypothesis and a new proposal for grounding conceptual content," *Journal of Physiology of Paris*, *102*, 59–70.

PART 1

Historical Underpinnings

1

PHENOMENOLOGY AND EMBODIED COGNITION

Shaun Gallagher

As this volume makes clear, research on embodied cognition draws from a number of disciplines and is supported by a variety of methodological strategies. In this chapter I focus on what phenomenology has contributed to our understanding of embodied cognition. I take 'phenomenology' to mean the philosophical tradition initiated in the 20th century by Edmund Husserl and developed by a variety of philosophers, including Martin Heidegger, Maurice Merleau-Ponty, Jean-Paul Sartre, and numerous others. More recently phenomenologists have been drawn into theoretical and empirical research in the cognitive sciences, and especially into discussions of enactive and embodied conceptions of the mind. I'll start by looking at some of the historical resources that define the phenomenology of the body. I'll then consider how phenomenology, as a methodology, relates to scientific investigations of embodied cognition, and finally go on to identify some of the insights that phenomenology provides about embodied cognition, agency, performance, and affectivity.

Historical resources

Husserl (1989) makes a phenomenological distinction between *Korper*, variously translated as the objective body or the body-as-object, and *Leib*, the lived body or body-as-subject. The body-as-object includes, for example, what one's body looks like in the mirror, or how it is considered in medical or scientific terms. In contrast, the body-as-subject refers to the perceiving (or experiencing) body, the agentive body that moves in action, where most of the experiencing is prereflective. In this regard, as I perceive the world around me, or as I engage in action, I do not experience my body as one object among others in the environment. Yet I am not completely unaware of my position or my movement – I have an immediate sense that I am sitting or running, for example. In this regard, Husserl (1997) provides an analysis of the role of kinesthesia (movement sense) in perception. For example, since extraocular motor processes help to control where we look, kinesthetic feedback from that movement correlates with perception of the visual field. Extraocular processes, however, are embedded in a motor system that controls head movement, and general body posture. Accordingly, kinesthetic patterns more generally are activated in correlation with perception. Husserl's analysis broadly anticipates the contemporary neuroscience of motor

 DOI: 10.4324/9781003322511-3

resonance understood as a kind of action-readiness when we perceive objects or other persons. He refers to this action-readiness as the 'I can,' contending that as I perceive objects around me, I perceive them in terms of the possibilities I have to interact with them. These action possibilities are not cognitive additions to perception, but are implicit in the way that I perceive the object – implicit in the intentional structure of perception. The concept of the *I can* is also taken up by Merleau-Ponty (2012), who in turn influenced both James Gibson (1979) in developing his notion of affordances, and the enactive approach to perception.

Merleau-Ponty was also influenced by Heidegger, and by his own readings in developmental psychology, psychiatry, and neurology. Heidegger (1962) has little to say about the body per se, but he does provide an influential account of a particular way of being-in-the-world that is implicitly embodied. His notion of the ready-to-hand (*Zuhanden*) involves a pragmatic conception of our ordinary stance towards the world. This analysis figures prominently in Hubert Dreyfus's work on embodied coping and expertise (Dreyfus 2000).

Of all the phenomenologists Merleau-Ponty is best known as the philosopher of embodiment. He was able to integrate his study of psychology and neurology into his phenomenology of perception where the notions of lived body and body schema play a central role. For Merleau-Ponty (2012), perception involves both sensory and motor processes. He provides an analysis of kinesthesia, phantom limbs, and other such topics by drawing heavily and with a critical eye on the neuroscience/neurology and psychology of his time.[1] He distinguishes the spatiality of the surrounding environment from the spatiality of the body; the latter organized in a proprioceptive order where my hand is not next to me in the same way that the cup is next to some other object (2012: 100–101). The body schema is ambiguous since it allows me to control my intentional movements, but it also seems to operate on its own in a way that is not explicitly under my control. Moreover, a body schema is not something produced by an association of partial images or sensations, but is rather a whole which governs my movement – it's the law or principle of movement rather than the immediate product of movement. It dynamically organizes bodily movement in terms of the agent's projects. The spatiality of the body, then, is not an objective spatiality measurable by a ruler, but a "spatiality of situation" in which the body and the world form a practical system.

Sartre (1956) introduced a different set of considerations by distinguishing between the body-for-itself (that is, the body-as-subject) and the body-for-others.[2] For Sartre, the body-for-others is first of all an observed object – it falls under the gaze of the other person and in most cases is objectified or reified. The other sees me first as an object, and this defines the initial encounter that I then have to work through in my intersubjective dealings with that other. Importantly, this adds a certain dimension to the subject's experience of her own body. Not only is my body seen by the other; it is experienced by me as seen by the other. This initiates an exterior perspective that I have on myself, and contributes to the constitution of an objective sense of self.

Critical phenomenology of the body

Merleau-Ponty and Sartre's ideas about body schema and the body-for-others were influential in analyses of race and gender in the work of critical phenomenologists like Franz Fanon (1986) and Iris Marion Young (1980). According to Fanon, "[i]n the white world the man of color encounters difficulties in the development of [or in elaborating] his body schema" (1986: 82). He experiences his body from a third-person perspective as a negative.

Fanon acknowledges what seems to be the ordinary workings of the body schema. He uses the example of reaching for his cigarettes and matches. His postural adjustments are quite specific to accomplish the task, and the body schema works as a kind of implicit know-how. "Such seems to be the schema. It does not impose itself on me; it is, rather, a definitive structuring of the self and of the world—definitive because it creates a real dialectic between my body and the world" (Fanon 1986: 83). Yet, for a black person there is something else going on – something that Merleau-Ponty's analysis does not capture – the idea that social distortions can impinge on the body schema. Fanon refers to this as a historico-racial schema woven "out of a thousand details, anecdotes, stories" (1986: 84).

Social distortions (bias, racial prejudice) can impinge on the body schema, mediated by a forced self-consciousness of my body derived from my awareness of how others (white colonizers) perceive my black body. I become self-conscious of my body under the other's gaze, which then may lead to awkward, stilted or constrained, or in some cases, reactive movements and gestures. An historico-racial schema, rather than a sanitized and neatly delineated, physiological body schema of the sort described by Merleau-Ponty, can be shaped by forces of oppression, by cultural practices and the normative systems that reflect power structures tied to race.

Young's classic 1980 essay, "Throwing like a girl," challenges the straightforward phenomenology of the body offered by philosophers like Merleau-Ponty and Husserl. The lived experience of movement, for example, is not always a matter of an 'I can.' Rather, for girls and women, it is often a matter of 'I cannot,' or 'I should not' – a case of "inhibited intentionality." In contrast to Erwin Straus, a phenomenological anthropologist and psychiatrist, who thinks that girls throw a ball differently from boys because of biological differences, Young argues that the difference is due to culture and the way girls are raised, which imposes a normative regime that involves cultural and social limitations. Young carefully notes that what she says about the way a girl or woman moves does not necessarily apply to all females universally. Drawing on Simone de Beauvoir's account of women's experiences, Young argues that culture defines the woman as Other, as a correlate to the male, and as an object, thereby denying her subjectivity, autonomy, and creativity, all of which shows up in 'the modalities of feminine bodily comportment, motility, and spatiality' (Young 1980: 141).

Young also provides an influential analysis of intersubjective existence and the fact that women are defined as objects by the gazes of others, which also infects their own self-perception. A woman is always living with the possibility that she will be gazed upon as a mere body, as a potential object of another's intentions and manipulations. Importantly, this also has an effect on a woman's attitude towards her own body. She "often actively takes up her body as a mere thing. She gazes at it in the mirror, worries about how it looks to others, prunes it, shapes it, molds and decorates it" (1980: 154). Again, culture imposes such normative constraints on women in a way that defines their situation.

Phenomenology in science

One might think that phenomenology, on its own, is limited to an analysis of the consciousness of the body – the way that we are aware of the body – since strictly speaking phenomenology is not able to penetrate beyond our experience of how things seem to us – the way the world appears, or the way one's body appears in consciousness. While phenomenology can certainly provide this kind of analysis, it can also go beyond it in at least two ways.

First, in the phenomenological analysis of action, for example, I can discover, in a negative way, what I either *do not* or *cannot* experience. For example, when I reach to grasp something I am not aware of the precise shaping of my grasp, which, on the basis of certain subpersonal processes and my pragmatic relation to the particular object, is different from the detailed shape of my grasp when the object is smaller or larger, or shaped differently, or positioned differently, or when my intention (what I want to do with the object) is different, etc. This shaping of the grasp happens in a non-conscious way. Although I am not aware of the details of such body-schematic processes or how they work, this lack of awareness can be the subject of phenomenological reflection. More generally, informed by scientific studies, I can reflectively understand how elements of body-schematic motor control integrate with and modulate conscious and intentional aspects of perception, attention, and action.

One might argue that behavioral studies can already tell us this. But in some important way this kind of negative phenomenology is an initial part of any behavioral study of this sort. If, for example, a scientist were studying for the very first time the simple action of reaching to grasp something, it would be important to know what the agent is conscious of during the action. Is the agent entirely unconscious of everything pertaining to the action; or is the agent entirely conscious of all aspects of her movement? When the agent reports that she is or is not conscious of a particular aspect of the action (if indeed she is asked) she is giving a phenomenological report (and with some training she may be better able to say what she is or is not conscious of). If the agent is not asked to provide such a report, there is likely some implicit or explicit assumption made by the behavioral scientist based on her own experience, or on previous empirical knowledge about how such things work. Even in the latter case, there is still some phenomenological fact of the matter, established in previous work and likely built into the design of the experiment. More generally, questions about what a subject is conscious of or not conscious of, what they know or don't know about the experiment, whether they are focused or not focused on what they are asked to focus on, etc., are important ones in many behavioral experiments.

Second, even if many of the effects of bodily processes on cognition happen on the subpersonal or neuronal level, phenomenology can still be relevant to working out a causal explanation. Since the investigation of subpersonal processes is often meant to be explanatory for cognitive operations that also have a person-level dimension – assuming that remembering, imagining, deciding, solving problems, dreaming, etc. are in some regards part of a person's conscious experience – it seems important to understand the nature of the person-level explanandum to even know what type of subpersonal processes to look for, or how such processes can be explanatory. Without the phenomenology, in fact, neuroscience would be hard-pressed to know what to look for; it would be working in the dark.

Consider the study of phantom limbs. Whether the neuroscientist discovers a neuromatrix involved in the phenomenal presence of the limb (Melzack 1990), or that neural plasticity is responsible for phantom pain, such explanations would make no sense at all without some reference to the subject's experience. Likewise for any number of pathological or experimentally induced phenomena – somatoparaphrenia, Anarchic Hand Syndrome, delusions of control, Rubber Hand Illusion, whole-body displacement, the Pinocchio effect, etc.

To be clear, there is not necessarily a one-to-one correlation between the phenomenology and specific brain and bodily processes. But cognition researchers are able to point to specific processes only in reference to person-level phenomena. To put this more strongly, it is not only that what happens on a phenomenologically accessible personal level can give us some clue to what may be happening on the subpersonal level, but the phenomenology may count as part of the explanation of subpersonal processes. The explanation has to go in at least two ways between first-person and third-person accounts. A cognitive neuroscientist who explains that neurons in area F5 are activated must give some indication of what this activation correlates to on the personal level of experience or behavior. In regard to cognitive neuroscientific methodology, if subjects are not in a specific personal-level situation (e.g., engaged in an intentional action, or watching another person engage in an intentional action, or imagining the doing or observing of an action) there is no expectation that specific neurons in area F5 will significantly activate. Neuroscientists thus need to appeal to personal-level practices and phenomenological experiences in setting up their experiments, and in many cases the only way to define the *explanandum* is in terms of phenomenology. In any particular case, if the neuroscientist is investigating brain processes that correlate with X (on an experiential or behavioral level) she cannot simply depend on a wild guess about what the experience of X is, or what behavioral situations might elicit it.

The phenomenology of agency and the sense of body ownership

One example of how phenomenology can inform experimental science concerns the experiences of agency and body ownership. Phenomenologists describe a sense of "mineness" or "ipseity" that is built into every experience, that is, a sense of ownership (SO), where ownership means not some external relation of *having* something (as in ownership of property), but rather signifies the intrinsic mineness of experience, an aspect of the experience that makes it subjectively *my* experience. SO, as such, holds not only with regard to experiences of my body or my body parts, e.g., the sense that it is *my* arm that is reaching and *my* hand that is grasping, when I reach and grasp something, but also in regard to my experiences of self-movement and action – SO not only for my arm, but also for my action. SO is directly tied to the phenomenological idea of prereflective self-awareness, i.e., when we consciously think, or perceive, or act, we are prereflectively aware that we are doing so, and this prereflective awareness is a structural feature of experience itself, part of the concurrent structure of any conscious process.

When I am engaged in intentional action, however, prereflective self-awareness may also involve a sense of agency (SA), which is conceptually distinct from SO (Gallagher 2000). SA can be defined as the prereflective experience that I am the one who is causing or generating a movement or action. In the case of involuntary movement, for example, if someone pushes me from behind, I experience the initial movement as something happening to me, as something that I am experiencing, and so have an experience of ownership for the movement. I do not claim that it is someone else who is moving, since I have an immediate sense that I am the one moving. At the same time, however, I can say that I have no experience of self-agency for this movement. I did not cause it; someone else pushed me. Accordingly, in the case of involuntary movement (as well as in reflex movement) SA and SO come apart. In the case of voluntary action, on the other hand, they seem tightly fitted and indistinguishable in prereflective experience.

Neuropsychologists have found this distinction useful for clarifying their studies of SO in perceptual illusions, for example, the Rubber Hand Illusion (e.g., Baum et al. 2022), and the loss of SA in schizophrenia (e.g., Kozáková et al. 2020). Experimenters have tried to identify the neural correlates for SA. Let's think again about involuntary movement. In the case of involuntary movement there is SO for the movement but no SA. The neuroscience suggests that awareness of my involuntary movement is generated in reafferent sensory feedback. In the case of involuntary movement there are no initial motor commands (no efferent signals). Thus, it seems possible that in both involuntary and voluntary movement SO is generated by sensory feedback, and that in the case of voluntary movement SA is generated by efferent signals (see Liesner, Hinz and Kunde 2021, for a recent review).

On this view SA is conceived as generated in neural processes related to motor control. But this may not be the whole story. SA, in addition to involving a sense of controlled embodied movement, also involves a sense of controlling events in the external world. We can distinguish phenomenologically between an experience of agency generated in motor control processes, and an experience of agency associated with perceptual monitoring of what one actually accomplishes by the action. Both these aspects, the *motor control aspect* (my sense that I am causing or controlling my bodily movement, linked to efferent processes), and the *intentional aspect* (my sense of what I accomplish, or fail to accomplish, by my action) enter into SA. Haggard (2005) confirms a consistency between the neuroscience and the phenomenology. That is, in both neuroscience and phenomenology one can find evidence for the same distinctions between SA taken as a sense of bodily control, and SA taken as a sense of controlling what one accomplishes in the world.

This distinction, however, has not always been clear in the experimental literature. For example, in an fMRI experiment designed to find the neural correlates of SA, subjects were asked to manipulate a joystick to drive a colored circle moving on a screen to specific locations on the screen (Farrer and Frith 2002). In some instances the subject causes this movement and in others the experimenter or computer does. The subject is asked to discriminate self-agency (when they feel they are in charge of the movement) and other-agency (when they feel the other person is in charge of the movement). Farrer and Frith, citing the distinction between SA and SO, associate SA with the intentional aspect of action, i.e., whether I am having some kind of effect with respect to the goal or intentional task (or what happens on the screen). When the subject reports having SA for the action on the screen, the anterior insula is activated bilaterally.

Although Farrer and Frith define SA as something tied to the intentional aspect of action rather than to mere bodily movement or motor control, when it comes to *explaining why* the anterior insula should be involved in generating SA, they frame the explanation entirely in terms of motor control. In the protocol of the experiment, and then in the explanation of the results, the distinction between the two aspects of SA (motor control *versus* intentional aspect) gets lost. In cases like this, phenomenology can be put to good use in clarifying this distinction and refining experimental design.

Phenomenologists can also show that there is more to SA than just the prereflective elements delineated here. In actions that involve reflective deliberation or retrospective evaluation, these more reflective aspects of action, which may also bring into play social norms and forces that are not reducible to processes confined to individual brains, may enter into the experience of agency (Gallagher 2010). In this regard, phenomenology tends to support a non-reductionist approach to the naturalistic study of human agency, regarding the sense of agency as complex – something that involves both prereflective and reflective aspects, and is influenced by social and cultural factors that may include race and gender.

The phenomenology of performance

How much detail can phenomenology explicate within the prereflective sense of agency? One might be able to make legitimate conceptual or theoretical distinctions between awareness of a goal, awareness of an intention to act, awareness of initiation of action, awareness of movements, sense of activity, sense of mental effort, sense of physical effort, sense of control, experience of authorship, experience of intentionality, experience of purposiveness, experience of freedom, and experience of mental causation.

(Pacherie 2007: 6)

The question is whether all these distinctions show up as such in one's actual first-order experience. Or whether they are simply the product of theoretical reflection on first-order experience?

The relationship between prereflective and reflective phenomenologies is explored in the study of skilled or expert performance. Dreyfus developed a well-known phenomenological analysis of expertise outlining the stages involved in achieving skilled performance (Dreyfus and Dreyfus 1980). A novice will be more aware of some of the details of her bodily movement than an expert performer (in music, dance, sports, etc.) who knows what to do without having to monitor her movements. On Dreyfus's account, engagement in embodied practice leads to habit formation to the point where acting does not require reflection or thought. Indeed, according to Dreyfus, reflective consciousness of one's action may disrupt the performance. Accordingly, he characterizes expert performance as 'mindless' and accompanied by very thin and undetailed senses of ownership and agency.[3]

More recently a number of theorists have argued against the Dreyfus view. Performance may be guided and even improved by varying degrees of reflective ability (e.g., Montero 2015). Performers can shift across the full register of reflective control and prereflective consciousness, improvising in some cases to adjust their attunement to changing conditions. In some cases, self-awareness during performance may be a prereflective, pragmatic, or performative self-awareness that does not take the body as an intentional object (Legrand 2007). One reason that performative or explicit forms of self-awareness can improve performance is due to the inaccuracy and the recessive nature of proprioception. Prereflective body awareness of posture and movement, based on proprioception and kinesthesia, may provide a general sense that I am sitting, or I am running, but it does not necessary include postural detail. "I may think I am keeping my head down when swinging a golf club, though an observer will easily see I do not. I may believe I am sitting straight when my back is rounded" (Shusterman 2008: 64). Training can improve one's performative awareness, and in this sense expert performance may involve more subtle, sophisticated, and detailed awareness of bodily comportment.

Affectivity

Although a good amount of the phenomenology of embodiment has focused on questions about motor control and action, bodily experience involves a rich set of affective processes that influence perception and cognition and generate interoception. Affectivity can be understood in a wide sense to include not just emotions, but a variety of bodily phenomena involving hunger/satiation, pain/pleasure, fatigue/high energy, etc. These are phenomena without which we would have a difficult time explaining passion, desire, and the motives that drive our actions and move us toward or away from one another. Affective phenomena also help to define individual perspective in cognitive processes. A broad spectrum of affective circumstances may be brought to bear on perception, judgment, memory, imagination, and so on.

Bodily affect, for example, significantly contributes to (either limiting or enabling) our contact with the world, our attentive outlook, our perceptual (including social perceptual) interests. Affect may or may not reach the threshold of conscious awareness. Consider the case of boredom (Heidegger 1995). Boredom is more than potentially related to action, in the case where we might try to overcome boredom. More importantly, boredom already modulates one's viewing or listening behavior, and it shows up in the way one arranges one's body, perhaps without even noticing, in a bored manner; or in the way one begins to fidget, widen one's eyes, give vent to an exasperated breath, etc. Such bodily expressions are moments of the affective phenomenon of boredom – part of the pattern of boredom that can be observed in bodily behavior. In boredom one finds oneself immediately embodying a certain stance towards one's situation, a pull that resonates with and perhaps already prepares, any further course of action.

Affect can motivate a sense of perceptual interest or investment, denoting a measure of the stakes or the costs involved in exchanges with one's environment. If perception involves the pragmatic 'I can' of affordances, one still might not feel 'up to the task,' or inclined to do the work it might involve. The task may be boring, or it may not be worth doing. These affective nuances shape my interest and the way that I experience the world. Affect is thus tightly interwoven with perception and action.[4]

Since we are flesh-and-blood creatures equipped with beating hearts, and since we are not brains in vats, we could point to many other examples of how the affective condition of the body shapes cognition.[5] Typically, our embodied condition does not reflect a simple, isolated affect—rather, our affective state is a mix of experiential factors. At the end of a long hike, for example, one's perception may be informed by a combination of hunger, pain, fatigue, troubled respiration, feelings of dirtiness, and the kinesthetic difficulty involved in climbing. At this point a mountain path will look steeper than after a good night's sleep. Having hiked up the mountain, my physical state may be felt as an over-whelming fatigue, or it may contribute to a feeling of deep satisfaction. Such affective aspects color my perception and more generally constrain my way of being in the world.

Conclusion

Phenomenology can point to a number of aspects of experience that demonstrate the embodied nature of cognition, including basic perceptual processes. Phenomenology can examine the explicitly reflective and the less explicit prereflective experiences of embodi-ment, but it can also point to those embodied processes that are more implicit, and in some cases non-conscious, but that nonetheless have an evidential effect on our perceptual and cognitive life. The phenomenological analyses of movement and action, self-consciousness, performance, intersubjectivity, and affect constitute only a limited number of issues in a broader range of embodied phenomena that are open to phenomenological investigation and confirmation in empirical scientific studies.

Notes

1 The 1930s and 1940s. In a central chapter of his *Phenomenology of Perception*, he introduces the concept of the body schema, which he finds in the work of Henry Head, and then famously reworks the concept by reinterpreting the case of Schneider, a brain-damaged patient treated by Kurt Goldstein.

2 For both Merleau-Ponty and Sartre, embodied processes of perception and action involve an important dimension of intersubjectivity. In this regard, Merleau-Ponty emphasized the notion of intercorporeity – a kind of intertwining of two embodied subjects in perceptual and interactive contact; a concept that supports more recent discussions of interaction in social cognition.

3 Although Dreyfus draws on Merleau-Ponty for the notion of a mindless absorbed coping, Merleau-Ponty actually defends the idea of a *minded* coping where the notion of mind is not the traditional disembodied notion, but rather an embodied mind. For him, mind and reason are not excluded from movement, but redefined as the expression of an embodied intelligence, somewhere between blind mechanism and explicit intellectual behavior (Merleau-Ponty 1963: 45).

4 Merleau-Ponty emphasized the role of affectivity in erotic perception, which, he contends, is always more than a *cogitatio*, representation, propositional attitude, or inference that links belief and behavior, and even more than an "I can" – it's rather a form of affective intentionality, which, as he suggests, brings to view 'the vital origins of perception' (2012: 158–160).

5 For example, we perceive features of the world according to whether we are fatigued or carrying weight (see, e.g., Proffitt et al. 2003). Hunger can shape, and perhaps even distort, judgment and rational decision. For example, whether a judge is hungry or satiated may play an important role her decisions about sentencing (Danziger et al. 2011).

References

Baum, K., Hackmann, J., Pakos, J., Kannen, K., Wiebe, A., Selaskowski, B., Pensel, M.C., Ettinger, U., Philipsen, A. and Braun, N. (2022) "Body transfer illusions in the schizophrenia spectrum: A systematic review," *Schizophrenia*, 8(1): 1–14.

Danziger, S., J. Levav, L. Avnaim-Pesso (2011) "Extraneous factors in judicial decisions," *PNAS* 108(17): 6889–6892.

Dreyfus, H. (2000) "Could anything be more intelligible than everyday intelligibility?" in J. Faulconer and M. Wrathall (eds), *Appropriating Heidegger*, Cambridge: Cambridge University Press, pp. 155–170.

Dreyfus, S. E. and Dreyfus, H. L. (1980) *A five-stage model of the mental activities involved in directed skill acquisition*, California University, Berkeley, Operations Research Center.

Fanon, F. (1986) *Black Skin, White Masks*, trans. C. L. Markmann, London: Pluto Press.

Farrer, C. and Frith, C.D. (2002) "Experiencing oneself vs. another person as being the cause of an action: the neural correlates of the experience of agency," *NeuroImage* 15: 596–603.

Gallagher, S. (2010) "Multiple aspects of agency," *New Ideas in Psychology* 30: 15–31.

——— (2000) "Philosophical conceptions of the self: implications for cognitive science," *Trends in Cognitive Science* 4(1): 14–21.

Gibson, J. J. (1979) *The Ecological Approach to Visual Perception*, Boston: Houghton-Mifflin.

Haggard, P. (2005) "Conscious intention and motor cognition," *Trends in Cognitive Sciences* 9(6): 290–295.

Heidegger, M. (1995) *The Fundamental Concepts of Metaphysics*, trans. W. McNeill and N. Walker, Bloomington: Indiana University Press.

——— (1962) *Being and Time*, trans. by J. Macquarrie and E. Robinson, London: SCM.

Husserl, E. (1997) *Thing and Space: Lectures of 1907*, trans. R. Rojcewicz, Dordrecht: Kluwer Academic Publishers.

——— (1989) *Ideas Pertaining to a Pure Phenomenology and to a Phenomenological Philosophy. Second Book*, trans. R. Rojcewicz and A. Schuwer. Dordrecht: Kluwer Academic Publishers.

Kozáková, E., Bakštein, E., Havlíček, O., Bečev, O., Knytl, P., Zaytseva, Y. and Španiel, F. (2020) "Disrupted sense of agency as a state marker of first-episode schizophrenia," *Frontiers in Psychiatry* 11: 570570.

Legrand, D. (2007) "Pre-reflective self-consciousness: On being bodily in the world," *Janus Head*, 9(2): 493–519.

Liesner, M., Hinz, N.-A. and Kunde, W. (2021) "How action shapes body ownership momentarily and throughout the lifespan," *Frontiers Human Neuroscience* 15: 697810.

Melzack, R. (1990) "Phantom limbs and the concept of a neuromatrix," *Trends in Neuroscience*, 13: 88–92.

Merleau-Ponty, M. (2012) *Phenomenology of Perception*, trans. D. A. Landes, New York: Routledge.
⸻ (1963) *The Structure of Behavior*, trans. A. L. Fisher, Pittsburgh: Duquesne University Press.
Montero, B. (2015) "Thinking in the zone: The expert mind in action," *The Southern Journal of Philosophy* 53: 126–140.
Pacherie, E. (2007) "The sense of control and the sense of agency," *Psyche* 13(1): np.
Proffitt, D., J. Stefanucci, T. Banton, and W. Epstein (2003) "The role of effort in perceiving distance," *Psychological Science* 14(2): 106–112.
Sartre, J.-P. (1956) *Being and Nothingness: An Essay on Phenomenological Ontology*, trans. H. E. Barnes, New York: Philosophical Library.
Shusterman, R. (2008) *Body Consciousness: A Philosophy of Mindfulness and Somaesthetics*, Cambridge: Cambridge University Press.
Young, I. M. (1980) "Throwing like a girl: A phenomenology of feminine body comportment, motility and spatiality" *Human Studies* 3(2): 137–156.

Further reading

De Jaegher, H., Di Paolo, E. and Gallagher, S. (2010). "Does social interaction constitute social cognition?" *Trends in Cognitive Sciences* 14(10): 441–447 – explicates an enactive approach to intersubjectivity drawing on Merleau-Ponty. Dreyfus, H. (2002). "Intelligence without representation – Merleau-Ponty's critique of mental representation," *Phenomenology and the Cognitive Sciences* 1: 367–383 – Dreyfus's interpretation of Merleau-Ponty on skilled performance. Dreyfus, H. (1973). *What Computers Can't Do*, New York: Cambridge, MA: MIT Press – classic work developing a phenomenological critique of AI. Gallagher, S. (2005). *How the Body Shapes the Mind*, New York: Oxford University Press, a phenomenological approach to embodied cognition. Gallagher, S. (2020). *Action and Interaction*. Oxford: Oxford University Press – a phenomenological-enactive explanation of action and intersubjective/social interaction.
Gallagher, S. and Zahavi, D. (2020). *The Phenomenological Mind*, 3rd ed. London: Routledge – a work that explores issues in philosophy of mind and cognitive science from a phenomenological perspective. Kelly, S. D. (2004). Merleau-Ponty on the Body. In M. Proudfoot, ed. *The Philosophy of the Body*, 62–76. London: Blackwell – an exploration of sensory-motor processes from the perspective of Merleau-Ponty. Thompson, E. (2007). *Mind in Life: Biology, Phenomenology, and the Sciences of Mind*, Cambridge, MA: Harvard University Press – an explication of enactivist philosophy informed by phenomenology. Varela, F., E. Thompson, and E. Rosch (1991). *The Embodied Mind: Cognitive Science and Human Experience*, Cambridge, MA: MIT Press – a classic text on embodied and enactive views highly informed by phenomenology.

2

A TEN COMMANDMENTS FOR ECOLOGICAL PSYCHOLOGY

Claire F. Michaels and Zsolt Palatinus

The ecological approach to perception and action evolved in the 1950s and 1960s, and major principles had been outlined by the time of the publication of J. J. Gibson's *The Senses Considered as Perceptual Systems* in 1966: ecological optics, invariants, exploration, direct perception, affordances, the education of attention, and the intimacies of perception and action, and of organism and environment, to name a few. In the intervening half century, these concepts have been experimented on and elaborated, and three new, related emphases have gained prominence: a concern with the coordination of action, adoption of the dynamical systems perspective, and embrace of what has been termed *physical psychology*, the attempt to make psychology continuous with physical science. Ecological psychology is arguably the original embedded, embodied cognition, so as the field that bears those names moves forward, the ecological approach should remain a valuable touchstone for evaluating principles, concepts, and theories.

In this chapter, we express the various historical and modern threads of ecological psychology as ten commandments. Obviously there are no 'official' ten commandments that serve as the final authority for evaluating constructs or tools. The ones presented here are the result of a self-imposed intellectual exercise. It is with mixed feelings that we adopt the label 'ten commandments.' The danger is that it will bolster the view held by some that ecological psychologists—Gibsonians—are more like religious fanatics than the conservative, open-minded scientists that we are. We brave that danger to make the point that just as observant Jews and Christians ought not pick and choose which commandments they follow, advocates of ecological psychology (or of genuinely embedded and embodied cognitive science) should see our commandments as a package deal. Some psychologists select their principles and concepts cafeteria-style, adopting ideas they like and leaving others behind, and even declare that being eclectic is a virtue. Unfortunately, the major principles of ecological psychology are deeply connected and intertwined. To subscribe to some and discard the others always entails contradiction.

There are two more preliminaries before the enumeration begins. First, note that the chapter is global and intuitive, rather than detailed and precise. It would take several hundred pages to include details, cite relevant research, and identify variations on themes.

DOI: 10.4324/9781003322511-4

Second, we will use the outfielder problem to illustrate various ideas, so we start with presenting the problem, which also can serve as a quick diagnostic test of how ecological one is.

The outfielder problem

The outfielder problem—how a centerfielder, say, can catch a ball that is hit precisely in the sagittal plane—brings home various emphases in the ecological approach. Assuming that the problem and its solution are not too old hat, trying to formulate a solution is a useful diagnostic tool for identifying one's own (perhaps tacit) theories of perception and or action. We ask the reader to submit to this test: think through how you believe the outfielder gets to the right place at the right time to catch the ball. We can keep it simple: one-eyed and deaf outfielders can catch balls, and at 100 meters, optical expansion of the image of a just-hit baseball is below threshold. Go!

The usual response is that the outfielder perceives the initial part of the trajectory, extrapolates that trajectory to estimate the time and place of the upcoming landing, and runs to that place by that time. The explanatory details vary from person to person: about the optical pattern that informs the perception of early trajectory, for example, or about how extrapolation operates (e.g., what is stored in memory and how the right trajectory is recognized or computed). If accounting for these details becomes the scientist's goal, the enumerated steps (information detection, pattern recognition, extrapolation, and action planning) become *the* constructs and processes that the theorist tries to embed and embody. However, as we shall see, it would already be too late to come to a good understanding of catching. Notice a few things about the account. The problems of perception and action are handled separately and sequentially, with the perceptual intermediaries including perceived trajectory, perceived (extrapolated, or inferred) landing time and landing place. Further, the to-be-perceived quantities dictate the kind of optical information one should look for—presumably the catcher needs information about both spatial and temporal components.

A more ecological solution to the outfielder problem—and for current purposes, we lump a number of related theories together—is that outfielders do not perceive trajectories, make predictions about when and where, and then act. Instead they run in such a way as to create an appropriate optical pattern. For example, the Chapman strategy (1968) proposes that a fielder runs so as to keep the rate of change of the tangent of the optical angle of the ball constant. The goal, to oversimplify, is to bring optical acceleration to zero and keep it there. This strategy puts the eye and the ball on intersecting paths; the catcher gets to the right place at the right time without perceiving the trajectory, or knowing either the time or place of intersection.

With these preliminaries in place, we now work through the major points of ecological science, organized into an admittedly arbitrarily ten commandments.

Commandment 1: Thou shalt not separate organism and environment

Historically, psychology and philosophy have treated the skin as the boundary of their territory and thereby embraced an organism-environment (O-E) dualism. In O-E dualism, things inside the skin constitute one domain and things outside the skin another, and the two domains are approached independently. The alternative, ecological view is O-E mutuality—the O-E system is taken as the minimal unit of analysis in the behavioral and cognitive sciences and ought not to be disjointed into separate areas of inquiry.

One consequence of emphasizing O-E mutuality is for ontology. A characterization of the environment that is not mindful of the organism is left to classical physicists and is therefore defined and measured with the metrics of physics. Take the approaching fly ball. It has diameter, mass, velocity, spin, drag, etc., can be located in Cartesian coordinates of space and time, and captured by Newtonian laws. Thus, anticipating a landing location requires either that the perceiver matches an input trajectory with stored trajectories, or applies some algorithm that approximates the physical laws. If, on the other hand, one attends to the O-E (catcher-ball) relation, problem and solution come together: the relevant optical information specifies how to modulate running so as to create and maintain a catcher-ball relation that puts them on a collision course.

Just as mid-twentieth-century biologists described and measured the environment as a home for life, ecological psychologists describe and measure the environment as a home for perceiving and acting. And just as we appreciate that ecologists' niches, dens, predators, and so forth constitute a bona fide ontology—real (objective, measurable) things that constitute the environment—so too are ecological psychologists' measurements of the environment (e.,g. affordances); for both, the characteristics of the organism shape the property of the environment.

A number of key ecological concepts follow in whole or in part from the tenet of O-E mutuality. One is *affordances*, the possibilities for action that can be engaged in with respect to some object, event, place, etc. These are, as noted above, organism-referential properties of the environment, and because of that they have 'ready-made' meaning. *Information*, too, is radically altered by a commitment to O-E mutuality. Descriptions and measurements of the energy patterns detected in perception are wrested from physics. Physical optics is replaced by ecological optics; physical acoustics is replaced by ecological acoustics, etc. The optical and acoustical structures relevant to perception and action cannot be captured in a one-size-fits-all description.

The new emphasis on environmental properties such as affordances does not mean that they are driving the show, as seems to be the inference that some thinkers draw when they liken ecological theory to behaviorism. Behaviorism did not at all respect O-E mutuality; it respected the skin boundary and sought explanations from the outside. As we shall see later, the ecological approach holds that intentions are central determinants of what is perceived and acted on.

Commandment 2: Thou shall not take the name information in vain

The term *information* serves many masters in science and engineering, but ecological psychology singles out a particular meaning and uses it in this restrictive sense. Information is a pattern in space and time that specifies a state of affairs of the O-E system. By 'specifies' is meant 'relates to uniquely' or 'relates to 1:1.' Specificity is an ecological, not a mathematical, concept; information is specific in the context of the O-E system. This means that information depends on global constraints (natural laws) and local constraints and circumstances. As an example, the law of universal gravitation captures the relation between masses, distances, and attractive force. The circumstances of the earth's mass and radius entail that a dropped object will accelerate at 9.8 meters/second per second. This local constraint, in turn, entails that in the optic array structured by the dropped object, the size and distance of the object, and its surrounds are specified. Local constraints contrived by a social and linguistic community can similarly constitute a basis for specification.

In addition to information-environment specificity, there is a second important specificity relation—that between perception and information. These two specificity relations together entail that perception is direct: because information is specific to an environmental state of affairs and perception is specific to the information, perception is specific to the environmental state of affairs – that is, direct.

Gibson's concept of information was a radical departure from the assumption of perception theorists from the Greeks through Helmholtz, Wundt, Titchener, the Gestaltists, and their modern counterparts in cognitive (neuro)science. The Helmholtzean view assumes that the information to the senses is non-specifying—indeed, impoverished—and, therefore, requires that the perceiver engage in computational, comparative, and memorial processes that serve to embellish the input.

Commandment 3: Thou shalt regard perception as the detection of information

This commandment is another way of formalizing and emphasizing the point just made that perception is specific to information. The premise is simple: if information patterns specify the objects and events, then perception of those objects and events is simply a matter of detecting the information. The scientist who wants to understand perception of some property hypothesizes a candidate information variable and asks whether that variable accounts for the systematic variance in reports about perception. Given the apparent detection of a variable, one could then ask how detection is embodied, that is, how tissue might be arranged (by evolution or by learning) such that it detects or resonates to that information, in analogy to how an antenna might be transparent to certain wavelengths of electromagnetic energy but not to others, and how neural firing might resonate to the information, in analogy to a radio.

If a candidate variable does not account for the variance in reports or actions, it is rejected and the search for a successful candidate continues: failure of a variable is simply that; it is not disproof of direct perception. Relatedly, conclusions about the success of a variable should always be tentative. The "real" information might be a covariate of the successful candidate. Even so, there is never proof that felicitous perception or action hasn't been achieved by virtue of computational and memorial processes. Dismissing this latter, conventional view must depend on other considerations, such as parsimony and which account has fewer unpaid loans of intelligence. In the ecological view, representation, calculation, comparison, and storage constitute such loans.

One might well ask why one variable and not some other is detected. This is by definition the realm of attention. How attention changes in learning is considered later, in commandment 10.

Commandment 4: Thou shalt not compute

The paradigmatic disembodied, unembedded device is the digital computer, which has served as a metaphor for a cognitive agent since the 1950s when flow charts were used to capture attentional and memorial processes. In distinguishing algorithmic and implementation levels, Marr (1982) sealed the deal on the legitimacy of disembodied computation. In the 1990s and 2000s, concern has shifted over to neurally embodied computation, but the computer metaphor—baldly, the consensual view of what the brain does—persists.

The alternative to a storage/comparison/computational metaphor is Runeson's (1977) *smart perceptual device*. A smart perceptual device detects information; it does not detect low-level stimulus properties and from them compute other properties, or embellish them with additional information from memory. Runeson offered the planimeter as a metaphor to make the idea of a smart perceptual device more intuitive. The planimeter is a simple machine consisting of a fixed point, two jointed arms, and a calibrated wheel. The fixed point is planted, and the end of the distal arm is traced around the perimeter of a regular or irregular figure, causing the wheel to roll and skid. The difference between the readings on the wheel before and after the tracing specifies the area circumscribed by the perimeter. So for a rectangle, one could put the wheel to zero, trace the perimeter, and read off the area. Seeing that the wheel indicates area, and given the conventional understanding that the area of a rectangle is the product of height and width, one might assume that the device measured the lengths, and multiplied. The construction of the planimeter, however, renders the outcome of the measuring act—tracing the perimeter—specific to area. The analogous expectation for a living system is that tissue is arranged (or, as we shall see later, rearranged) in a way that constitutes a smart device to register information.

Commandment 5: Thou shalt not separate perception and action

What is perception for? Michael Turvey (1977) argued that perception served the needs of the action system. This view followed 150 years of concern with perception itself and relative inattention to action. More generally, he charged the psychological community to ask how action is coordinated, which, he claimed, was every bit as theoretically rich and worthy of study as perception. The research community (though arguably not the teaching community) has risen to Turvey's challenges, and issues of coordination and perception-action relations are now heavily investigated.

The concept of affordances already reflects the intimacy of perception and action. Organisms perceive actions that they can enter into with respect to other organisms, objects, events, and places. Affordances, however, are only part of the perception-action story. Two other aspects deserve mention. One is exploration: perceivers engage in a variety of acts that make information available—looking, sniffing, savoring—but it is the haptic sense that most obviously depends on exploratory movements, such as palpating, rubbing, hefting, wielding, etc. Second, performatory actions also reveal information appropriate for their own guidance. This is illustrated once again in fly-ball catching. Recall that the rate of change of the tangent of the optical angle of horizon and ball specifies whether the catcher's velocity is appropriate to guarantee intersection of the eye and ball trajectories, and thus the bodily acceleration needed. Accelerating forward in response to optical deceleration decreases that deceleration. When the optical deceleration is nulled, the eye and ball will be on intersecting trajectories. Optics structured by an act can serve to refine it.

Commandment 6: Thou shalt have only one science before thee

What ought to be the relation between psychology and physical science? Are the phenomena of living and behaving systems so different from the phenomena of non-living and non-behaving systems that their respective sciences overlap little or not at all? The growing ecological view is more consonant with Iberall's dictum: "There is either one science or there is none." This commandment and the next two briefly address a scattering of themes that illustrate the idea of *physical psychology*, a budding discipline that exploits existing physical law and, where necessary, tries to crank up physical law to handle the phenomena of living and knowing. It emphatically does not try to crank *down* (reduce) the phenomena to a level that renders them explicable with physical law. One of the promising places to find lawfulness relevant for psychology is in the physics of self-organization.

One can think of scientific psychology as having the aim to explain the origins of the *patterns* over space and time that are manifested in experience and behavior: a sentence, guiding a car through traffic, a dance, groupings of Gestalt figures, groupings of people, personalities, seeing or recognizing a face, organization in recall—and the list goes on. We cannot think of an explanandum in psychology that is not some sort of pattern. There are three possible origins of patterns: other patterns, plans (algorithms, recipes, and blueprints), and self-organization. Only the last of these does not beg the question of origins. Using principles of self-organization to move one's science forward is difficult. First, one needs to emphasize the dynamics of a system, its evolution over time. States and statistics computed about states will not do the job. One needs to capture changes in states. Second, one can look at how patterns arise in self-organizing physical systems, and ask whether the same or analogous processes are observed at the behavioral level. The paradigmatic example is that the same principles that capture the coupling of neighboring pendulums also capture inter-limb coordination in humans, as when a person oscillates two fingers (Haken, Kelso, and Bunz 1985). In both cases, only certain phase relations are stable. While the two coupling phenomena differ in a number of ways (e.g., mechanical vs. informational coupling), does one really need a new set of natural laws to explain the tendency for two fingers or limbs to oscillate in unison? And if it turns out that the limbs of two people show the same attraction (as it has turned out), does one need yet another natural law to explain the social version of the phenomenon? Instead, one ecological tack is to seek analogous phenomena in the physical world and to exploit the laws that explain them.

Commandment 7: Thou shalt not steal intelligence

The prior patterns and plans mentioned above as origins of to-be-explained patterns are obviously pure cheats as explanations; they just pass the buck. Less obvious are the theoretical concepts that ought to be considered members of this class of explanations: memory (representations) as the basis of recall and recognition, motor programs as the basis of coordination, priors in Bayesian learning, brain structures and firing patterns as the basis of patterns at the cognitive and behavioral levels, and so forth. Dennett (1978) used the term *loans of intelligence* to identify unaccounted-for knowledge that is needed to make cognitive systems work, but he was too nice. *Loan* connotes that it is understood as such, but it is usually the case that there is no acknowledgment either that the explanation is empty until the loan is repaid, or that repayment is even necessary. Until one can explain how the pre-existing pattern or recipe arose, the putative explanation is just a scientific shell game.

Commandment 8: Thou shalt honor, exploit, and enlarge physical law

The careful expansion of physics needed to handle knowing and acting is exactly what Shaw and his colleagues are doing in *intentional dynamics* (e.g., Shaw and Kinsella-Shaw, 1988). Concepts in physics are generalized and enlarged to include intention and information (in the specificational sense). And just as physical dynamics captures constraints on the propagation of the path of a particle in space-time, intentional dynamics captures constraints, including intentional and informational constraints, on the propagation of an animal's path to a goal.

Ecological psychologists are sometimes charged with ignoring intention, and organism-based constraints, in general. In fact, ecological psychologists have had much to say about intention, though here there is only space for outlines and suggestions for important resources. First, one needs to distinguish the role intention plays from the origin of intention. As to the former, intentions are "exceptional boundary conditions" on the operation of physical laws (Kugler and Turvey, 1987). An intention harnesses a perceptual system to detect information appropriate to guide the deployment of metabolic resources. For the outfielder, the intention to catch a fly ball, for example, sets up the perception-action system in such a way that optical acceleration continually informs the deployment of metabolic resources to create forces at the foot that yield anterior or posterior locomotor acceleration. The intention to escape a lobbed grenade would entail other set-ups.

The origins of intention are more of a puzzle, but for us the best to-be-exploited insights derive from Iberall's concept of action modes (e.g., Iberall and McCulloch, 1969). Iberall argued that living systems comprise a small collection of limit-cycle oscillators that require a squirt of energy at regular, though not fixed, intervals. An organism needs to forage, eat, sleep, void, mate, etc. Each of these oscillators is marginally stable, and the winding down of a particular oscillator invites goal selection to restore the oscillation's amplitude. Our image of this is a juggler spinning an array of plates on sticks. As the rotational velocity of one plate decreases and it begins to wobble, the juggler must inject energy. The juggler thereby moves though a space of attractors whose strengths reflect current stability levels. These individual action cycles, together with the thermodynamic principles that capture their origins and maintenance, suggest where we might have to work to pay the cost of having intention play more than a descriptive, vitalistic role in science.

A closely related gambit of physical psychology and one that also has origins in thermodynamics is Iberall and Soodak's (1987) claim that the same (non-linear) laws apply at many scales. When there is flow through a system (e.g., heat through a pan of spaghetti, water through a pipe, people evacuating a building or migrating across a continent, capital flowing through an economy) and the flow is higher than can diffuse through the medium, structures arise that increase the flow. A generalized Reynolds number predicts how the various patterns (convection cells, eddies, cliques, cities, wealth) arise. Nobody thinks that using these tools is easy, but surely it is a better way to start than by begging the question or proliferating whole sciences to explain patterns at each level. Honoring, exploiting, and enlarging physical law as it applies to behavioral and cognitive phenomena is, we think, a more promising strategy.

Commandment 9: Thou shalt not make unto thee any mental image or likeness of anything

As noted earlier, philosophy and psychology have separated organism and environment and erected barriers between them (e.g., impoverished stimuli). For contact to be had with the environment, it had to be recreated (represented) in the brain or mind. Also deemed inexistent is the past, so the only means by which it can affect perception and action is also to have remnants of it stored away for later use. While philosophers have already acknowledged that some processes are less representation-hungry than others (Clark, 1997), the ecological commitment is to stand its ground: no representations, period.

The ecological take is that both perceptual and memorial representations are solutions to pseudo-problems arising from philosophical assumptions. Instead, perception is of the world—that is, direct—and learning does not involve storage. Certainly in the English lexicon the terms learning and memory go hand in hand, but we ought not to let language dictate theoretical entities. Is there some better way to understand the benefits of experience?

Michaels and Carello (1981, p. 78) tried to drive a wedge between learning and memory using an evolutionary metaphor: think of learning as we think of evolution.

> If it is assumed that evolution leads to a *new* biological machine that is better suited anatomically and physiologically to the environment than its predecessors or extinct cousins, we might also assume that personal experiences lead to a new machine that is better suited to its particular, personal environment. It is better able to detect the environment's affordances. In this analysis, the consequence of personal experience is not that the old animal has new knowledge, but *that it is a new animal that knows better.*

It's time to graduate to an appreciation that the function of sensory and neural systems is to modulate animal actions at multiple timescales, in the case of humans, from milliseconds to decades. The fact that a clock might register an interval—even a long interval—between an environmental event and the subsequent modulation of behavior is no cause for panic.

The temporal evolution of any system—living or non-living, knowing or unknowing—is to be captured by laws and circumstances. This simple fact helps clarify a distinction between ecological and non-ecological approaches. Non-ecological approaches are inclined to emphasize circumstances over lawfulness: the current state of the brain or of cognitive structures—circumstances—serves as the primary explanation of phenomena. With this comes the view that the scientist's work ends with an account of circumstances that explains the variance in those phenomena. The ecological view is arguably more law-based, taking a longer view of the dynamics of cognition. Circumstances still play a critical role for the ecological approach. For example, we noted that information can derive specificity from terrestrial characteristics, but there is far more emphasis on uncovering a basis in natural law, for example, how surfaces structure light by reflection, how oscillators couple, or how flow through a system creates structure. In the final, upcoming commandment, we consider how lawfulness over a long timescale offers a different approach to learning than does storage.

Commandment 10: Thou shalt change with experience

The alternative to the thesis that experience yields representations is that experience yields change—a different way of doing things. This final commandment addresses how that might happen.

E. J. and J. J. Gibson used the terms *differentiation* and *the education of attention* to capture learning, and E. J. Gibson devoted her distinguished career to addressing learning and development (E. J. Gibson, 1969). Differentiation was understood as becoming more able to distinguish among similar things. It involved detecting dimensions of difference, and becoming more attentive to distinctive features. Emphasizing such dissociation during the heyday of associationism, where meaning came from connecting things, created a storm of criticism, and a legendary battle ensued over 'enrichment' theory. As forcefully as she argued against traditional views, E. J. Gibson's approach to learning, with its emphasis on features and its inclusion of representations, arguably did not do justice to J. J. Gibson's concept of information and to his theory of information pickup (as articulated in Chapter 13 of J. J. Gibson, 1966).

Jacobs and Michaels (2007) have tried their hand at elaborating a theory arguably more consistent with J. J. Gibson's view; they termed it *direct learning*. Direct learning is in some ways at odds with the third commandment—that perceivers always exploit specifying information. This departure was motivated by observations that sometimes more variance in novice perceivers' judgments is accounted for by non-specifying variables than by a specifying variable (see, e.g., Gilden and Proffitt, 1989). Indeed, Jacobs and Michaels (2007) proposed that perceivers in novel situations are likely to use such variables on their way to direct perception. So what was needed was a theory that explains how perceivers come to use specifying information. The theory does not abandon specificity, but invokes it at the level of learning rather than perception. While direct learning is not mainstream ecological theory, it is included here because it illustrates in a simple way, we hope, ecological concepts that have been continual sticking points for psychologists and philosophers: learning without storage, representation, or memory.

Three ideas constitute the core of direct learning. The first is the concept of *information space*, which is said to comprise all the information variables that perceiver-actors might use in some task. Loci in the space differ in how well they constrain perception or action to be appropriate: some are good; some are not so good. These information spaces are local; they are structured by both global and local constraints. Information space replaces ecological psychology's single, specifying invariant as the informational basis for some perception or action. The second core idea is that at any point in time (i.e., on the shortest timescale) a perceiver uses information identified by some locus in the space; systematic variance in perception (or action) is accounted for by this variable. We sometimes say that a perceiver 'occupies' a locus. Third, learning is understood as movement through the space, where the movement is guided by longer-timescale information—*information-for-learning* (to distinguish it from *information-for-perception* or *-action*). Information-for-learning is hypothesized to be specificational; it directs the learner from the currently occupied locus in information space to the most useful locus. Thus, direct learning surrenders veridical perception in the short term in favor of veridical perception in the long term. Again, the overarching theme is that information alters and improves the fit of situations and actions at many timescales.

To gain some intuition about how this longer-timescale information operates, consider how learning might proceed in a dynamic touch paradigm. A perceiver wields an unseen rod behind a curtain and is asked to report how long it is, which is followed by feedback on actual length. Previous research showed that two moments of inertia were relevant to this judgment. Michaels and colleagues (Michaels, Arzamarski, Isenhower, and Jacobs, 2008) created a one-dimensional space of these variables ranging from complete reliance on one moment of inertia to complete reliance on the other, with their products and ratios occupying loci on the line. One area permitted excellent performance; other areas permitted poorer performance. We found that perceivers often started at suboptimal loci and moved toward more useful loci. We derived a candidate information-for-learning variable—the correlation between the error (reported length–actual length) and the mass of the wielded object. Using information at different loci in the space yielded errors that correlate differently with mass, and those correlations, represented as a vector field in the space, pointed to the optimal. The vector field constitutes an existence proof that information useful for directing change in information use is available at a locus (i.e., does not require comparison of neighboring loci). While one might counter that traditional cue combination could achieve the same changes as were observed in Michaels et al.'s (2008) participants, analysis of exploratory movements revealed that perceivers learned to 'combine' the inertial moments differently by wielding the rods differently. They learned how to explore so as to detect the optimal information for the task.

In addition to direct learning's success in a number of dynamic touch tasks, the approach has been applied to visual perception of kinetic properties, and to pole balancing. Importantly, the regularities on which the specificity of information-for-learning rest are not limited to those captured by natural law, but include circumstantial and social conventions. This more general view of the constraints that permit specificity and how they act on multiple scales should expand the range of applicability of the ecological approach.

Summary and conclusions

Ten do's and don'ts have been outlined. In many ways, they can be distilled down to one: respect the integrity of the system under investigation; it cannot be indiscriminately decomposed into parts. The backdrop is that the so-called parts depend for their nature and function on the other parts. While it may make sense to take a clock apart, describe the parts, and assess their functions and interrelations, the same cannot be said of living and knowing systems. If one nevertheless persists in decomposition, then the task is to re-embody the part or parts and re-embed them in a context. These endeavors are not necessary tasks for cognitive science; they are paying for one's mistakes. Our ten commandments are meant to promote a more unitary view, both of the organism–environment system and of the natural science with which we study it.

References

Chapman, S. (1968). Catching a baseball. *American Journal of Physics, 36*, 868–870.

Clark, A. (1997). *Being there*, Cambridge, MA: MIT Press.

Dennett, D. I. (1978). *Brainstorms: Philosophical essays on mind and psychology*, Montgomery, VT: Bradford Books.

Gibson, E. J. (1969). *Principles of perceptual learning and development.* New York: Appleton-Century-Crofts.

Gibson, J. J. (1966). *The senses considered as perceptual systems.* New York: Houghton-Mifflin.

Gilden, D. L., and Proffitt, D. R. (1989). Understanding collision dynamics. *Journal of Experimental Psychology: Human Perception and Performance, 15*, 372–383.

Haken, H., Kelso, J. A. S., and Bunz, H. (1985). A theoretical model of phase transitions in human hand movements. *Biological Cybernetics, 51*, 347–356.

Iberall, A. S., and McCulloch, W. S. (1969). The organizing principle of complex living systems. *Journal of Basic Engineering, 19*, 290–294.

Iberall, A. S., and Soodak, H. (1987). The physics of complex systems. In F. E. Yates (Ed.), *Self-organizing systems: The emergence of order* (pp. 521–540). New York: Plenum.

Jacobs, D. M., and Michaels, C. F. (2007). Direct-learning. *Ecological Psychology, 19*, 321–349.

Kugler, P. N., and Turvey, M. T. (1987). *Information, natural law, and the self-assembly of rhythmic movement.* Hillsdale, NJ: Erlbaum.

Marr, D. (1982). *Vision.* Cambridge, MA: MIT Press.

Michaels, C. F., Arzamarski, R., Isenhower, R., and Jacobs, D. M. (2008). Direct learning in dynamic touch. *Journal of Experimental Psychology: Human Perception and Performance, 34*(4), 944–957.

Michaels, C. F., and Carello, C. (1981). *Direct perception.* Englewood Cliffs, NJ: Prentice-Hall.

Runeson, S. (1977). On the possibility of "smart" perceptual mechanisms. *Scandinavian Journal of Psychology, 18,* 172–179.

Shaw, R., and Kinsella-Shaw, J. (1988). Ecological mechanics: A physical geometry for intentional constraints. *Human Movement Sciences, 7,* 155–200.

Turvey, M. T. (1977). Preliminaries to a theory of action with reference to vision. In R. E. Shaw and J. Bransford (Eds.), *Perceiving, acting, and knowing* (pp. 211–265). Hillsdale, NJ: Erlbaum.

Further reading

A. Chemero, *Radical embodied cognitive science* (Cambridge, MA: MIT Press, 2009) (an informed, philosophical consideration of the ecological approach to cognitive science); and M. J. Richardson, K. Shockley, B. R. Fajen, M. A. Richardson, and M. T. Turvey, "Ecological psychology: Six principles for an embodied-embedded approach to behavior," in P. Calvo and T. Gomila (Eds), *Handbook of cognitive psychology: An embedded approach* (New York: Elsevier, 2008), pp. 161–87 (an extended treatment of the implications of ecological psychology for embedded, embodied cognition).

PART 2

Perspectives on Embodied Cognition

3

FIRST-ORDER EMBODIMENT, SECOND-ORDER EMBODIMENT, THIRD-ORDER EMBODIMENT

Thomas Metzinger

Introduction: the self grounding problem

This chapter focuses on the relationship between embodiment and the phenomenology of selfhood. Specifically, it looks at the notion of *minimal phenomenal selfhood* (MPS; see pp. 000–00, below), which defines the research target of isolating the minimal set of conditions constituting the conscious experience of "being a self," relative to a given class of systems. In preparation, I will introduce three new working concepts: "first-order embodiment" (1E), "second-order embodiment" (2E), and "third-order embodiment" (3E).[1] Each of these concepts picks out a rather well-defined class of systems: 1E systems are reactive, adaptive systems, achieving intelligent behavior without explicit computation; 2E systems increase their level of causal self-control by explicitly and holistically representing themselves *as* embodied; and 3E systems integrate certain aspects of their body model into a unified ontology, thereby elevating them to the level of conscious experience. A normal, conscious human being walking down the street in an ordinary, non-pathological state of consciousness is a member of all three classes at the same time. This may be interestingly different, or not true at all, in certain alternative configurations like dreamless sleep, epileptic absence seizures, dreaming, or experimentally induced full-body illusions (FBIs) (Metzinger, 2013b). Here, my goal lies in drawing attention to a new version of the mind-body problem: How, precisely, do we describe the *grounding relations* holding between 1E, 2E, and 3E? In analogy to the "symbol grounding problem" one might also call this the "self grounding problem" (Harnad, 1990; Barsalou, 2008). It is the problem of describing the abstract computational principles as well as the implementational mechanics by which a system's phenomenal self-model (PSM; cf. Metzinger, 2003a, 2007) is anchored in low-level physical dynamics, in a maximally parsimonious way, and without assuming a single, central module for global self-representation.

1E, 2E, and 3E

First-order embodiment can be found, for instance, in bio-robotics and in all "bottom-up approaches" to artificial intelligence. Conceptually, this class of systems can be defined on

DOI: 10.4324/9781003322511-6

a microfunctionalist or dynamicist level of description (Clark, 1993; Chemero, 2009). The basic idea is to investigate how intelligent behavior and other complex system properties, which we previously termed "mental," can naturally evolve out of the dynamical, self-organizing interactions between the environment and a purely physical, reactive system that does not possess anything like a central processor, "software," or explicit computation of the different behaviors. Here, a leading theoretical intuition is that explicit representation is not necessary to generate complex forms of behavior, because the "the body is its own best model" (Brooks, 1991) and behaviors may emerge from the cooperation of low-level procedures, including properties of the environment. For research aimed at 1E, the relevant questions are: How was it possible for the very first forms of pre-rational intelligence to emerge in a physical universe? How could we *acquire* a flexible, evolvable, and coherent behavioral profile in the course of natural evolution? How is it possible to gradually generate intelligent behavior without explicit computation?

Second-order embodiment means that a system *represents* itself as embodied. Conceptually, this class of systems is picked out on the representationalist level of description because the emergence of 2E is determined by *representational* properties, namely, the possession of a body model. Second-order embodiment is a property that can be ascribed to any system that satisfies the following three conditions: first, we can successfully understand the intelligence of its behavior and other seemingly "mental" properties by describing it as a *representational* system; second, this system has a single, explicit, and coherent self-representation of itself *as being an embodied agent*; and, third, the way in which this system *uses* this explicit internal model of itself as an entity possessing and controlling a body helps us understand its intelligence and its psychology in functional terms. Typically, an unconscious body schema used in motor control could serve as the functional vehicle for realizing 2E. For example, some advanced robots, many primitive animals on our planet, and possibly sleepwalking human beings or patients showing complex behavior during certain epileptic absence seizures are plausible examples of 2E. However, the traditional notion of a "body schema" is vague (Gallagher, 2005, p. 17; de Vignemont, 2010; Alsmith and de Vignemont, 2012, p. 3). Currently, it has become the target of a fresh approach by modern cognitive neuroscience and robotics (e.g., Maravita, Spence, and Driver, 2003; Haggard and Wolpert, 2005; Hoffmann *et al.*, 2010).

In evolutionary bio-robotics, resilient systems have been developed that evolve continuous control of effectors with the help of a topological bodily self-model, indirectly inferring their own morphology through self-directed exploration and then using the resulting self-models to synthesize new behaviors (e.g., Gloye, Wiesel, Tenchio, and Simon, 2005; Bongard, Zykov, and Lipson, 2006; Schmidhuber, 2007). An excellent recent example of 2E can be found in the work of Holk Cruse and Malte Schilling (e.g., Schilling and Cruse, 2012). Their MMC-body model holistically encodes kinematic relationships between body parts in a recurrent neural network and can be used for prediction, sensor fusion, or inverse modeling ("MMC" stands for a specific principle of integration, the "mean of multiple computation"; see Cruse and Steinkühler, 1993; Cruse, Steinkühler, and Burkamp, 1998). In itself the body model cannot, of course, initiate or actively "construct" any behaviors (like the proverbial little man in the head), but in the context of the system as a whole it can function as a new tool – namely a grounded, predictive body model that continuously filters data in accordance with geometrical, kinematic, or dynamic boundary conditions. On a certain level of functional granularity, this type of core representation might also describe the generic, universal geometry which is *shared* by all members of a biological species. Therefore, it is conceivable how such a body model could support unconscious social cognition via 2E: an integrated body model is a new window into the social world (Metzinger, 2003a, 2009, ch. 9; Metzinger and Gallese, 2003). A second interesting feature demonstrated by this specific example is that 2E systems can in principle *alternate* between physical and virtual behavior. A body model could be used in simulating and predicting potential new solutions to a problem posed by the environment, with the physical body then testing various new behavioral solutions. Whereas a 1E system could be adaptive, only a 2E system could truly learn, because a self-model seems to be strictly necessary for the development of new behavioral patterns, just as a world model is necessary for the evaluation of causal structures (Ay and Zahedi, 2013, p. 502; Zahedi, Ay, and Der, 2010). Learning, in this sense, directly increases the level of causal self-control. This clearly is a new level of embodied intelligence, because it adds flexibility and sensitivity to a wider temporal context, plus a new possibility for actively exploring and appropriating the causal structure of the world, thereby considerably increasing the volume of the system's space of possible behaviors. This is a new *order* of embodiment, because the very fact of embodiment *as such* is now explicitly represented in the system itself.

Third-order embodiment is the special case in which a physical system not only explicitly models itself *as* an embodied being, but also maps some of the representational content generated in this process onto the level of conscious experience. This third-order embodiment is found in conscious human beings in ordinary wake states, in dreams, but also during naturally occurring altered states like out-of-body experiences (OBEs) or experimentally induced full-body illusions (FBIs; see p. 000, below; Metzinger, 2009, 2010, for an accessible introduction). It is plausible to assume that many higher animals are also frequent examples of 3E: they would then have an online model of their own body as a whole, elevated to the level of global availability and integrated with a single spatial situation model plus a virtual window of presence. Therefore, they can have the conscious experience of being situated as bodily selves while *owning* affective or sensorimotor states.[2]

Consequently, to fully understand 3E, one ultimately needs a comprehensive theory of consciousness (Metzinger, 1995, 2000). But what is conscious experience? Here is one very short answer: it is the functional level of granularity on which an information-processing system first generates a unified ontology, that is, an explicit and integrated set of assumptions about what exists and what does not, a single and integrated world model under which it now operates. In 3E systems, the body has become a part of this unified ontology. Third-order embodiment means that a given system consciously *experiences* itself as embodied, that the body is for the first time explicitly represented as *existing*, that a given organism or robot possesses a specific type of phenomenal self-model (Metzinger, 2003a, 2007).

The functional reason why we experience our own bodies as untranscendably real is that the bodily partition of our PSM is transparent. "Transparency" is here used to refer to an exclusive property of phenomenal states, meaning that the fact of their being *representational* states is inaccessible to introspective attention. Metaphorically speaking, the construction process is "invisible" on the level of phenomenal experience itself (Metzinger 2003a, §3.2.7; 2003b, p. 354). Phenomenal transparency explains why we *identify* with the content given via 3E. One of the main challenges in describing the step from conscious body representation to the phenomenal property of "selfhood" includes the subjective sense of identification, which also assigns a unique role to *this* body among all the other bodies potentially represented on the level of conscious experience as well. Those proprio- and interoceptive layers of the PSM that are constantly active may play a decisive role here (Seth, Suzuki, and Critchley, 2012; Seth, 2013). The central defining characteristic of 3E refers to the class of systems generating the phenomenology of body identification (i.e., the subjective sense of being identical with the contents of one specific body model, even if there is a social scene including other models of embodied agents[3]).

Equally important is a given conscious system's capacity for self-location in a spatio-temporal frame of reference. The phenomenal target property that has to be grounded is not only *my body* (consisting of identity as passively experienced, plus the implicit potential for active ownership via global control), but *my body here and now*. Conceptually, three conditions are central. First, the relevance of the phenomenological level of analysis: only 3E systems possess bodily self-consciousness, and as 1E and 2E systems do not possess the relevant set of phenomenal properties, no relevant phenomenological truths can be expressed about them.[4] Second, a whole set of new and interesting functional properties emerges, such as the availability of global properties for attention: the system can now for the first time turn the body *as a whole* into an object of self-directed attention, thereby making its own *global* properties the target of computational resource allocation, second-order statistics, selective motor control, or self-directed concept formation. The capacity for explicit self-location in a single, integrated spatio-temporal frame of reference, and on the level of global availability,[5] enables more flexible and context-sensitive forms of global self-control in the motor domain, but also for cognitive tasks (such as remembering past states or planning future goal states of the system *as a whole*, now importantly assuming trans-temporal identity, e.g., that action consequences like future reward events will be related to the *same* organism). Third, the functional integration of spatio-temporal self-location and the pre-reflective identification with the content of a currently active body model generate a specific new phenomenal property: we can now conceptualize the simplest form of self-consciousness as "transparent situatedness in time and space," namely the phenomenology of *Anwesenheit*, of being-present-as-an-embodied-self.

Example 1: "Visual attentional agency"

At this point, it is particularly interesting to introduce a first set of empirical data points. We must acknowledge the fact that body representation can be absolutely minimal while a robust, stable sense of selfhood is preserved: empirical research on OBEs and particularly on dreaming demonstrates that transparent self-location is enough to bring about a minimal form of self-consciousness.[6] That said, more complex forms of 3E can, and frequently do, arise in dreams and OBEs, raising the question of how they are grounded in 1E and 2E. But data clearly show that there exists a *limiting case* of 3E, namely a minimal, yet robustly self-conscious form of self-location without explicit embodiment in any interesting sense. This limiting case may be important for grounding the PSM. Let me illustrate the relevance of these findings by giving an example from my own work. In earlier publications, I have claimed that the dream state, which is accompanied by sleep paralysis, is often an example of explicit body representation (we experience a dream body), but in the absence of 1E, because the physical body is inert and fully paralyzed. Dreamers, therefore, are not fully embodied agents (e.g., Metzinger 2003a, p. 256; 2009). The functional disembodiment hypothesis (cf. Windt, in press) says that the dream state is characterized by a functional disconnection from the sleeping body such that real-body inputs do not enter into the dream and internally experienced dream movements are not enacted by the sleeping body.

However, I also pointed out a single, highly interesting exception, namely the reliable directional correspondence between dream eye movements and real eye movements: there is at least one sense in which the phenomenal dream self is not completely disembodied in the functional sense (Metzinger, 2003a, p. 261). For example, the spatial correlation between eye movements in the dream body and the physical body has served as the foundation for a number of ingenious studies homing in on the neural correlate of "lucidity" (i.e., the rare occurrence of realizing that one is dreaming during the dream state itself; see LaBerge, Stephen, Nagel, Dement, and Zarcone, 1981; Voss, Holzmann, Tuin, and Hobson, 2009; Voss, Schermelleh-Engel, Windt, Frenzel, and Hobson, 2013; Dresler *et al.*, 2012 – for discussion see Metzinger, 2003a; Windt and Metzinger, 2007; Windt, in press). In these experiments, lucid dreamers actively send signals to the experimenter via deliberate eye movements, which can be read off the EOG (electrooculogram) and are retrospectively confirmed by the dreamers themselves. This discovery is theoretically important, because it gives us a first candidate for a fine-grained *grounding relation* connecting 3E (the conscious dream body) with low-level physical dynamics (measurable, local neural activity controlling eye movements), plausibly mediated via 2E (i.e., a specific aspect of an unconscious body model mediating the active exploration of visual space). Phenomenal self-consciousness and self-related cognition can be grounded in different ways, including neurally realized simulations, bodily processes, and situated action (Barsalou, 2008, p. 619). Interestingly, here we find all three of them: gaze control in the lucid dream state clearly is a form of virtually situated action involving motor control plus attentional resource allocation in a virtual environment; it uses an internal simulation of the body-as-visually-attending (the PSM of the dream state; see Windt and Metzinger, 2007, and Windt, in press, for details); and it has dynamic, structure-preserving bodily correlates. The successful control of gaze direction in the lucid dream state is what anchors selective, high-level visual attention (including the conscious sense of "attentional agency," cf. Metzinger, p. 8) in low-level, non-representational features of bodily movement. Here we have an example of a specific and functionally persistent grounding relation connecting 1E, 2E, and 3E in a situation where most of these relations only hold between 2E and 3E and most functions of self-consciousness are not grounded in 1E.

The *generalized* version of the functional disembodiment claim, however, has now been refuted, as it can be shown that more than one minimal form of functional embodiment is preserved during REM (rapid eye movement)-sleep dreams (cf. Windt, in press). Real-body stimulation (e.g., sprays of water on the skin, Dement and Wolpert, 1958; electric stimulation, Koulack, 1969; blood-pressure-cuff stimulation on the leg, Nielsen, 1993; Sauvageau, Nielsen, Ouellet, and Montplaisir, 1993; Nielsen, Ouellet, and Zadra, 1995; Sauvageau, Nielsen, and Montplaisir, 1998; vestibular stimulation, Hoff, 1929; Hoff and Plötzl, 1937; Leslie and

Ogilvie, 1996) is frequently incorporated in dreams, and indeed it has been suggested that many typical dream themes – such as dreams of flying, falling, or being unable to move or flee from a pursuer – can be explained in terms of illusory own-body perception (Schönhammer, 2004, 2005), and the same may be true for sleep-paralysis nightmares during sleep onset (Cheyne, Rueffer, and Newby-Clark, 1999; Cheyne, 2003, 2005). An early predecessor of this view of dreams as *weakly functionally embodied* states (Windt, in press) is the *Leibreiztheorie*, promoted by nineteenth-century researchers and extensively discussed and rejected by Freud (1899/2003, pp. 38–56). On the output side, there is also ample evidence for dream-enactment behavior in healthy subjects (e.g., Nielsen, Svob, and Kuiken, 2009) and patients with RBD (REM-sleep behavior disorder; see Schenck, 2005, 2007), as well as some evidence from lucid dreaming suggesting that dream movements are accompanied by measurable muscle twitches in the corresponding limbs and changes in heart and respiration rate (LaBerge *et al.*, 1981; LaBerge and Dement, 1982; LaBerge, Greenleaf, and Kedzierski, 1983; Fenwick *et al.*, 1984; Schredl and Erlacher, 2008).

Are there any empirical examples of bodily experience in dreams being created completely offline, in the absence of 1E and 2E? At the very least, it would be hard to see how there could be any empirical evidence for saying that such instances of functionally disembodied 3E exist in dreams: state-of-the-art studies investigating the sensory input blockade (Hobson *et al.*, 2000), or, as Dang-Vu *et al.* more aptly call it, the "reduced sensitivity to external salient stimuli" (Dang-Vu *et al.*, 2005, p. 417; Dang-Vu *et al.*, 2007) during REM sleep not only explicitly acknowledge that the degree of sensory incorporation is weakened rather than completely absent in REM sleep, but also use stimulus incorporation as an important means of *studying* the underlying mechanisms in the first place. This suggests that the most plausible and parsimonious explanation of bodily experience in dreams, as well as the most effective methods used in its study, will appeal to its real-bodily basis. Of course, none of this is to say that 3E in the absence of 1E and 2E is impossible; but it is to say that its existence would be hard to establish empirically and sheds doubt on my own original claim that dreams are a real-world and empirically well-established example of bodily experience arising during a functionally disembodied state.

Grounding relations connecting 1E, 2E, and 3E

What is a "grounding relation"? A grounding relation connects a given intentional and/or phenomenal target property with the situated, low-level physical dynamics of a given type of cognitive and/or conscious system, for example by specifying a computational model that allows us to understand the transition from the representational or phenomenological level of description to the one of physical microdynamics. Such a grounding relation may span many levels of description and may therefore be decomposable into subrelations connecting descriptions on different levels of granularity and in widening domains. If we accept the modeling component as methodologically essential, we may speak of "computationally grounded cognition" and think of a corresponding cascade involving the local grounding of a given mental target property via neural dynamics, embodiment, and situatedness (Pezzulo *et al.*, 2013, p. 4). From a philosophy-of-science perspective, three steps have to be taken. First, in dealing with phenomenal properties like "selfhood," these have to be analyzed as *representational* structures (e.g., "transparency," "self-location," "egocentric frame of reference," etc.). Second, we have to develop a computational model or other formalism that allows these structures to "bottom out." This means that we need a better understanding of representationality as a *graded* property, as something that is not an all-or-nothing affair but permits degrees of constraint satisfaction. Such constraints could be spelled out in terms of stimulus correlation, decouplability, degrees of statistical covariance with body or environment, structural resemblance to the causal structure of the world, minimized prediction error, etc. Third, and perhaps most importantly, we must carefully distinguish between causally enabling and metaphysically necessary conditions, between the acquisition history and those properties *constituting* our respective target phenomenon (Blanke and Metzinger, 2009, Box 1; Weber and Vosgerau, 2012, p. 60). Grounding is about constitution. For phenomenal properties (like "selfhood" or "identification") we can expect a strictly local grounding, for example in contemporaneous states of the brain, and we know that local supervenience ultimately collapses into identity.[7] For intentional, representational, or semantic properties, the system's interaction history – in some cases even including social interactions within a linguistic community – plausibly will play a stronger role.

Let us now briefly look at the relationship between 1E, 2E, and 3E, while keeping our first example of a specific, to-be-grounded target property in mind. First-order embodiment describes a different class of systems than 2E and 3E. Therefore, it would be logically possible to have systems exhibiting 2E and/or 3E, but not 1E. In our world, however, 3E and 2E "ride" on 1E. Our first phenomenal target property ("visual attentional agency") is determined by a complex functional property, which in turn is locally realized by a specific bodily process. Consciously experienced eye movements are grounded in this process, which can be computationally modeled. The next logical step will have to be a formal specification spanning all three levels of description, a computational model that describes the PSM in the dream and wake states, plus the role of the unconscious body model in *linking* virtual and physical control of eye movements, as well as the dynamics in the local neural correlate, generating testable predictions. This then would be what Barsalou (2008, p. 635) has called "transitioning from demonstration experiments to analytic experiments." As soon as the target phenomenon has been well documented, we want to reveal the underlying formal principles.

Obviously, in our world, there are many systems exhibiting pure 1E, and probably many biological systems belong to the conjunction of 1E and 2E (like the stick insects that are the modeling target of Cruse and Schilling). But is it logically possible to have 3E and 2E in the absence of 1E? Perhaps we could imagine Cartesian souls in heaven, constantly misrepresenting themselves as embodied, dreaming the dream of incarnation. But their dreams and their misrepresentations would then be ungrounded in any sort of physical history or dynamics, and it may be difficult to understand how they could be *about* spatial and temporal properties in the first place, how ungrounded semantic content is possible. The existence of such systems might be logically possible – but even so, it doesn't seem conceivable how we could have observable and replicable scientific evidence for their disembodied existence. However, 1E, 2E, and 3E are here primarily meant to be used as epistemic notions, conceptual instruments developed for philosophy of cognitive science; and in the context of empirical research programs, this possibility is irrelevant.

But maybe one could have conscious embodiment in the absence of representation. Would it be logically possible to have 3E without 1E or 2E? In a specific kind of idealist metaphysics, one might assume that only phenomenal properties are real, and that ultimately neither physical nor representational properties exist. Third-order embodiment would then be pure appearance, a stand-alone phenomenal configuration. Here – if everything is phenomenal – the problem is to specify what the term "phenomenal" would mean. However, an example of a much more interesting, and heuristically fruitful, question would be the following: In our world, could there be *self-consciousness without representation*? Above, I have stipulated that 3E involves a mapping of representational content to consciousness. But perhaps scientific progress will ultimately allow us to drop this metatheoretical assumption in order to arrive at an even more parsimonious conceptual framework: Can 1E and 3E be simultaneously instantiated in a single system, can we have bodily self-consciousness without any form of representation? Or is an integrated body model strictly (nomologically) necessary?

However, the three notions of 1E, 2E, and 3E are primarily supposed to function as epistemic concepts, not as metaphysical ones. I believe that, if properly viewed as windows into different layers of embodiment, they might make a contribution as instruments possessing fecundity, in terms of helping us understand what exactly the real issues are – at this specific point in time, during this phase of scientific progress. Using the conceptual tools of 1E, 2E, and 3E, one can now formulate many relevant questions in a more precise way: Under the laws of nature holding in our universe (leaving logically possible worlds aside for a moment), what are the relevant, necessary and sufficient grounding relations connecting 1E, 2E, and 3E? How exactly is explicit, but unconscious, body representation grounded in the self-organizing, low-level microdynamics of local interaction between elements; and how exactly is the holistic phenomenology of bodily self-consciousness grounded in second-order embodiment? As indicated above, my own recommendation would be not to throw the baby out with the bath-water, but to mathematically describe "representationality" as a property that is graded, allowing the PSM to naturally "bottom out" into non-representational dynamics. The best indicator of progress will be the disappearance of Yes-or-No answers to questions like "Is bodily self-consciousness representational or not?" or "Is 3E possible in the absence of 2E?" These questions themselves are misleading.

One background assumption behind the conceptual distinction I have offered is that an ordinary human being, inattentively walking along the street "on autopilot," clearly exhibits 1E and 2E all of the time, whereas 3E is a fluctuating property, coming in different degrees and strengths. To be sure, we use physical properties of our bodies when generating the controlled form of falling we call "walking," and certainly there is an unconscious body schema supporting us when we walk through the streets with a wandering mind (e.g., Haggard and Wolpert, 2005; Schilling and Cruse, 2012; Metzinger, 2013c). But if we take our own body phenomenology seriously, we rarely have the body as a whole, it is more like "body islands" emerging and capturing our attention – an itch, a sudden sense of effort, a short loss of balance (e.g., Smith, 2009, pp. 89–90). There is a constant sense of identification with the body, but the actual conscious content is highly variable, task and context dependent. For a Zen monk walking extremely slowly and mindfully, say, during the practice of *kinhin* (walking) meditation, the phenomenological profile may be very different. Perhaps 3E is strongly expressed in terms of a dynamically stable, globally integrated body phenomenology, perhaps 3E is completely absent, because identification has been shifted to the situation model as a whole, or to the unity of consciousness as such.

Example 2: Full-body illusions and the concept of "minimal phenomenal selfhood"

What is the absolutely essential, the most central grounding relation that we find in *all* those cases where a system exhibits 1E, 2E, and 3E at the same time? Clearly, there will be no single, universal answer to this question: Bodily self-awareness will be extremely different in different types of systems (say, robots instantiating synthetic phenomenology, or dolphins, or humans), and the specific grounding relations for their respective PSMs will vary greatly (Shapiro, 2012, p. 143). Again, the search for an "essence" may be misguided. If we limit our intended class of systems to human beings in non-pathological waking states, then the question becomes: Is there a simplest, absolutely minimal form of self-consciousness, a fundamental form of phenomenal selfhood that underlies all other configurations and kinds of grounding? To answer this question we need to isolate the domain-specific, minimal form of phenomenal selfhood. For example, we might ask: Can there be conscious body representation without *own*-body representation – that is, bodily awareness without the phenomenology of ownership and bodily selfhood (Martin, 1995, pp. 269–70)? Can the two components of selfhood and body representation be functionally dissociated? This leads to the question of "minimal phenomenal selfhood" (Blanke and Metzinger, 2009). MPS is a new research target, namely, the attempt to isolate the minimal conditions for self-consciousness to appear in a given class of information-processing systems.

One important distinction is the one between local and global ownership (Blanke and Metzinger, 2009, p. 9; Petkova *et al.*, 2011). For example, in a disorder that has been called somatoparaphrenia, the phenomenology of ownership for a body part may break down following damage to the right temporoparietal cortex (Vallar and Ronchi, 2009). Somatoparaphrenic patients most often misattribute their contralesional hand as belonging to another mostly familiar person such as their doctor, nurse, a hospital neighbor, or friend. Other somatoparaphrenic patients suffer from the opposite pattern and self-attribute other people's hands when these are presented in their contralesional hemispace. Somatoparaphrenia affects only the contralesional (mostly left) hand (or foot) and never ipsilesional body parts. Somatoparaphrenia must be distinguished from other bodily symptoms reflecting disturbed partial ownership and/or agency such as xenomelia (the oppressive feeling that one or more limbs of one's body do not belong to one's self, sometimes also termed "body integrity identity disorder"; see, e.g., Hilti *et al.*, 2013), anosognosia for a paralyzed limb, asomatognosia, alien hand syndrome, or supernumerary phantom limbs. We must do justice to the fact that a complex set of phenomenological constraints has to be satisfied by any convincing theory, since there is a high-dimensional, variable landscape in bodily self-consciousness. This implies that phenomenological aspects like "identification" and "ownership" cannot be captured by a simple global/local distinction, but have to be described in their fine-grained variance (Longo, Schüür, Kammers, Tsakiris, and Haggard, 2008; Tsakiris, 2010; Longo and Haggard, 2012).

Global aspects of 3E as well as unconscious mechanisms of spatial self-location can be manipulated in a predictable fashion. In a now classic study (Lenggenhager, Tadi, Metzinger, and Blanke, 2007), a protocol similar to that in the rubber-hand illusion (RHI; Botvinick and Cohen, 1998) was extended to the full body, inducing FBIs. A video camera with a 3D encoder was placed behind the subject and relayed to a head-mounted display. Tactile stimulation (stroking) was applied on the back and the visual information related to this stimulation was systematically manipulated by displaying it either synchronously or asynchronously with the tactile sensation. Under these conditions, two measures were acquired: questionnaire scores to quantify self-identification and drift to quantify self-location. When the participants saw their body in front of themselves, being stroked synchronously on their own back, they sometimes felt as if the virtual body was their own (illusory self-identification) and showed drift towards it (illusory self-location). Both FBI measures were also observed for a fake body, but not, or to a weaker degree, for a rectangular object. The FBI (which generally is a weaker effect than the RHI) was abolished during asynchronous stroking. Henrik Ehrsson (2007) used a similar set-up, but stroked subjects on their chests (hidden from the view of the camera). In this FBI version, subjects saw the synchronous stroking in front of the camera, inducing the experience of being at the position of the camera that was behind the subjects' body. Research on FBIs, virtual and robotic re-embodiment is now a burgeoning interdisciplinary field in which new experimental techniques like the combination of virtual reality and fMRI are explored (see Blanke, 2012, for review). For the self grounding problem, all these new data may turn out to be decisive, because they demonstrate how the target property of phenomenal selfhood can in principle be grounded via the agency-independent property of passive body identification, which in turn can be selectively controlled and experimentally manipulated. What we currently lack is an adequate computational model *specifying* the grounding relations between 3E, 2E, and 1E.

MPS can be analyzed on phenomenological, representational, and functional levels of description. Central defining features are (1) a globalized form of identification with the body as a whole (as opposed to ownership for body parts), (2) spatio-temporal self-location, and (3) a first-person perspective (1PP). It is important to differentiate between a weak and at least two stronger readings of 1PP. MPS is the central enabling condition on the weak reading; it is a necessary (but not sufficient) condition on both stronger readings. A weak 1PP is a purely geometrical feature of a perceptual or imagined model of reality and has formed the target of empirical studies investigating visuospatial perspective-taking (Pfeiffer *et al.*, 2013). For example, in the human case a unimodal (e.g., visual) weak 1PP typically includes a spatial frame of reference, plus a global body representation, with a perspective originating *within* this body representation. There exists a center of projection, which functions as the geometrical origin of the "seeing" organism's passive perspective. Another important example is the sense of balance automatically provided by the vestibular system, whereas the sense of smell arguably may already present us with an intrinsically active modality, because the conscious detection of odorants involves top-down attention, however minimal. This is not to be confused with the warning system of the trigeminal nerve in the nasal cavity. The conscious experience of smells as perceived without being attended to are likely to be mediated by this warning system and not by the olfactory system (see Keller, 2011, p. 10). One conceptual difficulty here is that in *multimodal* experience "egocentric space seems unified in ways that resist neat characterization in terms of a privileged point of origin" (Smith, 2010, pp. 37, 39).

A stronger 1PP appears when the system as a whole is internally represented and actively *directed* at an object component, for example a perceptual object, an action goal, or perhaps the body as a whole. Conscious robots or other artificial systems might gradually develop their own kind of perspectivalness (Kuniyoshi *et al.*, 2007), but in human beings, we find the attentional 1PP and the cognitive 1PP. The property of "visual attentional agency" provided above is a good example, because the strong 1PP often involves the additional experience of controlling the focus of attention. From a philosophical perspective, attentional agency is one of the most interesting properties of all, because it marks the transition from passive identification with a body image to the stronger sense of selfhood generated in the process of active self-control. A strong 1PP is exactly what makes consciousness *subjective*: the fact that a system represents itself not only as a self, but as an epistemic agent. The capacity to represent oneself as an entity that actively seeks knowledge and is dynamically directed at *epistemic* goal states is, of course, not confined to the visual modality – a subjective perspective can also involve the sense of smell, auditory experience, or the introspective, inward-directed exploration of proprioception, of interoceptive feelings, or emotional states. Importantly, this also means that the organism represents itself *as representing*, because it co-represents the representational relation during the ongoing process of representation: a phenomenal self *as subject* appears exactly when the organism possesses a phenomenal model of the intentionality relation (Metzinger, 2003a, 2007). Perhaps there is an even stronger 1PP, which implies the possession of the *concept* of a subject of experience (an abstract "amodal self symbol"), and the additional ability of a given system to mentally apply this concept to itself. Such a "cognitive 1PP" is something I will not discuss here, because at present it is mostly of interest to philosophers and still outside the scope of empirical research programs.

Having MPS is a necessary condition for the strong (i.e., attentional and/or cognitive) 1PP, but not for the weak 1PP, because the weak 1PP is itself a constituting factor for MPS. The notion of "embodiment" is of central relevance for MPS and finding out how critical global bodily properties like self-identification, self-location, and 1PP can be grounded and functionally anchored in the brain. In standard configurations, the conscious body model defines a volume within a spatial frame of reference (the dimension of "self-location") within which the origin of the weak 1PP is also localized. Self-location possesses a variable internal structure: the bodily self is phenomenally represented as inhabiting a *volume* in space, whereas the weak 1PP is projected from an extensionless point, the geometrical origin of our perspectival visual model of reality (remember the example of visual attentional agency during some lucid dreams or asomatic OBEs). Normally this point of origin is embedded *within* the volume defined by self-location. Because this conscious body model is transparent, that is, because it cannot introspectively be recognized *as* a model, we fully identify with its representational content and enjoy the phenomenology of presence as bodily selves. But as we have seen above, it may be possible to *integrate* conditions (1) and (2), because more recent research has demonstrated the high prevalence of asomatic OBEs and dreams in which the sense of selfhood remains stable. MPS could then be transparent self-location in a spatio-temporal frame of reference (Windt, 2010).

In ordinary wake states, and on the representationalist level of description, the content of MPS has the function of indicating that a specific state in the system's internal neural dynamics has been reached, namely an integrated functional state that makes the body available for attention and global control. MPS, characterized by self-identification, self-location, and the weak 1PP, is the conscious representation of this achievement – and it is exactly the property that emerges when we wake up in the morning, when we suddenly "come to" ourselves. The simplest form of selfhood is a representation not of ongoing motor behavior or perceptual and attentional processing directed at single body parts, but of the entire body as being *functionally available* for global control. MPS thereby is a form of abstract (yet non-propositional) knowledge about oneself, information about newly acquired causal properties.

How can MPS be grounded with the help of a computational model? One might argue that MPS appears if and only if an organism has made such global properties of its own body available for flexible, high-level control and represents this very fact to itself. It is also important to understand that MPS as well as more complex forms of self-representation are not static internal copies of some mysterious thing or individual substance ("the" self), but only ongoing processes of tracking and controlling global bodily properties – for example with the help of an explicit, integrated body model. "Global control" is a process in which a system controls global properties of itself (as opposed to local properties). A global property is one that can only meaningfully be ascribed to a given system as a whole, often because it requires a new level of analysis defined by a different logical subject plus a corresponding set of predicates. A drop of water is wet, but none of the individual H_2O molecules has the property of "wetness." Global properties of the human body are, for example, the specific shape of the entire body surface or the whole body's translational properties as opposed to partial properties such as the skin of the fingertip or hand translation. The possession of MPS, of a weak, strong, or even cognitive 1PP, is also the possession of global properties; no individual part can have them. Third-order embodiment and self-consciousness more generally are properties of the system as a whole.

In conclusion, the self grounding problem can be viewed as an interesting set of conceptual and empirical issues that we discover when looking at a certain kind of system from the outside, from a third-person perspective, and with the eyes of a philosopher or scientist. It can be solved by formally specifying the grounding relations that hold between constitutive elements on different levels of embodiment, for example by describing degrees of representationality, local neural correlates (for phenomenal properties), or more extended dynamic interactions (for semantic properties). However, it is at least equally interesting to note how the solution to this problem can also be viewed from the perspective of the continuously evolving individual system itself, namely, as the acquisition of an extremely relevant set of *functional properties*: it is one thing to develop an explicit body model, eventually leading to a PSM, but it is quite another to reliably ground it in the process of controlling a real, physical body and to successfully embed it in a dense mesh of successful interactions – not only with the current situation, but also in the context of internally generated virtual environments and extended social ontologies. Passive identification through MPS is not the same as active body ownership via situated global self-control. Third-order embodiment and PSM have to become *functionally adequate* aspects of a much larger process. Any system that has achieved this to a sufficiently high degree has individually solved the self-grounding problem (now spelled with a hyphen), because it has grounded *itself* in a new way, by ascending to higher levels of embodiment. Perhaps future research can even interestingly connect such higher levels of embodiment with traditional philosophical notions like "autonomy."

Acknowledgments

I am greatly indebted to Adrian J. T. Alsmith and Jennifer M. Windt for criticism, many fruitful discussions, and valuable help with the English version of this contribution. Nihat Ay, Holk Cruse, and Keyan Ghazi-Zahedi have supported me by offering a number of helpful comments.

Notes

1 I first introduced these three concepts in Metzinger (2006). The concept of MPS was first developed in Blanke and Metzinger, 2009; references for the notion of a phenomenal self-model (PSM) are given in the main text.

2 It is interesting to note how this fact is highly relevant for ethics, because it is the central necessary precondition for the capacity to suffer, and it is specified in a hardware-independent way. Therefore, 3E plus valence representation helps us to define the class of objects of ethical consideration, for example in robot ethics (cf. Metzinger, 2013a, p. 262).

3 The phenomenon of heautoscopy provides an interesting (but rare) example of a specific neurological disorder in which patients see a hallucinatory image of their *own* body in extracorporeal space, with the phenomenal "locus of identification" being ambiguous. Specifically, the patient's stable, subjective sense of being anchored in one single body dissolves into a feeling of bi-location or of jumping back and forth between two body representations (see Figure 1 and Box 2 in Blanke and Metzinger, 2009, p. 10). This demonstrates how the identification component and the self-location component in 3E can be selectively compromised *in non-social configurations*, with the only additional body model available on the level of conscious experience being a hallucinatory model of the patient's *own* body as visually perceived. Heautoscopy is also associated with depersonalization and vestibular disorders (see Heydrich and Blanke, 2013). Out-of-body experiences are an obvious example for a second relevant class of 3E states frequently occurring in the absence of any social situation or context. See Blanke and Mohr, 2005, and Blanke, 2012, for review and further references.

4 Introducing this conceptual distinction enables us to ask new research questions more precisely, by drawing attention to the logical possibility of conscious systems not exhibiting 3E: Could there be conscious systems that (a) lack any conscious body model whatsoever, or (b) systems that possess body phenomenology, but selectively lack the passive sense of identification? Simple biological organisms, or patients suffering from severe cases of depersonalization disorder or Cotard syndrome, might be examples of such phenomenal state classes.

5 Here, the concept of "global availability" functions as a placeholder for "conscious processing"; see Metzinger, 2003a, pp. 30 and 117, for details and additional constraints.

6 See Metzinger, 2013a, for details. Empirical studies on so-called "asomatic" OBEs seem to show that not only are about 29 percent of OBEs characterized by an indefinite spatial volume of the body, but that another 31 percent seem to be "bodiless" altogether – while preserving a stable sense of selfhood – because they are experienced as bodiless and include an externalized visuospatial perspective only (e.g., Wolfradt, 2000). In dream research we find similar data showing how spatial self-location can be independent of bodily experience (though it will still involve the experience of being an extensionless point in space; cf. Windt, 2010). For reports of phenomenal selfhood lacking the phenomenology of embodiment, see Occhionero, Cicogna, Natale, Esposito, and Bosinelli, 2005; LaBerge and DeGracia, 2000; for a philosophical discussion of such experiences in dreams, see Windt, 2010, in press.

7 One of the weaknesses of supervenience theory generally speaking is that it is a *non-explanatory relationship*, because ultimately it does not tell us anything about the inner nature of psychophysical correlations. However, for every *local* supervenience relation that allows us to understand how supervenient causation is possible, there will be a nomologically equivalent, coextensive base property relative to the specific physical system we are looking at – and nomological coextensionality is an identity condition for properties. So local grounding will eventually go along with either a domain-specific reductive explanation or an elimination of phenomenal target properties like "selfhood" or "identification." See Kim, 1989, n. 29.

References

Alsmith, A. J., and de Vignemont, F. (2012). Embodying the mind and representing the body. *Review of Philosophy and Psychology*, *3(1)*, 1–13.

Ay, N., and Zahedi, K. (2013). Causal effects for prediction and deliberative decision making of embodied systems. In Y. Yamaguchi (Ed.), Advances in Cognitive Neurodynamics: Vol. 3. Proceedings of the Third International Conference on Cognitive Neurodynamics–2011 (pp. 499–506). Heidelberg: Springer.

Barsalou, L. W. (2008). Grounded cognition. *Annual Review of Psychology*, *59*, 617–645.

Blanke, O. (2012). Multisensory brain mechanisms of bodily self-consciousness. *Nature Reviews Neuroscience*, *13(8)*, 556–571.

Blanke, O., and Metzinger, T. (2009). Full-body illusions and minimal phenomenal selfhood. *Trends in Cognitive Sciences*, *13(1)*, 7–13.

Blanke, O., and Mohr, C. (2005). Out-of-body experience, heautoscopy, hallucination of neurological and autoscopic origin implications for neurocognitive mechanisms of corporeal awareness and self-consciousness. *Brain Research Reviews*, *50(1)*, 184–199.

Bongard, J., Zykov, V., and Lipson, H. (2006). Resilient machines through continuous self-modeling. *Science*, *314(5802)*, 1118–1121.

Botvinick, M., and Cohen, J. (1998). Rubber hands "feel" touch that eyes see. *Nature*, *391(6669)*, 756.

Brooks, R. A. (1991). Intelligence without representation. *Artificial Intelligence*, *47(1–3)*, 139–159.

Chemero, A. (2009). *Radical embodied cognitive science*. Cambridge, MA: MIT Press.

Cheyne, J. A. (2003). Sleep paralysis and the structure of waking-nightmare hallucinations. *Dreaming*, *13*, 163–179.

——— (2005). Sleep paralysis episode frequency and number, types, and structure of associated hallucinations. *Journal of Sleep Research*, *14*, 319–324.

Cheyne, J. A., Rueffer, S. D., and Newby-Clark, I. R. (1999). Hypnagogic and hypnopompic hallucinations during sleep paralysis: Neurological and cultural construction of the night-mare. *Consciousness and Cognition*, *8*, 319–337.

Clark, A. (1993). *Microcognition: Philosophy, cognitive science, and parallel distributed processing* (4th ed.). Cambridge, MA: MIT Press.

Cruse, H., and Steinkühler, U. (1993). Solution of the direct and inverse kinematic problems by a common algorithm based on the mean of multiple computations. *Biological Cybernetics*, *69(4)*, 345–351.

Cruse, H., Steinkühler, U., and Burkamp, C. (1998). MMC–A recurrent neural network which can be used as manipulable body model. In From Animals to Animats 5: Proceedings of the Fifth International Conference on Simulation of Adaptive Behavior (pp. 381–389). Cambridge, MA: MIT Press.

Dang-Vu, T.T., Desseilles, M., Albouy, G., Darsand, A., Gals, S., Rauchs, G., Schabus, M., Sterpenich, V., Vandewalle, G., Schwartz, S., and Maquet, P. (2005). Dreaming: A neuroimaging view. *Swiss Archives of Neurology and Psychiatry*, *156*, 415–425.

Dang-Vu, T. T., Desseilles, M., Petit, D., Mazza, S., Montplaisir, J., and Maquet, P. (2007). Neuroimaging in sleep medicine. *Sleep Medicine*, *8(4)*, 349–372.

Dement, W. C., and Wolpert, E. (1958). The relation of eye movements, body motility, and external stimuli to dream content. *Journal of Experimental Psychology*, *55*, 543–553.

Dresler, M., Wehrle, R., Spoormaker, V. I., Koch, S. P., Holsboer, F., Steiger, A., (2012). Neural correlates of dream lucidity obtained from contrasting lucid versus non-lucid REM sleep: A combined EEG/fMRI CASE Study. *Sleep*, *35(7)*, 1017–1020.

Ehrsson, H. H. (2007). The experimental induction of out-of-body experiences. *Science*, *317(5841)*, 1048.

Fenwick, P., Schatzman, M., Worsley, A., Adams, J., Stone, S., and Baker, A. (1984). Lucid dreaming: Correspondence between dreamed and actual events in one subject during REM sleep. *Biological Psychology*, *18*, 243–252.

Freud, S. (1899/2003). *Die Traumdeutung*. Frankfurt am Main: Fischer Taschenbuch.

Gallagher, S. (2005). *How the Body Shapes the Mind* (Oxford Scholarship Online). Oxford: Oxford University Press.

Gloye, A., Wiesel, F., Tenchio, O., and Simon, M. (2005). Verbesserung der Fahreigenschaften von fußballspielenden Robotern durch Antizipation [Reinforcing the driving quality of soccer-playing robots by anticipation]. *IT–Information Technology*, *47*(5), 250–257.

Haggard, P., and Wolpert, D. M. (2005). Disorders of body scheme. In H. J. Freund, M. Jeannerod, M. Hallett, and R. Leiguarda (Eds), *Higher-order motor disorders*. Oxford: Oxford University Press.

Harnad, S. (1990). The symbol grounding problem. *Physica D: Nonlinear Phenomena*, *42(1–3)*, 335–346.

Heydrich, L., and Blanke, O. (2013). Distinct illusory own-body perceptions caused by damage to posterior insula and extrastriate cortex. *Brain*, *136*(3), 790–803.

Hilti, L. M., Hänggi, J., Vitacco, D. A., Kraemer, B., Palla, A., Luechinger, R., (2013). The desire for healthy limb amputation: Structural brain correlates and clinical features of xenomelia. *Brain 136*(1), 318–329.

Hobson, J. A., Pace-Schott, E. F., and Stickgold, R. (2000). Dreaming and the brain: Toward a cognitive neuroscience of conscious states. *Behavioral and Brain Sciences*, *23*(6), 793–842.

Hoff, H. (1929). Zusammenhang von Vestibularfunktion, Schlafstellung und Traumleben. *Monatsschrift für Psychiatrie und Neurologie*, *71*(5–6), 366–372.

Hoff, H., and Plötzl, O. (1937). Über die labyrinthären Beziehungen von Flugsensationen und Flugträumen. *Monatsschrift für Psychiatrie und Neurologie*, *97*(4), 193–211.

Hoffmann, M., Marques, H. G., Hernandez Arieta, A., Sumioka, H., Lungarella, M., and Pfeifer, R. (2010). Body schema in robotics: A review. *IEEE Transactions on Autonomous Mental Development*, *2*(4), 304–324.

Keller, A. (2011). Attention and olfactory consciousness. *Frontiers in Psychology*, *2*(380), 1–12.

Kim, J. (1989). The myth of nonreductive materialism. *Proceedings and Addresses of the American Philosophical Association*, *3*, 31–47.

Koulack, D. (1969). Effects of somatosensory stimulation on dream content. *Archives of General Psychiatry*, *20*(6), 718–725.

Kuniyoshi, Y., Yorozu, Y., Suzuki, S., Sangawa, S., Ohmura, Y., Terada, K., (2007). Emergence and development of embodied cognition: A constructivist approach using robots. *Progress in Brain Research*, *164*, 425–456.

LaBerge, S., and DeGracia, D. J. (2000). Varieties of lucid dreaming experience. In R. G. Kunzendorf and G. Wallace (Eds), *Individual differences in conscious experience* (pp. 269–307), Amsterdam: John Benjamins.

LaBerge, S., and Dement, W. C. (1982). Voluntary control of respiration during lucid REM dreaming. *Sleep Research*, *11*, 107.

LaBerge, S., Greenleaf, W., and Kedzierski, B. (1983). Physiological responses to dreamed sexual activity during REM sleep. *Psychophysiology*, *19*, 454–455.

LaBerge, S., Stephen, P., Nagel, L. E., Dement, W. C., and Zarcone, V. P. (1981). Lucid dreaming verified by volitional communication during REM sleep. *Perceptual and Motor Skills*, *52*, 727–732.

Lenggenhager, B., Tadi, T., Metzinger, T., and Blanke, O. (2007). Video ergo sum: Manipulating bodily self-consciousness. *Science 317*(5841), 1096–1099.

Leslie, K., and Ogilvie, R. D. (1996). Vestibular dreams: the effect of rocking on dream mentation. *Dreaming*, *6*(1), 1–16.

Longo, M. R., and Haggard, P. (2012). What is it like to have a body? *Current Directions in Psychological Science*, *21*(2), 140–145.

Longo, M. R., Schüür, F., Kammers, M. P., Tsakiris M., and Haggard, P. (2008). What is embodiment? A psychometric approach. *Cognition*, *107*(3), 978–998.

Maravita, A., Spence, C., and Driver, J. (2003). Multisensory integration and the body schema: Close to hand and within reach. *Current Biology*, *13*(13), R531–39.

Martin, M. G. (1995). Bodily awareness: A sense of ownership. In J. L. Bermúdez, and A. J. Marcel (Eds), *The body and the self* (pp. 267–289). Cambridge, MA: MIT Press.

Metzinger, T. (1995). *Conscious experience*. Exeter: Imprint Academic.

———— (2000). *Neural correlates of consciousness: Empirical and conceptual questions*. Cambridge, MA: MIT Press.

———— (2003a). *Being no one: The self-model theory of subjectivity*. Cambridge, MA: MIT Press.

———— (2003b). Phenomenal transparency and cognitive self-reference. *Phenomenology and the Cognitive Sciences*, 2(4), 353–393.

———— (2006). Different conceptions of embodiment. *Psyche*, 12(4), 1–7. Retrieved from http://www.philosophie.uni-mainz.de/Dateien/Metzinger_PSYCHE_2006.zip

———— (2007). Self models. *Scholarpedia*, 2(10), 4174.

———— (2009). Why are out-of-body experiences interesting for philosophers? *Cortex*, 45(2), 256–258.

———— (2010). *The EGO tunnel: The science of the mind and the myth of the self* (1st ed.). New York: Basic Books.

———— (2013a). Two principles for robot ethics. In E. Hilgendorf and J.-P. Günther (Eds), *Robotik und Gesetzgebung*. Baden-Baden: Nomos.

———— (2013b). Why are dreams interesting for philosophers? The example of minimal phenomenal selfhood, plus an agenda for future research. *Frontiers in Psychology*, 4(746).

———— (2013c). The myth of cognitive agency: Subpersonal thinking as a cyclically recurring loss of mental autonomy. *Frontiers in Psychology*, 4(931).

Metzinger, T., and Gallese, V. (2003). The emergence of a shared action ontology: Building blocks for a theory. *Consciousness and Cognition*, 12(4), 549–571.

Nielsen, T. A. (1993). Changes in kinesthetic content of dreams following somatosensory stimulation of leg during REM sleep. *Dreaming*, 3, 99–113.

Nielsen, T. A., Ouellet, L., and Zadra, A. L. (1995). Pressure stimulation during REM sleep alters dream limb activity and body bizarreness. *Sleep Research*, 24, 134.

Nielsen, T. A., Svob, C., and Kuiken, D. (2009). Dream-enacting behaviors in a normal population. *Sleep*, 32(12), 1629–1636.

Occhionero, M., Cicogna, P., Natale, V., Esposito, M. J., and Bosinelli, M. (2005). Representation of self in SWS and REM dreams. *Sleep and Hypnosis*, 7(2), 77–83.

Petkova, V. I., Björnsdotter, M., Gentile, G., Jonsson, T., Li, T. Q., and Ehrsson, H. H. (2011). From part- to whole-body ownership in the multisensory brain. *Current Biology*, 21(13), 1118–1122.

Pezzulo, G., Barsalou, L. W., Cangelosi, A., Fischer, M. H., McRae, K., and Spivey, M. J. (2013). Computational grounded cognition: A new alliance between grounded cognition and computational modelling. *Frontiers in Psychology*, 3(612).

Pfeiffer, C., Lopez, C., Schmutz, V., Duenas, J. A., Martuzzi, R., and Blanke, O. (2013). Multisensory origin of the subjective first-person perspective: Visual, tactile, and vestibular mechanisms. *PLoS One*, 8(4), e61751.

Sauvageau, A., Nielsen, T. A., and Montplaisir, J. (1998). Effects of somatosensory stimulation on dream content in gymnasts and control participants: Evidence of vestibulomotor adaptation in REM sleep. *Dreaming*, 8, 125–134.

Sauvageau, A., Nielsen, T. A., Ouellet, L., and Montplaisir, J. (1993). Eye movement density and amplitude after somatosensory stimulation during REM sleep: Effects on gymnasts and controls. *Sleep Research*, 22, 133.

Schenck, C. (2005). *Paradox lost: Midnight in the battleground of sleep and dreams*. Minneapolis, MN: Extreme Nights, LLC.

———— (2007). *Sleep: The mysteries, the problems, and the solutions*, New York: Avery.

Schilling, M., and Cruse, H. (2012). What's next: Recruitment of a grounded predictive body model for planning a robot's actions. *Frontiers in Psychology*, 3(383).

Schmidhuber, J. (2007). Prototype resilient, self-modeling robots. *Science*, 316(5825), 688c.

Schönhammer, R. (2004). *Fliegen, Fallen, Flüchten: Psychologie intensiver Träume*. Tübingen: DGVT.

———— (2005). "Typical dreams": Reflections of arousal. *Journal of Consciousness Studies*, 12(4–5), 18–37.

Schredl, M., and Erlacher, D. (2008). Do REM (lucid) dreamed and executed actions share the same neural substrate? *International Journal of Dream Research*, 1(1), 7–14.

Seth, A. K. (2013). Interoceptive inference, emotion, and the embodied self. *Trends in Cognitive Sciences*, 17(11), 565–573.

Seth, A. K., Suzuki, K., and Critchley, H. D. (2012). An interoceptive predictive coding model of conscious presence. *Frontiers in Psychology*, 2(395).

Shapiro, L. A. (2012). Embodied cognition. In E. Margolis, R. Samuels, and S. Stich (Eds), *The Oxford handbook of philosophy of cognitive science*. Oxford: Oxford University Press.

Smith, A. J. T. (2009). Acting on (bodily) experience. *Psyche*, *15(1)*, 82–99. Retrieved from http://www.theassc.org/files/assc/2581.pdf

———— (2010). Comment: Minimal conditions for the simplest form of self-consciousness. F. Fuchs, H. C. Sattel, and P. Hennington (Eds), *The embodied self: Dimensions, coherence and disorders* (pp. 35–42). Stuttgart: Schattauer.

Tsakiris, M. (2010). My body in the brain: A neurocognitive model of body-ownership. *Neuropsychologia*, *48(3)*, 703–712.

Vallar, G., and Ronchi, R. (2009). Somatoparaphrenia: A body delusion–A review of the neuropsychological literature. *Experimental Brain Research*, *192(3)*, 533–551.

de Vignemont, F. (2010). Body schema and body image–Pros and cons. *Neuropsychologia*, *48(3)*, 669–680.

Voss, U., Holzmann, R., Tuin, I., and Hobson, J. A. (2009). Lucid dreaming: A state of consciousness with features of both waking and non-lucid dreaming. *Sleep*, *32(9)*, 1191–1200.

Voss, U., Schermelleh-Engel, K., Windt, J., Frenzel, C., and Hobson, A. (2013). Measuring consciousness in dreams: The lucidity and consciousness in dreams scale. *Consciousness and Cognition*, *22(1)*, 8–21.

Weber, A. M., and Vosgerau, G. (2012). Grounding action representations. *Review of Philosophy and Psychology*, *3(1)*, 53–69.

Windt, J. M. (2010). The immersive spatiotemporal hallucination model of dreaming. *Phenomenology and the Cognitive Sciences*, *9(2)*, 295–316.

———— (in press). *Dreaming: A conceptual framework for philosophy of mind and empirical research*. Cambridge, MA: MIT Press.

Windt, J. M., and Metzinger, T. (2007). The philosophy of dreaming and self-consciousness: What happens to the experiential subject during the dream state? In D. Barrett and P. McNamara (Eds), *The new science of dreaming: Vol. 3. Cultural and theoretical perspectives* (pp. 193–247) (Praeger Perspectives). Westport, CT: Praeger Publishers; Greenwood Publishing Group.

Wolfradt, U. (2000). Außerkörpererfahrungen (AKE) aus differentiell-psychologischer Perspektive. *Zeitschrift für Parapsychologie und Grenzgebiete der Psychologie*, *1(42–43)*, 65–108.

Zahedi, K., Ay, N., and Der, R. (2010). Higher coordination with less control–A result of information maximization in the sensorimotor loop. *Adaptive Behavior*, *18(3–4)*, 338–355.

4

EXTENDED COGNITION

Ken Aizawa

What takes place in the environment clearly influences cognitive processing. Children raised around speakers of English typically learn to understand English, whereas children raised around speakers of German typically learn to understand German. Accountants using calculators will typically know that accounts are balanced more quickly than those who use pencil and paper. Extended cognition goes beyond such pedestrian observations. Rather than causal dependency relations between cognitive processes and environmental processes, extended cognition postulates a constitutive dependence between cognitive processes and processes in brain, body, and environment. Cognitive processes are realized not just in the brain, but also in the body and world.

This brief chapter will focus on two types of arguments for extended cognition inspired by Clark and Chalmers (1998). First, there has been the thought that cognition extends when processes in the brain, body, and world are suitably similar to processes taking place in the brain. We might describe these as cognitive equivalence arguments for extended cognition. Second, there has been the thought that, when there is the right kind of causal connection between a cognitive process, and bodily and environmental processes, cognitive processes come to be realized by processes in the brain, body, and world. We might describe these as coupling arguments for extended cognition. What critics have found problematic are the kinds of similarity relations that have been taken to be applicable or suitable for concluding that there is extended cognition and the conditions that have been offered as providing the right kind of causal connection.

Cognitive equivalence arguments

The best-known cognitive equivalence argument is Andy Clark and David Chalmers' "Inga-Otto" thought experiment.[1] In this experiment, Inga is a normal human being who hears about an exhibit at the Museum of Modern Art. She decides that she wishes to see it, then pauses to recollect where the museum is. When she remembers, she heads out to 53rd Street. Next consider Otto, an individual suffering from the early stages of Alzheimer's disease. In order to cope with the loss of his biological memory, he turns to a notebook in which he keeps useful information, such as the location of the museum. When he hears

DOI: 10.4324/9781003322511-7   54

about the exhibit, he decides he wishes to see it, and then flips through his notebook until he finds the address. When he does, he heads out to 53rd Street.

Clark and Chalmers claim that the information stored in their respective brainy and papery resources constitutes memory for both Inga and Otto. They claim that

> in relevant respects the cases are entirely analogous: the notebook plays for Otto the same role that memory plays for Inga. The information in the notebook functions just like the information constituting an ordinary non-occurrent belief; it just happens that this information lies beyond the skin.
>
> *(Clark and Chalmers, 1998, p. 13)*

Further, "Certainly, insofar as beliefs and desires are characterized by their explanatory roles, Otto's and Inga's cases seem to be on a par: the essential causal dynamics of the two cases mirror each other precisely" (ibid.). And, finally, "To provide substantial resistance, an opponent has to show that Otto's and Inga's cases differ in some important and relevant respect. But in what deep respect are the cases different?" (Clark and Chalmers, 1998, pp. 14–15).[2]

Substantial resistance through non-derived content?

Critics have offered a number of proposals providing the kind of resistance that Clark and Chalmers demand. One contention has been that Inga's informational resources bear non-derived content, where Otto's informational resources bear derived content.[3] Non-derived content does not depend upon previously existing content, whereas derived content does. Stereotypically, non-derived content arises from social conventions. So, the meaning of a red traffic light, the meaning of a white flag, and the meaning of written words are paradigmatic instances of non-derived content.

It is sometimes claimed that cognitive states necessarily bear non-derived content, so that the fact that the letters and numerals in Otto's notebook presumably bear only derived content suffices to show that the letters and numerals are not constituents of any of Otto's cognitive states. Of course, bearing non-derived content may be important to cognition, even if it is not a strictly necessary property of a cognitive state. Perhaps cognitive states are natural kinds on the model of homeostatic property clusters.[4] On this analysis, cognitive states lack necessary or essential properties, such as bearing non-derived content, but they nevertheless tend to have a stable set of similarities, among which may be that they bear non-derived content. Thus, bearing derived content makes the inscriptions in Otto's notebook less like paradigmatic cognitive states. What this shows is that, in principle, there is more than one metatheoretical means by which to recognize the importance of non-derived content to being cognitive.

Dennett (1986), Clark (2005, 2010), Menary (2010), and Fisher (2009) argue that the derived/non-derived distinction is neither important nor relevant to cognitive status. Prior to the debate over extended cognition, Dennett (1986) gave a multifaceted challenge to the hypothesis of non-derived (or "original") content. He claimed that there is no distinction between derived and non-derived content, that humans lack non-derived content, and that there is no such thing as original intentionality. Furthermore, in opposition to the view that cognitive content is non-derived, he noted that organisms have the minds they do by virtue of evolution by natural selection. This means that there is a kind of derivation of human minds, hence, Dennett believes, a kind of derivation of the content in their minds. Relating this to the debate over extended cognition, we can see that if all content is derived, then the content in Inga's brain is derived, just as is the content in Otto's notebook. So, the derived/non-derived distinction is irrelevant.

Clark (2005) has inspired a different line of attack on the need for cognitive states to bear non-derived content. He invites us to imagine the discovery of a Martian whose brain manipulates bitmapped images of texts, so that the Martian would be manipulating texts in its brain. Clark claims that we would not hesitate to say that the Martian is doing cognitive processing with items bearing only non-derived content, so that we can see that cognitive processing does not necessarily traffic in only non-derived representations.[5] Clark (2010) brings the Martian example down to earth by proposing that certain human "memory masters" have the ability to recall image-like representations of texts. Were they to use their image-like representations on texts, then they would be performing cognitive operations on derived representations. Menary (2010) pursues this further by offering cases of "thinking in English." Words of natural language are paradigms of items bearing derived content, so insofar as "thinking in English" is literally thinking in English, we have cases of cognitive processing that involves trafficking in derived content.

Fisher (2009) argues that it is a mistake to propose that cognitive content must be non-derived, since there are numerous plausible cases of derived cognitive content. He suggests that the contents of thoughts, memories, and imaginational states derive from the contents of perceptual states. Given that the condition cannot hold of Inga's informational resources, it is too much to demand that it hold of Otto's.[6]

Substantial resistance from cognitive psychology?

A second potential source of substantial resistance to equating Inga and Otto comes from cognitive psychology. Rupert (2004) draws attention to two features of human memory: the phenomenon of negative transfer and the generation effect.[7] In the first phase of a typical negative transfer experiment, participants are presented with pairs of items, such as a male name (A) paired with the name of their significant other (B), and trained to a criterion to respond with a B item when probed by an A item. In the second phase of the experiment, participants are told that the relations of all the A individuals have changed. Now, John is not married to Mary, but is married to Sue, and so forth. Thus, participants must learn a new set of A–C associations that replace the prior A–B associations. In this second phase, the new A–C associations are more difficult to learn that the initial A–B associations. This is the negative transfer effect. *Ex hypothesi* Inga will perform as a typical participant in one of these experiments. By contrast, Otto using his notebook will probably not. In the first phase, Otto will write down all the A–B pairings on a single page. This will, presumably, enable Otto to reach criterion on the first pass, performance that is quite different from Inga's. In the second phase, Otto will presumably write all the A–C pairings on a new page. This will enable Otto to reach criterion again on the first pass, thereby differing dramatically from Inga's performance. Finally, we see that, with Otto, there is no negative transfer. Learning the A–B list does not inhibit learning of the A–C list.[8]

In a typical generation effect experiment, there are two groups of participants. In the first group, participants are given a list of A–B pairs to memorize; in the second group, participants generate a list of A–B pairs by reading a sentence, such as "The cow chased the ball." In both groups, participants develop a list of A–B pairs, such as "cow–ball," but participants who generate the pairs by reading sentences have better memory recall. This again applies straightforwardly to the Inga–Otto case. If we suppose that Inga is a normal human being, then *ex hypothesi* she will perform better when she is in the group that generates its *A–B* list by sentence reading than when she is in the group that is given the *A–B* list. By contrast, whichever group Otto is in, he will write down the items in the *A–B* list, then recall as necessary later. He will perform just as well in the generation condition as in the non-generation condition.

The generation effect and negative transfer effect seem to show that Clark and Chalmers are mistaken in their contention that Inga and Otto are in all important and relevant respects the same. Notice, as well, that this line of response can go beyond merely showing that Clark and Chalmers overstated their case for the similarity between Inga and Otto. We can draw attention to many other features of memory to argue, as does Rupert (2004), that external "memory" processing differs so dramatically from internal memory processing that these should not be treated as instances of a single natural kind. In advancing this argument, we do not have to say that any one feature, such as the negative transfer effect or the generation effect, is a necessary feature of memory. As noted above, we may, instead, propose that the particular features of memory that cognitive psychologists have so far discovered are elements in a much larger, perhaps poorly understood, homeostatic property cluster that constitutes human long-term memory as a natural kind. Thus, the more Inga and Otto differ in the properties that scientists have come to associate with long-term memory, the stronger is the case for saying that Inga and Otto do not have the same kind of "memory."

As emphasized above, Clark and Chalmers apparently believed that Inga and Otto are in *all* important and relevant respects the same.[9] Nevertheless, advocates of extended cognition need not take such a strong position. They can instead propose that Inga and Otto are in *some* important and relevant respects the same. If that were the case, there could be some sort of cognition that extends. This, in fact, seems to have become the favored defense of extended cognition.

So, what kind of important and relevant cognition is extended? There is no single answer. One proposal from Clark (2009) is that something like *folk psychology* is extended. Folk psychology consists of a largely implicit theory people have about the way humans perform in various situations. Perhaps, therefore, we could say that the hypothesis of extended *folk* cognition is true, important, and relevant, while conceding that the hypothesis of extended *scientific* cognition is false. Rowlands (2009) thinks that some form of *liberal functionalism* fits the bill.

> It is generally accepted that the arguments for EM [extended mind] presuppose functionalism. More than that, they presuppose a peculiarly *liberal* form of functionalism. Indeed, there is a way of understanding functionalism according to which EM emerges as a straightforward, almost *trivial*, consequence. In its more liberal forms, functionalism is based on a *principled* indifference to the details of the physical structures that realize mental processes. What is crucial to a mental state or process is its functional role, not its physical realization. For the liberal functionalist: if it walks like a duck, and talks like a duck, then it is a duck. *How* it manages to walk and talk like a duck is not directly relevant. To this, EM simply adds: neither does it matter where it walks and talks like a duck.
>
> (Rowlands, 2009, pp. 56–57)

Following Rowlands, then, we may say that the hypothesis of *liberal functionalist* cognition is true, important, and relevant, while conceding that the hypothesis of *scientific* cognition is false. Of course, whatever version of this approach we adopt, be it Clark's, or Rowlands', or some other, we do want some explanation of the importance of these forms of cognition and their extension and what relevance they have to scientific and philosophical projects.

Coupling arguments

Far more prevalent than cognitive equivalence arguments are a group of so-called "coupling arguments." So, to return to Clark and Chalmers' discussion, they argue that:

> It is not just the presence of advanced external computing resources which raises the issue, but rather the general tendency of human reasoners to lean heavily on environmental supports. Thus consider the use of pen and paper to perform long multiplication …, the use of physical re-arrangements of letter tiles to prompt word recall in Scrabble …, the use of instruments such as the nautical slide rule …, and the general paraphernalia of language, books, diagrams, and culture.
>
> *(Clark and Chalmers, 1998, p. 8)*

Then, somewhat later, they write

> In these cases, the human organism is linked with an external entity in a two-way interaction, creating a *coupled system* that can be seen as a cognitive system in its own right. All the components in the system play an active causal role, and they jointly govern behavior in the same sort of way that cognition usually does. If we remove the external component the system's behavioral competence will drop, just as it would if we removed part of its brain. Our thesis is that this sort of coupled process counts equally well as a cognitive process, whether or not it is wholly in the head.
>
> *(Ibid., pp. 8–9)*

These passages invite the following interpretation: when a process X has a causal influence on a cognitive process Y, then we may infer that the entire X–Y process is a cognitive process. This interpretation is reinforced if we bear in mind the introduction to Clark and Chalmers (1998), where they write, "We advocate a very different sort of externalism: an *active externalism*, based on the active role of the environment in driving cognitive processes" (ibid., p. 7).

While there are texts that suggest this line of argumentation, it is now common ground among advocates and critics of extended cognition that this simple argument is fallacious.[10] Just because a process X causally influences a cognitive process Y does not seem to be a sound basis upon which to infer that the whole X–Y process is cognitive. Consider this kind of reasoning in another context. Let X be the process of evaporative cooling found in a typical home air conditioning system. In a normal working system, this process is causally coupled to a process Y of deformation in the shape of a bimetallic strip in a thermostat in one room of the house. This causal linkage between X and Y does not make the entire X–Y process a process of shape deformation. For that matter, it does not make the whole X–Y process a matter of evaporative cooling.

While many advocates of extended cognition admit that there is this "coupling-constitution fallacy," they also sometimes suggest that this is not a mistake anyone has committed and leave the matter at that. Alternatively, they take the argument to be that cognition extends when there is the *right kind* of causal connection between brainy cognitive processes, and bodily and environmental processes. The simplistic coupling-constitution fallacy sketched above does not speak to this more subtle claim.

These replies, however, underestimate the challenge of moving from causal claims to constitutive claims. Rather than viewing the simple coupling-constitution fallacy as the end of a story, we should take it to be a starting point. It should lead us to ask how to refine the mistaken, simplistic account into a correct, sophisticated account. There are, however, two challenges lurking here. First, if we propose that additional conditions, $C_1, ..., C_n$, are needed in order for coupling relations to suffice to establish constitutive relations, then we must bear the burden of determining and theoretically validating those additional conditions $C_1, ..., C_n$. Second, once we establish a valid set of conditions, if we subsequently wish to show that we have an actual instance of extended cognition, as when using pen and paper to perform a long multiplication, then we will have to show that the putative actual instance satisfies $C_1, ..., C_n$. Moreover, the challenges interact. The more restrictive the set of theoretically valid conditions we develop, the greater the argumentative burden that will be needed in order to establish that they apply in any particular putative instance. Moreover, the more restrictive the set of theoretically valid conditions we develop, the fewer real-world instances we are likely to find to satisfy them.

To get a sense of this, let us consider a relatively trivial strengthening of the causal conditions that might be thought to suffice for a constitutive relation. Perhaps we should say that when a process X has a *reliable* causal influence on a cognitive process Y, then we may legitimately infer that the entire $X–Y$ process is cognitive. Clark and Chalmers seem to have such an idea in mind when they write,

> for coupled systems to be relevant to the core of cognition, *reliable* coupling is required. It happens that most reliable coupling takes place within the brain, but there can easily be reliable coupling with the environment as well. If the resources of my calculator or my Filofax are always there when I need them, then they are coupled with me as reliably as we need. ... If the relevant capacities are generally there when they are required, this is coupling enough.
>
> *(Clark and Chalmers, 1998, p. 8)*

Now return to the two challenges. In the first place, is a reliable causal connection really enough to warrant the conclusion that there is an extended cognitive process? Revisit the example of an air conditioning system. Let the process X of evaporative cooling be *reliably* causally coupled to the process Y of deformation in the shape of a bimetallic strip. This does not seem to make a difference. This reliable causal linkage between X and Y does not make the entire $X–Y$ process into a process of shape deformation. In this instance, reliable causal connection does not seem to determine the character of a process. So, the addition of the reliability condition does not seem to suffice to circumvent the coupling-constitution fallacy.[11] In the second place, reflect on the implications of the reliability condition. With this condition, not all uses of pen and paper for long multiplication will be instances of extended cognition. Cases in which an agent always has pen and paper at hand to do long multiplication will count as instances of extended cognition, whereas cases in which those implements are only occasionally available will not. This means that there are likely to be fewer instances of extended cognition than Clark and Chalmers may have led us to expect.

For a second illustration of the interaction between the two challenges, we could consider a set of more stringent conditions proposed by Clark and Chalmers:

> First, the notebook is a constant in Otto's life—in cases where the information in the notebook would be relevant, he will rarely take action without consulting it. Second, the information in the notebook is directly available without difficulty. Third, upon retrieving information from the notebook he automatically endorses it. Fourth, the information in the notebook has been consciously endorsed at some point in the past, and indeed is there as a consequence of this endorsement.
>
> *(Clark and Chalmers, 1998, p. 11)*

One may think that these conditions adequately meet the first challenge by yielding correct results for cases such as Otto's use of his notebook, but they also appear to rule out instances of bona fide memory. They appear to disallow cases of "alienation" from one's own cognitive resources. So, suppose that, for whatever reason, Dotto comes to the conclusion that he should not trust his memory to correctly recall people's names. Although he always does correctly recall the name of a person he sees, he does not trust his memory. Rather than take a chance on misidentifying someone, he either avoids the person or asks someone nearby to confirm his recollection. In this scenario, Dotto violates the first and third of Clark and Chalmers' conditions, suggesting that Dotto's memory is not really involved in cognitive processing.[12]

These sorts of examples, of course, do not prove that it is impossible to meet the two challenges. They do not show that it is impossible to find actual cases in which cognition extends when there is the *right kind* of causal connection between internal cognitive processes and bodily and environmental processes. Instead, they evidently establish the coupling-constitution fallacy as a provocation to further investigation.[13]

Conclusions

This chapter has focused on two prominent types of arguments for extended cognition: cognitive equivalence arguments and coupling arguments. These are perhaps best thought of as families of arguments. The members of the cognitive equivalence family differ among themselves regarding the standard of cognitive equivalence – for example, equivalence in all important and relevant respects, or equivalence in one or another respect. The members of the coupling family differ among themselves regarding what conditions, over and above a simple causal connection, warrant the conclusion that some process external to the brain constitutes a cognitive process. Insofar as we are concerned with the conditions under which there might be extended cognition, these appear to be the core approaches.[14]

Notes

1 The only other well-known cognitive equivalence argument is Clark and Chalmers' thought experiment with the video game Tetris. This argument was inspired by Kirsh and Maglio (1995).
2 In a similar bold spirit, Mark Rowlands claims "there is no sound theoretical reason for setting up a dichotomy between internal memory processes and external aids to those processes" (Rowlands, 1999, p. 121).

3 See, for example, Adams and Aizawa, 2001, 2008; and Fodor, 2009.
4 See, for example, Boyd, 1999a, 1999b.
5 For further discussion, see Clark, 2010.
6 For further discussion, see Adams and Aizawa, 2008; and Aizawa, 2010.
7 See Adams and Aizawa, 2008 for other examples of this sort.
8 Of course, we might try to modify the original Otto example in such a way as to display the negative transfer effect. Perhaps Otto does not write the A–C pairings on a new sheet of paper, but imperfectly erases the B entries and writes the C entries where the old B entries were. This way of entering the pairings may make it harder for Otto to write them correctly on the first try. And maybe this will make it harder for Otto to read the A–C pairings, which might explain why it takes him longer to get the A–C pairings right.
9 Also recall Rowlands' claim that "there is no sound theoretical reason for setting up a dichotomy between internal memory processes and external aids to those processes" (1999, p. 121).
10 See, for example, Clark, 2009; Fisher, 2009; and Wilson, 2010.
11 Notice that the reciprocal causal interaction between X and Y does not appear to make a difference. And, would it make a difference if the interaction between X and Y were non-linear?
12 For other examples in this vein, see Adams and Aizawa, 2008, ch. 7.
13 Other sets of condition on coupling will be found in van Gelder (1995) and Haugeland (1998). More recently, Chemero (2009) and Froese, Gershenson, and Rosenblueth (2013) have proposed that cognition extends when there is a non-linear coupling between brain processes and environmental processes, where Roberts (2012) has proposed that true cognitive extension occurs only when the subject takes responsibility for the contribution made by a non-neural resource.
14 For an alternative to causal coupling arguments, see Gillett, 2013, and the commentary in Aizawa, 2013.

References

Adams, F., and Aizawa, K. (2001). The bounds of cognition. *Philosophical Psychology*, *14*(1), 43–64.
——— (2008). *The bounds of cognition*. Malden, MA: Blackwell Publishers.
Aizawa, K. (2010). The boundaries still stand: A reply to Fisher. *Journal of Mind and Behavior*, *31*(1–2), 37–47.
——— (2013). Introduction to "The material bases of cognition". *Minds and Machines*, *23*(3), 277–286.
Boyd, R. (1999a). Homeostasis, species, and higher taxa. In R. Wilson (Ed.), *Species: New interdisciplinary essays* (pp. 141–185). Cambridge, MA: MIT Press.
——— (1999b). Kinds, complexity and multiple realization: Comments on Millikan's "Historical kinds and the special sciences". *Philosophical Studies*, *95*(1), 67–98.
Chemero, A. (2009). *Radical embodied cognitive science*. Cambridge, MA: MIT Press.
Clark, A. (2005). Intrinsic content, active memory and the extended mind. *Analysis*, *65*(1), 1–11.
——— (2009). *Supersizing the mind: Embodiment, action and cognitive extension*. New York: Oxford University Press.
——— (2010). Memento's revenge: The extended mind, extended. In R. Menary (Ed.), *The extended mind* (pp. 43–66). Cambridge, MA: MIT Press.
Clark, A., and Chalmers, D. (1998). The extended mind. *Analysis*, *58*(1), 7–19.
Dennett, D. C. (1986). The myth of original intentionality. In K. A. Mohyeldin Said, W. H. Newton-Smith, R. Viale, and K. V. Wilkes. (Eds), *Modeling the mind* (pp. 43–62). Oxford: Oxford University Press.
Fisher, J. (2009). Critical notice of the book *The bounds of cognition*, by F. Adams and K. Aizawa. *Journal of Mind and Brain*, *29*(4), 345–357.
Fodor, J. (2009). Where is my mind? *London Review of Books*, *31*(2), 13–15.
Froese, T., Gershenson, C., and Rosenblueth, D. A. (2013). The dynamically extended mind: A minimal modeling case study. Paper presented at the IEEE Congress on Evolutionary Computation, CEC 2013, Evolutionary Robotics track, Cancun, Mexico, June.

van Gelder, T. (1995). What might cognition be, if not computation? *Journal of Philosophy, 92,* 345–381.

Gillett, C. (2013). Constitution, and multiple constitution, in the sciences: Using the neuron to construct a starting framework. *Minds and Machines, 23(3),* 309–337.

Haugeland, J. (1998). Mind embodied and embedded. In J. Haugeland (Ed.), *Having thought: Essays in the metaphysics of mind* (pp. 207–237). Cambridge, MA: Harvard University Press.

Kirsh, D., and Maglio, P. (1995). Some epistemic benefits of action: Tetris, a case study. Proceedings of the Fourteenth Annual Conference of the Cognitive Science Society. Hillsdale, NJ: Lawrence Erlbaum Associates.

Menary, R. (2010). The holy grail of cognitivism: A response to Adams and Aizawa. *Phenomenology and the Cognitive Sciences, 9(4),* 605–618.

Roberts, T. (2012). You do the maths: Rules, extension, and cognitive responsibility. *Philosophical Explorations, 15(2),* 133–145.

Rowlands, M. (1999). *The body in mind: Understanding cognitive processes,* New York: Cambridge University Press.

——— (2009). Enactivism and the extended mind. *Topoi, 28(1),* 53–62.

Rupert, R. (2004). Challenges to the hypothesis of extended cognition. *Journal of Philosophy, 101(8),* 389–428.

Wilson, R. (2010). Extended vision. In N. Gangopadhyay, M. Madary, and F. Spicer (Eds), *Perception, action and consciousness: Sensorimotor dynamics and two visual systems* (pp. 277–290). Oxford: Oxford University Press.

5

COMPLEX DYNAMICAL SYSTEMS AND EMBODIMENT

Michael J. Richardson and Anthony Chemero

Although dynamical systems have been used by cognitive scientists for more than a decade already (e.g., Kugler, Kelso, and Turvey 1980), dynamical systems first gained widespread attention in the mid-1990s (e.g., Kelso 1995; Port and van Gelder 1995; Thelen and Smith 1994). Dynamical systems theory was then, and continues to be, a crucial tool for embodied cognitive science. The word *dynamical* simply means "changing over time" and thus a *dynamical system* is simply a system whose behavior evolves or changes over time. The scientific study of dynamical systems is concerned with understanding, modeling, and predicting the ways in which the behavior of a system changes over time. In the last few decades, thanks to increasing computational power, researchers have begun to investigate and understand the dynamic behavior of complex biological, cognitive, and social systems, using the concepts and tools of non-linear dynamical systems. In the next section, we will describe the key concepts of modern dynamical systems theory (complexity, self-organization, soft assembly, interaction dominance, and non-linearity). In the second section, we briefly discuss some dynamical analysis techniques used in the cognitive sciences. In the third, we give some examples of the application of complex dynamical systems theory and analysis in cognitive science. In the last, we sketch some consequences of the widespread applicability of dynamical approaches to understanding neural, cognitive, and social systems.

Complex dynamical systems

Complex dynamical systems exhibit three key characteristics (Gallagher and Appenzeller 1999). First, they consist of a number of interacting components or agents. These components can be homogeneous or heterogeneous. A collection of cortical areas or simple artificial agents can comprise a homogeneous, complex dynamical system; a brain in a body in an environment can comprise a heterogeneous, complex dynamical system. A second property is that these systems exhibit *emergent* behavior in that their collective behavior exhibits a coherent pattern that could not be predicted from the behavior of the components separately. Third, and most importantly, this emergent behavior is *self-organized* in that it does not result from a controlling component agent. These three characteristics can be seen clearly in phenomena such as bird flocking. Starlings, for example, gather in flocks of

DOI: 10.4324/9781003322511-8

hundreds to thousands known as "murmurations." Starling murmurations exhibit striking, globally unified behavior, in which large numbers of starlings move as a single, dark blob that changes shape as it moves across the sky. Murmurations are a coordination phenomenon in which interactions between individuals produce collective, large-scale patterns. Starling murmurations, and bird flocks more generally, exhibit all the key features of complex dynamical systems and have been modeled as such (Cavagna *et al.* 2010).

Self-organization

The term "self-organization" is used to refer to behavioral patterns that emerge from the interactions that bind the components of a system into a collective system, without a centralized controller. A murmuration's behavior is emergent and self-organized: murmurations form when sufficient numbers of starlings gather, without a head starling leading the way. In fact, in order to model the velocity of individual birds in a murmuration, Cavagna *et al.* (2010) start with the velocity of the murmuration as a whole, and work inward from there to model the velocities of individual birds. Starling flocking highlights how coordinated social behavior can result spontaneously from the interactions of agents. Coordinated, collective behavior among herds of mammals and schools of fish is self-organized in the same way, as is the nest-building behavior of ants, bees, and termites. In each of these cases, no individual animal or subset of the whole controls the behavior of the group (Camazine *et al.* 2001).

Soft assembly

Murmurations are temporary coalitions of starlings that are put together in a fluid and flexible manner. It doesn't matter which particular bird ends up in which position in the flock, and each bird will take up many different positions as the flock moves and takes shape. The behavior of the birds that are the components in the flock is context dependent. Dynamical systems that exhibit this kind of emergent, context-dependent behavior are often referred to as *softly assembled* systems, in that the behavioral system reflects a temporary coalition of coordinated entities, components, or factors. The term *synergy* is sometimes used to refer to softly assembled systems—a functional grouping of structural elements that are temporarily constrained to act as a single coherent unit (Kelso 2009). In contrast, most non-biological systems or machines are hard-molded systems. A laptop computer, for example, is a hard-molded system, in that it is composed of a series of components, each of which plays a specific, predetermined role in the laptop's behavior. Coordinated behavior in social animals, including humans, is often softly assembled.

Interaction-dominant dynamics

Softly assembled systems exhibit interaction-dominant dynamics, as opposed to component-dominant dynamics. For component-dominant dynamical systems, system behavior is the product of a rigidly delineated architecture of system modules, component elements, or agents, each with predetermined functions. For softly assembled, interaction-dominant dynamical systems, system behavior is the result of *interactions between* system components, agents, and situational factors, with these intercomponent or interagent interactions altering the dynamics of the component elements, situational factors, and agents themselves (Anderson, Richardson, and Chemero 2012; Van Orden, Kloos and Wallot 2011). As noted above, to model the behavior of individual starlings in a murmuration, Cavagna *et al.* (2010) began with the behavior of the flock as a whole. Within the murmuration, the behavior of any bird is primarily determined by the behavior of the whole murmuration, even though the murmuration is nothing other than the collection of individual birds. If one were to examine the relationship between any two levels of an interaction-dominant dynamical system, one would observe that elements or agents at the lower level of the system modulate the macroscopic order of the higher level, and at the same time are structured by the macroscopic order of the system. For interaction-dominant systems, it is difficult, and often impossible, to assign precise causal roles to particular components. It is also difficult, and often impossible, to predict the behavior of components within interaction-dominant systems from their behavior in isolation.

Non-linearity

A non-linear system is one in which the system's output is not directly proportional to the input, as opposed to a linear system in which the output can be simply represented as a weighted sum of input components. Complex dynamical systems are non-linear in this sense, so their behavior is never merely the sum of the behavior of the components (Van Orden, Holden, and Turvey 2003). Non-linearity cuts two ways. On one hand, the non-linearity of complex dynamical systems makes them much more difficult to understand. In fact, non-linear systems are non-decomposable, in that you cannot isolate components of the system and predict their behavior. On the other hand, it is only because complex dynamical systems are non-linear that they can exhibit complex behavior.

Dynamical analysis

Central to identifying the causal structures or processes that underlie and shape the physical and cognitive behavior of complex biological agents is time-series analysis. Substantial advances in the types of *non-linear* analysis techniques that have occurred in recent years, combined with the increasing availability of these techniques (i.e., via open-source software packages and code sharing), has further compounded their importance. In fact, it is becoming increasingly clear that non-linear time-series analysis is essential for understanding how the ordered regularity of human behavior and cognition can emerge and be maintained. The advantage of these methods over the traditional statistical techniques commonly employed in cognitive psychology is that they can handle the time dependence of behavior and are not restricted to making linear assumptions about behavioral organization. Indeed, contemporary methods of non-linear dynamics embrace the complexity of self-organized behavior and, accordingly, can provide deep insights about the behavior of real-world time-evolving processes. Here we discuss two methods of non-linear time-series analysis that have had a transformative impact on our ability to classify and understand a wide range of embodied cognition, namely recurrence analysis and fractal analysis.

Recurrence analysis

Recurrence analysis is a phase-space method that allows one to determine the dynamical structure of a recorded time series, no matter how complex the time series is, nor the number of state dimensions needed to capture the time series within its corresponding state space. The beauty of recurrence analysis, in comparison to other time-series methods, is that it does not require one to make any assumptions about the structure of the time series being investigated: it can be stationary, non-stationary periodic, stochastic, discrete, or categorical.

Essentially, recurrence analysis identifies the dynamics of a system by discerning (a) whether the states of system behavior recur over time and, if states do recur, (b) the deterministic regularity of the patterning of recurrences. Conceptually, performing recurrence analysis on behavioral data is relatively easy to understand; one simply plots whether recorded points, states, or events in a time series are revisited or reoccur over time on a two-dimensional plot, called a recurrence plot. This plot provides a visualization of the patterns of revisitations in a system's behavioral state space and can be quantified in various ways in order to identify the structure of the dynamics that exist (see Marwan, 2008 for details). The plots in Figure 5.1 are examples of what recurrence plots look like for a categorical (left plot) and continuous (right plot) behavioral time series.

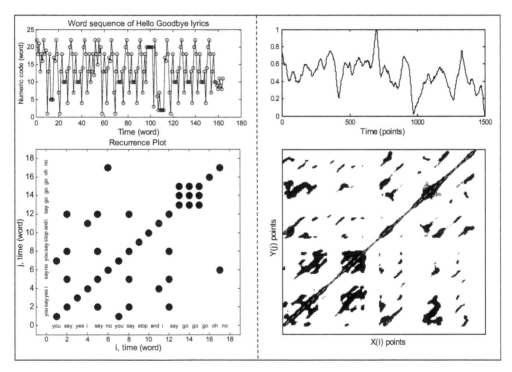

Figure 5.1 Categorical and continuous recurrence analysis. (Left top) The full time series of words extracted from the lyrics of "Hello, Goodbye" by the Beatles. The y-axis represents the numeric identifier to which a word is assigned, and the x-axis represents word-by-word unfolding of this "lexical" time series. (Left bottom) A recurrence plot of the first 20 words in the lyrics. Each point on the plot represents a relative point (i, j) in the lyrics at which a word is recurring (see, e.g., Dale and Spivey 2005, 2006). (Right top) The anterior-posterior postural sway movements of a single individual standing and listening to another person speak for 30 seconds. (Right bottom) A recurrence plot of the first 10 seconds of postural data. Despite the non-periodic nature of the postural movement, the recurrence plot reveals deterministic structure. (Adapted from Richardson et al. 2014.)

Recurrence analysis can also be extended to uncover the dynamic similarity and coordinated structure that exists between two different behavioral time series. This latter form of recurrence analysis is termed *cross-recurrence analysis* and is performed in much the same way as standard (auto-)recurrence analysis. The key difference is that recurrent points in cross-recurrence correspond to states or events in two time series that are recurrent with each other. Cross-recurrence analysis can therefore be employed to quantify the co-occurring dynamics of two behavioral time series.

Fractal analysis

Researchers in cognitive and behavioral psychology commonly collapse repeated measurements into summary variables, such as the mean and standard deviation, under the assumption that the measured data contain uncorrelated variance that is normally distributed. Real-time behavior and cognition, however, are rarely static and thus summary statistics often reveal little about how a system evolves over time. Indeed, time-series recordings of human performance and cognition typically contain various levels of correlated variance or non-random fluctuations that are not normally distributed (Stephen and Mirman, 2010) and, moreover, are structured in a *fractal* or *self-similar* manner (Gilden 2001, 2009; Van Orden *et al*. 2003; Van Orden *et al*. 2011). Indexing the correlated and self-similar variance within a behavioral time series requires the use of fractal methods of analysis, sometimes called *fractal statistics*.

A fractal or self-similar pattern is simply a pattern that is composed of nested copies of itself and looks similar at different scales of observation. A fractal time series is therefore a time series that contains nested patterns of variability (Figure 5.2). That is, the patterns of fluctuation over time look similar at different scales of magnification. The time series displayed in Figure 5.2 is a good example, with the self-similarity of its temporal fluctuations revealed by zooming in on smaller and smaller sections. At each level of magnification the temporal pattern looks similar (Holden 2005).

A fractal time series is characterized by an inverse proportional relationship between the power (P) and frequency (*f*) of observed variation. That is, for a fractal time series there exists a proportional relationship between the size of a change and how frequently changes of that size occur, with this relationship remaining stable across changes in scale. It is in this sense that the pattern of variability in a repeatedly measured behavior is self-similar; large-scale changes occur with the same *relative* frequency as small-scale changes. The degree to which a data set approximates this ideal relationship between power and frequency, $P = 1/f^{\alpha}$, is summarized in the scaling exponent, α. If one plots the power of the different spectral frequencies that make up a time series on double-logarithmic axes, α is equivalent to the slope of the line that best fits the data (Figure 5.3). That is, α captures the relationship between size and frequency of fluctuations in the time series of behavior. Random fluctuations (i.e., white noise) produce a flat line in a log-log spectral plot with a slope close to 0, which indicates that changes of all different sizes occur with approximately the same frequency. Alternatively, fractal fluctuations, often referred to as pink or $1/f$ noise, produce a line in a log-log spectral plot that has a slope closer to -1, which indicates the scale-invariant scaling relationship characteristic of fractal patterns.

The import of determining whether a behavioral time series contains fractal or $1/f$ variability is highlighted by a growing body of research demonstrating that most human behaviors exhibit fractal structure. For example, numerous studies have demonstrated how the

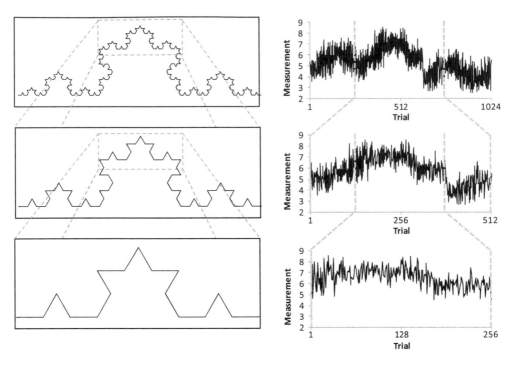

Figure 5.2 Example geometric and temporal fractal patterns (i.e., containing self-similar structure at different magnitudes of observation). (Left) Koch Snowflake at three levels of magnification. (Right) Fractal time series at three levels of magnification. (Adapted from Holden, 2005.)

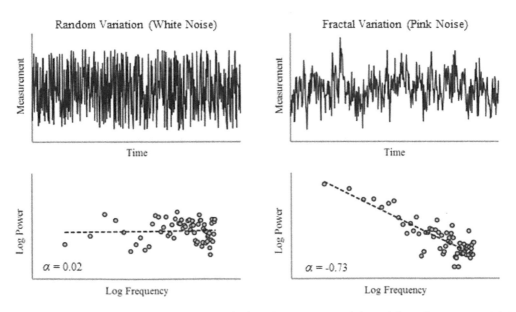

Figure 5.3 Examples of time series composed of random variation (left) and fractal variation (right) and the associated log-log spectral plots.

fluctuations in time series of ongoing stimulus-response activity, time estimation, cognitive performance, postural control, and eye movements exhibited fractal structure (see Delignières *et al.* 2006; Gilden 2009; Holden 2005). Even the flow of social interaction and behavior has a fractal structure (e.g., Delignières, Fortes, and Ninot 2004; Newtson 1994). Of particular relevance for the current discussion, however, is that this research has also demonstrated that the degree to which fluctuations within a behavioral time series are fractal (i.e., pink) or not (i.e., white), can provide evidence about whether a behavior is non-linear and the result of interaction-dominant dynamics (Van Orden *et al.* 2003).

Complex, dynamical cognitive systems

The above analysis techniques have been applied widely at all spatial scales relevant to cognitive science, from brain areas to embodied behavior, to agent–environment systems, and to social interaction. Although recurrence analysis is still relatively new, there is now substantial evidence to suggest that it is potentially one of the most generally applicable methods for assessing the dynamics of biological and human behavior (e.g., Marwan and Meinke 2002; Zbilut, Thomasson, and Webber 2002). This is due to the fact that recurrence analysis provides researchers with a way of determining whether the nested fluctuations and complex time-evolving patterns within almost any type of behavioral time series are deterministic and interrelated, or stochastic and disconnected (i.e., the degree a behavioral structure is the result of interaction-dominant dynamics). For instance, auto- and cross-recurrence analysis has already been employed to uncover the non-obvious changes that goal constraints produce on the synergistic dynamics of postural movements (Riley, Balasubramaniam, and Turvey 1999), the noise structure of limb movements (e.g., Pellecchia, Shockley, and Turvey 2005; Richardson, Schmidt, and Kay 2007c), the intermitted perceptual-motor synchrony that occurs between people interacting (Richardson and Dale 2005; Richardson, Marsh, and Schmidt 2005; Richardson, Marsh, Isenhower, Goodman, and Schmidt 2007b; Shockley, Santana, and Fowler 2003; Shockley, Baker, Richardson, and Fowler 2007), the deterministic structure inherent in eye movements and stimulus-response reaction-time data (e.g., Cherubini, Nüssli, and Dillenbourg 2010; Pannasch, Helmert, Müller, and Velichkovsky 2012), and even semantic similarity during conversation (Angus, Smith, and Wiles 2011) and the vocal dynamics of children during development (Warlaumont *et al.* 2010). In each case, recurrence analysis was able to reveal whether the observed dynamics were the result of nested physical, neural, and informational couplings that bound cognition and action to each other and to the relevant objects (individuals) and events within the task environment.

As noted above, the presence of $1/f$ scaling and complex patterns of recurrent structure in a cognitive and behavioral phenomenon is evidence that the softly assembled system is interaction dominant. Complex patterns of recurrent behavior and $1/f$ scaling has been observed in the brain, and in a wide variety of cognitive and behavioral tasks, from tapping to key pressing, to word naming, and many others (Van Orden *et al.* 2011). This indicates that softly assembled coalitions of components encompassing portions of the participants' brain and body were responsible for the performance of the experimental task. That the portions of the cognitive system that engage in tasks such as these are not fully encapsulated in the brain is perhaps not surprising, since each has a strong motor component. But we also see time-evolving recurrent structures and $1/f$ scaling in "purely cognitive" phenomena. In one example, Stephen, Dixon, and Isenhower (2009) have shown that problem-solving inference is accomplished by an interaction-dominant system. Using fractal statistics and recurrence analysis, they found that learning a new strategy for solving a problem coincides with changes in the complexity and amount of recurrent activity in an individual's eye movements. This indicates that even leaps of insight do not occur in the brain alone—the eye movements are part of the interaction-dominant system that realizes the cognitive act. Findings such as this impact not only the extent of the biological resources required for cognitive faculties, but also the separation of cognitive faculties from one another. Finding that moving eyes are components of the interaction-dominant system that has the problem-solving insight makes it more difficult to separate cognition from motor control.

There is reason to think that this expansion of the cognitive system does not stop at the boundaries of the biological body. For example, Dotov, Nie, and Chemero (2010) describe experiments designed to induce and then temporarily disrupt an extended cognitive system. Participants in these experiments play a simple video game, controlling an object on a monitor using a mouse. At some point during the 1-minute trial, the connection between the mouse and the object it controls is disrupted temporarily before returning to normal. Dotov *et al.* found $1/f$ scaling at the hand-mouse interface while the mouse was operating normally, but not during the disruption. As discussed above, this indicates that, during normal operation, the computer mouse is part of the smoothly functioning interaction-dominant system engaged in the task; during the mouse perturbation, however, the $1/f$ scaling at the hand-mouse interface disappears temporarily, indicating that the mouse is no longer part of the extended interaction-dominant system. These experiments were designed to detect, and did in fact detect, the presence of an extended cognitive system, an interaction-dominant system that included both biological and non-biological parts. The fact that such a mundane experimental set-up (using a computer mouse to control an object on a monitor) generated an extended cognitive system suggests that extended cognitive systems are quite common. These, of course, are not the only examples of interaction dominance in cognition (for a review, see Van Orden *et al.* 2011).

The phenomena of $1/f$ scaling and recurrent dynamics are ubiquitous in the brain as well. Heterogeneous coupling and multiscale dynamics are widespread features of the brain. Brain connectivity is organized on a hierarchy of scales ranging from local circuits of neurons to functional topological networks. At each scale the relevant neural dynamics are determined not just by processes at that scale, but by processes at other smaller and larger scales as well. Such multilevel clustered architectures promote varied and stable dynamic patterns via criticality and other dynamical and topological features. There is therefore also growing evidence that neural circuits are interaction dominant. Several recent studies have found evidence of $1/f$ scaling in human neural activity (e.g., Freeman, Rogers, Holmes, and Silbergeld 2000; Bullmore *et al.* 2001; Freeman 2009). Research on the dynamics of brain activity using recurrence analysis has also produced evidence that the dynamic behavior of the brain is characteristic of an interaction-dominant system. For example, Acharya and colleagues have employed recurrence analysis to uncover the non-linear and interaction-dominant dynamics of EEG singles during various sleep cycles and for individuals with epilepsy (e.g., Acharya, Faust, Kannathal, Chua, and Laxminarayan 2005).

Finally, the dynamics of many social behaviors are interaction dominant and characterized by complex recurrent patterns and $1/f$ scaling. For instance, Shockley *et al.* (2003) employed cross-recurrence analysis to examine the postural dynamics of two co-present participants completing a conversational task together. The experiment included two key manipulations. The first manipulation was whether the two participants were performing the task together, or whether the participants were co-present but performed the task with a confederate. The second manipulation was whether the participants were positioned facing each other or back to back. The analysis revealed that the postural activity of the two participants was more similar when performing the puzzle task together (i.e., conversing with each other) compared to when performing the task with the confederate. Surprisingly, the interpersonal postural dynamics were not influenced by vision, in that the same magnitude of recurrent activity was observed irrespective of whether the participants could see each other or not. Thus, the findings not only demonstrated how an individual's postural dynamics are spontaneously influenced by interactions with other conspecifics, but also how conversation alone can couple the behavioral dynamics of interacting individuals.

The fact that the physical and informational interactions that characterize social interaction operate to shape behavior (often spontaneously and without awareness) means that the behavioral dynamics of social activity are inherently interaction dominant. In addition to the postural work of Shockley *et al.* (2003), other studies investigating various forms of social movement coordination have produced findings that demonstrated that the dynamics of social behavior are interaction dominant (see Riley, Richardson, Shockley, and Ramenzoni 2011; Richardson, Marsh, and Schmidt 2010; Schmidt and Richardson 2008). The implication is that co-acting individuals form a synergy, whereby the behavioral order of the individuals involved is enslaved by the functional order of the group or team as a whole. Accordingly, the behavioral performance of interacting individuals is not simply an additive function of each individual's cognitive or behavioral capabilities and, moreover, cannot be understood by studying the individuals in isolation from each other or the social setting. Ramenzoni (2008) highlighted this point, using cross-recurrence analysis to demonstrate how the informational interaction that occurs during joint action results in the dimensional compression of each individual's behavioral degrees of freedom and the formation of a low-dimensional reciprocally compensating synergy. Similar findings have been made by Richardson, Dale, and colleagues in studies investigating social eye coordination and language comprehension (Richardson, Dale, and Tomlinson 2009). Using categorical cross-recurrence analysis, they have demonstrated across several studies that a shared task context results in synergistic eye movements and that the coordinated stability of such eye movements reflects how well two people comprehend each other (Richardson and Dale 2005), the strength of their shared knowledge, and how much two people converge in language use (Richardson, Dale, and Spivey 2007a).

With respect to $1/f$ scaling and the fractal nature of social behavior, Delignières *et al.* (2004) have demonstrated that fractal processes underlie the dynamics of self-esteem and physical self. Twice a day, for 512 consecutive days, they collected data about the global self-esteem of four individuals. Consistent with a conception of self-perception as an emergent product of an interaction-dominant dynamical system, an analysis of the resulting time series found converging evidence of $1/f$ scaling in the behavioral series. At a more local level, Malone and colleagues (Malone, Castillo, Holden, Kloos, and Richardson 2013) recently employed a social Simon stimulus-response compatibility task to demonstrate how the mere presence of another actor constrains the fractal variability of an individual's response behavior. The results revealed how the presence of another actor alters a task setting and, as such, the ongoing dynamics of individual behavior (even if the co-present individual is engaged in an independent task). Eiler, Kallen, Harrison, and Richardson (2013) have uncovered preliminary evidence that social stereotypes and gender salience can influence the fractal structure of an individual's cognitive and behavioral performance. Perhaps most compelling is the work by Correll (2008), which has shown that participants who are trying to avoid racial bias show decreased fractal signature in their response latencies in a video game. In light of characterizing social perception and other processes as a system of many intertwined dependencies—as processes of an interaction-dominant dynamical system—these findings suggest that the behavioral fluctuations of socially situated performance reflects the distributed influence of positive and negative perceptions and judgments, and the cultural regulations that define them.

Consequences

The complexity and unpredictability of human behavior has led many cognitive scientists to attempt to understand cognitive systems as complex dynamical systems, and to approach them using complex dynamical analysis. The result of this has been the widespread recognition of interaction-dominant dynamics in the brain and in individual and social cognition. This recognition has consequences both for the nature of cognition and for the practice of cognitive science. Here we focus on consequences concerning modularity and extended cognition (see Chemero, in press).

Modularity

An *interaction-dominant system* is a highly interconnected system, each of whose components alters the dynamics of many of the others to such an extent that the effects of the interactions are more powerful than the intrinsic dynamics of the components. In an interaction-dominant system, inherent variability (i.e., fluctuations or noise) of any individual component propagates through the system as a whole, altering the dynamics of the other components. In interaction-dominant systems one cannot treat the components of the system in isolation: because of the widespread feedback in interaction-dominant systems, one cannot isolate components to determine exactly what their contribution is to particular behavior. And because the effects of interactions are more powerful than the intrinsic dynamics of the components, the behavior of the components in any particular interaction-dominant system is not predictable from their behavior in isolation or from their behavior in some other interaction-dominant system. Interaction-dominant systems, in other words, are not *modular*. They are in a deep way *unified* in that the responsibility for system behavior is distributed across all of the components. Given the rapid pace at which cognitive systems have been shown to be interaction dominant in the twenty-first century, there is good reason to think that cognitive systems are not, in general, modular (Anderson *et al.* 2012; Chemero, in press).

Extended cognition

We have seen that not just neural and brain-body systems are interaction dominant; so too are human-tool cognitive systems and social cognitive systems. Because interaction-dominant systems are unified, we should identify the cognitive systems in these cases with human-tool and social systems as a whole. That is, the cognitive system in question is not encapsulated within an individual brain or even an individual body. This supports the hypothesis of extended cognition. According to the hypothesis of extended cognition, cognitive systems sometimes include portions of the non-bodily environment (Clark and Chalmers 1998; Chemero 2009). When human-tool or social cognitive systems are complex dynamical systems with interaction-dominant dynamics, they are extended cognitive systems. Moreover, these studies support extended cognition empirically, and not with a priori philosophical argumentation.

References

Acharya, U. R., Faust, O., Kannathal, N., Chua, T. L., and Laxminarayan, S. (2005) "Non-linear analysis of EEG signals at various sleep stages," *Computer Methods and Programs in Biomedicine*, 80, 37–45.

Anderson, M. L., Richardson, M. J., and Chemero, A. (2012) "Eroding the boundaries of cognition: Implications of embodiment," *Topics in Cognitive Science*, 4, 1–14.

Angus, D., Smith, A., and Wiles, J. (2011) "Conceptual recurrence plots: Revealing patterns in human discourse," *IEEE Transactions on Visualization and Computer Graphics*, 18, 988–997.

Bullmore, E., Long, C., Suckling, J., Fadili, J., Calvert, G., Zelaya, F., Carpenter, T. A., and Brammer, M. (2001) "Colored noise and computational inference in neurophysiological (fMRI) time series analysis: Resampling methods in time and wavelet domains," *Human Brain Mapping*, 12, 61–78

Camazine, S., Deneubourg, J. L., Franks, N. R., Sneyd, J., Theraulaz, G., and Bonabeau, E. (2001) *Self-organization in biological systems*, Princeton, NJ: Princeton University Press.

Cavagna, A., Cimarelli, A., Giardina, I., Parisi, G., Santagati, F., Stefanini, F., and Viale, M. (2010) "Scale-free correlations in starling flocks," *Proceedings of the National Academy of Sciences of the United States of America*, 107, 11865–11870.

Chemero, A. (2009) *Radical embodied cognitive science*, Cambridge, MA: MIT Press.

Chemero, A. (in press) "The architecture of cognition: Rethinking Fodor and Pylyshyn's systematicity challenge," in P. Calvo Garzon and J. Symons (eds), *Systematicity and the cognitive architecture*, Cambridge, MA: MIT Press.

Cherubini, M.-A. Nüssli, M.-A., and Dillenbourg, P. (2010) "This is it!: Indicating and looking in collaborative work at distance," *Journal of Eye Movement Research*, 3, 1–20.

Clark, A., and Chalmers, D. J. (1998) "The extended mind," *Analysis*, 58, 7–19.

Correll, J. (2008) "1/f noise and effort on implicit measures of racial bias," *Journal of Personality and Social Psychology*, 94, 48–59.

Dale, R., and Spivey, M. J. (2005) "Categorical recurrence analysis of child language," in B. Bara, L. Barsalou, and M. Bucciarelli (eds), *Proceedings of the 27th Annual Meeting of the Cognitive Science Society* (pp. 530–535) Mahwah, NJ: Lawrence Erlbaum.

Dale, R., and Spivey, M. J. (2006) "Unraveling the dyad: Using recurrence analysis to explore patterns of syntactic coordination between children and caregivers in conversation," *Language Learning*, 56, 391–430.

Delignières, D., Fortes, M., and Ninot, G. (2004) "The fractal dynamics of self-esteem and physical self," *Nonlinear Dynamics in Psychology and Life Science*, 8, 479–510.

Delignières, D., Ramdani, S., Lemoine, L., Torre, K., Fortes, M., and Ninot, G. (2006) "Fractal analysis for short time series: A reassessment of classical methods," *Journal of Mathematical Psychology*, 50, 525–544.

Dotov, D., Nie, L., and Chemero, A. (2010) "A demonstration of the transition from readiness-to-hand to unreadiness-to-hand," *PLoS One*, 5(3), e9433.

Eiler, B. A., Kallen, R. W., Harrison, S. J., and Richardson, M. J. (2013) "Origins of order in joint activity and social behavior," *Ecological Psychology* 25(3), 316–326.

Freeman, W. J. (2009) "Deep analysis of perception through dynamic structures that emerge in cortical activity from self-regulated noise," *Cognitive Neurodynamics*, 3, 105–116.

Freeman, W. J., Rogers, L. J., Holmes, M. D., and Silbergeld, D. L. (2000) "Spatial spectral analysis of human electrocorticograms including the alpha and gamma bands," *Journal of Neuroscience Methods*, 95, 111–121.

Gallagher, R. and Appenzeller, T. (1999) "Beyond reductionism," *Science*, 284, 79.

Gilden, D. L. (2001) "Cognitive emissions of 1/f noise," *Psychological Review*, 108, 33–56.

Gilden, D. L. (2009) "Global model analysis of cognitive variability," *Cognitive Science*, 33, 1441–1467.

Holden, J. G. (2005) "Gauging the fractal dimension of response times from cognitive tasks," in M. A. Riley and G. C. Van Orden (eds), *Contemporary nonlinear methods for behavioral scientists: A webbook tutorial* (pp. 267–318) Retrieved 8 April 2005, from http://www.nsf.gov/sbe/bcs/pac/nmbs/nmbs.jsp

Kelso, J. A. S. (1995) *Dynamic patterns*, Cambridge, MA: MIT Press.

Kelso, J. A. S. (2009) "Synergies: Atoms of brain and behavior," in D. Sternad (ed.), *Progress in motor control* (pp. 83–91) Heidelberg: Springer.

Kugler, P. N., Kelso, J. A. S., and Turvey, M. T. (1980) "On the concept of coordinative structures as dissipative structures, I: Theoretical lines of convergence," in G. E. Stelmach and J. Requin (eds), *Tutorials in motor behavior* (pp. 3–47) Amsterdam: North Holland.

Malone, M., Castillo, R. D., Holden, J. D., Kloos, H., and Richardson, M. J. (2013) "Dynamic structure of joint-action stimulus-response activity," in M. Knauff, M. Pauen, N. Sebanz, and I. Wachsmuth (eds), *Proceedings of the 35th Annual Conference of the Cognitive Science Society* (pp. 172–177) Austin, TX: Cognitive Science Society.

Marwan, N. (2008) "A historical review of recurrence plots," *European Physical Journal*, 164, 3–12.

Marwan, N., and Meinke, A. (2002) "Extended recurrence plot analysis and its application to ERP data," *International Journal of Bifurcation and Chaos*, 14, 761–771.

Newtson, D. (1994) "The perception and coupling of behavior waves," in R. Vallacher and A. Nowak (eds), *Dynamical systems in social psychology* (pp. 139–167) San Diego, CA: Academic Press.

Pannasch, S., Helmert, J. R., Müller, R., and Velichkovsky, B. M. (2012) "The analysis of eye movements in the context of cognitive technical systems: Three critical issue," *Lecture Notes in Computer Science: Cognitive Behavioural Systems*, 7403, 19–34.

Pellecchia, G., Shockley, K., and Turvey, M. (2005) "Concurrent cognitive task modulates coordination dynamics," *Cognitive Science*, 29, 531–557.

Port, R., and van Gelder, T. (1995) *Mind as motion*, Cambridge, MA: MIT Press.

Ramenzoni, V. C. (2008) *Effects of joint task performance on interpersonal postural coordination* (Unpublished doctoral dissertation) University of Cincinnati, Cincinnati, OH.

Richardson, D. C., and Dale, R. (2005) "Looking to understand: The coupling between speakers' and listeners' eye movements and its relationship to discourse comprehension," *Cognitive Science*, 29, 1045–1060.

Richardson, D. C., Dale, R., and Spivey, M. J. (2007a) "Eye movements in language and cognition," in M. Gonzalez-Marquez, I. Mittelberg, S. Coulson, and M. J. Spivey (eds), *Methods in cognitive linguistics* (pp. 328–341) Amsterdam; PA: John Benjamins.

Richardson, D. C., Dale, R., and Tomlinson, J. M. (2009) "Conversation, gaze coordination, and beliefs about visual context," *Cognitive Science*, 33, 1468–1482.

Richardson, M. J., Dale, R., and Marsh, K. L. (2014) "Complex Dynamical Systems in Social and Personality Psychology: Theory, modeling and analysis," in H. T. Reiss and C. M. Judd (eds), *Handbook of Research Methods in Social and Personality Psychology*, 2nd Edition. New York, NY: Cambridge University Press.

Richardson, M. J., Marsh, K. L., Isenhower, R., Goodman, J., and Schmidt, R. C. (2007b) "Rocking together: Dynamics of intentional and unintentional interpersonal coordination," *Human Movement Science*, 26, 867–891.

Richardson, M. J., Marsh, K. L., and Schmidt, R. C. (2005) "Effects of visual and verbal information on unintentional interpersonal coordination," *Journal of Experimental Psychology: Human Perception and Performance*, 31, 62–79.

Richardson, M. J., Marsh, K. L., and Schmidt, R. C. (2010) "Challenging egocentric notions of perceiving, acting, and knowing," in L. F. Barrett, B. Mesquita, and E. Smith (eds), *The mind in context* (pp. 307–333) New York, NY: Guilford.

Richardson, M. J., Schmidt, R. C., and Kay, B. A. (2007c) "Distinguishing the noise and attractor strength of coordinated limb movements using recurrence analysis," *Biological Cybernetics*, 96, 59–78.

Riley, M. A., Balasubramaniam, R., and Turvey, M. T. (1999) "Recurrence quantification analysis of postural fluctuations," *Gait and Posture*, 9, 65–78.

Riley, M. A., Richardson, M. J., Shockley, K., and Ramenzoni, V. C. (2011) "Interpersonal synergies," *Frontiers in Psychology*, 2(38), 1–7.

Schmidt, R. C., and Richardson, M. J. (2008) "Dynamics of interpersonal coordination," in A. Fuchs and V. Jirsa (eds), *Coordination: Neural, behavioural and social dynamics* (pp. 281–308) Heidelberg: Springer.

Shockley, K., Santana, M. V., and Fowler, C. A. (2003) "Mutual interpersonal postural constraints are involved in cooperative conversation," *Journal of Experimental Psychology: Human Perception and Performance*, 29, 326–332.

Shockley, K. D., Baker, A. A., Richardson, M. J., and Fowler, C. A. (2007) "Verbal constraints on interpersonal postural coordination," *Journal of Experimental Psychology: Human Perception and Performance*, 33, 201–208.

Stephen, D., Dixon, J., and Isenhower, R. (2009) "Dynamics of representational change: Entropy, action, cognition," *Journal of Experimental Psychology: Human Perception and Performance*, 35, 1811–1822.

Stephen, D. G., and Mirman, D. (2010) "Interactions dominate the dynamics of visual cognition," *Cognition*, 115, 154–165.

Thelen, E., and Smith, L. B. (1994) *A dynamic systems approach to the development of cognition and action*, Cambridge, MA: MIT Press.

Van Orden, G. C., Holden, J. G., and Turvey, M. T. (2003) "Self-organization of cognitive performance," *Journal of Experimental Psychology: General*, 132, 331–350.

Van Orden, G. C., Kloos, H., and Wallot, S. (2011) "Living in the pink: intentionality, wellbeing, and complexity," in C. A. Hooker (ed.), *Philosophy of complex systems: Handbook of the philosophy of science* (pp. 639–684) Amsterdam: Elsevier.

Warlaumont, A. S., Oller, D. K., Dale, R., Richards, J. A., Gilkerson, J., and Dongxin, X. (2010) "Vocal interaction dynamics of children with and without autism," in S. Ohlsson and R. Catrambone (eds), *Proceedings of the 32nd Annual Meeting of the Cognitive Science Society* (pp. 121–126) Austin, TX: Cognitive Science Society.

Zbilut, Joseph P., Thomasson, Nitza, and Webber, Charles L. (2002) "Recurrence quantification analysis as a tool for nonlinear exploration of nonstationary cardiac signals," *Medical Engineering & Physics*, 24(1), 53–60.

6
EMBEDDED AND SITUATED COGNITION

Michael R. W. Dawson

Embodied cognitive science reacts against more established traditions within cognitive science (Clark 1997; Dawson 2013; Dawson et al. 2010; Shapiro 2019; Gibson 1979). Shapiro identifies three main themes which separate the embodied approach from other traditions. According to *conceptualization*, an agent's understanding of its world depends critically upon the agent's body. According to *replacement*, an agent's interactions with the world replace the need for mental representations. According to *constitution*, an agent's world and body are constituents of (and not merely causally related to) an agent's mind.

The current chapter explores what is meant when cognitive scientists describe cognition as *embodied, embedded* or *situated* (Chemero 2009; Clancey 1997; Clark 1997, 1999, 2003; Dawson et al. 2010; Dourish 2001; Shapiro 2019; Varela et al. 1991). The chapter contrasts these ideas with some traditional foundations of standard cognitive science (Dawson 1998; Dawson 2013).

Underdetermination in Perception

Humans take seeing for granted. When we look at the world, we automatically experience seeing it in high detail (Noë 2002, 2004), as if human eyes are like video cameras for delivering visual information. However, when researchers failed in attempts to program seeing computers, they realized the video camera theory was inadequate because the human visual system effortlessly solves complex information-processing problems. Primary visual data (the proximal stimulus on the retina) does not contain enough information to determine a unique and correct visual interpretation: instead, a single proximal stimulus is consistent with an infinite number of different interpretations (Marr 1982). We call this the *problem of underdetermination*, or, borrowing a term from linguistics (Chomsky 1965) the *poverty of the stimulus*. Problems of underdetermination are notoriously difficult, but human visual processing solves such problems effortlessly.

How might problems of underdetermination be solved? Standard cognitive science appeals to *unconscious inference* (Bruner 1957; Helmholtz 1868/1968; Rock 1983). According to unconscious inference, perception is identical to cognition; knowledge-driven

DOI: 10.4324/9781003322511-9

inferential processing adds information to disambiguate the proximal stimulus and produce the correct interpretation.

The cognitive view continues to dominate modern theories of perception, which assume sensation provides information for creating a mental model (Pylyshyn 2003). However, completing the mental model also requires thinking (e.g., unconscious inference) to supplement information from sensation. Once created, the seer uses the mental model to plan and to act. The cognitive view places thinking as a necessary intermediary between sensing and acting, producing the *sense-think-act cycle* or the *classical sandwich* (Hurley 2001).

However, what if perception does not build mental models, but instead directly controls actions on the world? Embodied cognitive science replaces the sense-think-act cycle with the *sense-act cycle* (Brooks 1999; Clark 1997; Pfeifer and Scheier 1999). *Direct* links between sensing and acting exist in a sense-act cycle. What are the implications of replacing the sense-think-act cycle with the sense-act cycle? Consider an example from comparative psychology.

Case Study: Echolocation

In the sense-think-act cycle, agents passively receive information. In contrast, perception is active in the sense-act cycle, because perceivers constantly explore and act upon the world. One example of active sensing is *echolocation*, in which bats use self-generated energy to probe the world (Nelson and MacIver 2006). Many bat species hunt by emitting ultrasonic sounds and by using echoes of their sounds to detect targets. Echolocation enables bats to discover and intercept prey as small as fruit flies or mosquitos from distances of between 50 and 100cm (Griffin et al. 1960).

Echolocation consists of three stages (Griffin et al. 1960). In the *search phase*, bats fly relatively straight and emit sounds at a relatively slow rate of repetition. When the bat first detects an insect during the search phase, an *approach phase* begins: the bat turns towards the detected insect while progressively increasing the signaling rate, presumably to locate the target more accurately. When close enough to the target, the bat moves into a *terminal phase* and produces sounds at a high rate – an ultrasonic buzz – to enable the bat to close in and capture the quarry.

However, moths do not simply wait to become meals. The scales of moth wings absorb sounds at the frequencies of bat ultrasonics, dampening a moth's echo (Zeng et al. 2011). Some moths can hear bat echolocation signals (Fenton and Fullard 1979; Roeder and Treat 1961; Rydell et al. 1995). As soon as such a signal is heard, a moth executes a power dive towards the ground: evasive maneuvers including tight turns, loops, and climbs (Roeder and Treat 1961). In addition, some moth species also emit ultrasonic sounds, causing bats to turn away from their prey (Dunning and Roeder 1965) either because the moth's signal indicates that the moth is inedible or because the moth signal interferes with bat echolocation (Fenton and Fullard 1979; Fullard et al. 1994; Hristov and Conner 2005; Rydell et al. 1995).

Moth counter measures to echolocation are themselves countered by bats. Some bats use ultrasonic frequencies beyond the range of moth hearing, or hunt silently and listen for the sounds generated by their prey (Rydell et al. 1995). Bats also learn from echolocation encounters, changing behavior to discriminate different types of targets (Griffin et al. 1965). In short, a dynamic relationship exists between a single echolocating bat and an individual moth which hears and attempts to evade the predator.

Situating Echolocation

Cyberneticists recognized the intrinsic coupling between agents and environments, because an agent's actions can change the world, which in turn influences the agent's future actions. Cyberneticists called such coupling *feedback* (Ashby 1956; Wiener 1948).

Feedback exists between an echolocating bat and the bat's environment. The bat's actions – its flight pattern and the sounds it generates – depend upon the distance between the bat and its prey. When a moth detects an attack and begins evasive maneuvers, the maneuvers represent a change in the world caused by the bat's ultrasonic probing. In turn, the change in the world changes the bat's behavior, as it alters its flight path to foil the evasion.

Critically, the coupling between the actions of the bat and the actions of its prey occurs over drastically short periods of time (Griffin et al. 1960). Bats usually hunt targets less than a meter away, fly at speeds of 1 to 6m/s, and therefore have only a few milliseconds to process the echo from any given target (Horiuchi 2005). As a result, bat flight is adjusted by neurons that only have enough time to generate one or two action potentials.

Embodied cognitive science aims for theories capable of controlling action under severe time restrictions. One reason researchers hypothesize the sense-act cycle is to decrease processing time by eliminating the 'thinking bottleneck.' The neuroscience of bat echolocation reveals a circuitry consistent with sense-act processing. For instance, auditory processing in the bat brain is tightly coupled with motor processing, particularly with motor circuits responsible for bat vocalizations (Moss and Sinha 2003). Such coupling reflects a sense-act system for modulating ultrasonic signals as a function of echolocation feedback; we saw earlier the signals produced by bats vary throughout an attack sequence. Similarly, VLSI circuits for modeling the neural circuitry of echolocation, and which use the output of this circuitry to control movements directly, can successfully steer robots through complex obstacle courses (Horiuchi 2005).

Adequate echolocation theories must consider the coupling between the bat and its world. Bats detect small, moving targets, do so while flying in three dimensions at high speeds, and detect (and react to) changes in target location in a matter of milliseconds. The dynamic relationship between the bat and the world in which it hunts places constraints on echolocation theories.

To say an adequate theory of echolocation must consider the coupling of a bat and its environment is to say such a theory must be *embedded* or *situated*. When researchers describe cognition as being embedded or situated (Beer 2003; Clancey 1993; Clancey 1997; Pylyshyn 2000; Roy 2005), they emphasize the coupling of agents with a dynamic world (Shapiro 2019). The explanatory force of an embedded or situated theory comes from appealing to properties of the world, or to properties of the world–agent interface (Ashby 1956; Grey Walter 1963; Simon 1969).

Underdetermination and Embodiment

Standard cognitive scientists argue (Vera and Simon 1993, 1994) that their theories have long included environmental influences, citing Simon's parable of the ant (Simon 1969) as a famous example. However, standard cognitive scientists also admit they emphasize 'thinking' within the classical sandwich at the expense of both sensing and acting (Anderson et al. 2004; Newell 1990). In embedded or situated cognition, the environment is more than just a source of inputs. When an agent is situated, its experience of the world depends crucially upon not only its sensory mechanisms, but also upon the shape of its body and the potential of its body to affect the world. "It is often neglected that the words *animal* and *environment* make an inseparable pair" (Gibson 1979: 8).

Embodied cognitive science's interest in embedded or situated theories provides a link to theories developed in other disciplines. Biologist Jakob von Uexküll coined the term *Umwelt* to denote the "island of the senses" produced by the unique way an organism perceptually engages with its world (Uexküll 2001). One can only describe an *Umwelt* by describing the properties of both a world and an agent. Psychologist James Gibson proposed the ecological theory of perception (Gibson 1966; Gibson 1979). Gibson's theory focused upon the coupling between an agent and the world, and emphasized that this coupling depends upon the nature of an agent's body. Gibson argued perception's goal is to deliver *affordances*.

Affordances are the possibilities for action a particular object offers to a particular agent. Affordances require an integral relationship between an object's properties and an agent's abilities to act. Furthermore, an agent's abilities to act depend upon the structure of its body: doorknobs do not offer the affordance of 'turnability' to dogs and their paws. In short, affordances are defined in relation to an agent's body.

The previous section on situating echolocation argued that if perception is embedded or situated, then a theory of perception must refer to the dynamic coupling between an agent and the world. The current section implies that a theory of perception must also refer to the nature of the agent's body. For an example, let us return to bat echolocation.

In echolocation, the difference in time between the echo's arrival to a bat's left and right ears uniquely determines the *horizontal* position of a prey insect. However, this difference in time is not sufficient to determine the target's *vertical* position. How does the bat's echolocation system solve underdetermination of vertical position?

Bats are noted for the extravagant shapes of the pinna and tragus of their external ears. Evidence suggests such amazing ear shapes help bats determine a target's vertical position. For instance, gluing the tragus of its ear forward severely impairs a bat's vertical discrimination ability (Chiu and Moss 2007; Lawrence and Simmons 1982).

Why does bat ear shape matter? The shape causes returning echoes to strike the ear at different angles of entry, distorting the sound signal (Muller et al. 2008; Obrist et al. 1993; Reijniers et al. 2010). These distortions provide additional auditory cues which vary systematically with the vertical position of the target (Wotton et al. 1995; Wotton and Simmons 2000). In other words, the shape of a bat's ear alters sound in such a way to add information about a target's vertical dimension to the incoming signal.

Claiming the shape of a bat's ear solves a problem of underdetermination radically departs from claiming that unconscious inference deals with the poverty of the stimulus. In the case of bat echolocation, the bat's body removes the problem of vertical underdetermination before auditory signals reach the bat's brain!

Degrees of Embodiment

In viewing cognition as embedded or situated, embodied cognitive science emphasizes feedback between an agent and the world. An agent's body influences feedback, because an agent's body places constraints on how the world is experienced (*Umwelt*) as well as on how the world is acted upon (affordance). Consequently, we can describe agents with different kinds of bodies as having differing degrees of embodiment (Fong et al. 2003).

Embodiment can be defined as the extent to which an agent can alter its environment. For instance, Fong et al. (2003: 149) argue "embodiment is grounded in the relationship between a system and its environment. The more a robot can perturb an environment, and be perturbed by it, the more it is embodied." An agent which is more embodied becomes immersed in more complex feedback.

However, we cannot assess degrees of embodiment without considering an agent's *Umwelt*. For instance, from the perspective of the human *Umwelt*, bats are not very embodied, because they do not (for instance) move large objects around. However, from the perspective of the bat, bat echolocation causes dramatic environmental changes by altering the movements of flying insects attempting to avoid predators. Similarly, famous social robots like Kismet (Breazeal 2002) seem weakly embodied because they are only heads, and have no arms to manipulate the world and no legs to move through it. However, in Kismet's social *Umwelt*, changes in facial expression and in head posture produce dramatic changes in expression, posture, and vocalizations of humans interacting with the social robot.

The more embodied the agent, the more interesting are the potential architectures that can account for its cognitive processing. For instance, entomologists have long been interested in explaining how social insects can produce large and complex structures such as termite mounds. These mounds range from 2 to 7 meters in height, (von Frisch 1974), and a single mound may exist for decades. A colony's mound extends in space and time far beyond the life expectancy of the individual termites who help build it.

Some researchers propose that *stigmergy* controls termite mound construction (Grassé 1959; Theraulaz and Bonabeau 1999). The term comes from the Greek *stigma*, meaning sting, and *ergon*, meaning work, capturing the notion the environment is a stimulus which causes particular work (behavior) to occur. Grassé demonstrated termites' building behavior is not regulated by the insects themselves, but is instead controlled externally by the termite mound. The appearance of a part of the mound serves as a stimulus to cause termites to alter that part of the mound in a particular way. The change in the mound becomes a new stimulus to cause new, future mound-changing behaviors.

Stigmergy is an example of how embodied cognitive science can offer alternatives to standard cognitive science. Most cognitive theories include internal control mechanisms for choosing which primitive operation to execute at any given moment. With concepts like stigmergy, embodied cognitive science counters the standard approach by exploring the possibility the external world provides control (Downing and Jeanne 1988; Holland and Melhuish 1999; Karsai 1999; Susi and Ziemke 2001; Theraulaz and Bonabeau 1999).

Importantly, notions like stigmergy are not merely appeals to external sources of information. The degree to which stigmergy controls an agent depends upon the agent's coupling with the world, and therefore depends upon an agent's body, as well as the potential changes to the world that agent's body makes possible. The more embodied an agent is, the more capable it is of altering the world around it, and of modifying the affordances the world makes available.

Active Externalization

In spite of repeated warnings during its formative years (Hayes et al. 1994; Miller et al. 1960; Norman 1980), standard cognitive science has steadfastly underemphasized the role of the environment. It has been argued (Dawson 2013) that the root of this stubborn stance is cognitivism's reaction against behaviorism; cognitivists were concerned that behaviorists viewed humans as passive responders to the environment (Gardner 1984). By rejecting the environment, standard cognitivism excluded a central plank of behaviorism.

Importantly, the notion of degrees of embodiment prevents embedded or situated cognition from devolving back into behaviorism. Humans are perhaps the most embodied agents on the planet, in the sense we actively strive to manipulate our environment (Bronowski 1973). As a result, humans can exploit their coupling with the world to deliberately extend or externalize their cognitive processes. Using external structures to support cognition is *cognitive scaffolding* (Clark 1997).

Research on practical cognition, or mind in action (Scribner 1985; Scribner and Beach 1993; Scribner and Tobach 1997) reveals that humans are masters of cognitive scaffolding. For example, Scribner discovered a reliable difference between expert and novice dairy workers: the experts were more likely to use environmental resources to scaffold their activities. For instance, expert workers used the visual appearance of dairy crates to determine how to fill orders of different amounts of dairy products.

The external world not only provides information storage, but can also manipulate stored information. A variety of navigational tools permit the results of computations to simply be inspected after data is recorded on them (Hutchins 1995). "It seems that much of the computation was done by the tool, or by its designer. The person somehow could succeed by doing less because the tool did more" (Hutchins 1995: 151).

Critically, our ability to alter the environment does not decouple us from it. Humans actively manipulate and create their world, but dynamically respond to it too. Cognitive scaffolding is not without constraints. Artifacts, equipment, or technologies which provide scaffolding exist at the interface between a person and the world. Successful scaffolding reflects such embedding; a scaffold succeeds because it is appropriate to the actions available to the person taking advantage of it. It would seem, then, that an examination of the artifacts which are pervasive in human societies should reveal a great deal about human cognition.

In other words, embodied cognitive science could flourish as a science of design. Viewing cognitive science as a science of design is not a novel idea. Simon's (1969) famous monograph *The sciences of the artificial* argued design was central to studying cognition. However, Simon viewed the science of design from the perspective of standard cognitive science: a problem-solving process which searched for optimal designs using representational techniques.

More modern approaches to design (Dourish 2001; Norman 1998, 2002, 2004; Schön 1992; Visser 2006; Winograd and Flores 1987) are more sympathetic to embodied cognitive science. In modern design, the relationship between artifacts and agents is central: the more aware an agent is of an artifact's affordances (and the less aware of the artifact as an object), the better is the artifact's design. "A device is easy to use when there is visibility to the set of possible actions, where the controls and displays exploit natural mappings" (Norman 2002: 25). Embodied cognitive science departs from standard cognitive science by examining design as the coupling between agents and environments. "Man – or at least the intellective component of man – may be relatively simple; most of the complexity of his behavior may be drawn from his environment, from his search for good designs" (Simon 1969: 83).

References

Anderson, J. R., Bothell, D., Byrne, M. D., Douglass, S., Lebiere, C. and Qin, Y. L. (2004) "An Integrated Theory Of The Mind", *Psychological Review*, 111, 1036–1060.

Ashby, W. R. (1956) *An Introduction To Cybernetics*, London, Chapman and Hall.

Beer, R. D. (2003) "The Dynamics Of Active Categorical Perception," in An Evolved Model Agent, *Adaptive Behavior*, 11, 209–243.

Breazeal, C. L. (2002) *Designing Sociable Robots*, Cambridge, MA, MIT Press.

Bronowski, J. (1973) *The Ascent Of Man*, London, British Broadcasting Corporation.

Brooks, R. A. (1999) *Cambrian Intelligence: The Early History Of The New AI*, Cambridge, MA, MIT Press.

Bruner, J. S. (1957) "On Perceptual Readiness," *Psychological Review*, 64, 123–152.

Chemero, A. (2009) *Radical Embodied Cognitive Science*, Cambridge, MA, MIT Press.

Chiu, C. and Moss, C. F. (2007) "The Role Of The External Ear In Vertical Sound Localization In The Free Flying Bat, Eptesicus Fuscus," *Journal of The Acoustical Society of America*, 121, 2227–2235.

Chomsky, N. (1965) *Aspects Of The Theory Of Syntax*, Cambridge, MA, MIT Press.

Clancey, W. J. (1993) "Situated Action: A Neuropsychological Interpretation Response," *Cognitive Science*, 17, 87–116.

—— (1997) *Situated Cognition*, Cambridge, UK, Cambridge University Press.

Clark, A. (1997) *Being There: Putting Brain, Body, And World Together Again*, Cambridge, MA, MIT Press.

—— (1999) "An Embodied Cognitive Science?" *Trends in Cognitive Sciences*, 3, 345–351.

—— (2003) *Natural-Born Cyborgs*; Oxford, New York, Oxford University Press.

Dawson, M. R. W. (1998) *Understanding Cognitive Science*, Oxford, UK, Blackwell.

—— (2013) *Mind, Body, World: Foundations Of Cognitive Science*, Edmonton, Alberta, Athabasca University Press.

Dawson, M. R. W., Dupuis, B. and Wilson, M. (2010) *From Bricks To Brains: The Embodied Cognitive Science Of Lego Robots*, Edmonton, Alberta, Athabasca University Press.

Dourish, P. (2001) *Where The Action Is: The Foundations Of Embodied Interaction*, Cambridge, MA, MIT Press.

Downing, H. A. and Jeanne, R. L. (1988) "Nest Construction By The Paper Wasp, *Polistes* - A Test Of Stigmergy Theory," *Animal Behaviour*, 36, 1729–1739.

Dunning, D. C. and Roeder, K. D. (1965) "Moth Sounds And Insect Catching Behavior Of Bats," *Science*, 147, 173–174.

Fenton, M. B. and Fullard, J. H. (1979) "Influence Of Moth Hearing On Bat Echolocation Strategies," *Journal of Comparative Physiology*, 132, 77–86.

Fong, T., Nourbakhsh, I. and Dautenhahn, K. (2003) "A Survey Of Socially Interactive Robots," *Robotics And Autonomous Systems*, 42, 143–166.

Fullard, J. H., Simmons, J. A. and Saillant, P. A. (1994) "Jaming Bat Echolocation: The Dogbane Tiger Moth *Cycnia Tenera* Times It Clicks To The Terminal Attack Calls Of The Big Brown Bat *Eptesicus Fuscus*," *Journal of Experimental Biology*, 194, 285–298.

Gardner, H. (1984) *The Mind's New Science*, New York, Basic Books.

Gibson, J. J. (1966) *The Senses Considered As Perceptual Systems*, Boston, MA, Houghton Mifflin.

—— (1979) *The Ecological Approach To Visual Perception*, Boston, MA, Houghton Mifflin.

Grassé, P. P. (1959) "La Reconstruction Du Nid Et Les Coordinations Interindividuelles Chez *Bellicositermes Natalensis* Et *Cubitermes Sp."* La Théorie De La Stigmergie: Essai D'interprétation Du Comportement Des Termites Constructeurs Insectes Sociaux*, 6, 41–80.

Grey Walter, W. (1963) *The Living Brain*, New York, NY, W.W. Norton and Co.

Griffin, D. R., Friend, J. H. and Webster, F. A. (1965) "Target Discrimination By Echolocation Of Bats," *Journal of Experimental Zoology*, 158, 155-and.

Griffin, D. R., Webster, F. A. and Michael, C. R. (1960) "The Echolocation Of Flying Insects By Bats," *Animal Behaviour*, 8, 141–154.

Hayes, P. J., Ford, K. M. and Agnew, N. (1994) "On Babies And Bathwater: A Cautionary Tale," *AI Magazine*, 15, 15–26.

Helmholtz, H. (1868/1968) "The Recent Progress Of The Theory Of Vision," *in*: Warren, R. M. and Warren, R. P. (eds), *Helmholtz On Perception: Its Physiology And Development*. New York: John Wiley and Sons.

Holland, O. and Melhuish, C. (1999) "Stigmergy, Self-Organization, And Sorting In Collective Robotics," *Artificial Life*, 5, 173–202.

Horiuchi, T. K. (2005) "'Seeing' In The Dark: Neuromorphic Vlsi Modeling Of Bat Echolocation," *IEEE Signal Processing Magazine*, 22, 134–139.

Hristov, N. I. and Conner, W. E. (2005) "Sound Strategy: Acoustic Aposematism In The Bat-Tiger Moth Arms Race," *Naturwissenschaften*, 92, 164–169.

Hurley, S. (2001) "Perception And Action: Alternative Views," *Synthese*, 129, 3–40.

Hutchins, E. (1995) *Cognition In The Wild*, Cambridge, MA, MIT Press.

Karsai, I. (1999) "Decentralized Control Of Construction Behavior In Paper Wasps: An Overview Of The Stigmergy Approach," *Artificial Life*, 5, 117–136.

Lawrence, B. D. and Simmons, J. A. (1982) "Echolocation In Bats: The External Ear And Perception Of The Vertical Positions Of Targets," *Science*, 218, 481–483.

Marr, D. (1982) *Vision*, San Francisco, CA, W.H. Freeman.

Miller, G. A., Galanter, E. and Pribram, K. H. (1960) *Plans And The Structure Of Behavior*, New York, Henry Holt and Co.

Moss, C. F. and Sinha, S. R. (2003) "Neurobiology Of Echolocation In Bats," *Current Opinion in Neurobiology*, 13, 751–758.

Muller, R., Lu, H. W. and Buck, J. R. (2008) "Sound-Diffracting Flap In The Ear Of A Bat Generates Spatial Information," *Physical Review Letters*, 100.

Nelson, M. E. and Maciver, M. A.(2006) "Sensory Acquisition In Active Sensing Systems," *Journal of Comparative Physiology A-Neuroethology Sensory Neural and Behavioral Physiology*, 192, 573–586.

Newell, A. (1990) *Unified Theories Of Cognition*, Cambridge, MA, Harvard University Press.

Noë, A. (2002) "Is The Visual World A Grand Illusion?" *Journal of Consciousness Studies*, 9, 1–12.

—— (2004) *Action In Perception*, Cambridge, MA, MIT Press.

Norman, D. A. (1980) "Twelve Issues For Cognitive Science," *Cognitive Science*, 4, 1–32.

—— (1998) *The Invisible Computer*, Cambridge, MA, MIT Press.

—— (2002) *The Design Of Everyday Things*, New York, Basic Books.

—— (2004) *Emotional Design: Why We Love (Or Hate) Everyday Things*, New York, Basic Books.

Obrist, M. K., Fenton, M. B., Eger, J. L. and Schlegel, P. A. (1993) "What Ears Do For Bats: A Comparative Study Of Pinna Sound Pressure Transformation In Chiroptera," *Journal of Experimental Biology*, 180, 119–152.

Pfeifer, R. and Scheier, C. (1999) *Understanding Intelligence*, Cambridge, MA, MIT Press.

Pylyshyn, Z. W. (2000) "Situating Vision In The World," *Trends in Cognitive Sciences*, 4, 197–207.

—— (2003) *Seeing And Visualizing: It's Not What You Think*, Cambridge, MA, MIT Press.

Reijniers, J., Vanderelst, D. and Peremans, H. (2010) "Morphology-Induced Information Transfer In Bat Sonar," *Physical Review Letters*, 105.

Rock, I. (1983) *The Logic Of Perception*, Cambridge, MA, MIT Press.

Roeder, K. D. and Treat, A. E. (1961) "The Detection And Evasion Of Bats By Moths," *American Scientist*, 49, 135–148.

Roy, D. (2005) "Grounding Words In Perception And Action: Computational Insights," *Trends in Cognitive Sciences*, 9, 389–396.

Rydell, J., Jones, G. and Waters, D. (1995) "Echolocating Bats And Hearing Moths: Who Are The Winners?" *Oikos*, 73, 419–424.

Schön, D. A. (1992) "Designing As Reflective Conversation With The Materials Of A Design Situation," *Knowledge-Based Systems*, 5, 3–14.

Scribner, S. (1985) "Knowledge At Work," *Anthropology and Education Quarterly*, 16, 199–206.

Scribner, S. and Beach, K. (1993) "An Activity Theory Approach To Memory," *Applied Cognitive Psychology*, 7, 185–190.

Scribner, S. and Tobach, E. (1997) *Mind And Social Practice: Selected Writings Of Sylvia Scribner*, Cambridge; New York, Cambridge University Press.

Shapiro, L. A. (2019) *Embodied Cognition*, New York, Routledge.

Simon, H. A. (1969) *The Sciences Of The Artificial*, Cambridge, MA, MIT Press.

Susi, T. and Ziemke, T. (2001) "Social Cognition, Artefacts, And Stigmergy: A Comparative Analysis Of Theoretical Frameworks For The Understanding Of Artefact-Mediated Collaborative Activity," *Journal of Cognitive Systems Research*, 2, 273–290.

Theraulaz, G. and Bonabeau, E. (1999) "A Brief History Of Stigmergy," *Artificial Life*, 5, 97–116.

Uexküll, J. V. (2001) "An Introduction To Umwelt," *Semiotica*, 134, 107–110.

Varela, F. J., Thompson, E. and Rosch, E. (1991) *The Embodied Mind: Cognitive Science And Human Experience*, Cambridge, MA, MIT Press.

Vera, A. H. and Simon, H. A. (1993) "Situated Action: A Symbolic Interpretation," *Cognitive Science*, 17, 7–48.

———— (1994) "Reply To Touretzky And Pomerlau: Reconstructing Physical Symbol Systems," *Cognitive Science*, 18, 355–360.

Visser, W. (2006) *The Cognitive Artifacts Of Designing*, Mahwah, NJ, L. Erlbaum Associates.

Von Frisch, K. (1974) *Animal Architecture*, New York, Harcourt Brace Jovanovich.

Wiener, N. (1948) *Cybernetics: Or Control And Communciation In The Animal And The Machine*, Cambridge, MA, MIT Press.

Winograd, T. and Flores, F. (1987) *Understanding Computers and Cognition*, New York, Addison-Wesley.

Wotton, J. M., Haresign, T. and Simmons, J. A. (1995) "Spatially Dependent Acoustic Cues Generated By The External Ear Of The Big Brown Bat, *Eptesicus Fuscus*," *Journal of the Acoustical Society of America*, 98, 1423–1445.

Wotton, J. M. and Simmons, J. A.(2000) "Spectral Cues And Perception Of The Vertical Position Of Targets By The Big Brown Bat, Eptesicus Fuscus," *Journal Of The Acoustical Society Of America*, 107, 1034–1041.

Zeng, J. Y., Xiang, N., Jiang, L., Jones, G., Zheng, Y. M., Liu, B. W. and Zhang, S. Y. (2011) "Moth Wing Scales Slightly Increase The Absorbance Of Bat Echolocation Calls," *PLOS One*, 6 (11): e27190.

7

THE ENACTIVE APPROACH

Ezequiel A. Di Paolo and Evan Thompson

Embodied approaches in cognitive science hold that the body is crucial for cognition. Yet despite many decades of research,[1] what this "embodiment thesis"[2] amounts to remains unclear (Shapiro 2011). The meaning of the embodiment thesis depends on how we interpret its key terms, *body* and *cognition*, as well as on what exactly it means to say that the body is *crucial* for cognition (Kyselo and Di Paolo 2015). In recent years, the term *embodied* has been used elastically to refer to anything from ideas about how bodily action provides a format for neuronal representations (Goldman and de Vignemont 2009; Gallese 2010; Goldman 2012) or helps to reduce computational load (Clark 2008; Wheeler 2005, 2010; Wilson 2004), to a variety of "radical embodiment" proposals (Clark 1999; Thompson and Varela 2001)—for example, that kinesthetic body schemas are a constitutive part of mental skills (Lakoff and Johnson 1999; Núñez 2010), that sensorimotor know-how is constitutive of perceptual experience (O'Regan and Noë 2001; Noë 2004), that bodily life regulation is constitutive of phenomenal consciousness and its extended neurophysiological substrates (Thompson and Varela 2001; Thompson and Cosmelli 2011), and that social interaction is constitutive of social cognition and language (De Jaegher, Di Paolo, and Gallagher, 2010; Di Paolo, Cuffari, and De Jaegher 2018). In some cases, these radical embodiment proposals are based on the "enactive" view that the mind depends constitutively on the living body, understood as an autonomous system (Varela, Thompson, and Rosch 1991; Thompson 2007; Di Paolo 2009; Froese and Ziemke 2009). Our aim in this chapter is to explain this key enactive notion of *autonomy*. This is a key technical concept, a necessary idea to offer a genuine alternative to traditional functionalist and cognitivist views. We cannot do justice to the variety of applications of the enactive approach that connect to this idea, but we mention a few examples and provide pointers for further reading.

Bodies as autonomous

A key attribute of the living body is its individuation, the process by which it makes itself distinct from its immediate surroundings. More precisely, bodies are *self-individuating*—they generate and maintain themselves through constant structural and functional change.

DOI: 10.4324/9781003322511-10

Yet many of the systems we study in science—particles, rivers, communities, galaxies—we typically individuate from the outside by convention and as a matter of convenience. In other words, what counts as one system as distinct from another typically depends on conventional criteria; such criteria include considerations of convenience, perceptual biases, relative timescales of change, semi-arbitrary definitions, and historical or practical use. In many areas of study, this practice works fine. To this day, functionalism in cognitive science identifies cognitive systems in this way, that is, by convention: a robot, a body, or an agent is specified as the system it is according to some tacit agreement. Many embodied approaches to the mind also proceed in this way. Thus, references to the *body* are understood contextually as references to a given anatomical structure or physiological function, to the details of a given sensorimotor system, or to being situated in a given world of habits, norms, skills, and so on. Yet, regardless of the conventional criteria we may use to individuate bodies externally, they nonetheless possess the peculiar attribute of being self-individuating: they produce themselves and they actively generate and maintain a distinction between themselves and their environment. A guiding idea of the enactive approach is that any adequate description of how bodies can be or instantiate a cognitive system must take account of this fact of self-individuation.

This point brings us to the principal concept that differentiates the enactive approach from other embodied approaches to the mind—the concept of *autonomy*. By making use of this technical concept— which, as we will see, explains how bodies are self-individuating— we can give operational criteria for distinguishing cognitive systems from non-cognitive systems.

The idea of autonomy has roots in Maturana and Varela's (1980) theory of autopoiesis. This theory has strongly influenced enactive thinking to the point that work based on the notion of autonomy has sometimes been branded "autopoietic enactivism" (Hutto and Myin, 2013). This label is misleading: key theoretical developments in this area concern various extensions *and* some departures from the original autopoietic framework (see Di Paolo 2009, 2018; Thompson 2011a, 2011b). These elaborations should become clear in this section for the case of autonomy (the same goes for other concepts in the enactive framework not discussed here in full, such as adaptivity, sense-making, and agency; see Di Paolo 2005, 2009; Thompson 2007, 2011a, 2011b).

Autonomy was initially conceived as a generalization of the concept of autopoiesis. This idea describes a central aspect of the organization of living systems, namely that the processes that make up an organism relate to each other in such a way that the same organization is constantly regenerated by the activities of the processes themselves. This continues to happen despite variations across time. Varela (1979) extended the idea of autopoiesis into other domains, calling it *autonomy*. He identified a similar organizational logic in other systems such as the nervous system and immune networks, and he hinted at the application of the concept of autonomy to other domains, such as communication networks.

We define an autonomous system as an *operationally closed* and *precarious* system.

To unpack these technical terms, it may help to introduce an intuitive procedure. Let's consider the following situation. A scientist is observing, recording, and intervening in various processes that she finds of interest in a lab. She observes and measures variables and their relations, takes notes of events, and attempts to establish the connections between her observations. To some extent, what she observes is a matter of choice, as are the procedures she follows. She may be interested in the fact that some temperature measurements are relatively constant throughout the day in spite of the varying temperatures outside. Or she may be looking at some chemical reactions and measuring the speed with which they happen. To keep things to a general level, let's say that she is observing *processes*. How each of these processes is identified is not our main issue here; the means of identification will likely depend on the observer's history, skills, tools, and purposes.

As the scientist actively intervenes in the various processes she is observing, she takes note of regular effects. For example, she changes a setting in a thermostat and the room temperature is now maintained at a higher value. Or she observes that the chemical reactions are now happening faster, and so on. Eventually, she may be able to establish various relations between the observed processes. Some of these relations indicate merely contextual effects—the observed process is altered in some way by intervening on a different process; other relations are stronger and indicate enabling conditions—the observed process disappears or stops if a particular intervention is made on a different process (for more on the difference between contextual and enabling conditions, see De Jaegher, Di Paolo, and Gallagher 2010). Thus, changing the thermostat setting brings the desired room temperature to a cooler or warmer value, but unplugging the air conditioning simply prevents any temperature regulation from happening at all. Temperature regulation as such has stopped as a process. Such enabling relations, of course, depend on the circumstances and may change over time.

We use Figure 7.1 to depict this situation. The circles represent the processes being observed by the scientist. Whenever an enabling relation is established, we draw an arrow from the process that is perturbed to the process that stops or disappears as a consequence. An arrow going from process *A* to process *B* indicates that the operation of *A* is an enabling condition for *B* to occur. Of course, there may be several enabling conditions affecting a given process. We do not assume that the scientist is mapping all of them, only those that she finds relevant or can uncover with her methods.

As the mapping of enabling conditions proceeds, the scientist may notice something interesting. It may happen that a set of processes relate to each other with a special topological property. These processes are marked in black in the figure. If we look at any process in black, we observe that it has some enabling arrows *arriving at* it that originate in other processes in black, and that it has some enabling arrows *coming out of it* that end up also in other processes in black. When this condition is met, the black processes form a closed network of enabling relations; this topological property is what we mean by *operational closure*.

Notice that this form of closure does *not* imply the independence of the network from other processes that are not part of it. There may be enabling dependencies on external processes that are not themselves enabled by the network; for example, plants can photosynthesize in the presence of sunlight as an enabling condition, but the sun's existence is independent of plant life on Earth. Similarly, there may be processes that are made possible only by the activity of the network but that do not themselves "feed back" any enabling relations toward the network itself. Moreover, arrows describe links of enabling dependence, but other links may exist too, such as interactions that have only contextual effects. In short, an operationally closed system should not be conceived as in any way isolated from dependencies or from interactions with other processes. In fact, such "external" dependencies and interactions *define* the network's environment, which is, *ipso facto*, always relative to the system.

Notice too that although the choice of processes under study is more or less arbitrary and subject to the observer's history, goals, and methods, the topological property of closure unraveled in this way (if one is present) is *not* arbitrary. The property of being an

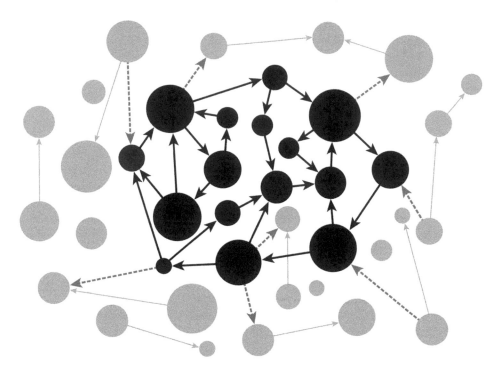

Figure 7.1 A schematic illustration of the concept of operational closure. Circles are observed processes and arrows indicate enabling conditions. The black circles form part of an operationally closed network of enabling relations. Each black circle has at least one arrow arriving at it and at least one arrow coming from it, respectively originating or terminating in another black circle. Dashed arrows indicate enabling relations between processes in the operationally closed network and processes in the environment. (Copyright Ezequiel Di Paolo, 2013. This work is licensed under a Creative Commons Attribution-NonCommercial-ShareAlike 3.0 Unported License.)

operationally closed network is not a matter of ascription, convention, or opinion. While it exists, the operationally closed system is self-asserting and this only changes if its enabling conditions change.

A living cell is an example of an operationally closed network. The closed dependencies between constituent chemical and physical processes in the cell are very complex, but it is relatively easy to point to some of them. For example, the spatial enclosure provided by a semipermeable cell membrane is an enabling condition for certain autocatalytic reactions to occur in the cell's interior, otherwise the catalysts would diffuse into the medium and the reactions would occur at very different rates or not at all. Hence there is an enabling arrow going from the membrane to the metabolic reactions. But the membrane is not a given; it is also a process that depends, among other things, on the repair components that are generated by the cellular metabolism. So, there is an enabling arrow coming back from metabolic reactions to the membrane. Hence, we have already identified one of many closed loops between cellular processes. If the scientist chooses not to observe the membrane in relation to the metabolic reactions, she would probably miss the topological relation between them. Operational closure—cellular life in this case—can be missed if we choose to focus elsewhere, but it is not an arbitrary property if we observe it at the right scale.

Is autonomy the same as operational closure? Although it seems to have been the same for Varela (1979)—at least in terms of his formal definition of an autonomous system—we have argued in other writings that operational closure is not sufficient to capture certain important implications of the wider sense of the term "autonomy"—implications conveyed by notions such as "spontaneity," "immanent purposiveness," "intrinsic teleology," and the "self-generation of norms" (see Di Paolo 2005; Thompson 2007). Given the above definition of operational closure, various "trivial" examples of such closure may exist. For example, in cellular automata, the regeneration of an equilibrium state in each cell mutually depends on the equilibrium state in others, making the dependencies into a closed network.

We need an additional condition to make operational closure more specific of living organization, and this is the condition of *precariousness*. Of course, all material processes are precarious if we wait long enough. The fact that the operational relations of closure may break down and the network lose its topology already points to a kind of systemic fragility (see Beer and Di Paolo 2023). In the current context, however, what we mean by "precariousness" is the following processual condition: in the absence of the enabling relations established by the operationally closed network, a constituent process will stop or run down at a timescale similar to or faster than that of the network's operation. And this applies to all constituent processes.

It might seem at first that this condition is redundant. Isn't precariousness implied in the fact that a black circle in Figure 7.1 is always enabled by other black circles? Surely if the enabling relations disappear, that process should stop. This need not be the case. There may also be redundancies among the enabling relations affecting a given process (more than one arrow may come into a circle, and this could mean that all of the arrows are needed simultaneously or that different subsets of the incoming arrows are sufficient for the process to continue). An enabling relation, as we stated above, in principle holds only in given circumstances. If a process is enabled by the operationally closed network *and* by external processes as well, it may be the case than when the network is removed the process remains thanks to the external support. Such a process would not be precarious. A precarious process is such that, whatever the complex configuration of enabling conditions, if the dependencies on other processes in the operationally closed network are removed, the process stops. In other words, it is not possible for a precarious process in an operationally closed network to exist on its own in the circumstances created by the absence of the network, other conditions being equal.

A precarious, operationally closed system is literally self-enabling, and thus it sustains itself in time partially due to the activity of its own constituent processes. Moreover, because these processes are precarious, the system is always decaying. The natural tendency for each constituent process is to run down, a fate the activity of the other processes prevents. The system is sustained on a double negation. The impermanence of each individual process tends to affect the network negatively if unchecked. It is only the effect of other processes that curb such negative tendencies. This contrasts with the way we typically conceive of organic processes as contributing positively to sustaining life; if any constituent processes were to run unchecked, in contrast, it would kill the organism. As a consequence, a precarious, operationally closed system is inherently restless. In order to sustain itself despite its intrinsic tendencies towards internal imbalance, it requires energy, matter, and other relations with the outside world. Hence, the system is not only self-enabling, but must also show some spontaneity in its interactions due to a constitutive need to constantly "buy time" against the negative tendencies of its own constituent parts.

The simultaneous requirements of operational closure and precariousness are the defining properties of autonomy.[3] With this concept we can begin to answer the opening question in this section about the individuation of bodies. A body is understood as such an autonomous system, i.e., as precarious and continuously self-individuating in necessary interaction with its environment. Moreover, since we have not made any claims about the specific kinds of processes that enter into a relation of precarious closure, this perspective allows for the possibility that bodies need not be constituted exclusively by biochemical or physiological processes (Di Paolo, Buhrman, and Barandiaran 2017; Di Paolo et al. 2018; Thompson and Stapleton 2009; Kyselo and Di Paolo 2015).

What we have provided in this section is a principled, step-by-step procedure to answer the question of whether a system is autonomous. The enactive concept of autonomy is entirely operational in this sense and therefore naturalistic, though not reductionist. It is not a concept that could be captured by functionalism. Autonomy illustrates a fundamental difference between enactive and functionalist approaches to the mind. As we have seen, autonomy entails precariousness, but precariousness is not a positive property, but rather an unavoidable aspect of materiality. In the current context, precariousness is the insufficient permanence of any positive property that might play a functional role in sustaining the autonomous system in the absence of the system's closed organization. There is no utility function for precariousness. Yet its negative effects are what the system is constantly acting against and will in large part define, contextually, how the system should operate to continue to exist. For this reason, precariousness might be modeled (Beer and Di Paolo 2023), but never fully captured in functionalist terms, as the conditions that satisfy any functional approximation (for instance, a decay function affecting various parameters) should themselves be precarious if the system were really autonomous.

In this way, the enactive concept of autonomy captures individuation as a non-arbitrary ongoing process as well as the spontaneity of living bodies. The concept also leads to various other developments, such as a naturalistic way to account for what Kant described as the intrinsic teleology or immanent purposiveness that appears to belong to living beings by virtue of being self-organizing (Weber and Varela 2002; Di Paolo 2005; Thompson 2007).

Autonomy is closely linked to two other key enactive concepts: *adaptivity* and *sense-making* (Di Paolo 2005, 2009; Thompson 2011a, 2011b). Adaptivity refers to the capacity of some autonomous systems to regulate their own processes and their relation to the environment when conditions tend towards loss of viability (Di Paolo 2005). This ability for adaptive regulation is inextricably linked to autonomy. This is because what is regulated is the continuation of the system's own way of existing. Sense-making describes activity in relation to norms that the system itself brings forth or incorporates on the basis of its adaptive autonomy. Sense-making is an active form of non-indifference, or caring, which is common to all kinds of minded activity. An adaptive autonomous system produces and sustains its own identity in precarious conditions, registered as better or worse, and thereby establishes a perspective from which interactions with the world acquire a normative status. Certain interactions contribute to the viability of the systems and other interactions degrade it. In Merleau-Ponty's words, "each organism, in the presence of a given milieu, has its optimal conditions of activity and its proper manner of realizing equilibrium," and each organism "modifies its milieu according to the internal norms of its activity" (Merleau-Ponty 1963: 148, 154).

For the enactive approach, a system is cognitive when its activity is governed by the norms of the system's own continued existence and flourishing; in other words, when it is a sense-maker. Under these conditions of autonomy, adaptivity, and normativity, we also speak of *agency* (Di Paolo et al. 2017).[4] Cognition, in this view, is not a matter of representing states of affairs but rather of establishing relevance through the need to maintain an identity that is constantly facing the possibility of disintegration. This identity is given by precarious autonomy, which may be realized not only in the organic, but also in the sensorimotor and social domains. From this perspective, the body is not just the means but also an end of being a cognitive system, the vantage point from which the world is meaningful. To put the point another way, cognition at its basis is more a matter of adaptive self-regulation in precarious conditions than abstract problem solving. The point here is not to deny that we can and do engage in high-level problem solving. Rather, it is to say that this kind of narrow cognition presupposes the broader and more basic activity that we call sense-making.

Application of enactive ideas

As mentioned, there is a wide variety of questions where progress is being made by applying enactive ideas, not just within the sciences of the mind, as in explanations of brain function, perceptual learning, and language (e.g., Fuchs 2018; Gallagher 2017; Di Paolo and De Jaegher 2012; Di Paolo et al. 2017, 2018), but also in the areas of psychiatry (De Jaegher 2013; de Haan 2020; Fuchs 2018), musicology (van der Schyff, Schiavio, and Elliott 2022), education science (Abrahamson 2022; Maiese 2017), health sciences (Stilwell and Harman 2019; Arandia and Di Paolo 2021), AI and robotics (Froese and Ziemke 2009; Zebrowski and McGraw 2022), the cognitive humanities (Caracciolo 2014; Popova 2015), and the arts (Gallagher and Gallagher 2020; Murphy 2019; Welch 2022). A survey of these applications is beyond the scope of this chapter, so we limit ourselves to discussing two examples where the idea of autonomy plays crucial but distinct roles.

Modeling autonomy: bacterial chemotaxis

Because of the operational character of the idea of autonomy, it should be possible to construct models of autonomous systems to explore some of the implications of this concept.

We begin with a couple of clarifications. First, by a *model* we mean a formal or material system that instantiates *some* aspects of an autonomous system that are relevant in a particular context. By its nature, a model is a simplification and not a realization of the modeled system. In other words, a model of an autonomous system is not, in itself, an autonomous system, nor is it meant to be. A fluid dynamics model of a river is not a river. The second clarification concerns the question of whether, given a modeling approach, it is possible to capture all key aspects of autonomy. This is an open question, but we can at least say that given our claim that precariousness cannot be captured as a positive function, it is difficult to model full autonomy in traditional computational terms, and this includes dynamical systems models. Some aspects of precariousness can find analogous correspondence in relation to the substrate of the model (see Beer and Di Paolo 2023). But, to repeat, these correspondences within a model do not amount to a realization of autonomous processes. It may be the case that modeling some aspects of autonomy requires a material implementation to further approximate the relations of precarious operational closure. Computers don't typically work in this way, although the limitations of what may be captured computationally are still being explored. A computational model may approximate with sufficient accuracy those aspects that are relevant to the question at hand. This way of proceeding is no different from other kinds of scientific models; such models have a limited range of validity outside which the grounding assumptions fail.

Matthew Egbert and colleagues have explored a series of dynamical systems models of autonomy in the context of bacterial behavior (Egbert, Barandiaran, and Di Paolo 2010; Egbert 2013). These models explore the relation between autonomy and sense-making in its most basic forms (bacterial chemotaxis is a canonical example of sense-making, often used in the enactive literature; Varela et al. 1991; Thompson 2007, 2011c).

For decades, the chemotactic behavior of bacteria has been investigated as if it did not depend on their metabolic state. Whether bacteria are "hungry" or "satiated," it is often assumed that they will always follow a chemical gradient towards sources of nourishment, as if governed by a blind mechanism. Evidence shows, however, that the assumption of metabolism independence often fails (Alexandre and Zhulin 2001). For example, in some species of bacteria, non-metabolizable chemical analogs of metabolizable attractants are not themselves attractants. Even though they excite chemical sensors in the same way, bacteria ignore them. In addition, the inhibition of the metabolic pathways to process a chemical attractant completely stops chemotaxis to this attractant and only this attractant. In short, there seems to be a deep link between metabolism (the process of self-individuation) and behavior (the regulation of interactions with the world) as expected from the relation between autonomy and sense-making. By modeling metabolism as a cycle of autocatalytic reactions far from thermodynamic equilibrium, thus capturing some aspects of precarious operational closure, and by modeling behavior regulation as modulated by metabolism, Egbert and colleagues have managed to replicate various empirically observed behaviors of bacteria. These behaviors are chemotaxis towards metabolic resources and away from metabolic inhibitors, inhibition of chemotaxis in the presence of abundant resources, cessation of chemotaxis to a resource due to inhibition of the metabolism of that resource, sensitivity to metabolic and behavioral history, and integration of simultaneous complex environmental "stimuli."

Participatory sense-making

Another area where enactive ideas have made an impact is social cognition and intersubjectivity research. This area has been a concern of enactivists for some time (Thompson 2001, 2007; Gallagher 2009). As a result of De Jaegher and Di Paolo's (2007) introduction of the concept of *participatory sense-making*, the enactive approach has ramified into fields as varied as animal behavior, psychiatry, social neuroscience, dance, music, literary studies, education sciences, and embodied linguistics.

The enactive account of intersubjectivity calls attention to participatory and relational processes beyond individuals, unlike traditional approaches where social understanding is reduced to the skull-bound inferences or simulations a typically passive observer can make about the mental state of others based on their behavior. By giving social interaction a more central role, enactivists reject methodological individualism. De Jaegher and Di Paolo (2007) use the idea of autonomy, but this time applied to the relational processes that often take place in the encounter of two or more participants. Sometimes these encounters take on a life of their own and the actions of the agents involved, or their intentions, do not fully determine the outcome of the encounter, which also depends on its own relational and dynamic constituent processes. In these cases, where relational patterns emerge as autonomous and the participants themselves remain autonomous, we are in the presence of a *social interaction*, which can be thus defined formally (De Jaegher and Di Paolo 2007: 493). The processes involved are patterns of intercorporeal coordination at various levels—imitative gestures, regulation of personal distance, posture and orientation, heart rates and brain activity, attunement to conversation or walking rhythms, and so on.

Given that sense-making is an embodied process of active regulation of the coupling between agent and world, social interaction—through patterns of bodily coordination, breakdown, and recovery— opens the possibility of this process being co-authored by the participants. Participatory sense-making is this form of sense-making in social interaction. It can vary in kind and degrees, from orientation of individual sense-making (someone draws our attention to an aspect of the world we have ignored) to joint sense-making (a co-authored piece of work literally created together through a process that would not be possible by the individuals involved on their own).

This proposal has important empirical implications. De Jaegher, Di Paolo, and Gallagher (2010) show that making the scientific study of interaction more explicit can offer parsimonious hypotheses about the processes sustaining a cognitive performance, and it frees researchers from postulating complicated mechanisms in the individual brain that duplicate what the interactive dynamic configuration already brings about on its own. Paying more attention to interactive factors comes at a time when empirical methods in psychology and neuroscience (such as hyperscanning, thermal imaging, motion energy analysis, and second-person methodologies) have been developing to the point that live and relatively unconstrained interactions can be directly investigated. These sciences can now move away from the individualistic and observational paradigms. It is even possible to propose broad empirical hypotheses about the relation between individual brain mechanisms, the development of interactive skills, and interactive history (Di Paolo and De Jaegher 2012).

Through participatory sense-making, the enactive approach brings into play pre-existing empirical and practical knowledge that has often been neglected by mainstream theoretical frameworks. This is particularly the case in psychiatry, where the social dimension of the etiology, diagnosis, and intervention for disorders such as schizophrenia or autism has been well known in practice and to a large extent well documented, and yet cognitivist or neurocentric approaches tend to downplay this dimension. Explanations in mental health can be reconsidered from a non-individualistic enactive perspective (e.g., Bervoets et al. 2023; de Haan 2020; De Jaegher 2013, 2021). Such reconsideration does not imply positing either the individual or the interactive levels as fundamental, but rather understanding the mutually enabling relations between the two (Fuchs 2018; De Jaegher and Di Paolo 2013). The ethical and existential implications of this work have continued to be elaborated in enactive accounts of personhood, *languaging*, and human becoming (Candiotto and De Jaegher 2021; Di Paolo et al. 2018; Di Paolo 2021; Di Paolo and De Jaegher 2022; Dierckxsens 2022; Fourlas and Cuffari 2022).

Conclusion

We can use the concepts sketched here to offer responses to the three questions that any embodied perspective should be able to provide about the embodiment thesis. If the body is crucial for cognition, we should be able to say: (1) What is meant by *body*? (2) What is meant by *cognition*? (3) What is meant by *crucial*?

1 The enactive approach provides a principled definition of bodies as self-individuating systems. The concept of autonomy is what allows us to provide this definition. Thus, what is meant by *body*, for the enactive approach, is not the body as a functional system defined in terms of inputs and outputs (as it is for functionalist cognitive science), nor the body as a set of anatomical structures and physiological systems, but rather the concrete body as an adaptive autonomous system.[5]

2 Cognition, in its most general form, is sense-making—the adaptive regulation of states and interactions by a body with respect to the consequences for the body's own viability. It is manifested as an active form of non-indifference.

3 Without a body, there is no sense-making. Sense-making is a bodily process of adaptive self-regulation. The link between the body and cognition is accordingly constitutive and not merely causal. To be a sense-maker is, among other things, to be autonomous and precarious, that is, to be a situated body, in the precise sense of *body* that the enactive approach proposes.

Notes

1 Dreyfus (1972) is probably the earliest statement of what is now known as embodied cognitive science. Yet this work was largely critical. Constructive theories and models of embodied cognition started to arrive in the mid-1980s, in works by Winograd and Flores (1986), Lakoff (1987), and Johnson (1987).

2 Wilson and Foglia (2011, n.p.) state the embodiment thesis as follows: "Many features of cognition are embodied in that they are deeply dependent upon characteristics of the physical body of an agent, such that the agent's beyond-the-brain body plays a significant causal role, or a physically constitutive role, in that agent's cognitive processing."

3 Autonomy, defined in terms of operational closure, has been a central idea in organizational approaches in biology. For instance, Moreno and Mossio (2015) present a more elaborate picture of closure by introducing distinctions between timescales and between processes and constraints. Their emphasis is on thermodynamic, rather than processual precariousness.

4 One may draw parallels between the enactive perspective and other approaches proposing a connection between the conservation of systemic identity and relating to the environment in cognitive terms. An example is the recent work applying the "free energy principle" to biological and cognitive systems (e.g., Wiese and Friston 2021). Despite repeated claims and superficial resemblances, this proposal turns out to be very different from the ideas of autopoiesis and enaction discussed here. For a detailed exploration of the tensions and incompatibilities between these approaches see Di Paolo, Thompson, and Beer 2022.

5 Note that the human body as a whole comprises a number of overlapping autonomous systems, such as the nervous system and the immune system, and that these systems can incorporate extra-organic elements (e.g., neural prosthetics) into their operationally closed networks of enabling processes (Di Paolo, 2009; Di Paolo et al. 2017; Thompson and Stapleton 2009). For discussion of the relation between these systemic characterizations of the body and the phenomenological or subjective and experiential aspects of the body, see Thompson 2007.

References

Abrahamson, D. (2022) "Enactive perception as mathematics learning," in M.-C. Shanahan, B. Kim, M. A. Takeuchi, K. Koh, A. P. Preciado-Babb, & P. Sengupta (eds), *The Learning Sciences in conversation: Theories, methodologies, and boundary spaces* (pp. 153–170). London: Routledge.

Alexandre, G., and Zhulin, I. B. (2001) "More than one way to sense chemicals," *Journal of Bacteriology*, 183, 4681–4686.

Arandia, I. R. and Di Paolo E. A. (2021) "Placebo from an enactive perspective," *Frontiers in Psychology. 12*, 660118. https://doi.org/10.3389/fpsyg.2021.660118

Beer, R. D. and Di Paolo, E. A. (2023) "The theoretical foundations of enaction: Precariousness," *BioSystems*, [online first] https://doi.org/10.1016/j.biosystems.2022.104823

Bervoets, J., Beljaars, D., and De Jaegher H. (2023) "Letting Tourette's be: The importance of understanding lived experience in research and the clinic," *Developmental Medicine and Child Neurology*, [online first]. https://doi.org/10.1111/dmcn.15545

Candiotto, L., and De Jaegher, H. (2021) "Love In-Between," *Journal of Ethics 25*, 501–524. https://doi.org/10.1007/s10892-020-09357-9

Caracciolo, M. (2014) *The Experientiality of Narrative: An Enactivist Approach*, Berlin: De Gruyter.

Clark, A. (1999) "An embodied cognitive science?" *Trends in Cognitive Sciences, 3*, 345–351.

——— (2008) *Supersizing the mind: Embodiment, action, and cognitive extension*, New York: Oxford University Press.

de Haan, S. (2020) *Enactive Psychiatry*, Cambridge: Cambridge University Press.

De Jaegher H. (2013) "Embodiment and sense-making in autism," *Frontiers in Integrative Neuroscience, 7*, 15. https://doi.org/10.3389/fnint.2013.00015

De Jaegher, H. (2021) "Seeing and inviting participation in autistic interactions," *Transcultural Psychiatry*. [online first]. https://doi.org/10.1177/13634615211009627

De Jaegher, H., and Di Paolo, E. A. (2007) "Participatory sense-making: An enactive approach to social cognition," *Phenomenology and the Cognitive Sciences, 6*(4), 485–507.

——— (2013) "Enactivism is not interactionism," *Frontiers in Human Neuroscience, 6*(345).

De Jaegher, H., Di Paolo, E. A., and Gallagher, S. (2010) "Can social interaction constitute social cognition?" *Trends in Cognitive Sciences, 14*(10), 441–447.

Di Paolo, E. A. (2005) "Autopoiesis, adaptivity, teleology, agency," *Phenomenology and the Cognitive Sciences, 4*, 97–125.

——— (2009) "Extended life," *Topoi, 28*, 9–21.

——— (2018) "The enactive conception of life," in A. Newen, S. Gallagher, L. de Bruin (eds), *The Oxford Handbook of 4E Cognition: Embodied, Embedded, Enactive and Extended*, Oxford University Press. pp 71–94.

Di Paolo, E. A., and De Jaegher, H. (2012) "The interactive brain hypothesis," *Frontiers in Human Neuroscience, 6*, 163.

Di Paolo, E. A. (2021) "Enactive becoming," *Phenomenology and the Cognitive Sciences, 20*, 783–809. https://doi.org/10.1007/s11097-019-09654-1

Di Paolo, E. A. and De Jaegher, H. (2022) "Enactive ethics: Difference becoming participation," *Topoi, 41*, 241–256. doi:10.1007/s11245-021-09766-x

Di Paolo, E. A., Buhrmann, T., & Barandiaran, X. E. (2017) *Sensorimotor life: An enactive proposal*. Oxford: Oxford University Press.

Di Paolo, E. A., Cuffari, E. C., and De Jaegher, H. (2018) *Linguistic bodies: The continuity between life and language*. Cambridge: MIT Press.

Di Paolo, E. A., Thompson, E. and Beer, R. D. (2022) "Laying down a forking path: Tensions between enaction and the free energy principle," *Philosophy and the Mind Sciences, 3*. https://doi.org/10.33735/phimisci.2022.9187

Dierckxsens, G. (2022) "Introduction: Ethical dimensions of enactive cognition—Perspectives on enactivism, bioethics and applied ethics," *Topoi 41*, 235–239 (2022). https://doi.org/10.1007/s11245-021-09787-6

Dreyfus, H. (1972) *What computers can't do*, New York: Harper & Row.

Egbert, M. D. (2013) "Bacterial chemotaxis: Introverted or extroverted? A comparison of the advantages and disadvantages of basic forms of metabolism-based and metabolism-independent behavior using a computational model," *PloS One, 8*(5), e63617.

Egbert, M. D., Barandiaran, X. E., and Di Paolo, E. A. (2010) "A minimal model of metabolism-based chemotaxis," *PloS Computational Biology, 6*(12), e1001004.

Fourlas, G.N., Cuffari, E.C. (2022) "Enacting ought: Ethics, anti-racism, and interactional possibilities," *Topoi 41*, 355–371. https://doi.org/10.1007/s11245-021-09783-w

Froese, T., and Ziemke, T. (2009) "Enactive artificial intelligence: Investigating the systemic organization of life and mind," *Artificial Intelligence, 173*(3–4), 466–500.

Fuchs, T. (2018) *Ecology of the brain: The phenomenology and biology of the embodied mind*, Oxford: Oxford University Press.

Gallagher, S. (2009) "Two problems of intersubjectivity," *Journal of Consciousness Studies, 16*, (6-8), 289–308.

———— (2017) *Enactivist interventions: Rethinking the mind*, Oxford: Oxford University Press.

Gallagher, S. and Gallagher, J. (2020) "Acting oneself as another: An actor's empathy for her character," *Topoi*, 39, 779–790, doi: 10.1007/s11245-018-9624-7

Gallese, V. (2010) "Embodied simulation and its role in intersubjectivity," in T. Fuchs, H. C. Sattel, and P. Henningsen (eds), *The embodied self: Dimensions, coherence and disorders* (pp. 78–92). Stuttgart: Schattauer.

Goldman, A. (2012) "A moderate approach to embodied cognitive science," *Review of Philosophy and Psychology, 3*(1), 71–88.

Goldman, A., and de Vignemont, F. (2009) "Is social cognition embodied?" *Trends in Cognitive Sciences, 13*(4), 154–159.

Hutto, D., and Myin, E. (2013) *Radicalizing enactivism: Basic minds without content*, Cambridge, MA: MIT Press.

Johnson, M. (1987) *The body in the mind: The bodily basis of meaning, imagination, and reason*, Chicago: University of Chicago Press.

Kyselo, M., and Di Paolo, E. (2015) "Locked-in syndrome: A challenge for embodied cognitive science," *Phenomenology and the Cognitive Sciences*, 14, 517–542. doi:10.1007/s11097-013-9344-9

Lakoff, G. (1987) *Women, fire, and dangerous things: What categories reveal about the mind*, Chicago: University of Chicago Press.

Lakoff, G., and Johnson, M. (1999) *Philosophy in the flesh: The embodied mind and its challenge to Western thought*, New York: Basic Books.

Maiese, M. (2017) "Transformative learning, enactivism, and affectivity," *Studies in Philosophy and Education, 36*(2), 197–216.

Maturana, H., and Varela, F. (1980) *Autopoiesis and cognition: The realization of the living*, Dordrecht: D. Reidel Publishing Co.

Merleau-Ponty, M. (1963) *The structure of behavior* (A. Fisher, Trans.). Pittsburgh, PA: Duquesne University Press.

Moreno, A., and Mossio, M. (2015) *Biological autonomy: A philosophical and theoretical enquiry*, Berlin: Springer.

Murphy, M. (2019) *Enacting Lecoq: Movement in theatre, cognition, and life*, Cham: Palgrave Macmillan.

Noë, A. (2004) *Action in perception*, Cambridge, MA: MIT Press.

Núñez, R. (2010) "Enacting infinity: Bringing transfinite cardinals into being," in J. Stewart, O. Gapenne, and E. Di Paolo (eds), *Enaction: Towards a new paradigm in cognitive science* (pp. 307–333). Cambridge, MA: MIT Press.

O'Regan, K., and Noë, A. (2001) "A sensorimotor account of vision and visual consciousness," *Behavioral and Brain Sciences, 24*, 939–1031.

Popova, Y. B. (2015) *Stories, meaning, and experience: Narrativity and enaction*, London: Routledge.

Shapiro, L. (2011) *Embodied cognition*, New York: Routledge.

Stilwell, P., Harman, K. (2019) "An enactive approach to pain: beyond the biopsychosocial model," *Phenomenology and the Cognitive Sciences*, 18, 637–665. https://doi.org/10.1007/s11097-019-09624-7

Thompson, E. (2001) "Empathy and consciousness," *Journal of Consciousness Studies, 8*(5–7), 1–32.

———— (2007) *Mind in life: Biology, phenomenology, and the sciences of mind*, Cambridge, MA: Harvard University Press.

———— (2011a) "Précis *of Mind in Life*, by E. Thompson," *Journal of Consciousness Studies, 18*, 10–22.

———— (2011b) "Reply to commentaries," *Journal of Consciousness Studies*, 18, 176–223.

———— (2011c) "Living ways of sense-making," *Philosophy Today 55, (SPEP Suppl.)*, 114–123.

Thompson, E., and Cosmelli, D. (2011) "Brain in a vat or body in a world? Brainbound versus enactive views of experience," *Philosophical Topics*, 39, 163–180.

Thompson, E., and Stapleton, M. (2009) "Making sense of sense-making: Reflections on enactive and extended mind theories," *Topoi*, 28, 23–30.

Thompson, E., and Varela, F. (2001) "Radical embodiment: Neural dynamics and consciousness," *Trends in Cognitive Sciences*, 5, 418–425.

van der Schyff, D., Schiavio, A., and Elliott D. J. (2022) *Musical bodies, musical minds. Enactive cognitive science and the meaning of human musicality*, Cambridge, MA: The MIT Press.

Varela, F. J. (1979) *Principles of biological autonomy*, New York: Elsevier; North Holland.

Varela, F. J., Thompson, E., and Rosch, E. (1991) *The embodied mind: Cognitive science and human experience*, Cambridge, MA: MIT Press.

Weber, A., and Varela, F. J. (2002) "Life after Kant: Natural purposes and the autopoietic foundations of biological individuality," *Phenomenology and the Cognitive Sciences*, 1, 97–125.

Welch, S. (2022) *Choreography as embodied critical inquiry: Embodied cognition and creative movement*, Palgrave Macmillan.

Wheeler, M. (2005) *Reconstructing the cognitive world: The next step*, Cambridge, MA: MIT Press.

——— (2010) "In defense of extended functionalism," in Richard Menary (ed.), *The extended mind*. Cambridge, MA: MIT Press.

Wiese, W., & Friston, K. J. (2021) "Examining the continuity between life and mind: Is there a continuity between autopoietic intentionality and representationality?" *Philosophies*, 6(1), 18. https://doi.org/10.3390/philosophies6010018

Wilson, R. A. (2004) *Boundaries of the mind: The individual in the fragile sciences – Cognition*, Cambridge: Cambridge University Press.

Wilson, R. A., and Foglia, L. (2011) "Embodied cognition." In E. N. Zalta (ed.), *The Stanford encyclopedia of philosophy* (Fall 2011 ed.). Retrieved from http://plato.stanford.edu/archives/fall2011/entries/embodied-cognition/

Winograd, T., and Flores, F. (1986) *Understanding computers and cognition: A new foundation for design*, Norwood, NJ: Ablex.

Zebrowski, R.L. and McGraw, E. B. (2022) "Carving up participation: Sense-making and sociomorphing for artificial minds," *Frontiers in Neurorobotics*, 16, 815850. doi: 10.3389/fnbot.2022.815850

PART 3

Embodied Cognition and Predictive Processing

8

INTEGRATING EMBODIED COGNITION AND PREDICTIVE PROCESSING

Elmarie Venter

Introduction

In this chapter, I consider the prospects of compatibility and integration of two accounts that have gained much popularity in the last two decades: predictive processing (PP) and embodied cognition (EC). Some argue that the two views are inconsistent, making contradictory claims, and that the only way to integrate them is to reduce the claims of one to the assumptions of the other (Hohwy 2018). Others think that the views are compatible and consistent and nothing more needs to be done to defend compatibility (Clark 2017). There is thus no sight of agreement on the compatibility and integration of these two accounts (Clark 2015a, 2017; Anderson 2018; Hohwy 2018; Kirchhoff 2018; Venter 2021).

Attempts at integration face a challenge because both approaches have variations that are well defended and consequently, perhaps ironically, they can be ambiguous in their commitments. This issue may not be easily resolved and thus any answer to the question concerning the compatibility and integration of EC and PP depends on the particular version one is committed to. In this chapter, I propose that the debate concerning integration of PP and EC is based on the assumptions of weak EC which is committed to the view that the body plays some important role in cognition but also that 'real' cognitive processes occur only in the neural domain. The commitment to weak EC in PP seems to be a natural result of the distinction between perceptual and active inference – a distinction which, I propose, leads to an inadequate explanation of cognition. Given that weak EC assigns a *causal* role for the body, it may be the obstacle in the way of an integrated account of PP and EC. What happens if we integrate PP and *strong* EC, i.e., the view that the body is a constituent element of cognition? Strong EC has gained much support in recent research and is a worthy contender that may overcome some challenges faced by its weaker counterpart. In this chapter, I consider the outcome of integrating strong EC with PP, arguing that it is a good starting point for a comprehensive and insightful picture of the mind.

The chapter is structured as follows. I first discuss the key tenets of various interpretations of PP. Given that the spectrum of PP varies greatly, I evaluate how three interpretations stand in relation to EC. I then develop my proposal of an integrated account. The upshot of the integration is that prediction error is minimized through the process of

 DOI: 10.4324/9781003322511-12

sensorimotor inference – a process of prediction that couples the agent and world in such a way that the whole embodied agent instantiates a model of the world. Building on the idea of continuous reciprocal processing between brain, body, and world, I illustrate how agents embody structural regularities from the environment in their morphology and internal dynamics. Finally, I show how these claims lead to the supposition that prediction error is more widely minimized than the neural domain. Instead of reconstructing a rich internal model of the world, the environment and body *guide* an agent through space, minimizing prediction error on the fly. My proposal entails that the neural domain is part of a larger system in which cognitive states and processes are found and serves an important, albeit not unprecedented, role.

PP and EC – from specter to spectrum

The key tenet of PP is that cognition consists in inferences at various levels of the relevant system in which higher levels of the system attempt to predict bottom-up input on the basis of models encoding the causal structure of the world (Friston and Stephan 2007; Clark 2013, 2016; Hohwy 2013). This is typically explained by the metaphor of the brain as a prediction machine (Hohwy 2013). The view is that brains are fundamentally tasked with minimizing the discrepancy (i.e., surprisal or prediction error) between top-down predictions and incoming sensory stimulation (Clark 2017). The system is hierarchical and the precision weighting (i.e., the degree of certainty) at each level of the hierarchy determines the error minimizing strategy to be employed. Each level of the hierarchy predicts activity at that level and the level below, receives prediction errors, and transmits the error back so that the next predictions are more accurate (Hohwy 2020).[1] This process involves an interplay between evidence, i.e., input through the sensory organs, and predictions generated by the model in the brain to ultimately reduce prediction error in the long run. This view exemplifies the conservative side of the PP spectrum in which the neural domain plays an unprecedented role and prediction error is minimized in that either the "brain perceives by minimizing prediction error between its hypotheses about the world through updating the parameters of those hypotheses" (i.e., perceptual inference) or "the brain acts by changing its sensory input so it is less erroneous (more accurate) with respect to its hypotheses about the world" (i.e., active inference) (Hohwy 2016).

Importantly, this is not only an explanation of perception but also of motor action (Friston, Thornton, and Clark 2012; Miller and Clark 2017; Clark 2020). Proprioceptive predictions generate motor commands when a need for action arises. One way in which prediction error is minimized is to move the body in such a way that predictions about action are met, i.e., through active inference. Action thus depends on 'systemic misrepresentation' of the bodily state (Wiese 2017). One implication of this is that prediction error minimization – be it through perceptual or active inference – is limited to processes in the neural domain and as such "becomes an affirmation of simple Cartesian skepticism" (Hohwy 2016).

Despite (or, as I will argue, because of) the distinction between perceptual and active inference, the approach is committed to weak readings of EC. Weak EC claims that the body plays a *causal* role in cognitive processing and can be differentiated from strong EC which posits a *constitutive* role for the body in cognition. The commitments of weak EC entail that interaction with the world activates bodily representations understood as either representations of bodily states or representations in the "distinctively bodily (i.e., sensory or motor) cortex" (Rupert 2011). In other words, the body is important only insofar as it is treated as a hidden cause of sensory input. This implies that "cognitive states are not extended into the body" (Hohwy 2016) and "the involvement of the body and of action in cognition can be described in wholly neuronal, internal, inferential terms" (Hohwy 2016).

In response to the richly reconstructive interpretation of PP described above, many have opted for more embodied interpretations of PP. Clark, for example, sees PP as a "thoroughly dynamical story that highlights self-organization and complex brain-body-world interactions" (Clark 2017). This makes PP a good partner for EC.[2] A generative model need only update a few parameters when receiving new sensory input – it need not reconstruct the sensory input entirely. Clark refers to this as "productive laziness" (Clark 2015b), i.e., the processes involved in encoding and updating the generative model are economic and efficient. Notice that this implies that perception is entangled with cognitive, contextual, and motor factors in a non-sequential fashion (Clark 2015b), meaning that the fundamental boundary between perception and action becomes obsolete (Clark 2015a). Notwithstanding the coupled nature of perception and action, Clark still relies heavily on the "inner processing economy" to do the work. Even in his most recent work, he maintains that "predictive brains explain and *make possible* the looping sensorimotor encounters that build extended minds" (Clark 2022; my emphasis). Consequently, Clark's seemingly embodied approach only provides a more conservative interpretation of PP that seems more aligned with weak EC than strong EC. As such it does not yet represent the other side of the PP spectrum. This honor goes to enactivist interpretations of PP.

Bruineberg, Rietveld, and Kiverstein (2018), for example, posit a constitutive role for the body in generating predictive models, rejecting the reconstructive function of the brain, and thereby avoiding the troubles of Cartesian skepticism faced by conservative interpretations. They draw upon the free energy principle which posits that an organism can maintain its organization by keeping itself within a certain range of states, i.e., by minimizing any 'surprisal' (discrepancy from a viable range of states). This range of states is determined by the embodiment of the agent which in turn is constrained by the environmental conditions (Bruineberg, Rietveld, and Kiverstein 2018). From this they conclude that what needs to be minimized is embodied surprisal and this can only be done by means of action, i.e., perceptual inference is not sufficient for minimizing 'embodied' surprisal.

Anticipating the kinds of interactions with the environment that contribute to flourishing is the most important objective for the agent. This leads the enactivist to understand the function of the generative model to be *mediating* (rather than reconstructing) the agent's interaction with the environment. Though the mediation component seems similar to Clark's proposal, 'generative model' takes on a different meaning for the enactivist. The generative model is not a reconstruction in the brain of the world as it happens to be but an *embodiment* of longer-term regularities between agent and environment (Bruineberg, Rietveld, and Kiverstein 2018). In many ways, the agent's body echoes the structure of the environment and thus "an agent does not *have* a model of its world, [but rather] it *is* a model" (Friston 2013; emphasis in original). The enactivist sees this as a virtue because the organization of the whole embodied agent constitutes the cognitive system. Enactivist interpretations of PP thus provide us with a taste of what an integrated account of strong EC and PP could look like.

At the same time, however, it is worth highlighting that Bruineberg *et al.* propose that what is minimized by the system is not prediction error in the inferential sense but free energy.[3] Given this, they claim, it is unnecessary to appeal to 'mental' structures that represent and encode long-term information about the causal structure of the world (Bruineberg, Rietveld, and Kiverstein 2018). The question, then, is: how can more sophisticated cognitive capacities such as decision making, language processing, and memory in human agents be explained? They prefer to think "in terms of affordance-related states of action readiness" and propose that higher cognitive capacities can be explained in those terms (Bruineberg, Rietveld, and Kiverstein 2018). For them, affordances are possibilities for action provided to the agent by the environment and a "state of action readiness" is a phenomenon somewhere between overt action and the ability to act (Bruineberg and Rietveld 2014). Mental representations have no place in enactivist interpretations of PP which appeal rather to direct interaction with the environment. This leads to bodily chauvinism, implying that every cognitive process can only be explained by appeal to bodily and environmental changes. Ideally, we want an account that does not grant the neural domain an unprecedented role in cognition and, at the same time, does not disregard the important role of the mental. This seems to be a challenge for the philosopher of mind; one that I propose can be overcome if the distinction between perceptual and active inference is replaced by a single strategy, namely sensorimotor inference.

Embodied predictive processing (EPP)

Notice that on the PP spectrum, the role of the body varies greatly in the strategies that minimize prediction error. Whereas Hohwy allocates an unprecedented role to the neural domain in both perceptual and active inference, Clark posits a strong coupling between perceptual and active inference, granting a more important role to the body and interaction with the world. Both these interpretations, at the very least, have in common that perceptual and active inference are taken to be distinct strategies even when the processes involved are similar. This, I believe, is a natural consequence of the commitment to weak EC. Bruineberg *et al.*, on the other hand, argue that the notions of active inference and perceptual inference, as they are derived in the literature, are incompatible: "it is *action* that does the work of actually minimizing surprisal" (Bruineberg, Rietveld, and Kiverstein 2018; emphasis in original). For the enactivist, perceptual inference seems unnecessary because sensations are not impoverished given that the agent can pick up on environmental regularities directly in the world (Bruineberg, Rietveld, and Kiverstein 2018).

In short, we seem to have either a distinction between perceptual and active inference or an elimination of one of the strategies. In the following subsections, I consider the upshots of an integrated account of PP and strong EC, starting with the natural consequence that agents minimize prediction error using a single strategy, namely sensorimotor inference. Sensorimotor inference takes perception and action to be a single constitutive process that couples the agent to the environment. My proposal departs from the enactivist view, in that I uphold the conceptual definition of the generative model used by Clark and Hohwy and maintain that the neural domain (perhaps through the use of mental representations) has a role in minimizing prediction error, albeit not the unprecedented role the conservative theorist would posit. The alternative proposal differs from the conservative views, in that prediction error is minimized by the body, brain, and interaction with the world.

Looking at the bare bones of PP, we find that the key tenet is that the system *models* the causal structure of the world. This much seems to be agreed upon across the spectrum even when the exact details of implementation differ. These models are *hierarchically structured*, perhaps nested, and the function of the system is to *minimize discrepancies* between inferences and reality. Any additional assumptions are a result of integration with a particular theory or framework (see Kersten 2023). I have not said much about the adequacy of the various accounts I have outlined; the debate between these philosophers is vast and they provide good criticisms of one another. Likewise, the debate concerning weak and strong EC is ongoing, but it is widely accepted that strong EC shows promise. The aim of this chapter is not to evaluate and criticize the various accounts but simply to point out that there is a gap to be filled: more needs to be done to analyze how *strong* EC and PP can be integrated.

Prediction error is minimized by a single process: sensorimotor inference

The first upshot of an integrated account is that prediction error is minimized using a single strategy, what I call "sensorimotor inference." The idea is that inferences are generated about the world in virtue of embodied action and the possible future states the body may find itself in. This makes a distinction between perceptual and active inference superfluous. In other words, perception and action do not come apart, not even in terms of inferences. An agent's relation to the world is determined by how she moves and consists in the inference that by moving her body, the world is made available to her. The notion of sensorimotor inference shares similarities with some claims of sensorimotor enactivism, including the idea that the cognitive processes are *causally* dependent on what happens in the brain (Noë 2004). It departs from the view, however, in that sensorimotor inference entails a model instantiated in the whole embodied agent. This commitment is explained in the next subsection.

To further illustrate sensorimotor inference, consider the following example adapted from Noë (2004). An agent perceives a cube consisting of six sides, twelve edges, and eight vertices. From any perspective, the agent only has visual access to three sides of the cube. How can we then say she perceives a cube? If we do not opt for the orthodox representational account which posits that she has a mental representation of cubes or that she has a generative model that implies it is a cube, one alternative is that inferences are generated about the causal structure of the world contingent on embodied action, i.e., that the object is a cube because of how its appearance changes as she moves. The key tenet is that the agent actively moves through and engages with the environment and thereby the inferences are generated.

If this is correct, the process of generating inferences and minimizing the resulting prediction error consist in being sensitive to embodied action – these processes cannot be separated, and it is only when operating in tandem that the function of cognition is fulfilled. How the world changes when an agent acts on it (and vice versa) crucially determines the inferences about the causal structure of the world. This is true in the long and short term and involves a circular causality typical of PP explanations (Bruineberg and Rietveld 2014; Pezzulo 2014; Veissière *et al.* 2020). Circular causality implies a *continuous (and nonlinear) reciprocal* causation between brain, body, and world (Clark 1998) and in this sense a form of constitutive causation (see Kirchhoff 2017). Sensorimotor inference seems to naturally involve such circular causality. Noë (2004: 63) captures this in his example of seeing a cat behind a fence: "My sense of the perceptual presence, now, of that which is now hidden behind a slat in the fence, consists in my expectation that by moving my body I can produce the right sort of 'new cat' stimulation" (Noë 2004).

The whole embodied agent encodes the causal structure of the world

The notion of inference is central in PP and entails that a model exists which generates the inferences. It is often assumed that such a model must be representational and limited to the neural domain (Hohwy 2013, 2016). Though the model may take on a representational form, it is not necessarily limited to brain and need not entail *mental* representations. The embodied structure of the agent is a good candidate for recapitulating the causal structure of the world (Calvo and Friston 2017) because the generative model is obtained from the environment (Bruineberg and Rietveld 2014) and is as such "an achievement, rather than a given" (Ramstead *et al.*, 2021). There is no a priori reason why the model might not consist of neural processes, the body, *and* the environment.

Consider the case of sensory augmentation devices, such as the feelSpace belt. The feel-Space belt is a wearable device that provides an agent with information about magnetic north via vibrotactile simulation (König and König 2016). It works by using a series of vibrating motors arranged around the waist which receive data from a built-in compass sensor that detects the Earth's magnetic field. As the agent changes direction, the motors vibrate in different patterns and intensities, providing haptic feedback that recapitulates the structure of the world. In this sense, it serves as a form of spatial orientation. The feelSpace belt has been shown to improve agents' sense of direction and spatial awareness (Kaspar *et al.* 2014) and leads to subjective changes in how the world is perceived (König and König 2016).

Cases like these are indicative of how embodiment and cognitive capacities, such as spatial navigation, are constitutively related insofar as the body obtains and encodes a model of the world through movement. The agent has direct access to the haptic feedback from the belt and uses this access to navigate the belt. Furthermore, it is only through embodied action that the haptic feedback is received and encoded. This may very well be compatible with weak EC, were it not for the constitutive dependence of bodily movement. Additionally, mental representation and modeling of sensory information is not sufficient for explaining how the causal structure of the world is modeled and runs into what Noë (2004) calls *the fundamental problem for visual theory*. This problem calls for an explanation of how we see the world, given imperfections of sensory input. The conservatives may think they have solved this problem by appealing to perceptual inference, but this alone does not explain why we continuously direct our attention to the world to gather information. The answer is simple: the world is directly available to us; we simply need to move around to obtain it. That said, generating models of the world may depend *causally* on mental activity (i.e., mental representations or a generative model encoded with inferences), but it is only through yielding the constitutive dependence of the body and world that we get an adequate explanation of how an agent interacts with and navigates the complex world.

Prediction error is minimized more widely than the neural domain

The previous two sections lead us to the supposition that prediction error minimization is not limited only to the brain and constitutively depends on the embodiment of the agent and interaction with the world. Sensorimotor inferences concern how an agent coordinates action within a complex environment rather than reconstructing the world. These inferences are encoded in the organization of the whole embodied agent and any discrepancy between the inferences and the environment needs to be minimized. It is agreed upon that all the components making up the nested, hierarchical system contribute constitutively to minimizing prediction error. Given the commitments of strong EC, this implies that the generative model is made up of brain, body, and interaction with the world – a condition which is supported by some literature on predictive processing. Friston, for example, states that what we take to be a model needs to be more inclusive, "combining interpretive dispositions, morphology, and neural architecture" (Friston, Thornton, and Clark 2012).

Consider the artistic gymnast striving for smoothness while swinging between two parallel bars. She requires precise awareness of spatiality and timing to execute the movements and prediction error needs to be minimized at a remarkable speed. The space and position in which she is executing the exercise is encoded in terms of her movements. Her brain and body are "not merely ways of implementing a spatial perception and action algorithm, they are elements in the computations themselves" (Noë 2004: 26). As she holds her swing in an upside-down position, physiological changes are taking place to help maintain balance; the vestibular system detects and encodes the angular and linear components of her movements, and based on this she can shift her weight by moving one leg further forward than the other. The gymnast need not build up a detailed mental representation of her movements in space, generating inferences and motor commands to minimize prediction errors; instead, the environment and her body *guide* her through space, minimizing prediction error on the fly. Prediction error minimization at the level of motor movements and reflexes is necessary for ongoing prediction error in the neural domain, and vice versa.

This comes with an important implication, namely that it shifts the so-called 'evidentiary boundary.'[4] Hohwy sees this as a challenge to strong readings of EC, but this is misguided because it is not the case that the brain must constantly infer the nature of the world based on impoverished sensory inputs. Instead, we act on the world in ways that test 'hypotheses,' e.g., we move around the cube to confirm or gain insight that it is in fact a cube, we shift our weight to maintain balance (i.e., to confirm that we are upright or upside down). This aligns with a commitment that has been implied throughout this chapter, namely that cognition (generating inferences, encoding models, minimizing prediction error) is for coordinating and mediating interaction with the world rather than for reconstructing a model of the world based on some sensory inputs alone.

Conclusion

There are substantial variations in both embodied cognition (EC) and predictive processing (PP) and depending on one's exact commitments, the compatibility of the two views will differ. This is illustrated in the various attempts at integrating PP and EC, ranging from conservative approaches embracing only weak EC (Hohwy 2013, 2015, 2016, 2018) to more embodied interpretations (Clark 2015b, 2015a, 2017, 2022) and, finally, enactivist interpretations (Bruineberg and Rietveld 2014; Bruineberg, Rietveld, and Kiverstein 2018; Kiverstein, Miller, and Rietveld 2019). This chapter considered what an integrated account of strong EC and PP would look like. I have not said much about strong EC, but it is widely accepted on this view that the body is a constituent of cognition and that the whole embodied agent is coupled to the environment. If these commitments are integrated with the key tenets of PP (i.e., that the system, which is hierarchically structured, models the causal structure of the world and minimizes prediction error), we get the following view. Prediction error is minimized using a single strategy: sensorimotor inference. Sensorimotor inferences concern embodied action and the possible future state the body may find itself in when interacting with the world. Given the constitutive dependence of the body on generating inferences, the causal structure of the world is encoded by the whole embodied agent and as such also minimizes prediction error. This is by no means a fully developed account of integration between PP and strong EC, but there is a gap that needs to be filled and these ideas can serve as guidelines for the further development of EPP.

Notes

1 There is a relevant debate here on overfitting and underfitting of generative models which I do not discuss. Interested readers can refer to Hohwy's (2020) review.
2 This is Clark's claim; he does not distinguish between weak and strong EC.
3 The conceptual relation between prediction error and free energy is controversial and beyond the scope of this chapter. Put in simple terms, one can assume that prediction error is a form of free energy that must be minimized, and thus free energy is a broader term for disattunement to be decreased relevant to the whole (living) system (Bruineberg, Rietveld, and Kiverstein, 2018).
4 The basic idea of the evidentiary boundary is that it draws a circle around e_i and h_i, on the one hand, and the hidden causes of e_i, on the other – where e_i stands for evidence and h_i for hypothesis. Hohwy (2016) deals with this at length.

References

Anderson, M. (2018) "The body in action: Predictive processing and the embodiment thesis," in A. Newen, L. de Bruin, and S. Gallagher (eds), *The Oxford Handbook of 4E Cognition*. Oxford: Oxford University Press, pp. 243–260.

Bruineberg, J. and Rietveld, E. (2014) "Self-organization, free energy minimization, and optimal grip on a field of affordances," *Frontiers in Human Neuroscience*, 8(August), pp. 1–14.

Bruineberg, J., Rietveld, E., and Kiverstein, J. (2018) "The anticipating brain is not a scientist: the free-energy principle from an ecological-enactive perspective," *Synthese*, 195(6), pp. 2417–2444.

Calvo, P. and Friston, K. (2017) "Predicting green: Really radical (plant) predictive processing," *Journal of the Royal Society Interface*, 14, p. 20170096.

Clark, A. (1998) *Being There. Putting Brain, Body, and World Together Again*. Cambridge: MIT Press.

——— (2013) "Whatever next? Predictive brains, situated agents, and the future of cognitive science," *Behavioral and Brain Sciences*, 36(3), pp. 181–204.

——— (2015a) "Embodied prediction," in T. Metzinger and J. Windt (eds), *Open MIND*. Frankfurt am Main: MIND Group.

——— (2015b) "Radical predictive processing," *Southern Journal of Philosophy*, 53(S1), pp. 3–27.

——— (2016) *Surfing Uncertainty*. New York: Oxford University Press.

——— (2017) "Busting out: Predictive brains, embodied minds, and the puzzle of the evidentiary veil," *Nous*, 51(4), pp. 727–753.

——— (2020) "Beyond desire? Agency, choice, and the predictive mind," *Australasian Journal of Philosophy*, 98(1), pp. 1–15.

——— (2022) "Extending the predictive mind," *Australasian Journal of Philosophy* [Preprint].

Friston, K. (2013) "Active inference and free energy," *Behavioral and Brain Sciences*, 36, pp. 212–213.

Friston, K. and Stephan, K. (2007) "Free-energy and the brain," *Synthese*, 159(3), pp. 417–458.

Friston, K., Thornton, C., and Clark, A. (2012) "Free-energy minimization and the dark-room problem," *Frontiers in Psychology*, 3, pp. 1–7.

Hohwy, J. (2013) *The Predictive Mind*. Oxford: Oxford University Press.

——— (2015) "The neural organ explains the mind," in T. Metzinger and J. Windt (eds), *Open MIND*. Frankfurt am Main: MIND Group.

——— (2016) "The self-evidencing brain," *Nous*, 50(2), pp. 259–285.

────── (2018) "Predictive processing hypothesis," in A. Newen, L. de Bruin, and S. Gallagher (eds), *The Oxford Handbook of 4E Cognition*. Oxford: Oxford University Press, pp. 127–146.

────── (2020) "New directions in predictive processing," *Mind and Language*, 35(2), pp. 209–223.

Kaspar, K., König, S., Schwandt, J., & König, P. (2014) "The experience of new sensorimotor contingencies by sensory augmentation," *Consciousness and Cognition*, 28(1), pp. 47–63.

Kersten, L. (2023) "A Model Solution: On the Compatibility of Predictive Processing and Embodied Cognition," *Minds and Machines*, 33(1), pp. 113–134

Kirchhoff, M. (2018) "The body in action: predictive processing and the embodiment thesis," in A. Newen, L. de Bruin, and S. Gallagher (eds), *The Oxford Handbook of 4E Cognition*. Oxford: Oxford University Press, pp. 243–260.

────── (2017) "From mutual manipulation to cognitive extension: challenges and implications," *Phenomenology and the Cognitive Sciences*, 16(5), pp. 863–878.

Kiverstein, J., Miller, M., and Rietveld, E. (2019) "The feeling of grip: novelty, error dynamics, and the predictive brain," *Synthese*, 196(7), pp. 2847–2869.

König, P. and König, S. (2016) "Learning a new sense by sensory augmentation," in *4th International Winter Conference on Brain-Computer Interface, BCI 2016*. Institute of Electrical and Electronics Engineers Inc.

Miller, M. and Clark, A. (2017) "Happily entangled: Prediction, emotion, and the embodied mind," *Synthese*, 195(6), pp. 2559–2579.

Noë, A. (2004) *Action in Perception*. Cambridge: MIT Press.

Pezzulo, G. (2014) "Why do you fear the bogeyman? An embodied predictive coding model of perceptual inference," *Cognitive, Affective & Behavioral Neuroscience*, 14, pp. 902–911.

Ramstead, M., Kirchhoff, M., Constant, A., & Friston, K. (2021) "Multiscale integration: beyond internalism and externalism," *Synthese*, 198, pp. 41–70.

Rupert, R. (2011) "Embodiment, Consciousness, and the Massively Representational Mind," *Philosophical Topics*, 39(1), pp. 99–120.

Veissière, S., Constant, A., Ramstead, M., Friston, K., & Kirmayer, L. (2020) "Thinking through other minds: a variational approach to cognition and culture," *Behavioral and Brain Sciences*, 43, p. e90.

Venter, E. (2021) "Toward an embodied, embedded predictive processing account of cognition," *Frontiers in Psychology*, 12(543076).

Wiese, W. (2017) "Action is enabled by systematic misrepresentations," *Erkenntnis*, 82(6), pp. 1233–1252.

9

PREDICTING THE BODY OR EMBODIED PREDICTION?

New Directions in Embodied Predictive Processing

Luke Kersten

In its broadest form, embodied cognition (EC) proposes that cognitive science is at a significant disadvantage when it fails to acknowledge the formative role played by the body in perception and cognition. When construed slightly more narrowly, it suggests that the real-time, dynamic contributions of the body and its interactions constitute or deeply influence the character of cognitive and perceptual processes. For many, EC has proven a haven from the more reconstructionist and neurocentric tendencies in cognitive science (Maturana and Varela 1991; Chemero 2009; Shapiro 2011).

Recently, a new of vision of cognition has begun to attract increasing attention within cognitive science. Emerging from converging work in cognitive and computational neuroscience, "predictive processing" (PP) suggests that the brain/mind does not have direct access to the world but, rather, must infer hidden causes from ongoing sensory input. By virtue of being inferentially secluded, cognitive systems, such as the brain, are constantly tied up in a process of trying to minimise the difference between incoming sensory inputs and prior expectations about the world, what is called "prediction error minimization" (PEM). For many, PP delivers a simple yet compelling story for a wide range of perceptual and cognitive processes and abilities, from vision and attention to consciousness and imagination (Clark 2013; Hohwy 2013).

Not surprisingly, several thinkers have begun to wonder how compatible these two influential approaches might be. Clark (2015, 2016, 2017), for instance, has suggested that PP and EC are not only compatible, but that they form a unifying vision of cognition. Hohwy (2016, 2018, 2019), on the other hand, has remained more sceptical, arguing that PP eschews stronger forms of embodiment in favour of a more inferential and representational picture of the mind. The task of sussing out the issue of compatibility is an important one. Not only have PP and EC been hailed as "paradigm shifts" and "revolutions" within cognitive science, but they have also stimulated a wealth of new research, including work on conceptual knowledge (Gallese and Lakoff 2005), emotion (Colombetti 2017), music cognition (Kersten and Wilson 2016) and consciousness (Deane 2021). Given its importance, this chapter looks to weigh in on the growing discussion surrounding PP–EC

DOI: 10.4324/9781003322511-13

110

compatibility. I begin by providing a brief overview of recent discussion, and then turn to articulating two outstanding issues. I conclude by pointing in the direction of some fruitful lines of future development.

Predicting the Body or Embodied Prediction?

As mentioned, two authors have featured prominently in recent discussions of PP–EC compatibility: Andy Clark and Jakob Hohwy.[1] Each has argued at considerable length for what they see as the correct vision of the relationship.

Hohwy's (2016, 2018, 2019) view begins from the premise that the brain/central nervous system is constantly trying to provide its best "hypotheses" for incoming sensory data. In line with the standard PP story, there are two general ways it can do this. One is to update its expectations about the world (change its predictive or *generative* model); the other is to act on the world so as to bring it in line with its expectation (*active inference*). The former reduces the mismatch between prior expectations and incoming sensory signals via model updating, while the latter reduces mismatch via aligning the world with prior expectations. Both strategies minimise the same sensory prediction error, albeit through different means. If Hohwy is right, then the brain is trying to constantly infer the shape and structure of a distal realm on the basis of partial and fragmentary information. The brain's access to the world is limited by the flow of information from an individual's sensory surfaces, whether that is visual, auditory, or motor.

But importantly, PEM takes place behind what Hohwy calls an 'evidentiary boundary' (EE). The idea is that when some evidence becomes an indispensable part of the evidential basis for a hypothesis, an evidentiary boundary is formed, one which draws a circle around e_i and h_j, on the one hand, and the hidden causes of e_i, on the other. For example, following Hempel (1965), Hohwy offers the case of seeing footprints in the snow. While seeing footprints may give rise to the hypothesis that there is a potential burglar lurking nearby, the strength of the footprints acting as evidence for the burglar hypothesis rests on how well the burglar hypothesis, in turn, explains the evidence.

The evidentiary boundary is important, Hohwy thinks, because it can be used to demarcate the boundaries of cognition – that is, whether or not something qualifies as part of a cognitive process or state depends on what side of the evidentiary boundary it finds itself. This spells trouble for strong versions of EC (i.e., ones that view the body as constitutive of cognition), because it looks like only sensory states of the nervous system are appropriately placed to stand in for evidence. As Hohwy explains:

> [W]hat is actually part of the EE-circle determined by our prediction error minimizing systems? The answer to this question is that it is brains and sensory states (i.e., the states of the sensory organs) that form the EE-circle. There is no good reason to include anything else in the EE-circle.
>
> *(2016, p. 269)*

The trouble is that while we regularly interact with bodies such that we form hypotheses or models about them via predicting the sensory inputs they cause, we do not do so with our sensory organs. Given this, it seems that features of the body fall outside the evidentiary boundary.

The implication is that EC can be accommodated by PP but only from within the strictures of the self-evidencing brain. As Hohwy (2016) makes the point:

> [T]here is no fundamental difference between types of inference that rely on the body and types that don't: they all consist just of inner representations of interacting, hidden causes and generation of expected sensory inference on the basis of these representations. Embodied cognition boils down to the fact that one of these modeled causes is the agent's own body.
>
> *(p. 275)*

It is inference and inference alone which secures evidence for the hypotheses the brain uses to guide action. It is inference which puts the brain in a position to match sensory inputs with expected outputs in the first place; a process which is wholly internal, and brain bound. So, while it is true to say that the body plays a role in cognition for Hohwy, it operates only as a useful parameter for PEM within the internal generative model of the brain.

In contrast, Clark (2015, 2016, 2017) envisages a more constructive relationship between PP and EC. Recall that on Clark's view EC and PP are not only compatible, they form a unifying picture of cognition. Clark offers both negative and positive arguments for this position, though for reasons of simplicity and space I focus largely on the presentation provided in Clark (2017).

On the negative side, Clark attempts to show there is no direct link between PP and neuro-centric visions of the mind. He suggests, for instance, that there is an ambiguity in how some authors use the concept of "inference" within PP. One way to understand inference, he thinks, in line with Hohwy's take, is as a *reconstructive* process. On this interpretation, the brain is trying to piece together an internal model of the world based on impoverished incoming sensory data. This, Clark suggests, is what gives rise to the impression that the brain is secluded from the world, so that one has to infer the world from limited sensory input. However, another way to interpret the concept is as a process that enables different strategies for co-ordinating behaviour. On this *non-reconstructive* interpretation, long-term prediction error minimisation is actually an action-involving process. The reason for this is that it is often simpler and more efficient to enact certain behaviours and shape the sensory flow than it is to try and create costly internal representations. As Clark (2017) puts it: "The task of PP systems is not to infer the best description of the world given the sensory evidence. The fundamental task, using prediction errors as the lever, is to find the neuronal activity patterns that most successfully accommodate (in action, and in readiness for action) current sensory states" (p. 734). For Clark, talk of inferring the right "hypotheses" is unnecessarily reconstructivist. While initially couched in neurocentric terms, concepts such as inference are not inherently biased against EC. An equally viable interpretation, one compatible with the PP story, is that inference involves a way of structuring ongoing interactions with the world.[2]

This idea of structuring ongoing, fluid interactions with the world in the service of PEM leads Clark to a more positive proposal. Because agents engage in iterative, dynamic perception-action cycles, they often offload computational work onto their environment, which allows them to minimise prediction error more cost effectively. One illustrative example comes from the outfielder problem. The outfielder problem asks how a baseball player (an outfielder) is able to catch a fly ball while on the run. One suggestion, in line with the reconstructivist view, is that agents engage in a form of internal replica building via inference, estimating and tracking the ball's trajectory using rich, internal representations. However, an alternative, more cost-efficient method, is that agents keep the image of the ball stationary on their retina in order to keep the flow of sensory information within a certain range. On this second approach, behavioural success is achieved not by reconstructing costly inner replicas but simply by maintaining invariant relations between the agent and the world. For Clark, the key insight is that agents often use low-cost, action-driven strategies to minimise prediction error; they engage in a form of "productive laziness". In so doing, they create temporary neural-body-world ensembles to solve context-dependent problems, such as catching the fly ball. These temporary problem-solving ensembles emerge and dissolve out of local necessity and are driven by action-perception cycles.

There are two important ideas here. The first is that in order to sculpt the flow of sensory information for real-time, ongoing use, agents must often engage in bouts of action-perception cycles (see, e.g., Clark 2015). These are circular, casual interactions between the organism and its environment, ones which spread the computational workload from the brain to the non-neural body and world, what is sometimes called "cognitive scaffolding". This process creates a "motor-informational weave", as Clark calls it, which is necessary to sustain the creation of "transient extended cognitive systems" (or TECs) (Clark 2008, 2016, 2017). The idea is that agents can sometimes get by with purely internal neural assemblies, and sometimes they need to call on external non-neuronal resources, such as the body, to form larger problem-solving wholes.

The second is that many of the same basic rules and principles that govern inner neural coalitions, such as efficacy and efficiency, also govern TECs – Clark points to optical acceleration cancellation (the strategy of keeping the ball's image on the retina) as an example of how systems trade off efficacy and efficiency. There is no real difference, according to Clark, in how coalitions of internal neural assemblies and body-spanning ones select actions to solve specific problems. Crucial to both is the ability to make task-specific information available for fast, fluid use. This means that PP actually fleshes out the computational story behind why TECs are formed: they are one strategy amongst others for minimising prediction error.

The takeaway is that PP is not only opposed to more "reconstructive" interpretations, but it also accommodates key ideas from EC, such as cognitive scaffolding and productive laziness. This more "radical" reading offers a systematic way of combining deep, model-based flexibility of PP with the frugal, environmentally exploitative actions of EC.

Two Outstanding Issues

There is much to be said for Hohwy's and Clark's proposals. Both authors offer instructive and nuanced discussions of various aspects of the PP–EC relationship, such as the relationship between active inference and perception-action. However, despite their informative character, there are still several outstanding issues that need to be addressed if discussion of PP–EC compatibility is to progress.[3]

One issue concerns the conceptual status of PP and EC. The trouble is that it is often unclear what types of unit of analysis PP and EC are supposed to denote within philosophic and scientific theorising. For instance, while some have suggested that PP is a unifying "theory" (Hohwy 2013, 2020; Litwin and Miłkowski 2021), others have contended it is a research "framework" or "paradigm" (Sprevak 2021; Michel 2022). Similarly, while some have suggested that EC is a "thesis" or "hypothesis" (Meteyard et al. 2012; Wilson and

Golonka 2013; Mahon 2015), others have claimed it is a "research programme" or "research tradition" (Shapiro 2007; Shapiro and Spaulding 2021; Miłkowski and Nowakowski 2021). A wide, and largely distinct, array of terms has been applied to discussions of PP and EC, and not always in consistent ways.

This "status" problem is important because different theoretical units carry with them different standards of comparison and modes of relation. For example, while behaviourism and cognitivism are arguably incompatible when cast at the level of theory, each offering rival attempts to explain a specific phenomenon such as language acquisition, the same cannot be said when viewed at the level of a research programme. While theories can be in direct tension with one another, it is less clear the same is true of theories and research programmes (Moore 1997). Because different theoretical units can vary with respect to level of abstractness and function, the character of compatibility between PP and EC can change depending on the type of conceptual unit being compared. If PP denotes, for instance, a "theory-like" structure, while EC picks out a "research programme-like" structure, then the question of compatibility may arise in a different form than it would if they referred to the same structure. Without first getting clear on the theoretical status of PP and EC, any discussion of compatibility may prove premature.

A second issue concerns the theoretical commitments of PP and EC. The trouble this time is that it is unclear which theoretical commitments are supposed to be central to PP and EC. For instance, in various places Clark (2015, 2017) points to "cognitive scaffolding" and "productive laziness" as key elements of EC, whereas Hohwy (2018) singles out "tight agent-environment coupling" and "fast and frugal processing". A similar point holds in the case of PP. For instance, Michel (2022) suggests that the central tenet of PP is that the "mind entertains a probabilistic, hierarchical generative model", while Sprevak (2021) rejects such a characterisation in favour of a cluster of claims about the computational, algorithmic and implementational details of cognition (see Sprevak (2021) for details). There is little agreement, even at a very general level, about the core ontological and methodological commitments of PP and EC. As Miłkowski (2019) ably puts the point in the context of EC: "While most surveys, defences, and critiques of embodied cognition proceed by treating it as a neatly delineated claim, such an approach soon becomes problematic due to the inherent plurality of this perspective on cognition" (p. 221).

This "commitment" problem is again important because a lack of consensus could spell trouble for the scope of any account of compatibility. If the commitments are spelled out too narrowly, then compatibility might be achieved but only at the cost of sacrificing wider insight. For example, if, as Clark suggests, PP and EC are compatible with respect to cognitive scaffolding, but not, as Hohwy suggests, constitutive embodiment, then Clark's account, while illuminating, would only have limited scope. It would only demonstrate compatibility for specific formulations of EC, such as those pertaining to cognitive scaffolding, but it would remain silent on how PP relates to other (potential) core commitments of EC. If we are not clear about which commitments are central to EC and PP, then a given account could exclude other relevant commitments. Conversely, if the commitments are defined too broadly, then compatibility could become trivial. For example, if, as is sometimes suggested, EC is simply the commitment to a "crucial role for the body" (Meteyard et al. 2012) and PP is simply the idea that brain is a "prediction machine" (Venter 2021), then the two views may be compatible but this compatibility is not particularly informative. What we need is a way of making sense of the diversity of commitments found within PP and EC, but such that it does not sacrifice the informativeness of the account of compatibility.

So, to summarise, there are two outstanding issues impeding progress on thinking about PP–EC compatibility. The first concerns the theoretical status of PP and EC, while the second concerns how to specify the theoretical commitments of PP and EC. To be clear, I raise these issues not as specific criticisms of existing proposals but, rather, as invitations for further development.

New Directions in Embodied Predictive Processing

In this final section, I want to say a bit about how to tackle the two outstanding issues. The proposal, in short, is that discussions of compatibility will benefit from more explicit engagement with the resources of philosophy of science.

To begin, consider that there is a general distinction within philosophy of science between two types of units of analysis or scientific representations (Lakatos 1970; Laudan 1977). On the one hand, there are the more detailed, concrete units, ones which attempt to explain and predict specific phenomena, such as optical occlusion in visual perception or the phenology of hibernation. These units usually march under the banner of terms like "theory" or "model", with examples including Maxwell's theory of electromagnetism or Baddeley's model of working memory. On the other hand, there are broader, more abstract units, ones which operate above the level of individual theory or model and often guide and constrain theory or model formation; examples include Hutton's uniformitarianist theory in geology or Gibson's ecological approach in psychology. These units are sometimes referred to as "research programmes", "paradigms", or "frameworks".[4]

Now the question of how these two types of units or representations relate is a subtle and complex one. Fortunately, for present purposes, we can sidestep this issue and focus instead on how PP and EC have been more generally characterised in discussions. This is interesting because many authors see PP and EC as falling into either one or the other category. For example, Shapiro (2007) maintains that: "the point of labelling EC a research programme, *rather than* a theory, is to indicate that the commitments and subject matters of EC remain fairly nebulous" (my emphasis). In a similar vein, Sprevak (2021) suggests of PP that: "it is more accurate to think of predictive coding [PP] as a research programme *rather than* as a mature theory" (my emphasis). For both authors, PP and EC are best thought of as *either* concrete, testable units or abstract, research-guiding units, but not both. What I want to suggest, though, is that we should also favour the abstract interpretation of PP and EC, and that interesting possibilities begin to open up when we do so. There are two main reasons for this.

The first is the characteristic function of PP and EC within scientific practice and theorising. In a broad sense, research programmes, paradigms, and frameworks all aim to motivate and guide theory or model development. They do so by providing high-level schematic proposals for how to implement and interpret various principles or concepts. This is in keeping with how PP and EC generally function within scientific and philosophic discourse (see, e.g., Shapiro 2007, 2011; Miłkowski 2019; Sprevak 2021; Michel 2022). For example, while many descriptions of PP express a commitment to the idea that precision weighting is important for optimising prediction error minimisation (e.g., Clark, 2013; Hohwy, 2013), the question of how precision weighting is actually implemented in the dynamics of neurotransmitters is often left unspecified.[5] This makes sense if PP operates as a broader, more abstract unit of analysis. The implementational details are left open because PP is not trying to provide specific, testable claims. Rather, PP aims to guide and constrain specific theory and model construction through the articulation of general principles and concepts. The same is also true of EC. It is better to talk of PP and EC as unifying frameworks or research programmes, rather than unifying theories.

The second reason is that PP and EC possess a wide array of ontological and methodological commitments. For example, as mentioned, PP regularly employs talk of generative models, probabilistic inference, efficient neural coding, prediction error minimisation, and top-down effects; while EC invokes talk of sensorimotor contingencies, action-perception cycles, exploitative representations, and temporally extended dynamic systems. The easiest way to accommodate this range of concepts and principles is to conceptualise them as organising or guiding commitments for research. Research programmes, paradigms, and frameworks all specify, in very general terms, the basic types of fundamental entities that exist within a domain, and the methods used for conducting inquiry. Or, to frame the point in more Marrian terms, PP and EC provide sets of concepts and principles that guide and constrain further algorithmic and implementation-level accounts. While individual theories and models also exhibit various ontological and methodological commitments, it is the diversity and generality of the commitments found in PP and EC that speak in favour of their interpretation as more abstract units of analysis.

If it is right to say that PP and EC are best understood as broader, more abstract units, then this opens up interesting possibilities when it comes to addressing the theoretical commitment issue. This is because there is already a well-established literature dealing with the character and function of abstract units within philosophy of science (see, e.g., Lakatos, 1970; Laudan, 1977). One point often made in these discussions is that the same general commitments can be implemented in a variety of ways with particular theories or models – for example, to develop a theory of the motion of a compass when near a current-carrying wire a researcher must go beyond the general commitments of Newtonian physics, such as the claim that all non-rectilinear motions should be treated as cases of centrally directed forces.

This provides one potential explanation for why it has proven so difficult to clarify the commitments of PP and EC: one cannot read off the commitments of abstract units from their associated theories or models, nor vice versa. If one were to survey embodied theories of semantics, for instance, one would be forgiven for thinking that a notion of "representation" is common to EC; talk of the sensory and motor information in cognitive representations is a constant theme in discussions of embodied semantics (see, e.g., Lakoff 2012; Dove 2022). However, as is well known, a number of distinct EC theories of vision, such as Noë (2004, 2009), explicitly eschew talk of representations in favour of explanations involving the action dynamics of an agent. Because different theories or models have different ways of implementing the more general commitments of abstract units, attempting to infer the core commitments from a survey of associated theories or models is not only unlikely to succeed but also potentially misleading. One implication is that researchers should avoid making inferences about core commitments solely on the basis of an abstract unit's associated theories or models. Instead, they must provide a rich, detailed study of the unit's history.

Whether or not this particular point about the relationship between abstract and concrete units is correct is less important than the example it provides. For it shows how the resources of philosophy of science can fruitfully be brought to bear in discussions of compatibility. The toolkit provided by philosophy of science better positions researchers to identify the core commitments of PP and EC, and thereby make progress on the question of compatibility.

So, taking stock, this chapter has attempted to weigh in on the growing discussion surrounding PP–EC compatibility. It did so by, first, surveying two prominent proposals from Clark and Hohwy and, second, articulating two outstanding issues. The positive proposal was that both outstanding issues could be fruitfully addressed by drawing on the resources of philosophy of science. The significance of the analysis, as I see it, lies not only in the specific proposals it makes, but in the general direction it sets for discussion. It raises a number of interesting further questions, such as: What *specific* types of units of analysis are PP and EC? Are they research programmes, research traditions, or frameworks? Are there important differences depending on which we choose? Is there a particular model of science that we should adopt when thinking about compatibility? Lakatos (1970) or Laudan (1977)? And under what conditions is integration possible? The answers to some (or all) of these questions could notably reshape the form of compatibility the PP–EC relationship takes going forward.

Acknowledgements

Some passages in this chapter have been adapted with revision from Kersten (2022, 2023).

Notes

1 For other interesting discussions of PP–EC compatibility, see also Anderson (2017), Kirchhoff (2018), and Venter (2021).
2 While I cannot go into detail for reasons of space, it is worth noting that Hohwy (2019) does respond to Clark's (2017) critique, arguing in turn that Clark's embodied-friendly interpretation of PEM as "accommodation" is equally problematic, and that only an inferential interpretation coheres with PP.
3 To qualify slightly, while I am placing scientific units broadly into two categories, I do not think these are the only categories possible for scientific units. I acknowledge, for example, that there is an important difference between "models"' and "theories". Nevertheless, I think this omission is largely justified at present because the taxonomy marks at least one important distinction with respect to function and abstractness of different units.
4 For a more detailed discussion, see Kersten (2022, 2023).
5 Precision weighting describes the "gain" as it applies to components of the prediction error. Errors that have a high precision weighting are prioritised during a task; errors that have a low precision weighting are given a lower priority or even partly discounted.

References

Anderson, M. L. (2017) "Of Bayes and Bullets: An embodied, situated, targeting-based account of predictive processing," in T. Metzinger and W. Wiese (eds), *Philosophy and Predictive Processing: 4*. MIND Group.
Chemero, A. (2009) *Radical Embodied Cognitive Science*, The MIT Press.
Clark, A. (2008) *Supersizing the Mind: Embodiment, Action, and Cognitive Extension*, Oxford University Press.
——— (2013) "Whatever next? Predictive brains, situated agents, and the future of cognitive science," *Behavioral and Brain Sciences*, 36(3), 181–204.
——— (2015) "Radical predictive processing," *The Southern Journal of Philosophy*, 53(S1), 3–27. https://doi.org/10.1111/sjp.12120

———— (2016) *Surfing Uncertainty: Prediction, Action, and the Embodied Mind*, Oxford University Press.

———— (2017) "Busting out: Predictive brains, embodied minds, and the puzzle of the evidentiary veil," *Noûs*, *51*(4), 727–753.

Colombetti, G. (2017) "The Embodied and Situated Nature of Moods," *Philosophia*, 45, 1437–1451. https://doi.org/10.1007/s11406-017-9817-0

Deane, G. (2021) "Consciousness in active inference: Deep self-models, other minds, and the challenge of psychedelic-induced ego-dissolution," *Neuroscience of Consciousness*, 2021(2), niab024.

Dove, G. (2022) *Abstract Concepts and the Embodied Mind: Rethinking Grounded Cognition*, Oxford University Press.

Gallese, V., & Lakoff, G. (2005) "The brain's concepts: The role of the sensory-motor system in conceptual knowledge," *Cognitive Neuropsychology*, *22*(3/4), 455–479.

Hempel, C.G. (1965) *Aspects of Scientific Explanation* (Vol. 1). New York: Free Press.

Hohwy, J. (2013) *The predictive mind*, Oxford University Press.

———— (2016) "The self-evidencing brain," *Nous*, *50*(2), 259–285.

———— (2018) "The Predictive Processing Hypothesis," in A. Newen, L. De Bruin, & S. Gallagher (eds), *The Oxford Handbook of 4E Cognition* (pp. 129–145) Oxford University Press.

———— (2019) "Quick 'n' Lean or Slow and Rich?: Andy Clark on Predictive Processing and Embodied Cognition," in M. Colombo, E. Irvine, and M. Stapleton (eds), *Andy Clark and His Critics* (pp. 191–205) Oxford University Pres. https://doi.org/10.1093/oso/9780190662813.003.0015

———— (2020) "New directions in predictive processing," *Mind & Language*, 35, 209–223.

Kersten, L. (2022) "A new mark of the cognitive? Predictive processing and extended cognition," *Synthese*, *200*(281), 1–25. https://doi.org/10.1007/s11229-022-03674-2

———— (2023) "A Model Solution: On the Compatibility of Predictive Processing and Embodied Cognition," *Minds and Machines*, *33*(1), 117–134. https://doi.org/10.1007/s11023-022-09617-7

Kersten, L., & Wilson, R. (2016) "The sound of music: Externalist style," *American Philosophical Quarterly*, *53*(2), 139–154.

Kirchhoff, M. (2018) "The Body in Action: Predictive Processing and the Embodiment Thesis," in A. Newen, L. De Bruin, and S. Gallagher (eds), *The Oxford Handbook of 4E Cognition* (pp. 243–260) Oxford University Press.

Lakatos, I. (1970) "Falsification and the methodology of scientific research programmes," in I. Lakatos and A. Musgrave (eds), *Criticism and the growth of knowledge: Proceedings of the international colloquium in the philosophy of science*, Cambridge University Press.

Lakoff, G. (2012) "Explaining embodied cognition results," *Topics in Cognitive Science*, *4*(4), 773–785. https://doi.org/10.1111/j.1756-8765.2012.01222.x

Laudan, L. (1977) *Progress and its problem: Towards a theory of scientific growth*, University of California Press.

Litwin, P., & Miłkowski, M. (2021) "Unification by fiat: Arrested development of predictive processing," *Cognitive Science*. https://doi.org/10.1111/cogs.12867

Mahon, B. Z. (2015) "The burden of embodied cognition," *Canadian Journal of Experimental Psychology*, *69*(2), 172–178. https://doi.org/10.1037/cep0000060

Maturana, H. R., & Varela, F. J. (1991) *Autopoiesis and cognition: The realization of the living*. Dordrecht: D. Reidel Publishing Company.

Meteyard, L., Rodriguez, S., Bahrami, B., & Vigliocco, G. (2012) "Coming of age: A review of embodiment and the neuroscience of semantics," *Cortex*, *48*(7), 788–804.

Michel, C. (2022) "Scaling up predictive processing to language with construction grammar," *Philosophical Psychology*. https://doi.org/10.1080/09515089.2022.2050198

Miłkowski, M. (2019) "Fallible heuristics and evaluation of research traditions. The case of embodied cognition," *Ruch Filozoficzny*, *75*(2), 223–236. https://doi.org/10.12775/rf.2019.031

Miłkowski, M., & Nowakowski, P. (2021) "Representational unification in cognitive science: Is embodied cognition a unifying perspective?" *Synthese*, *199*(Suppl 1), 67–88.

Moore, J. (1997) "On the relation between behaviorism and cognitive psychology," *The Journal of Mind and Behavior*, *17*(4), 345–367.

Noë, A. (2004) *Action in Perception*, MIT Press.

———— (2009) *Out of Our Heads: Why you are not your Brain, and other lessons from the Biology of Consciousness*, Hill and Wang.

Shapiro, L., and Spaulding, S. (2021) "Embodied Cognition," The Stanford Encyclopaedia of Philosophy, Edward N. Zalta (ed.) https://plato.stanford.edu/archives/win2021/entries/embodied-cognition/. Accessed 11 October 2022.

Shapiro, L. A. (2007) "The embodied cognition research programme," *Philosophy Compass*, 2(2), 338–346. https://doi.org/10.1111/j.1747-9991.2007.00064.x

——— (2011) *Embodied cognition*, Routledge.

Sprevak, M. (2021) "Predictive coding II: The computational level," TBC. [Online access].

Venter, E. (2021) "Toward an embodied, embedded predictive processing account," *Frontiers in Psychology*, 12, 543076. https://doi.org/10.3389/fpsyg.2021.543076

Wilson, A. D., & Golonka, S. (2013) "Embodied cognition is not what you think it is," *Frontiers in Psychology*. https://doi.org/10.3389/fpsyg.2013.0005

10

PREDICTIVE PROCESSING AND EMBODIMENT IN EMOTION

Fiorella Del Popolo Cristaldi, Suzanne Oosterwijk, and Lisa Feldman Barrett

Introduction

Imagine that you are cycling home. Suddenly you see a right-turning car from the corner of your eye. The car will hit you if you don't act. Your brain immediately prepares your body for action: your heart pumps faster; your hands grip the bars of the bicycsle. You squeeze the brakes and skid to a full stop. You feel scared. The car turns without noticing you. You feel anger.

In this chapter we will introduce the theory of constructed emotion (Barrett 2017b, 2022; Barrett and Lida, 2024), a brain-based, context-sensitive theory of emotion that hypothesizes that past experience (e.g., of cycling around the city) is continuously being used to plan action (e.g., the viscero- and skeletomotor movements for braking) and predict experience (e.g., the incoming sense data from the body and the world that result in the percept of a car), including the creation of instances of emotion (e.g., fear, anger). We explain that all actions and experiences begin as prediction signals that are, in effect, ad hoc conceptual categories that the brain constructs in a situated, embodied way. Incoming sense data from the body and the world help select and confirm prediction signals, in effect categorizing those signals. Every instance of emotion, like every mental event, is a combination of these embodied concepts (i.e., the remembered past) and incoming signals to the brain (i.e., the sensory present). We also discuss how interoception (i.e., the brain's modeling of the sensory state of the body) is related to the affective features of consciousness and gives instances of emotion their characteristic affective feel (e.g., pleasure, discomfort, activation). Finally, we address how perceiving instances of emotion in others (e.g., observing someone else being almost hit by a car and perceiving them as being afraid) is produced by the same embodied predictive process.

A predictive model of emotion

Predictive processing and the theory of constructed emotion

The theory of constructed emotion (Barrett 2017b, 2022; Barrett and Lida, 2024) is a predictive processing account of brain function (e.g., Clark 2013; Seth and Friston 2016;

Hutchinson and Barrett 2019) hypothesizing that past experience is continuously being used to predictively guide action and construct experience. In order to reduce uncertainty and conserve metabolic resources for growth, survival and reproduction, the brain runs an internal model of actions coupled with continuously arriving signals from the body's sensory surfaces (e.g., retina, cochlea, glucose receptors, etc.) to anticipate the body's energetic needs and try to meet them before they arise (called allostasis; Sterling 2012; Barrett 2017b; Pezzulo, Zorzi and Corbetta 2021). Running an internal model of the body in the world, thus, serves to regulate that body in the world.

Predictive processing accounts dismiss the idea of a reactive brain that processes all incoming information bit by bit, because such a system would quickly drain all metabolic resources (e.g., Sterling and Laughlin 2015). A predictive brain, instead, minimizes the processing costs of new information by using previous experience (based on features of equivalence) to generate visceromotor and skeletomotor control signals that plan upcoming, situated action as well as predict the sensory consequences of those actions. Incoming sensory signals are thought to confirm or correct the sensory predictions as a means of coordinating and controlling action. Discrepancies between ongoing prediction signals and incoming sensory signals (i.e., *prediction errors*) provide the brain with an opportunity to update its internal model (i.e., learn) (Den Ouden, Kok and De Lange 2012; Clark 2018). In part, the decision to update or adjust ongoing predictions depends on *precision signals* (i.e., attentional control) that modulate the strength of the prediction signals (as priors) as well as the incoming sensory prediction errors with regard to their relevance for allostasis (e.g., reward-prediction errors).

The theory of constructed emotion (Barrett 2017b) draws on the predictive computational architecture of the brain as the core biological substrate in which instances of emotions (as well as other mental phenomena) unfold. Emotions are not represented in distinct, dedicated neural circuits, but are hypothesized to be created through the activation of multiple spatiotemporal neural patterns serving the general purpose of predicting and correcting to maintain allostasis and skeletomotor control (Barrett and Simmons 2015; Chanes and Barrett 2016; Barrett 2017b; Kleckner *et al.* 2017; Katsumi *et al.* 2022, 2023). A crucial and paradigm-shifting consequence of these assumptions is that instances of emotion can no longer be considered "reactions to the world". People are active constructors of their emotions rather than passive receivers of sensory inputs (Barrett 2017a).

Predictions as concepts

When a brain constructs prediction signals, it is in effect constructing an *ad hoc, situated* and *embodied* conceptual category (see Barrett 2017a, 2017b for a discussion of ad hoc categories; see Barsalou 1983; Barsalou *et al.* 2003; Casasanto and Lupyan 2015). A category consists of a reassembly of a group of past events that share features of equivalence with the current state of the body and the world (Radulescu, Shin and Niv 2021). The brain continuously constructs these complex assemblies of prediction signals in order to coordinate and control motor actions, thereby explaining the cause of those actions and disambiguating the meaning of associated sensory signals (Barrett 2017a, 2017b and references therein). Precision signals and incoming sensory signals help to select (or correct) this assembly of prediction signals. In other words, based on past experiences with similar features, the brain runs an internal model to estimate the state of its body in the present world, thereby constructing situated categories tailored to the goals and functional requirements of the present.

Categories can be assemblies of low-level sensory and motor features with high dimensionality or assemblies of compressed, multi-modal summaries of those sensory and motor features, i.e., abstract mental features (for discussion, see Barrett 2017b, 2022; Barrett and Finlay 2018). Abstract conceptual categories, such as emotion categories, are constructed when the brain assembles abstract mental features of equivalence, such as "protect against threat" (i.e., a multi-modal summary of past events with a similar goal to protect oneself) and "arousal" (i.e., a multi-modal summary of past events similarly experienced as arousing) (for neural details, see these papers and references therein: Barrett and Simmons 2015; Chanes and Barrett 2016; Barrett 2017a, 2017b; Hutchinson and Barrett 2019; Katsumi *et al.* 2021, 2022). It is these abstract mental features that make instances of an emotion similar across situations. Abstract mental features can reflect plans for visceromotor and motor action (i.e., abstract action concepts; Barrett and Finlay 2018), but also the goals associated with actions (e.g., to protect yourself), appraisals of the situation (e.g., novelty) and affective features (e.g., feeling aroused). An instance of an emotion is thus a mental event, in which the brain has selected a pattern of features (i.e., an emotion category constructed specifically for that situation) that confirms (or corrects) incoming sensory signals, thereby guiding action and giving psychological meaning to those incoming signals.

Previous experiences begin to be assembled as multi-modal, compressed, embodied representations of "the body in the world" (Barrett and Simmons 2015) and then become decompressed as they cascade along various architectural gradients in the brain to create the motor and sensory particulars of a situation-specific representation (for a review, see Barrett 2017b; Katsumi *et al.* 2022, 2023, and references therein). Part of this process involves predicting and integrating ascending signals from the visceral organs, the immune system and endocrine system, referred to as *interoception* (Critchley *et al.* 2004; Craig 2015; Kleckner *et al.* 2017). Thus, the brain not only predicts incoming signals from the external world (creating what you see, hear, smell and so on), but also generates interoceptive predictions about how the body reacts to the world. These embodied predictions have both sensory and motor aspects: they make up part of a brain's efforts to maintain allostasis while at the same time the efferent copies of those allostatic (i.e., visceromotor) control signals are sensory "simulations" (Barrett 2017b; Katsumi *et al.* 2022).

Let's apply this to our cycling example. As you are cycling home, your brain is continually reassembling (i.e., remembering) events from the past that are similar to the present (e.g., past experiences of cycling around the city, watching other people cycle or hearing stories about cycling) as a way of predicting what to do next. If predictions come from past instances of *fear* that you have experienced, read or heard about, then your brain is constructing an ad hoc, situated conceptual category for *fear*. These predictions take the form of visceromotor plans that may change your physiology (e.g., accelerate your heart rate, quicken your breath, release cortisol) to support planned skeletomotor movements, and sensory prediction signals that anticipate what you will see (the car), hear (screeching tires) and feel (activated). These prediction signals (e.g., what will happen if the car hits you), when confirmed by the incoming signals from the body's sensory surfaces, give psychological meaning to those sensory signals, including the abstract mental features (e.g., a goal to protect yourself) that are commonly experienced in similarly situated instances of fear. If predictions are constructed from prior instances of *anger* (including, for example, the abstract mental feature to punish someone), then the resulting sensations and actions are experienced as a situated instance of *anger*.

Importantly, in our predictive approach, it is the brain's preparation for action that guides perception (the visual percept of a car coming too close) and experience (the subjective experience of anger and fear). Thus, perception and experience *arise from* action (Barrett 2022). Even before you see the car, your brain is preparing actions to handle the situation. This information is sent to sensory regions of the brain, predicting the sensory consequences of those skeletomotor changes. If there is a car dangerously approaching you, the predictions are confirmed and the motor plans to handle the situation are executed. If the car stays in its lane, your brain might ignore the prediction error and execute the motor plans anyway, particularly in this situation where your life may be at stake. If the brain encodes the prediction error, you might have a slight swerve and keep going, or keep pedaling with no change in speed, but might feel the affective changes nonetheless, because the ascending interoceptive prediction error to correct the interoceptive predictions is slow.

A predictive functional architecture of the brain

One of the main strengths of the theory of constructed emotion is that it is based on the structural and functional architecture of the brain (for reviews, see Barrett and Simmons 2015; Kleckner *et al.* 2017; Katsumi *et al.* 2021, 2022). It leans on evidence demonstrating that there is no consistent one-to-one mapping between specific emotion categories and any neural and physiological correlates (Lindquist *et al.* 2012; Touroutoglou *et al.* 2015; Siegel *et al.* 2018; Westlin *et al.* 2023). Instead, situated variation in the sensory and motor features of instances within the same emotion category is a core feature of our framework (Barrett 2009, 2017b, 2022; for a discussion, see Barrett and Satpute 2019).

Here we will introduce three large-scale, distributed brain networks that are suggested as the neural substrates for the construction of embodied predictions (Seth and Friston 2016; Barrett 2017b; Katsumi *et al.* 2022). First, we hypothesize that the *default mode network* (DMN) constructs compressed, multi-modal summaries (i.e., prediction signals with a relatively high level of abstractness). This role of the DMN is supported by meta-analyses showing consistent activation of this network during emotional experience (Lindquist *et al.* 2012; Satpute and Lindquist 2019), emotion regulation (Wager *et al.* 2008) and subjective affective ratings (Wilson-Mendenhall, Barrett and Barsalou 2013). These summaries then cascade and become particularized into signals that predict specific sensory and motor details. Second, we hypothesize that the *salience network* estimates the precision for prediction errors relative to which are most relevant for allostasis and which can safely be ignored as noise (for discussion, see Barrett 2017b; Katsumi *et al.* 2022). This function of the salience network is consistent with its general role in interoception (Critchley *et al.* 2004), and with its common involvement in emotion perception and experience (Lindquist *et al.* 2012; Oosterwijk *et al.* 2012; Zaki, Davis and Ochsner 2012; Touroutoglou *et al.* 2015). Third, we hypothesize that the *frontoparietal control network* is involved in generating precision signals that estimate the priors of prediction signals (Barrett 2017b). It also tunes internal models with prediction errors by supporting top-down control activity in response to feedback. Therefore, we hypothesize that all these regions and networks, and the functions they support, play a pivotal role in upholding embodied prediction construction (Katsumi *et al.* 2022).

It is important to note that the brain networks presented here are domain general. That is, these networks serve general psychological functions across a range of mental phenomena, including emotion, (social) cognition, perception and memory. For example, the DMN plays a role in emotion, but also in other instances of the mind (see for an overview Buckner and DiNicola 2019), including self-relevant thought (e.g., Northoff *et al.* 2006), internal mentation (Andrews-Hanna *et al.* 2010), and understanding the minds of other people (Spreng and Grady 2010). We argue that what unifies these different psychological domains is the general role of these networks in the construction of embodied predictions in the service of allostasis.

The fundamental role of context

If emotions derive from *ad hoc*, *situated* and *embodied* conceptual categories, it follows that the specific situation in which they unfold, as well as what the brain is doing in the meantime, may influence how an embodied prediction yields an instance of an emotion. Simply put, emotions cannot be understood separately from the context in which they occur. Crucially, by "context" we mean not only what happens *outside* the brain while an emotion is being constructed (i.e., the *external context*), but also what happens *inside* (i.e., the *internal* or *neural context*).

The impact of the *external context* is well illustrated by research demonstrating that neural activation for the same emotion category differs as a function of the situation in which the emotion is experienced. For example, Wilson-Mendenhall *et al.* (2011) found that anger and fear showed different patterns of neural activation depending on the situational context in which they were categorized (e.g., situations describing physical danger engaged the salience network more than situations involving social evaluation). Furthermore, recent work has shown that experiencing certain vs. uncertain stimuli predictability (that is, probabilistic context) modulates pre- and post-stimulus cortical processing of positive and negative affective pictures (Del Popolo Cristaldi *et al.* 2021). In addition, external contextual factors related to previous experience were found to shape subjective affective ratings (see Del Popolo Cristaldi, Gambarota and Oosterwijk 2022b). The *neural or internal context* (i.e., what the brain is doing while an instance of emotion is constructed) is another crucial factor shaping the way in which an instance of emotion is constructed. Within this view lies evidence suggesting that the brain's functional connectivity at rest may predict affective processes such as the construction of affective predictions (Del Popolo Cristaldi *et al.* 2022a), emotional face processing, social cognition and the expression of emotions (Kong *et al.* 2019), and even pain sensitivity (Spisak *et al.* 2020). Further, bodily states measured as peripheral physiological activity may also modulate embodied predictions and the associated subjective experience of emotion (e.g., MacCormack and Lindquist 2019; for a comprehensive review, see Pace-Schott *et al.* 2019).

Prediction and embodiment in emotion perception

If subjective emotional experience can be understood as the product of a predictive process, then predictions may also be fundamental to representing emotion in perception (e.g., perceiving fear in someone else; Chanes *et al.* 2018), cognition (e.g., thinking about your partner's anger), memory (e.g., retrieving a happy memory), imagination (e.g., imagining a threatening situation; Oosterwijk *et al.* 2017) and language (e.g., reading about a disgusting experience; Oosterwijk *et al.* 2015). Indeed, several recent perspectives have positioned predictive processing as central to social cognitive processes (e.g., Gallagher and Allen 2018; Tamir and Thornton 2018; Shamay-Tsoory *et al.* 2019). Moreover, predictive processing may not only be fundamental in understanding the emotional states of other people, but also in aligning one's own emotional state with the state of psychologically close others (Shamay-Tsoory *et al.* 2019).

The idea that embodied predictions underlie social cognition resonates with embodied simulation theories that propose that observing actions, sensations and emotions in other people engages the same neural circuits as experiencing actions, sensations and emotions in the self (e.g., Bastiaansen, Thioux and Keysers 2009). Furthermore, it is consistent with views that propose that the conceptual system for emotion is grounded in sensorimotor and bodily states (Barsalou 1999; Niedenthal 2007; see for empirical support Oosterwijk *et al.* 2009, 2015; see for an overview Winkielman, Coulson and Niedenthal 2018). According to these views, multi-modal systems in the brain and body *simulate* experiential states in order to represent online instances of emotion (e.g., observing someone who is frightened) and offline instances of emotion (e.g., reading about a frightening event), even in the absence of direct sensory or bodily stimulation. Similar to "embodied cognition" accounts, we propose that people explain the external world, including the thoughts, feelings and actions of the other people in it, by constructing embodied predictions that anticipate the sensory signals that arise from the actions or words of others. In other words, we use our own internal model of our body in the world to predict what other people think, feel and do.

Neuroimaging work supports the idea that predictions based on an individual's own lived experience lie at the core of understanding other people. For example, neuroimaging experiments demonstrate neural overlap when people experience and observe emotions (Jabbi, Bastiaansen and Keysers 2008) or pain in other people (Zaki *et al.* 2016). Furthermore, vicarious experience is seen as an important component of empathy (Keysers and Gazzola 2014) and involves activation in the previously discussed salience network (e.g., Decety 2011; Fan *et al.* 2011). Moreover, there is an abundance of findings in the social neuroscience literature that demonstrates that the DMN network is involved when people make attributions about the content of other people's mental state (e.g., Van Overwalle and Baetens 2009; Yeshurun, Nguyen and Hasson 2021) or engage in other tasks that require a high level of abstraction (Satpute and Lindquist 2019).

To illustrate how a predictive process lies at the core of different emotion phenomena, we give an example from our own lab (Oosterwijk *et al.* 2017). In this study, participants imagined emotion-related actions (e.g., pushing someone away), interoceptive sensations (e.g., an increased heart rate) and situations (e.g., being alone in a park at night); and engaged in other-focused understanding of emotion-related actions (i.e., how does this person express his/her emotions?), interoceptive sensations (i.e., what does this person feel in their body?) and situations (i.e., why does this person feel an emotion?). Consistent with the idea that embodied predictions underlie imagery (Barrett 2017b), we found that imagining actions, interoceptive sensations and situations involved the salience network and DMN. Furthermore, using a classifier trained on the imagery task, we could accurately decode whether participants focused on actions, interoceptive sensations or situations when understanding the emotions of other people. Thus, the brain generates similar embodied predictions when imagining "experiencing" an action (or sensation or situation) and when understanding an action (or sensation or situation) in someone else.

Future directions

In summary, our constructionist framework connects a range of emotional phenomena by proposing that emotional experience and perception share a predictive process that dynamically adapts to the context at hand. Although some progress has been made in answering questions about how instances of emotion are grounded in the brain, body and situational context, there are still many questions that call for further investigation.

First of all, we know relatively little about how cultural differences impact the generation and implementation of predictions, even though people from different cultures differ in emotional expression and experience (e.g., Boiger and Mesquita 2012; Jack *et al.* 2012). Future research could focus on how culturally shared and culturally different emotion knowledge guides embodied predictions in interactive social contexts. A second topic for future research is the development of predictions across the lifespan. Although there is work that emphasizes the importance of shared allostatic experiences between children and parents in fine-tuning the internal model of "the body in the world" (e.g., Atzil and Gendron 2017), we know relatively little about how people continue to update their internal model in adulthood. For example, it is an open question how people build predictions not only on their own lived experience, but also on the lived experience of other people, for example through the consumption of TV shows, movies and books (see Hoemann and Barrett 2019). And finally, in order to capture emotions as they unfold in real life, affective research should start coming out of the labs and design more ecologically valid studies that can complement and overcome the limitations of traditional lab-based experiments. In the effort to do so, we call for a combined investigation of the neural, behavioural and subjective level in the experience of emotion, with the end goal of explaining emotion in all its complexity.

Acknowledgments

We thank Dr Antonio Maffei who read and/or made invaluable comments on an earlier draft of this chapter.

References

Andrews-Hanna, J.R. *et al.* (2010) "Evidence for the default network's role in spontaneous cognition," *Journal of Neurophysiology*, 104(1), pp. 322–335. Available at: https://doi.org/10.1152/jn.00830.2009

Atzil, S. and Gendron, M. (2017) "Bio-behavioral synchrony promotes the development of conceptualized emotions," *Current Opinion in Psychology*, 17, pp. 162–169. Available at: https://doi.org/10.1016/j.copsyc.2017.07.009

Barrett, L.F. (2009) "Variety is the spice of life: A psychological construction approach to understanding variability in emotion," *Cognition and Emotion*, 23(7), pp. 1284–1306. Available at: https://doi.org/10.1080/02699930902985894

——— (2017a) *How Emotions Are Made: The Secret Life of the Brain*. Houghton Mifflin Harcourt.

——— (2017b) "The theory of constructed emotion: an active inference account of interoception and categorization," *Social Cognitive and Affective Neuroscience*, 12(1), pp. 1–23. Available at: https://doi.org/10.1093/scan/nsw154

——— (2022) "Context reconsidered: Complex signal ensembles, relational meaning, and population thinking in psychological science.," *American Psychologist*, 77(8), p. 894. Available at: https://doi.org/10.1037/amp0001054

Barrett, L.F. and Finlay, B.L. (2018) "Concepts, goals and the control of survival-related behaviors," *Current Opinion in Behavioral Sciences*, 24, pp. 172–179. Available at: https://doi.org/10.1016/j.cobeha.2018.10.001

Barrett, L. F. and Lida, T. (2024) "Constructionist approaches to emotion in psychology and related fields." In A. Scarantino (Ed.), *Emotion Theory: The Routledge Comprehensive Guide Volume I: History, Contemporary Theories, and Key Elements*. Routledge.

Barrett, L.F. and Satpute, A.B. (2019) "Historical pitfalls and new directions in the neuroscience of emotion," *Neuroscience Letters*, 693, pp. 9–18. Available at: https://doi.org/10.1016/J.NEULET.2017.07.045

Barrett, L.F. and Simmons, W.K. (2015) "Interoceptive predictions in the brain," *Nature Reviews Neuroscience*, 16(7), pp. 419–429. Available at: https://doi.org/10.1038/nrn3950

Barsalou, L.W. (1983) "Ad hoc categories," *Memory and cognition*, 11(3), pp. 211–227.

——— (1999) "Perceptual symbol systems," *Behavioral and Brain Sciences*, 22(4), pp. 577–660. Available at: https://doi.org/10.1017/S0140525X99002149

Barsalou, L.W. *et al.* (2003) "Grounding conceptual knowledge in modality-specific systems," *Trends in Cognitive Sciences*, 7(2), pp. 84–91.

Bastiaansen, C.J., Thioux, M. and Keysers, C. (2009) "Evidence for mirror systems in emotions," *Philosophical Transactions of the Royal Society B: Biological Sciences*, 364(1528), pp. 2391–2404. Available at: https://doi.org/10.1098/rstb.2009.0058

Boiger, M. and Mesquita, B. (2012) "The Construction of Emotion in Interactions, Relationships, and Cultures," *Emotion Review*, 4(3), pp. 221–229. Available at: https://doi.org/10.1177/1754073912439765

Buckner, R.L. and DiNicola, L.M. (2019) "The brain's default network: updated anatomy, physiology and evolving insights," *Nature Reviews Neuroscience*, 20(10), pp. 593–608. Available at: https://doi.org/10.1038/s41583-019-0212-7

Casasanto, D. and Lupyan, G. (2015) "All concepts are ad hoc concepts," In Margolis E. & Laurence S. (Eds.), *Conceptual Mind: New Directions in the Study of Concepts*, pp. 543–566. MIT Press.

Chanes, L. *et al.* (2018) *"Facial expression predictions as drivers of social perception," Journal of Personality and Social Psychology*, 114, pp. 380–396. Available at: https://doi.org/10.1037/pspa0000108

Chanes, L. and Barrett, L.F. (2016) "Redefining the role of limbic areas in cortical processing," *Trends in Cognitive Sciences*, 20(2), pp. 96–106. Available at: https://doi.org/10.1016/j.tics.2015.11.005

Clark, A. (2013) "Whatever next? Predictive brains, situated agents, and the future of cognitive science," *Behavioral and Brain Sciences*, 36(3), pp. 181–204. Available at: https://doi.org/10.1017/S0140525X12000477

——— (2018) "A nice surprise? Predictive processing and the active pursuit of novelty," *Phenomenology and the Cognitive Sciences*, 17(3), pp. 521–534. Available at: https://doi.org/10.1007/s11097-017-9525-z

Craig, A.D. (2015) *How Do You Feel? An Interoceptive Moment with Your Neurobiological Self, How Do You Feel?* Princeton University Press.

Critchley, H.D. *et al.* (2004) "Neural systems supporting interoceptive awareness," *Nature Neuroscience*, 7(2), pp. 189–195. Available at: https://doi.org/10.1038/nn1176

Decety, J. (2011) "Dissecting the neural mechanisms mediating empathy," *Emotion Review*, 3(1), pp. 92–108. Available at: https://doi.org/10.1177/1754073910374662

Del Popolo Cristaldi, F. *et al.* (2021) "What's next? Neural correlates of emotional predictions: A high-density EEG investigation," *Brain and Cognition*, 150, p. 105708. Available at: https://doi.org/10.1016/j.bandc.2021.105708

——— (2022a) "Unbalanced functional connectivity at rest affects the ERP correlates of affective prediction in high intolerance of uncertainty individuals: A high density EEG investigation," *International Journal of Psychophysiology*, 178, pp. 22–33. Available at: https://doi.org/10.1016/j.ijpsycho.2022.06.006

Del Popolo Cristaldi, F., Gambarota, F. and Oosterwijk, S. (2022b) "Does your past define you? The role of previous visual experience in subjective reactions to new affective pictures and sounds," *Emotion* [Preprint]. Available at: https://doi.org/10.1037/emo0001168

Den Ouden, H., Kok, P. and De Lange, F. (2012) "How Prediction Errors Shape Perception, Attention, and Motivation," *Frontiers in Psychology*, 3. Available at: https://www.frontiersin.org/articles/10.3389/fpsyg.2012.00548 (Accessed: 17 February 2023).

Fan, Y. *et al.* (2011) "Is there a core neural network in empathy? An fMRI based quantitative meta-analysis," *Neuroscience and Biobehavioral Reviews*, 35(3), pp. 903–911. Available at: https://doi.org/10.1016/j.neubiorev.2010.10.009

Gallagher, S. and Allen, M. (2018) "Active inference, enactivism and the hermeneutics of social cognition," *Synthese*, 195(6), pp. 2627–2648. Available at: https://doi.org/10.1007/s11229-016-1269-8

Hoemann, K. and Barrett, L.F. (2019) "Concepts dissolve artificial boundaries in the study of emotion and cognition, uniting body, brain, and mind," *Cognition and Emotion*, 33(1), pp. 67–76. Available at: https://doi.org/10.1080/02699931.2018.1535428

Hutchinson, J.B. and Barrett, L.F. (2019) "The power of predictions: An emerging paradigm for psychological research," *Current Directions in Psychological Science*, 28(3), pp. 280–291. Available at: https://doi.org/10.1177/0963721419831992

Jabbi, M., Bastiaansen, J. and Keysers, C. (2008) "A common anterior insula representation of disgust observation, experience and imagination shows divergent functional connectivity pathways," *PLOS ONE*, 3(8), p. e2939. Available at: https://doi.org/10.1371/journal.pone.0002939

Jack, R.E. *et al.* (2012) "Facial expressions of emotion are not culturally universal," *Proceedings of the National Academy of Sciences of the United States of America*, 109(19), pp. 7241–7244. Available at: https://doi.org/10.1073/pnas.1200155109

Katsumi, Y. *et al.* (2021) "Functional connectivity gradients as a common neural architecture for predictive processing in the human brain". bioRxiv, p. 2021.09.01.456844. Available at: https://doi.org/10.1101/2021.09.01.456844

——— (2022) "Allostasis as a core feature of hierarchical gradients in the human brain," *Network Neuroscience*, 6(4), pp. 1010–1031. Available at: https://doi.org/10.1162/netn_a_00240

——— (2023) "Correspondence of functional connectivity gradients across human isocortex, cerebellum, and hippocampus," *Communications Biology*, 6(1), pp. 1–13. Available at: https://doi.org/10.1038/s42003-023-04796-0

Keysers, C. and Gazzola, V. (2014) "Dissociating the ability and propensity for empathy," *Trends in Cognitive Sciences*, 18(4), pp. 163–166. Available at: https://doi.org/10.1016/j.tics.2013.12.011

Kleckner, I.R. *et al.* (2017) "Evidence for a large-scale brain system supporting allostasis and interoception in humans," *Nature Human Behaviour*, 1(5), pp. 1–14. Available at: https://doi.org/10.1038/s41562-017-0069

Kong, R. *et al.* (2019) "Spatial topography of individual-specific cortical networks predicts human cognition, personality, and emotion," *Cerebral Cortex*, 29(6), pp. 2533–2551. Available at: https://doi.org/10.1093/cercor/bhy123

Lindquist, K.A. *et al.* (2012) "The brain basis of emotion: A meta-analytic review," *Behav Brain Sci*, 35(3), pp. 121–143. Available at: https://doi.org/10.1017/S0140525X11000446

MacCormack, J.K. and Lindquist, K.A. (2019) "Feeling hangry? When hunger is conceptualized as emotion," *Emotion*, 19, pp. 301–319. Available at: https://doi.org/10.1037/emo0000422

Niedenthal, P.M. (2007) "Embodying Emotion," *Science*, 316(5827), pp. 1002–1005. Available at: https://doi.org/10.1126/science.1136930

Northoff, G. *et al.* (2006) "Self-referential processing in our brain—A meta-analysis of imaging studies on the self," *NeuroImage*, 31(1), pp. 440–457. Available at: https://doi.org/10.1016/j.neuroimage.2005.12.002

Oosterwijk, S. *et al.* (2009) "Embodied emotion concepts: How generating words about pride and disappointment influences posture," *European Journal of Social Psychology*, 39(3), pp. 457–466. Available at: https://doi.org/10.1002/ejsp.584

——— (2012) "States of mind: Emotions, body feelings, and thoughts share distributed neural networks," *NeuroImage*, 62(3), pp. 2110–2128. Available at: https://doi.org/10.1016/J.NEUROIMAGE.2012.05.079

——— (2015) "Concepts in context: Processing mental state concepts with internal or external focus involves different neural systems," *Social Neuroscience*, 10(3), pp. 294–307. Available at: https://doi.org/10.1080/17470919.2014.998840

——— (2017) "Shared states: using MVPA to test neural overlap between self-focused emotion imagery and other-focused emotion understanding," *Social Cognitive and Affective Neuroscience*, 12(7), pp. 1025–1035. Available at: https://doi.org/10.1093/scan/nsx037

Pace-Schott, E.F. *et al.* (2019) "Physiological feelings," *Neuroscience and Biobehavioral Reviews*, 103, pp. 267–304. Available at: https://doi.org/10.1016/j.neubiorev.2019.05.002

Pezzulo, G., Zorzi, M. and Corbetta, M. (2021) "The secret life of predictive brains: what's spontaneous activity for?," *Trends in Cognitive Sciences*, 0(0). Available at: https://doi.org/10.1016/j.tics.2021.05.007

Radulescu, A., Shin, Y.S. and Niv, Y. (2021) "Human representation learning," *Annual Review of Neuroscience*, 44(1), pp. 253–273. Available at: https://doi.org/10.1146/annurev-neuro-092920-120559

Satpute, A.B. and Lindquist, K.A. (2019) "The default mode network's role in discrete emotion," *Trends in Cognitive Sciences*, 23(10), pp. 851–864. Available at: https://doi.org/10.1016/j.tics.2019.07.003

Seth, A.K. and Friston, K.J. (2016) "Active interoceptive inference and the emotional brain," *Philosophical Transactions of the Royal Society B: Biological Sciences*, 371(1708), p. 20160007. Available at: https://doi.org/10.1098/rstb.2016.0007

Shamay-Tsoory, S.G. *et al.* (2019) "Herding brains: A core neural mechanism for social alignment," *Trends in Cognitive Sciences*, 23(3), pp. 174–186. Available at: https://doi.org/10.1016/j.tics.2019.01.002

Siegel, E.H. *et al.* (2018) "Emotion fingerprints or emotion populations? A meta-analytic investigation of autonomic features of emotion categories," *Psychological Bulletin*, 144(4), pp. 343–393. Available at: https://doi.org/10.1037/bul0000128

Spisak, T. *et al.* (2020) "Pain-free resting-state functional brain connectivity predicts individual pain sensitivity," *Nature Communications*, 11(1), p. 187. Available at: https://doi.org/10.1038/s41467-019-13785-z

Spreng, R.N. and Grady, C.L. (2010) "Patterns of brain activity supporting autobiographical memory, prospection, and theory of mind, and their relationship to the default mode network," *Journal of Cognitive Neuroscience*, 22(6), pp. 1112–1123. Available at: https://doi.org/10.1162/jocn.2009.21282

Sterling, P. (2012) "Allostasis: A model of predictive regulation," *Physiology and Behavior*, 106(1), pp. 5–15. Available at: https://doi.org/10.1016/j.physbeh.2011.06.004

Sterling, P. and Laughlin, S. (2015) *Principles of neural design*. MIT Press.

Tamir, D.I. and Thornton, M.A. (2018) "Modeling the predictive social mind," *Trends in Cognitive Sciences*, 22(3), pp. 201–212. Available at: https://doi.org/10.1016/j.tics.2017.12.005

Touroutoglou, A. *et al.* (2015) "Intrinsic connectivity in the human brain does not reveal networks for "basic" emotions," *Social Cognitive and Affective Neuroscience*, 10(9), pp. 1257–1265. Available at: https://doi.org/10.1093/scan/nsv013

Van Overwalle, F. and Baetens, K. (2009) "Understanding others' actions and goals by mirror and mentalizing systems: A meta-analysis," *NeuroImage*, 48(3), pp. 564–584. Available at: https://doi.org/10.1016/j.neuroimage.2009.06.009

Wager, T.D. *et al.* (2008) "Prefrontal-subcortical pathways mediating successful emotion regulation," *Neuron*, 59(6), pp. 1037–1050. Available at: https://doi.org/10.1016/j.neuron.2008.09.006

Westlin, C. *et al.* (2023) "Improving the study of brain-behavior relationships by revisiting basic assumptions," *Trends in Cognitive Sciences*, 27(3), pp. 246–257. Available at: https://doi.org/10.1016/j.tics.2022.12.015

Wilson-Mendenhall, C.D. *et al.* (2011) "Grounding emotion in situated conceptualization," *Neuropsychologia*, 49(5), pp. 1105–1127. Available at: https://doi.org/10.1016/J.NEUROPSYCHOLOGIA.2010.12.032

Wilson-Mendenhall, C.D., Barrett, L.F. and Barsalou, L.W. (2013) "Neural evidence that human emotions share core affective properties," *Psychological Science*, 24(6), pp. 947–956. Available at: https://doi.org/10.1177/0956797612464242

Winkielman, P., Coulson, S. and Niedenthal, P. (2018) "Dynamic grounding of emotion concepts," *Philosophical Transactions of the Royal Society B: Biological Sciences*, 373(1752), p. 20170127. Available at: https://doi.org/10.1098/rstb.2017.0127

Yeshurun, Y., Nguyen, M. and Hasson, U. (2021) "The default mode network: where the idiosyncratic self meets the shared social world," *Nature Reviews Neuroscience*, 22(3), pp. 181–192. Available at: https://doi.org/10.1038/s41583-020-00420-w

Zaki, J. *et al.* (2016) "The anatomy of suffering: Understanding the relationship between nociceptive and empathic pain," *Trends in Cognitive Sciences*, 20(4), pp. 249–259. Available at: https://doi.org/10.1016/j.tics.2016.02.003

Zaki, J., Davis, J.I. and Ochsner, K.N. (2012) "Overlapping activity in anterior insula during interoception and emotional experience," *NeuroImage*, 62(1), pp. 493–499. Available at: https://doi.org/10.1016/j.neuroimage.2012.05.012

11

VISUAL EXPERIENCE

Michael Madary

In this chapter I will discuss a number of empirical approaches to conscious visual experience that fall under the general framework of embodied cognition. I will organize the chapter by treating the following topics in order: embedded and situated vision, extended vision, enactive vision, dynamical systems approaches to vision, and the neuroscience of vision with a focus on predictive processing. In the first five sections of the chapter, I will present each approach along with some common objections. In the final section of the chapter, I will indicate questions for future investigation. As one might expect, there will be some overlap between the different approaches.

Embedded and situated vision

An embedded and situated approach to visual experience would place emphasis on the details of the embodiment of the visual system. This emphasis marks a clear departure from the orthodox computational approach to vision, an approach heavily influenced by David Marr (1983), in which the implementation of the visual system is thought to be of little importance. Embedded and situated approaches to vision, in contrast, suggest that the bodily details are crucial for understanding visual experience.

The details of embodiment reveal that human vision typically involves continuous eye and body movements. Action and visual perception seem to be interrelated in some important way. Eye tracking devices show that humans typically saccade, which is to make a ballistic eye movement, three to four times per second (Findlay and Gilchrist 2003). Even when we deliberately try to keep from saccading, we make involuntary eye movements described as drifts, tremors, or microsaccades (Martinez-Conde et al. 2009). When precise devices are used to stabilize the retinal image by counteracting saccades, subjects experience temporary blindness (Riggs and Ratliff 1952). Eye tracking studies have shown that we naturally saccade towards areas in a visual scene which are rich in information relevant for our current goals.[1]

In addition to these discoveries about eye movements, there are at least three other lines of evidence suggesting an important role for action in visual perception. The first involves

DOI: 10.4324/9781003322511-15

selective rearing (Held and Hein 1963), the second involves distorting goggles (Kohler 1961, Taylor 1962), and the third involves sensory substitution (Bach-y-Rita 1972). Kevin O'Regan and Alva Noë (2001) have suggested that these lines of evidence indicate that human visual perception requires an understanding of "sensorimotor contingencies," which are the way appearances change due to self-generated movement.

In the remainder of this section, I will discuss two main objections to the claim that action is tightly connected with visual experience. The first main objection is that the claim itself is not clear. Is it the strong claim that token actions are necessary for vision to occur, or is it something weaker? And if it is something weaker, who would deny it? Ken Aizawa (2007), for instance, has attributed the stronger claim to Alva Noë (2004). Aizawa challenges Noë's view by presenting examples of individuals under complete paralysis during surgery who reported having visual experiences while paralyzed (2010: 23). These cases look to provide a counterexample to the stronger thesis about action and visual perception.

A second main objection to the connection between action and visual perception comes from what is known as the two-visual-systems hypothesis (Block 2005, Jacob and Jeannerod 2003). Human visual processing involves two physiologically distinct processing streams in cortex. The dorsal stream projects from primary visual cortex to posterior parietal cortex, and the ventral stream projects from primary visual cortex to inferotemporal cortex. According to the best-known version of the hypothesis (Milner and Goodale 1995), dorsal processing is devoted to "vision for action" and is not available for consciousness. Ventral processing, in contrast, is devoted to "vision for perception" and can enter consciousness. In humans, the evidence for the hypothesis comes from lesion studies as well as the existence of illusions that affect conscious perception but not visually guided grasping. If vision for action is both unconscious and distinct from vision for perception, then the purported tight connection between action and visual perception may not be so tight after all.

Without entering into the details, here are two quick points about this objection. First, it seems obvious that conscious visual experience *can* guide action. But it is not clear that the hypothesis can accommodate this fact so long as we keep a strict distinction between vision for action and vision for perception (Briscoe 2009, Noë 2010). Second, another way to describe the differences between the two streams is to say that the dorsal stream is faster and devoted to peripheral vision, while the ventral stream is slower and devoted to central vision (Madary 2017, Chapter 7). This way of distinguishing the two streams accommodates the empirical evidence and avoids placing a wedge between action and visual perception (Gangopadhyay et al. 2010).

Extended vision

Much of the research on *extended* cognition has focused on the possibility that unconscious mental states are partially constituted by entities outside the brain (Clark and Chalmers 1998, Menary 2010). Some philosophers, however, have defended a thesis about the constitutive base of visual experience extending outside the brain. They have defended something like the following thesis:

Externalism about the Vehicles of Perceptual States (EVPS): The vehicles of human conscious visual states can sometimes include the body and environment in addition to the brain.

Both Susan Hurley and Alva Noë are known for defending EVPS. In this section, due to space limitations, I focus on Hurley's argument for EVPS.[2]

This is one way of formulating Hurley's argument in support of EVPS. I will discuss each premise in turn.

1 The subpersonal mechanisms of conscious vision are temporally extended.
2 Temporal extension can lead to spatial extension.
3 In the case of the human visual system, temporal extension does lead to spatial extension. Conclusion: EVPS

The main inspiration behind (1) is Daniel Dennett's attack on the "Cartesian theater." The Cartesian theater is his name for the particular place in the brain in which experience happens, where "it all comes together" (1991: 107). By appealing to results from visual masking experiments, Dennett makes the case that there is no Cartesian theater. Hurley picks up on this idea and attacks what she calls "temporal atomism," which is the view that each instant of visual consciousness is "carried by subpersonal processes moment by moment, snapshot by snapshot" (Hurley, 1998: 31). The alternative to temporal atomism is (1), or in other words, the idea that the subpersonal processes that enable visual experience are always dynamic by nature; a frozen snapshot of neural activity does not determine any visual state (also see Noë 2004: 218).

I take premise (2) from a passage of Hurley's published posthumously:

> Temporal extension leads to spatial extension; Dennett (1991) famously made the intracranial version of this point in his arguments against a Cartesian theater, but the point extends promiscuously across the boundaries of skull and body.
>
> *(Hurley, 2010: 111)*

What I take Hurley to mean here is that some systems have the following structure: if causal influences are traced over time, then we find an expanding spatial area which is a part of that system. As a matter of empirical fact, according to Hurley, human vision is such a system. Hurley's support for (3) is that, if "we track the causal arrow through time" in the human visual system, we find feedback loops at multiple spatial and temporal scales (1998: 307). Some feedback loops are neural, and some include the active body (Hurley 1998, Chapter 10).[3] Further support for (3) can be found in dynamical systems approaches to vision, which I will cover below.

One main objection to EVPS is that its proponents fail to distinguish causation from constitution (Block 2005, Prinz 2006, Adams and Aizawa 2008).[4] All parties agree that the body and the environment play an important causal role in conscious visual perception. But the opponents of EVPS see no need to make the further claim that the body and environment partially constitute the substrate of visual experience. It is tempting for proponents of EVPS to reject the distinction between causation and constitution, but note that this move may not be available: EVPS itself seems to depend on there being such a distinction. Hurley indicated that she would rather frame EVPS in terms of explanation than constitution versus "mere" causation (2010: 113–14). Don Ross and James Ladyman (2010) have made a strong contribution to the debate by arguing that the causal/constitutive distinction has no place in the mature sciences.

Enactive vision

"Sense-making" is a central theme within the *enactive* approach to cognition.[5] Roughly, the idea is that meaning and significance emerge out of the interaction between an organism and its environment. This theme raises interesting issues for our understanding of visual experience. On one hand, the received view is that the content of visual experience is a representation of the objective world. On the other hand, according to the enactivist's commitment to sense-making, one's environment is always partially determined by the interests and goals of the perceiver. To put the disagreement bluntly: do we see the world, or do we see the emergent result of our particular interaction with the world? In this section I will outline some of the enactivist's reasons for rejecting the received view.

The received view in the philosophy and science of perception is that vision has the task of representing the world around us more or less as it really is (Lewis 1980: 239, Marr 1983). Evan Thompson has described the received view as the "objectivist" view of representation (2007: 52). One of the main motivations for the objectivist view is that it is reasonable to think that our visual representations must be accurate if they are to guide behavior in a successful way.

The enactivist, in contrast, rejects the supposition that an organism represents features of an objective world. Following Merleau-Ponty (1963), Hans Jonas (2001), and others, Thompson asserts that living organisms create meaning based on their own autonomous metabolic structure. A simple example of this process can be found in the behavior of bacterial cells. Some bacteria respond to sugar gradients in a solution by swimming against the gradient towards areas of greater sucrose concentration. Thompson elaborates:

> While sucrose is a real and present condition of the physicochemical environment, the status of sucrose as a nutrient is not. Being a nutrient ... is enacted or brought forth by the way the organism, given its autonomy and the norms its autonomy brings about, couples with the environment.
>
> *(2007: 74)*

If the interaction between organism and environment is one of "sense-making," as enactivism suggests, then there should be implications for human vision.

One way in which we might apply the enactivist concept of "sense-making" to vision would be to claim that the content of visual perception is always informed in some way by our own goals and interests. According to this claim, we do not simply see the objective world; we do not merely seek "to know what is where by looking" (Marr 1983/2002: 229). Instead, what we see depends in some way on the details of our own situation, similar to the way in which the nutritional status of sucrose depends on the metabolism of the bacterium. There are a number of lines of empirical evidence which can be cited in support of this claim. First, and perhaps most obviously, the evidence for task dependence on saccade patterns, sketched above, could be used. Another line of support would be evidence that sociocultural factors can influence visual experience (Bruner and Goodman 1947, Boduroglu et al. 2009). A third line of evidence available to the enactivist comes from neuroscience, which I discuss below.

One objection to this aspect of enactivism has been raised by Dennett, who claims that there is nothing new or revolutionary about enactivist sense-making:

> As I and others have argued, all meaning in organisms is constructed by self-regarding processes that gerrymander the 'given' categories of physics to suit their purposes.
>
> *(2011: 30)*

He goes on to suggest that this idea can be found in Sellars, Quine, and "most AI systems" (ibid.). Thompson has replied that sense-making, as he intends it, can only be carried out by a system that has a particular kind of autonomy, a kind not found in most AI systems (2011: 189). Is enactivist sense-making a new and radical idea, or is it already widely accepted? I leave this question open.

The dynamical systems approach to vision

Modeling cognitive processes as *dynamical* systems has met with success in a number of areas of cognitive science (Port and van Gelder 1995, Thelen and Smith 1994, Spivey 2007). One main way in which dynamical systems are relevant for vision will be familiar from our discussion above on extended cognition; dynamical models of the physical substrate of visual experience might provide a motivation for EVPS, for the claim that the physical substrate of vision expands beyond the brain, and perhaps even the body.

Recall that EVPS is the thesis that the vehicles of perceptual states can sometimes extend beyond the brain, into the body and environment. One of Hurley's main motivations behind EVPS was that tracing the causal arrow over time leads to extended spatial boundaries of the system (premise (3) from the argument above). This idea can also be found in dynamical systems models. One common feature of dynamical systems is that the parts of the system do not always correspond to macroscopic physical boundaries. If those features can be found in the causal interactions between brain, body, and environment in visual perception, then we can construct dynamicist models which will include body and environment as a part of the system.

What remains to be seen is whether our best models of vision will be these kinds of dynamicist models. The main alternative would be internalist mechanistic models of the visual brain. Proponents of mechanistic explanation have voiced some of the most important objections to dynamical systems models of the mind. Carl Craver (2007), for instance, has argued that neuroscientific explanations should be mechanistic, that differential equations alone leave out something essential for the explanation. Apart from general worries about explanation with dynamical systems, one might also object to the practice of using dynamical systems theory in order to motivate claims about the spatial boundaries of physical systems. Recent work has gestured towards possible ways to reconcile the mechanistic explanatory framework with some of the features of dynamical systems modelling (Bechtel 2009). It remains unclear where this conciliatory strategy leads on the question of the boundaries of the physical basis of visual consciousness.

The embodied neuroscience of vision

Embodied approaches to visual experience all emphasize the fact that the body is active – that we typically see by actively exploring our environment. In neuroscience, the sort of work that is friendly to embodied approaches takes seriously the fact that the brain itself is active. Instead of thinking about neural processing as the passive reception of outside stimuli, we can emphasize that the brain is active with its own ongoing dynamics.[6] By far the most impactful version of this way to think about the brain in recent years has been the predictive processing approach. Before discussing predictive processing, let us first consider the active brain as a motivation for rejecting the objectivist view mentioned.

The objectivist maintains that the task of vision is to represent the objective world, without variation due to context or embellishment of other kinds. The neuroscientific tradition which most strongly supports this position dates back to the Nobel Prize-winning work of David Hubel and Torsten Wiesel (1959). They used single-cell recordings to demonstrate that particular neurons in the cat brain fired strongly in response to particular visual stimuli. This method has since been widely used in support of the idea that visual neurons function as feature detectors. If visual neurons are strictly in the business of representing objective features in the world, then objectivism looks to be correct.

But if we take into account the ongoing activity of the brain, we can note that neural processing is strongly context sensitive. On this view, the response of visual neurons depends only partly on the nature of the visual stimulus. The response of visual neurons also depends on other factors such as the ongoing endogenous dynamics within cortex (Arieli et al. 1996, perhaps also including what is known as the "default mode network," Raichle et al. 2001), the task that the organism is trying to accomplish (Cohen and Newsome 2008), and bodily states of the organism (Horn and Hill 1969, Abeles and Prut 1996 as cited in Noë and Thompson 2004). Amos Arieli and colleagues illustrate the main idea in a study on this theme as follows: "Thus, the effect of a stimulus [on cortex] might be likened to the additional ripples caused by tossing a stone into a wavy sea" (1996: 1869).

Before moving on to the models of predictive processing, I will make two quick comments about how context sensitivity might connect with some of the topics covered above. First, the ongoing dynamics of cortex could be used as support for premise (1) in my reconstruction of Hurley's argument for EVPS. Second, in the debate between objectivism and enactivism, the objectivist can appeal to the evidence which shows visual neurons to be feature detectors, and the enactivist can appeal to the evidence for context sensitivity in visual neuronal response.[7]

The predictive processing approach to cognitive neuroscience has exploded in popularity over the past decade with a vast and growing body of literature.[8] The basic idea is that the brain actively predicts the incoming sensory signal in a probabilistic manner and seeks to minimize predictive error – either through perceptual inference or action. An early overview of the neuroscientific evidence that motivates this theme can be found in Kestutis Kveraga et al. (2007), who cover both neurophysiological evidence and mathematical models. The important neurophysiological features of cortex include two well-established facts. First, there are distinct visual pathways from the retina that process information at different speeds. This fact underlies the hypothesis that the faster processing enables anticipatory feedback to the slower pathway (Bullier 2001). Second, there is massive feedback connectivity in the mammalian visual areas (Rockland and Van Hoesen 1994). The traditional understanding of the feedback connections is that they are "merely" modulatory, but the newly emerging understanding of them is that they are predictive (Rao and Ballard 1999, Friston and Kiebel 2009).

In order to see how predictive processing fits with embodied approaches to vision more generally, recall the concept of sensorimotor contingencies from the beginning of this chapter. The sensory input to our eyes is contingent upon our ongoing motor movements. As we develop, we learn these sensorimotor contingencies; we learn how appearances ought to change as we move. Predictive processing can be incorporated at this point with the suggestion that the brain actively predicts the sensory (visual) consequences of self-generated movement. For additional development of the connection between the sensorimotor and predictive processing approaches to vision, see Seth (2014) and Madary (2017).

This way of thinking about visual processing has led researchers to questions having to do with conscious visual experience. Most generally, we might ask: if the visual processing is predictive and probabilistic at the neural level, is this structure reflected at the level of conscious visual experience? Is visual consciousness predictive and probabilistic? For the question of whether there is predictive (or anticipatory) content in visual consciousness, see Siegel (2010a) and Madary (2017). For the question of whether visual consciousness has a probabilistic or indeterminate character, see Madary (2012b), Block (2018), Clark (2018), Siegel (2022), Nave (2022), and Britten-Neish (2022).

Future directions for embodied approaches to visual experience

This final section of the chapter raises three areas of future research for embodied approaches to visual experience. These areas involve the nature of visual consciousness, the role of the brain for embodied approaches, and the question of visual representation.

The first area of future research has to do with the nature of visual consciousness itself, as indicated at the end of the previous section. The orthodox view in the philosophy of perception is that, if visual experience has any content at all, then it is propositional content of some kind (Siegel 2010b). Often this content is described using natural language, as in Searle (1983: 41). It is not obvious that this way of describing visual content is compatible with some of the themes explored in this chapter. In particular, it is not clear that everyday linguistic reports can capture the content of visual experience if that content is anticipatory, probabilistic, closely bound up with action, dynamic, and enacted (as in sense-making). Future work will determine whether and to what extent there is a real tension here.

The second area for future research has to do with the role of the brain. Perhaps owing to the influence of J. J. Gibson, embodied approaches to vision have sometimes urged a limited role for neuroscience as a way of explaining vision (O'Regan and Noë 2001, Noë 2004, O'Regan 2011). On the other hand, as explained above, some current trends in neuroscience seem to converge on themes that are important to embodied vision researchers. Of particular interest here are Bayesian predictive coding models of neural processing (Friston and Kiebel 2009, Hohwy 2013, Clark 2013; 2019). Do these kinds of models support the theories of embodied vision researchers, or will the charge remain that the brain is the wrong place to look for understanding conscious vision? Will the current fashion for predictive processing stand the test of time?

The third area for future research has to do with visual representation. Traditionally, a representation refers to an information state with correctness conditions (Fodor 1987, Dretske 1995). Will our best models of vision include representations? There are a number of related questions here. For instance, one might distinguish between personal and subpersonal representations. Does it make sense to posit representations at one level and not the other? There has been a good deal of debate over whether dynamical systems models of the mind involve representations (van Gelder 1995, Bechtel 1998). As long as we use dynamical systems to model vision, then this debate may be relevant. Similarly, the disagreement between objectivist and enactivist stances is relevant here. If the enactivist is correct that our visual experience is partly determined by our own interests and so forth, then can such an experience be described in terms of personal-level representational content? In other words, can there be correctness conditions for content which is the result of enactivist sense-making? Is there hope for, as Clark (2015) has predicted, lasting peace in "the representation wars?"

Notes

1 The classic early studies were carried out by Alfred Yarbus (1967). Due to the nature of early eye trackers, Yarbus' experiments were confined to the laboratory. In the 1990s, Michael Land and colleagues used mobile lightweight trackers to confirm the influence of task on eye movements in natural environments (see Land et al. 1999, for example). Along the same lines, Dana Ballard and colleagues have shown that subjects use eye movements for "pointing" purposes as an efficient strategy for completing cognitive tasks (Ballard et al. 1997). Excellent overviews can be found in Findlay and Gilchrist (2003, Chapter 7) and Hayhoe and Ballard (2005).
2 Some of this material is covered in Madary (2012a) in detail.
3 For a critique of the view that the basis of visual consciousness can extend outside of the brain, see Clark (2009) and a response by Ward (2012). For a treatment of the larger question of boundaries of the mind from the view of predictive processing, see Hohwy (2016).
4 There are at least two other objections to be found in the literature. The first is that brain stimulation alone is sufficient for visual experiences (Penfield and Jasper 1954, Prinz 2006). The second objection is that dreaming involves visual experiences without the active body. For Noë's defense of EVPS against these objections, see his (2004: 209–215).
5 The term "enactivism" has been used in slightly different ways in the literature. Here I understand the term to reflect an approach to the mind associated with the works of Humberto Maturana, Francisco Varela, and Evan Thompson. I regard Thompson's (2007) to be the most comprehensive expression of this approach.
6 An early pioneer of this way to think about the brain is Walter Freeman (1999).
7 For a non-visual neurophysiological case against objectivism, see Kathleen Akins (1996), who focused on the human thermoreceptive system.
8 Some of the important texts include: Rao and Ballard (1999), Friston and Stephan (2007), Friston (2013), Clark (2013) and (2015), Hohwy (2013).

References

Abeles, M. and Prut, Y. "Spatio-temporal firing patterns in the frontal cortex of behaving monkeys" *Journal of Physiology* 90 (1996) 249–250.

Adams, F. and Aizawa, K. *The Bounds of Cognition*. Blackwell, 2008.

Aizawa, K. "Understanding the embodiment of perception" *The Journal of Philosophy* 104 (2007) 5–25.

Akins, K. "Of sensory systems and the 'aboutness' of mental states" *The Journal of Philosophy* 93 (1996) 337–372.

Arieli, A., Sterkin, A., Grinvald, A., Aertsen, A. "Dynamics of ongoing activity: Explanation of the large variability in evoked cortical responses" *Science* 273 (1996) 1868–1871.

Bach-y-Rita, P. *Brain Mechanisms in Sensory Substitution*. Academic Press, 1972.

Ballard, D., Hayhoe, M., Pook, P., and Rao, R. "Deictic codes for the embodiment of cognition" *Behavioral and Brain Sciences* 20 (1997) 723–767.

Bechtel, W. "Representations and cognitive explanations: Assessing the dynamicist challenge in cognitive science" *Cognitive Science* 22 (1998) 295–318.

——— "Looking down, around, and up: Mechanistic explanation in psychology" *Philosophical Psychology*, 22(5), (2009) 543–564. https://doi.org/10.1080/09515080903238948

Block, N. "Review of Alva Noë *Action in Perception*" *Journal of Philosophy* 5 (2005) 259–272.

——— "If perception is probabilistic, why does it not seem probabilistic?" *Philosophical Transactions of the Royal Society B: Biological Sciences*, 373 (1755), (2018) 1–10. https://doi.org/10.1098/rstb.2017.0341

Boduroglu, A., Shah, P., and Nisbett, R. "Cultural differences in allocation of attention in visual information processing" *Journal of Cross Cultural Psychology* 40 (2009) 349–360.

Briscoe, R. "Egocentric spatial representation in action and perception" *Philosophy and Phenomenological Research*, 2 (2009) 423–460.

Britten-Neish, G. "Are basic actors brainbound agents? Narrowing down solutions to the problem of probabilistic content for predictive perceivers" *Phenomenology and the Cognitive Sciences*, 21 (2), (2022) 435–459. https://doi.org/10.1007/s11097-021-09736-z

Bruner, J. and Goodman, C. "Value and Need as Organizing Factors in Perception" *Journal of Abnormal and Social Psychology*, 42 (1947) 33–44.

Bullier, J. "Feedback connections and conscious vision" *Trends in Cognitive Sciences* 5 (2001) 369–370.

Clark, A. and Chalmers, D. "The extended mind" *Analysis* 58 (1998) 10–23.

Clark, A. "Spreading the joy? Why the Machinery of Consciousness is (Probably) Still in the Head" *Mind*, 118 (472), (2009) 963–993. https://doi.org/10.1093/mind/fzp110

——— "Whatever Next? Predictive Brains, Situated Agents, and the Future of Cognitive Science" *Behavioral and Brain Sciences* 36 (2013) 181–204.

——— "Predicting Peace: The End of the Representation Wars-A Reply to Michael Madary" *Open MIND.* (2015) https://doi.org/10.15502/9783958570979

——— *Surfing Uncertainty: Prediction, Action, and the Embodied Mind.* Oxford University Press, 2019.

——— "Beyond the 'Bayesian blur': predictive processing and the nature of subjective experience" *Journal of Consciousness Studies* 25 (3–4), (2018) 71–87.

Cohen, M. and Newsome, W. "Context-Dependent Changes in Functional Circuitry in Visual Area MT" *Neuron* 60 (2008) 162–173.

Craver, C. *Explaining the Brain* Oxford University Press, 2007.

Dennett, D. *Consciousness Explained.* Little, Brown, 1991.

——— "Shall We Tango? No, but Thanks for Asking" *Journal of Consciousness Studies* 18 (2011) 23–34.

Dretske, F. *Naturalizing the Mind.* MIT Press, 1995.

Findlay, J. M. and Gilchrist, I. *Active Vision* Oxford, 2003.

Fodor, J. *Psychosemantics.* MIT Press, 1987.

Freeman, W. *How Brains Make Up Their Minds.* Weidenfeld & Nicolson, 1999.

Friston, K. "Life as we know it" *Journal of The Royal Society Interface*, 10 (86), (2013). https://doi.org/10.1098/rsif.2013.0475

Friston, K. and Kiebel, S. J. "Predictive coding under the free-energy principle" *Philosophical Transactions of the Royal Society B*, 364 (2009) 1211–1211.

Friston, K. J., and Stephan, K. E. Free-energy and the brain. *Synthese*, 159 (3) (2007) 417–458. https://doi.org/10.1007/s11229-007-9237-y

Gangopadhyay, N., Madary, M. and Spicer, F. (eds) *Perception, Action, Consciousness: Sensorimotor Dynamics and Two Visual Systems.* Oxford University Press, 2010.

Hayhoe, M. and Ballard, D. "Eye Movements in Natural Behavior" *Trends in Cognitive Science* 9 (2005) 188–194.

Held, R. and Hein, A. "Movement produced stimulation in the development of visually guided behavior" *Journal of Comparative and Physiological Psychology* 56 (1963) 873–876.

Hohwy, J. *The Predictive Mind.* Oxford University Press, 2013.

——— "The Self-Evidencing Brain" *Noûs*, 50 (2), (2016) 259–285. https://doi.org/10.1111/nous.12062

Horn, G. and Hill, R. "Modifications of the receptive field of cells in the visual cortex occuring spontaneously and associated with bodily tilt" *Nature* 221 (1969) 185–187.

Hubel, D. and Wiesel, T. "Receptive Fields of Singles Neurones in the Cat's Striate Cortex" *Journal of Physiology* 148 (1959) 574–591.

Hurley, S. *Consciousness in Action.* Harvard University Press, 1998.

Hurley S. "The Varieties of Externalism" in *The Extended Mind*, Menary, ed. MIT Press, 2010.

Jacob, P. and Jeannerod, M. *Ways of Seeing: The Scope and Limits of Visual Cognition* Oxford University Press, 2003.

Jonas, H. *The Phenomenon of Life: Toward a Philosophical Biology*. Northwestern University Press, 2001.

Kohler, I. "Experiments with Goggles" *Scientific American* 206 (1961) 62–86.

Kveraga, K., Ghuman, A., and Bar, M. "Top-down predictions in the cognitive brain" *Brain and Cognition* 65 (2007) 145–168.

Land, M., Mennie, N., and Rusted, J. "The roles of vision and eye movements in the control of activities of everyday living" *Perception* 28 (1999) 1311–1328.

Lewis, D. "Veridical Hallucination and Prosthetic Vision" *Australasian Journal of Philosophy* 58 (1980) 239–249.

Madary, M. "Showtime at the Cartesian Theater? Vehicle externalism and dynamical explanations" in *Consciousness in Interaction*, F. Paglieri, ed. John Benjamins Publishing, 2012a.

——— "How would the world look if it looked as if it were encoded as an intertwined set of probability density distributions?" *Frontiers in Psychology*, (2012b) 3. https://doi.org/10.3389/fpsyg.2012.00419

——— *Visual Phenomenology*. MIT Press, 2017.

Marr, D. *Vision*. W. H. Freeman and Sons, 1983.

Martinez-Conde, S., Macknik, S., Troncoso, X., and Hubel D. "Microsaccades: a neurophysiological analysis" *Trends in Neuroscience* 9 (2009) 463–475.

Menary, R. (ed.) *The Extended Mind*. MIT Press, 2010.

Merleau-Ponty, M. *The Structure of Behavior*, trans. A. Fisher. Dusquesne University Press, 1963.

Milner, A. D., and Goodale, M. A. *The Visual Brain in Action*. Oxford, 1995.

Nave, K. "Visual experience in the predictive brain is univocal, but indeterminate" *Phenomenology and the Cognitive Sciences*, 21 (2), (2022) 395–419. https://doi.org/10.1007/s11097-021-09747-w

Noë, A. *Action in Perception*. MIT Press, 2004.

——— "Vision without representation" in N. Gangopadhyay et al., Oxford University Press, 2010, 245–256.

Noë, A. and Thompson, E. "What is a Neural Correlate of Consciousness?" *The Journal of Consciousness Studies*, 11 (2004) 3–28.

O'Regan, K. and Noë, A. "A sensorimotor account of vision and visual consciousness" *Behavioral and Brain Sciences* 24 (2001) 939–1031.

O'Regan, K. *Why Red Doesn't Sound Like a Bell*. Oxford University Press, 2011.

Penfield, W. and Jasper, H. *Epilepsy and the Functional Anatomy of the Human Brain*. Little, Brown, 1954.

Port, R. and van Gelder, T. (eds) *Mind as Motion*. MIT Press, 1995.

Prinz, J. "Putting the Breaks on Enactive Perception" *Psyche* 12 (2006).

Raichle, M. et al. "A default mode of brain function" *PNAS* 98 (2001) 676–682.

Rao, R. P. N. and Ballard, D. "Predictive coding in the visual cortex: a functional interpretation of some extra-classical receptive-field effects" *Nature Neuroscience* 2 (1999) 79–87.

Riggs, L. A. and Ratliff, F. "The Effects of Counteracting the Normal Movements of the Eye" *Journal of the Optical Society of America* 42 (1952) 872–873.

Rockland, K. and Van Hoesen, G. "Direct Temporal-Occipital Feedback Connections to Striate Cortex?(V1) in the Macaque Monkey" *Cerebral Cortex* 4 (1994) 300–313.

Ross, D. and Ladyman, J. "The Alleged Coupling-Constitution Fallacy and the Mature Sciences" in *The Extended Mind*, R. Menary, ed. MIT Press. 2010.

Searle, J. *Intentionality*. Cambridge University Press, 1983.

Seth, A. K. "A predictive processing theory of sensorimotor contingencies: Explaining the puzzle of perceptual presence and its absence in synesthesia" *Cognitive Neuroscience*, 5 (2), (2014) 97–118. https://doi.org/10.1080/17588928.2013.877880

Siegel, S. *The Contents of Visual Experience*. Oxford University Press, 2010a.

——— "The contents of perception" *Stanford Encyclopedia of Philosophy* (2010b) http://plato.stanford.edu/entries/perception-contents/

——— "How can perceptual experiences explain uncertainty?" *Mind & Language*, 37 (2), (2022) 134–158. https://doi.org/10.1111/mila.12348

Spivey, M. *The Continuity of Mind*. Oxford University Press, 2007.

Taylor, J. *The Behavioral Basis of Perception*. Yale University Press, 1962.

Thelen, E. and Smith, L. *A Dynamic Systems Approach to the Development of Cognition and Action*. MIT Press, 1994.

Thompson, E. *Mind in Life* Harvard University Press, 2007.

——— "Reply to commentaries" *Journal of Consciousness Studies*, 18 (2011) 176–223.

van Gelder, T. "What might cognition be if not computation?" *Journal of Philosophy*, 92 (1995) 345–381.

Ward, D. "Enjoying the spread: Conscious externalism reconsidered" *Mind*, 121 (483), (2012) 731–751. https://doi.org/10.1093/mind/fzs095

Yarbus, A. *Eye Movements and Vision*. Plenum Press, 1967.

PART 4

Perception

12

EXTENDED REALITY (XR) IN EMBODIED MUSICAL ART AND SCIENCE

Pieter-Jan Maes, Bavo van Kerrebroeck, Mattia Rosso, Ioulia Marouda, and Marc Leman

Introduction

Musical art and science have always flourished in the evolving relationship between humans and technologies, and have been situated within broader historical and sociocultural contexts. Music technologies continuously reshape the human ability to explore, express, communicate and augment human sensitivities. They allow us to regulate emotions and feelings, tighten social bonds, develop cognitive and sensorimotor capacities, and create out-of-the-ordinary experiences and narratives that spring from creative imagination. Throughout history and across cultures, the character and development of musical instruments and spaces have strongly influenced the sound of, and interaction with, music. The advent of electronic and digital technologies in the 20th century revolutionized musical instruments and spaces in unprecedented ways, radically expanding the possibilities for music creation and experience. The sheer excitement of the practically endless possibilities – from the early experiments by Leon Theremin in the 1930s (Smirnov 2013), to the analog synthesizers of Robert Moog in the 1960s (Moog 1965), to the networked performances in COVID-19 times (Onderdijk, Acar and Van Dyck 2021) – demonstrated that the human body is an important mediator between technology and human musical expression. This realization fueled musicology to further deepen the study of the body and the 'lived musical experience' as core aspects of music interaction and sense-making (Shove and Repp 1995; Mead 1999; Leman 2007). Apart from stimulating reflection on the role of the body in action-perception processes and musical sense-making from a fundamental theoretical perspective, electronic and digital technologies innovated possibilities for empirical musicology at the methodological level. The access to motion-capture technologies, (neuro)physiological sensors and imaging techniques, as well as computational hard- and software for analysis purposes, offered a wide pallet of quantitative means to uncover the principles underlying embodied music interaction.

Extended reality (XR) is an umbrella term for a continuum of immersive technologies, including virtual (VR), augmented (AR) and mixed reality (MR), that merge our naturalistic world with computer-generated worlds to some degree. Although early development and experimentation with XR dates back to the 1960s, it is only recently that we have witnessed

DOI: 10.4324/9781003322511-17

a rapid acceleration of its development and adoption into many societal domains. In this chapter, we consider the role of XR technologies in the field of musical art and science, specifically in relation to the concept of musical embodiment. We will argue that XR technologies can intervene in the coupled action-perception processes that regulate human interaction with music. By extending the human sensorimotor capacities into (partly) computer-generated environments, we argue that XR is a technological medium with the potential to realize genuine *virtual embodiment* (Clark 2003; Kilteni, Groten and Slater 2012; Pint 2012; Beaufils and Berland 2022). In addition to exploring the exciting novel possibilities for music experience and performance practice, we will focus on the potential of XR for empirical research in the domain of embodied music interaction, both on the theoretical and methodological levels.

To understand the potential of XR at these levels, it is worthwhile to first address the nature of XR at the technological level, covering immersive multisensory displays and bodily interfaces. We then argue, from a theoretical perspective, that the functioning of XR technologies supports the notions of virtual embodiment and presence. These concepts form the essential psychological aspects of the user experience. Further, we formulate the idea that XR facilitates designing new musical *spaces* for innovation in musical art and science. In our research, we specifically define three types of XR musical spaces: spaces for empirical research in the domain of embodied music interaction ('*research labs* of the future'), spaces for artistic-creative interaction, ('*concert halls* of the future'), and spaces for human interaction with cultural heritage ('*museums* of the future'). To conclude the chapter, we describe several cases that illustrate the potential of these new XR musical spaces for musical art and science.

Extended reality – a technological perspective

As the human experience of XR from an embodied point of view is closely intertwined with its technological realization, it is worthwhile to zoom in first on its technological underpinning. We argue that the XR experience depends on the complementary working of two main categories of technologies, namely immersive multisensory displays and bodily interfaces.

Immersive multisensory displays

XR offers a diverse set of immersive displays that add computer-generated and 3D multisensory stimuli to a user's environment, either in combination with the physical environment (cf. augmented or mixed reality, AR/MR), or as full virtual reality (VR) (Scarfe and Glennerster 2019). The combination of visual, auditory, tactile and other sensory displays may render virtual simulations of existing (physical) stimuli and environments, or create new imaginary worlds and sensations. As argued earlier by Grau (2003), rather than viewing immersive XR as a totally new *phenomenon*, it may be better conceived as a novel technological *medium* that is part of a long history of immersion and illusion in the arts. As a technological medium, XR was already being explored in the 1960s by pioneers like Morton Heilig and Ivan Sutherland (Sutherland 1968; Damer and Hinrichs 2014; Lanier 2017). Yet it was only recently, under the impetus of innovations in online video gaming and the metaverse concept (Ball 2022; Turchet 2023), that XR technology rapidly gained traction, and is increasingly accessible and relevant for various societal domains. What sets XR immersive displays apart from traditional displays, like a 2D screen or stereo audio, for instance, is the explicit user-centered approach of the stimuli presentation. Whether it concerns visual objects, sound sources, tactile or olfactory sensations, XR displays are consistently rendered from, and adapted to, the perspective of users. This 'first-person perspective' means that, in principle, users can wander freely into computer-generated environments and experience these with all their senses from the inside out. A core requirement of such immersive experience is the ability to track users' body movement, rotation and displacement. Therefore, immersive displays need to be complemented with a second category of technologies, which we capture under the common denominator 'bodily interfaces.'

Bodily interfaces

Digital technologies require interfaces to translate active human input and information to (abstract) digital code and processing. The history of interfaces within the domain of human–computer interaction can be characterized as a history of *shifting interfaces* (Hove et al. 2018). In the early days of *digital history*, active user input was mediated primarily through keyboard and mouse actions. Since then, interfaces have shifted from being manifest and explicit to being more transparent, less visible, multimodal and embodied. In that sense, interfaces today evolve rapidly towards unobtrusive wearables that capture information and naturalistic (inter)action patterns "completely weaved into the fabric of the everyday lives of users" (Hove et al. 2018). In the domain of XR, the primary function of bodily interfaces is to make multisensory displays adaptable to the users' perspective, by reliably mapping bodily actions and neurophysiological activation to corresponding changes in the virtual environment. Interestingly, bodily interfaces may also be used to measure and acquire knowledge about human behavior and responses within XR environments. This makes XR relevant as a methodological tool within the sciences, as will be detailed below.

Extended reality – a human embodied perspective

We take the concept of *virtual embodiment* as an extension of the concept of embodiment as it is understood in embodied music cognition theory and the sensorimotor theory (O'Regan and Noë 2001; Leman 2007). These accounts hold that music perception, sense-making, and emotion are rooted in an active engagement with musical environments, including sounds, musical instruments, other musicians and audiences. Through repeated interactions with(in) musical environments, patterns and lawful relationships of sensorimotor dependences become established, providing a basis for musical experience and performance. This direct action-environment coupling at the level of action-perception processes is specifically relevant in view of the XR technologies under consideration here. These technologies allow for a direct and principled (re)mapping of user movements to changes in the XR musical environments, and these mappings are perceived from a first-person perspective. In that regard, XR technologies may appear to intervene seemingly *transparently* into the action-perception processes that regulate our interactions with the world and extend these processes into computer-generated virtual worlds. This idea of extending the direct coupling of action and perception into computer-generated, virtual worlds is foundational to our notion of virtual embodiment (Figure 12.1).

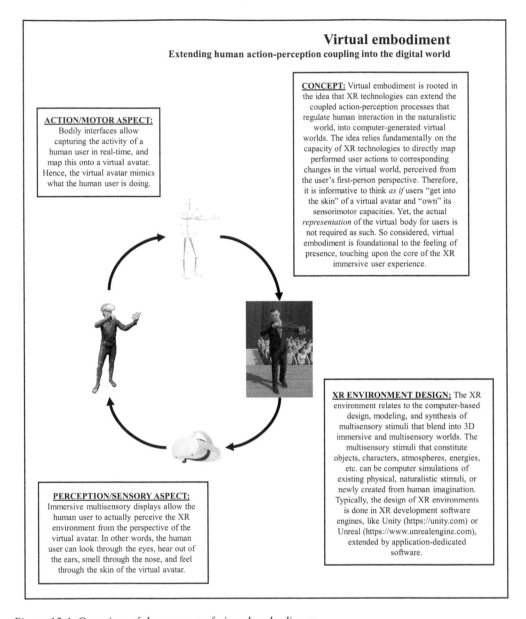

Figure 12.1 Overview of the concept of virtual embodiment.

In turn, virtual embodiment subserves a core psychological dimension for the user experience in XR, namely the feeling of *presence* (Lombard and Ditton 1997; Slater 2009; Cummings and Bailenson 2016). In Lombard and Ditton's (1997) seminal article, presence was formally defined as "the perceptual illusion of nonmediation." This concept of presence encompasses multiple categories related to the physical environment, users' own bodies or their social environment. The first category – physical presence, or telepresence – pertains to the illusory feeling for users of actually being present in an environment other than the one they are physically in (Minsky 1980; Slater and Sanchez-Vives 2016). The other categories – self-presence, co-presence and social presence – are rooted in the capacity of XR to map the physical body movements of users onto moving bodies of virtual avatars. Self-presence relates to the illusory feeling for a user of owning, controlling and being inside a body other than one's physical body (Braun et al. 2018; Matamala-Gomez et al. 2020). In addition, within a social context, one may experience co-presence or social presence in relation to the sense of being together (co-presence) or bodily interacting (social presence) with other embodied avatars or agents (Short, Williams and Christie 1976; Parsons, Gaggioli and Riva 2017).

In our view, virtual embodiment is connected essentially to the idea that XR technologies provide a direct and apparently *nonmediated* relationship between action and perception for users within computer-generated environments. Yet, we can distinguish different *degrees* of virtual embodiment, linked to available bodily interfaces ('action' component) and immersive displays ('perception' component). The minimal requirement for establishing virtual embodiment is the availability of trackers for the head orientation and displacement typically available for users in head-mounted displays (HMDs). This allows users to automatically adapt and match the multisensory display perspective to their corresponding actions to direct gaze and attention. More bodily interfaces can be added – such as for hand, face and full-body tracking – to provide users with additional sensorimotor control and interaction in their XR environment. The total set of available bodily interfaces defines what Slater (2009: 3550) calls the *valid (sensorimotor and effectual) action*s that users can perform to effect changes in their XR environment. A similar range of possibilities could equally be identified for immersive displays, particularly related to the modality they add to the XR experience. Apart from the more traditional visual and auditory displays, the XR experience may be significantly strengthened by including modalities such as tactile, force feedback and even olfactory sensing. Together, available bodily interfaces and multisensory displays define the level of (technological) immersion, which correspondingly relates to the degree of (psychological) presence experienced by users.

Extended reality – new spaces for musical art and science

Music has always been shaped by the space and environment in which it is performed and experienced. As David Byrne insightfully argues in his book *How music works* (2012), musical spaces and surroundings fundamentally set the possibilities and constraints for composers and artists to canalize their musical goals, skills and creativity. Think about how the musical properties of medieval plainchant neatly fit the acoustics of the churches in which it was performed, or how the punk music of David Byrne fits the low reverberation CBGB club in New York City. And think about what would happen if you exchanged the venues of both genres of music...

In our work, we are interested in exploring how XR technologies create new spaces for human embodied interaction with and via music. To orient our art and science work, we define three main categories of musical XR spaces, linked to the archetypical institutions we know in musical art, science and culture: the research lab, the concert hall and the museum (Figure 12.2).

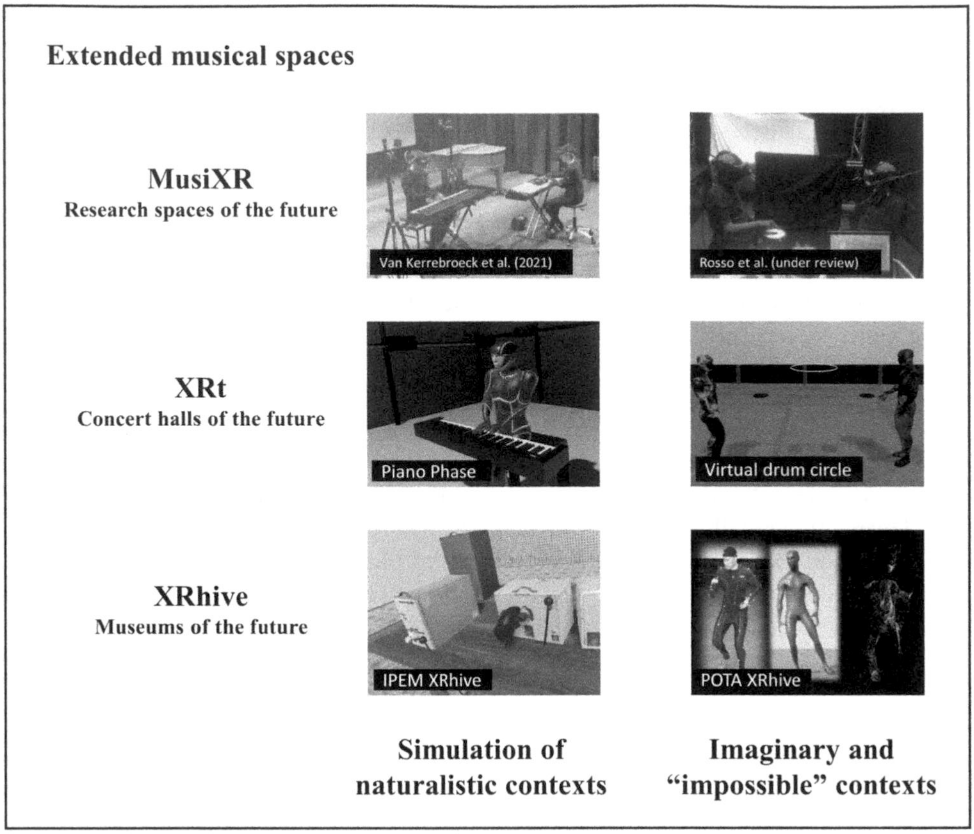

Extended musical spaces

MusiXR
Research spaces of the future

Van Kerrebroeck et al. (2021)

Rosso et al. (under review)

XRt
Concert halls of the future

Piano Phase

Virtual drum circle

XRhive
Museums of the future

IPEM XRhive

POTA XRhive

**Simulation of
naturalistic contexts**

**Imaginary and
"impossible" contexts**

Figure 12.2 Overview of the types of new musical spaces XR has to offer. The pictures illustrate different cases discussed below.

MusiXR: Research spaces of the future – bridging ecological validity and experimental control

Empirical research on embodied music interaction often confronts a thorny divide between *ecological validity* on the one hand and *experimental control* on the other. Ideally, embodied music interactions are studied "in the wild," that is, in *real* musical contexts. Yet, research is often conducted in the "safer" environment of a research laboratory, where stimuli are more controlled and measurement technologies are available for assessing human behavior and responses. The positive aspects of both situations are evident, yet their limitations are substantial, often hampering robust and reliable research outcomes. Since the early days of XR, experimental research in the human sciences picked up on its potential to bridge ecological validity and experimental control (Van Kerrebroeck, Caruso and Maes 2021). By bringing in (real-world) musical contexts through immersive XR displays, ecological validity can be *simulated* into controlled laboratory settings. The concepts of virtual embodiment and presence hold significant importance. They allow participants to experience the illusory feeling of actually being within simulated spatial and social contexts, such as concert environments and music classrooms, among others. In addition to *simulated ecological validity*, a secondary complementary merit relates to the controllability of the XR environment. Whether it is full virtual reality (VR) or partly augmented or mixed reality (AR/MR), no matter how complex the XR environment is, the experience is realized through computer-generated data. This means that the variables of the XR environment become fully under the control of the researchers, enabling the empirical testing of specific hypotheses and scenarios in a systematic way. For instance, in the study of collaborative music playing, we could accurately model the timing behavior of interactive computational agents displayed as 3D holograms, or reliably manipulate their communicative cues within live interactions with subjects. Interestingly, the plethora of possible manipulations may even generate "impossible" contexts that could not be tested by existing physical means. Inducing multimodal incongruencies, bodily perception illusions or changes of the visual perspective are only a few examples that can be exploited to deepen knowledge of the embodied (musical) mind and its interactions. Hence, from the viewpoint of XR as a new research space, it is exactly the bridging of simulated ecological validity and extended experimental control that fosters valuable opportunities to innovate methodologies and experimental paradigms in humanities and (neuro)scientific research.

XRt: Concert halls of the future – innovating artistic-creative music interaction

What is the consequence when virtual embodiment allows us to feel *present* in computer-generated spaces and bodies? We here consider the practical interest for musical expression, experience, interaction and imagination, towards the development of what we call *concert halls of the future*. XR invites us to rethink the concept of a concert hall as being a specific physical venue that people need to travel to at a specific moment in time in order to experience music. The moment XR realizes *presence*, in particular physical and social presence, it becomes possible for people to experience music, free from time constraints, while situated in physically remote locations. It becomes particularly interesting when live, three-dimensional and embodied virtual avatars (EVAs) are used to bring together musicians and their audiences. In contrast to traditional digital mediation of social interaction via two-dimensional screens, EVAs allow the capture of fine-grained bodily articulations inherent to the expression and communication of musical intentions and emotions (Van Kerrebroeck et al. 2021; Van Kerrebroeck, Crombé, Willain, Leman, and Maes, n.d. under review). But more than simulating known, naturalistic musical contexts, we are interested in exploring novel possibilities that XR offers. For instance, XR may realize unique personalized experiences for audience members, allowing people to walk around on stage, getting close to their favorite musician, or even experience a concert from the musician's point of view. Musicians may practice or improvise with artificially intelligent computer-controlled agents or play on the stage of their favorite concert hall. Further, one may think about multisensory imaginary environments, spatial objects, and avatars and agents leading to novel networked and collaborative musical experiences and interactions. The possibilities are limited only by the artist-researcher's imagination and XR design expertise. In that regard, XR may contribute to many of the challenges raised in the domains of art, science and technology (e.g., https://smcnetwork.org/index.html#roadmap), to the development of the concept of the musical *internet of things* (IoT) and the musical *metaverse* (Turchet, Hamilton and Çamci 2021; Turchet 2023) and to the development of novel business models for the cultural and creative sector.

XRhive: Museums of the future – living archives for embodied interaction

Traditionally, preservation of cultural heritage adheres to the curation of documents, such as texts, audio recordings and video. These documents are typically exhibited and stored within the confined environment of museums, archives and the like. Digital tools are hence of increasing importance, especially at the service of digitalization of the documents, facilitating their storage, exhibition, distribution, searchability and analysis. In our research however, we explore how XR can help to realize a complementary paradigm in heritage preservation, which puts human embodied interaction at the center of attention (Leman and Six 2018). In this interaction-based paradigm, heritage is embedded and (re-)valued in a living culture of human embodied interaction and experience: what we call a *living archive*. XR technologies like 3D scanners, motion-capture systems, volumetric video and XR design software thereby allow the transfer of cultural artifacts, sceneries, and music and dance performances into their 3D immersive virtual counterparts. As physical materials are turned into digital data, they become of use to the arts, science and technology communities, where they can be reconstituted and augmented into diverse kinds of XR spaces. In turn, these invite embodied user experience, participation and interaction, connecting users to the cultural past, as living archives. In addition to living archives as a finalized outcome, there is major value in the design process itself. The whole process of 3D virtualization and interactive digital contextualization and storytelling invites us to dig deeper into the past and bring together voices in an interdisciplinary dialog. It is exactly in that process of reconstituting the past in interactive XR spaces that materials are revitalized and knowledge re-activated. Hence, XR living archives provide the possibility not only of augmenting interactions with cultural heritage and increasing its accessibility, but also of supporting an innovative methodology to acquire and preserve historical knowledge in a living culture of interaction.

XR-based art and science case studies

Based on the conceptual definitions of virtual embodiment, and of the related novel musical spaces that XR has to offer, we describe in the following several concrete cases and applications that illustrate the potential of these spaces for music and science. Visualizations of the cases can be found in Figure 12.2.

MusiXR cases

The first pair of studies aimed to empirically validate a basic assumption underlying the notion of virtual embodiment and the use of XR as new research space (Van Kerrebroeck et al. 2021). Specifically, we wanted to investigate whether musicians can effectively play music together, and experience feelings of *social presence*, when their interaction is fully mediated via 3D EVAs. For that purpose, the experiments operationalized the scheme presented in Figure 12.1 within the context of live joint music making. In this research, we developed a pragmatic methodological approach to reliably measure social presence in XR-mediated interactions. According to the approach, social presence in XR contexts is established when musicians behave and respond similarly to how they would in corresponding naturalistic contexts. In the analysis of musicians' behavior and responses, we defined a layered framework that distinguishes three levels of joint music interaction:

(1) the music-technical aspects of the music performance; (2) the musicians' embodied co-regulation of intentions and expression; and (3) the musicians' subjectively felt quality of experience. Hence, by comparing naturalistic music performances with their simulated XR counterparts across these levels, we obtained a measure for the degree of social presence experienced by musicians in XR environments. We applied this methodological framework in two empirical studies.

In the first experiment by Van Kerrebroeck et al. (2021), we invited a 'subject pianist' to play the piano duet *Piano Phase* (1967) composed by Steve Reich together with a 'confederate pianist' in three conditions. The first condition involved a traditional performance in which the subject pianist saw the confederate pianist in a naturalistic, physical manner. In the second condition, the subject pianist saw the confederate pianist as EVA (using a VR HMD), while playing live together. In the third condition, the subject pianist played together with a pre-made recording of the virtual avatar of the confederate pianist, which was automatically phase aligned by a computational model to the playing of the subject pianist, according to the score instructions. The results of this first case study demonstrated that the subject pianist experienced a strong feeling of social presence – as evidenced on all three analysis levels – when playing live together with the confederate pianist observed as EVA (condition 2). In contrast, even though the music-technical performance when playing with the computer-modeled virtual avatar in condition 3 was successful, we noted that embodied co-regulation and the subjectively felt quality of experience were seriously disturbed.

For a second experiment by Van Kerrebroeck et al. (under review), an XR platform was developed that allowed networked and polyrhythmic music performance using full-body interaction as EVAs between two players in AR. A central element was the use of a virtual 'drum circle' that coupled players together and offered visual cues as 3D spheres on how to perform a polyrhythm together. Sixteen duos were invited to play the virtual drum circle in an experimental design. Again, we aimed to assess the social presence of 3D avatar-mediated interaction by comparing this condition with naturalistic, physical interaction, and interaction without seeing and only hearing each other. The results showed, again, that performative and experiential dynamics were maintained in the avatar-mediated interaction. In addition, results also showed that performers moved more energetically and had stronger prosocial feelings of shared agency and self–other integration when seeing each other as fully embodied virtual avatars as compared to not seeing each other.

Together, the above two studies provide empirical support for the potential and value of musical interactions mediated via full-body EVAs. Results suggest that live avatar-mediated interactions allow musicians to successfully perform music together. This was not only reflected in the successful musical output, but also in the successful co-regulation of intentions via bodily gestures and cues, and in the positive quality of experience felt by the musicians.

In another empirical study, conducted by Rosso et al. (2023), we shifted the focus from the investigation of social presence towards the use of XR to provide stimuli and apply manipulations that are not possible in naturalistic conditions. In particular, we explored the role of visual perspective in joint coordination of dyads engaged in a musical tapping task. We hypothesized that the tendency for spontaneous joint synchronization would be strengthened when two subjects of a dyad perceive the movements of the other from the other's first-person perspective, as compared to when subjects perceive the movements of the other from a naturalistic second-person perspective. The required visual perspective manipulations were realized in XR by swapping the visual scenes perceived by two individuals looking at the back of their own hand and streaming them into the partner's VR headset. The manipulation resulted in a partial body-swap, wherein the visual percept of the hand was rotated into the partner's egocentric frame of reference. The drifting metronomes paradigm for dyadic entrainment (Rosso, Maes and Leman 2021) was adopted to quantify the overall strength and dynamics of interpersonal synchronization, while neural activity and subjective ratings of embodiment and agency were recorded respectively via electroencephalography (EEG) hyperscanning (Rosso et al. 2022) and questionnaires. Overall, we found that dyads' joint coordination was indeed significantly more oriented towards synchronized behavior when subjects observed the movements of their partner from the partner's first-person perspective, compared to the naturalistic face-to-face context. Relying on the possibilities of XR and the concept of virtual embodiment, this study could contribute to knowledge on the sensorimotor principles underlying human musical coordination.

XRt cases

Based on the scientific studies described above (Van Kerrebroeck et al. 2021; Van Kerrebroeck et al., under review), we further explored the artistic-creative potential of the research outcomes, in support of the development of our concept of *concert halls of the future*. Specifically, both experiments were demonstrated as public music performances with performers and a hybrid, online and offline, audience sharing a musical XR space. As in the first experiment, the *Piano Phase* performance involved a full-body, motion-tracked pianist who performed the piece as avatar with the algorithmically controlled agent, based on pre-made recordings of herself (Caruso 2022). Pianist and audience shared a physical and a virtual space, the latter mediated through a VR HMD and a 2D screen projection. Central to the performance was the notion of a "virtual mirror," a technologically mediated form of biofeedback on expressive gestures for artistic practice improvement (Caruso, Nijs and Leman 2021). The second experiment led to a hybrid performance in which real-time and remote full-body interaction, XR instruments and musical objects in the form of a virtual drum circle were core ideas ("Onze (on)bekabelde cultuur" 2022). Performers were separated by over 100 meters, shared a virtual space with an offline and online audience, and wore AR HMDs to rhythmically interact with shared virtual objects and each other. The performance successfully demonstrated an approach to disentangle performance space and embodied physicality as well as introduce novel affordances in the form of audiovisual couplings. Together, these performances exemplify how the digital and flexible nature of XR further blurs the line between simulated music scenarios in the lab and the public domain, opening a musical XR space fertile for continued artistic and scientific music research.

XRhive cases

IPEM-XRhive: Founded in 1963 in Ghent, Belgium, the Institute of Psychoacoustics and Electronic Music (IPEM) played a pioneering role worldwide in the development of electronic and electro-acoustic music. In the *avant-la-lettre* art, science and technology approach, new analog, electronic sound modules were designed for sound recording, processing and playback. The Musical Instruments Museum (MIM, https://www.mim.be) in Brussels exhibits many sound modules and instruments from that early history of IPEM.

Despite the considerable attention paid to this heritage, it is difficult for visitors to the MIM to imagine the possibilities of such instruments, as well as the context in which they were used. With the IPEM-XRhive project, we want to bring these instruments back to life, using XR technology, and let people enter the immersive environment of the IPEM sound lab of the 1960s, and play the sound modules and instruments of that time. To this end, 3D scans were made of the physical sound modules and simulated as virtual objects that people can operate and explore, by turning knobs and connecting modules via cables. In addition, we filled the immersive XR space with other artifacts that provide more historical context to these instruments. Throughout the process, the development of the IPEM-XRhive permitted us to bring together people from various disciplines and backgrounds, to explore and re-activate historical knowledge, as well as to restore sound modules back to their original condition. In addition, we investigated how this application can be valuable for pedagogical purposes and innovative trends within the museum's operation and policy (De Graeve 2022).

Odin Teatret-XRhive: Odin Teatret was founded in 1964 by Eugenio Barba in Oslo, Norway, as an *avant-garde* theater company for actor training and performance (https:// odinteatret.org). The Odin Teatret Archive holds the almost 60-year-long history of Odin Teatret through a collection of paper and audiovisual documents like photographs, videos, letters, sketches and notes, among others. Many of these archive materials provide information about actor training exercises, which play a vital role at Odin Teatret as they aim towards the development of embodied knowledge and technical skills, foundational to actors' *scenic presence*. The project *Practicing Odin Teatret Archive* (POTA) is a project about archiving this embodied knowledge into an experiential network of XR environments, in which users become interactively and creatively engaged in the production of knowledge about theater training practices (La Selva and Marouda 2022; Marouda et al., 2023). Central to the project is the notion of translation, in particular the translation of corporeal energies and techniques by abstracting their intrinsic qualities and subsequently creating multisensory XR renderings with them. This process started with the selection of exercises and the recording of practitioners performing them using motion capture and other physiological sensors. Examples of such exercises are vocal and breathing training, rhythm work and physical comedy or energetic work, all of them part of the Odin Teatret tradition and its genealogy. Through this, we developed a mesh of different translation layers. Specifically, we identified three layers: 1) the skin layer, or the representation of the performer's figure; 2) the energy layer, or the inner drive which carries the performance; and 3) the interaction layer between participant and environment, which allows for experimentation and dynamic exchange, opening possibilities for shifts in behavior. This entanglement of different layers of translation renegotiates the learning process and creates space for new ways of experiencing and extending one's own action repertoire while developing a sense of scenic presence.

Conclusion

We are witnessing a rapid acceleration of development and adoption of XR technologies across the whole of society. In this chapter, we considered their role in the domain of art and science. Central to the chapter is the argument that XR technologies intervene in the coupled action-perception processes that regulate human interaction with the naturalistic "analog" world and extend these into computer-generated digital worlds. This argument is fundamental to our notion of virtual embodiment and foundational to the notion of presence, being the illusory feeling for users of being physically present while interacting within computer-generated environments. Further, we have argued that, in their capacity to create that sense of presence for their users, XR technologies have the potential to constitute new *spaces* for musical art and science. For science, XR provides "not just external props and aids," to borrow the words of Andy Clark (2003: 5–6), but are "deep and integral parts of problem-solving systems we now identify as human intelligence." For the arts, XR provides new spaces to extend human expression, imagination and interaction. We are only at the beginning of the mind-dazzling times ahead of us.

References

Ball, M. (2022) *The metaverse: and how it will revolutionize everything*, New York, NY: Liveright Publishing.

Beaufils, K. and Berland, A. (2022) "Avatar embodiment: from cognitive self-representation to digital body ownership," *Hybrid. Revue des Arts et Médiations Humaines*, 9, pp. 1–17.

Braun, N. *et al.* (2018) "The senses of agency and ownership: a review," *Frontiers in Psychology*, 9(535), pp. 1–17.

Byrne, D. (2012) *How music works*, San Francisco, CA: McSweeney's.

Caruso, G. (2022) Piano Phase performance at Cremona Musica Festival. Retrieved from www.pianostreet.com/blog/articles/avatar-piano-duet-in-metaverse-11921/

Caruso, G., Nijs, L. and Leman, M. (2021) ""My avatar and me": technology-enhanced mirror in monitoring music performance practice," in Hepworth-Sawyer, R., Paterson, J., and Toulson, R. (eds), *Innovation in Music: Future Opportunities*. New York, NY: Routledge, pp. 355–369.

Clark, A. (2003) *Natural-born cyborgs: minds, technologies and the future of human intelligence*, Oxford, UK: Oxford University Press.

Cummings, J. J. and Bailenson, J. N. (2016) "How immersive is enough? A meta-analysis of the effect of immersive technology on user presence," *Media Psychology*, 19(2), pp. 272–309.

Damer, B. and Hinrichs, R. (2014) "The virtuality and reality of avatar cyberspace," in Grimshaw, M. (ed.), *The Oxford handbook of virtuality*, Oxford, UK: Oxford University Press, pp. 17–41.

De Graeve, M. (2022) *Het museum van de toekomst: een wisselwerking tussen educatie en technologie*, Ghent, Belgium: Ghent University.

Grau, O. (2003) *Virtual art: from illusion to immersion*, Cambridge, MA: MIT Press.

Hove, S. V. *et al.* (2018) "Human-computer interaction to human-computer-context interaction: towards a conceptual framework for conducting user studies for shifting interfaces," in *International Conference of Design, User Experience, and Usability*. Cham: Springer, pp. 277–293.

Kilteni, K., Groten, R. and Slater, M. (2012) "The sense of embodiment in virtual reality," *Presence: Teleoperators and Virtual Environments*, 21(4), pp. 373–387.

Lanier, J. (2017) *Dawn of the new everything: encounters with reality and virtual reality*, New York, NY: Henry Holt and Co.

Leman, M. (2007) *Embodied music cognition and mediation technology*, Cambridge, MA: MIT Press.

Leman, M. and Six, J. (2018) "Beyond documentation: the digital philology of interaction heritage," *Journal of New Music Research*, 47(4), pp. 309–320.

Lombard, M. and Ditton, T. (1997) "At the heart of it all: The concept of presence," *Journal of Computer-Mediated Communication*, 3(2), JCMC321.

Marouda, I., La Selva, A. and Maes, P.-J. (2023) "From capture to texture: affective environments for theatre training in virtual reality (VR)," *Theatre and Performance Design*, 9(1–2), pp. 52–73.

Matamala-Gomez, M. *et al.* (2020) "Body illusions for mental health: A systematic review," *PsyArXiv Preprints*.

Mead, A. (1999) "Bodily hearing: physiological metaphors and musical understanding," *Journal of Music Theory*, 43(1), pp. 1–19.

Minsky, M. (1980) "Telepresence," *OMNI Magazine*, 2(9), pp. 44–52.

Moog, R. A. (1965) "Voltage-controlled electronic music modules," *Journal of the Audio Engineering Society*, 13(3), pp. 200–206.

Onze (on)bekabelde cultuur. (2022) Retrieved from https://www.youtube.com/watch?v=90gtGwnTvKU

Onderdijk, K. E., Acar, F. and Van Dyck, E. (2021) "Impact of lockdown measures on joint music making: playing online and physically together," *Frontiers in Psychology*, 12, p. 642713.

O'Regan, J. K. and Noë, A. (2001) "A sensorimotor account of vision and visual consciousness," *Behavioral and Brain Sciences*, 24(5), pp. 55–68.

Parsons, T. D., Gaggioli, A. and Riva, G. (2017) "Virtual reality for research in social neuroscience," *Brain Sciences*, 7(4), pp. 1–21.

Pint, K. (2012) "The avatar as a methodological tool for the embodied exploration of virtual environments," *CLCWeb: Comparative Literature and Culture*, 14(3), pp. 1–9.

Rosso, M. *et al.* (2022) "Mutual beta power modulation in dyadic entrainment," *NeuroImage*, 257, p. 119326.

———— (2023) "Embodied perspective-taking enhances interpersonal synchronization. A body-swap study,"*iScience*, 108099, pp. 1–16.

Rosso, M., Maes, P.-J. and Leman, M. (2021) "Modality-specific attractor dynamics in dyadic entrainment," *Scientific Reports*, 11, pp. 1–13.

Scarfe, P. and Glennerster, A. (2019) "The science behind virtual reality displays," *Annual Review of Vision Science*, 5(18), pp. 1–20.

Short, J., Williams, E. and Christie, B. (1976) *The social psychology of telecommunications*, Hoboken, NJ: John Wiley and Sons.

Shove, P. and Repp, B. H. (1995) "Musical motion and performance: theoretical and empirical perspectives," in Rink, E. (ed.) *The Practice of Performance*, Cambridge, UK: Cambridge University Press, pp. 55–83.

Slater, M. (2009) "Place illusion and plausibility can lead to realistic behaviour in immersive virtual environments," *Philosophical Transactions of the Royal Society B: Biological Sciences*, 364(1535), pp. 3549–3557.

Slater, M. and Sanchez-Vives, M. (2016) "Enhancing our lives with immersive virtual reality," *Frontiers in Robotics and AI*, 3(74), pp. 1–47.

Smirnov, A. (2013) *Sound in Z: experiments in sound and electronic music in early 20th century Russia*, London, UK: Koenig Books Limited.

Sutherland, I. E. (1968) "A head-mounted three dimensional display," in *AFIPS '68 (Fall, part I): Proceedings of the Fall Joint Computer Conference*, pp. 757–764.

Turchet, L. (2023) "Musical metaverse: vision, opportunities, and challenges," *Personal and Ubiquitous Computing*, Published.

Turchet, L., Hamilton, R. and Çamci, A. (2021) "Music in extended realities," *IEEE Access*, 9, pp. 15810–15832.

Van Kerrebroeck, B. *et al.* (n.d. under review) "The virtual drum circle: polyrhythmic music interactions in mixed reality," *Journal of New Music Research*. https://doi.org/10.48550/arXiv.2308.01889

Van Kerrebroeck, B., Caruso, G. and Maes, P.-J. (2021) "A methodological framework for assessing social presence in music interactions in virtual reality," *Frontiers in Psychology*, 12, p. 663725.

13

ENACTIVE VISION

Erik Myin and Farid Zahnoun

Enactivism and the Sensorimotor Account

Enactivism, ever since Varela, Thompson, and Rosch's (1991) influential formulation, has always promoted a concept of cognition as being fundamentally embodied and embedded. Enactivists further developing this view have placed the living body, as a self-individuating and autonomous system, at the core of cognition. Cognition is then seen as a form of adaptive regulation of interactions living bodies have with their environments. By actively regulating these interactions, living bodies show their sensitivity to the norms of their own viability (see also the chapter by Di Paolo and Thompson in this book). Enactivists of this stripe have always stressed the open-ended character of cognition, characterizing it as something perpetually "in the making"—a path laid down in walking, in terms of Antonio Machado's metaphor they have adopted (see Varela, Thompson and Rosch 1991, Chapter 11; Di Paolo, Thompson and Beer 2022). By proposing this approach to minds, enactivists in this tradition explicitly oppose cognitivism: they propose that interactions and their histories do not complement, but instead *replace* cognitivist characterizations and explanations of mentality expressed in terms of mental representation and computation.

In the domain of perception, the term "enactivism" has become associated with the so-called sensorimotor contingency approach that O'Regan and Noë (2001) present. Vision, according to the sensorimotor approach, is something we do, rather than something that happens in us (see O'Regan and Noë 2001; see also Noë 2004). The approach rejects the view of vision as aimed at producing a "faithful metric-preserving replica of the outside world inside the head" (O'Regan 1992: 463). This is not to say that the sensorimotor theorists don't agree that seeing provides access to the spatially extended outside world, or that the outside world becomes visually available in seeing. Rather, their claim is that such access is best understood as achieved in "exploratory activity." Perceiving visually occurs through moving about in a world and using one's eyes, head, and body to find out about shapes, colors, scenes, or, in short, everything that can be seen. Such activity *constitutes* seeing; it is not a mere causal prelude to the formation of a visual percept—an effect of the activity that would form the proper substrate of seeing.

DOI: 10.4324/9781003322511-18

The sensorimotor approach rejects the idea that the additional formation of a percept would enhance our understanding of perception or perceptual experience beyond what is provided by an analysis of perception in terms of active engagement and so-called sensorimotor contingencies. Sensorimotor contingencies are ways in which sensory stimulation changes with movement—such as when a retinal image changes when one walks around an object. Seeing, on the sensorimotor approach, is comparable to feeling a surface or object by exploring it with the hand, where the experience is of the whole surface or object, despite the fact that momentary tactile stimulation is limited to the fingertips making contact only at particular places.

Sensorimotor theorists have defended the idea that vision should be understood as temporally extended interaction by virtue of the insights it provides into the nature and character of perceptual experiences. According to the sensorimotor approach, perceptual experiences owe their character to the patterns of sensorimotor contingencies typical of the kinds of organism–environment interactions in which those experiences normally arise. For example, determining tactile feelings of hardness or softness are the particular patterns of sensorimotor contingencies one has when engaging in activities such as squishing a sponge or pushing a brick wall. Similarly, on this view, experiences of seeing differ as a class from experiences of hearing by virtue of the differential patterns of sensorimotor contingencies specific to vision and audition. For instance, in seeing, but not in hearing, stimulation from a particular source ceases when turning one's head sideways or closing one's eyes.

Findings on adaptation to distorting or inverting glasses as well as findings of experiments with sensory substitution devices (Hurley and Noë 2003; Noë 2004; O'Regan 2011) support the crucial role that patterns of sensorimotor contingency play in shaping perceptual experience. For it seems that experiential change here follows on the heels of adaptation to patterns of sensorimotor contingencies.

The sensorimotor approach faces strong opposition and criticism, often formulated as criticism of enactivist approaches to perception generally (e.g., Block 2005; Prinz 2006, 2009). Critics of the sensorimotor approach have been puzzled, both by general claims about the role of sensorimotor contingencies in shaping experience and by the appeal to phenomena such as sensory substitution and distorted vision. Some critics have reached the verdict that these phenomena do nothing to support the sensorimotor approach. They have further held that the sensorimotor approach's claims regarding the determination of experiential quality fly in the face of the simplest observations about experience in imagery, dreaming, or paralysis, in which experience seems radically disconnected from any presently obtaining sensorimotor interaction.

In what follows, we will discuss the sensorimotor approach in the light of the broader enactivism we sketched above. Trading in a relatively narrow view of relevant interactions for a wider one allows the sensorimotor contingency theory to silence prominent objections that critics have raised, including those that invoke experiences in minimally interactive contexts, such as in dreams or hallucinations.

Sensorimotor Contingency Theory: The Basics

Let us first return to the sensorimotor contingency account, originally presented in O'Regan and Noë (2001). "Vision," they said, is "a mode of exploration of the world, mediated by knowledge of ... sensorimotor contingencies" (p. 940), which they characterized as "the structure of the rules governing the sensory changes produced by various motor actions" (p. 941). They emphasized that the knowledge involved is "implicit," leading to a view of perception as a "skillful activity." On O'Regan and Noë's view, the sensorimotor approach opposes theories according to which "vision consists in the creation of an internal representation of the outside world whose activation somehow generates visual experience" (p. 940). In order to get a firmer grip on the sensorimotor approach, it is helpful to look in some more detail at how O'Regan and Noë apply the sensorimotor approach to a number of perceptual phenomena (O'Regan and Noë 2001; Noë 2004; O'Regan 2011).

First, consider expanded vision, which refers to the kind of visual experience one has as when looking at a large screen, or when holding a book open in one's hand and having the experience of seeing both pages. Expanded vision is characterized by the experienced spatial and temporal continuity of what is seen. Essentially, visually experiencing a scene is having the feeling of being in roughly simultaneous visual contact with a stretch of one's environment.

Though expanded vision comes very naturally to us, some well-known facts prevent a straightforward explanation of it. First, subjects are not continuously engaging with the whole scene in the same way, due to such factors as differences in the spatial distribution of receptors in the retina, and the presence of the blind spot (O'Regan 1992, 2011). Second, results from studies on change blindness and inattentional blindness highlight the absence of homogeneous simultaneous contact, for they show that large changes in a scene can go unnoticed, for example when other changes are particularly prone to grabbing one's attention.

One way to explain expanded vision in the face of these facts is to relegate the homogeneity of experience to something like the "internal representation of the outside world" (reiterating O'Regan and Noë 2001). A non-homogeneous and gappy retinal image would be "filled in" to produce a homogeneous, complete representation, apparently the fitting substrate for an experience of spatial continuity. The sensorimotor approach, however, denies such an inner simulacrum is needed or useful. It is not useful, because it is not solving the problem it was invoked for: explaining the homogeneity of experience. For why would the presence of a homogeneous substrate give rise to an experience of homogeneity? Further, there would have to be a scientific story to be told of how a visual system characterized by non-homogeneities gives rise to this homogeneous representation. A bridge has to be build between non-homogeneity and homogeneity. But that just duplicates the original problem of moving from non-homogeneous interactions to a smooth experience. Any positing of a smooth intermediary—like the complete representation—just re-invokes the same bridging task. The intervening homogenous representation, so the sensorimotor theorists plead, is the middleman that should be cut out. Once this is done, it can be seen that non-homogeneities of the visual apparatus are not a bug, but a feature. That is, local non-homogeneities of the retina, or the existence of a blind spot, create opportunities that are exploited in how we come to see. Such facts do not compromise the possibility of continuous perception. On the contrary, sensorimotor theorists claim, it is the changes the environment creates on the non-homogeneous and gappy retina that enable perceivers to experience a spatially continuous world. It is because of patterns in these changes that we perceive what we perceive. For example, that the stimulation disappears during and reappers after a blink shouldn't mislead into thinking that experience must disappear for a brief moment. On the contrary, the sensorimotor contingencies linked to blinking enable the experience of a surrounding environment. If it were somehow possible to artificially sustain, during blinks, the stimulation that would be had if one did not blink, different sensorimotor contingencies would obtain and, so the sensorimotor account claims, one would not have the experience of an outside world (O'Regan and Noë 2001: 968). If it were somehow possible to compensate for the retinal irregularities by "correcting" the arriving stimulation—so that a red stimulus would have the same effects all over the retina—visual experience would be abnormal, because now sensorimotor contingencies would occur that would be specific not to the actual environment, but to a different environment—one in which there would be brighter reds, for example.

So perceiving an expanded scene requires sensitivity to patterns of sensorimotor contingencies that exist because of the ways light, objects, and our sensing body interact. Sensorimotor patterns that re-occur bear the signature of what happens out there. Facing an expanded scene comes with its own specific sensorimotor patterns, and we experience scenes as expanded because we are sensitive to these patterns. A sensorimotor pattern that is for expanded vision, according to the sensorimotor approach, is that perceivers are set up to react to sudden changes in visual characteristics, so that normally, any such significant change will lead the perceiver to focus on it. A light suddenly flashes, initially in the corner of our eye, but then we quickly move our gaze to it. The trick to a successful change-blindness experiment is to tamper with this "grabbiness" or "alerting capacity" of environmental changes (O'Regan, Myin, and Noë 2005), by introducing an even larger visual alteration such as a blank screen between two pictures of a scene before and after changes. The usual pattern of interaction is disturbed, and we don't see what we would see were the sudden masking change not introduced.

Next, consider the experience of seeing an ordinary, three-dimensional object. Sensorimotor theorists, following Donald MacKay, have compared the visual experience in object vision to the tactile experience of holding a bottle. The actual tactile contact with the bottle is limited to where the fingers touch the bottle. Nevertheless, the experience is of a bottle and not of disconnected bits of hard material. Again, one could invoke a homogeneous representation to account for the experience of the whole object. However, the sensorimotor approach proposes that such a theoretical construct is not necessary. To account for the perception of an object, it suffices to invoke the way perceivers are able to perceptually explore the object. A perceiver will touch and explore the bottle in certain ways, acquired through previous explorations of bottles. For example, she moves along the surface of the body and is not surprised that, when the bottle's shoulder is reached, her fingers move inwards, to move along a line again at the neck. The perceiver is "attuned" to a sensorimotor pattern (O'Regan and Noë 2001). Put differently, her history of interactions has shaped her perceptual anticipations. The crucial claim of the sensorimotor approach is that experience of feeling the whole bottle results from attunement to patterns of changes in stimulation that will occur during active exploration.

Thirdly, take sensory qualities, such as colors, sounds, or smells. Sensorimotor theorists have argued that here as well, an analysis in terms of specific ways of interaction offers an account for experience. The experience of tactile qualities, such as softness or hardness, are offered as paradigmatic examples. Feeling the softness of a sponge, so the claim goes, consists in squeezing it and finding out that it offers no resistance. In contrast, a hard object resists being compressed in the way a sponge can be. What goes for tactile sensations also holds for visual sensations, such as the experience of different colors. That is, different colors are equally associated with different sensorimotor contingencies. Reds interact with light in different ways than greens or yellows. When a color patch moves, when a light source moves, or when a perceiver moves with respect to them, differently colored surfaces will bring about a specific change in how light is reflected from it after the movement. Such signature patterns have a temporal dimension too. Different colors come with different ways of changing the light reflected from them. In short, being capable of seeing colors consists of being attuned to chromatic profiles, or to the changes in stimulation one would receive under various circumstances. As O'Regan and Noë put it: "Red" is knowing the structure of the changes that "red" causes (O'Regan and Noë 2001; 951; see also Philipona and O'Regan 2006 for a very detailed sensorimotor treatment of color).

This way of conceiving of color perception illustrates the overall sensorimotor take on the qualitative character of perceptual experience. The sensorimotor approach claims that both the character of sensory qualities within a modality, such as the difference between softness and hardness, as well as differences between the character of modalities as a whole, are determined by differences in classes of sensorimotor contingencies typical of perceptual interactions. The experiential quality of softness differs from the quality of hardness, because of the different effects of pressing or squeezing. Similarly, touch differs from vision, among other things, because tactile, but not visual experience of an object comes to an end when immediate bodily contact is lost. Again, they argue their approach shows that adding a further element or process over and above interaction cannot do additional work in accounting for experience. They explicitly target, for instance, the historical doctrine of specific nerve energies (O'Regan and Noë 2001: 940). Johannes Müller, in his pioneering work in "physiological optics," invoked "specific nerve energies" typical for activity in the neural pathways associated with the different perceptual modalities, as the source of the way the felt quality of seeing differed from the quality of hearing. Sensorimotor theorists argue that Müller's hypothesized mechanisms are mysterious and unnecessary. They don't explain anything by themselves. They can and should be replaced by reference to differences in interactions. The scope of the sensorimotor critique of "specific nerve energies" goes beyond that historic doctrine, and applies to more recent ways of accounting for the phenomenal feel of sensory experience by positing a non-interactive property, such as a specific "visual quale" for the feel of the visual modality, or "red quale" for the feel of red (O'Regan and Noë 2001: 961–962).

Supporting Evidence

Sensorimotor theorists have appealed to various sources of evidence for their position. Amongst many other findings they have referred to research about adaptation to distorting glasses or about sensory substitution. Critics of the sensorimotor approach to perception and perceptual awareness have challenged it on this front, claiming that neither findings about distorting glasses nor those about sensory substitution confirm the sensorimotor approach (Block 2005; Prinz 2006; Klein 2007). What are these findings?

By means of lenses or prisms, the light entering the eyes can be inverted in a left-right and/or an above-below dimension. This introduces systematic changes in the perceiver's visual sensorimotor interaction with the environment. It has been reported that after extensive wearing of inverting glasses (within 6–10 days), visual abilities can be reacquired and one may once again be able to see where things are (e.g., Stratton 1896, 1897; Taylor 1962; Kohler 1964; Dolezal 1982; but see for example Linden, Kallenbach, Heinecke, Singer, and Goebel 1999, for negative findings).

Subjects often report that on first wearing inverting glasses, the stability of visual experience breaks down with head movements, as if the scene moves in front of one's eyes. This confirms that visual experience depends on sensorimotor contingencies, or on the relation between sensory stimulation and bodily movement (Taylor 1962), and not on sensory stimulation alone. For since sensory stimulation is only spatially inverted, dependence on sensory stimulation only predicts inverted, but not unstable experience. Over the days, free-moving subjects adapt to the new situation and head movements no longer disrupt visual stability. The subject has become attuned to the novel sensorimotor contingencies, so that environmental movements lead to a distinctively visual experience of movement in the scene, while movement of the perceiver's own point or direction of view does not.

Further evidence for the crucial role of sensorimotor contingencies is the finding that when subjects use a chin rest to avoid head movement, adaptation is very restricted. Indeed, it seems that only adaptation of proprioceptive experiences—and no adaptation of visual experience—takes place when subjects perform actions without head movements (for some examples, see Harris 1965). We can make sense of this by distinguishing kinds of sensorimotor contingency. We could distinguish those related to exploratory activities such as looking, from those related to performatory activities, such as grasping (Gibson 1964): genuinely visual adaptation to wearing inverting glasses depends strongly on active visual exploration.

It is also clear that the distortion brought about by glasses affects different kinds of sensorimotor contingencies differently. Since the early reports of Stratton (1896, 1897), the focus of analysis in inversion studies has often been on the altered relation between vision on the one hand, and touch or bodily experiences on the other. However, inverting glasses introduce a conflict within spatial vision itself (Degenaar 2014). Head movements and eye movements involve different patterns of sensorimotor contingencies, some of which change and some of which remain unaffected under the distortion. A subject wearing the glasses has to adapt to the altered patterns while leaving the existing attunement to the unaltered patterns intact. Instead of leading to a prediction of a complete "inversion of experience" (Klein 2007), a sensorimotor position thus leads to the expectation that experience, while certainly changing in systematic ways, will also retain continuities with experience before the goggles were put on. Sensorimotor theorists have emphasized that the sensorimotor view of vision naturally allows for partial adaptation, noting that wearers of distorting goggles might have learned to see the positions of moving cars correctly, while still seeing the license plates as in a mirror (O'Regan and Noë, 2001; O'Regan 2011).

Partial adaptation challenges the idea that vision is based on a unitary image or representation in the brain. It is thinking of vision in this distinctively non-sensorimotor way which leads to an expectation of "re-inversion" of experience. The contrast between this way of thinking and a sensorimotor approach becomes even stronger when the latter is of the enactivist variety, for an enactivist sensorimotor approach is more fully, or at least more explicitly, non-representational. Indeed, at least when it comes to the knowledge of sensorimotor contingencies, O'Regan and Noë still rely on a form of representationalism, as we'll see further.

Next, let's look at research involving so-called sensory substitution devices. Sensory substitution devices enable a new mode of interaction with the environment, for example, by transforming an image recorded by a camera into a pattern of tactile stimulation on the subject's skin (e.g., Bach-y-Rita, 1984) or into a pattern of auditory stimulation (e.g., Auvray, Hanneton, Lenay, and O'Regan 2005; Auvray, Hanneton, and O'Regan 2007; Meijer 1992; Ward and Meijer 2010). After practice with such visual-to-tactile or visual-to-auditory substitution devices, some blind or blindfolded subjects report the experience of objects in distal space and describe vision-like experiences, such as that objects increase in apparent size on approach. Furthermore, following a training period, persons using a sensory substitution device have been found to acquire such capacities as involved in locomotor guidance, object localization, and object categorization (see Auvray and Myin 2009 for further information and pointers to the literature). Crucially, however, as in the adaptation to inverting glasses, *active exploration* is required: subjects must be able to control the camera in order to develop this kind of spatial experience (Bach-y-Rita 1984; Auvray et al. 2005). Sensorimotor theorists have referred to this adaptation as evidence for their approach because it shows the pivotal role of sensorimotor contingencies in visual behavior and attunement. If a set of sensorimotor contingencies—such as those concerning change in size upon approach or retreat—are transferred from vision to touch, then they seem to enable vision-like behavior and experience once the subject is attuned to the contingencies. It is this positive point which is key: Despite the novel modality these contingencies become embedded in, strikingly, they are able to entrain behavioral and experiential change. In other words, they seem to be, at least to some degree, independent from the sensory modalities with which they are ordinarily associated.

Critics of the sensorimotor approach have always been keen to point out that many, or at least some, aspects of experience remain linked to the modality the sensorimotor patterns are transferred to (e.g., Block 2005; Prinz 2006, 2009). For example, Prinz (2006: 5) claims that persons who successfully use a tactile-to-visual sensory substitution device still have tactile experience. They infer automatically where objects are located in space and have visual imagery related to that, but do not enjoy visual perceptual experience. So perceptual experience and the ability to interact visually are not coupled in the way the sensorimotor theorists envisage. Such an objection to the sensorimotor approach disregards the fact that the approach, just as was the case for inverting glasses, predicts a mixture of continuity and change in experience after learning to perceive with a sensory substitution device. Sensory substitution devices add to the sensorimotor repertoire of the stimulated sense without destroying the repertoire already present. Existing functionality—existing attunement to sensorimotor contingencies—remains in place. To the extent that aspects of the experiential character remain those of the "old" modality, this can be explained by the persistent attunement to the "old" sensorimotor contingencies. In other words, the sensory modality onto which the device is grafted can show a level of "tenacity" (Myin, Cooke, and Zahidi 2014), or a lack of deference to the new sensorimotor context (Hurley and Noë 2003).

Explicating Attunement

In the different applications of the sensorimotor approach surveyed above, the notion of "being attuned to sensorimotor contingencies" has played a prominent role. This raises questions about its precise meaning. What does it mean that a person is attuned to the sensorimotor contingencies of "red" or "softness?" O'Regan and Noë's (2001) answer appeals to the exercise of the "mastery" or "knowledge" of sensorimotor contingencies, building on the already mentioned characterization of "vision as exploratory activity mediated by knowledge of sensorimotor contingencies." A problem with an appeal to knowledge, however, is that it allows a representational interpretation. On such an interpretation, having knowledge about sensorimotor contingencies involves representing those sensorimotor contingencies. Appealing to knowledge, understood in terms of representation, to explain sensorimotor attunement ignores the lesson from the previous discussion of vision: positing an inner representation of external phenomena is neither necessary nor explanatory. Perhaps the specification, in O'Regan and Noë (2001) and elsewhere, that the knowledge is meant to be "implicit," is aimed at excluding such an interpretation in favor of an approach based on practical know-how, or skills. However, Daniel Hutto points out, insisting that knowledge is meant to be "implicit" is difficult to reconcile with supposing that the knowledge plays a "mediating" role (Hutto 2005). It is unclear how an appeal to mediating knowledge does not imply commitment to an intermediating representational stage. And indeed, in at least one place in a canonical expression of the sensorimotor theory, such a representational view is explicitly endorsed: "our view relies on the existence of representations. Knowledge of the laws of sensorimotor contingency themselves must surely be represented. We readily grant this." (O'Regan and Noë 2001:1017)

We can avoid such representational commitments by construing "attunement" in purely interactive ways. An organism is attuned to sensorimotor contingencies of, for example, an object if its interactions with that object are appropriate with respect to the sensorimotor contingencies interaction with the object involves. For example, when facing an object with an unseen backside, the organism will make the right movements when it wants to explore it further visually. When it wants to grasp it, it will initiate a grip fit for the full object, not just the side of it that it sees. Such an organism might perhaps be said to display practical knowledge of sensorimotor contingencies. Such practical knowledge can be thought of as an acquired way of interacting with the environment. Past dealings with its surroundings have left their marks on how the organism interacts with it now—and current interaction shapes future interaction. In such a view attunement is embodied in how current capacities for interactions are molded by past interactions. There is no logical need to invoke a representation of history in order to conceive of current interactions as historically shaped. All that matters is that what currently happens is different, given a different history.

In this vein, attunement to sensorimotor contingencies is a way of interacting with the environment. But "interaction" remains a very general term. For example, is a mechanical device whose movements are driven by input from a camera engaging in interactions characterized by sensorimotor contingencies? And if it is, does the sensorimotor approach claim that such a device is enjoying conscious visual experiences? We think that sensorimotor enactivism can avoid over-ascribing experience by teaming up with the broader enactivism in the Varela tradition. In this tradition, experience is restricted to organisms—perhaps more generally "systems" that are structurally like living beings—because of features such as self-individuation, autonomy, and precariousness (see chapter by Di Paolo and Thompson in this volume; see also Di Paolo et al. 2017).

Internalism Might Still Be the Case: Empirical Considerations

An oft-heard objection to the sensorimotor approach is that it runs counter to the observation that we often *do* have sensory experiences without any dynamic interactions at all. In many cases, visual experience, for instance, does not seem to necessitate action at all. Such cases include visual imagery, visual hallucinations, visual experiences in paralyzed people and, of course, dreaming. Various authors have pointed out that these phenomena indicate that neural activity suffices for the generation of perceptual experience, requiring no inter-action in principle. According to O'Brien and Opie, for instance, "[s]uch experiences pro-vide compelling evidence that neural activity is sometimes sufficient for visual awareness" (O'Brien and Opie 2001). Similarly, by drawing from "incontestable evidence from dream research," Revonsuo claims: "the brain might be entirely sufficient for producing experi-ences" (Revonsuo 2001: 1000). In other words, perceptual experience might still be all in the head after all.

This so-called internalism rests on both empirical and logical arguments. Staying with the example of dreaming for a minute, some authors have argued that, since visual experi-ence in both waking and dreaming is qualitatively identical, and since no action, but only neural activity, is involved in dreaming, we have no reason to assume that neural activity also doesn't suffice for ordinary visual perception. This argument does not work for several reasons. First of all, it is contentious to claim that "the form of dream experience is identical to that of waking experience" (Revonsuo 2001: 1000). If this were the case, then why is it that we have no problem whatsoever distinguishing between dreams and reality? The ina-bility to distinguish dreaming experience from waking experience is the exception, not the rule (for a reply along these lines, see Noë 2004: 213–215). Rather than emphasizing the similarities, we have at least as much reason for emphasizing the many differences between both kinds of experiences (e.g., difference in detail, stability, coherence...). And to account for these differences, the sensorimotor theorist might have just the right story to tell. For it might very well be the case that the difference between ordinary visual perception and the visual experience in dreams—which is in an important sense precisely not perceptual, i.e., in the sense of having experiences of one's environment—is to be accounted for in terms of sensorimotor activity. Visual experience associated with perception might differ from visual experience associated with dreaming, precisely because the latter does not, but the former *does* involve extra-neural activity. In this sense, the example from paralysis strengthens rather than weakens the sensorimotor proposal. For the suggestion that paralyzed people still have visual experiences, and that this example invalidates the sensorimotor proposal, runs counter to the experimentally confirmed fact that one's visual perception disappears almost instantaneously after the eyes are artificially rendered immobile (see Martinez-Conde, Macknik, and Hubel 2004 for a review). Visual perception, then, requires move-ment, if only eye movement.

The second reason it is empirically unwarranted to treat perception and dreaming on an equal footing is that the latter is clearly dependent on the former, but not the other way around. The visual experience one has in dreaming depends asymmetrically on, and is constrained by, the visual experience one has had in perception. For instance, the fact that it is impossible to dream (or imagine or hallucinate) a field of vision of 360° has to be explained in light of the fact that human visual perception is limited to (almost) 180°, something which itself needs to be accounted for in relation to the specifics of our embodi-ment (eyes in the front). This raises a question for the internalist: if perception is really just in the brain, then why is it structured and constrained the way it is? In any case, the fact that we sometimes have visual experiences without co-occurring interactions with the envi-ronment does not mean that visual experience does not presuppose any active environmen-tal interactions at all. Clearly, without a history of such interactions, one would not be dreaming the way one does.

Third, the idea that dreaming involves only neural activity, and that no interactions are involved whatsoever, is itself far from obvious. On the one hand, at the whole organism level, it is true that there is no ordinary exploratory interaction going on between organism and environment. But that doesn't mean that one is absolutely detached from one's environment whilst sleeping. There is still interaction going on, which in some cases clearly affects the subject's dream state (as when one dreams one is drowning while one's head is tangled up in the bed sheets). On the other hand, there are also interactions going on, not between whole body and environment, but within the body itself. In an important sense, it is simply not true that there is only neural activity involved in dreaming. This neural activity is interactive as well, as it continuously interacts with other bodily states and processes. Certain medication tends to induce nightmares, and so does eating large quantities of cheese before going to bed. So mere neural activity can't be enough.

Internalism Might Still Be the Case: Logical Arguments

In light of these empirical considerations, the neurocentric internalist ("neural activity is enough") might turn to logical arguments. According to Clark (2013), for instance, a fundamental flaw of sensorimotor theory is that it mislocates experience. Whereas the sensorimotor theorists locate experience within the dynamics of the organism–environment interactions—which of course involves neural activity—Clark argues that these interactions might not necessarily themselves constitute experience. The sensorimotor regularities which these interactions lay bare can just be seen as "training and tuning the neural systems" (Clark 2013: 218). Once the brain is trained, we have no longer reason to see the sensorimotor interactions as constitutive of the experience. Logically speaking, we could conceive of a brain which is tuned just right, not via a history of interactions, but via some artificial means which don't involve exploratory movements at all. We have no logical reason to suspect that such an artificially tuned brain would not give rise to precisely the same kind of perceptual experiences as one trained by a history of interactions characterized by sensorimotor regularities, or so Clark tells us. Hence, perceptual experience in principle does not rely on bodily interactions. Logically speaking, neural activity might suffice. Similarly, in discussing Cosmelli and Thompson's claim that we "cannot simply "carve off" the neural elements from the rest of the body," Clark replies: "Intuitively, visual experience may still at each moment depend solely on the complex brain activity caused by the ongoing engagements with body and world." All we have to do, Clark adds, is "imagine that the various body-involving loops matter only insofar as they "report information back" to the brain" (Clark 2013: 222). Finally, Clark argues that, even if we accept that the neural states supporting a given experience must have evolved in some specific way, i.e., via a history of organism–environment interactions, this still does not defeat internalism. As he puts it:

> Here too it is tempting to defend the internalist intuition by arguing that whatever this signature evolution may be, it is surely an evolution of neural states; and so all we need to do is somehow or other to bring about that very same state evolution, thus ensuring (purely internally) that the experience occurs.
>
> *(Clark 2013: 223)*

Varying Intuitions

What Clark presents as tempting and intuitive here might perhaps be so for someone who is already convinced of the truth of internalism. The enactivist, however, starts with other intuitions. On closer inspection, the point Clark is making is always the same: as long as we can logically conceive of the brain as the sufficient condition for experience, all possible alternatives are at best incomplete (they require, as Clark puts it, "one last ingredient" (Clark 2013: 222)). However, this argument from conceivability is not very convincing in a discussion about empirical matters. Countering an empirical claim by pointing out that one can still (intuitively or not) conceive of the claim being false is not really an argument at all; it is a truism. Furthermore, the internalist alternative Clark makes against the enactivist proposal simply denies one of the core tenets of the enactivist proposal, namely that one can't simply isolate the brain from the larger organism–environment system. Saying that "visual experience may still at each moment depend solely on the complex brain activity caused by the ongoing engagements with body and world" only supports internalism in an argumentative way if one is at the same time entitled to claim that these ongoing engagements with body and world are nothing but a contingency that can in principle be dispensed with. But this is precisely what the discussion is about. As such, Clark's hypotheses are simply a logical denial of the enactivist's claim to the contrary. More importantly, however, it becomes clear here just how much the internalism at issue relies on conceptual, rather than empirical considerations. For saying that "visual experience might solely depend on brain activity caused by ongoing engagements with body and world" is, from an empirical point of view, an argument *pro*, rather than *contra* the enactivist. If the brain activity causally depends on the larger body–environment interactions, then we have reason to assume that visual experience also depends on these interactions, and not solely on neural activity. There seems to be no other reason to accept the internalist alternative here besides the fact that we can *imagine* it to be true. Or, as Clark repeatedly puts it: it might still be the case.

Conclusion

The sensorimotor account of perception and vision in particular remains a viable theoretical option. Especially when coupled to the theoretical tenets of a broader enactivism, it can withstand common criticisms. For instance, the enactive sensorimotor approach has the advantage of offering a reading of "attunement to sensorimotor contingencies" which is consistent with the anti-representationalism present in the original sensorimotor analyses of expanded vision, object-seeing, and the experience of qualitative properties such as softness or color. Furthermore, its coherence does not depend on appeals to any kind of mediating knowledge, implicit or otherwise.

Of course, the theoretical basis of the approach requires further clarification and elaboration. The work of Di Paolo, Buhrmann, and Barandiaran on the key concept of sensorimotor contingencies (Buhrmann, Di Paolo, and Barandiaran 2013; Di Paolo, Buhrmann, and Barandiaran 2017) offers a good start. Moreover, the approach remains rooted in new empirical research that continues to expand, often along the line spelled out in the original sensorimotor formulation (see, for instance, König et al. 2016; see also Witzel et al. 2022). The above makes clear that the sensorimotor approach offers a strong, substantive, and fruitful perspective on perception, for vision as well as for other modalities.

Acknowledgments

This work was supported by the Research Foundation Flanders, Project G049619N "Facing the Interface"(Myin and Zahnoun) and the Alexander von Humboldt Foundation (Zahnoun).

References

Auvray, M., Hanneton, S., Lenay, C., and O'Regan, J. K. (2005) "There is something out there: Distal attribution in sensory substitution, twenty years later," *Journal of Integrative Neuroscience*, 4(4), 505–21.

Auvray, M., Hanneton, S., and O'Regan, J. K. (2007) "Learning to perceive with a visuo-auditory substitution system: Localisation and object recognition with "The vOICe"," *Perception*, 36, 416–30.

Auvray, M., and Myin, E. (2009) "From sensory substitution to sensorimotor extension," *Cognitive Science*, 33(7), 1036–58.

Bach-y-Rita, P. (1984) "The relationship between motor processes and cognition in tactile vision substitution," in W. Prinz and A. F. Sanders (eds), *Cognition and motor processes*. Berlin: Springer, pp. 149–60.

Block, N. (2005) "Review of the book Action in perception, by Alva Noë," *Journal of Philosophy*, 102, 259–72.

Buhrmann, T., Di Paolo, E., and Barandiaran, X. (2013) "A dynamical systems account of sensorimotor Contingencies," *Frontiers in Psychology*, 4, 285.

Clark, A. (2013) *Mindware: An Introduction to the Philosophy of Cognitive Science* (2nd ed.). Oxford University Press.

Degenaar, J. (2014) "Through the inverting glass: First-person observations on spatial vision and imagery," *Phenomenology and the Cognitive Sciences* 13 (2):373–393

Di Paolo, E. A., Buhrmann, T., and Barandiaran, X. (2017) *Sensorimotor life: An enactive proposal.* Oxford University Press.

Di Paolo, E. A., Thompson, E., and Beer, R. D. (2022) "Laying down a forking path: Tensions between enaction and the free energy principle," *Philosophy and the Mind Sciences* 3. https://doi.org/10.33735/phimisci.2022.9187

Dolezal, H. (1982) *Living in a world transformed: Perceptual and performatory adaptation to visual distortion.* New York: Academic Press.

Gibson, J. J. (1964) "Introduction," *Psychological Issues*, 3(4), 5–13.

Harris, C. S. (1965) "Perceptual adaptation to inverted, reversed, and displaced vision," *Psychological Review*, 72(6), 419–44.

Hurley, S. L., and Noë, A. (2003) "Neural plasticity and consciousness," *Biology and Philosophy*, 18, 131–68.

Hutto, D. D. (2005) "Knowing what? Radical versus conservative enactivism," *Phenomenology and the Cognitive Sciences*, 4, 389–405.

Klein, C. (2007) "Kicking the Kohler habit," *Philosophical Psychology*, 20(5), 609–19.

Kohler, I. (1964) "The formation and transformation of the perceptual world," *Psychological Issues*, 3(4), 19–173.

König, S. U., Schumann, F., Keyser, J., Goeke, C., Krause, C., Wache, S., and König, P. (2016) "Learning new sensorimotor contingencies: Effects of long-term use of sensory augmentation on the brain and conscious perception," *Plos One*, 11(12): e0166647.

Linden, D. E. J., Kallenbach, U., Heinecke, A., Singer, W., and Goebel, R. (1999) "The myth of upright vision: A psychophysical and functional imaging study of adaptation to inverting spectacles," *Perception*, 28, 469–81.

Martinez-Conde, S., Macknik, S. L., and Hubel, D. H. (2004) "The role of fixational eye movements in visual perception," *Nature Reviews Neuroscience*, 5(3), 229–240

Meijer, P. B. L. (1992) "An experimental system for auditory image representations," *IEEE Transactions on Biological Engineering*, 39(2), 112–121

Myin, E., Cooke, E., and Zahidi, K. (2014) "Morphing senses," in M. Matthen, D. Stokes, and S. Biggs (eds), *Perception and its modalities*. New York: Oxford University Press.

Noë, A. (2004) *Action in perception*. Cambridge, MA: MIT Press.

O'Brien, G., & Opie, J. (2001) "Connectionist vehicles, structural resemblance, and the phenomenal mind," *Communication & Cognition*, 34(1–2).

O'Regan, J. K. (1992) "Solving the "real" mysteries of visual perception: The world as an outside memory," *Canadian Journal of Psychology*, 46(3), 461–88.

——— (2011) *Why red doesn't sound like a bell: Understanding the feel of consciousness.* New York: Oxford University Press.

O'Regan, J. K., Myin, E., and Noë, A. (2005) "Sensory consciousness explained (better) in terms of "corporality" and "alerting capacity"" *Phenomenology and the Cognitive Sciences*, 44, 369–87.

O'Regan, J. K., and Noë, A. (2001) "A sensorimotor account of vision and visual consciousness," *Behavioral and Brain Sciences*, 24, 939–73.

Philipona, D. L., and O'Regan, J. K. (2006) "Color naming, unique hues, and hue cancellation predicted from singularities in reflection properties," *Visual Neuroscience*, 23, 331–39.

Prinz, J. (2006) "Putting the brakes on enactive perception," *Psyche*, 12(1). Retrieved from http://psyche.cs.monash.edu.au/

——— (2009) "Is consciousness embodied? "in P. Robbins and M. Aydede (eds), *Cambridge handbook of situated cognition* (pp. 419–36). Cambridge: Cambridge University Press.

Revonsuo, Antti (2001) "Dreaming and the place of consciousness in nature," *Behavioral and Brain Sciences* 24 (5):1000–1001.

Stratton, G. M. (1896) "Some preliminary experiments on vision without inversion of the retinal image," *Psychological Review*, 3, 611–17.

——— (1897) "Vision without inversion of the retinal image," *Psychological Review*, 4, 341–60 and 463–81.

Taylor, J. G. (1962) *The behavioral basis of perception*, New Haven, CT: Yale University Press.

Varela, F. J., Thompson, E., and Rosch, E. (1991) *The Embodied Mind: Cognitive science and Human Experience*, Cambridge, MA: MIT Press.

Ward, J., and Meijer, P. B. L. (2010) "Visual experiences in the blind induced by an auditory sensory substitution device," *Consciousness and Cognition*, 19(1), 492–500

Witzel, C., Lübbert, A., O'Regan, J. K., Hanneton, S., Schumann, F. (2022) "Can perception be extended to a "feel of north"? Tests of automaticity with the NaviEar," *Adaptive Behavior*, 31(3): 239–264. https://doi.org10.1177/10597123221130235

14

PERCEPTION AND/FOR/WITH/AS ACTION

Cedar Riener and Jeanine Stefanucci

Perception _____ Action

What is the nature of the relationship between perception and action? This is an enduring question in psychology with no definitive answer. Does perception *serve* action? Can actions occur *without* perception? In other words, are their underlying processes shared? Some have argued perceptual processes are cognitively impenetrable and may operate outside of cognitive and motor processes (Pylyshyn 1999). Others believe perception and action are intimately linked and do not operate on their own (cf. Gibson). The question of whether and how perception and action are represented in the brain has also been central to these debates. Finally, questions of purpose in psychology inevitably include theories about the connection between perception and action.

In the following review, we summarize several approaches to understanding perception and action by considering the words that could connect "perception" to "action." The categorical boundaries implied by "and," "for," "with," and "as" are surely not definitive, and some theories could fit into several of these categories. However, we believe that this framework usefully compares the different approaches used to study perception and action. Moreover, we discuss how these categories relate to arguments about how perception and action are represented (or not) for each of these approaches. If readers are interested in neurobiological evidence for relationships between perception and action, we point them to other reviews. For example, Creem-Regehr and Kunz (2010) include neurobiological as well as behavioral evidence in their review. We review approaches to perception and action focusing on behavioral evidence and propose that these approaches may overlap, but not entirely.

We begin with perception AND action, which may seem to be a neutral default, but an even pairing is in itself a claim about the nature of their connection. After briefly exploring this approach, we follow with perception FOR action, which suggests that action is the primary constraint on perception; as if the goal of perception is to enable effective action. Then we explore approaches which posit a clear connection between these constructs, in which perception exists in a constant dynamic feedback loop WITH action. Finally, we

 DOI: 10.4324/9781003322511-19

describe approaches that conceptualize most boundaries between the functions of perception and action as semantic. In these cases, perception is seen AS a type of action.

Perception AND Action

The phrase "perception and action" implies that perception and action are separable, distinct functions. This approach is best represented by the information-processing approach Marr (1982) describes, in which stages of visual processing take raw stimulus features and combine them to pass them on to later stages such as action and decision making. Pylyshyn (1999) expanded on Marr, claiming that vision is "cognitively impenetrable." In other words, early stages of vision are entirely separate and distinct from processes which receive information ("outputs") or visual representations. According to this view, the outputs of perception are unaffected by the processes receiving them (such as action or cognition).

For this view, perception is not embodied, but is separate from the body, in which case researchers can study perception without considering the body and action. While early vision is described as cognitively impenetrable, it is also accepted that actions (other than head movement) do not meaningfully affect early vision. One can thereby study vision and action separately. Since this is not an embodied view of perception, an extensive review of it is not appropriate here.

Perception FOR Action

Research in the tradition of "perception FOR action" proposes that perceptual mechanisms and representations take into account both constraints on action and particular goals of action. Early pioneers of this approach (Ungerleider and Mishkin 1982; Goodale and Milner 1992, 2008) argued for two separate visual systems of processing in the brain. The dorsal or "how" stream supports visual guidance of action, while the ventral or "what" stream supports conscious object recognition and visual representation. Evidence for this approach came first from neuropsychological patients who had one system preserved (both functionally and neurologically) but the other severely damaged. These patients showed that one system could function without access to the representations of the other. For example, patient DF (Milner and Goodale 2008) could not identify objects following a lesion to the ventral stream but could accurately grasp and act on them.

Healthy individuals judging or acting on visual illusions have produced more evidence in favor of the two visual streams approach. For example, Aglioti, DeSouza, and Goodale (1995) investigated size perception in both streams by using the Ebbinghaus illusion, an illusion in which two identical circles appear to differ in size because they are surrounded by either larger circles or smaller circles. The researchers suggested that the "what" stream provided the information for size judgments given that they were conscious. However, when asked to reach out to grasp the inner circles, participants' grips were similar across the two contexts, suggesting that the "how" or visually guided action stream was unaffected by the illusion. This work, as well as that done on other illusions such as the Muller–Lyer (Westwood, Heath, and Roy 2000; Wraga, Creem, and Proffitt 2000) and Ponzo (Stöttinger and Perner 2006), suggests a dissociation between the "what" and "how" streams. The former is specialized for understanding details and features in a visual scene, while the latter is responsible for determining spatial locations and guidance of action.

It is important to note, though, that the evidence for the two visual streams has been controversial (Glover 2004; Schenk and McIntosh 2010) and also recently updated. Milner and Goodale (2008) reappraised their approach to emphasize that the two systems have many connections, and that, for example, actions may require information from the ventral stream (for a recent review, see Goodale and Milner, 2018). In addition, other researchers propose the dorsal stream contributes to object perception tasks even when no action is needed. Advances in presenting real objects as stimuli in fMRI scanning experiments reveal that dorsal processing occurs during depth perception (Orban, 2011), perceiving structure from motion (Erlikman et al. 2018), and shape processing (Freud, Culham, Plaut, and Behrmann 2017). Freud, Behrman, and Snow (2020) conclude a review of this evidence by suggesting that the dorsal stream is not merely for online perceptual processing serving action, but is also sensitive to action-relevant features of objects, even when not immediately acting upon them. The more recent evidence against a total dissociation suggests to us that a characterization of perception FOR action is more accurate than describing perception and action as separate, as the original proposal of the two visual streams suggested.

A different perception FOR action approach is one Proffitt and Linkenauger (2013) call the perception-as-phenotype approach. They (and colleagues) argue that conscious visual awareness rescales visual information about spatial layout of the environment to metrics of the body. These "body units" then support decisions about possible actions. In other words, to be functional, perception must be scaled by some unit or ruler. They argue that the units are derived from the observers' bodies and action capabilities. Such an explanation makes evolutionary sense, given observers always have their bodies with them to scale the world.

A growing body of literature provides support for this approach. For example, in studies of near distances (within or just outside of reach), observers judged targets that were just beyond reach as closer when they held a tool (Witt and Proffitt 2008). Further, right-handed individuals perceived distances to be closer when reaching with their right hand than with their left (Linkenauger, Witt, Bakdash, Stefanucci, and Proffitt 2009). According to the perception-as-phenotype approach, participants' increased facility with their dominant hand leads to a different unit for scaling of the space relevant to that hand. Other effects of scaling with the body have been observed in spaces farther from the body. Stefanucci and Geuss (2009) showed that the width of the body may be used to estimate the size of apertures, such that changes in body size result in changes in perceptual estimates. For reviews of this approach as well as one that shows effects of action on perception, see Proffitt (2006; 2008) and Witt (2011). Overall, the approach suggests that perceptual representations are constructed for the purpose of future action and thus are grounded in the body that will be performing the action.

Perception WITH Action

The perception WITH action approach emphasizes that perception and action are inseparable. In this approach, both perception and action have direct contact with the environment. In other words, perceptual representations are not constrained or scaled by actions, but rather the environment constrains each.

The ecological approach that Gibson (1966, 1979) proposed is an example of perception arising from the detection of sensory information *WITH* action. In other words, perception and action are inseparable because they rely on one another. However, Gibson's approach does not require representations. Instead, he argues that perception is *direct*. Specifically, he claimed that the properties of the perceived environment (mostly those related to the guidance of action) are specified without the need of processing when taking into account movement and action. Thus, as the observer moves around, the structure of the light will be revealed along with the properties of the environment (Michaels and Carello 1981; Shaw, Turvey, and Mace, 1982; Wagman and Blau, 2020). Indeed, Fajen, Riley, and Turvey (2008) state that this allows observers to "achieve direct epistemic contact with their environments; that is, that they can know their environments in a way that is unmediated by internal representations" (p. 80). This approach contrasts with the idea that information for perception is ambiguous and so requires inference to arrive at a three-dimensional representation of the world. In the latter case, perception is not direct; it is an *indirect* interpretation of the environment based on sensory information acquired by the retina and cognitive inferential processes applied to the stimulus.

Although indirect theories of perception can explain visual illusions and other phenomena, they do not provide a model for how perception and action may dynamically interact. Such dynamic interaction must take place given that action requires movement, which leads to changing stimulus information for the eye. For example, David Lee and colleagues (Lee and Lishman 1977) examined the changes in optical information ("arrays") that occur when observers act, thereby allowing them to discover ways to perform complex actions like catching and hitting balls. To catch an object, observers must anticipate when the object will come into contact with them. Lee (1976) found that time to contact (TTC) can be perceived by focusing on the size of the object and the change in its size over time (optical expansion). Estimations of speed and distance were not necessary to execute a successful catch. Though more recent work has contested the sole use of TTC in actions like catching (Hecht and Savelsbergh 2004; Tresilian 1999), Lee's work inspired others to search for invariants in the optical array that could lead to coordinated behaviors without need for representation.

In addition to TTC, subsequent work suggests that to make a successful catch, one must also detect the passing distance of the ball (Gray and Sieffert 2005). Researchers in this domain have also argued that simply wielding or hefting an object conveys information about the object's size, length, weight, and more, given the haptic deformations of the muscles, tendons, and skin as well as the joint angles that result from that interaction (Turvey and Carello 1995). Dynamic touch information can be used to guide actions and calibrate them over time, even when vision is unavailable (Withagen and Michaels 2004). Constant across these examples is the investigation of perception–action relationships in *dynamic* settings. It is also important to note that for skilled actions like catching, observers may not be *tuned* to the appropriate information to pick up in the environment when they begin to learn that skill. However, with practice, they can begin to identify which optical variables are most useful for guiding their actions (Jacobs and Michaels, 2006; van der Kamp, Savelsbergh, and Smeets 1997), which is especially important in the context of sports (Fajen, Riley, and Turvey 2008).

Also related to the study of spatial perception and action is Gibson's notion of *affordances* (1977). Perhaps the most well-known aspect of the ecological approach, affordances are the opportunities for action relative to a perceiver's intentions. For example, a chair affords sitting when an observer needs a place to rest and a tree affords climbing if an observer needs to flee. Like the rest of the optical array, Gibson proposed that affordances can be directly perceived in the light reflecting from the environment. Moreover, they are dependent upon the observer's size and shape as it relates to the properties of the environment. A five-foot tall observer may not be able to climb a tree where the lowest branch is six feet. Further, affordances can be "perceived" via dynamic touch or interaction with objects (and without vision) as briefly described above (Michaels, Weier, and Harrison 2007) Thus, affordances readily demonstrate the perception *WITH* action characterization, given that they rely on properties of both the observer and the environment to be perceived.

A large body of empirical work supports the notion of affordances. Here, we discuss just a few studies related to the perception of affordances at farther distances. To begin, Warren (1984) showed that people report being able to step onto an object if it is less than 0.88 times their leg length. Mark (1987) found that people could adjust to changes in their height (achieved by asking people to wear blocks under their shoes) when estimating what they could sit on. Stefanucci and Geuss (2010) found that adding similar blocks to observers' feet also affected their judgments of what they could walk under. Warren and Whang (1987) asked participants to decide whether they could walk through apertures of different sizes without rotating their shoulders. They found that both body size and eye height information contributed to their decisions about what was passable. Moreover, these judgments can be made in virtual environments where visual cues can be manipulated to determine their effect on perceived affordances. Geuss et al. (2010) found no difference in judgments of whether an aperture afforded passage in a real environment as compared to a visually matched virtual environment. Fath and Fajen (2011) systematically manipulated the availability of eye height information and dynamic information (head sway and stride length) for passing through apertures in virtual environments. They found that performance was no different across various cue availability manipulations, suggesting that affordances for passage may rely on cues other than just eye height.

Perception AS Action

The final approach is perception AS a form of action. Drawing inspiration from Merleau-Ponty (1962), Gibson (1979), and Ballard (1996), Alva Nöe provides a modern summary of this enactive approach: "Think of a blind person tap-tapping his or her way around a cluttered space, perceiving that space by touch, not all at once, but through time, by skillful probing and movement. This is, or at least ought to be, our paradigm for what perceiving is." (Noë 2004, p. 1). O'Regan and Noë (2001) argue that perception is a form of sensorimotor bodily skill. They cite cases of experiential blindness, in which surgery restores sight to congenitally blind patients. However, patients are unable to understand their newly found sensations such as experiences of lights, colors, and edges, suggesting that this surgery restores visual sensations but not perception. Instead, perceptual meaning is derived from the sensorimotor significance of these patterns of light. As behavioral evidence for this phenomenon, Nöe cites the effects of left-right inverting prism glasses in people with normal vision. With these prism goggles, what would normally be seen on the right side of space is sent to the right side of the retina (instead of the left, which is the normal case). Instead of an inversion of visual experience, observers experience a kind of blindness, such that they are temporarily unable to connect the pattern of light to sensorimotor significance.

Another clear example of the perception AS action approach is the theory of event coding (TEC), or the common coding approach proposed by Prinz, Hommel, and colleagues

(Hommel 2019; Hommel, Müsseler, Aschersleben, and Prinz 2001). In their framework, perception and action are virtually inseparable because they share a common representational code. To be fair, the proponents of this approach do not claim to have a theory explaining all potential perception and action phenomena, but rather what they call late perception and early action (i.e., action planning). Indeed, early critics of the approach noted that there was no explanation for how these common representational codes might interact with control processes. Despite this, one might consider this approach as also fitting into the perception *FOR* action section. The TEC framework is clearly different than the ecological approach because it supports representations as underlying perception and action. However, it does not adhere to traditional information-processing models (i.e., those most often considered representational), because these models generally separate representations used for perception and action and study these phenomena in isolation. Although both ecological and information-processing models contributed to the TEC framework, they are clearly different.

The main tenet of the TEC approach is that perception and action planning share a common representational code. Thus, perceived and produced events are related through interaction between their representations, and perception is considered functional in that it produces adaptive actions. Also, the progression from perceptual representation to executed action plan is not thought to be linear. So, important to this framework is the notion that perception may even require action. We must move around the world to acquire more sensory input and information, which then leads to sensorimotor coordination also resulting from the intentions of the observer/actor. This means that both action and perception codes are related in that they are concerned with distal (also termed "extrinsic") events. However, they are interactive only when they are both related to a specific extrinsic feature of those distal events. Situational demands may drive the overlap of perceptual and action representations by weighting features that are particularly relevant for a given task, regardless of code. In perception, feature weighting likely occurs through attention, whereas with action, feature weighting is related to the intention of the observer. Both result in the anticipation of and preparation for upcoming important events.

Support for this framework in spatial perception derives from many paradigms of research, including both behavioral and neuroscience work. Early evidence supporting TEC came from work on spatial, stimulus–response (S–R) compatibility paradigms (Simon 1967; 1969; Wallace 1971; 1972). In these studies, participants are asked to respond to stimuli that correspond to the spatial location of the response. For instance, a stimulus that appears to the right of the participant (either auditory or visual) will be responded to more quickly if the location of the to-be-executed response is also on the right. Importantly, this effect is not driven by the location of the effector (e.g., the right hand). Instead, it is the location of the response that matters most. Even when participants crossed their hands to make their responses (i.e., the right hand is responding to the stimuli on the left), the correspondence between the stimulus and the response location produced the fastest responses. This is true even if responding when holding sticks rather than using one's fingers (Riggio, Gawryszewski, and Umilta 1986).

These S–R compatibility effects are not limited to static stimuli. Michaels (1988) displayed stimuli that were either on the right- or left-hand side of a screen. One object would then begin moving to the opposite side of the screen, which would signal the observer to respond. If the object's movement direction corresponded to the response location, then responses were facilitated, suggesting that dynamic properties of events can activate feature codes that enhance responses. When observers are asked to respond by making a particular hand gesture, work by Sturmer, Aschersleben, and Prinz (2000) shows that conflicting gestures presented before cueing the response may interfere with the time that it takes participants to act. For instance, when observers see static images of a non-corresponding hand gesture (a grasp) and then are asked to produce a finger movement in response, they will be slower to act. This interference also occurs if a dynamic movie of a hand gesturing is played prior to the cue to respond. End state of the response action was achieved at a faster rate when the image or action viewed on the screen corresponded to the response action goal state. This enhancement in performance was predicted by TEC when the end state representation was associated with the action code. However, it is also important to note that when representations completely overlap or are mostly shared, it may be harder to synchronize them (Aschersleben and Prinz 1995).

Summary and Conclusions

In this review, we describe a novel strategy for categorizing the many ways in which perception and action have been studied, namely, by using prepositions to label the nature of the relationship as it has been investigated across the various approaches. However, we acknowledge that these categories may overlap. For example, Gibson's ecological approach is categorized as a perception WITH action approach, but it also has some connection to the work proposed in the perception FOR action section (e.g., the perception-as-phenotype approach), or the perception AS action section, given Gibson's view of perception as direct. Likewise, the TEC framework in the perception AS action section is not easily dissociable from the perception-as-phenotype approach in the perception FOR action section. If the body is being used to scale perception, which is then used for action, then a common coding system could underlie both perception and action. Nevertheless, we believe that thinking about the nature of the relationship between perception and action is important, given the lack of a unified approach, and hope that our categorizations may help reveal commonalities and differences among these approaches.

References

Aglioti, S., DeSouza, J. F., and Goodale, M. A. (1995) "Size-Contrast Illusions Deceive the Eye but not the Hand," *Current Biology*, 5(6), 679–685.

Aschersleben, G., and Prinz, W. (1995) "Synchronizing Actions with Events: The Role of Sensory Information," *Perception And Psychophysics*, 57(3), 305–317.

Ballard, D. H. (1996) "On the Function of Visual Representation," in *Perception: Volume 5, Vancouver Studies in Cognitive Science*, ed. Kathleen Akins, 111–131. New York: Oxford University Press. Reprinted in *Vision and Mind: Selected Readings in the Philosophy of Perception*, A. Noë and E. Thompson, (eds) (pp. 459–479). Cambridge MA: The MIT Press, 2002.

Creem-Regehr, S. H., and Kunz, B. R. (2010) "Perception and Action," *Wiley Interdisciplinary Reviews: Cognitive Science*, 1(6), 800–810.

Fajen, B. R., Riley, M. A., and Turvey, M. T. (2008) "Information, affordances, and the control of action in sport," *International Journal of Sport Psychology*, 3590(1), 79–107.

Fath, A. J., and Fajen, B. R. (2011) "Static and Dynamic Visual Information About the Size and Passability of an Aperture," *Perception*, 40(8) 887–904.

Freud, E., Behrmann, M., & Snow, J. C. (2020) "What does dorsal cortex contribute to perception?" *Open Mind*, 4, 40–56.

Freud, E., Culham, J. C., Plaut, D. C., & Behrmann, M. (2017) "The large-scale organization of shape processing in the ventral and dorsal pathways," *elife*, 6, e27576.

Gibson, J. J. (1966) *The Senses Considered as Perceptual Systems*, Boston: Houghton Mifflin.

Gibson, J.J. (1977) "The Theory of Affordances," in R. Shaw and J. Bransford (eds). *Perceiving, Acting, and Knowing: Toward an Ecological Psychology*, (pp. 67–82). Hillsdale, NJ: Lawrence Erlbaum.

Gibson, J. J. (1979) *The Ecological Approach to Visual Perception*, Hillsdale, NJ: Lawrence Erlbaum.

Glover, S. (2004) "Separate Visual Representations in the Planning and Control of Action," *Behavioral and Brain Sciences, 27,* 3–78.

Goodale, M. A., and Milner, A. D. (1992) "Separate Visual Pathways for Perception and Action," *Trends in Neurosciences, 15*(1), 20–25.

——— (2018). Two visual pathways—Where have they taken us and where will they lead in future? *Cortex, 98,* 283–292.

Gray, R., and Sieffert, R. (2005) "Different Strategies for Using Motion-in-Depth Information in Catching," *Journal of Experimental Psychology: Human Perception and Performance, 31*(5), 1004–1022.

Hecht, H., and Savelsbergh, G. J. P. (2004) "Theories of Time-to-Contact Judgment," in H. Hecht and G. Savelsbergh (eds), *Advances in Psychology, Vol 135: Time-to-contact* (pp. 1–11).

Hommel, B. (2019) "Theory of Event Coding (TEC) V2. 0: Representing and controlling perception and action," *Attention, Perception, and Psychophysics, 81,* 2139–2154.

Hommel, B., Müsseler, J., Aschersleben, G., and Prinz, W. (2001) "The Theory of Event Coding (TEC): A Framework for Perception and Action Planning," *Behavioral and Brain Sciences, 24,* 849–878.

Jacobs, D. M., and Michaels, C. F. (2006) "Lateral Interception I: Operative Optical Variables, Attunement, and Calibration," *Journal of Experimental Psychology: Human Perception and Performance, 32*(2), 443–458.

Lee, D. N. (1976) "A Theory of Visual Control of Braking Based on Information About Time to Collision," *Perception, 5,* 437–459.

Lee, D. N., and Lishman, R. (1977) "Visual Control of Locomotion," *Scandinavian Journal of Psychology, 18*(3), 224–230.

Linkenauger, S. A., Witt, J. K., Bakdash, J. Z., Stefanucci, J. K., and Proffitt, D. R. (2009) "Asymmetrical Body Perception: A Possible Role for Neural Body Representations," *Psychological Science, 20*(11), 1373–1380.

Mark, L. S. (1987) "Eyeheight Scaled Information About Affordances: A Study of Sitting and Stair Climbing," *Journal of Experimental Psychology: Human Performance and Perception, 13,* 371–383.

Marr, D. (1982) *Vision*, New York: W.H. Freeman and Sons.

Merleau-Ponty, M. (1962) *Phenomenology of Perception*, London: Routledge and Kegan Paul.

Michaels, C. F. (1988) "SR compatibility between response position and destination of apparent motion: evidence of the detection of affordances," *Journal of Experimental Psychology: Human perception and performance, 14*(2), 231.

Michaels, C. F., and Carello, C. (1981) *Direct Perception*, New York: Prentice-Hall.

Michaels, C. F., Weier, Z., and Harrison, S. J. (2007) "Using vision and dynamic touch to perceive the affordances of tools," *Perception, 36*(5), 750–772.

Milner, A. D., and Goodale, M. A. (2008) "Two Visual Systems Re-viewed," *Neuropsychologia, 46*(3), 774–785.

Noë, A. (2004) *Action in Perception*, Cambridge: MIT Press.

Orban, G. A. (2011) "The extraction of 3D shape in the visual system of human and nonhuman primates," *Annual Review of Neuroscience, 34,* 361–388. https://doi.org/10.1146/annurev-neuro-061010-113819

O'Regan J. K., and Noë, A. (2001) "A Sensorimotor Approach to Vision and Visual Consciousness," *Behavioral and Brain Sciences, 24*(5), 939–973.

Proffitt, D. R. (2006) "Embodied Perception and the Economy of Action," *Perspectives on Psychological Science, 1*(2), 110–122.

——— (2008) "An Action-Specific Appraoch to Spatial Perception," in R. L. Klatsky, M. Behrmann, and B. MacWinney (eds), *Embodiment, ego-space, and action* (pp. 177–200). Mahwah, NJ: Erlbaum.

Proffitt, D. R., and Linkenauger, S. A. (2013) "Perception Viewed as a Phenotypic Expression," in W. Prinz, M. Beisert, and A. Herwig (eds), *Tutorials In Action Science*, Cambridge: MIT Press.

Pylyshyn, Z. (1999) "Is Vision Continuous with Cognition? The Case for Cognitive Impenetrability of Visual Perception," *The Behavioral and Brain Sciences*, 22(3), 341–365; discussion 366–423.

Riggio, L., Gawryszewski, L. G., and Umilta, C. (1986) "What is Crossed in Crossed-Hand Effects?" *Acta Psychologica*, 62, 89–100.

Schenk, T., and McIntosh, R. D. (2010) "Do We Have Independent Visual Streams for Perception and Action?" *Cognitive Neuroscience*, 1(1), 52–62.

Shaw, R. E., Turvey, M. T., and Mace, W. M. (1982) "Ecological Psychology: The Consequence of a Commitment to Realism," in W. Weimer and D. Palermo (eds), *Cognition and the symbolic processes*, 2, 159–226.

Simon, H. A. (1967) "An information-processing explanation of some perceptual phenomena," *British Journal of Psychology*, 58(1–2), 1–12.

Simon, J. R. (1969) "Reactions Toward the Source of Stimulation," *Journal of Experimental Psychology*, 81, 174–176.

Stefanucci, J. K., and Geuss, M. N. (2009) "Big People, Little World: The Body Influences Size Perception," *Perception*, 38(12), 1782–1795.

Stefanucci, J. K., and Geuss, M. N. (2010) "Duck! Scaling the height of a horizontal barrier to body height," *Attention, Perception, & Psychophysics*, 72(5), 1338–1349.

Stöttinger, E., and Perner, J. (2006) "Dissociating Size Representation for Action and for Conscious Judgment: Grasping Visual illusions Without Apparent Obstacles," *Consciousness and Cognition: An International Journal*, 15(2), 269–284.

Sturmer, B., Aschersleben, G., and Prinz, W. (2000) "Correspondence Effects with Manual Gestures and Postures: A Study of Imitation," *Journal of Experimental Psychology: Human Performance and Perception*, 26(6), 1746–1759.

Tresilian, J. R. (1999) "Abstract Levels of Motor Control in Prehension: Normal and Pathological Performance," *Human Movement Science*, 18(2–3), 219–239.

Turvey, M. T., and Carello, C. (1995) "Dynamic touch," *Perception of Space and Motion*, 401–490. https://doi.org/10.1016/B978-012240530-3/50013-4

Ungerleider, L. G., and Mishkin, M. (1982) "Two Cortical Visual Systems," in D. J. Ingle, M. A. Goodale, and R. J. W. Mansfield (eds), *Analysis of Visual Behavior* (Vol. 549, pp. 549–586). MIT Press.

Van der Kamp, J., Savelsbergh, G., and Smeets, J. (1997) "Multiple Information Sources in Interceptive Timing," *Human Movement Science*, 16(6), 787–821.

Wagman, J. B., and Blau, J. J. (2020) *Perception as information detection: Reflections on Gibson's ecological approach to visual perception.* Routledge/Taylor and Francis Group.

Wallace, R. J. (1971) "SR compatibility and the idea of a response code," *Journal of Experimental Psychology*, 88(3), 354.

Wallace, R. J. (1972) "Spatial SR compatibility effects involving kinesthetic cues," *Journal of Experimental Psychology*, 93(1), 163.

Warren, W. H. (1984) "Perceiving Affordances: Visual Guidance of Stair Climbing," *Journal of Experimental Psychology: Human Perception and Performance*, 10(5), 683–703.

Warren, W. H., and Whang, S. (1987) "Visual Guidance of Walking Through Apertures: Body-Scaled Information for Affordances," *Journal of Experimental Psychology: Human Perception and Performance*, 13(3), 371–383.

Westwood, D. A., Heath, M., and Roy, E. A. (2000) "The Effect of a Pictorial Illusion on Closed-Loop and Open-Loop Prehension," *Experimental Brain Research*, 134(4), 456–463.

Withagen, R., & Michaels, C. F. (2004) "Transfer of calibration in length perception by dynamic touch," *Perception & Psychophysics*, 66, 1282–1292.

Witt, J. K., and Proffitt, D. R. (2008) "Action-Specific Influences on Distance Perception: A Role for Motor Simulation," *Journal of Experimental Psychology Human Perception and Performance*, 34(6), 1479–1492.

Witt, J. K. (2011) "Action's Effect on Perception," *Current Directions in Psychological Science*, 20(3), 201–206.

Wraga, M., Creem, S. H., and Proffitt, D. R. (2000) "Perception-Action Dissociations of a Walkable Müller-Lyer Configuration," *Psychological Science*, 11(3), 239–243.

PART 5

Language

15

BODILY RELATIVITY

Daniel Casasanto

Introduction

Our bodies are an ever-present part of the context in which we use our minds. Thinking depends on context. Therefore, our bodies can exert myriad influences on how and what we think. How can we identify ways in which our bodily interactions with the environment are shaping our brains and minds? One strategy is to investigate whether people with different kinds of bodies think differently, in predictable ways. This chapter reviews research exploring ways in which the particulars of people's bodies shape their words, thoughts, feelings, and choices, and ways in which our habits of body–world interaction determine how thoughts and feelings are implemented in our brains.

This research is motivated by the *body-specificity hypothesis* (Casasanto, 2009, 2011): to the extent that the content of the mind depends on our interactions with our environment, people with different kinds of bodies – who interact with the environment in systematically different ways – should tend to form correspondingly different neural and cognitive representations. The body-specificity hypothesis has now been validated by more than two dozen experiments, conducted in a variety of populations on four continents, using methods that range from questionnaires (e.g., Casasanto, 2009) and reaction time tasks (e.g., de la Vega, de Filippis, Lachmair, Dudschig, and Kaup, 2012) to analyses of spontaneous gesture (Casasanto and Jasmin, 2010), memory tasks (Brunyé, Gardony, Mahoney, and Taylor, 2012), lesion-outcome studies (e.g., Casasanto and Chrysikou, 2011), visual hemifield (VHF) manipulations (Brookshire and Casasanto, 2013), functional magnetic resonance imaging (fMRI; e.g., Willems, Hagoort, and Casasanto, 2010), electroencephalography (EEG; Brookshire and Casasanto, 2012), and transcranial direct current stimulation (tDCS; Brookshire, Graver, and Casasanto, 2013). The mental processes and cognitive domains that exhibit body specificity include action verb understanding (Willems, Toni, Hagoort, and Casasanto, 2010), idiom comprehension (de la Vega, Dudschig, Lachmair, and Kaup, in press), motor imagery (Willems, Toni, Hagoort, and Casasanto, 2009), emotional valence (e.g., Casasanto, 2009), and affective motivation (Brookshire and Casasanto, 2012).

In light of the amount and diversity of the data, these studies that support the body-specificity hypothesis can be considered to be the first wave of evidence for a theory of

 DOI: 10.4324/9781003322511-21

bodily relativity (Casasanto, 2011), which can be described by analogy to a theory of linguistic relativity. Language and the body are two particularly stable and omnipresent
aspects of the context in which we do our thinking, both of which act as crucial points of
interface between the mind and the world, and thereby shape the way we think. Just as
speakers of different languages come to think differently in various ways, via a variety of
mechanisms (Boroditsky, 2011; Casasanto, 2012; Lupyan, 2012), so do people with different kinds of bodies think differently, in various ways, via a variety of mechanisms that can
have subtle or dramatic effects on brain and behavior.

Body specificity of action language and motor imagery

Initial tests of the body-specificity hypothesis used handedness as a "fruit fly": a simple
model system for testing broad principles. Unlike actual fruit flies, the hands are indispensable in our daily lives, mediating countless interactions between people and their environment – and importantly, different people use their hands differently, in some ways that are
easy to observe and quantify.

Right- and left-handers often perform the same actions differently. When people throw
a ball, sign a check, or grasp a coffee mug they usually use their dominant hand. Do differences in how people perform actions influence the way they imagine actions and process
action language? To find out, my collaborators and I used fMRI to compare right- and
left-handers' brain activity during motor imagery and action verb understanding.

Imagined actions

In one experiment, participants were asked to imagine performing actions while lying perfectly still in the fMRI scanner. They imagined some actions that are usually performed with
the dominant hand (scribble, toss) and some actions performed with other parts of the body
(kneel, giggle). Mental imagery for hand actions corresponded to different patterns of activity in right- and left-handers' motor systems. Left-hemisphere motor areas were activated in
right-handers, but right-hemisphere motor areas were activated in left-handers (Willems
et al. 2009). People with different kinds of bodies imagine the same actions differently, in
this case using opposite hemispheres of the brain.

Motor action and verb meaning

A similar pattern was found when people read words for actions they usually perform with
their dominant hands or with other parts of the body. When right-handers read words for
hand actions they preferentially activated the left premotor cortex, an area used in planning
actions with the right hand. Left-handers showed the opposite pattern, activating right-
hemisphere premotor areas used for planning left-hand actions (Willems, Hagoort, and
Casasanto, 2010). This was true even though they were not asked to imagine performing the
actions, or to think about the meanings of the verbs. Further fMRI experiments confirmed that activation during action verb reading was not due to conscious imagery of
actions (Willems, Toni, Hagoort, and Casasanto, 2010).

Do the *meanings* of action verbs differ between right- and left-handers? One way to
address this question is to determine whether the motor areas that show body-specific patterns of activation play a functional role in verb processing. We used theta-burst repetitive

transcranial magnetic stimulation (rTMS) to modulate neural activity in the premotor hand areas identified in our earlier fMRI study. Participants' ability to distinguish meaningful manual action verbs from pseudo-words was affected by rTMS to the premotor cortex in the hemisphere that controls their dominant hand, but not in the other hemisphere. The rTMS to the hand areas had no effect on processing non-manual action verbs, which served as a control. These data suggest that, when people read words like *grasp*, neural activity in the premotor area that controls the dominant hand is not an epiphenomenon, or a downstream consequence of semantic processing. Rather, body-specific activation of the motor system plays a functional role in processing language about hand actions (Willems, Labruna, D'Esposito, Ivry, and Casasanto, 2011). People tend to understand verbs as referring to actions they would perform with their particular bodies – not to a Platonic ideal of the action, or to the action as it is performed by the majority of language users. In this sense, people with different bodies understand the same verbs to mean something different.

These results are also informative about the kind of experience that people simulate when understanding action verbs: seeing actions or performing actions. Following Pulvermüller (2005), numerous studies have shown effector-specific activity cued by action verbs: hand areas respond selectively to hand-related verbs, foot areas to foot-related verbs, etc. Based on previous studies, however, it was not clear to what extent the motor component of action word meanings reflects actions we have observed others performing with their bodies (*allocentric simulation*) or actions we have performed ourselves (*egocentric simulation*). The allocentric possibility predicts that neurocognitive representations of manual action word meanings should be similar in right- and left-handers, since presumably everyone observes about the same proportion of right- and left-handed actions by other people. The discovery that motor activity associated with manual action words is body specific supports the egocentric possibility and suggests that, at least by default, people implicitly simulate their own prior or potential actions when understanding action words.

Body specificity of emotion

Abstract concepts of things we can never perceive with the senses or act upon with the muscles are the hard case for any theory that foregrounds the role of bodily experience in constructing the mind. Beyond the concrete domain of action, how might bodily experience shape mental representations of more abstract ideas like *goodness* and *badness, victory* and *loss, deceit* and *honesty*? Like many abstract concepts, these notions carry either positive or negative emotional valence. Affective valence (i.e., positivity or negativity) and motivation (i.e., the predisposition to approach or withdraw from physical and social situations) appear to be grounded in patterns of body-specific motor experience.

Emotional valence: choosing sides

Across languages and cultures, good things are often associated with the right side of space and bad things with the left. This association is evident in positive and negative idioms like *my right-hand man* and *two left feet*, and in the meanings of English words derived from the Latin for "right" (*dexter*) and "left" (*sinister*).

Beyond language, people also conceptualize good and bad in terms of left–right space, but not always in the way linguistic and cultural conventions suggest. Rather, people's implicit associations between space and valence are body specific. When asked to decide which of two products to buy, which of two job applicants to hire, or which of two alien creatures looks more trustworthy, right- and left-handers respond differently. Right-handers tend to prefer the product, person, or creature presented on their right side but left-handers tend to prefer the one on their left (Casasanto, 2009). This pattern persists even when people make judgments orally, without using their hands to respond. Children as young as five years old already make evaluations according to handedness and spatial location, judging animals shown on their dominant side to be nicer and smarter than animals on their non-dominant side (Casasanto and Henetz, 2012).

The implicit association between valence and left–right space influences people's memory and their motor responses, as well as their judgments. In one experiment, participants were shown the locations of fictitious positive and negative events on a map, and asked to recall the locations later. Memory errors were predicted by the valence of the event and the handedness of the participant: right-handers were biased to locate positive events too far to the right and negative events too far to the left on the map, whereas left-handers showed the opposite biases (Brunyé *et al.*, 2012). In reaction time tasks, right- and left-handers were faster to classify words as positive when responding by pressing a button with their dominant hand, and faster to classify words as negative when responding with their non-dominant hand (de la Vega *et al.*, 2012).

Left-handers have no choice but to use verbal idioms that suggest the right side is the good side: lefties cannot use *two left feet* to mean graceful, or refer to the correct answer as *the left answer*. Yet, one experiment suggests that left-handers process these idioms differently than right-handers. Left-handers responded slower than right-handers when asked to judge highly conventional good-is-right and bad-is-left idioms, but there was no difference between groups when participants judged literal left-right expressions or handedness-irrelevant metaphors (de la Vega *et al.*, in press).

Beyond the laboratory, the association of "good" with the dominant side can be seen in left- and right-handers' spontaneous speech and gestures. In the final debates of the 2004 and 2008 US presidential elections, positive speech was more strongly associated with right-hand gestures and negative speech with left-hand gestures in the two right-handed candidates (Bush, Kerry), but the opposite association was found in the two left-handed candidates (McCain, Obama; Casasanto and Jasmin, 2010). Body-specific associations between space and valence have visible consequences for the way people communicate about positive and negative ideas.

How using your hands can change your mind

Why do right- and left-handers think differently in this way? These results cannot be predicted or explained by conventions in language and culture, which consistently associate "good" with "right" and "bad" with "left." Instead, implicit associations linking valence with left–right space appear to be created as people interact with their physical environment. In general, greater motor fluency leads to more positive feelings and evaluations: people like things better when they are easier to perceive and interact with (e.g., Ping, Dhillon, and Beilock, 2009). Bodies are lopsided. Most of us have a dominant side and a non-dominant side, and therefore interact with the physical environment more fluently on one side of space than on the other. As a consequence right-handers, who interact with their environment more fluently on the right and more clumsily on the left, come to implicitly associate "good" with "right" and "bad" with "left," whereas left-handers form the opposite association (Casasanto, 2009).

To test this proposal, Evangelia Chrysikou and I studied how people think about "good" and "bad" after their dominant hand has been handicapped, either due to brain injury or to something much less extreme: wearing a bulky ski glove. One experiment tested space–valence mappings in stroke patients with hemiparesis (weakness or paralysis) on either their right or left side following damage to the opposite hemisphere of the brain. The patients, who had all been right-handed prior to brain injury, performed a task known to reveal body-specific space–valence associations in healthy participants. Patients who lost the use of their left hand post stroke showed the usual right-is-good pattern. By contrast, patients who had lost the use of their right hand associated "good" with "left," like natural left-handers.

A similar reversal was found in healthy university students who performed a motor fluency task while wearing a cumbersome glove on either their left hand (which preserved their natural right-handedness), or on their right hand, which turned them temporarily into left-handers. After about twelve minutes of lopsided motor experience, participants removed the glove and performed a test of space–valence associations, which they believed to be unrelated. Participants who had worn the left glove still thought "right" was "good," but participants who had worn the right glove showed the opposite left-is-good bias, like natural lefties (Casasanto and Chrysikou, 2011).

Motor experience plays a causal role in shaping abstract thoughts. Even a few minutes of acting more fluently with the left hand can change right-handers' implicit associations between space and emotional valence, causing a reversal of their usual judgments. People generally have the impression that their judgments are rational and their concepts are stable. But if wearing a glove for a few minutes can reverse our usual decisions about what is good and bad, the mind may be more malleable than we thought.

The effects of short-term motor asymmetries are presumably temporary, but the same associative learning mechanisms that changed people's judgments in the laboratory training task may result in the long-term changes we found in stroke patients, and may shape natural right- and left-handers' space–valence associations in the course of ordinary motor experience. Using our asymmetrical bodies, and therefore interacting with the physical environment more fluently on one side of space than the other, may serve as a kind of natural "motor training."

Is valence differently lateralized in right- and left-handers' brains?

The discovery of body-specific associations between space and valence motivates a re-evaluation of an influential model of emotional valence in the brain, according to which the left hemisphere is specialized for positive emotions and the right hemisphere for negative emotions (e.g., Davidson and Sutton, 1995). Dozens of studies have used lateralized stimulus or response tasks to investigate the hemispheric correlates of valence, most typically VHF manipulations in which positive and negative stimuli (e.g., happy/sad faces) were presented briefly to the right or left of a central fixation point, to send visual information to the contralateral hemisphere. Studies manipulating the right-vs.-left VHF have been interpreted as showing that positive emotions are processed in the left hemisphere and negative emotions in the right hemisphere (e.g., Reuter-Lorenz and Davidson, 1981). At least this appears to be the case in right-handers. Over the past three decades, there have been occasional reports of deviations from this well-established pattern when VHF emotion studies have been conducted in left-handers (e.g., Everhart,

Harrison, Crews, 1996; Natale, Gur, and Gur, 1983). The left-handers' data have been somewhat inconsistent, and have been largely interpreted as noise, but they raise the possibility that hemispheric specialization for valence could vary with handedness. An alternative possibility, however, is that only *responses* in VHF emotion studies could vary with handedness.

Although the goal of these VHF studies has been to determine hemispheric organization of emotion, there are reasons to reconsider whether they can be interpreted with respect to that goal – and whether valence is differently lateralized in right- and left-handers' brains (or, indeed, lateralized at all). Body-specific space–valence associations provide an alternative explanation for *all* previous VHF emotion experiments, and for related experiments using lateralized auditory or haptic presentation of emotional stimuli (e.g., McFarland and Kennison, 1989) or lateralized manual outputs (e.g., Kong, 2013; Root, Wong, and Kinsbourne, 2006). Stimuli presented to the right VHF appear on the participant's right side of space; stimuli presented to the left VHF appear on the participant's left side. Therefore, presenting positive and negative stimuli on a participant's "good" and "bad" side could produce "VHF effects" even if participants were not selectively processing the stimuli in one hemisphere or the other. Many of the space–valence experiments reviewed above show that laterally presented stimuli can activate space–valence associations even when the stimuli are processed slowly and presumably *bi-hemispherically*. Therefore, there is no need to posit hemispheric specialization for emotion to account for emotional VHF effects.

In short, in light of what we have learned in this program of research so far, it appears that decades of emotional VHF experiments may have been drastically misinterpreted. If emotional VHF effects are, in fact, due to body-specific associations in memory, created by habitual asymmetries in manual motor fluency, then two predictions follow. First, right- and left-handers should show opposite patterns of responses on an emotional VHF task. Second, response patterns should *reverse* with motor training that temporarily reverses hand dominance (as in Casasanto and Chrysikou, 2011).

A test of this proposal supported both of these predictions. First, in a version of a classic VHF experiment on emotional face judgments, right-handers were more likely to judge neutral faces to be positive when they appeared on the right of fixation and to be negative when they appeared on the left – but left-handers showed the opposite pattern (Brookshire and Casasanto, 2013). The strength of the body-specific judgment bias varied parametrically with the participant's degree of handedness, as measured by participants' scores on the Edinburgh Handedness Inventory (EHI; Oldfield, 1971). Right- and left-handers showed opposite emotional VHF effects.

In a second experiment, right-handers performed the ski-glove training task (Casasanto and Chrysikou, 2011) before the VHF face task. After training, participants who had worn the glove on their right hand (becoming transiently left-handed in the relevant regard) were more likely to judge neutral faces to be positive when they appeared on their left of fixation and to be negative when they appeared on the right – like natural left-handers. Twelve minutes of motor experience can completely reverse the emotional VHF effect typically found in right-handers (in our study and in many others like it). It is more likely that this twelve-minute training intervention was able to alter fluency-based associations between space and valence in participants' memory than to completely reverse any gross hemispheric specialization for valance.

Summary of body-specific space–valence associations

Right- and left-handers form the opposite implicit associations between left-right space and positive and negative emotional valence. Each group tends to associate "good" with their dominant side of space and "bad" with their non-dominant side. For right-handers, these associations accord with linguistic and cultural conventions that link "good" with "right," but left-handers' implicit associations contradict these conventions. These implicit associations appear to be formed as people interact with their environment more fluently on their dominant side of space and more clumsily on their non-dominant side, as evidenced by stroke patients and laboratory participants who have their naturally dominant hand impaired (permanently or transiently) and show a corresponding reversal of their space–valence association.

This discovery suggests that numerous behavioral studies previously interpreted as evidence for hemispheric specialization of positive and negative valence should be reinterpreted. The results of VHF emotion tasks (and other lateralized stimulus-and-response tasks) can be explained in terms of previously undocumented mnemonic associations between space and valence. These data do not require an explanation in terms of hemispheric specialization, which seems very unlikely to be correct in light of evidence that responses on a VHF valence task can be completely reversed by a few minutes of motor training. Reinterpreting VHF emotion tasks in terms of body-specific space–valence associations – rather than hemispheric specialization – reconciles a large body of behavioral data with newer neuroimaging data that cast doubt on the seemingly well-supported "valence model," according to which positive and negative valence were thought to be differently lateralized in the hemispheres (Berkman and Lieberman, 2010; Harmon-Jones, Gable, and Peterson, 2010), thus clarifying theories of the cortical substrates of emotion.

Motivation and motor action: the sword and shield hypothesis

Neuroimaging studies that have called the hemispheric laterality of *emotional valence* into question have, at the same time, strengthened the evidence for hemispheric specialization of *affective motivation* (Berkman and Lieberman, 2010; Coan and Allen, 2003; Harmon-Jones, 2003). More than seventy EEG studies show approach and avoidance motivational states are differently lateralized in the frontotemporal cortices (Harmon-Jones *et al.*, 2010). At least this is true in right-handers. Decades after the first EEG motivation study in right-handers was published, there were no tests in left-handers.

Why might a test of motivational asymmetries in left-handers' brains be fruitful? It is important to state that testing for handedness-related differences in hemispheric specialization is not necessarily of theoretical interest, per se: many of the hemispheric differences that have been documented were weak, unpredicted, unexplained, and their implications for scientific theorizing remain unclear. In the case of affective motivation, however, we had a focused reason for investigating whether the well-established hemispheric asymmetry in right-handers is also found in left-handers.

Emotional states are intimately linked to actions and to the hands people use to perform them. In centuries past, sword fighters wielded the sword in the dominant hand to approach an enemy, and raised the shield with the non-dominant hand to avoid attack. The tendency to *approach* with the dominant hand and *avoid* with the non-dominant hand is evident in more ordinary motor actions, as well, including reflex actions. When startled, people reflexively raise the non-dominant hand to defend themselves (Coren, 1992), keeping the more skilful dominant hand out of harm's way, and leaving it free for more complex approach actions.

In right-handers, the left hemisphere is specialized for approach emotions, and the right hemisphere for avoidance emotions (Harmon-Jones *et al.*, 2010). This means that, for right-handers, approach motivation is co-lateralized with the neural circuits primarily responsible for control of the dominant hand, and avoidance motivation with the circuits responsible for control of the non-dominant hand. This may be no mere coincidence. Approach motivation may be co-lateralized with dominant-hand motor control *because* the dominant "sword hand" is used preferentially for approach actions. Likewise, avoidance motivation may be co-lateralized with non-dominant-hand motor control because the non-dominant "shield hand" is used for avoidance actions. This is the *sword and shield hypothesis* (SSH; Brookshire and Casasanto, 2012; Casasanto, 2009).

This proposal makes a clear prediction: the hemispheric laterality of approach and avoidance motivation found previously in right-handers should reverse in left-handers, for whom cortical control of the "sword hand" and "shield hand" is reversed. To test this prediction, Geoffrey Brookshire and I measured alpha-band power (an inverse index of neural activity) in right- and left-handers during resting-state EEG, and analyzed hemispheric alpha-power asymmetries as a function of the participants' trait approach motivational tendencies (measured by the BAS [behavioral activation system] scale; Carver and White, 1994). Stronger approach motivation was associated with more left-hemisphere activity in right-handers, but with more *right*-hemisphere activity in left-handers – indicating a complete reversal of hemispheric specialization for approach motivation (Brookshire and Casasanto, 2012).

A further study confirmed these EEG results using tDCS (which delivers a weak electrical current to the brain through the skull) to manipulate the level of neural activity in participants' left and right frontal lobes (Brookshire, Graver, and Casasanto, 2013). This study showed that the degree to which approach motivation is lateralized in the left-vs.-right hemisphere covaries continuously with the strength and direction of the participants' hand dominance, as measured by the EHI.

According to the "motivation model" of hemispheric specialization, which is supported by more than a hundred behavioral and neuroimaging studies, the left hemisphere is specialized for approach motivation and the right hemisphere specialized for avoidance motivation. But this conclusion – a cornerstone of affective neuroscience – appears to be incorrect: it appears to be a sampling artifact that resulted from the common practice of testing only strong right-handers in neuroimaging studies. The data demonstrating the body specificity of approach motivation suggest that there is no "approach hemisphere" and no "avoidance hemisphere." Rather, approach motivation appears to be distributed across both hemispheres, consistent with (and perhaps because of) handedness-related differences in hemispheric specialization for manual motor control.

Conclusions

People with different kinds of bodies think differently, in predictable ways. Even highly abstract thoughts depend, in part, on the ways people interact with the physical environment using their particular bodies. The body shapes the mind on various timescales. To the extent that habits of body–world interaction are stable, the habits of mental representation they encourage should be stable over time; to the extent that they change, mental representations may change accordingly. Many other contextual factors influence the representations people form and the judgments they make, as well, and other factors may override body-specific influences at times. But the body is an ever-present part of the context in which we use our minds, and therefore has pervasive influences on the neurocognitive activity that constitutes our thoughts.

These first tests of the body-specificity hypothesis focused on how handedness, genetic or induced, influences brain and mind. On the basis of this bodily attribute, right- and left-handers tend to form systematically different mental images, create different word meanings, arrive at opposite judgments about the same objects in the world, and have a radically different cortical organization of affective motivation. Our hands are particularly important for interfacing with the physical and social environment, but there may be nothing special about the mechanisms by which using our hands shapes our brains and minds (e.g., associative learning), and body-specificity effects should extend beyond the initial test bed of handedness. The ways in which cognitive scientists might discover that bodily differences lead to cognitive differences are limited only by our imaginations.

Like research on linguistic relativity and cultural relativity, investigations of bodily relativity elucidate how patterns of experience give rise to corresponding habits of thinking, feeling, and communicating: how experience shapes our brains and minds. A further challenge is to determine how influences of linguistic, cultural, and bodily experiences combine to shape our mental lives.

Acknowledgments

Research supported in part by a James S. McDonnell Foundation Scholar Award (No. 220020236) and by an NSF grant (BCS-1257101). Portions of this text are excerpted or adapted from the article "Different bodies, different minds: The body specificity of language and thought," published in *Current Directions in Psychological Science*, 20 (6) (2011), 378–83, by Daniel Casasanto, and are used here with permission of the author/copyright holder and Sage Publications.

References

Berkman, E., and Lieberman, M. (2010). Approaching the bad and avoiding the good: Lateral prefrontal cortical asymmetry distinguishes between action and valence. *Journal of Cognitive Neuroscience*, 22(9), 1970–1979.

Boroditsky, L. (2011). How language shapes thought. *Scientific American*, 304(February), 63–65.

Brookshire, G., and Casasanto, D. (2012). Motivation and motor control: Hemispheric specialization for approach motivation reverses with handedness. *PLoS One*, 7(4), e36036.

———— (2013). Brief motor experience reverses visual hemifield effects for emotional faces. Poster presented at the 25th Annual Convention of the Association for Psychological Science, Washington, DC.

Brookshire, G., Graver, C., and Casasanto, D. (2013). Motor asymmetries predict neural organization of emotion. In M. Knauff, M. Pauen, N. Sebanz, and I. Wachsmuth (Eds), *Proceedings of the 35th Annual Conference of the Cognitive Science Society* (pp. 245–250). Austin, TX: Cognitive Science Society.

Brunyé, T., Gardony, A., Mahoney, C. R., and Taylor, H. A. (2012). Body-specific representations of spatial location. *Cognition*, 23(2), 229–239.

Carver, C. S., and White, T. L. (1994). Behavioral inhibition, behavioral activation, and affective responses to impending reward and punishment: The BIS/BAS scales. *Journal of Personality and Social Psychology*, 67, 319–333.

Casasanto, D. (2009). Embodiment of abstract concepts: Good and bad in right- and left-handers. *Journal of Experimental Psychology: General, 138*(3), 351–367.

——— (2011). Different bodies, different minds: The body specificity of language and thought. *Current Directions in Psychological Science, 20*(6), 378–383.

——— (2012). Whorfian hypothesis. In *Oxford Bibliographies online: Anthropology*. New York: Oxford University Press.

Casasanto, D., and Chrysikou, E. G. (2011). When left is "right": Motor fluency shapes abstract concepts. *Psychological Science, 22*(4), 419–422.

Casasanto, D., and Henetz, T. (2012). Handedness shapes children's abstract concepts. *Cognitive Science, 36*, 359–372.

Casasanto, D., and Jasmin, K. (2010). Good and bad in the hands of politicians. *PLoS One, 5*(7), e11805.

Coan, J. A., and Allen, J. J. B. (2003). Frontal EEG asymmetry and the behavioral activation and inhibition systems. *Psychophysiology, 40*(1), 106–114.

Coren, S. (1992). *The left-hander syndrome: The causes and consequences of left-handedness*. New York: Random House.

Davidson, R. J., and Sutton, S. K. (1995). Affective neuroscience: The emergence of a discipline. *Current Opinion in Neurobiology, 5*, 217–224.

de la Vega, I., de Filippis, M., Lachmair, M., Dudschig, C., and Kaup, B. (2012). Emotional valence and physical space: Limits of interaction. *Journal of Experimental Psychology: Human Perception and Performance, 38*(2), 375–385.

de la Vega, I., Dudschig, C., Lachmair, M., and Kaup, B. (in press). Being someone's *right hand* doesn't always feel right: Bodily experiences affect metaphoric language processing. *Language and Cognitive Processes, 29*(10), 1227–1232.

Everhart, D., Harrison, D., and Crews, W., Jr. (1996). Hemispheric asymmetry as a function of handedness: Perception of facial affect stimuli. *Perceptual and Motor Skills, 82*, 264–266.

Harmon-Jones, E. (2003). Clarifying the emotive functions of asymmetrical frontal cortical activity. *Psychophysiology, 40*, 838–848.

Harmon-Jones, E., Gable, P., and Peterson, C. (2010). The role of asymmetric frontal cortical activity in emotion-related phenomena: A review and update. *Biological Psychology, 84*, 451–462.

Kong, F. (2013). Space-valence associations depend on handedness: Evidence from a bimanual output task. *Psychological Research, 77*(6), 773–779.

Lupyan, G. (2012). Linguistically modulated perception and cognition: the label feedback hypothesis. *Frontiers in Cognition, 3*(54).

McFarland, R. A., and Kennison, R. (1989). Handedness affects emotional valence asymmetry. *Perceptual and Motor Skills, 68*, 435–441.

Natale, M., Gur, R. E., and Gur, R. C. (1983). Hemispheric asymmetries in processing emotional expressions. *Neuropsychologia, 21*(5), 555–565.

Oldfield, R. C. (1971). The assessment and analysis of handedness: The Edinburgh Inventory. *Neuropsychologia, 9*, 97–113.

Ping, R. M., Dhillon, S., and Beilock, S. L. (2009). Reach for what you like: The body's role in shaping preferences. *Emotion Review, 1*, 140–150.

Pulvermüller, F. (2005). Brain mechanisms linking language and action. *Nature Reviews Neuroscience, 6*(7), 576–582.

Reuter-Lorenz, P. A., and Davidson, R. J. (1981). Differential contributions of the two cerebral hemispheres to the perception of happy and sad faces. *Neuropsychologia, 19*, 609–613.

Root, J. C., Wong, P. S., and Kinsbourne, M. (2006). Left hemisphere specialization for response to positive emotional expressions: A divided output methodology. *Emotion, 6*(3), 473–483.

Willems, R. M., Hagoort, P., and Casasanto, D. (2010). Body-specific representations of action verbs: Neural evidence from right- and left-handers. *Psychological Science, 21*(1), 67–74.

Willems, R. M., Labruna, L., D'Esposito, M., Ivry, R., and Casasanto, D. (2011). A functional role for the motor system in language understanding: Evidence from theta-burst TMS. *Psychological Science, 22*(7), 849–854.

Willems, R. M., Toni, I., Hagoort, P., and Casasanto, D. (2009). Body-specific motor imagery of hand actions: Neural evidence from right- and left-handers. *Frontiers in Human Neuroscience, 3*(39), 1–9.

——— (2010). Neural dissociations between action verb understanding and motor imagery. *Journal of Cognitive Neuroscience, 22*(10), 2387–2400.

16

EMBODIED APPROACHES TO LANGUAGE COMPREHENSION

Michael P. Kaschak, Michael Long, and Julie Madden

Embodied approaches to language comprehension are based on the idea that linguistic meaning arises from sensorimotor simulations of the content of the linguistic input (e.g., Glenberg and Gallese 2012; Zwaan 2014). The understanding of a sentence such as *Michael gave Meghan a birthday cake* might involve perceptual simulation (the sight of the cake and candles; Stanfield and Zwaan 2001), motor simulation (the action of presenting the cake; Bub, Masson and Cree 2008), and emotional simulation (the joy of receiving a cake; Havas et al. 2007). The simulations are generated by activating patterns of neural activity that occur when real objects, actions, events, and emotions are perceived (Barsalou 1999; Pulvermüller 2018). In other words, linguistic simulations are built using traces of our experience perceiving and acting in the world.

The *symbol grounding problem* (e.g., Harnad 1990) was a key impetus in the development of embodied approaches to language comprehension. Embodied approaches began to appear in the psycholinguistics literature in the mid-1990s. At this time, major theories of language comprehension were based on arbitrary symbols of the sort that supported computation in digital computers (e.g., Kintsch 1988; MacDonald et al. 1994). The theories did not propose any specific mapping between the symbols and the world that they were meant to reference (e.g., how does the word *cake* relate to the perceptual and motor experience of interacting with cakes?). Harnad (1990) argued that arbitrary symbols of this sort were not sufficient to give rise to meaning. To be meaningful, the symbols must be grounded in something that is meaningful to the comprehender; they must be connected to the world. The symbol grounding argument was taken as a sign that extant theories of comprehension were lacking as accounts of meaning.

Glenberg (1997) suggested that linguistic symbols (such as words and phrases) become meaningful through their grounding in our bodies' systems of perception and action planning. Barsalou (1999) similarly proposed that our conceptual system was grounded in perception and action, and developed the notion of simulation which became a core component of the embodied approach to language comprehension. Embodied approaches thus constituted a proposal for how the symbol grounding problem could be resolved in a linguistic system, and thereby offered a promising new account of language comprehension. In the following years, there was much debate over the symbol grounding problem, the extent to

DOI: 10.4324/9781003322511-22

which "traditional" psycholinguistic accounts provided a sufficient account of meaning, and the extent to which embodied approaches provided an adequate resolution of the symbol grounding problem (see chapters in de Vega et al. 2012; Mahon 2015; Glenberg 2015).

This chapter provides an overview of the embodied approach to language comprehension that has developed over the past quarter century. We discuss the empirical evidence for embodiment (concentrating on behavioral studies), consider critiques of embodied theories of comprehension, and conclude with a look toward the future.

Action Simulation in Language Comprehension

Embodied theories of language comprehension make a strong commitment to the nature of the representations that underlie linguistic meaning – specifically, these theories claim that sensorimotor representations are at the core of the comprehension process. The challenge for researchers exploring the embodied approach is to find ways to demonstrate that a) sensorimotor representations are recruited during the comprehension process, and b) the recruitment of sensorimotor representations is essential to the comprehension process. The main strategy for doing so has been to design experiments that ask participants to engage in different perceptual or motor tasks while processing language in order to demonstrate interplay between the content of the perceptual/motor task and the language processing.

The Action-sentence Compatibility Effect (ACE; Glenberg and Kaschak 2002) was an early demonstration of the role of motor information in sentence comprehension. Participants were asked to read sentences such as *Art passed the note to you* (action toward the body) or *You passed Art the note* (action away from the body). Participants indicated that the sentence was sensible by moving their arm toward (or away from) their body to push a response button. The key finding from the study was that participants were faster to generate the response action (toward or away from the body) when the direction of the action matched the direction of the action described in the sentence. For example, *Art passed the note to you* would elicit a faster response toward the body and *You passed Art the note* would elicit a faster response away from the body.

The claim that processing of sentences about action involves the recruitment of motor information was strengthened by several subsequent studies. Borreggine and Kaschak (2006) replicated the ACE in a slightly different paradigm, and Ibanez et al. (2013) demonstrated that the ACE is impaired in patients with early Parkinson's disease. Zwaan and Taylor (2006) introduced a new motor compatibility effect task that involved the manual rotation of a knob while processing sentences about rotation actions (e.g., turning a door knob). They found that the execution of actions was facilitated when the direction of the rotation in the sentence matched the direction of the rotation required for the experiment task (see also Taylor and Zwaan 2008). Bub and Masson (2012; Bub et al. 2008) employed a paradigm in which participants were trained to execute a range of actions (e.g., a pinching grip; a whole-hand grip). The actions could relate to *functional* dimensions of an object (e.g., you typically act on a calculator by poking at its buttons) or *volumetric* dimensions of an object (e.g., you use a whole-hand grip to pick up a calculator). Across a series of studies, Bub, Masson and colleagues demonstrated that the processing of words and sentences leads to the activation of both functional and volumetric information (with functional information typically activated before volumetric information; Bub et al. 2008), and that the action information activated during the processing of language can affect the execution of motor acts with the hands (e.g., Till et al. 2014). Finally, Olmstead et al. (2009) demonstrated the activity of the motor system during language comprehension by showing that the processing of action sentences affected participants' performance on a bimanual coordination task.

The aforementioned studies provide evidence for the claim that processing action-relevant language elicits motor activity. Another line of research has attempted to extend these findings to the comprehension of language about abstract concepts such as time. It has been suggested that time is understood in terms of space (e.g., the future is in front of you, and the past is behind you), and that movement through time is understood as movement through space (e.g., Casasanto and Boroditsky 2008). The mapping of time to space along the front-back, up-down, or left-right axis varies from culture to culture, and may be affected by factors such as the reading direction used in that culture (e.g., the mental time-line might run left to right in cultures with a left-to-right reading direction, and might run in the opposite direction in cultures with a right-to-left reading direction; Furhman and Boroditsky 2010; Ouellet et al. 2010). Sell and Kaschak (2011) report a motor compatibility effect when participants comprehend sentences about time shifts – they are faster to respond to sentences about a shift to the future when they respond with an arm movement away from their body (future in front) and faster to respond to sentences about a shift to the past with an arm movement toward their body (future behind; Scheifele et al. 2018, replicate this effect). Nevertheless, several other studies have failed to find evidence for response compatibility effects when processing language related to time (e.g., Ulrich and Maienborn 2010; Ulrich et al. 2012). A recent meta-analysis (von Sobbe et al. 2019) suggests that a key factor in eliciting motor compatibility effects in response to sentences about time is the extent to which time is relevant to the judgment that participants are making. Response compatibility effects are larger in cases where participants are making explicit judgments about time than in cases where the temporal information is incidental to the judgments that are made.

The inconsistent observation of motor compatibility effects when processing language about shifts in time suggests that whereas spatial and motoric representations may be useful for representing time under some circumstances, space and action are not necessary for understanding language about time. A similar suggestion has been made about motor compatibility effects in general (e.g., Mahon and Caramazza 2008; Mahon 2015). Just as response compatibility effects are not reliably observed when processing language about time, there is growing evidence that compatibility effects are not reliably observed when processing language about concrete action. Both Papesh (2015) and Morey et al. (2022) report failures to replicate the ACE. Echoing von Sobbe et al.'s (2019) conclusions about temporal language, Papesh (personal communication) reports that the ACE is stronger when participants are made aware of the motor compatibility effect under study than when they are unaware of the importance of action to the experiment. Furthermore, a recent meta-analysis (Winter et al. 2022) demonstrates that the magnitude of the ACE may depend on the timing of the motor response relative to the processing of the sentence.

At present, the extant literature suggests that motor representations play a role in language comprehension, at least under some conditions. We need to learn more about the conditions under which these effects arise in order to assess whether the strongest forms of the embodied approach to language comprehension are viable.

Perceptual Simulation in Language Comprehension

The literature reviewed in the previous section suggests that motor representations may play a role in the comprehension process. A similar body of literature has explored the extent to which perceptual representations support language comprehension. Some of the earliest work suggesting the role of perceptual simulation in language comprehension comes from Stanfield and Zwaan (2001; see also Zwaan et al. 2002). The experiments used a sentence–picture verification procedure. Participants first processed a sentence such as *The eagle is in the sky* or *The eagle is in the nest*. The sentences named objects or animals that would have different shapes or orientations across situations. For example, an eagle in the sky would have outstretched wings but an eagle in the nest would have its wings folded in. After processing the sentence, participants saw a picture and needed to indicate whether the picture depicted an entity from the preceding sentence. Critically, the picture could either match the preceding sentence (*The eagle is in the sky* followed by a picture of an eagle with outstretched wings) or mismatch the preceding sentence (*The eagle is in the sky* followed by a picture of an eagle with folded-in wings). Both pictures would get a *yes* response because they depicted an eagle. However, participants were faster to respond to the picture of the eagle when the eagle was presented in a shape or orientation that matched the situation depicted in the preceding sentence. Zwaan and colleagues interpreted these results as suggesting that participants had constructed a perceptual simulation of the events described in the sentence. Simulating a flying eagle subsequently facilitated the processing of a picture of a flying eagle.

Variations on Stanfield and Zwaan's (2001) sentence–picture paradigm have been used to examine different aspects of perceptual simulation. As one example, Connell (2007) asked participants to process sentences such as *The steak was cooked/raw* before viewing and responding to a picture. The picture of the steak would depict the steak as brown (matching the cooked steak, but mismatching a raw steak) or red (matching the raw steak, but mismatching the cooked steak). Connell (2007) reported that response times were faster for the mismatching pictures (e.g., the picture of a red steak following *The steak was cooked*). Connell (2007) interpreted these data as support for the idea that the visual simulation of an object during sentence processing involves the simulation of its color. However, it is worth noting that Zwaan and Pecher's (2012) replication of this study resulted in the opposite result: participants responded to pictures of the objects more quickly when the color of the object matched the color of the object implied by the preceding sentence (e.g., the picture of a red steak following *The steak was raw*). The reason for the discrepant results has not been resolved. Nevertheless, studies using other paradigms (e.g., Richter and Zwaan 2009; Connell and Lynott 2009; Hoeben Mannaert et al. 2017) appear to converge on the finding that participants respond to visual stimuli faster when the color implied by the preceding linguistic content matches the color of the visual stimulus than when the color implied by the preceding linguistic content mismatches the color of the visual stimulus.

The aforementioned studies suggest that static perceptual properties such as orientation and color are represented during language comprehension. Evidence also suggests that dynamic properties such as motion are also represented during the comprehension. Zwaan et al. (2004) asked participants to process sentences such as *The pitcher threw the ball to you*. Subsequent to this, participants saw two pictures of the critical object (in this case, a ball) presented in rapid succession. The size of the ball would either be bigger in the second picture than in the first (as would be the case if the ball approached you) or smaller in the second picture than the first (as would be the case if the ball was moving away from you). Participants were faster to respond when the sequence of pictures matched the motion that was implied by the preceding sentence (e.g., seeing a sequence in which the second ball was bigger after the sentence *The pitcher threw the ball to you*). Kaschak et al. (2005) and Meteyard et al. (2007) provide further evidence for the simulation of motion during sentence processing. Kaschak et al. (2005) asked participants to listen to sentences such as *The car approached you* while simultaneously viewing an image depicting motion toward or away from the participant. They found that participants were faster to respond to the sentences when the visual motion mismatched the motion implied by the sentence (seeing motion away from the participant while processing *The car approached you*). They interpret this mismatch advantage as indicative of a resource-sharing problem: the visual system is processing an external stimulus depicting motion toward the participant, and these perceptual resources are less available to simulate the motion of the car toward the participant. Like Kaschak et al. (2005), Meteyard et al. (2007) presented visual and linguistic stimuli simultaneously. They report that the processing of verbs implying upward or downward motion affects participants' ability to detect upward or downward motion in visual stimuli. Meteyard et al. (2007) likewise show that the perception of visual motion affects the processing of motion verbs (e.g., responding to *rise* is faster when viewing upward motion than when viewing downward motion). Thus, it appears that the perception of visual motion affects language processing, and that the processing of language affects the perception of visual motion (see Kaschak et al. 2006, for a demonstration of similar effects with the perception of auditory motion).

Another set of studies has demonstrated that language comprehenders' simulation of motion represents the speed at which the motion takes place (e.g., Speed and Vigliocco 2014; Van Dam et al. 2017). Speed and Vigliocco (2014) asked participants to listen to sentences while viewing a visual scene. Their pattern of eye movements on the visual scene (particularly looking time) was affected by the speed of the action described in the sentence. Van Dam et al. (2017) further suggest that the nature of the simulation of speed may depend on how quickly the depicted event unfolds. Scenes involving faster motion appear to be grounded in a visual simulation, and scenes involving slower motion appear to be grounded in motor simulations.

Language comprehension appears to involve the simulation of perceptual features of the event being described, at least in the case of visual and auditory features (see Speed and Majid 2020, for evidence that simulation of perceptual information from other senses – smell, touch, and taste – is weak or absent during the comprehension process). Comprehension also appears to cue participants' attention to spatial locations. Dudschig et al. (2012) demonstrated that processing words such as *cloud* (an object typically observed above the participant) and *shoe* (an object typically observed below the participant) cued the participants' attention to upper and lower locations on a computer screen. Dudschig et al. (2012) further demonstrated that processing *up* or *down* words facilitated the execution of upward or downward eye movements, respectively. Ostarek and Vigliocco (2017) provide a qualification to these effects, suggesting that the perceptual effects occur around 250 msec (but not earlier or later) after processing words implying *up* or *down* locations.

Earlier, we discussed recent findings that cast doubt on the claim that motor representations are a central or essential component of the comprehension process under all circumstances. Similar work has been done in the domain of visual perception. As one example, Ostarek et al. (2019) suggest that match effects of the sort observed by Stanfield and Zwaan

(2001) are not modulated by viewing visual noise during the comprehension process. Because viewing the noise should attenuate the participants' ability to generate a visual simulation during the comprehension of the sentence (the basis of the match effect), an embodied account would need to explain why this manipulation does not interfere with the match effect. In addition, Rommers et al. (2013) suggest that perceptual information most strongly affects performance in tasks such as Stanfield and Zwaan's (2001) when participants are explicitly engaging in a visual imagery strategy during the processing of the sentence (but see Zwaan 2014, for a reply). As in the case of the motor compatibility effects, it appears that more work needs to be done to determine how and when perceptual information is recruited during sentence processing, and the role that such information plays in constructing the meaning of the sentence.

Embodiment: Challenges, and A Look to the Future

Our chapter focused on findings that support the claims of the embodied approach to comprehension. Nevertheless, it seems that the strongest form of the embodiment hypothesis –that sensorimotor simulations are a necessary part of language comprehension – is not consistent with the extant literature. We mentioned demonstrations suggesting that perceptual (e.g., Ostarek et al. 2019) and motor (e.g., von Sobbe et al. 2019) simulations are not necessary for comprehending some types of language. Mahon and Caramazza (2008) discuss findings from neuroscience which they interpret as evidence against the claim that sensorimotor simulations are necessary for comprehension. They argue that the recruitment of perceptual or motor areas of the cortex during comprehension does not entail that the comprehension process is embodied. These observations have led some to propose hybrid embodied-symbolic approaches to language comprehension. On these accounts, comprehension can be achieved through both abstract, symbolic linguistic representations (e.g., the co-occurrences of particular words and phrases) and perceptual simulations (see Mahon and Caramazza 2008, Zwaan 2014, and Connell 2019, for examples of such approaches). Abstract, symbolic representations make contact with sensorimotor representations (Mahon and Caramazza 2008), but access to the sensorimotor representations is not required for comprehension.

One response to these criticisms of embodied approaches to language is to note that the version of "embodiment" that they attack is incomplete. The theoretical adversary assumed in many of these critiques is one in which embodied language is entirely conflated with the comprehension-as-simulation view (e.g., Mahon and Caramazza 2008). The empirical record makes it clear that criticism of the comprehension-as-simulation view is warranted, but this is not the only way in which language could (or should) be viewed as embodied. Language is action, both in a physical sense (the movement required to generate a linguistic signal) and a social sense (what social acts are we performing when we use language?; Clark 1996; Brown and Levinson 1987). Pickering and Garrod (2013) argue that we can think of embodiment as both *embodiment of form* (the perceptual and motor information that informs our production and perception of the linguistic signal) and *embodiment of content* (akin to the comprehension-as-simulation idea). This broader perspective on what it might mean for language to be embodied may provide a theoretical framework through which the full range of sensorimotor contributions to language use can be understood. We see this is a crucial direction for development in the embodiment program (see Wilson and Golonka 2013).

Another direction for development in the embodiment research program is methodological. As noted earlier, there are published reports suggesting that well-known "embodiment" effects are not as reliable as they initially appeared (e.g., Rommers et al. 2013; Morey et al. 2022). Part of the replicability issue may be that experiments in this area of research suffered from the same general flaws that afflicted experiments in many areas of psychology – for example, low sample sizes and behavioral measures that did not have good psychometric properties. Another part of the issue is likely that embodied theories of language do not fully specify the nature of the mechanisms involved in the comprehension process. For example, several studies report that the magnitude of the ACE varies based on the timing of the motor response relative to the processing of the language (see Winter et al. 2022, for a discussion). Nevertheless, we lack a precise theory to explain the source of these timing-based differences and when we should expect them to appear. It is our sense that the solutions to these issues are intertwined. As we develop more precise theories of embodied language comprehension, it will be possible to generate more precise and reliable tests of the role of sensorimotor processes in language comprehension.

In the quarter century since embodied approaches to language arrived in the field, much progress has been made to delineate the contributions that sensorimotor information makes to the comprehension process. We are excited to see what the next quarter century brings as research on embodiment moves from its youthful exuberance to a more mature phase of theorizing and empirical investigation.

References

Barsalou, L. W. (1999) Perceptual symbol systems. *Behavioral and Brain Sciences*, 22, 577–660.

Borreggine, K. L., and Kaschak, M. P. (2006) "The action–sentence compatibility effect: It's all in the timing," *Cognitive Science*, 30, 1097–1112.

Brown, P., and Levinson, S. C. (1987) *Politeness theory: Some universals in language usage*, Cambridge University Press.

Bub, D. N., and Masson, M. E. J. (2012) "On the dynamics of action representations evoked by names of manipulable objects," *Journal of Experimental Psychology: General*, 141, 502–517.

Bub, D. N., Masson, M. E. J., and Cree, G. S. (2008) "Evocation of functional and volumetric gestural knowledge by objects and words," *Journal of Memory and Language*, 106, 27–58.

Casasanto, D., and Boroditsky, L. (2008) "Time in the mind: Using space to think about time," *Cognition*, 106, 579–593.

Clark, H. H. (1996) *Using language*, Cambridge University Press.

Connell, L. (2007) "Representing object color in language comprehension," *Cognition*, 102, 476–485.

——— (2019) "What have labels ever done for us? The linguistic shortcut in conceptual processing," *Language, Cognition and Neuroscience*, 34, 1308–1318.

Connell, L., and Lynott, D. (2009) "Is a bear white in the woods? Parallel representation of implied color during language comprehension," *Psychonomic Bulletin and Review*, 16, 573–577.

de Vega, M., Glenberg, A. M., and Graesser, A. C. (eds) (2012) *Symbols and embodiment: Debates on meaning and cognition*, Oxford University Press.

Dudschig, C., Lachmair, M., de la Vega, I., de Fillipis, M., and Kaup, B. (2012) "From top to bottom: Spatial shifts of attention caused by linguistic stimuli," *Cognitive Processing*, 13, 151–154.

Furhman, O., and Boroditsky, L. (2010) "Cross-cultural differences in mental representations of time: Evidence from an implicit non-linguistic task," *Cognitive Science*, 34, 1430–1451.

Glenberg, A. M. (1997) "What memory is for," *Behavioral and Brain Sciences*, 20, 1–55.

——— (2015) "Few believe the world is flat: How embodiment is changing the scientific understanding of cognition," *Canadian Journal of Experimental PSychology*, 69, 165–171.

Glenberg, A. M., and Gallese, V. (2012) "Action-based language: A theory of language acquisition, comprehension, and production," *Cortex*, 48, 905–922.

Glenberg, A. M., and Kaschak, M. P. (2002) "Grounding language in action," *Psychonomic Bulletin and Review*, 9, 558–565.

Harnad, S. (1990) "The symbol grounding problem," *Physica D*, 42, 335–346.

Havas, D. A., Glenberg, A. M., and Rinck, M. (2007) "Emotion simulation during language comprehension," *Psychonomic Bulletin and Review*, 14, 436–441.

Hoeben Mannaert. L. N., Dijkstra, K., and Zwaan, R. A. (2017) "Is color an integral part of a rich mental simulation?" *Memory and Cognition*, 45, 974–982.

Ibanez, A., Cardona, J. F., dos Santos, Y. V., Blenkmann, A., Aravena, P., Roca, M., Hurtado, E., Nerguizian, M., Amoruso, L., Gomez-Arevalo, G., Chase A., Burbovsky, A., Gershanik, O., Kochen, S., Glenberg, A., Manes, F., Bekinschtein, T. (2013) "Motor-language coupling: Direct evidence from early Parkinson's disease and intracranial cortical recordings," *Cortex*, 49, 968–984.

Kaschak, M. P., Madden, C. J., Therriault, D. J., Yaxley, R. H., Aveyard, M. E., Blanchard, A. A., and Zwaan, R. A. (2005) "Perception of motion affects language processing," *Cognition*, 94, B79–B89.

Kaschak, M. P., Zwaan, R. A., Aveyard, M., and Yaxley, R. H. (2006) "Perception of auditory motion affects sentence processing," *Cognitive Science*, 30, 733–744.

Kintsch, W. (1988) "The role of knowledge in discourse comprehension: A construction-integration model," *Psychological Review*, 95, 163–182.

MacDonald, M. C., Pearlmutter, N. J., and Seidenberg, M. S. (1994) "Lexical nature of syntactic ambiguity resolution," *Psychological Review*, 101, 676–703.

Mahon, B. Z. (2015) "The burden of embodied cognition," *Canadian Journal of Experimental Psychology*, 69, 172–178.

Mahon, B. Z., and Caramazza, A. (2008) "A critical look at the embodied cognition hypothesis and a new proposal for grounding conceptual content," *Journal of Physiology-Paris*, 102, 59–70.

Meteyard, L., Bahrami, B., and Vigliocco, G. (2007) "Motion detection and motion verbs," *Psychological Science*, 18, 1007–1013.

Morey, R. D., Kaschak, M. P., Díez-Álamo, A. M., Glenberg, A. M., Zwaan, R. A., Lakens, D., Ibáñez, A., García, A., Gianelli, C., Jones, J. L., Madden, J., Alifano, F., Bergen, B., Bloxsom, N. G., Bub, D. N., Cai, Z. G., Chartier, C. R., Chatterjee, A., Conwell, E., Cook, S. W., Davis, J. D., Evers, E., Girard, S., Harter, D., Hartung, F., Herrera, E., Huettig, F., Humphries, S., Juanchich, M., Kühne, K., Lu, S., Lynes, T., Masson, M. E. J., Ostarek, M., Pessers, S., Reglin, R., Steegen, S., Thiessen, E. D., Thomas, L. E., Trott, S., Vanderkerckhove, J., Vanpaemel, W., Vlachou, M., Williams, K., and Ziv-Crispel, N. (2022) "A pre-registered multi-lab non-replication of the Action-sentence Compatibility Effect (ACE)," *Psychonomic Bulletin and Review*, 29, 613–626.

Olmstead, A. J., Viswanathan, N., Aicher, K. A., and Fowler, C. A. (2009) "Sentence comprehension affects the dynamics of bimanual coordination: Implications for embodied cognition," *Quarterly Journal of Experimental Psychology*, 62, 2409–2417.

Ostarek, M., Joosen, D., Ishag, A., de Nijs, M., and Huettig, F. (2019) "Are visual processes causally involved in "perceptual simulation" effects in the sentence-picture verification task?" *Cognition*, 182, 84–94.

Ostarek, M., and Vigliocco, G. (2017) "Reading sky and seeing a cloud: On the relevance of events for perceptual simulation," *Journal of Experimental Psychology: Learning, Memory, and Cognition*, 43, 579–590.

Ouellet, M., Santiago, J., Israeli, Z., and Gabay, S. (2010) "Is the future the right time?" *Experimental Psychology*, 57, 308–314.

Papesh, M. H. (2015) "Just out of reach: On the reliability of the action-sentence compatibility effect," *Journal of Experimental Psychology: General*, 144, 116–141.

Pickering, M. J., and Garrod, S. (2013) "An integrated theory of language production and comprehension," *Behavioral and Brain Sciences*, 36, 329–392.

Pulvermüller, F. (2018) "Neural reuse of action perception circuits for language, concepts and communication," *Progress in Neurobiology*, 160, 1–44.

Richter, T., and Zwaan, R. A. (2009) "Processing of color words activates color representations," *Cognition*, 111, 383–389.

Rommers, J., Meyer, A. S., and Huettig, F. (2013) "Object shape and orientation do not routinely influence performance during language processing," *Psychological Science, 24*, 2218–2225.

Scheifele, E., Eikmeier, V., Alex-Ruf, S., Maienborn, C., and Ulrich, R. (2018) "A replication of "Processing Time Shifts Affects the Execution of Motor Responses (Sell and Kaschak, 2011, Experiment 1)", *The Quantitative Methods for Psychology, 14*, 8–11.

Sell, A. J., and Kaschak, M. P. (2011) "Processing time shifts affects the execution of motor responses," *Brain and Language, 117*, 39–44.

Speed, L. J., and Majid, A. (2020) "Grounding language in the neglected senses of touch, taste, and smell," *Cognitive Neuropsychology, 37*, 363–392.

Speed, L. J., and Vigliocco, G. (2014) "Eye movements reveal the dynamic simulation of speed in language," *Cognitive Science, 38*, 367–382.

Stanfield, R. A., and Zwaan, R. A. (2001) "The effect of implied orientation derived from verbal context on picture recognition," *Psychological Science, 12*, 153–156.

Taylor, L. J., and Zwaan, R. A. (2008) "Motor resonance and linguistic focus," *Quarterly Journal of Experimental Psychology, 61*, 896–904.

Till, B. C., Masson, M. E. J., Bub, D. N., and Driessen, P. F. (2014) "Embodied effects of conceptual knowledge continuously perturb the hand in flight," *Psychological Science, 25*, 1637–1648.

Ulrich, R., Eilmeier, V., de la Vega, I., Fernandez, S. R., Alex-Ruf, S., and Maienborn, C. (2012) "With the past behind and the future ahead: Back-to-front representation of past and future sentences," *Memory and Cognition, 40*, 483–495.

Ulrich, R., and Maienborn, C. (2010) "Left-right coding of past and future in language: The mental timeline during sentence processing," *Cognition, 117*, 126–138.

van Dam, W. O., Speed, L. J., Lai, V. T., Vigliocco, G., and Desai, R. H. (2017) "Effects of motion speed in action representations," *Brain and Language, 168*, 47–56.

von Sobbe, L., Scheifele, E., Maienborn, C., and Ulrich, R. (2019) "The space-time congruency effect: A meta-analysis," *Cognitive Science, 43*, e12709.

Wilson, A. D., and Golonka, S. (2013) "Embodied cognition is not what you think it is," *Frontiers in Psychology, 4*, 58.

Winter, A., Dudschig, C., Miller, J., Ulrich, R., Kaup, B. (2022) "The action-sentence compatibility effect (ACE): Meta-analysis of a benchmark finding for embodiment," *Acta Psychologica, 230*, 103712.

Zwaan, R. A. (2014) "Embodiment and language comprehension: Reframing the discussion," *Trends in Cognitive Sciences, 18*, 229–234.

Zwaan, R. A., Madden, C. J., Yaxley, R. H., and Aveyard, M. E. (2004) "Moving words: Dynamic representations in language comprehension," *Cognitive Science, 28*, 611–619.

Zwaan, R. A., and Pecher, D. (2012) "Revisiting mental simulation in language comprehension: Six replication attempts," *PLoS One, 7*, e51382.

Zwaan, R. A., Stanfield, R. A., and Yaxley, R. H. (2002) "Language comprehenders mentally represent the shape of objects," *Psychological Science, 13*, 168–171.

Zwaan, R. A., and Taylor, L. J. (2006) "Seeing, acting, understanding: Motor resonance in language comprehension," *Journal of Experimental Psychology: General, 135*, 1–11.

17

THE GROUNDING OF CONCRETE AND ABSTRACT LANGUAGE

Consolidated evidence, open issues, and new challenges

Claudia Scorolli and Claudia Mazzuca

Embodied view of language

Embodied perspectives on concepts (Barsalou, 1999) emphasize that cognition is shaped by both the physical properties of the world (i.e., "grounded") and the physical constraintsw of our body (i.e., "embodied"); they also underline that cognitive processing strongly depends on current constraints and task demands (i.e., "situated"; Pezzulo, et al. 2013). Behavioral and brain-imaging studies collected in the last 20 years converge in suggesting that seeing an object, for example a Lego brick, activates motor information (Ellis and Tucker 2000).[1] Importantly, the physical context, namely the actual possibility of reaching the object (Ambrosini et al. 2012), as well as the social and affective relations it affords, seem to modulate this motor information (Scorolli 2019). To illustrate, recent proposals (Caravà and Scorolli 2020) stress the importance of the affective dimension in object–agent interactions, emphasizing the role affective and emotional components of objects have in motor responses triggered by visual recognition of those objects.

Just as viewing an object such as a plastic construction toy activates contextually specific motor information, the processing of nouns ("Lego") or verbs ("assembling") referring to that object recruits the same brain areas involved when perceiving and interacting with it. Thus, words can be conceived as surrogates for more direct interactions with the environment (Glenberg 1997). From cognitive linguistics to neuroscience, empirical evidence has shown that language comprehension results in embodied representations encoding action or perception tendencies related to linguistic referents, that is in *simulations* of experiences with things in the world (Gallese and Goldman 1998; Glenberg and Kaschak 2002).[2] The notion of simulation applied to the understanding of a verb–noun combination as "interlocking Legos" refers to the activation of the same sensorimotor neural correlates[3] involved when we previously executed that specific action (Gallese 2008; Gallese and Sinigaglia 2011).

Concrete words: the specificity of Simulation

The mental simulation of motor actions that occurs during language processing invokes specific sensorimotor experiences. In the understanding of words referring to concrete

DOI: 10.4324/9781003322511-23

entities or processes (e.g., "ball," "throwing the ball") many different aspects might drive simulations—also depending on task demands. The sections below present an overview of some of the simulation effects that have been reported in the literature, according to specific properties of concrete referents.

Object properties

Embodied simulations are sensitive to differences pertaining to intrinsic object properties, such as shape (Zwaan et al. 2002), size (Glover and Dixon 2002), and color (Connell 2007), and extrinsic properties,[4] such as orientation (Stanfield and Zwaan 2001) and distance (Winter and Bergen 2012). In a simple sentence-picture verification task, participants read a sentence implying different orientations (or shapes/colors) of an object (e.g., "John put the pencil in the cup" *vs.* "in the drawer"). Immediately after, they are presented with pictures of objects whose properties match or mismatch the ones evoked by the sentence (vertical *vs.* horizontal axis of symmetry). The task consists in judging whether the object presented was mentioned in the sentence or not. Even if object visual properties are irrelevant to the task, participants' responses are faster in case of agreement between the orientation suggested in the sentence and the orientation of the depicted object.[5] Further evidence shows that the simulation triggered by language understanding is also sensitive to implied directions, as participants are faster when the linguistically evoked motion unfolds in a direction opposite to that of the simultaneously presented visual stimuli (Kaschak, et al. 2005). Taken together, this evidence suggests perceptual and conceptual processes are strictly interwoven and dynamically interact in language understanding. However, the direction of the influence of perception on language has been a matter of debate—as sometimes perceptual simulations have been found to facilitate language comprehension (e.g., Stanfield and Zwaan 2001), while sometimes they interfered with it (e.g., Kaschak et al. 2005). To account for facilitation and interference effects, two complementary explanations have been provided: the first based on the temporal overlap between perceptual stimulation and conceptual task, the second on the extent to which the perceptual stimulation can be integrated into the simulation constructed during language comprehension.[6]

Although the examples above refer to the visual modality, it is worth noting that simulations triggered by language processing also engage the auditory (Pecher et al. 2003),[7] tactile, gustatory, and olfactory systems (although evidence for sensorimotor simulation in touch, taste, and smell is weaker; see Speed and Majid 2020).

Relational properties

Conceptual knowledge guides action in the world: Embodied simulations are consistently sensitive to the properties of objects, conveyed through different modalities referred to by language, but also to the reciprocal dynamic relation between agents and objects. For instance, Borghi, Glenberg, and Kaschak (2004) presented participants with sentences describing objects or locations from an inside (e.g., "You are eating in a restaurant") or an outside (e.g., "You are waiting outside a restaurant") perspective, followed by a target word that could be either a part of the object or not. Importantly, the parts of the objects could typically be found inside (e.g., "table") or outside (e.g., "sign"). Participants were asked to verify whether the target word was a part of the object. Results show that response latencies in pressing a key are affected by the inside *vs.* outside perspective induced by language (e.g., "table" and "sign" are respectively advantaged by "You are eating in a restaurant" and "You are waiting outside a restaurant"). When manipulating the motor response required for participants to answer, namely an upward *vs.* a downward movement, there was an advantage if the final movement position was compatible with the typical location of the mentioned object part (e.g., upward movement for "hair" as part of the "doll").

Likewise, participants are faster and more accurate in judging the sensibility of sentences referring to oppositely directed actions in case of correspondence between the direction implied by language and the one required to respond (e.g., button near the body for "Put your finger under your nose") rather than in the case of non-correspondence (button far from the body).[8] This has been called the *action–sentence compatibility effect* (ACE, Glenberg and Kaschak 2002), and has been taken as further evidence supporting the grounding of language in bodily actions (see Table 17.1).

Effectors and action goal

The semantics of action verbs can refer to different body parts, as in "grasping" (hand) or "kicking" (foot), and to a specific final goal, as in "grasping the toffee to eat it" or "grasping the eggplant to cook it." Empirical studies have investigated the processing of hand, foot, or mouth actions presenting single verbs (Pulvermüller et al. 2001; Buccino et al. 2005) or verbs embedded in sentences (Scorolli and Borghi 2007). Depending on the method, analyses were performed on event-related potentials, on motor-evoked potentials from hand muscles, or on response latencies collected from different effectors. Findings converge in demonstrating that action words referring to different effectors elicit neurophysiological activity with different cortical topographies. Consistently, behavioral evidence shows a timing modulation determined by the possible matching, or mismatching,[9] between the effector referred to by language and the one used to respond (e.g., responses with feet for verb–noun combinations like "throwing the ball" *vs.* "kicking the ball").

Action plans are encoded not just at a proximal, but also at a distal level (Hommel et al. 2001). Indeed, the simulation entailed by language processing was also found to be sensitive to the final goal expressed by the sentence. For example, Borghi and Scorolli (2009) reported a similar dominant-right hand responses advantage for verb–noun pairs referring to manual actions and mouth actions, but not for pairs referring to foot actions. This is consistent with the fact that an action performed with the mouth (e.g., eating a slice of bread), but not with the foot, usually implies a previous action with the hand (e.g., slicing the bread and bringing it to the mouth). So, these results suggest that language is capable of triggering simulations of complex relational motor schema, like the ones entailed in a composite action like eating. In addition, this pattern of results is also consistent with evidence indicating that at the neural level hand and mouth actions activate contiguous regions (Pulvermüller et al. 2001)—supporting striking proposals suggesting that language could have evolved from gestures (Corballis 2002; Arbib 2005).

Grammatical features

The evidence reviewed so far suggests that simulation is affected by content words, like nouns and verbs. Nonetheless, grammar also affects language-driven mental simulations. The meaning of noun/verb specifies which kind of object/action to simulate; grammar

Table 17.1 Some evidence on the specificity of the simulation activated by concrete words.

Evidence on concrete words and the specificity of the simulation

Semantic features				Relational properties		Grammatical categories and constructions			
Object properties							Focus on different aspects		
Intrinsic object features		Extrinsic object features		Perspective	Action sentence compatibility	Effectors	Agent	Action	Object
Shape	Size	Orientation	Object motion — Direction	Physical perspective	ACE effect	Kind — Hand, foot, mouth	Pronoun	Adjective vs. Adverb	Adjective vs. Adverb
Zwaan, Stanfield, and Yaxley 2002.	Glover and Dixon 2002; Borghi and Riggio 2009.	Stanfield and Zwaan 2001; Borghi and Riggio 2009.	Zwaan, Madden, Yaxley, and Aveyard 2002. Kaschak, Madden, Therriault, Yaxley, Aveyard, Blanchard, and Zwaan 2005.	Borghi, Glenberg, and Kaschak 2004. Brunyé, Ditman, Mahoney, Augustyn, and Taylor 2009. Sato and Bergen 2013;	Glenberg and Kaschak 2002. Glenberg, Sato, Cattaneo, Riggio, Palumbo, and Buccino 2008. Bergen and Wheeler 2010.	Pulvermüller, Härle, and Hummel 2001. Buccino, Riggio, Melli, Binkofski, Gallese, and Rizzolatti 2005. Scorolli and Borghi 2007. Kemmerer and Gonzalez Castillo 2010.	Brunyé, Ditman, Mahoney, Augustyn, and Taylor 2009. Sato and Bergen 2013.	Gentilucci, Benuzzi, Bertolani, Daprati, and Gangitano 2000.	Gentilucci, Benuzzi, Bertolani, Daprati, and Gangitano 2000.

Color	Mass-weight	Distance	Social perspective	Right, left hand	Adjective vs. Verb — Action	Adjective vs. Verb — Verb
Connell 2007.	Scorolli, Borghi, and Glenberg 2009.	Winter and Bergen 2012.	Gianelli, Scorolli, and Borghi 2013.	Borghi and Scorolli 2009.	Gentilucci 2003 Madden and Zwaan 2003. Kemmerer and Gonzalez Castillo 2010. Bergen and Wheeler 2010.	Gentilucci, 2003. Bergen and Wheeler 2010.

specifies higher-order characteristics of the simulation (Glenberg and Gallese 2012; Sato et al. 2013). Bergen and Wheeler (2010) found that progressive aspect drives readers to mentally simulate the central process of a described motor event, while perfect aspect does not. These "second-order effects" operate over the representations evoked by content words, for example modulating the specific part of simulation readers focus on. In "Virginia is brushing her teeth," progressive aspects accentuate the internal structure of an event, while in "Virginia has brushed her teeth," perfect aspects highlight the resulting end state (Dowty 1977).

To summarize, research investigating the motor and perceptual underpinnings of language comprehension showed that modality-specific simulations can be triggered by different aspects of linguistic constructions. The entanglement between perception, action, and language seems rather straightforward in the case of words whose referents are things that can be perceived through the five senses. In the following sections, instead, we will address this relation looking at words whose referents cannot be experienced only through sensory and perceptual modalities, i.e., abstract words.

The issue of Abstractness

The evidence above strongly supports the main claim of standard embodied accounts: concepts are grounded in perception and action systems, and therefore they are modal. However, all these empirical studies focus on words with concrete referents (e.g., highly imageable words whose referents can be perceived through the five senses) and have limited reach with respect to abstract concepts (Louwerse and Jeuniaux 2010; Borghi and Cimatti 2009; 2012; Dove 2009; Mahon and Caramazza 2008). While many studies have been devoted to this important topic, from an embodied and grounded perspective the issue of abstractness remains puzzling (Borghi 2023; Borghi et al. 2017; Mazzuca et al. 2021; Conca et al. 2021; Dove 2022).Indeed, while the representation and processing of concrete words can be explained through modality-specific simulations, the extent to which these can be elicited by words with a looser grip on perception and action is still a matter of debate.

To tackle the issue of abstractness, different proposals have been advanced. Some studies showed that abstract words refer metaphorically to concrete referents (Lakoff and Johnson 1999; Casasanto and Boroditsky 2008), that abstract sentences too recruit the motor system (Glenberg et al. 2008; Glenberg and Gallese 2012), and that abstract concepts elicit situations and simulations of internal states (Barsalou and Wiemer-Hastings 2005). This research, though compelling, refers only to a limited subset of phenomena (see Table 17.2).

In an effort to generalize these results, a first step could be to study the abstract–concrete dimension as a continuum (Wiemer-Hastings et al. 2001). In a cross-cultural study, Scorolli et al. (2011) combined a concrete verb with both a concrete and an abstract noun, and an abstract verb with the same concrete and abstract nouns. Participants evaluated the sensibility of the combinations. To account for differences in grammatical features, two syntactically different languages were considered: German and Italian. In German, nouns precede verbs, whereas Italian exhibits the opposite pattern. The processing of mixed combinations (concrete–abstract) was slower than that of compatible ones, and it was modulated by the specific language. Regardless of the grammatical class, the first concrete word sped up responses. Findings from mixed combinations are consistent with the claim that both abstract and concrete words are represented modally and activate parallel systems: concrete words are thought to rely more on perception and action areas, while abstract words more

Table 17.2 Proposals and evidence on abstract concepts and words

Proposals and evidence on abstract concepts and words

'Aspecific' proposals			Continuum	Multiple types of representations theories			Specificity of abstract words					Linguistic diversity and relativity
Recruitment of motor system	Conceptual metaphors	simulations of internal states	Abstract-concrete	LASS	representational pluralism	WAT	Acquisition of abstract words	Emotional Aspects	Intra-categories differences	Numbers	Linguistic and social information	
Glenberg, Sato, Cattaneo, Riggio, Palumbo, and Buccino 2008. Glenberg and Gallese 2012.	Lakoff and Johnson 1999. Casasanto and Boroditsky 2008.	Barsalou and Wiemer-Hastings 2005.	Wiemer-Hastings et al. 2001. Scorolli, Binkofski, Buccino, Nicoletti, Riggio, and Borghi 2011. Scorolli, Jacquet, Binkofski, Nicoletti, Tessari, and Borghi 2012. Sakreida, Scorolli, Menz, Heim, Borghi, and Binkofski 2013.	Barsalou, Santos, Simmons and Wilson 2008.	Dove 2009.	Borghi and Cimatti 2010. Scorolli, Daprati, Nico, and Borghi 2016. Borghi, Binkofski, Castelfranchi, Cimatti, Scorolli, and Tummolini 2017. Borghi, Barca, Binkofski, Castelfranchi, Pezzulo, and Tummolini 2019.	Lund, Sidhu and Pexman 2019. Ponari, Norbury, and Vigliocco 2018. Bellagamba, Borghi, Mazzuca, Pecora, Ferrara, and Fogel 2022. 'Novel' words Borghi, Flumini, Cimatti, Marocco and Scorolli 2011. Granito, Scorolli, and Borghi 2014.	Vigliocco, Kousta, Della Rosa, Vinson, Tettamanti, Devlin, and Cappa 2014. Barca, Mazzuca, and Borghi 2017. Buccino, Colagè, Silipo, and D'Ambrosio 2019.	Villani, Lugli, Liuzza, and Borghi 2019. Kiefer and Harpaintner 2020. Mazzuca and Santarelli 2022.	Fischer 2012. Fischer and Shaki 2018.	Fini, Era, Da Rold, Candidi, and Borghi 2021. Borghi 2022. Diveica, Pexman, and Binney 2022. Mazzuca, Falcinelli, Michall, Tummolini, and Borghi 2022.	Borghi, Barca, Binkofski, and Tummolini 2018. Davis and Yee 2021. Kemmerer 2022. See also Henrich, Heine, and Norenzayan 2010.

on sensorimotor linguistic areas (Paivio 1986). The greater difficulty in processing abstract words—indicated by their slower response times—is accounted for by their later acquisition (Borghi et al. 2017).

The same paradigm was also used in studies involving both transcranial magnetic stimulation (Scorolli et al. 2012) and functional magnetic resonance (Sakreida et al. 2013). They converged in showing that both concrete and abstract multi-word expressions engage core areas of the sensorimotor neural network. While phrases containing concrete verbs imply a direct early activation of modality-specific systems (in this case hand-related motor areas, as concrete items featured graspable objects and related motor verbs), the activation of the same system is delayed in the case of phrases containing abstract verbs: the processing of abstract verbs could first engage mouth-related motor areas that later affect the contiguous areas (hand areas). Furthermore, the processing of abstract noun–abstract verb combinations has been linked to a pronounced activation in the left anterior middle temporal gyrus, an area close to the language processing system (Price 2010).

Acquisition of new words

The findings reported in the previous section suggest concrete and abstract concepts elicit different motor patterns, because they might be acquired through different mechanisms. Intuitively, in acquiring concrete words, we first experience concrete entities (e.g., pencil), and then we tag them using linguistic labels (we learn the name "pencil"). With abstract words, we might initially learn a word (the label) and then "tag" it with our sensorimotor experience, that is, we use the word to assemble a set of experiences (e.g., we probably put together different experiences of freedom once we have learned the word "freedom"). Abstract words refer to more varied experiences (i.e., they have lower "situational systematicity"; see Davis, Altmann, and Yee 2020) than concrete words, and language might be a necessary tool to keep all these (bodily and social) experiences together. Consistently, abstract word meanings rely more than concrete word meanings on the social experience of language. Indeed, it has been proposed that concrete words are acquired earlier than abstract words because they rely on sensorimotor experiences, while more complex and abstract meanings emerge later with the refinement of linguistic abilities (Buccino et al. 2019; Lund, Sidhu, and Pexman 2019). Recent findings confirm this, showing for example that under the age of four, less than 10% of children's vocabulary is composed of abstract words, whereas this percentage increases to more than 40% by the age of 12 (Ponari, Norbury, and Vigliocco 2018). Other studies focused on the longitudinal process of acquisition of abstract words, showing that these emerge progressively in children's vocabulary over the second year of age (Bellagamba et al. 2022)—with major leaps between 12 and 15 months, and 22 and 24 months.

If one of the core differences between concrete and abstract words is to be found in their peculiar acquisition mechanisms,[10] simulating the acquisition of new concrete and abstract words should lead to findings symmetrical to the ones obtained with existing words. With the aim of verifying this prediction, Borghi et al. (2011) performed four experiments in which they simulated the acquisition of new words. First, participants acquired new concepts by manipulating novel objects (concrete concepts) or by observing groups of objects interacting in novel ways (abstract concepts). Then they were provided with a category label. To assess if novel abstract and concrete words differed along the same dimensions of existing abstract and concrete ones, participants performed a feature production task in which they were asked to list properties of the objects. Crucially, association score analyses showed that concrete words evoked more perceptual properties, as typically found with existing concrete words (Borghi and Caramelli 2001). Participants were also asked to decide which of the exemplars could be named with a given verbal label. Errors results showed that it was more difficult to form abstract than concrete categories. Finally, participants performed a color verification task (on the known stimuli) with manual/verbal responses. Interestingly, for abstract words microphone use was easier for subjects than keyboard use. Consistent with the predictions, (new) concrete words evoked more manual information, while (new) abstract words elicited more verbal information (for similar results see also Granito et al. 2015; Borghi and Zarcone 2016; Mazzuca et al. 2018).

Multiple types of representations

Attempts to sketch a unitary framework to address both concrete and abstract word representation suggest that multiple representational systems[11] are activated during conceptual processing. Some of these proposals adopt an embodied perspective.[12] Barsalou et al. (2008) propose the Language and Situated Simulation Theory (LASS), claiming that linguistic forms and situated simulations interact continuously: Different mixtures of the two systems underlie a wide variety of tasks. The linguistic system (left hemisphere) is involved mainly during superficial linguistic processing, whereas deeper conceptual processing requires the activation of the sensorimotor system (bilateral posterior areas). In a similar vein, Borghi and Binkofski (2014: Words As Tools, WAT; see also Borghi et al. 2017, 2018) propose to extend the embodied view of cognition in order to consider not only language grounding, but also the role that language plays in shaping our experience. In contrast to LASS, WAT claims that the linguistic system does not simply involve a form of superficial processing. The novelty of approaches such as the WAT proposal thus consists in conceiving words not as mere signals of something (Lupyan and Lewis 2019), but also as "social tools." In addition, WAT makes specific predictions concerning abstract and concrete word representations: While both engage the sensorimotor neural network, abstract words specifically activate the linguistic neural network due to their different acquisition mechanisms.

Notwithstanding broadly distinguishable characteristics of abstract and concrete conceptual knowledge, theories of abstract concepts are recently converging on the idea that the abstract–concrete distinction might be an artificial oversimplification (Barsalou, Dutriaux and Scheepers 2018). Multiple Representation Theories (MRTs), for instance, propose that concepts are embedded in a multidimensional space composed of varying dimensions that might be more or less relevant for the grounding of specific concepts (Borghi et al. 2019; Banks et al. in press). Specifically, two main novelties characterize these accounts. First, the distinction between abstract and concrete concepts as traditionally intended is called into question. In fact, recent studies show that sensorimotor and perceptual components do not uniquely characterize concrete concepts but might also be salient for representation of abstract concepts (e.g., Connell and Lynott 2012a,b; Banks and Connell 2023). For example, Banks and Connell (2023) examined the members of categories produced by participants for a set of 117 categories, spanning from more concrete ones (e.g., "furniture") to more abstract ones (e.g., "social relationships") and identified their sensorimotor and perceptual components. Their results show that although overall more concrete categories exhibited higher rates of sensorimotor components, many abstract categories were comparable in their mean sensorimotor strength with other concrete categories. As for the modalities they elicited, concrete categories were found to be more related to touch, whereas abstract categories were more related to hearing and interoception.

The second novelty introduced by MRTs underlines the heterogeneity of the category of abstract concepts. While traditional accounts of abstract conceptual knowledge sharply distinguished abstract and concrete concepts on the basis of their conceptual representation (i.e., perceptual vs linguistic; see Paivio 1986; Brysbaert et al. 2014), recent insights suggest this distinction might conceal important intra-categorical differences (see Villani et al. 2019; Kiefer and Harpaintner 2020). Abstract concepts are thus now understood as a variegated category, encompassing exemplars for which emotional aspects are more central (Vigliocco et al. 2014; Barca, Mazzuca, and Borghi 2017) as well as exemplars more grounded in perceptual and sensorimotor experiences (e.g., numbers; see Fischer 2012; Fischer and Shaki 2018). To illustrate, the association between number knowledge and space is now well established, giving rise to SNARC effects (Spatial-Numerical Association of Response Codes; see Fischer 2012), where smaller numbers are associated with left and bigger numbers with right. Furthermore, recent research strands are now starting to explore more deeply the role that linguistic and social information and experiences have in shaping abstract concepts—suggesting that social interaction constitutes one of the most important grounding sources for specific kinds of abstract concepts (Borghi 2022; Diveica, Pexman, and Binney 2022; Fini et al. 2021). For example, processing social concepts like "sociality" or "lawyer" has been consistently linked to the activation of a large network of brain regions associated with social cognition processing, with a predominant role for ATL (specifically, superior anterior temporal lobes; see review in Conca et al. 2021) Among these concepts, those related to political or politicized referents might be particularly relevant (Mazzuca and Santarelli 2022) for understanding the intertwinement between personal, perceptual experiences, and social and linguistic aspects (see also Mazzuca et al. 2021). For instance, in a study comparing free associations to the word "gender" across groups with different sex/gender experiences, Mazzuca et al. (2020) found that cisgender, monosexual participants consistently mentioned words related to perceptual and biological aspects (e.g., female, male, sex), whereas gender-diverse, non-monosexual participants frequently mentioned words related to sociocultural aspects (e.g., queer, fluidity, construction).

To conclude, recent advances in the study of abstract concepts suggest it is time to go beyond the classical distinction between abstract and concrete concepts. Abstract concepts are heterogeneous, and investigating them thoroughly requires acknowledging fine-grained nuances that might be hidden behind traditional classifications.

Language to act

Cultural and social features

As we have seen, a critical problem faced by embodied views is the issue of how abstract words are represented. According to recent proposals, both sensorimotor and linguistic information play a role in conceptual representation (Barsalou et al. 2008; Borghi et al. 2017, 2018; Davis and Yee 2021). The WAT proposal advanced the idea that language is not only affected by our previous experience, but also actively shapes speakers' perceptions of the world (see also Boroditsky and Ramscar 2002; Gentner 2003; see also the Sapir–Whorf hypothesis).

In keeping with this hypothesis, some studies suggest that different languages can differently carve up our experience. For example, in a behavioral study, Scorolli et al. (2011) found differences between speakers of two languages that differ grammatically: German participants were faster with abstract verbs while Italian ones were slower with the same kind of verbs (regardless of the kind of noun that preceded or followed the verb). Similarly, Bergen and Chan Lau (2012) tested native speakers of English, Mandarin Chinese from mainland China, and Mandarin Chinese from Taiwan: the writing direction for the first two groups is left to right and then top to bottom; for the third group, writing direction is predominantly top to bottom and then right to left. When asked to order cards describing different stages of temporal development, participants replicated differences in their native writing systems, supporting the idea that the axis used to represent time in terms of space is affected by language experience. In a related study Pesciarelli et al. (2019) tested Italian participants with an unmasked/masked priming paradigm to verify if gender stereotypes conveyed by language affected the processing of third-person pronouns in conjunction with role nouns. Results on event-related brain potentials showed that stereotypical knowledge is unconsciously activated by linguistic stimuli. Importantly they also found that female (e.g., teacher) and male (e.g., driver) stereotypes affected the processing of pronouns differently. Recently, the argument on linguistic diversity and its implications for conceptual representations has gone as far as to claim that embodied and grounded cognition *entails* linguistic relativity (see Kemmerer 2019, 2022).

The attention on the *social* aspects of language has suggested a focus not only on cultural differences[13] but also on the effects of having another person in the scene (Knoblich and Sebanz 2008; Goldman and de Vignemont 2009), with or without a collaborative attitude (see Scorolli et al. 2012; Tomasello 2009; Becchio et al. 2012). Gianelli et al. (2013) investigated whether the reach-to-grasp movement towards an object was influenced by the presence of a second person. This person could be either a friend or a non-friend and was either invisible (behind) or located in different positions with respect to the agent and the object. While only the agent performed the physical action, both the participants could be (in turn) the speaker. Before movement initiation, the speaker pronounced a sentence referring to her own action (e.g., "*I* grasp") or to the same action performed by the other (e.g., "*You* grasp"). Interestingly, the agent's grasping component of the movement was influenced by the kind of relationship between her and the other person, as well as by their relative physical positions. Most crucially, the overall reaching time showed an interaction between the speaker and the used pronoun: participants reached for the object more quickly when the other spoke, particularly if she used the "*I*" pronoun.

This evidence supports the idea of two forms of *social perspective*: the physical perspective, conveyed by both the other's body position and the distance from the object; and the perspective induced by language. Speaking, and particularly assuming the first-person perspective (linguistically conveyed by the first-person pronoun) evokes a potential action, consistently with the claim that words can be intended as kinds of actions. In a similar vein, Scorolli et al. (2016) showed that effective use of words, like an effective use of physical external auxiliaries such as tools (Farnè, Iriki, and Làdavas 2005), can determine an extension of the peripersonal space (Borghi et al. 2017, 2010; Clark 2008). Along the same lines, research shows that actively thinking in a different language (L2) can impact decision outcomes, for instance reducing biases and anti-utilitarian choices. This is known as Foreign

Language Effect (FLE; for a metanalysis see Del Maschio et al. 2022), and it has been proposed to be a cognitive "nudge" that can directly contribute to well-being and to the promotion and enforcement of sustainable practices (e.g., eating insects or drinking recycled water; see McFarlane, Cipolletti Perez, and Weissglass 2020). Interestingly, while much evidence supporting this claim is based on cross-cultural studies targeting native vs foreign languages, it has been recently shown that this effect also extends to different varieties of the same language (Miozzo et al. 2020).

Taken together, these findings suggest that language processing is not simply a matter of computation. Rather, sociocultural and personal experiences sedimented and encoded in linguistic cues are actively retrieved during language comprehension, and impact cognitive processes in accordance with features that are more or less salient in a given language or situation.

Extended mind

Nowadays we badly need further evidence to complement this big picture,[14] particularly empirical data on normal language development[15] (see Bergelson and Swingley 2013) as well as on developmental disorders (for a good review see Marcus and Rabagliati 2006).

Nevertheless, evidence collected so far clearly argues in favor of 1) a mind that is not "brainbound" (e.g., Clark 2008; Noë 2009; Wilson and Golonka 2013), but distributed also beyond the body's edges; 2) a language that cannot be conceived only in its referential aspects, but also in its social and public features (Borghi et al. 2013, 2017); and 3) body edges that are not static, but that can be plastically re-arranged (Tsakiris 2010; Longo and Serino 2012). This suggests that an embodied-grounded view of cognition should be integrated with the extended mind view (Clark and Chalmers 1998)[16]: the combination of these two perspectives promises to shed new light not only on language processing, but also on the actual potentialities of language.

New challenges and future directions: the reproducibility crisis

Over the last decade, the scientific community has witnessed a major shift of awareness towards reproducibility issues. Psychological findings in particular have been subjected to thorough examinations after the Open Science Collaboration report (2015) drew attention to the so-called *replication crisis*. Specifically, the project conducted replications of 100 experimental and correlational studies, 97% reporting significant results. Among the entire pool of replications, only 36% significantly replicated the original results (for similar results see also Youyou, Yang, and Uzzi 2023). Questions have been raised also regarding the extent to which results that are thought to be robust might replicate in non-Western educated industrialized rich democratic (WEIRD) societies (Henrich, Heine, and Norenzayan 2010), thus making the issue of generalizability of psychological findings even more problematic. Likewise, over-reliance on English in cognitive science has been recently criticized, exposing how it contributed to underestimate the impact of language(s) on cognition more widely (Blasi et al. 2022).

Against this backdrop some scholars have started to embrace new research practices in an attempt to overcome—or potentially limit—reproducibility issues hampering scientific progress. Among these there are preregistrations, registered reports, collaborative projects, and open online repositories enabling the sharing of data, materials, and analysis codes and scripts (e.g., Munafò et al. 2017; Moshontz et al. 2018).

Like other well-established effects in psychology, results supporting embodied cognition stances on the interplay between language and perception and action have also been a matter of critical re-examination. Morey et al. (2022) attempted a pre-registered, multi-lab replication of the ACE effect, with 18 different labs recruiting a total of 1,278 participants. Surprisingly, none of the labs were able to replicate the original effect, and the meta-analytic effect size was close to zero (see also Papesh 2015 for similar findings). Other classic embodied cognition findings on language comprehension, such as those reporting participants' simulation of the orientation and shape of objects described in sentences, were instead successfully replicated by Zwaan and Pecher (2012), but not in a following study by Rommers, Meyers, and Huettig (2013).

While these failures are certainly important to acknowledge, they do not in and of themselves markedly undermine the major tenets of embodied accounts of language. Indeed, as argued elsewhere (see e.g., Kaschak and Madden 2021; Zwaan 2021; Barsalou 2020), replication failures might be the result of multiple factors interacting with each other, like the general lack of precision in theorizing, hypothesis formulation, context sensitivity, weak power, or construct validity (see also Ostarek and Bottini 2021; Ostarek and Huettig 2019; Muthukrishna and Henrich 2019; Flake and Fried 2020; Barsalou 2020). Over the last two decades, insights gained from embodied-grounded research programs have changed the way in which we understand, among other things, language, concepts, and memory. As science evolves and scientific practices change, research programs have the chance of refining their methods and reconsidering their findings in light of the newly available evidence. It is therefore of vital importance for the future developments of embodied accounts of language—and in general for embodied cognition as a scientific program—to pursue the aim of reproducibility, transparency, and generalizability.

Notes

1 See the chapter on Dynamical Cognition by Anthony Chemero
2 For an alternative perspective see also Tomasino and Rumiati 2013.
3 As to Neuroscientific Bases of Embodiment, Chapter xx by Laila Craighero.
4 I.e., properties that depend on object's relationship with the agent or with other objects.
5 For controversial results as to color, see Zwaan and Pecher 2012.
6 For a discussion on interference and facilitation effects, see Borreggine and Kaschak (2006), and Connell and Lynott (2012a).
7 Winter and Bergen (2012) contrast the visual modality (e.g., "You are looking at the milk bottle across the supermarket" vs. "You are looking at the milk bottle in the fridge") with the auditory one (e.g., "Someone fires a handgun in the distance" vs. "Right next to you, someone fires a handgun") and find that mental simulation of objects' distance occurs in both conditions.
8 For kinematic evidence, see also Gentilucci et al. 2000; Scorolli et al. 2009.
9 For a discussion on embodied models explaining interference and facilitation effects see Borghi, Gianelli, and Scorolli (2010).
10 For a close examination of the mode of acquisition, MOA, construct see Wauters, Tellings, Van Bon and Van Haaften (2003); as to Concept acquisition, see also Chapter XX by Daniel Casasanto.
11 See also the Dual-coding Theory, Paivio (1986).
12 For a "non-embodied" version of this view see Dove (2009)
13 For an in-depth discussion see Chapter xx on Cultural Differences by Arthur Glenberg.
14 See Chapter XX on Future Prospects by Michael Wheeler.
15 See Chapter xx on Language Acquisition by Chen Yu.
16 See Chapter XX on Extended Cognition by Ken Aizawa.

Cross-references

Aizawa (Chapter 4): Extended cognition
Casasanto (Chapter 15): Concept acquisition
Richardson and Chemero (Chapter 5): Dynamical cognition
Craighero (Chapter 36): Neuroscientific bases of embodiment
Soliman and Glenberg (Chapter 30): Cultural differences
Shapiro (Introduction): Embodied cognition – A new paradigm?
Yu (Chapter 18): Language acquisition
Wheeler (Chapter 42): Future prospects

References

Ambrosini, E., Scorolli, C., Borghi, A.M., and Costantini, M. (2012) "Which body for embodied cognition? Affordance and language within actual and perceived reaching space," *Consciousness and Cognition*, 21, 1551–1557.

Arbib, M. A. (2005) "From monkey-like action recognition to human language: An evolutionary framework for neurolinguistics," *Behavioral and Brain Sciences*, 28, 105–124.

Banks, B., and Connell, L. (2023) "Multi-dimensional sensorimotor grounding of concrete and abstract categories," *Philosophical Transactions of the Royal Society B*, 378(1870), 20210366.

Barca, L., Mazzuca, C., and Borghi, A. M. (2017). "Pacifier overuse and conceptual relations of abstract and emotional concepts," *Frontiers in Psychology*, 8, 2014.

Barsalou, L. W. (1999) "Perceptual symbol systems," *Behavioral and Brain Sciences*, 22, 577–609.

Barsalou, L. W. (2020) "Challenges and opportunities for grounding cognition," *Journal of Cognition*, 3(1), 1–24.

Barsalou, L. W., Santos, A., Simmons, W. K., and Wilson, C. D. (2008) "Language and simulation in conceptual processing," in *Symbols, embodiment, and meaning*, (eds) M. De Vega, A. M. Glenberg, and A. C. Graesser (pp. 245–284). Oxford, UK: Oxford University Press.

Barsalou, L.W., and Wiemer-Hastings, K. (2005) "Situating abstract concepts," in D. Pecher and R. Zwaan (eds), *Grounding cognition: The role of perception and action in memory, language, and thought* (pp. 129–163), New York: Cambridge University Press.

Barsalou, L. W., Dutriaux, L., and Scheepers, C. (2018) "Moving beyond the distinction between concrete and abstract concepts," *Philosophical Transactions of the Royal Society B: Biological Sciences*, 373(1752), 20170144.

Becchio, C., Cavallo, A., Begliomini, C., Sartori, L., Feltrin, G., and Castiello, U. (2012) "Social grasping: From mirroring to mentalizing," *Neuroimage*, 61, 240–248.

Bellagamba, F., Borghi, A. M., Mazzuca, C., Pecora, G., Ferrara, F., and Fogel, A. (2022) "Abstractness emerges progressively over the second year of life," *Scientific Reports*, 12(1), 20940

Bergelson, E. and Swingley, D. (2013) "The acquisition of abstract words by young infants," *Cognition*, 127, 391–397.

Bergen, B.K. and Chan, Lau T.T. (2012) "Writing direction affects how people map space onto time," *Frontiers in Psychology*, 3: 109.

Bergen, B., and Wheeler, K. (2010) "Grammatical aspect and mental simulation," *Brain and Language*, 112, 150–158.

Blasi, D. E., Henrich, J., Adamou, E., Kemmerer, D., and Majid, A. (2022) "Over-reliance on English hinders cognitive science," *Trends in Cognitive Sciences* 26(12), 1153–1170.

Borghi, A. M. (2023) *The Freedom of Words. Abstractness and the power of language*, Cambridge: Cambridge University Press.

Borghi, A. M. (2022) "Concepts for which we need others more: the case of abstract concepts," *Current Directions in Psychological Science*, 31(3), 238–246.

Borghi, A. M., Barca, L., Binkofski, F., and Tummolini, L. (2018) "Varieties of abstract concepts: development, use and representation in the brain," *Philosophical Transactions of the Royal Society B: Biological Sciences*, 373(1752), 20170121.

Borghi, A. M., and Binkofski, F. (2014) *Words as social tools: An embodied view on abstract concepts*, Vol. 2, New York: Springer.

Borghi, A.M., Binkofski, F., Castelfranchi, C., Cimatti, F., Scorolli, C., and Tummolini, L. (2017) "The challenge of abstract concepts," *Psychological Bulletin*, 143, 263–292.

Borghi, A., and Caramelli, N. (2001) "Taxonomic relations and cognitive economy in conceptual organization," in (eds.) J. D. Moore and K. Stenning, *Proceedings of 23rd meeting of the cognitive science society* (pp. 98–103) London: Erlbaum.

Borghi, A. M., Barca, L., Binkofski, F., Castelfranchi, C., Pezzulo, G., and Tummolini, L. (2019) "Words as social tools: Language, sociality and inner grounding in abstract concepts," *Physics of Life Reviews*, 29, 120–153.

Borghi, A. M., and Cimatti, F. (2009) "Words as tools and the problem of abstract word meanings," *Proceedings of the Annual Meeting of the Cognitive Science Society*, 31(31).

Borghi, A. M., and Cimatti, F. (2010) "Embodied cognition and beyond: acting and sensing the body," *Neuropsychologia*, 48, 763–773.

Borghi, A., Flumini, A., Cimatti, F., Marocco, D. and Scorolli, C. (2011) "Manipulating objects and telling words: A study on concrete and abstract words acquisition," *Frontiers in Psychology* 2, 15.

Borghi, A.M., Gianelli, C., and Scorolli, C. (2010) "Sentence comprehension: Effectors and goals, self and others. An overview of experiments and implications for robotics," *Frontiers in Neurorobotics*, 4, 3.

Borghi, A.M., Glenberg, A.M., and Kaschak, M.P. (2004) "Putting words in perspective," *Memory and Cognition*, 32, 863–873.

Borghi, A.M., and Riggio, L. (2009) "Sentence comprehension and simulation of object temporary, canonical and stable affordances," *Brain Research*, 1253, 117–128.

Borghi, A.M., and Scorolli, C. (2009) "Language comprehension and hand motion simulation," *Human Movement Science*, 28, 12–27.

Borghi, AM, Scorolli, C, Caligiore, D, Baldassarre, G, and Tummolini, L (2013) "The embodied mind extended: Using words as social tools," *Frontiers in Psychology*, 4:214.

Borghi, A. M., and Zarcone, E. (2016) "Grounding abstractness: abstract concepts and the activation of the mouth," *Frontiers in Psychology*, 7, 1498.

Boroditsky, L. and Ramscar, M. (2002) "The Roles of Body and Mind in Abstract Thought," *Psychological Science*, 13, 185–188.

Borreggine, K.L., and Kaschak, M. (2006) "The Action-sentence Compatibility Effect: It's all in the timing," *Cognitive Science*, 30, 1097–1112.

Brunyé, T. T., Ditman, T., Mahoney, C. R., Augustyn, J. S., and Taylor, H. A. (2009) "When you and I share perspectives: Pronouns modulate perspective taking during narrative comprehension," *Psychological Science*, 20, 27–32.

Brysbaert, M., Warriner, A. B., and Kuperman, V. (2014) "Concreteness ratings for 40 thousand generally known English word lemmas," *Behavior Research Methods*, 46, 904–911.

Buccino, G., Colagè, I., Silipo, F., and D'Ambrosio, P. (2019) "The concreteness of abstract language: an ancient issue and a new perspective," *Brain Structure and Function*, 224(4), 1385–1401.

Buccino G., Riggio L., Melli G., Binkofski F., Gallese V., and Rizzolatti G. (2005) "Listening to action-related sentences modulates the activity of the motor system: A combined TMS and behavioral study," *Cognitive Brain Research*, 24, 355–363.

Caravà, M., and Scorolli, C. (2020) "When affective relation weighs more than the mug handle: investigating Affective Affordances," *Frontiers in Psychology*, 11, 1928.

Casasanto, D., and Boroditsky, L. (2008) "Time in the mind: Using space to think about time," *Cognition*, 106, 579–593.

Clark, A. (2008) *Supersizing the mind. Embodiment, action, and cognitive extension*, Oxford: Oxford University Press.

Clark, A. and Chalmers, D. (1998) "The extended mind," *Analysis*, 58, 7–19.

Connell, L. (2007) "Representing object colour in language comprehension," *Cognition* 102, 476–485.

Connell, L. and Lynott, D. (2012a) "When does perception facilitate or interfere with conceptual processing? The effect of attentional modulation," *Frontiers in Psychology* 3, 474.

Connell, L., and Lynott, D. (2012b) "Strength of perceptual experience predicts word processing performance better than concreteness or imageability," *Cognition*, 125(3), 452–465.

Corballis, M. C. (2002) *From hand to mouth. The origins of language*, Princeton: Princeton University Press.

Davis, C. P., Altmann, G. T., and Yee, E. (2020) "Situational systematicity: A role for schema in understanding the differences between abstract and concrete concepts," *Cognitive Neuropsychology*, 37(1–2), 142–153.

Davis, C. P., and Yee, E. (2021) "Building semantic memory from embodied and distributional language experience," *Wiley Interdisciplinary Reviews: Cognitive Science*, 12(5), e1555.

Del Maschio, N., Crespi, F., Peressotti, F., Abutalebi, J., and Sulpizio, S. (2022) "Decision-making depends on language: A meta-analysis of the Foreign Language Effect," *Bilingualism: Language and Cognition*, 25(4), 617–630.

Diveica, V., Pexman, P. M., and Binney, R. J. (2022) "Quantifying social semantics: An inclusive definition of socialness and ratings for 8388 English words," *Behavior Research Methods*, 55, 1–13.

Dove, G. (2009) "Beyond perceptual symbols: a call for representational pluralism," *Cognition*, 110, 412–431.

Dove, G. (2022) *Abstract concepts and the embodied mind: Rethinking grounded cognition*, Oxford: Oxford University Press.

Dowty, D. (1977) "Toward a semantic analysis of verb aspect and the English "imperfective" progressive," *Linguistics and Philosophy*, 1, 45–77.

Ellis, R. and Tucker, M. (2000) "Micro-affordance: the potentiation of components of action by seen objects," *British Journal of Psychology*, 91, 451–471.

Farnè, A, Iriki, A, and Làdavas, E. (2005) "Shaping multisensory action-space with tools: evidence from patients with cross-modal extinction," *Neuropsychologia*, 43, 238–248.

Fini, C., Era, V., Da Rold, F., Candidi, M., and Borghi, A. M. (2021) "Abstract concepts in interaction: The need of others when guessing abstract concepts smooths dyadic motor interactions," *Royal Society Open Science*, 8(7), 201205.

Fischer, M. H. (2012) "A hierarchical view of grounded, embodied, and situated numerical cognition," *Cognitive Processing*, 13, 161–164.

Fischer, M. H., and Shaki, S. (2018) "Number concepts: Abstract and embodied," *Philosophical Transactions of the Royal Society B: Biological Sciences*, 373(1752), 20170125.

Flake, J. K., and Fried, E. I. (2020) "Measurement schmeasurement: Questionable measurement practices and how to avoid them," *Advances in Methods and Practices in Psychological Science*, 3(4), 456–465.

Gallese, V. (2008) "Mirror neurons and the social nature of language: The neural exploitation hypothesis," *Social Neuroscience*, 3, 317–333.

Gallese, V. and Goldman, A. (1998) "Mirror neurons and the simulation theory of mind-reading," *Trends in Cognitive Sciences*, 12, 493–501.

Gallese V., and Sinigaglia C. (2011) "What is so special with Embodied Simulation," *Trends in Cognitive Sciences*, 15, 512–519.

Gentilucci, M. (2003) "Object motor representation and language," *Experimental Brain Research*, 153, 260–265.

Gentilucci, M., Benuzzi, F., Bertolani, L., Daprati, E., and Gangitano, M. (2000) "Language and motor control," *Experimental Brain Research*, 133, 468–490.

Gentner, D. (2003) "Why we're so smart," in D. Gentner and S. Goldin-Meadow (eds), *Language in mind: Advances in the study of language and cognition* (pp. 195–236). Cambridge, MA: MIT Press.

Gianelli, C., Scorolli, C., and Borghi, A.M. (2013) "Acting in perspective: The role of body and language as social tools," *Psychological Research*, 77, 40–52.

Glenberg, A. M. (1997) "What memory is for," *Behavioral and Brain Sciences*, 20, 1–55.

Glenberg, A.M. and Gallese, V (2012) "Action-based language: a theory of language acquisition, comprehension, and production," *Cortex*, 48, 905–922.

Glenberg, A. M., and Kaschak, M. P. (2002) "Grounding language in action," *Psychonomic Bulletin and Review*, 9, 558–565.

Glenberg, A.M., Sato, M., Cattaneo, L., Riggio, L., Palumbo, D., and Buccino, G. (2008) "Processing abstract language modulates motor system activity," *Quarterly Journal of Experimental Psychology*, 61, 905–919.

Glover, S., and Dixon, P. (2002) "Semantics affects the planning but not the control of grasping," *Experimental Brain Research*, 146, 383–387.

Goldman, A.I. and de Vignemont, F. (2009) "Is social cognition embodied?" *Trends in Cognitive Sciences*, 13, 154–159.

Granito, C., Scorolli, C., and Borghi, A.M. (2015) "Naming a Lego world. The Role of Language in the Acquisition of Abstract Concepts," *PLoS ONE*, 10 (1): e0114615.

Henrich, J., Heine, S. J., and Norenzayan, A. (2010) "The weirdest people in the world?" *Behavioral and Brain Sciences*, 33(2–3), 61–83.

Hommel, B., Müsseler, J., Aschersleben, G., and Prinz, W. (2001) "The theory of event coding (TEC): A framework for perception and action planning," *Behavioral and Brain Sciences*, 24, 849–878.

Kaschak, M. P., and Madden, J. (2021) "Embodiment in the Lab: Theory, Measurement, and Reproducibility," in *Handbook of embodied psychology* (pp. 619–635). Springer, Cham.

Kaschak, M. P., Madden, C. J., Therriault, D. J., Yaxley, R. J., Aveyard, M., Blanchard, A. A., and Zwaan, R. A. (2005) "Perception of motion affects language processing," *Cognition*, 94, 79–89.

Kemmerer, D. (2019) *Concepts in the brain: The view from cross-linguistic diversity*, Oxford: Oxford University Press.

Kemmerer, D. (2022) "Grounded cognition entails linguistic relativity: a neglected implication of a major semantic theory," *Topics in Cognitive Science*, 15, 615–647.

Kemmerer, D., and Gonzalez Castillo, J. (2010) "The Two-Level Theory of verb meaning: An approach to integrating the semantics of action with the mirror neuron system," *Brain and Language*, 112, 54–76.

Kiefer, M., and Harpaintner, M. (2020) "Varieties of abstract concepts and their grounding in perception or action," *Open Psychology*, 2(1), 119–137.

Knoblich, G., and Sebanz, N. (2008) "Evolving intentions for social interaction: from entrainment to joint action," *Philosophical Transactions of the Royal Society, Biological Sciences*, 363, 2021–2031.

Lakoff, G. and Johnson, M. (1999) *Philosophy in the flesh: The embodied mind and its challenge to western though*. New York: Basic Books

Longo, MR., and Serino, A. (2012) "Tool use induces complex and flexible plasticity of human body representations, commentary on Vaesen, K.," *Behavioral Brain Sciences*, 35, 229–230.

Louwerse, M. M., and Jeuniaux, P. (2010) "The linguistic and embodied nature of conceptual processing," *Cognition*, 114, 96–104.

Lund, T. C., Sidhu, D. M., and Pexman, P. M. (2019) "Sensitivity to emotion information in children's lexical processing," *Cognition*, 190, 61–71.

Lupyan, G., and Lewis, M. (2019) "From words-as-mappings to words-as-cues: The role of language in semantic knowledge," *Language, Cognition and Neuroscience*, 34(10), 1319–1337.

Madden, C. J., and Zwaan, R. A. (2003) "How does verb aspect constrain event representations?" *Memory and Cognition*, 31, 663–672

Mahon, B.Z., and Caramazza, A. (2008) "A critical look at the Embodied Cognition Hypothesis and a new proposal for grounding conceptual content," *Journal of Physiology-Paris*, 102, 59–70

Marcus, G.F. and Rabagliati, H. (2006) "What developmental disorders can tell us about the nature and origins of language," *Nature Neuroscience*, 9, 1226–1229.

Mazzuca, C., Falcinelli, I., Michalland, A. H., Tummolini, L., and Borghi, A. M. (2022) "Bodily, emotional, and public sphere at the time of COVID-19. An investigation on concrete and abstract concepts," *Psychological Research*, 86(7), 2266–2277.

Mazzuca, C., Lugli, L., Benassi, M., Nicoletti, R., and Borghi, A. M. (2018) "Abstract, emotional and concrete concepts and the activation of mouth-hand effectors," *PeerJ*, 6, e5987.

Mazzuca, C., and Santarelli, M. (2022) "Making it abstract, making it contestable: politicization at the intersection of political and cognitive science," *Review of Philosophy and Psychology*, 14, 1–22.

Mazzuca, C., Majid, A., Lugli, L., Nicoletti, R., and Borghi, A. M. (2020) "Gender is a multifaceted concept: evidence that specific life experiences differentially shape the concept of gender," *Language and Cognition*, 12(4), 649–678.

McFarlane, S., Cipolletti Perez, H., and Weissglass, C. (2020) "Thinking in a Non-native Language: A New Nudge?" *Frontiers in Psychology*, 11, 549083.

Miozzo, M., Navarrete, E., Ongis, M., Mello, E., Girotto, V., and Peressotti, F. (2020) "Foreign language effect in decision-making: How foreign is it?" *Cognition*, 199, 104245.

Morey, R. D., Kaschak, M. P., Díez-Álamo, A. M., Glenberg, A. M., Zwaan, R. A., Lakens, D., ... and Ziv-Crispel, N. (2022) "A pre-registered, multi-lab non-replication of the action-sentence compatibility effect (ACE)," *Psychonomic Bulletin and Review*, 29(2), 613–626.

Moshontz, H., Campbell, L., Ebersole, C. R., IJzerman, H., Urry, H. L., Forscher, P. S., ... Chartier, C. R. (2018) "The Psychological Science Accelerator: Advancing psychology through a distributed collaborative network," *Advances in Methods and Practices in Psychological Science*, 1(4), 501–515.

Munafò, M. R., Nosek, B. A., Bishop, D. V., Button, K. S., Chambers, C. D., Percie du Sert, N., ... and Ioannidis, J. (2017) "A manifesto for reproducible science," *Nature Human Behaviour*, 1(1), 1–9.

Muthukrishna, M., and Henrich, J. (2019) "A problem in theory," *Nature Human Behaviour*, 3(3), 221–229.

Noë, A. (2009) *Out of our heads. Why you are not your brain, and other lessons from the biology of consciousness*. New York: Hill and Wang.

Open Science Collaboration. (2015) "Estimating the reproducibility of psychological science," *Science*, 349(6251), aac4716.

Ostarek, M., and Bottini, R. (2021) "Towards strong inference in research on embodiment–possibilities and limitations of causal paradigms," *Journal of Cognition*, 4(1), 1–21.

Ostarek, M., and Huettig, F. (2019) "Six challenges for embodiment research," *Current Directions in Psychological Science*, 28(6), 593–599.

Paivio, A. (1986) *Mental representations: A dual coding approach*. New York, NY: Oxford University Press.

Papesh, M. H. (2015) "Just out of reach: On the reliability of the action-sentence compatibility effect," *Journal of Experimental Psychology: General*, 144(6), e116.

Ponari, M., Norbury, C. F., and Vigliocco, G. (2018) "Acquisition of abstract concepts is influenced by emotional valence," *Developmental Science*, 21(2), e12549.

Pecher, D., Zeelenberg, R., and Barsalou, L.W. (2003) "Verifying Different-Modality Properties for Concepts Produces Switching Costs," *Psychological Science*, 14, 119–124.

Pesciarelli, F., Scorolli, C., and Cacciari, C. (2019) "Neural correlates of the implicit processing of grammatical and stereotypical gender violations: A masked and unmasked priming study," *Biological Psychology*, 146:107714.

Pezzulo, G., Barsalou, L.W., Cangelosi, A., Fischer, M.H., McRae, K., and Spivey, M.J. (2013) "Computational Grounded Cognition: a new alliance between grounded cognition and computational modeling," *Frontiers in Psychology* 3:612.

Price, C. J. (2010) "The anatomy of language: a review of 100 fMRI studies published in 2009," *Annals of the New York Academy of Sciences*, 1191, 62–88.

Pulvermüller, F., Härle, M., and Hummel, F. (2001) "Walking or talking? Behavioral and electrophysiological correlates of action verb processing," *Brain and Language*, 78, 143–168.

Rommers, J., Meyer, A. S., and Huettig, F. (2013) "Object shape and orientation do not routinely influence performance during language processing," *Psychological Science*, 24(11), 2218–2225.

Sakreida, K., Scorolli, C., Menz, M.M., Heim, S, Borghi, A.M. and Binkofski, F. (2013) "Are abstract action words embodied? An fMRI investigation at the interface between language and motor cognition," *Frontiers in Human Neurosciences*, 7, 125.

Sato, M. and Bergen, B. (2013) "The case of the missing pronouns: Does mentally simulated perspective play a functional role in the comprehension of person?" *Cognition*, 127, 361–374.

Sato, M., Schafer, A. and Bergen, B. (2013) "One word at a time: Mental representations of object shape change incrementally during sentence processing," *Language and Cognition*, 5, 345–373.

Scorolli, C. (2019) "Re-enacting the Bodily Self on Stage: Embodied Cognition meets Psychoanalysis," *Frontiers in Psychology*, 10, 492.

Scorolli, C., and Borghi, A.M. (2007) "Sentence comprehension and action: Effector specific modulation of the motor system," *Brain Research*, 1130, 119–124.

Scorolli, C., Borghi, A.M., and Glenberg, A. (2009) "Language-Induced Motor Activity in bi-manual Object Lifting," *Experimental Brain Research*, 193, 43–53.

Scorolli, C., Binkofski F., Buccino G., Nicoletti R., Riggio L. and Borghi A.M. (2011) "Abstract and concrete sentences, embodiment, and languages," *Frontiers in Psychology*, 2: 227.

Scorolli, C., Daprati, E., Nico, D., and Borghi, A. (2016) "Reaching for Objects or Asking for them: Distance Estimation in 7- to 15-Years-Old Children," *Journal of Motor Behavior*, 48, 2, 183–191.

Scorolli, C., Jacquet, P.O., Binkofski, F., Nicoletti, R., Tessari, A., and Borghi, A.M. (2012) "Abstract and concrete phrases processing differentially modulates Cortico-Spinal excitability," *Brain Research*, 1488, 60–71.

Scorolli, C., Miatton, M., Wheaton, L.A., and Borghi, A.M. (2012) "When a glass calls: anatomy of a toast," *Cognitive Processing*, Special Issue, 13, pp. S69–S70, Springer Heidelberg, Germany.

Speed, L. J., and Majid, A. (2020) "Grounding language in the neglected senses of touch, taste, and smell," *Cognitive Neuropsychology*, 37(5–6), 363–392.

Stanfield, R.A., and Zwaan, R.A. (2001) "The effect of implied orientation derived from verbal context on picture recognition," *Psychological Science*, 121, 153–156.

Tomasello M. (2009) *Why we cooperate*, Cambridge, MA: MIT Press.

Tomasino, B and Rumiati, RI (2013) "At the mercy of strategies: the role of motor representations in language understanding," *Frontiers in Psychology* 4, 27.

Tsakiris, M. (2010) "My body in the brain: a neurocognitive model of body-ownership," *Neuropsychologia*, 48, 703–712.

Vigliocco, G., Kousta, S. T., Della Rosa, P. A., Vinson, D. P., Tettamanti, M., Devlin, J. T., and Cappa, S. F. (2014) "The neural representation of abstract words: the role of emotion," *Cerebral Cortex*, 24(7), 1767–1777.

Villani, C., Lugli, L., Liuzza, M. T., and Borghi, A. M. (2019) "Varieties of abstract concepts and their multiple dimensions," *Language and Cognition*, 11(3), 403–430.

Wauters, L. N., Tellings, A. E. J. M., van Bon, W. H. J., and van Haaften, A. W. (2003) "Mode of acquisition of word meanings: The viability of a theoretical construct," *Applied Psycholinguistics*, 24, 385–406.

Wiemer-Hastings, K., Krug, J., and Xu, X. (2001) "Imagery, context availability, contextual constraints and abstractness," *Proceedings of 23rd Annual Meeting of the Cognitive Science Society* (pp. 1106–1111). Hillsdale, N.J.: Lawrence Erlbaum Associates.

Wilson, A.D., and Golonka, S. (2013) "Embodied cognition is not what you think it is," *Frontiers in Psychology*, 4, 58.

Winter, B. and Bergen, B. (2012) "Language comprehenders represent object distance both visually and auditorily," *Language and Cognition*, 4, 1–16.

Youyou, W., Yang, Y., and Uzzi, B. (2023) "A discipline-wide investigation of the replicability of Psychology papers over the past two decades," *Proceedings of the National Academy of Sciences*, 120(6), e2208863120.

Zwaan, R. A. (2021) "Two challenges to "embodied cognition" research and how to overcome them," *Journal of Cognition*, 4(1), 1–9.

Zwaan RA, and Pecher D (2012) "Revisiting Mental Simulation in Language Comprehension: Six Replication Attempts," *PLoS ONE* 7, e51382.

Zwaan, R.A., Stanfield, R.A., and Yaxley R.H. (2002) "Language comprehenders mentally represent the shapes of objects," *Psychological Science*, 13, 168–171.

Further reading

Dove, G. *Abstract concepts and the embodied mind: rethinking grounded cognition.* (Oxford: Oxford University Press, 2022) offers a compelling review of abstract concepts and embodied cognition, touching upon recent developments.

Borghi, A. M., *the freedom of words. Abstractness and the power of language* (Cambridge: Cambridge University Press, 2023) provides an overview of up-to-date evidence on the impact of language and social interaction in the acquisition and representation of abstract concepts.

Malt, B. C. and Wolff, P. (Eds), *Words and the mind: how words capture human experience*. (Oxford: Oxford University Press, 2010) summarizes findings concerned with cross-linguistic and cross-cultural variation, and how these affect concepts of different domains.

Kemmerer, D., *Concepts in the brain: The view from cross-linguistic diversity* (Oxford: Oxford University Press, 2019) inspects the relation between grammar, semantics, and sensorimotor systems, reconciling neuroscientific findings with semantic typology.

18

LINKING WORDS TO WORLD

An embodiment perspective

Chen Yu

Introduction

Children begin to comprehend words at nine months. They say their first word at around 12 months. The pace with which children add new words to receptive and productive vocabulary then accelerates such that by 24 to 30 months, children are adding words at the staggering rate of five to nine new words a day (Bloom, 2000). Just as in many other cognitive learning tasks, a critical problem in word learning is the uncertainty and ambiguity in the learning environment – young word learners need to discover correct word-referent mappings among many possible candidate words and many possible candidate referents from potentially many objects that are simultaneously available. For example, Quine (1960) famously presented the core problem for learning word meanings from their co-occurrence with perceived events in the world. He imagined an anthropologist who observes a speaker saying "gavagai" while pointing in the general direction of a field. The intended referent (rabbit, grass, the field, or rabbit ears, etc.) is indeterminate from this example.

Past work has shown that the social context plays a key role in young learners' prowess in disambiguating cluttered learning situations. The literature provides many powerful demonstrations of how social-interactional cues guide infants' word learning, and in many cases, these seem essential to successful learning (Baldwin, 1993; Tomasello and Akhtar, 1995; Woodward and Guajardo, 2002; Bloom, 2000). Often the importance of social cues is interpreted in terms of children's understanding that words are used with an "intent to refer." Thus children's early dependence on social cues is seen as a diagnostic marker of their ability to infer the intentions of the speaker. This kind of social cognition is called "mindreading" by Baron-Cohen (1997) or more generally "theory of mind" (Wellman and Liu, 2004). Consistent with these ideas, studies have shown that very young learners map nouns to objects only when the speaker is intentionally attending to the named object and not, for example, when there is an accidental co-occurrence of object and name (Tomasello, 2000). Such results point to the importance of understanding the social structure of learning experiences. However, there is much that is still not understood:

DOI: 10.4324/9781003322511-24

1 At the behavioral level, most studies have examined early word learning in constrained experimental tasks with only one or two objects in view. The adult partner (usually the experimenter) is focused on the child, on effective teaching, and provides clear and repeated signals of her attention to the object being named. In this way, the attentional task is simple, and easily described in discrete and categorical terms (the attended object vs. the distractor). These contexts are not at all like the real world in which word learning is embedded in *a stream of activity* – in which parents both react to and attempt to control toddler behaviors and in which toddlers react to, direct, and sometimes ignore parents as they pursue their own goals. If we are going to understand the role of social cues in real-world word learning, we need to study social interactions and learning as they unfold in real time in dynamically complex and cluttered contexts.

2 At the theoretical level, the focus on macro-level behaviors and folk-psychological constructs does not connect easily to the real-time events in which learning happens. Current theoretical models explain the role of social cues in word learning via *internal* computations – mental models about the intentional states of the social partner and inferences about the goals and plans of the other (Breazeal and Scassellati, 2000). It is not at all clear that such abstract logic-like inferences about the internal states of others can happen *fast enough* to explain the exquisite real-time "dance" of social interactions in which effective adjustments within the dyad happen in fractions of seconds.

3 At the computational level, the analysis of the learning task has been based on an *adult's* – and *third person's* – view of the learning environment. Experimenters and theorists of children's word learning are adults with a mature and developed view of the structure of the learning task and of the attentional and intentional states of the learner. As observers, we watch interactions between child and parent and we interpret these interactions from a vantage point that sees both the causes and effects of each action on each participant. It is seductively easy to describe such events in folk-psychological terms that sound like explanations: "the mother tried to elicit the child's attention by waving the toy," "the child wanted the toy and so reached for it." There are many philosophical, methodological, and theoretical problems with this (Pfeifer and Scheier, 1999). One straightforward problem is that the third-person observer's view (the experimenter's view, etc.) of the learning task is not the learner's view. Instead, what the learner sees – moment to moment – is a dynamic event that depends on the learner's own momentary interests and *bodily orientation*. Recent studies using head-mounted cameras indicate that the adult view of the learning task *does not align at all with the dynamic first-person view of toddlers*, and is, therefore, a poor basis for theorizing about underlying processes.

> (Pereira, Smith, and Yu, in press; Smith, Yu, and Pereira, 2011;
> Yu, Smith, Shen, Pereira, and Smith, 2009)

In brief, traditional theories of learning and intelligence (and many contemporary theories of development, learning, and social interaction) concentrate on internal representations and inferences from those representations, paying little attention to the body and to the ways intelligence is affected by and affects the physical world. More recently, there has been a shift toward ideas of embodiment, that intelligence emerges in the interaction of an agent *and its body* with an environment (Brooks and Stein, 1994; Clark, 2008;

Ballard, Hayhoe, Pook, and Rao, 1997; Pfeifer and Scheier, 1999; Gibbs, 2006; Shapiro 2011; Spivey, 2007). In these analyses, the body – its morphology and its own intrinsic dynamics – plays just as important a role as the internal cognitive system and physical environment. Beer (1995) provided a principled theoretical analysis of these ideas in which behavior and cognition are understood as arising from the dynamical interaction between a brain (or cognitive system), body, and environment which critically includes other brain-body-environment systems as shown in Figure 18.1 (left). From this perspective, the behavior and cognition *of an individual* may be conceptualized as arising from the closed-loop interaction of the cognitive system with the body and the environment in which it is embedded, rather than as the sole product of any one component of this coupled system, such as the brain or internal representations. The behavior and collaboration of several individuals – for instance, word learning from child–parent social interaction – may be conceptualized as the *coupling* of these two systems, as illustrated in Figure 18.1 (right).

Further, the critical role of embodiment has been demonstrated empirically and computationally in various behavioral science fields. For example, Ballard *et al.* (1997) proposed a model of "embodied cognition" that operates at timescales of approximately one-third of a second and uses subtle orienting movements of the body during a variety of cognitive tasks as input to a computational model. At this "embodiment" level, the constraints of the body determine the nature of cognitive operations, and the body's pointing movements are used as deictic (pointing) references to bind objects in the physical environment to variables in cognitive programs of the brain. In our studies of child word learning, we emphasize the dependencies between the learner's *own actions* and the learner's internal cognitive state. Accordingly, understanding how the sensorimotor dependencies in the child affect cognition and learning – how, for example, looking at an object or holding it may engage and maintain attention – is viewed as critical. These sensorimotor-cognition couplings also mean that the momentary sensorimotor actions of the learner are likely to be indicative of the learner's internal state (Yu, Ballard, and Aslin, 2005). The basic idea behind our research is that the body – and its momentary actions – are crucial to social collaboration. Toward this goal, we seek to simultaneously measure multiple streams of behaviors and then to use data mining and machine learning

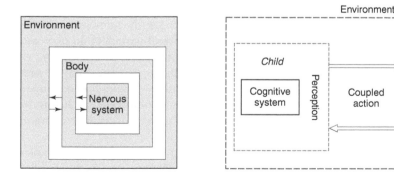

Figure 18.1 Overview of embodied social interaction. (Left) The brain-body-environment system in Beer (1995). (Right) Our proposed coupled embodied framework of child–parent interaction and communication.

techniques to *discover* patterns that support smooth interactions and word learning. We concentrate on measuring multiple streams of sensorimotor data because ultimately it is these coupled real-time behaviors that create the learning input and the learning environment.

A case study: multimodal word learning

Experiment

Here we describe a general experimental context that has been developed and used to understand word learning through parent–child interaction (Yu and Smith, 2012; Smith *et al.*, 2011). The experimental task is unconstrained tabletop play between a toddler (children between 15 and 20 months of age) and a parent. We chose the context of parent and child playing with toys on a tabletop as our naturalistic context for three reasons: (1) it is a common everyday context in which parents and toddlers are jointly engaged and in which word learning takes place (Callanan, 1985, 1990); (2) it is attentionally complex in that there can be many objects on the table, multiple and competing goals, and many shifts in attention; and (3) the geometry of tabletop play is sufficiently constrained that we can measure the first-person view and the head and hand movements of each participant. Figure 18.2 shows the basic set-up. The interaction is recorded by three cameras: one head-mounted camera provides information about the scene from the child's point of view; a second head-mounted camera provides the parent's viewpoint; and a third from a top-down third-person viewpoint allows a clear observation of exactly what was on the table at any given moment (mostly the participants' hands and the objects being played with). We also measure both the child's and the parent's head and hand movements with a Polhemus 6 degrees-of-freedom motion-tracking system and also the parent's speech through a headset. A particularly important and novel component of our method is the recording of visual information from the *learner's point of view* via a lightweight mini-camera mounted on a sports headband and placed low on the forehead. The angle of the camera is adjustable, and has a visual field of approximately 90 degrees, horizontally and vertically.

Parents were told that their goal was simply to engage the child with the toys and that they should interact as naturally as possible. The experimental objects were simple novel objects with novel names. Parents were taught the names prior to the experiment. Besides that, there were no constraints on what parents (or the children) had to say or what they had to do. Parents were told to engage their child with objects, to use the names we supplied *if* they named them, and that we were interested in the dynamics of parent–child play with toys. There were three toy objects in each of the three trials. At the end of interaction, we also tested each child's knowledge of the names of the nine objects that they played with, using a standard forced choice procedure. In this way, we used – as described above – completely novel methods of collecting multiple streams of sensorimotor data during the course of the learning experiences but we tied these measures to well-documented, standard, and highly reliable measures of word learning.

Video, motion-tracking, and speech data were coded to extract sensorimotor variables, such as object size in view, holding activities from both participants, and head stability. Technical details can be found in Yu and Smith (2012); Yu *et al.* (2009). As a result, we have collected and extracted multiple time series that capture visual, motor, and speech

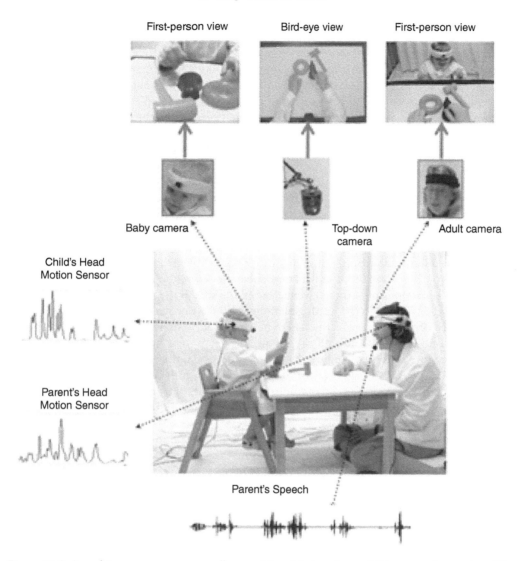

Figure 18.2 A multisensory system to collect multimodal data from child–parent interaction. The young word learner and the language teacher play with a set of objects at a table. Two mini cameras are placed onto the child's and the parent's heads respectively to collect visual information from two first-person views. Note that these two views are dramatically different. A third camera mounted high above the table records the bird's-eye view of the whole interaction. The participants also wore motion sensors to track their head and hand movements. A headset was used to record the caregiver's speech. In this way, we collected multimodal multistreaming data to analyze and detect interactive perception-action patterns from both the child and the parent that lead to successful word learning.

behaviors moment by moment from both the child and the parent. Those derived data were further analyzed to discover various sensory and motor patterns from child–parent interactions.

Results

During the play session, parents uttered on average 365 words (tokens). Each of the nine object names was produced by the parents on average only 5.32 times (standard deviation [SD] = 1.12). An object name was categorized as learned for an infant if his looking behavior at test indicated learning. The number of times parents named each object was negatively correlated with the likelihood that the infant learned the object name: 4.5 naming events for learned names and 6.5 per name for unlearned names. This may be due to parents' use of the name in attempts to engage children with specific objects that were not of interest to the child. At any rate, the lack of correlation reminds us that learning may depend on more than the mere frequency of heard names and more critically on the frequency with which naming coincides with the infant's visual selection of the named object. All parent naming events associated with learned object names were designated "successful" (n = 149). All other object-naming events were designated "unsucessful" (n = 136). Recall that objects were presented in three sets of three. Successful and unsuccessful naming events did not differ in duration, nor in any other noticeable property.

Our first hypothesis was that toddlers may solve the referential uncertainty problem at a sensory level. To test this hypothesis, we measured the size of the named target and the size of other *distractor* objects in the head-camera images. This provided a measure of the relative dominance of the referent of the object name and its visual competitors. The sizes of the target and other objects in both the infant and the parent head-camera views during naming events are shown in Figure 18.3. Consider first the pattern from the child's head-camera images. The image sizes of the named target in the child head-camera during *successful* naming events differed from non-naming events (mean object size, $M_{\text{Successful}}$ = 6.28% of pixels in the image; object size is measured as the total number of object pixels divided by the head-camera image size), but the target object sizes for unsuccessful naming events did not ($M_{\text{Unsuccessful}}$ = 4.07%). This provides direct support for the hypothesis that referential selection at *input*, at the sensory level, matters to successful object name learning by infants. However, parent naming versus not naming was not strongly associated with the visual dominance of the target object in the child's view. Parents produced nearly as many unsuccessful naming events as successful ones, and only successful naming events show the visual signature of target objects in the child's view. Notice also that the named target object was larger in the child's head-camera view for successful than for unsuccessful naming events ($M_{\text{Successful}}$ = 6.28%; $M_{\text{Unsuccessful}}$ = 3.88%). We also examined whether these differences changed over the course of the play session: it could be that infants learned some words early in the session and because they knew these words, they might interact with the objects differently or parents might name objects differently early versus later in play. Comparisons of the relative dominance of the named object for the first three versus second three play trials did not differ for either successful or unsuccessful naming events. These analyses provide strong support for the relevance of visual information at the moment an object name was heard for the learning of that name by 18-month-old infants.

Now consider these same measures for the parent head-camera images, also shown in Figure 18.3. The image size of the objects was always smaller (because the objects tend to be farther away) in the parent's than in the infant's head-camera images. However, the pattern of image size for the named object for successful versus unsuccessful naming events *is the same for parents and infants*. More specifically, for the parent head-camera images, the named target was larger in the parents' head-camera image during successful than

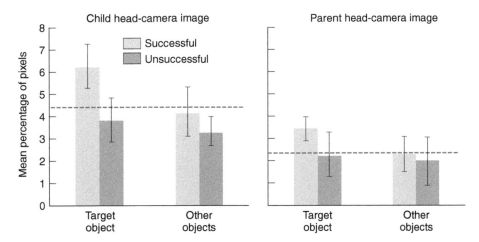

Figure 18.3 Mean object size (% pixels in image) for the named target, and for other objects in child's and parent's head-camera images during the naming event, for successful naming events that led to learning at post-test and for unsuccessful naming events that did not lead to learning as measured by test. Means and standard errors calculated with respect to trials. Dashed line indicates the mean object size during non-naming moments.

unsuccessful naming moments ($M_{\text{Successful}}$ = 3.46%; $M_{\text{Unsuccessful}}$ = 2.29%) and differed reliably from the comparison measure for non-naming events ($M_{\text{Non-naming}}$ = 2.36%). Considering that the target object was closer to the child (as established in the analyses of the child head-camera images), this pattern can happen *only* if parents move their head toward the named target (and child) during the naming event, thereby reducing the distance between the object and the head (and the head-camera). In brief, the target object was more visually dominant in *both* the infant's and the parent's view during successful but not unsuccessful naming events, indicating coordinated and joint attention during successful naming events.

Visual selection and the reduction of referential ambiguity at the sensory level, at input, must be accomplished by changing the physical relation between the potential visual targets and the eyes. Hand actions that move the object close to the head and eyes and the quieting of head movements that stabilize the view are thus potentially important components of visual selection. The left side of Figure 18.4 shows that infants were more likely to be holding the named object than other objects during both successful and unsuccessful naming events but holding was more strongly associated with successful than unsuccessful naming events. The object-holding behavior of parents, shown on the right side of Figure 18.4, was not reliably related to naming or to the learning of the object name. But notice there was a slight tendency for parents to be holding the named object during *unsuccessful* naming events; in the present task, parents did not often jointly hold the object that the child was holding and thus parent-holding is associated with not-holding by the child, which, in turn is associated with less visual dominance for the named target and with a decreased likelihood of learning the object name.

If sustained visual selection is critical to infant learning, then learning may also depend on the quieting of head movements to stabilize the selected object in the visual field. Figure 18.5 shows the percentage of time that infants and adults were moving their head during successful, non-successful, and non-naming events. For both head orientation and position and for both parents and infants, successful naming events are characterized by *less* head

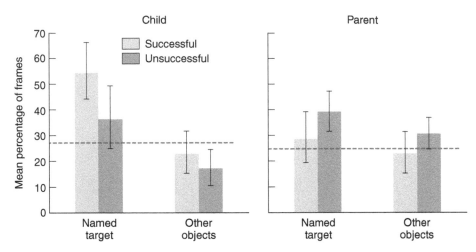

Figure 18.4 Mean percentage of frames in which the parent or child was holding the named object or another object for successful and unsuccessful naming events. Means and standard errors calculated with respect to trials. Dashed line indicates mean holding for children and parents during non-naming moments.

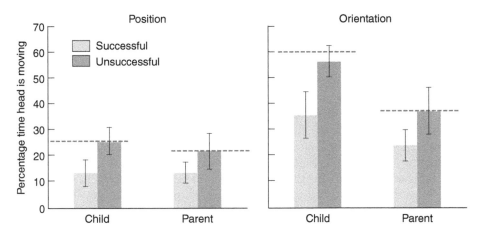

Figure 18.5 Mean percentage time with position and orientation head movements during successful and unsuccessful naming events for children and parents. Means and standard errors calculated with respect to trials. Dashed line indicates mean movements during non-naming moments.

movement, suggesting the importance of stabilized visual attention. The fact that both parents and infants stabilized attention on the named object during successful but not unsuccessful naming events again points to coordinated or joint attention at the sensorimotor level. Considering the evidence on hands and heads together, successful naming events in the present context appear to have the following properties. During successful naming events, infants tend to hold the target object and visually isolate that object for some time before and after it is named, and in doing so, they stabilize head movements, maintaining this visual dominance of the selected object. During successful naming events, parents tend, immediately prior to the naming event, to move their heads toward the named object and to hold the head steady at that moment, directed at the named object, but this increased visual dominance of the named object for the parent does not last and is localized to the naming event itself. Unsuccessful naming events have a different character, one in which both manual and visual attention on the part of the infant is more transient and one in which the visual field is more cluttered with other objects as large in the view as the named object. Both child's and parent's head movements may also reflect this greater clutter and more transient attention during non-successful naming events as infants and parents are less likely to move their heads toward the target object and less likely to stabilize the head.

General discussion

The problem of referential uncertainty, a fundamental one for learners who must learn words from their co-occurrence with scenes, is reduced if object names are provided when there is but one dominating object in the learner's view. The present results show that infants often create these moments through their own actions and that object naming during these visually optimal moments is associated with learning.

When infants bring objects close to their eyes and head, they effectively reduce the clutter and distraction in the visual field as close objects are visually large and block the view of potential distractors. This is a form of externally rather than internally accomplished visual selection and it highlights how the early control of attention may be tightly linked to sensorimotor behavior. This is a particularly interesting developmental idea because many cognitive developmental disorders involve attention and because there is considerable evidence of comorbidity of these cognitive disorders with early usual sensorimotor patterns (Hartman, Houwen, Scherder, and Visscher, 2010).

Experimental studies of adults show that the mature system can select and sustain attention on a visual target solely through internal means, without moving any part of the body and while eye gaze is fixated elsewhere (e.g., Müller, Philiastides, and Newsome, 2005; Shepherd, Findlay, and Hockey, 1986). However, visual attention is also usually linked to eye movements to the attended object's location (Hayhoe and Ballard, 2005). Moreover, eye movements (Grosbras, Laird, and Paus, 2005), head movements (Colby and Goldberg, 1992), and hand movements (Hagler, Riecke, and Sereno, 2007) have been shown to bias visual attention – detection and depth of processing – in the direction of the movement. This link between the localization of action and the localization of visual attention may be revealing of the common mechanisms behind action and attention as indicated by growing neural evidence that motor-planning regions play a role in cortical attentional networks (Hagler *et al.*, 2007). Perhaps for physically active toddlers, visual attention is more tightly tied to external action and with development these external mechanisms become more internalized.

The present study also raises a discussion on the level of understanding. Children learn the names of objects in which they are interested. Therefore, as shown in Figure 18.6(a), "interest," as a macro-level concept, may be viewed as a driving force behind learning (Bloom, Tinker, and Scholnick, 2001). Given this, what is the new contribution of the present study based on sensorimotor dynamics? One might argue that the main result is that infants learn object names when they are *interested* in those objects: that holding an object and a one-object view are merely indicators of the infant's interest in the object. That is, the cause of learning may not be the lack of visual clutter at the moment of object naming, but may be the child's interest in the object which happens to be correlated with the not

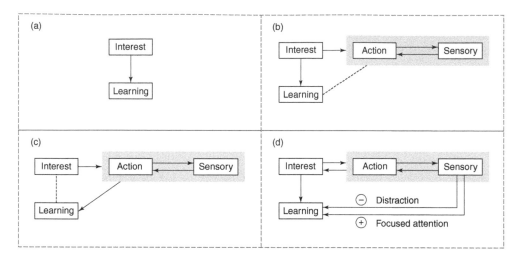

Figure 18.6 Four hypotheses on child's interest, learning, and sensorimotor behaviors. (a) Child's interest in target objects leads to learning. (b) Child's interest drives both learning and sensorimotor behaviors. Therefore, there are correlations between the two (the dashed line). (c) Child's interest leads to a sequence of actions on the interested object (e.g., holding and manipulating), which then lead to the visual dominance of that object. This clean visual input is fed into internal learning processes. In this way, child's interest is indirectly correlated to learning (the dashed line) because interest is implemented through child's perception and action which directly connect to learning. (d) Initially, child's interest directly influences both learning and sensorimotor behaviors. Thereafter, sensorimotor behaviors also directly influence learning (and maybe interest itself as well), as sustained attention to the target object may facilitate learning while distracting and messy sensory input may disrupt learning. In this way, both child's interest and sensorimotor behaviors jointly influence learning.

causally relevant one-object view. By this argument (as shown in Figure 18.6(b)), the results show only that infants learn the names of things in which they are interested more readily than the names of things in which they have little interest; visual selection at the sensory level is merely an associated attribute but not essential, nor contributory, to learning. From this perspective, the present study has gone to a lot of trouble and a lot of technology to demonstrate the obvious. Although we disagree with this view, the proposal that our measures of image size and holding are measures of infants' interest in the target object and that the results show that infants learn when they are interested in an object seems absolutely right to us. What the present results add to the macro-level construct of "interest" are two alternative explanations shown in Figure 18.6(c) and (d). First, the present study may provide a mechanistic explanation at a more micro level of analysis of why "interest" matters to learning. As proposed in Figure 18.6(c), interest in an object by a toddler may often *create* a bottom-up sensory input that is clean, optimized on a single object, and sustained. Interest may mechanistically yield better learning (at least in part) *because* of these sensory consequences. Therefore, at the macro level, one may observe the correlation between learning and interest; at the micro level, the effect of interest on learning may be implemented through clean sensory input, and through perceptual and action processes that directly connect to learning. Figure 18.6(d) provides a more integrated version of these ideas: interest may initially drive both learning (through a separate path) and the child's perception and action – which feed back onto interest and sustained attention and support learning. That is, interest may drive actions and the visual isolation of the object and thus increase interest. These sensorimotor behaviors may also directly influence learning by localizing and stabilizing attention and by limiting clutter and distraction. In brief, the micro-level embodied analyses presented here are not in competition with macro-level accounts but offer new and testable hypotheses at a finer grain of mechanism – moving forward from Figure 18.6(a) to 18.6(b), (c), and (d).

In conclusion, the main contribution of this research direction, then, is that it suggests a bottom-up embodied solution to word-referent learning by toddlers. Toddlers, through their own actions, often create a personal view that consists of one dominating object. Parents often (but not always) name objects during these optimal sensory moments and when they do, toddlers learn the object name.

Acknowledgments

I would like to thank Linda Smith as an incredible collaborator in the research discussed in this book chapter. I also thank Charlotte Wozniak, Amanda Favata, Alfredo Pereira, Amara Stuehling, and Andrew Filipowicz for collection of the data, Thomas Smith and Tian (Linger) Xu for developing data management and preprocessing software. This research was supported by National Science Foundation Grant 0924248 and AFOSR FA9550-09-1-0665.

References

Baldwin, D. (1993). Early referential understanding: Infants' ability to recognize referential acts for what they are. *Developmental Psychology, 29*, 832–843.

Ballard, D. H., Hayhoe, M. M., Pook, P. K., and Rao, R. P. N. (1997). Deictic codes for the embodiment of cognition. *Behavioral and Brain Sciences, 20*, 723–742.

Baron-Cohen, S. (1997). *Mindblindness: An essay on autism and theory of mind.* Cambridge, MA: MIT Press.

Beer, R. D. (1995). A dynamical systems perspective on agent-environment interaction. *Artificial Intelligence, 72*, 173–215.

Bloom, L., Tinker, E., and Scholnick, E. K. (2001). *The intentionality model and language acquisition: Engagement, effort, and the essential tension in development.* Malden, MA: Wiley-Blackwell.

Bloom, P. (2000). *How children learn the meaning of words.* Cambridge, MA: MIT Press.

Breazeal, C., and Scassellati, B. (2000). Infant-like social interactions between a robot and a human caregiver. *Adaptive Behavior, 8*, 49.

Brooks, R. A., and Stein, L. A. (1994). Building brains for bodies. *Autonomous Robots, 1*, 7–25.

Callanan, M. A. (1985). How parents label objects for young children: The role of input in the acquisition of category hierarchies. *Child Development*, 508–523.

———— (1990). Parents' descriptions of objects: Potential data for children's inferences about category principles. *Cognitive Development, 5(1)*, 101–122.

Clark, A. (2008). *Supersizing the mind: Embodiment, action, and cognitive extension.* Oxford: Oxford University Press.

Colby, C., and Goldberg, M. (1992). The updating of the representation of visual space in parietal cortex by intended eye movements. *Science, 255*, 90.

Gibbs, R. W. (2006). *Embodiment and cognitive science.* Cambridge: Cambridge University Press.

Grosbras, M. H., Laird, A. R., and Paus, T. (2005). Cortical regions involved in eye movements, shifts of attention, and gaze perception. *Human Brain Mapping, 25*, 140–154.

Hagler, D., Jr., Riecke, L., and Sereno, M. (2007). Parietal and superior frontal visuospatial maps activated by pointing and saccades. *Neuroimage, 35*, 1562–1577.

Hartman, E., Houwen, S., Scherder, E., and Visscher, C. (2010). On the relationship between motor performance and executive functioning in children with intellectual disabilities. *Journal of Intellectual Disability Research, 54*, 468–477.

Hayhoe, M., and Ballard, D. (2005). Eye movements in natural behavior. *Trends in Cognitive Sciences*, *9(4)*, 188–194.

Müller, J. R., Philiastides, M. G., and Newsome, W. T. (2005). Microstimulation of the superior colliculus focuses attention without moving the eyes. *Proceedings of the National Academy of Sciences of the United States of America*, *102(3)*, 524–529.

Pereira, A. F., Smith, L. B., and Yu, C. (in press). A bottom-up view of toddler word learning. *Psychological Bulletin and Review*.

Pfeifer, R., and Scheier, C. (1999). *Understanding intelligence*. Cambridge, MA: MIT Press.

Quine, W. (1960). *Word and object*. Cambridge, MA: MIT Press.

Shapiro, L. (2011). *Embodied cognition*. London: Taylor & Francis.

Shepherd, M., Findlay, J., and Hockey, R. (1986). The relationship between eye movements and spatial attention. *Quarterly Journal of Experimental Psychology Section A*, *38(3)*, 475–491.

Smith, L. B., Yu, C., and Pereira, A. F. (2011). Not your mother's view: The dynamics of toddler visual experience. *Developmental Science*, *14*, 9–17.

Spivey, M. (2007). *The Continuity of Mind*. New York: Oxford University Press.

Tomasello, M. (2000). The social-pragmatic theory of word learning. *Pragmatics*, *10*, 401–413.

Tomasello, M., and Akhtar, N. (1995). Two-year-olds use pragmatic cues to differentiate reference to objects and actions. *Cognitive Development*, *10*, 201–224.

Wellman, H. M., and Liu, D. (2004). Scaling of theory-of-mind tasks. *Child Development*, *75*, 523–541.

Woodward, A. L., and Guajardo, J. J. (2002). Infants' understanding of the point gesture as an object-directed action. *Cognitive Development*, *17*, 1061–1084.

Yu, C., Ballard, D. H., and Aslin, R. N. (2005). The role of embodied intention in early lexical acquisition. *Cognitive Science: A Multidisciplinary Journal*, *29*, 961–1005.

Yu, C., and Smith, L. B. (2012). Embodied attention and word learning by toddlers. *Cognition*, *125*, 244–262.

Yu, C., Smith, L. B., Shen, H., Pereira, A., and Smith, T. (2009). Active information selection: Visual attention through the hands. *IEEE Transactions on Autonomous Mental Development*, *2*, 141–151.

PART 6

Reasoning and Education

19

GESTURE IN REASONING

An embodied perspective

Martha W. Alibali, Rebecca Boncoddo, and
Autumn B. Hostetter

Introduction

Theories of embodied cognition claim that cognitive processes are rooted in interactions of the human body with the physical world. The core idea is that cognition depends on the specifics of the body and its actual or possible actions in the world. This embodied perspective is the basis for a diverse set of theoretical positions and specific claims regarding perception, cognition, and language (summarized in Anderson 2003; Nathan 2021; Shapiro 2011; Wilson 2002). In this chapter, we take an embodied perspective on *reasoning*, which we define as cognitive processing in the service of inference, judgment, or solving problems. We review research relevant to two central claims of the embodied cognition perspective: (1) reasoning is based in perception and action; and (2) reasoning is grounded in the physical environment.

A growing body of research shows that actions – including both physical actions that people perform and simulated actions that people imagine – can affect reasoning and problem solving. In this chapter, we focus on one special type of action – gesture. Gestures are movements of the hands and body that are integrally connected with thinking, and often, with speaking.

Many past studies have considered speakers' gestures as evidence that the knowledge expressed in those gestures is "embodied." Indeed, a recent theoretical account, the Gesture as Simulated Action (GSA) framework (Hostetter and Alibali 2008, 2019), holds that gestures derive from simulated actions. This view builds on the idea that mental simulations of actions and perceptual states activate the same neural areas that are used in actual actions and perception. According to the GSA framework, this activation is not always completely inhibited during speaking, and it can be expressed in gestures.

From this perspective, then, gestures yield evidence for the embodiment of cognition because they derive from simulated actions and perceptions. At the same time, gestures are also actions. As such, gestures may directly affect thought in many of the same ways that action can.

In this chapter, we focus on gesture and the role it plays in an embodied account of reasoning. We first address the distinction between action and gesture. We then consider

DOI: 10.4324/9781003322511-26

three broad claims regarding gesture and reasoning: (1) gesture production manifests embodied processes in reasoning; (2) gesture production plays a causal role in reasoning by raising activation on perceptual-motor information; and (3) gesture communicates information that affects listeners' reasoning.

What are gestures?

Actions are movements of parts of the body. As such, actions involve an interaction between an individual and the physical environment. In many cases, actions involve manipulating or moving objects. *Gestures* are a special form of action that typically do not involve acting on the environment or manipulating objects. Instead, gestures involve moving a part of the body (often the hands or arms) in order to express an idea or meaning. Gestures are not produced in order to act upon the world; instead, they are produced as part of the cognitive processes that underlie thinking and speaking.

The distinction between gestures and other actions is not always clear-cut (Novack, Wakefield, and Goldin-Meadow 2016). Gestures typically represent things without utilizing objects. However, in some cases people gesture with objects (e.g., pointers) or toward or on objects (e.g., tracing a feature of an object to represent that feature). Additionally, people sometimes hold up or manipulate objects when they speak or think about those objects, and those movements are also gesture-like, in that they highlight or direct attention to features of the objects or demonstrate actions on those objects. Some researchers consider only movements produced along with speech to be gestures (e.g., Goldin-Meadow 2003: 8), while others take a broader view that also includes movements produced when thinking in silence (e.g., Chu and Kita 2011). Our focus in this chapter is on gestures as a form of action, so we take a broader perspective. We consider gestures to be actions that are produced as part of the cognitive processes involved in speaking or thinking.

Several different classification systems for gestures have been proposed (e.g., McNeill 1992). Our focus in this chapter is primarily on *representational* gestures, which are gestures that depict some aspect of their meaning via hand shape or motion (e.g., moving the hand in a circle to represent *spin*). We also consider *pointing* gestures, a subtype of representational gestures that indicate objects or locations. These types of gestures can be distinguished from *beat* gestures, which are motorically simple, rhythmic movements, akin to beating time, and *interactive* gestures, which are used to regulate turn-taking and other aspects of interaction.

There are a number of contemporary theories about the cognitive processes that give rise to gestures (e.g., Clark 2016; Kita and Özyürek 2003; McNeill 2005). One perspective, the GSA framework (Hostetter and Alibali 2008, 2019), builds on an embodied perspective on language and cognitive processing, and makes explicit ties to action. Simply stated, the GSA framework proposes that gestures derive from simulated actions or perceptual states, which people utilize when thinking or when producing or comprehending language. These simulated actions and perceptual states activate corresponding motor and premotor areas of the brain (e.g., Hauk, Johnsrude, and Pulvermüller 2004). When activation in these areas exceeds a critical threshold, people may produce overt movements that we recognize as gestures.

Hostetter and Alibali (2010) tested the GSA framework's claim that gestures arise from highly activated simulations of action. In a series of experiments, they found that participants produced more gestures when describing information they acquired through physical actions than information they acquired visually. This evidence supports the central claim of the GSA framework, namely that gestures arise when speakers strongly simulate actions.

According to the GSA framework, gestures are particularly likely to occur along with speech, because the combined activation from speech production and mental simulation is likely to exceed the speaker's gesture threshold. However, producing speech is not necessary for a gesture to occur. In some cases, activation on action simulations can exceed the gesture threshold, even without the extra "boost" in activation provided by speech production. For example, when performing mental rotation tasks, some people spontaneously produce gestures, even when they do not speak aloud (Chu and Kita 2011). Similarly, when given a configuration of gears and asked to predict the movement of a specific gear, many participants spontaneously produce gestures depicting gear movements (Alibali, Spencer, Knox, and Kita 2011, Experiment 2). These studies suggest that people gesture when they engage in cognitive processing that involves highly activated simulations of actions or perceptual states, even if they are not also producing speech.

Gesture production manifests embodied processes in reasoning

The embodied cognition perspective holds that thought is based in perception and action. If gestures do, in fact, derive from simulated actions and perceptual states, as claimed by the GSA framework, then gestures provide *prima facie* evidence for this claim. When speakers express ideas that they mentally represent in simulations of actions and perceptual states, they naturally produce gestures, and these gestures manifest the embodied nature of those ideas.

Gestures that manifest simulated actions and perceptions commonly occur with the verbalizations that people produce during reasoning and problem-solving tasks. Not surprisingly, people often produce gestures when talking about *bodily actions* that they have performed (or could perform). For example, Kamermans and colleagues compared the gestures of participants who had learned about a shape via manual exploration (i.e., by touching a foam cut-out of the shape) and participants who had learned about the shape via vision (i.e., by seeing it). Those who learned via manual exploration gestured more than those who learned via vision, and they were more likely to produce gestures that depicted tracing the contour of the shape (Kamermans *et al.* 2019). Along similar lines, Cook and Tanenhaus (2009) compared the gestures of participants who had solved a Tower of Hanoi puzzle using physical objects (i.e., disks and pegs) and participants who solved the same puzzle on a computer. Participants in both conditions described moving the disks in speech and gestures, but participants in the real-objects condition produced a greater proportion of gestures that used grasping hand shapes, like the actions they produced when actually moving the disks, than participants in the computer condition. In both experiments, participants' gestures were aligned with the actual actions they had produced earlier in the experiment, which they presumably called to mind in subsequent tasks.

People also produce gestures when they engage in other forms of reasoning that involve simulated actions and perceptions, such as when they reason about physical forces (Roth 2002) or when they form or manipulate mental images of objects or scenes that are not physically present (Chu and Kita 2008; McNeill *et al.* 2001). For example, Singer, Radinsky, and Goldman (2008) described the gestures produced by children in a science class when discussing data about earthquakes and volcanoes. The children frequently produced representational gestures depicting the movements of tectonic plates, including rift, subduction, and buckling.

Perhaps most surprising is that people also use representational gestures when reasoning about *abstract ideas*. Several accounts of human cognition are compatible with the idea that simulations of actions and perceptual states are activated when thinking about abstract concepts (e.g., Barsalou, Simmons, Barbey, and Wilson 2003; Glenberg *et al.* 2008; Lakoff and Johnson 1980). Lakoff and Johnson (1980) argued that many abstract concepts are understood in terms of metaphors that are based in the body or in human experience. These metaphors are sometimes manifested in the gestures that people produce when speaking or reasoning about abstract concepts. For example, one conceptual metaphor that applies in early mathematics is ARITHMETIC IS COLLECTING OBJECTS (Lakoff and Núñez 2001), and this metaphor can also be observed in spontaneous gestures (Alcaraz-Carrión, Alibali, and Valenzuela 2022). For example, Marghetis, Bergen, and Núñez (2012) described a student who said, "Because you add the same numbers" while producing a gesture in which she brought her hands, in grasping hand shapes, together in front of her body, representing gathering two collections or masses. Thus, evidence from gestures suggests that adding abstract entities, such as numbers, may involve a mental simulation of the physical action of collecting objects. Even abstract notions, such as mathematical concepts, are rooted in bodily actions.

Thus far, we have focused on gestures that display elements of people's mental simulations of actions and perceptual states by virtue of their form (hand shape or motion trajectory). However, not all gestures depict semantic content in this way. Instead, some gestures express information by *pointing*. Pointing gestures index objects and locations in the physical world, and they have meaning by virtue of this indexing function (Glenberg and Robertson 2000). A pointing gesture may directly refer to the object or location that it indicates (e.g., pointing to a cup to refer to that cup), or it can refer indirectly to a related or perceptually similar object (e.g., pointing to a cup on one's desk to refer to a cup in one's cupboard; Butcher, Mylander, and Goldin-Meadow 1991). Pointing gestures can even refer metaphorically to abstract ideas by indicating "places" for those ideas (e.g., gesturing to one location to indicate "pros" of a decision, and to another location to indicate "cons"). Thus, pointing gestures manifest another of the core claims of many theories of embodied cognition, namely, the notion that cognition is grounded in the environment. Pointing gestures suggest that speakers utilize the environment as "part" of their cognitive system, by indexing present objects and locations, sometimes to represent non-present objects or locations, or even non-tangible ideas.

Thus, there are multiple ways in which gesture manifests embodied processes in human reasoning (see Alibali and Nathan 2012, for further discussion). First, representational gestures display elements of mental simulations of actions and perceptual states. Second, some representational gestures reveal body-based and experiential metaphors that are associated with, and may underpin, certain abstract concepts. Finally, pointing gestures index words and ideas to the physical world. Thus, gestures suggest that cognition is both rooted in perception and action, and grounded in the environment.

Gesture production plays a causal role in reasoning

We have argued that gestures *reflect* thoughts that are grounded in sensory and motor processes – thus, gestures manifest embodied thinking. However, gestures may also do more. In this section, we present evidence that producing gestures can *affect* thought by increasing activation on perceptual and motor information.

Several studies have demonstrated that *actions* can facilitate problem solving when they embody a problem's solution (e.g., Catrambone, Craig, and Nersessian 2006). For example, Thomas and Lleras (2007) asked participants to solve Duncker's (1945) radiation problem, in which a doctor tries to destroy a tumor with a ray. If the ray is directed at the tumor with enough intensity to destroy it, it will also destroy the healthy tissue it passes through. At lesser intensities, the ray can safely pass through healthy tissue, but it will not affect the tumor. How can the doctor use the ray to destroy the tumor, without destroying the healthy tissue around it? The solution is to split the ray into multiple, less intense rays that converge on the tumor. Participants worked on the radiation problem and took frequent breaks to do a seemingly unrelated eye-tracking task, in which they directed their eyes to a digit among an array of letters. In the critical condition, the location of the digits required that participants moved their eyes repeatedly from the periphery of the screen to the center. Participants who produced these seemingly unrelated eye movements were more likely to solve the radiation problem than participants who produced other eye movement patterns.

The effect of action is not limited to eye movements. Several studies have reported beneficial effects of directed hand movements for reasoning tasks. For example, Thomas and Lleras (2009) asked participants to solve Maier's (1931) two-string problem, which requires figuring out how to tie together two strings that are hanging from the ceiling sufficiently far apart that participants cannot simply reach both strings at the same time. The solution is to tie a pair of pliers that is available in the room to one string so that it will swing like a pendulum and come within arm's reach of the solver. Participants who took problem-solving breaks in which they engaged in arm-swinging "exercises" were more likely to solve the problem than were participants who engaged in stretching exercises, which did not embody the problem's solution. Moreover, this effect held even for participants who were not aware that there was a connection between their movements and the solution. Along similar lines, Nathan and colleagues found that directing participants to produce hand movements relevant to mathematical proofs supported participants in generating the core insights that underlay the proofs (Nathan *et al.* 2014). Likewise, Ginns and colleagues found that directing participants to make tracing actions over relevant features of worked mathematics problems was beneficial for participants' subsequent problem solving, both for problems that involved angle relationships in triangles and for problems that involved applying order of operations rules (Ginns, Hu, Byrne, and Bobis 2016).

These studies suggest that *actions* affect problem solving, but what about *gestures*? As discussed above, gestures are a special kind of action produced as part of the cognitive processes involved in speaking or thinking. In contrast to the arm-swinging movements produced by participants in Thomas and Lleras's (2009) study, gestures manifest specific ideas that people have in mind. According to the GSA framework, speakers produce gestures because they mentally simulate actions or perceptual states, and gestures represent salient or highly activated elements of those simulations.

Recent work suggests that, not only do gestures manifest elements of peoples' mental simulations, they can also affect those simulations, and thereby influence memory and problem solving (Cook, Yip, and Goldin-Meadow 2010; Wesp, Hess, Keutmann, and Wheaton 2001). Kita, Alibali, and Chu (2017) summarized the literature on gesture's effects in terms of four primary functions that affect the content of people's mental simulations: gesture serves to *activate*, *manipulate*, *package*, and *explore* perceptual and motor information for speaking and thinking. They further argued that these functions are shaped by gesture's propensity to *schematize* information, or to "focus on a small subset of available information that is potentially relevant to the task at hand" (p. 246).

Several sources of data indicate that gesture serves to *activate* perceptual and motor elements of mental simulations. In so doing, gesture highlights those elements as relevant and important for further processing (see Alibali and Kita 2010; Goldin-Meadow and Beilock 2010; Kita *et al*. 2017, for discussion). In support of this view, when people gesture about a task, scene, or event, they are especially likely to focus on perceptual elements of that task, scene, or event. For example, Alibali and Kita (2010) asked children to explain their solutions to Piagetian conservation problems, with gesture either allowed or prevented. Children were more likely to describe perceptually present information (e.g., perceptual features of the task objects, such as height, width, or length) when they were allowed to gesture. When they were prevented from gesturing, children were more likely to describe how the problem looked previously or how it might look in the future, rather than how it looked at that moment. Thus, gestures appear to ground speakers' thinking and speaking in perceptually present features of the current environment.

Gestures can activate perceptual and motoric aspects of problems, even when problems involve no perceptually available display. In one study, college students were asked to imagine sequences of varying numbers of gears, and for each sequence, to predict the direction of movement of the final gear, given the movement of the initial gear. Participants talked out loud as they solved the problems, and some participants were prevented from gesturing. Participants who were allowed to gesture were *less likely* to discover that odd-numbered gears turn in the same direction as the initial gear and even-numbered gears turn in the opposite direction (the *parity* rule) than were participants who were prevented from gesturing. Instead, participants who were allowed to gesture tended to simulate the actions of each gear to predict the movement of the final gear (Alibali *et al*. 2011, Experiment 1). Thus, gestures highlighted perceptual and motoric aspects of the task, even though those aspects were not perceptually present in the given problems.

In the gear task, focusing on perceptual and motor information actually *hindered* participants' performance, as it prevented them from generating the abstract, highly efficient parity rule. Studies of analogical problem solving have also revealed detrimental effects of gesture production on performance (Hostetter *et al*. 2016; Cooperrider and Goldin-Meadow 2014). Gesture's tendency to highlight perceptual information may actually make it more challenging for solvers who produce gestures to discern the more abstract problem structure that is key to analogical mapping – an idea that seems to contradict the claim that gesture's power comes from its ability to schematize information (Kita *et al*. 2017). Indeed, whether gesture helps or hinders problem solving may depend on whether perceptual and motor information is integral to the problem's solution, and on whether that information contributes to a helpful or an unhelpful schematization of the problem.

Gestures can also support people as they attempt to *manipulate* perceptual or motoric information for reasoning and solving problems. Evidence for this function comes from a variety of experimental tasks, including mental rotation (Chu and Kita 2011), abacus calculation (Hatano, Miyake, and Binks 1977), and "penetrative thinking," which involves reasoning about the internal structure of an object based on its visible surface (Atit, Gagnier, and Shipley 2015). As one example, Chu and Kita (2011) found that people solved mental rotation problems more accurately when they produced gestures compared to when they did not. Along similar lines, Hatano *et al*. (1977) found that many expert abacus operators moved their fingers as if manipulating an abacus while performing mental calculation, and they tended to calculate less accurately when they were prevented from moving their hands. With a larger sample of abacus experts, however, Brooks *et al.* (2018) found that being prevented from moving did not significantly impair performance, though motor interference (e.g., tapping) did (see also Kamermans *et al.* 2019). It may be that it is the ability to plan and imagine a gesture—rather than actually producing the gesture—that is most beneficial.

Gesture can also help people to *package* complex information into chunks or units suitable for verbalizing (Kita 2000) or problem solving (Kita *et al.* 2017). Evidence for this function comes from a study of children learning to solve equations such as $2 + 3 + 7 =$ __ $+ 7$ (Goldin-Meadow *et al.* 2009). Children were directed to gesture, either to parts of the equations that were directly relevant to a correct solution strategy (i.e., pointing to the $2 + 3$ and then the blank) or to units that were less directly relevant to a correct solution strategy (i.e., pointing to the $3 + 7$ and then the blank). Children who gestured to solution-appropriate units solved similar problems more successfully on a subsequent post-test than did children who gestured to less solution-appropriate units.

Gesture can also be used to *explore* perceptual and motor information relevant to a problem at hand. In so doing, gesture may generate new information that is not provided in the given problem. For example, Boncoddo, Dixon, and Kelley (2010) asked preschool children to solve gear-system problems, in which they had to determine in which direction a final gear would turn, given information about how an initial gear turned. Children often traced the alternating sequence of gears in gestures as they attempted to solve the problems. Moreover, the more children traced the sequence, the more likely they were to discover the new idea that adjacent gears turn in alternating directions. Note that the alternating movements were not actually present in the display – instead, children generated the notion of alternation in their gestures. Thus, gestures introduced new information into children's reasoning.

Research on people engaging in mathematical proof also supports the idea that people may explore problems with gestures, and that doing so may bring new information into people's reasoning. Pier and colleagues (2019) presented college students with two conjectures – a geometric conjecture that involved triangles, and a conjecture about the number system that involved odd/even numbers – and asked them to offer a justification for each. They coded participants' production of *dynamic gestures*, which they defined as gestures that represent transformations of mathematical objects (see Garcia and Infante 2012). For both conjectures, participants who produced dynamic gestures were more likely to express valid proofs than participants who did not produce dynamic gestures – compatible with the idea that producing gestures brought relevant information into their reasoning.

However, subsequent work by Walkington and colleagues (2019) casts some doubt on the idea that gesture plays a causal role in mathematical proof. They asked college students to generate proofs for geometric conjectures and prevented some participants from gesturing while doing so. They found no differences between participants who were allowed to gesture and participants who were prevented from gesturing in their proof generation. These null findings highlight the importance of understanding the tasks, conditions, and participant groups for which gestures are versus are not beneficial for reasoning.

In sum, although some studies have yielded null or mixed results, there is a considerable body of evidence that suggests that gesture production activates perceptual and motor information, supports people in manipulating and packaging such information, and is a means through which people explore perceptual and motor aspects of problems. In many cases, when people gesture, they are more likely to incorporate perceptual and motor information into their reasoning – both information that is available in the problem at hand, and novel information that they generate by exploring the problem space with gestures. Kita, Alibali, and Chu (2017) argued that these functions flow from gesture's ability to schematize perceptual and motoric information – thus, producing gestures can enhance the role of such information in reasoning. Further work is needed to better understand the cognitive mechanisms by which gesture influences reasoning, and to elucidate the boundary conditions on the causal effects of gestures.

Gesture communicates information that affects listeners' reasoning

Thus far, we have focused on gestures from the perspective of the individual who produces them. We have considered what gestures reveal about the cognitive processes of the gesturer, and we have discussed the role of gesture in shaping those cognitive processes. In this section, we consider the other side of the interactional "coin" – that is, we consider speakers' gestures from the perspective of the listener (or observer). We argue that gesture may affect *listeners'* cognitive processing in two main ways. First, speakers' gestures may help listeners to *grasp speakers' referential intentions*, by indexing their utterances to objects or locations in the physical and socially shared environment. Second, speakers' gestures can help listeners to grasp *speakers' semantic intentions*, by helping them to simulate the actions and perceptual states that speakers have in mind.

As discussed above, pointing gestures communicate because they index words and phrases to objects and locations in the physical world (Glenberg and Robertson 2000). Pointing gestures help listeners to make reference, especially when speech is ambiguous or degraded (Thompson and Massaro 1994). From an embodied perspective, this phenomenon suggests that speakers' pointing gestures help listeners to index the referents that speakers intend. Thus, in communicative settings, pointing gestures affect listeners' reasoning because they help listeners grasp speakers' referential intentions.

Like pointing gestures, representational gestures can also influence listeners' comprehension (for reviews, see Hostetter 2011; Dargue, Sweller, and Jones 2019). There are at least two possible pathways by which this can occur. First, observing a speaker's representational gestures might guide listeners in constructing corresponding action simulations in their own minds (Alibali and Hostetter 2011). When people observe others' actions, motor and premotor areas of their brains are activated in corresponding ways (Jeannerod 2001; Rizzolatti, Fogassi, and Gallese 2001; Wheaton, Thompson, Syngeniotis, Abbott, and Puce 2004). Put simply, "our motor system simulates under threshold the observed action in a strictly congruent fashion" (Fadiga, Craighero, and Olivier 2005, p. 213). Because gestures are a form of action, the same principles presumably apply in observing gestures. If gestures manifest simulated actions and perceptual states, then observing gestures may guide listeners to generate corresponding simulations in their own minds. Consistent with this idea, Wakefield and colleagues have shown that children who viewed a lesson about equations that included gesture as well as speech later showed more activation in motor regions of the brain when later solving equations than children who learned from a speech-only lesson (Wakefield, Congdon, Novack, Goldin-Meadow, and James 2019). Thus, speakers' representational gestures may help listeners to comprehend speakers' intended meanings by helping them construct comparable mental simulations.

Some evidence suggests that listeners may understand speakers' intended meanings better when speakers produce gestures that simulate actions than when they produce actual actions. Hostetter, Pouw, and Wakefield (2020) showed listeners videos of an actor either gesturing about how to move objects to different locations or actually moving the objects to the locations. The actor's movements depicted a rule about how to move the objects (e.g., objects picked up with one hand should be moved up). Hostetter *et al.* found that seeing the movements enacted in gesture led to better comprehension of the underlying rule than seeing the actual movements performed on the objects. These findings suggest that seeing gestures encouraged listeners to simulate specific details of the actions in their own minds, such that those details were then more available for later use.

Second, observing a speaker's gestures may encourage listeners to produce corresponding gestures themselves. That is, viewing a speaker's gestures may elicit overt mimicry of those gestures, and those gestures may in turn affect reasoning. A similar mechanism has been proposed for understanding facial expressions of emotion (the Simulation of Smiles model; Niedenthal, Mermillod, Maringer, and Hess 2010). According to this model, both mimicry and simulation contribute to perceivers' understanding of different types of smiles. In a parallel fashion, we suggest that both overt gestural mimicry and covert simulation of corresponding actions contribute to listeners' comprehension of gestures.

Do listeners overtly mimic speakers' gestures, either in silence during the speaker's turn, or in their own subsequent turns? Yes, such mimicry does occur. For example, children who received a math lesson in which the instructor gestured were themselves more likely to gesture when explaining math problems than children who received a similar lesson in which the instructor did not gesture (Cook and Goldin-Meadow 2006). Moreover, children's gestures tended to reproduce the form of the instructor's gestures. Children not only mimic the gestures of human teachers, but they also mimic the gestures produced by an animated teacher avatar (Vest, Fyfe, Nathan, and Alibali 2020).

Gestural mimicry is also evident in other discourse contexts, including conversation and narrative (Kimbara 2006; Lakoff and Núñez 2001). Moreover, people produce similar gestures more frequently when they can see one another than when they cannot (Holler and Wilkin 2011; Kimbara 2008), suggesting that gestural mimicry is purposeful, and not simply due to people using similar gestures when they talk about similar things. Holler and Wilkin (2011) argue that gestural mimicry fosters shared understanding between participants in dialog, in some cases by presenting semantic information that aligns with what the other had expressed on a previous turn, and at other times by displaying "acceptance" or comprehension of the other's communication.

However, despite evidence that gesture mimicry plays an important role in establishing shared understanding, overt mimicry of gestures is relatively rare (see, e.g., Holler and Wilkin 2011). It is also unusual to see listeners gesture *while* others are speaking. Therefore, it seems likely that most of gesture's contribution to comprehension comes from gesture guiding covert action simulations or facilitating reference via indexing.

In sum, there are multiple reasons why speakers' gestures may influence listeners' comprehension, and consequently their reasoning (Hostetter 2011). First, speakers' gestures help listeners to index speakers' utterances to the physical environment. Second, speakers' gestures help listeners to construct simulations that align with those of the speakers. They may do so via two distinct pathways – by encouraging overt mimicry of gestural actions, or by guiding construction of appropriate simulations.

Conclusion

In this chapter, we have provided evidence for three broad claims regarding gesture and reasoning. First, we argued that gestures manifest embodied processes in reasoning. In line with the GSA framework, we argued that *representational gestures* derive from mental simulations of actions and perceptual states. When speakers express ideas based in simulations of actions and perceptual states, they often produce gestures, and those gestures manifest the embodied nature of those ideas. Further, we argued that *pointing gestures* index objects and locations in the physical world. As such, pointing gestures provide evidence for the claim that cognition is grounded in the physical environment.

Second, we presented evidence that gesture plays a causal role in reasoning, and that it does so by highlighting perceptual and motor information, both in the environment and in people's mental simulations of tasks, events, or scenes. We reviewed evidence that gestures increase activation on perceptual and motor information, support people in manipulating and packaging perceptual and motor information, and are a means by which people can explore perceptual and motor aspects of a problem or situation. Because of these functions of gesture, people are more likely to incorporate perceptual and motor information into their reasoning when they produce gestures.

Finally, we argued that speakers' gestures affect listeners' reasoning. Speakers' gestures guide listeners' indexing of speakers' utterances to the physical environment. In addition, speakers' gestures may help listeners to construct simulations that align with speakers' simulations. This may occur via listeners' direct mimicry of speakers' gestures, or by listeners using information expressed in speakers' gestures to guide and constrain their own mental simulations.

In sum, it is becoming increasingly clear that gestures are more than simple "hand waving." Gestures offer researchers a valuable window on the embodied cognitive processes involved in reasoning. Moreover, as a form of action, gestures can also play a functional role in those processes. A deeper understanding of how and why people gesture is critical for scientific progress in understanding human reasoning. Better understanding of the mechanisms that underpin gesture production and comprehension will lead to greater insights into when, why, for whom, and in what contexts gesture contributes to reasoning.

References

Alcaraz-Carrión, D., Alibali. M. W., and Valenzuela, J. (2022) "Adding and subtracting by hand: Metaphorical representations of arithmetic in spontaneous co-speech gestures," *Acta Psychologica*, *228*, Article 103624. https://doi.org/10.1016/j.actpsy.2022.103624

Alibali, M. W., and Hostetter, A. B. (2011) "Mimicry and simulation in gesture comprehension," *Behavioral and Brain Sciences*, *33*, 433–434. (Commentary on Niedenthal, Maringer, Mermillod, and Hess, 2010.)

Alibali, M. W., and Kita, S. (2010) "Gesture highlights perceptually present information for speakers," *Gesture*, *10(1)*, 3–28.

Alibali, M. W., and Nathan, M. J. (2012) "Embodiment in mathematics teaching and learning: Evidence from students' and teachers' gestures," *Journal of the Learning Sciences*, *21(2)*, 247–286.

Alibali, M. W., Spencer, R. C., Knox, L., and Kita, S. (2011) "Spontaneous gestures influence strategy choices in problem solving," *Psychological Science*, *22(9)*, 1138–1144.

Anderson, M. L. (2003) "Embodied cognition: A field guide," *Artificial Intelligence*, *149(1)*, 91–130.

Atit, K., Gagnier, K., and Shipley, T. (2015) "Student gestures aid penetrative thinking," *Journal of Geoscience Education*, *63*, 66–72.

Barsalou, L. W., Simmons, W. K., Barbey, A. K., and Wilson, C. D. (2003) "Grounding conceptual knowledge in modality-specific systems," *Trends in Cognitive Sciences*, *7*(2), 84–91.

Boncoddo, R., Dixon, J. A., and Kelley, E. (2010) "The emergence of a novel representation from action: Evidence from preschoolers," *Developmental Science*, *13*(2), 370–377.

Brooks, N. B., Barner, D., Frank, M., and Goldin-Meadow, S. (2018) "The role of gesture in supporting mental representations: The case of mental abacus arithmetic," *Cognitive Science*, *42*(2), 554–575.

Butcher, C., Mylander, C., and Goldin-Meadow, S. (1991) "Displaced communication in a self-styled gesture system: Pointing at the nonpresent," *Cognitive Development*, *6*, 315–342.

Catrambone, R., Craig, D. L., and Nersessian, N. J. (2006) "The role of perceptually represented structure in analogical problem solving," *Memory and Cognition*, *34*(5), 1126–1132.

Chu, M., and Kita, S. (2008) "Spontaneous gestures during mental rotation tasks: Insights into the microdevelopment of the motor strategy," *Journal of Experimental Psychology: General*, *137*(4), 706–723.

———— (2011) "The nature of gestures' beneficial role in spatial problem solving," *Journal of Experimental Psychology: General*, *140*(1), 102–116.

Clark, H. H. (2016) "Depicting as a method of communication," *Psychological Review*, *123*(3), 324–347.

Cook, S. W., and Goldin-Meadow, S. (2006) "The role of gesture in learning: Do children use their hands to change their minds?" *Journal of Cognition and Development*, *7*, 211–232.

Cook, S. W., and Tanenhaus, M. K. (2009) "Embodied communication: Speakers' gestures affect listeners' actions," *Cognition*, *113*(1), 98–104.

Cook, S. W., Yip, T. K., and Goldin-Meadow, S. (2010) "Gesturing makes memories that last," *Journal of Memory and Language*, *63*(4), 465–475.

Cooperrider, K., and Goldin-Meadow, S. (2014) "The role of gesture in analogical problem solving.," in P. Bello, M. Guarini, M. McShane, and B. Scassellati (eds), *Proceedings of the 36th. Annual Conference of the Cognitive Science Society* (pp. 2068–2072) Austin, TX: Cognitive Science Society.

Dargue, N., Sweller, N., and Jones, M. P. (2019) "When our hands help us understand: A meta-analysis into the effects of gesture on comprehension," *Psychological Bulletin*, *145*(8), 765–784.

Duncker, K. (1945) "On problem solving" (L. S. Lees, Trans.) (Special issue) *Psychological Monographs*, *58*(270)

Fadiga, L., Craighero, L., and Olivier, E. (2005) "Human motor cortex excitability during the perception of others' action," *Current Opinion in Neurobiology*, *15*(2), 213–218.

Garcia, N., and Infante, N. E. (2012) "Gestures as facilitators to proficient mental modelers," in L. R. Van Zoest, J.-J. Lo, and J. L. Kratky (eds) *Proceedings of the 34th annual meeting of the North American chapter of the International Group for the Psychology of Mathematics Education* (pp. 289–295) Kalamazoo, MI: Western Michigan University.

Ginns, P., Hu, F., Byrne, E., and Bobis, J. (2016) "Learning by tracing worked examples," *Applied Cognitive Psychology*, *30*(2), 160–169.

Glenberg, A. M., and Robertson, D. A. (2000) "Symbol grounding and meaning: A comparison of high-dimensional and embodied theories of meaning," *Journal of Memory and Language*, *43*, 379–401.

Glenberg, A. M., Sato, M., Cattaneo, L., Riggio, L., Palumbo, D., and Buccino, G. (2008) "Processing abstract language modulates motor system activity," *Quarterly Journal of Experimental Psychology*, *61*(6), 905–919.

Goldin-Meadow, S. (2003) *Hearing gesture: How our hands help us think*, Cambridge, MA: Harvard University Press.

Goldin-Meadow, S., and Beilock, S. L. (2010) "Action's influence on thought: The case of gesture," *Perspectives on Psychological Science*, *5*(6), 664–674.

Goldin-Meadow, S., Cook, S. W., and Mitchell, Z. A. (2009) "Gesturing gives children new ideas about math," *Psychological Science*, *20*, 267–272.

Hatano, G., Miyake, Y., and Binks, M. G. (1977) "Performance of expert abacus operators," *Cognition, 5*, 47–55.

Hauk, O., Johnsrude, I., and Pulvermüller, F. (2004) "Somatotopic representation of action words in human motor and premotor cortex," *Neuron, 41*, 301–307.

Holler, J., and Wilkin, K. (2011) "Co-speech gesture mimicry in the process of collaborative referring during face-to-face dialogue," *Journal of Nonverbal Behavior, 35(2)*, 133–153.

Hostetter, A. B. (2011) "When do gestures communicate? A meta-analysis," *Psychological Bulletin, 137(2)*, 297–315.

Hostetter, A. B., and Alibali, M. W. (2008) "Visible embodiment: Gestures as simulated action," *Psychonomic Bulletin and Review, 15(3)*, 495–514.

—— (2010) "Language, gesture, action! A test of the Gesture as Simulated Action framework," *Journal of Memory and Language, 63*, 245–257.

—— (2019) "Gesture as Simulated Action? Revisiting the framework," *Psychonomic Bulletin and Review, 26*, 721–752.

Hostetter, A. B., Pouw, W., and Wakefield, E. M. (2020) "Learning from gesture and action: An investigation of where objects went and how they got there," *Cognitive Science, 44*, 1–24.

Hostetter, A. B., Wieth, M., Foster, K. D., Moreno, K., and Washinton, J. (2016) "Effects of gesture on analogical problem solving: When the hands lead you astray," in A. Papafragou, D. Grodner, D. Mirman, and J. C. Trueswell (Eds), *Proceedings of the 38th Annual Conference of the Cognitive Science Society* (pp. 1685–1690) Austin, TX: Cognitive Science Society.

Jeannerod, M. (2001) "Neural simulation of action: A unifying mechanism for motor cognition," *NeuroImage, 14*, S103–9.

Kamermans, K., Pouw, W. T. J. L., Fassi, L., Aslanidou, A., Paas, F., and Hostetter, A. B. (2019) "The role of gesture as simulated action in the reinterpretation of mental imagery," *Acta Psychologica, 197*, 131–142.

Kimbara, I. (2006) "On gestural mimicry," *Gesture, 6(1)*, 39–61.

—— (2008) "Gesture form convergence in joint description," *Journal of Nonverbal Behavior, 32(2)*, 123–131.

Kita, S. (2000) "How representational gestures help speaking," in D. McNeill (ed.), *Language and gesture* (pp. 162–185) Cambridge, UK: Cambridge University Press.

Kita, S., Alibali, M. W., and Chu, M. (2017) "How do gestures influence thinking and speaking? The Gesture for Conceptualization hypothesis," *Psychological Review, 124(3)*, 245–266.

Kita, S., and Özyürek, A. (2003) "What does cross-linguistic variation in semantic coordination of speech and gesture reveal? Evidence for an interface representation of spatial thinking and speaking," *Journal of Memory and Language, 48*, 16–32.

Lakoff, G., and Johnson, M. (1980) *Metaphors we live by*, Chicago: University of Chicago Press.

Lakoff, G., and Núñez, R. (2001) *Where mathematics comes from: How the embodied mind brings mathematics into being*, New York: Basic Books.

Maier, N. R. F. (1931) "Reasoning in humans, II: The solution of a problem and its appearance in consciousness," *Journal of Comparative Psychology, 12*, 181–194.

Marghetis, T., Bergen, B., and Núñez, R. (2012) "Metaphorical conceptualization of arithmetic: Evidence in gesture of the flexible deployment of complementary construals of abstract arithmetic," paper presented at the Fourth Annual Meeting of the UK Cognitive Linguistics Association, London, July.

McNeill, D. (1992) *Hand and mind: What gestures reveal about thought*, Chicago: University of Chicago Press.

—— (2005) *Gesture and thought*, Chicago: University of Chicago Press.

McNeill, D., Quek, F., McCullough, K. E., Duncan, S., Furuyama, N., Bryll, R., (2001) "Catchments, prosody, and discourse," *Gesture, 1(1)*, 9–33.

Nathan, M. J. (2021) *Foundations of embodied learning: A paradigm for education*, Routledge.

Nathan, M. J., Walkington, C. A., Boncoddo, R., Pier, E. A., Williams, C., and Alibali, M. W. (2014) "Actions speak louder with words: The role of actions and pedagogical language for grounding mathematical reasoning," *Learning and Instruction, 33*, 182–193.

Niedenthal, P. M., Mermillod, M., Maringer, M., and Hess, U. (2010) "The Simulation of Smiles (SIMS) model: Embodied simulation and the meaning of facial expression," *Behavioral and Brain Sciences, 33*, 417–480.

Novack, M. A., Wakefield, E. M., and Goldin-Meadow, S. (2016) "What makes a movement a gesture?" *Cognition, 146,* 339–348.

Pier, E., Walkington, C. A., Clinton, V. E., Boncoddo, R., Williams-Pierce, C., Alibali, M. W., and Nathan, M. J. (2019) "Embodied truths: How dynamic gesture contributes to mathematical proof practices," *Contemporary Educational Psychology, 58,* 44–57.

Rizzolatti, G., Fogassi, L., and Gallese, V. (2001) "Neurophysiological mechanisms underlying the understanding and imitation of action," *Nature Reviews Neuroscience, 2,* 661–670.

Roth, W. M. (2002) "From action to discourse: The bridging function of gestures," *Cognitive Systems Research, 3,* 535–554.

Shapiro, L. (2011) *Embodied cognition,* New York, NY: Routledge.

Singer, M. A., Radinsky, J., and Goldman, S. R. (2008) "The role of gesture in meaning construction," *Discourse Processes, 45,* 365–386.

Thomas, L. E., and Lleras, A. (2007) "Moving eyes and moving thought: On the spatial compatibility between eye movements and cognition," *Psychonomic Bulletin and Review, 14*(4), 663–668.

—— (2009) "Swinging into thought: Directed movement guides insight in problem solving," *Psychonomic Bulletin and Review, 16*(4), 719–723.

Thompson, L. A., and Massaro, D. W. (1994) "Children's integration of speech and pointing gestures in comprehension," *Journal of Experimental Child Psychology, 57,* 327–354.

Vest, N. A., Fyfe, E. R., Nathan, M. J., and Alibali, M. W. (2020) "Learning from an avatar video instructor: Gesture mimicry supports middle school students' algebra learning," *Gesture, 19,* 128–155.

Wakefield, E. M., Congdon, E. L., Novack, M. A., Goldin-Meadow, S., and James, K. H. (2019) "Learning math by hand: The neural effects of gesture-based instruction in 8-year-old children," *Attention, Perception, and Psychophysics, 81*(7), 2343–2353.

Walkington, C., Woods, D., Nathan, M. J., Chelule, G., and Wang, M. (2019) "Does restricting hand gestures impair mathematical reasoning?" *Learning and Instruction, 64.*

Wesp, R., Hess, J., Keutmann, D., and Wheaton, K. (2001) "Gestures maintain spatial imagery," *American Journal of Psychology, 114,* 591–600.

Wheaton, K. J., Thompson, J. C., Syngeniotis, A., Abbott, D. F., and Puce, A. (2004) "Viewing the motion of human body parts activates different regions of premotor, temporal, and parietal cortex," *NeuroImage, 22*(1), 277–288.

Wilson, M. (2002) "Six views of embodied cognition," *Psychonomic Bulletin and Review, 9,* 625–636.

20

THE EMBODIED DYNAMICS OF PROBLEM SOLVING

New structure from multiscale interactions

James A. Dixon, Damian G. Kelty-Stephen, Benjamin De Bari, and Jason Anastas

Problem solving has been a rich area for psychology. Nearly all major cognitive phenomena occur in the context of problem solving, including memory search (Hélie and Sun 2010), analogical mapping (Gick and Holyoak 1980), reasoning (Thibodeau and Boroditsky 2011), association (Grabner et al. 2009), abductive inference (Langley, Laird, and Rogers 2009), and priming (Slepian, Weisbuch, Rutchick, Newman, and Ambady 2010), as well as many social phenomena, such as group facilitation (Liker and Bókony 2009) and inhibition (Diehl and Stroebe 1987) effects. In a sense, problem solving provides us with a microcosm of the key issue for psychology: "How does an organism successfully engage in goal-directed action?" Indeed, if we had a fully worked out theory of problem solving, it would provide a foundation on which to build theories of cognition. Currently, however, psychology and cognitive science place little emphasis on problem solving as a major area in the field, although posing problems to organisms, typically humans, is the stock-in-trade of experimental psychologists. Most studies in psychology pose a problem to their participants, in the form of task instructions and constraints, with the hope that participants will solve the problem using the processes the researcher wishes to study. Missing from current practice is a theory (or even a reasonable hypothesis) about how an organism could configure itself into some novel spatio-temporal structure in a way that accomplishes a novel task. Of course, we recognize that experimental tasks might be considered graded in terms of their novelty at a particular moment in time. For example, recalling a list of words might be analogous to recalling items on a shopping list and thus weakly novel. Naming the color of ink in which words are written, while trying not to read the words (the classic "Stroop" task), might be considered somewhat more strongly novel. At the far end of this continuum, might be tasks that are explicitly intended to require an innovative solution, such as the mutilated checkerboard problem (Kaplan and Simon 1990) or traveling salesman problem (Applegate, Bixby, Chvatal, and Cook 2011).

Early giants in the field, such as Köhler (1947) and Duncker (1945), appreciated that an organism's ability to generate innovative solutions in the face of novel problems was a deep theoretical issue. Indeed, as we will argue below, taking this aspect of problem solving seriously provides a powerful constraint on how we should conceive of cognition, in general. Consider, for example, how an organism could know, in advance of actually doing it,

DOI: 10.4324/9781003322511-27

246

that configuring itself in a particular way would allow it to obtain a desired goal. Organisms from all five kingdoms are capable of this, but for now let us take the familiar example of a primate staring at a banana that is suspended from the ceiling, well out of reach. After trying out a few behaviors, such as jumping and climbing on objects, the primate stacks some nearby boxes, creating a platform from which he or she can reach the banana (Köhler 1956). Let us stipulate that, because this primate has been reared in controlled conditions, we can be quite certain of the novelty of the problem and the solution. The primate in this example has generated a new structure, the complex behavior of stacking the boxes and climbing upon them, in the service of a goal. The question is: how can a theory of cognition explain such an event?

First, we consider the ability of computationalism-representationalism to address novel cognitive structures. We then discuss embodied cognition as an emerging position that may provide an account of novelty in cognition. Finally, we illustrate how such an approach might begin to be fleshed out using examples from our own recent work.

Computation over representations

Clearly, the dominant theoretical framework for cognition assumes that cognition is the processing of "information," and that information processing must be computations over representations (Fodor 1981; Newell 1994). The assumptions of this framework are so deeply embedded in how cognitive scientists and psychologists currently think about cognition that it often appears that they are unaware that computationalism-representationalism (henceforth, CR) is actually a theoretical position, not a self-evident fact. At the risk of treading too-well-worn paths, recall that CR takes the strong position that representations are internal states of arbitrary form that stand in some relation to external events in the world, and that these states are operated on by a set of rules. The output of this process yields another symbol (or symbols), the meaning of which is relevant to the organism, e.g. "It's a frog," "Scratch your left ear," "She's not listening," etc. It is important to point out here that if one takes CR as a theoretical approach to explaining cognition, then the whole theory has to be fleshed out in representations and computations. For example, one cannot insert an intelligent agent at the back end of the process that interprets the symbol, provides the necessary background knowledge, decides what actions to take, or otherwise provides the intelligent, goal-directed behavior we set out to explain (Dennett 1981).

One of the many limitations of CR is that the symbols and the rules are fixed. That is, there's no natural way for the system to generate new symbols or new rules. No matter how many times a rule is invoked or a symbol used as input or output, novel rules and representations do not occur. This point is easy to appreciate, if one imagines the steps taken in the operation of a Turing machine: advance tape, read symbol, write symbol, advance tape. These operations are all there is to this form of computation. The machine can only read-write symbols it already knows and only execute rules it already has stored. Indeed, it is reasonable to think of computation as a highly efficient method of expressing what is already known (and encoded into the computing system).

Two major escape hatches might save CR from this seeming incompatibility with the facts of cognition. First, one might propose that the system actually contains all the rules it will ever use, but that they unfold over the life of the organism through some unspecified developmental process. Novelty here is just a mirage. The system already knows everything there is to know but rolls out that knowledge when the time is right. This would clearly be a miracle of very high order. But even if one accepts that biology and evolution might be capable of pulling off something so extraordinary, it seems obvious that this explanation only works for objects and situations with an evolutionary history. Humans, for example, both create and adapt to cultural artifacts (e.g., golf clubs, cars, keyboards), objects that have no history on an evolutionary timescale. Thus, our abilities to configure ourselves into a biomechanically efficient striker of a tiny white ball or a non-self-propelled controller of a complicated high-speed machine are clearly not going to be explainable this way.

The second way one might attempt to save CR from the conundrum of novelty is to suggest that the computational system essentially operates on itself (Goldberg and Holland 1988). This account proposes that there exists a class of symbols, call them second-order symbols, which stand in relation to the system's own internal rules or parts of those rules. For example, a rule such as "if C is true, then P" might be represented by two second-order symbols, X which would stand for the phrase "if C is true," and Y which would stand for "then P." These second-order symbols would then be manipulated by their own set of rules. The key role of these rules would be to recombine the second-order symbols into new combinations, thus allowing the system to invent new rules. Thus, the system might make a combination that specifies, "if C is true, then Q." While such a modification of CR is plausible, it is hopelessly underpowered. The size of the set of possible combinations is just the product of the number of unique phrases of each type. The second-order rules generate novel first-order rules, but from a limited and completely prescribed set.

Note that this approach cannot be expanded to generate new symbols (i.e., representations) that stand in relation to the objects, events, etc., in the environment. The reason is easy to appreciate. CR systems are only in touch with the environment through their current set of symbols. All elements in the environment that are not encoded by those symbols are undetectable for that system. They literally have no means of entry. So, in the absence of a special front-end, an explicitly non-CR front-end that knows about the environment in some other way, CR systems cannot generate new symbols. This point begins to sail close to the now standard (and quite devastating) critique of CR that emphasizes its failures in the realm of semantics (e.g., Bickhard 2009). While we appreciate the force of those arguments, here we have focused briefly on issues that bear more especially on the generation of new structure.

Embodied cognition

Unlike CR, embodied cognition does not yet have a rigorous definition, and thus evaluating its potential requires some speculation about what exactly it entails. At a minimum, embodied cognition proposes that the states and actions of the body play a causal role in processes that are traditionally considered cognitive.

Embodied cognition has the potential to offer a serious alternative to CR. However, realizing this potential requires a radical rethinking of the nature of cognition. If embodied cognition is to move the field beyond its current state, it must embrace the deep implications of cognition being a physical (i.e., embodied) system. Attempting to slide embodiment beneath CR, as a grounding for representations, will simply inherit all the problems of CR while resolving none of them.

One recently recognized problem with any attempt to embed cognitive representations in the body concerns the requirement that such representations be grounded in stable physical structures or processes. The physical structures that make up cells are themselves in constant flux (Nicholson 2019). For example, synapses, the most widely accepted candidate for storing information in CR approaches, undergo constant synthesis and degradation (Biever et al. 2019). At a more macro scale, regardless of what observable we choose, the body exhibits a concept from statistical physics called "weak ergodicity breaking." In statistical terms, ergodicity is the expectation that the average of an individual exemplar of system behavior over time resembles the average for a sample of exemplars (Mangalam and Kelty-Stephen 2021). The problem for cognitive theorizing is that ergodicity is the license for forecasting from prior events (e.g., via stored representations) to current events. For example, if during my walk today, my stride lengths are not predictable from the stride lengths from all my previous walks (i.e., stride length is not ergodic), then it seems self-evident that stride length is not being generated by a stable CR process. The simple empirical fact is that ergodicity is rare in biological variability, whether in generic cellular, specifically neural, or more molar musculoskeletal dynamics, as well as standard psychological measures like self-reported well-being (Olthof et al. 2020). The closer we look at physical processes in the body, the more we find poor conditions for grounding a computational-representational framework. Indeed, embodiment appears to undermine the stability necessary for a representational system.

The most likely source of ergodicity breaking is specifically a hierarchical sort of organization whose interactions across scales couch and contextualize events between molecular and molar, between part and whole. Failure of representativeness means that ergodicity-breaking systems cannot support any decomposition between, say, a stable part that wields the information (e.g., "the controller") and an unstable part to be controlled with that information ("the controlled").

How then can we handle the fact that cognition is the product of a physical system? We propose the following fundamental properties of biological systems as an initial starting place for understanding cognition.

Dissipative structures

All organisms, including humans, are ensembles of dissipative structures (Kondepudi et al. 2017). Dissipative structures are self-organizing systems that form and persist in response to the flow of energy and matter. That is, they emerge to degrade energy and their survival continually requires energy degradation. That biological entities are dissipative structures is non-controversial, although the theory has been primarily developed in physico-chemical systems. Importantly, dissipative structures have a number of properties that help get a theory of cognition off the ground. First, they occur spontaneously in living and non-living systems, so their origin is cashed out from first principles, that is, thermodynamic laws. One need not license their existence through appeals to special processes or hidden agents. Second, dissipative structures are exquisitely sensitive to changes in their environments. Any change in circumstance that changes the flow through the structure can have consequences for the whole structure, including generating new structures. Thus, explaining how a system can rapidly and seamlessly adjust to changes in the environment becomes a question of tracking how exogenous energy fluctuations impact the flow through the system. Inherently intractable issues such as "encoding," "sensory integration," and the like are rendered nugatory in this framework. Third, dissipative structures exhibit a rudimentary form of end-directedness; they form such that their spatio-temporal properties degrade energy and, perhaps, maximize the rate of entropy production. Thus, the question of how inert matter becomes active is answered directly by the theory of dissipative structures.

Non-equilibrium stability and intrinsic embodiment

Dissipative structures, unlike machines, are characteristically context sensitive, emerging only when subject to a flow of energy and/or matter. Consider how a fluid convection roll, a classic dissipative structure, requires a temperature gradient across the system and continuous energy exchanges with the environment (Nicolis 1989). In this way dissipative structures depend existentially on circumstances outside the system's boundaries. Given the dependence on energy fluxes, the system is intrinsically sensitive to and naturally responds to any perturbation to this flux. In an electrical dissipative structure (EDS), branching assemblages of metal beads (Figure 20.1) move through a shallow bath of oil and conduct electrical charges to ground (Kondepudi et al. 2017). These "trees" are sensitive to the embedding distribution of electrical charges which accumulate on the oil surface, tending to move in the direction of increasing charge density (De Bari et al. 2019). Empirical evidence and computational modeling have revealed that for a variety of different perturbations to the electrical flux, these trees consistently respond by modulating their morphology (Kondepudi et al. 2017), dynamics (De Bari et al. 2019), or both, facilitating an increase in the electrical current. Their dynamics are context sensitive, adapting to changing circumstances to maintain the sustaining flow.

Dissipative structures are sensitive to environmental context in a variety of ways. Dissipative structures emerge when systems are pushed through a critical point that drives instability-induced symmetry breaking and the transition to a new dynamic (Prigogine and Stengers 1984). Often, multiple equally probable dynamics exist (e.g., directional rotation of convective rolls), though only one is actualized. The "choice" is made through the amplification of microscopic fluctuations in the system and feedback across scales (Prigogine and Stengers 1984). Embedding electrical or gravitational (Kondepudi and Prigogine 1981) fields can bias the emergence of self-organized patterns in chemical media. Weak magnetic fields bias the morphological development of tree structures in the EDS (Kondepudi et al.,

Figure 20.1 The Electrical Dissipative Structure (EDS). Branching dissipative "tree" structures self-organize and serve as pathways for the conduction of charge.

2020). This *non-equilibrium sensitivity* is thought to underlie the gravitational sensitivity of microtubule growth in some cells (Bizzari et al. 2018) and is a candidate explanation for the non-obvious temperature dependence of some organisms (Ferguson and Joanen 1982; Partridge et al. 1994).

Rather than embodied context (body states, actions, environment) providing new symbols or information sources, dissipative structures are sensitive to context through reciprocal interactions. The EDS moves due to the distribution of electrical charges on the oil surface (De Bari et al. 2019) while continually absorbing these charges and conducting them to ground, thereby altering the same field of forces which guides it. Behaviors, including oscillation, synchronization, and coordination of multiple trees, are explained by the depletion and accumulation of charges (De Bari et al. 2021). In our view, dissipative structures are intrinsically embodied in this radical sense, and these rich context sensitivities are foundational to the embodied cognition of biology.

Existential problems, self-maintenance, and emergent normativity

Dissipative structures depend on irreversible entropy-producing processes to maintain self-organized dynamics, drawing energy from the environment. Some far-from-equilibrium systems are known to spontaneously reorganize in a way that facilitates their continued existence and are thus self-maintaining (Bickhard 2009). Because dissipative structures depend on energetic fluxes, they face an intrinsic existential problem of survival (Egbert 2022). Some behaviors, stabilizing or destabilizing, are functional for the system and thus intrinsically normative (Bickhard 2009) – stabilizing behaviors or circumstances are "preferred" and non-stabilizing behaviors or circumstances are "non-preferred." To the extent that a dissipative structure can be sensitive to and respond appropriately to contextual constraints on stability, they display a form of problem solving. Such problem solving need not involve computation over representations.

For example, when a tree structure in the EDS is placed in a region of relatively low charge density, it will reliably move to distal regions of higher charge density and remain there, resulting in a higher dissipation rate. Given that the intrinsic end is to maximize stability (dissipation), the system is initially presented with a problem in which, for the present circumstances, dissipation and stability could be greater. The system is intrinsically sensitive to the embedding context (charge distribution), and reciprocal effects between the tree activity and charge distribution guide the tree in the direction of greater charge density. Behaviors that increase or decrease dissipation are detected due to the reciprocal interaction of the tree and charge distribution (De Bari et al. 2019, 2021) without any traditional form of error detection via comparison of representations.

Multiscale nesting spread across hierarchical systems

The ensembles of dissipative structures that constitute organisms arrange themselves hierarchically across a wide range of spatio-temporal scales. These scales are nested such that smaller-scale structures comprise larger scales. In complex biological systems, the number of scales is not known and likely changes over time. Both the spatial structures (i.e., morphology) and temporal structures (i.e., behaviors) that are typically the focus of research in biology and psychology are embedded in the activity of the other scales of the system. Embedded here means that there are causal dependencies amongst structures at different scales. A class of formalisms has been developed to express these multiscale relations in complex systems in physics and related fields (Lovejoy and Schertzer 2013). It is important to keep in mind that our identification of the behavior (or aspect of morphology) in which we are interested, say the discovery of a new problem-solving strategy, is the application of a particular measurement frame on a continuous and extremely heterogeneous system. The act of measuring the system tempts us not only to reify the behavior, but also to treat it as if it were now a component part in a mechanical system. In psychology and cognitive science, this usually involves casting the behavior as a player on the stage of the general linear model, in which exogenous causes push and pull on non-causal outcome variables. However, the proper metaphysics for understanding biological behavior is dictated by the hierarchical nature of the system whose multiscale nestings produced the behavior, not the convenience and familiarity of the metaphysics of machines.

We have proposed that the energy flow through the hierarchical arrangement that constitutes the organism may provide a clearer portrait of embodied cognition. As it turns out, flows of energy through hierarchical constraints generate cascades (Lovejoy and Schertzer 2013), and cascades manifest in the power-law distribution, the exponents of which can vary with time, with space, and with different arrangements of hierarchical energy flows.

Rule induction in card sorting

Among the many amazing properties of human problem solvers is the ability to detect regularities embedded in sequences of temporal events. From our theoretical perspective, when any organism detects a regularity (i.e., a "rule"), it has reorganized itself such that it is now attuned to a new pattern of variation in the environment. This is a substantial and non-trivial event for the system, and thus we should be able to see evidence for it in the multiscale behavior of the system.

To test this overarching hypothesis, we asked college-age participants to perform a reduced version of the Wisconsin Card Sort Test (WCST) (Grant and Berg 1948). Participants were asked to sort cards into four categories, each defined by a guide card. After they placed each card, the experimenter provided them with feedback about whether or not that placement was correct. Participants had to induce the correct sorting rule for each of five trials. (In the classic WCST, but not here, the rule also changes within trial.) An example of this simple set-up is shown in Figure 20.2.

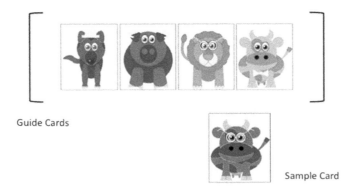

Guide Cards

Sample Card

Figure 20.2 Card-sorting task. A simple card-sorting task in which children are asked to sort along one dimension (e.g., type of animal), while ignoring the other dimensions.

As a comparison condition, we asked a second group of participants to sort cards according to the same rules, but in this condition the rules were stated explicitly. A new rule was given to the participants (as was the initial rule) at the start of each trial. Thus, this group sorted cards according to the same rules, but did not have to induce the rules. We call this the "explicit" condition, to denote the explicit stating of the rules, and the set-up described above, the "induction" condition (see Anastas, Stephen, and Dixon 2011 for details).

For both conditions, we tracked the motion of the participant's dominant hand (i.e., the hand used to sort the cards) at a high sampling rate (60 hertz) and with considerable precision (on the millimeter scale). We used the time series of the motion data to quantify multi-scale activity of the system.

A few words are probably in order here about why we think the motion of the hand tells us about activity of the cognitive system with respect to this task. Consider that inferring that a participant has a "rule" involves applying a particular measurement frame to the pattern of motions he or she generates, relative to the problem context. Relatively macro-scale temporal relations in the participant's motions are taken as evidence of having acquired the rule. While it is tempting to talk about "rules" and other cognitive structures as if they existed as disembodied entities, their measurement in scientific practice requires an instantiation in the physical world. (One might also note that a commitment to materialism makes a parallel argument for the physical instantiation of rules.) If rules are then to be embodied entities that are produced by real, multiscale physical structures, they should show interesting micro-scale behavior, especially during their formation. Because hand motions are intrinsic to the instantiation of the rules in the present task, they should provide a quantitative window onto the relevant system activity.

A rejoinder to this argument, it should be noted, is that hand motions are run by the motor system, and that a different system is in charge of cognitive structures such as rules. This second system tells the motor system what to do, in general terms, and the motor system works out the details. Implicit in this description of two systems (rather than one) is the idea that motor processes and cognitive processes are insulated from each other. The systems communicate over some channel but do their work independently. This strong architectural assumption, an implication of Simon's near-decomposability thesis (Simon 1962), is rarely tested, despite the fact that it is the essential licensure for all component approaches to cognition.

There are a few ways to empirically evaluate the component assumption. Some involve quite quantitatively advanced methods, usually in the realm of time-series analysis, such as iterative amplitude-adjusted Fourier transform (Ihlen and Vereijken 2010). Others are more pragmatic in that they simply ask whether the component that is proposed to be causally downstream (e.g., motor) is related to upstream components (e.g., cognitive) in unexpected ways. In a sense, most of the surprising effects in embodied cognition are of this latter type. We have examined both types of evidence for the card-sorting data. Although we focus on the latter type here, we note that more quantitatively advanced methods strongly suggest that card sorting is not the product of a component-dominant process (Stephen, Anastas, and Dixon 2012).

To explore the relationships between the microstructure of the motion of the hands and the phenomenon of induction, we briefly and non-technically consider a quantitative measure of hierarchically multiscale activity to tell the rest of the story. The motion data obtained during each participant's card sorting contain a remarkable amount of information about the activity of the system during the task. One analysis of interest directly estimates the hierarchical activity of the system as distributed over nested temporal scales. Physical systems that are composed of many interacting spatio-temporal scales will show a systematic power-law relationship between temporal scale (i.e., the length of time over which the measurement is taken) and the degree of activity. We used detrended fluctuation analysis (DFA) (Peng et al. 1994) to estimate the relationship between temporal scale and activity. This relationship is typically (and testably) a power law, quantified in DFA as a Hurst exponent (H). Values of H near 1 are consistent with long-term correlations in the time series and have been taken as an index of the degree to which the system is "poised" to respond to changes. Not too long ago, researchers began to find $H \sim 1$ in a wide variety of biological domains, suggesting that many processes in biology and psychology were not only poised to respond to changes, but appear to return repeatedly to that poised state (Bak 1999). A related body of work shows that as a complex system approaches a structural or functional change, it goes to a poised (or "critical") state, showing properties much like a phase transition (Hinrichsen 2006).

In the card-sorting task, the motion data from both the induction and explicit conditions had average Hurst exponents that suggested long-term correlations in the data. More importantly, we predicted that participants in the induction condition (who had to discover the rule) would show a pattern of increase and decrease in their Hurst exponents, indicative of the system becoming poised for a change (increasing H), and then settling into a stable regime (decreasing H). We also predicted that participants in the explicit condition (who were given the rules) would show a decrease in their Hurst exponents as they settled into a stable organization with the given rule. Figure 20.3 shows the average Hurst exponents for both conditions as a function of time (expressed as epochs; epochs are about 13 seconds in duration). Both these predictions were confirmed: the induction condition showed a strong peak in the Hurst exponent, and the explicit condition showed an overall decrease.

Note that in both these conditions participants were, from a motor perspective, doing much the same thing: sorting cards into four piles. The speed of their sorting motions, the duration of the trials, and a variety of other factors do not significantly differ between conditions, nor do they add predictive power to statistical models of the Hurst exponent trajectories. The difference between the time series generated in these two conditions is not reducible to some macro-scale difference. Rather, the difference in the trajectories of the Hurst exponents over time is consistent with the hypothesis that rule induction is an instance of self-organization in a multiscale system. The interactions across scales increase in the induction condition, allowing the system to reach a novel rule, and then decrease as the system stabilizes around that rule. Likewise, in the explicit condition, in which no discovery is necessary, the system just stabilizes as it repeatedly instantiates the rule. "Rule" here, we should emphasize, is a shorthand way of describing a particular, and quite complex, spatio-temporal organization of the system, rather than a simple conditional statement (e.g., "Put the card in the pile that matches on color"). While such a statement is enough to get a participant started sorting, his or her system still must organize to the many constraints of the task, such as spatial positions, variations across individual cards, etc. The rule that the system learns is the amalgamation of all the relevant task constraints.

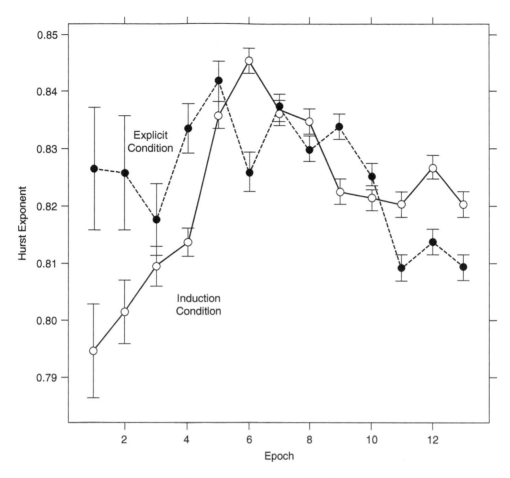

Figure 20.3 Hurst exponents over time during card sorting. The Hurst exponents (H) are shown as a function of epoch (time), with separate curves for the "induction" and "explicit" rule conditions. Errors bars show 1 standard error of the mean.

Focal tasks rest on interactions across scale cascade globally through the body

In the earlier edition of this chapter, the present account of a radical embodied cognition rooted in hierarchical energy flows began and ended with hands stirring up the focal aspects of a task environment. The foregoing work addressed embodied cognition through estimates of a power-law exponent describing hand movements in ongoing contact with the task environment. It was originally an existence proof that taking a statistical physics estimate of energy flow through a hierarchical arrangement of bodily constraints could pay dividends towards a more thoroughly representation-free, computation-free option. The embodied dynamics of so-called representation change showed us that what cognitive psychology calls representations might be fluid, contingent postures of a hierarchically ordered organism.

More recent work has sought to situate these initial existence proofs with the distributed hierarchical landscape afforded by the organism. After all, the organism is more than its parts and sooner spans a global, body-wide pre-tensed relationship amongst these parts. So, the organism is of course more than the point of a fingertip or the sweep of a card-sorting hand. And, as we have said, the organism is not a homogeneous soup. Heads wield eyes, hands wield fingers, and torsos wield heads while legs negotiate between torso and ground surface. Behind the immediate contact with the focal aspects of the task environment, (i.e., with the cards) there is a vast webbing of bodily activity, supporting and steering the focal contacts. The very neurons that less embodied approaches have put in the foreground will only operate as needed when they rest on a substrate maintaining proper mechanical tension—no tension, no action potential (Ingber 2006).

The tensional architecture we have just described predicts a proliferation of varied power-law exponents spread across the body. It is just such a proliferation of power-law exponents that we find across the body (discussed below), even as the organism engages with the task environment. As we focus our eyes on the text concluding this chapter, we may notice that it is not only our eyes doing the work. We may notice instead that we tilt our hand, reposition our torso in our chair, plant an elbow on the desk. When Köhler's primates sighted the banana, they stabilized their gaze and searched for the right box, picked it up and hefted it for size, and then stabilized their posture with careful footholds as they extended their reach towards the prize. In short, the focal task rests on a vast swarm of energy flows written across the tensions and compressions spread hierarchically through the body.

Elaboration of embodied cognition may lie in the recent findings that body-wide distributions of power-law exponents can predict solutions of the focal task. Power-law exponents can predict from head sway or eye movements how we attend to visual stimulation. Power-law exponents in hand fluctuations predict not just the evolution of card sorting but also of wielding handheld objects, e.g., a box, to explore their spatial extent (Kelty-Stephen and Dixon 2014). Feet cannot as easily draw cards, but power-law exponents at the foot appear to predict a similar capacity for wielding to perceive an object's shape and size, e.g., clambering up on a foothold. Power-law exponents in postural center of pressure predict how we solve the problem of unstable terrain or stance and also how we respond to changes in optic flow, e.g., stabilizing posture on a wobbly stack of boxes (Kelty-Stephen et al. 2021). Causal modeling shows that power-law exponents across the body spread among these disparate bodily contacts, showing subtle task sensitivity and promoting accuracy of perceptual judgments in the focal task (Mangalam et al. 2020).

Conclusions

We have argued that the dominant approach to cognition, CR, cannot handle the phenomenon of new structure, a fundamental aspect of the problem-solving behavior exhibited by humans and other organisms. Embodied cognition has the potential to provide an account of how new structures emerge. The implications of this account could radically reshape how we understand cognition. We propose that such an account must be grounded in thermodynamic laws, while capitalizing on what is already known about how those laws manifest themselves in complex, heterogeneous systems. The work we have reviewed above takes some initial steps in this direction, addressing the phenomenon of new macroscopic cognitive structure as a phase transition. Phase transitions are well understood theoretically and have been broadly demonstrated empirically in a wide variety of systems (e.g., Cortet, Chiffaudel, Daviaud, and Dubrulle 2010). Our work shows that the formation of new cognitive structures shows the same signatures as in other embodied, physical systems. That is, an increase in fluctuations as the transition point approaches, indexed by an increase in H (and followed by a decrease in those fluctuations). While it is, of course, possible to create long-term correlated time series using linear methods (and thus consistent with the near-decomposability assumption), it is not clear how such an approach would explain the observed pattern of changes in H. We note that our work shows that these patterns can be experimentally manipulated, as well as observed in spontaneous behavior. Finally, we note that, in our view, embodied cognition is poised at a critical juncture. It can become a side show in the CR cognition circus, an exhibition of somewhat perplexing and bemusing phenomena that run counter to expectation. But embracing the deep implications of its commitment to the physical implications of embodiment has begun to offer traction for a truly new approach to cognition in which minds are fluid, hierarchical organisms rather than just computing nervous systems.

References

Anastas, J. R., Stephen, D. G., and Dixon, J. A. (2011) "The scaling behavior of hand motions reveals self-organization during an executive function task," *Physica A: Statistical Mechanics and Its Applications*, 390(9), 1539–1545.

Applegate, D. L., Bixby, R. E., Chvatal, V., and Cook, W. J. (2011) *The traveling salesman problem: A computational study*, Princeton: Princeton University Press.

Bak, P. (1999) *How nature works: The science of self-organized criticality*, New York: Springer.

Bickhard, M. H. (2009) "The interactivist model," *Synthese*, 166. https://doi.org/10.1007/s11229-008-9375-x

Biever, A., Donlin-Asp, P. G., and Schuman, E. M. (2019) "Local translation in neuronal processes," *Current Opinion in Neurobiology*, 57, 141–148.

Bizzari M., Masiello M. G., Giuliani A., Cucina A. (2018) "Gravity constraints drive biological systems toward specific organization patterns," *BioEssays*, 40. https://doi.org/10.1002/bies.201700138

Cortet, P.-P., Chiffaudel, A., Daviaud, F., and Dubrulle, B. (2010) "Experimental evidence of a phase transition in a closed turbulent flow," *Physical Review Letters*, 105, 214501.

De Bari, B., Dixon, J. A., Kay, B. A., and Kondepudi, D. (2019) "Oscillatory dynamics of an electrically driven dissipative structure," *PLoS ONE*, 14(5), 1–22. https://doi.org/10.1371/journal.pone.0217305

De Bari, B., Paxton, A., Kondepudi, D. K., Kay, B. A., and Dixon, J. A. (2021) "Functional interdependence in coupled dissipative structures: Physical foundations of biological coordination," *Entropy*, 23(5), 1–21. https://doi.org/10.3390/e23050614

Dennett, D. C. (1981) *Brainstorms: Philosophical essays on mind and psychology*, Repr. Ed. Cambridge, MA: MIT Press.

Diehl, M., and Stroebe, W. (1987) "Productivity loss in brainstorming groups: Toward the solution of a riddle," *Journal of Personality and Social Psychology*, 53(3), 497–509.

Duncker, K. (1945) "On problem-solving," (L. S. Lees, Trans.) (*Special* issue). *Psychological Monographs*, 58(270).

Egbert, M. (2022) "Self-preserving mechanisms in motile oil droplets: A computational model of abiological self-preservation," *Royal Society of Chemistry*, 8. https://doi.org/10.1098/rsos.210534

Ferguson M. J. W., Joanen T. (1982) "Temperature of egg incubation determines sex in Alligator mississippiensis," *Nature*, 296(29), 850–853.

Fodor, J. A. (1981) *The mind-body problem*, New York: W. H. Freeman.

Gick, M. L., and Holyoak, K. J. (1980) "Analogical problem solving," *Cognitive Psychology*, 12(3), 306–355.

Goldberg, D. E., and Holland, J. H. (1988) "Genetic algorithms and machine learning," *Machine Learning*, 3(2), 95–99.

Grabner, R. H., Ansari, D., Koschutnig, K., Reishofer, G., Ebner, F., and Neuper, C. (2009) "To retrieve or to calculate? Left angular gyrus mediates the retrieval of arithmetic facts during problem solving," *Neuropsychologia*, 47(2), 604–608.

Grant, D. A., and Berg, E. (1948) "A behavioral analysis of degree of reinforcement and ease of shifting to new responses in a Weigl-type card-sorting problem," *Journal of Experimental Psychology, 38(4)*, 404–411.

Hélie, S., and Sun, R. (2010) "Incubation, insight, and creative problem solving: A unified theory and a connectionist model," *Psychological Review, 117(3)*, 994–1024.

Hinrichsen, H. (2006) "Non-equilibrium phase transitions," *Physica A: Statistical Mechanics and Its Applications, 369(1)*, 1–28.

Ihlen, E. A. F., and Vereijken, B. (2010) "Interaction-dominant dynamics in human cognition: Beyond 1/f α fluctuation," *Journal of Experimental Psychology: General, 139(3)*, 436.

Ingber, D. E. (2006) "Cellular mechanotransduction: putting all the pieces together again," *FASEB Journal, 20*, 811–827. https://doi.org/10.1096/fj.05-5424rev

Kaplan, C. A., and Simon, H. A. (1990) "In search of insight," *Cognitive Psychology, 22(3)*, 374–419.

Kelty-Stephen, D., and Dixon, J. A. (2014) "Interwoven fluctuations in intermodal perception: Fractality in head-sway supports the use of visual feedback in haptic perceptual judgments by manual wielding," *Journal of Experimental Psychology: Human Perception and Performance, 40*, 2289–2309. http://dx.doi.org/10.1037/a0038159

Kelty-Stephen, D. G., Lee, I. C., Carver, N. S., Newell, K. M., and Mangalam, M. (2021) "Multifractal roots of suprapostural dexterity," *Human Movement Science, 76*, 102771.

Köhler, W. (1947) *Gestalt psychology: An introduction to new concepts in modern psychology*, New York: Liveright Publishing.

——— (1956). *The mentality of apes*. New York: Vintage Books.

Kondepudi, D. K., and Prigogine, I., (1981) "Sensitivity of nonequilibrium systems," *Physica A, 107*.

Kondepudi, D. K., De Bari, B., and Dixon, J. A. (2020) "Dissipative structures, organisms, and evolution," *Entropy, 22(1305)*. https://doi.org/10.3390/e22111305

Kondepudi D. K., Kay B., Dixon J. A. (2017) "Dissipative structures, machines, and organisms: A perspective," *Chaos, 27(104607)*. https://doi.org/10.1063/1.5001195

Langley, P., Laird, J. E., and Rogers, S. (2009) "Cognitive architectures: Research issues and challenges," *Cognitive Systems Research, 10(2)*, 141–160.

Liker, A., and Bókony, V. (2009) "Larger groups are more successful in innovative problem solving in house sparrows," *Proceedings of the National Academy of Sciences of the United States of America, 106(19)*, 7893–7898.

Lovejoy, S., and Schertzer, D. (2013) *The Weather and Climate: Emergent laws and multifractal cascades*, Cambridge: Cambridge University Press.

Mangalam, M., and Kelty-Stephen, D. G. (2021)"Point estimates, Simpson's paradox, and nonergodicity in biological sciences," *Neuroscience and Biobehavioral Reviews, 125*, 98–107.

Mangalam, M., Carver, N. S., and Kelty-Stephen, D. G. (2020) "Multifractal signatures of perceptual processing on anatomical sleeves of the human body," *Journal of The Royal Society Interface, 17(168)*, 20200328.

Newell, A. (1994) *Unified theories of cognition*, Cambridge, MA: Harvard University Press.

Nicholson, D. J. (2019) "Is the cell really a machine?" *Journal of Theoretical* Biology, 477, 108–126. https://doi.org/10.1016/j.jtbi.2019.06.002

Nicolis, G. (1989) "Physics of far-from-equilibrium systems and self-organization," in P. Davies (Ed.), *The New Physics*, (pp. 316–347), Cambridge University Press.

Olthof, M., Hasselman, F., and Lichtwarck-Aschoff, A. (2020) "Complexity in psychological self-ratings: Implications for research and practice," *BMC Medicine, 18(1)*, 317. https://doi.org/10.1186/s12916- 020- 01727-2

Partridge L. Barrie B. Fowler, K. French, V. (1994) "Evolution and development of body size and cell size in Drosophila Melanogaster in response to temperature," *Evolution, 48*, 1269–1276.

Peng, C. K., Buldyrev, S.V., Havlin, S., Simons, M., Stanley, H. E., and Goldberger, A. L. (1994) "Mosaic organization of DNA nucleotides," *Physical Review E, 49(2)*, 1685–1689.

Prigogine, I., and Stengers, I. (1984) *Order out of chaos: Man's new dialogue with nature*, Bantam

Simon, H. A. (1962) "The architecture of complexity," *Proceedings of the American Philosophical Society, 106(6)*, 467–482.

Slepian, M. L., Weisbuch, M., Rutchick, A. M., Newman, L. S., and Ambady, N. (2010) "Shedding light on insight: Priming bright ideas.," *Journal of Experimental Social Psychology, 46(4)*, 696–700.

Stephen, D. G., Anastas, J. R., and Dixon, J. A. (2012) "Scaling in cognitive performance reflects multiplicative multifractal cascade dynamics," *Frontiers in Physiology, 3(102)*.

Thibodeau, P. H., and Boroditsky, L. (2011) "Metaphors we think with: The role of metaphor in reasoning," *PLoS One, 6(2)*, e16782.

Further reading

Bickhard, M. H., and Terveen, L. (1996) *Foundational issues in artificial intelligence and cognitive science: Impasse and solution*, Amsterdam: Elsevier.

Stephen, D. G., and Dixon, J. A. (2009) "The self-organization of insight: Entropy and power laws in problem solving," *Journal of Problem Solving, 2(1)*, 72–101.

Stephen, D. G., Dixon, J. A., and Isenhower, R. W. (2009) "Dynamics of representational change: Entropy, action, and cognition," *Journal of Experimental Psychology: Human Perception and Performance, 35(6)*, 1811–1832.

De Bari, B., Kondepudi, D. K., Kay, B. A., and Dixon, J. A. (2020) "Collective dissipative structures, force-flow Reciprocity, and the foundations of perception–action mutuality," *Ecological Psychology, 32(4)*, 153–180. https://doi.org/10.1080/10407413.2020.1820337

21

ADVANCES IN GROUNDED AND EMBODIED MATHEMATICAL REASONING

Theory, Technology, and Research Methods

Mitchell J. Nathan

The objective of this chapter is to complement and extend the information provided in Chapter 17 of the First Edition of the *Routledge Handbook of Embodied Cognition* about the varieties of mathematical reasoning (MR) from a grounded and embodied perspective (Nathan, 2014). Major developments in embodiment theory, research methods and technology since that publication have fueled enormous progress in our understanding of the role of the body in MR. These individual developments contribute synergistically to exciting advances in learning theory, mathematics education, and disciplinary practices.

An essential quality of mathematical reasoning is that people imbue symbolic notational systems and computational procedures with *meaning*. Mathematics as a discipline and a scholastic subject area is not merely a collection of facts, symbols, vocabulary terms, diagrams, and procedures. Even early topics, such as number sense, must impart connotations of *number* as more than just a visual string of numerals. For MR about numbers to be sensible, numbers must activate in people's minds (often simultaneously), location on a number line, cardinality (set size), properties such as parity and multiplicative factors, coded symbolic systems denoting place value, cultural associations, and so on.

Nathan (2014) characterizes MR along three dimensions: Mathematical content, including numbers and operations, arithmetic, algebra, and geometry; disciplinary practices for doing mathematics, such as performing computational procedures, finding patterns, using visual representations, and generalizing claims via proofs; and the psychological processes involved in reasoning about specific content while employing particular practices. Mathematically valid reasoning arises when these psychological processes engage grounded and embodied systems that include body states and embodied interactions with one's environment and other people in ways that enact the appropriate disciplinary practices. For example, people may be observed evoking such embodied resources as axial symmetry of the body and sensations of balance (Donovan and Alibali, 2021; Schenck and Nathan, 2021), spatial systems (e.g., Alcaraz-Carrión, et al., 2022; Schenck et al., 2022), manipulation of physical objects (Martin & Schwartz, 2005), and sociocultural participation (e.g., Nasir et al., 2018) to infuse meaning into mathematical ideas and explanations, computational procedures, and formal representations.

DOI: 10.4324/9781003322511-28

Nathan's (2021) Grounded and Embodied Learning (GEL) framework identifies four types of embodiment. First, intellectual behaviors (i.e., "online" cognition) may be performed with our bodies. *Body form and sensorimotor interactions in the world*, such as using touches to establish one-to-one correspondence between two collections of objects, highlight that ecologically situated intellectual behaviors (i.e., "online" cognition) are performed with our bodies. *Simulation processes* are a second type of embodiment that extend these experiences into intellectual behaviors by recruiting sensorimotor systems even when task stimuli are no longer present (so-called *off-line cognition*; Wilson, 2002). Some of the powerful ways simulation processes are activated during MR involve metaphor and conceptual blending, analogical mapping, and relational priming, hypothetico-deductive reasoning, and predictive processing, gestural insight, and gestural replays, each of which can support the transfer of knowledge to new mathematical topics and practices (Nathan & Alibali, 2021). *Gestures*, a third type, are ubiquitous, spontaneous movements of one's hands and arms that serve both social interaction (interpersonal processes) and thought (intrapersonal processes). A fourth type of embodiment is *materialist epistemology*, wherein objects, devices, instruments, and the like, carry out epistemic functions. It is likely that this embodied form applies to virtual as well as tangible objects (e.g., Walkington et al., 2023a).

The full GEL framework (Table 21.1) is built out by identifying the ways each type of embodiment interacts with various learning processes in service of MR. One such form of

Table 21.1 GEL Framework (Nathan, 2021) applied to MR.

Forms of Learning → Types of Embodiment	Grounding	Offloading	Action-Cognition Transduction	Participation
Body form, action, & perception **(Online cognition)**	Equal sign as body symmetry and balance	Finger counting	Sweeping hand to the right in indicate addition	Collaborative body formation of geometric shapes
Gesture	Linking gestures between algebra equations and graphs	Pointing to diagrams and neutral space	Dynamic depictive gestures for transformational proofs	Collaborative and dialogic gestures during math problem posing
Simulation (Off-line cognition)	Grounding conceptual metaphors of arithmetic	Right-hand rule for vector multiplication	Motor system activation during gestural replays of geometric transformations	Participatory simulation of complex systems
Materialist epistemology	World represents itself Instruments determine a concept (e.g., one cup)	Use real and virtual objects for modeling, e.g., cottage cheese	Operations on math manipulatives	Social norms of STEM talk in robotics clubs

learning is *grounding*, whereby a novel idea, abstraction, or formal symbol system, is mapped directly to a more concrete and familiar referent, such as an object, event, or lived perceptual experience (Barsalou, 2008; Glenberg, De Vega, & Graesser, 2008). The meaning of novel mathematical ideas and symbolic notations need not be directly embodied, and can be achieved using other grounding systems, such as language, cultural practices, and social interactions, as when algebraic operations are mapped onto narrative structures of events (Koedinger et al., 2008). Furthermore, people can build a grounded understanding of a new mathematics topic in terms of a well-understood topic, such as grounding *matrix algebra* to *algebra*, instituting a cumulative form of cultural and personal knowledge akin to the "ratchet effect" (Tomasello, 1999).

Another form of grounded and embodied learning is *offloading*, in which resources in the environment – including symbolic, tangible, and digital tools, as well as other people – extend one's cognitive capacities and enhance cognitive performance in the service of MR. *Action-cognition transduction* is a third form of grounded and embodied learning that describes how actions induce cognitive states. Transduction acknowledges a reciprocity between thinking and goal-directed movement. For example, transduction explains how task-relevant movements benefit MR, such as proof production by enabling more facile hypothetical-deductive thinking in support of generalization (Nathan & Walkington, 2017). A fourth form of learning occurs through *participation* by taking up the social norms, perceptual awareness, and cultural behaviors of communities of practice that engage in MR, as evidenced by membership in groups such as robotics teams (Michaelis & Nathan, 2014).

I selectively review ways that developments in three areas – theory of embodied cognition, research methods, and technology – have accelerated advances in grounded and embodied accounts of MR and are propelling innovations in the design and deployment of new classes of interventions for enhancing learning, teaching, knowledge assessment, and new disciplinary practices for the field of mathematics.

Developments in Embodiment Theory

Several major theoretical developments in grounded and embodied cognition have shaped and continue to influence ways scholars and educational practitioners think about and support MR. A general framework for these developments is "4e cognition," so named because of the prominence of four connected, though separate, viewpoints that each coincidently start (in the English language) with the letter *E* (Menary, 2010): Enactive, embodied, extended, and embedded cognition.

Perhaps their greatest point of convergence is that each offers compelling alternatives to an information-processing account of MR. The math education community, in particular, has had a complex relationship with information processing as the cornerstone of MR. Information processing plays an important role in theorizing about some aspects of MR, especially when describing individuals working in relative isolation from authentic contexts, other people, and cultural and scientific tools while tackling highly structured puzzles and academic problem solving of rather short durations (seconds to minutes) (e.g., Schoenfeld, 1987/2013). As learning research has broadened its scope, the mathematics education research community has come to recognize ways in which information-processing theory falls short of addressing authentic mathematical practices that occur outside the laboratory and beyond scholastic worksheets (e.g., Carraher et al., 1985; Hutchins, 1995;

Saxe, 1982). Indeed, reflecting on changes in education research over the past 100 years, Schoenfeld (2016, p. 514) highlights the ascent of embodiment research, noting that

> the term 'embodied cognition' did not appear in the index of the 2007 *Handbook* [*of Research on Mathematics Teaching and Learning*]; yet both embodied cognition (e.g., Nemirovsky & Ferrara, 2009) and embodied design (e.g., Abrahamson, 2009; Alibali & Nathan, 2012) are receiving increased attention in mathematics education.

Each 4e viewpoint also addresses different types of processes and each offers unique claims.

Enactivist viewpoints theorize that MR emerges from the self-organizing perceptuo-motor activity of autonomous agents driven toward sense-making via dynamical interactions with the environment that obviate the need for an apparatus for mental representation in order to "know" the world and operate within it competently (Chemero 2011; O'Regan & Noë, 2001; Thompson 2010). For example, a child striving to monitor and control movement of one hand at a ratio of 1:2 with their other hand will form a new perceptual structure (i.e., an "attentional anchor"; Abrahamson & Bakker, 2016) that supports development of multiplicative reasoning.

Embodied viewpoints theorize about the causal or physically constitutive roles the body plays in cognition (Shapiro, 2019), including spatial and physical metaphors and gestures (Alibali & Nathan, 2012; Lakoff & Johnson, 1980; Núñez et al., 1999). For example, both mathematics experts and non-experts generate *dynamic depictive gestures* (Garcia & Infante, 2012) that simulate object transformations alongside their MR (Nathan et al., 2020). Through action-cognition transduction, these actions are hypothesized to induce cognitive states that benefit mathematical insights (gist-level reasoning) and mathematically valid proofs that are logical, operational, and generalize over the entire class of mathematical objects under consideration (Kim & Nathan, 2022; Nathan et al., 2020).

Extended cognition (Clark & Chalmers, 1998) offers a viewpoint of MR that expands beyond one's skin, where knowledge and reasoning are "stretched over, not divided among – mind, body, activity and culturally organized settings" to form a distributed cognitive system (Lave 1988, p. 1). As an example, Flood (2018) observed tutors and students co-creating distributed knowledge systems when engaged in *dialogic gestures*, which enabled learners to connect emerging scientific concepts (e.g., rate of change) to co-operative action. Similarly, Walkington et al. (2019, 2020) showed students and teachers co-creating *collaborative gestures* that mirror one another's movements and even recruit the bodies of their colleagues, thus expanding the available resources for exploring mathematical properties of space and shape. They found that MR benefited significantly when in the presence of collaborative gestures, even above and beyond the significant benefits associated with producing non-collaborative dynamic gestures. Teachers' embodied learning experiences also improved their attitudes about gestures as beneficial for learning (Schenck et al., 2022), suggesting greater uptake and more lasting changes of embodied instructional practices.

The *embedded* viewpoint complements and contrasts with the extended view by acknowledging the fundamental role of culture, context, and social interactions in reasoning and intellectual development. Whereas extended cognition regards the external environment as a way to *replace* what might be done internally, embedded views assume that people's social and cultural interactions *alter* what individuals and communities can think about and how. One example is the embedded community-based practices at the African

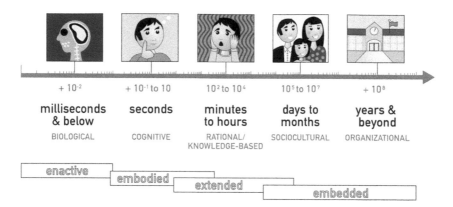

Figure 21.1 The Grounded and Embodied Learning (GEL) Framework depicting the timescales (using a $\log_{10}$ scale) in which processes of mathematical reasoning operate. Overlays the scope of each of the 4e's: enactive, embodied, extended, and embedded cognition. (Reproduced from Nathan, 2021).

American Male Achievement (AAMA) Initiative in the Oakland Unified School District (Nasir, Givens, & Chatmon, 2018). Families and caregivers learn together with young people to nurture students' self-identities as accomplished math and science learners and affirm the professional identities of the Black male teachers, all of which contribute to high rates of teacher retention and student academic performance (Dee & Penner, 2019).

An exemplary framework that brings the 4e viewpoints together is articulation of the *RISE Principles* (McKinney de Royston et al., 2020), which acknowledge four empirically established propositions of learning as: Rooted in basic biological and cognitive processes; Integrated with socioemotional and identity development; Situated in and shaped by social and cultural contexts; and Experienced as embodied and socially coordinated interactions. Collectively, the 4e viewpoints span the range of MR processes that are depicted in Nathan's (2021) grounded and embodied learning timescale continuum. This includes the fast neural and perceptual processes central to the enactivist viewpoint, cognitive processes associated with the embodied viewpoint, rational/knowledge-based processes characteristic of the extended viewpoint, all the way to sociocultural and organizational processes that align with the embedded viewpoint (Figure 21.1).

Predictive processing also interconnects the 4e viewpoints by acknowledging the need for situated, enactive, embedded minds to effectively navigate the world by capitalizing on its probabilistic regularities (Clark, 2015). Predictive processing shifts one's relationship with one's environment from a reactive to a proactive stance, emphasizing one's attunements to the affordances the environment offers (Gibson, 1977). For example, participants prompted to *predict* task-relevant movements aligned with geometric conjectures showed superior MR even beyond those who *produced* task-relevant movements, suggesting that predictive processing facilitated simulated actions that supported hypothetical-deductive thinking (Xia et al., 2022).

Developments in Technology

The past decade has seen a number of technological developments relevant to embodied mathematical reasoning that largely fall into four categories. This section looks at the first two: mathematical activity and data collection. Two other developments, advances in data analysis, and designs of technology-based learning interventions, appear in later sections.

Mathematical Activity

Technological developments can influence *how* people perform mathematics and also *what* mathematics they have access to. One of the most notable technological developments of the last decade is the availability of higher-bandwidth, lower-cost immersive, extended reality (XR) systems, a class of technologies that include motion capture, augmented reality (AR) and virtual reality (VR) systems delivered via handhelds, special environments (such as VR rooms), and head-mounted devices. XR environments provide direct experiences with mathematical phenomena. For example, students can use VR to perceive and directly manipulate holographic objects as "spatially inscribed realizations of mathematical figures" such as spheres and infinite planes to gain novel insights about their properties over time and from different viewpoints, including third-person, first-person, and interior perspectives (Dimmel et al., 2021, p. 123).

Walkington et al. (2021, 2022b, 2023a) demonstrate how shared AR (shAR) systems use the next generation of XR headsets, such as the Microsoft HoloLens 2®, to incorporate 3D manipulable holograms into students' actual physical spaces, such as mathematics classrooms. shAR systems are unique because they support *collaborative* construction of mathematical knowledge by engaging processes of embodied learning and extended cognition, since participants can make lasting alterations to holographic objects made by others in the shAR environment while also seeing one another's movements and gestures. As shAR technologies expand the range of mathematical phenomena that are part of the public substrate, interlocutors take up new forms of co-operative social organization. This, in turn, alters people's mathematical activity and their ways of thinking and communicating (Goodwin, 2013).

Data Collection

The "embodiment turn" (e.g., Abrahamson et al., 2020) in the philosophy of mind benefited greatly from the earlier emergence of instruments such as consumer-grade video recording equipment and laboratory eye trackers. Recent developments have greatly expanded the range of body movement data and the environments in which these data can be collected. Analytic methods for multimodal data (described below) draw on an ever-expanding range of movement, communication, and biometric data for their modeling (Blikstein & Worsley, 2016; Walkington et al., 2023a).

The processing capabilities of systems for collecting motion-capture data also continue to improve. These systems include dedicated sensor arrays and resident computer cameras coupled with specialized computer vision algorithms (such as Convolutional Pose Machines; Wei et al., 2016) that document real-time changes in locations at increasingly high (and dynamically adjustable) frame rates of a rapidly growing number of body-based landmarks. For example, the MediaPipe Holistic model provides *X*, *Y*, & *Z* coordinates of 33 points along the general skeletal frame of the human body, 21 points along each hand, and hundreds of facial landmarks. MediaPipe Holistic also reports visibility metrics (roughly, how certain the system is that it is capturing the position of the intended body landmark). Interactions with devices such as the Balance Number Line capture data on whole-body oscillatory movement (Tancredi et al., 2022).

The proliferation of portable eye tracking devices means that investigators – and more notably, their research participants – are no longer tethered to bite bars and screens in the lab, enabling these rich records of attention and pupillometry to be captured "in the wild." Dual eye trackers among collaborators identify joint visual attention (Schneider et al., 2021; Shvarts & Abrahamson, 2019). Other wearable sensors, such as Fitbit® and the Wayband®, record arm movement and swaying, global body location, velocity, and so on.

Developments in Research Methods

With a richer set of multimodal data comes the need for multimodal data analytic tools and research methods. A methodological commitment to multimodality rests on a central tenet derived from the social theory of communication (Halliday, 1978) that all modes of inter-action, including one's socially situated actions, contribute to meaning making and its inter-personal and intrapersonal expression.

The synchrony between gestures, speech, and mathematical inscriptions demonstrates ways "mathematical learning and teaching are multimodal interactions that occur in rich communicative contexts" (Alibali & Nathan, 2012, p. 276; also see de Freitas & Sinclair, 2014). This offers a compelling case for multimodal analytic methods to investigate ways MR is expressed and influenced by verbal and nonverbal behaviors (e.g., Blikstein & Worsley, 2016; Ochoa et al., 2017; Walkington et al., 2023a). For example, combined qualitative and quantitative analyses presented by Pier et al. (2019) suggest that some aspects of students' mathematical knowledge are expressed only in gestures, and incorpo-rating factors that measure gesture production reliably improves statistical models of stu-dents' geometry-proof performance, even when controlling for what students say, and factors such as their spatial reasoning and prior math achievement. *Dynamic depictive gestures*, in particular, have emerged as a powerful exhibition of simulated action in sup-port of MR.

Scholars (Beilock & Goldin-Meadow, 2010; Walkington et al., 2022a) have also observed the influential role of *gestural replays*, speakers' nonverbal re-instatements of cognitively relevant actions made during subsequent explanations. For example, Walkington et al. (2022a) found that occurrences of high school mathematics students' gestures – both replays and non-replays – made during their explanations after playing *The Hidden Village* motion-capture video game were associated with significantly more accurate mathematical insights and more mathematically valid proofs. Xia et al. (2023) extended this line of inquiry by demonstrating that gestural replays specifically benefited geometry-proof pro-duction, with the most likely cause due to higher rates of mathematically valid *operational thought*, where the prover progresses systematically through a goal structure, anticipating the outcomes of proposed transformations on imagined – and often gestured – mathemati-cal entities. These advantages were evident even when participants engaged different corre-sponding body parts in these replays, such as using hands or fingers to replay cognitively relevant arm movements. In each case, the effect was strongest when replaying *dynamic* depictive gestures. Both the Walkington and Xia studies interpret their findings in terms of the action-cognition transduction framework and conclude that dynamic gestural replays instantiate a form of simulated action that activated relevant cognitive states for substanti-ating participants' generalized reasoning about the universal properties of space and shapes.

Methods for studies of larger-scale movements – such as movements across one's neigh-borhood, and migration behaviors – have emerged with improved access to and accuracy of locative information from satellite-based global positioning systems (GPS) and cellular networks that provide generative ways for investigating MR (Hall, Ma, & Nemirovsky, 2014; Rubel & Nicol, 2020; Taylor, 2020). For example, *locative literacies* (Taylor, 2017) and *math walks* (Wang et al., 2021) are ways people occupy place-based representations of their movements, and even design purposeful patterns using their movements for others to analyze. Geo-spatial methods, combined with discourse and gesture analysis, enable scholars to study *embedded* learning during authentic activities in data science, geographic information systems (GIS), topology, and geometric reasoning. Such investigations reveal ways that adults and youth perceive and inhabit mathematical spaces and spatial relations in their daily lives. These investigations also raise critical discussions about Cartesian representations of lived spaces and movement and their implications for the equitable distribution of resources, such as access to public transportation and the integrity of neighborhoods.

Multimodal approaches may align with different general methodological frameworks. *Multimodal analysis (MA)* methods largely focus on human-interpretable data from sources like video recordings that analyze audio and visual records of behavior (Walkington et al., 2023a). Example resources are: MAXQDA, NVivo, V-note, Transana, ATLAS.ti, and Anotemos. One benefit of MA is the close relation of the analysis to the data and its ready interpretation in terms of human mathematical activity. *Multimodal learning analytics (MMLA)* methods strive to expand the available corpora to support holistic accounts of learning (Ochoa et al., 2017) that span the biological-to-institutional spectrum (Figure 21.2). For example, Alcaraz-Carrión (2022) used MMLA techniques on corpora of television news broadcasts to reveal consistent patterns of speakers' gestures when verbalizing addition and subtraction that conform to two core metaphors of arithmetic: as motion along a path, and as object collection. A tradeoff is that the raw data streams and resultant MMLA models may be of such complexity that they are not directly interpretable by humans without computational support (e.g., EZ-MMLA toolkit). MMLA and MA methods can be combined to capitalize on their relative strengths (e.g., Lee-Cultura et al., 2021).

A central methodological challenge for all multimodal methods is cross-modal integration to support a convergent interpretation. Integration is most typically performed through *triangulation*—a process that draws on independent data modalities to form a coherent interpretation (Sung et al., 2022). *Interleaving* is another integration method that focuses

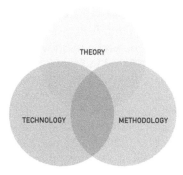

Figure 21.2 Developments in theory of embodied cognition, research methods, and technology-fueled advancements in grounded and embodied accounts of mathematical reasoning.

on the temporal structure of multimodal interactions during learning to form a cumulative structure of when, how, and what one learns (Sung et al., 2022). Huang et al. (2023) demonstrated the utility of a novel method for analyzing how learners orchestrate simultaneous and sequential relationships among modality-specific actions at micro and macro levels. They analyzed participants' interactions along four collaborative modalities of communication that are particularly salient in shared VR environments: actions on virtual objects, gestures, virtual (avatar) and physical body movements, and speech. Overall, emerging multimodal methods of analysis reveal the enactive, embodied, extended, and embedded nature of MR processes and continue to evolve along with developments in technology and theories of embodiment (Walkington et al., 2023a).

Co-Developments in Technology and Research Methods

As noted earlier, there is a reciprocity of sorts between the research methods for analyzing multimodal data and the technological developments in sensors, computing power and machine learning algorithms, and the nature of the mathematical activities afforded by technological platforms. MMLA tools often depend on machine learning algorithms and AI programs for multivariate feature detection, pattern matching over "windows" of input data, and probabilistic classification (Sharma & Giannakos, 2020) because these tasks often exceed human limits of attention and cognitive processing (Miller, 1956). AI programs can continuously monitor streams of human multimodal activity. However, it must be noted that these AI programs are instantiations of the very same *disembodied* symbol manipulation operations that characterize information-processing models of cognition – systems that I will collectively refer to as *disembodied AI* (dAI; Nathan, 2023). dAIs lack basic abilities to perceive the affordances of their environments, process stimuli in terms of grounded physiological and affective states, and interpret behaviors within sociocultural and historical contexts (Barsalou, 2008; Clark & Chalmers, 1998; Damasio 1999; Gallagher, 2017; Glenberg & Robertson, 2000; Hutchins, 1995; Newen et al., 2018; O'Regan & Noë, 2001). As such, dAIs are fundamentally incapable of making sense of embodied behaviors the ways that humans do regardless of the complexity of their training sets, size, and computing capacity (Harnad, 1990; Searle, 1980).

New developments in *augmented intelligence systems* (AIS) offer promising new approaches by augmenting the natural intelligence of humans with the artificial intelligence of dAIs. Specifically, AIS achieve this by integrating the capabilities of omnipresent dAI to detect complex patterns in multimodal data streams, with the capabilities of humans to meaningfully interpret people's embodied interactions. This enables AIS to achieve a balance between complexity, interpretability, and accountability for allocating education resources. The expansion of AIS to include body-based indicators of cognitive and affective processes shows tremendous promise (Nathan, Baker, Hutt, & Swart, 2022a). Learners commonly signal through posture, body movements, and facial expressions consequential cognitive and affective states such as "failure events" (Simpson et al., 2022) and "trouble spots" (Alibali et al., 2013), as well as signaling cognitive shifts from incorrect MR to correct insights (Laukkonen et al., 2021; Nathan et al., 2020). As one example, dAIs can be trained via machine learning methods to be targeted *detectors*, which continually monitor for body-based indicators of insights and trouble spots. Once body-based indicators of critical cognitive and affective states are detected (with sufficient likelihood), this alerts a human to conduct a detector-driven interview, which engages the human's capabilities to meaningfully interpret people's embodied interactions within the rich sociocultural contexts in which they occur (Baker et al., 2021; Hutt et al., 2022; Ocumpaugh et al., 2021). This *augments* human embodied intelligence with disembodied artificial intelligence in order to improve the investigation of fleeting, but consequential events that can help a research team to better understand learners' MR as it unfolds in real time within authentic settings.

Co-Developments in Technology and Theory

MR and mathematics education have historically benefited from – and depended on – technological achievements for the visual display of mathematical ideas. Developments that seem pedestrian today, such as high-resolution graphical displays and color printers, were pivotal to advancements in topics such as fractal geometry. The prior development of directly manipulable graphical objects through programmable digital multitouch systems ushered in new ways of conceptualizing and teaching a broad array of topics, including number, algebra, geometry, calculus, and functions through innovations such as TouchCounts (Sinclair & Pimm, 2014), GeoGebra (Hohenwarter et al., 2008), Cabri Geometry (Arzarello et al., 2014), and Graspable Math (Ottmar et al., 2015). Today, immersive extended reality (XR) has further expanded the ways people can experience mathematics. Motion capture using both specialized hardware and resident cameras on laptops and mobile devices has given rise to new platforms for embodied mathematics that are used in research and classrooms. AR and VR development has led to "spatially inscribed realizations of mathematical figures," offering a paradigmatic shift from 2D diagrams and touch-sensitive graphical displays (Dimmel et al., 2021, p. 123). Students can now have immersive, collaborative, embodied experiences of novel mathematical phenomena in their own classrooms. For example, students using XR can experience what it is like to be two-dimensional entities confined to movements on a Euclidean plane, as described in Abbott's (1884/1987) landmark novella *Flatland*. Students can then experience what it would be like when two-dimensional entities encounter three-dimensional entities that cannot be bound to a plane (Walkington & Nathan, 2020; cf. Valentine & Kopcha, 2020). XR activities of this sort can help learners to ground their understanding of *dimensionality* through embodied experiences and serve as a basis for how we, as three-dimensional beings, can conceptualize entities of four or more dimensions. Developments in XR, sometimes coupled with 3D printing, extend to post-secondary mathematics, including 3D vector operations, and calculus conceptualization and visualization (Lai & Cheong, 2022). Studies also show that XR interventions do not always support significant benefits in calculus learning compared to control conditions (Kang et al., 2020).

Theory-driven technological innovations prompt new perceptual and biomechanical ways of interacting with mathematical objects, collaborative embodied engagement, and multimodal discussions among learners, which cumulatively can tap into each of the 4e processes of enactivist, embodied, extended, and embedded cognition. The combined impact of developments in theory and technology has fostered an entirely new class of educational interventions based on a framework of *embodied design* (Abrahamson, 2009, 2014), "a theory-to-practice approach to mathematics education … [meant] to articulate integrated guidelines for building and facilitating pedagogical materials and activities" (Abrahamson et al., 2020, p. 1). These interventions instantiate several empirically validated principles of grounded and embodied mathematical cognition that advance both learning theories and future educational designs.

In sum, these principles hold that MR is fundamentally rooted in perceptuomotor processes, even when reading and manipulating traditional, static symbolic formalisms, such as equations and graphs. Designing technologies that engage students to enact cognitively relevant movements, perceptions, and talk, can lead to enhanced MR, greater learning gains, and more robust transfer to novel problems, new settings, and more advanced mathematics topics. Further, verbal and nonverbal behaviors can reveal emerging and transitional knowledge that may not be immediately obvious but may be identified by skilled observers (e.g., teachers trained to notice students' gestures) or by analyzing (e.g., using MMLA tools) large corpora of learners' multimodal behaviors.

Many current digital and tangible activities can readily adopt these effective grounding and embodied learning practices and provide the multimodal data for richer forms of learning assessments and scientific modeling of reasoning, learning, and cognitive development. A brief sampling of technology-based embodied interventions illustrates innovations that instantiate these design principles:

- Counting and arithmetic in *TouchCounts* (Sinclair & Heyd-Metzuyanim, 2014).
- Multiplicative reasoning using *The Mathematics Imagery Trainer for Proportion* (MIT-P; Howison et al. 2011) and *Rolly's Adventure* (Williams-Pierce & Thevenow-Harrison, 2021).
- Fractions learning through embodied video game play (Swart et al., 2016) and *The Fractions Tutor* (Rau et al., 2015).
- Instructional gestures for algebra produced by a computer-animated pedagogical avatar (Vest, Fyfe, Nathan, & Alibali, 2020).
- Algebra symbol manipulation using *Graspable Math* (Ottmar et al., 2015).
- Secondary-level geometric proof using *The Hidden Village* (Fogel et al., 2022; Nathan et al., 2022b), VR (Dimmel et al., 2021) and immersive shared AR (Huang et al., 2023 in press; Walkington et al., 2021, 2022b).
- Vectors arithmetic in *Magna-AR* (Vieyra & Vieyra, 2022) and embodied video game play (Zhao & Nathan, 2023).
- Quadratic reasoning with *The MIT-Parabola* (Shvarts & Abrahamson, 2019).
- Complex systems dynamics (Danish, 2014; Goldstone & Son, 2005; Tancredi et al., 2021).

Co-Developments in Theory and Research Methods

Learning scientists enter into educational settings with research methods chosen with the dual objectives of "use inspired basic research" (Stokes, 1997): to investigate theoretically driven questions about learning; *and of equal importance*, to inform the design and implementation of promising learning interventions (Nathan & Sawyer, 2022). Space considerations limit the focus here to two central topics (for a broader account, see Nathan, 2021): supporting abstraction and transfer, and assessing nonverbal ways of knowing.

Bridging from concrete, embodied experiences to mathematical abstractions and knowledge transfer requires reframing what is meant by "concrete," "abstract" and the "bridging" that takes place (e.g., Fyfe & Nathan, 2019). Notably, all "abstract representations" invoke perceptual affordances. Concreteness fading (Bruner, 1966) is a theory of instruction for fostering transfer using a *multi-step progression*. It starts with activating the affordances of a contextually embedded, grounded sensorimotor experience of a mathematical concept (e.g., balancing the weight of objects; the *enactive* stage). That experience is mapped to a decontextualized image-based depiction of the sensorimotor experience (images of objects on a pan balance; the *iconic* stage). The image is *faded* into a generic, idealized representation of that same concept (symbolic equations; the *symbolic* stage) that is chosen because it is used in discipline-specific practice by mathematicians and scientists. Research methods that integrate quantitative metrics (performance, response times), qualitative data (speech, gestures), and MMLA (arousal, grip) can help illuminate the internal processes operating at each stage. Such investigations can inform embodied theories of transfer (e.g., Day & Goldstone, 2011; Nathan & Alibali, 2021) that focus on the cohesion of learners' modes of perceiving and acting across physical instantiations and settings to reveal learners' awareness of invariant mathematical relations.

Assessing nonverbal ways of knowing becomes unavoidable when one acknowledges the embodied nature of MR. Avenues of expressing nonverbal forms of reasoning and knowledge alongside verbal knowledge assessments need to be offered to all learners, especially those with diverse linguistic and cultural backgrounds (Walkington et al., 2023b). However, summative assessment methods in schools traditionally privilege verbal and symbolic forms of knowledge expression. Presumably, this is because of efficiencies in test scoring, and epistemological viewpoints such as *formalisms first* among educators and test designers (Nathan, 2012), even if these approaches lead to systematic mischaracterizations in students' MR and the perpetuation of educational inequities. For example, verbal assessment methods, such as typing, simplify test administration and scoring but can disadvantage learners (i.e., compared to interviews and presentations) by restricting body-based behaviors such as gestures that might reveal nonverbal forms of knowledge. Typing also may inhibit the activation of action-cognition transduction that can enhance intellectual performance (Nathan & Martinez, 2015). Regardless of the challenges, multimodal forms of knowledge expression that include speech, gestures and distributed knowledge must become the gold standard because these provide the most veridical account of one's MR and intellectual development (e.g., Grondin et al., 2022). This is equally relevant when training formative assessment practices that inform teachers' real-time instructional accommodations when noticing multimodal indicators of students' reasoning, trouble spots, and readiness to learn (Alibali et al., 1997; Flood et al., 2022; Sung et al., 2021).

Overall Advancements in Grounded and Embodied Mathematical Reasoning and Areas for Future Development

Mutual developments in embodiment theory, technology, and research methods contribute to significant advances in understanding the nature of grounded and embodied mathematical reasoning and designing for its continual improvement. In the near term, we can expect to see particular impact in the design of embodied learning environments for fostering grounded MR for an ever broadening array of mathematics topics. For example, learners may have opportunities to directly experience and manipulate mathematical phenomena that are inaccessible due to natural limitations in people's spatial and cognitive capacities, such as 4-dimensional operations using quaternions (3blue1brown, 2018). These innovations are likely to spawn more inclusive approaches to teaching and assessment of verbal and nonverbal ways of knowing.

Theory, method, and technology mutually offer promising changes in the types of behaviors that can be documented, analyzed, and intepreted in ways that are likely to propel our scientific understanding of mathematical thinking and learning. This can support advances in areas such as the development of mathematical intuition, and the co-construction of distributed knowledge and collaborative problem solving.

Longer-term influences are likely to foster the emergence of new disciplinary practices for the field of mathematics, such as "publishing" multimodal proofs that are experienced in immersive XR environments (Walkington et al., 2023b). With continued development of theories and methods we may also witness support for more integrative psychological theories that acknowledge the interrelations of verbal and nonverbal cognitive and affective processes that are a natural outcome of embodied accounts of mathematical reasoning.

Related Topics

Chapter 4. Extended Cognition *Ken Aizawa*
Chapter 6. Embedded and Situated Cognition *M. R. W. Dawson*
Chapter 7. The Enactive Approach *Evan Thompson and Ezequiel A. Di Paolo*
Chapter 8. Integrating Embodied Cognition and Predictive Processing *Elmarie Venter*
Chapter 9. Predicting the Body or Embodied Prediction? New Directions in Embodied Predictive Processing *Luke Kersten*
Chapter 17. The Grounding of Concrete and Abstract Language: Consolidated Evidence, New Issues, and New Challenges *Claudia Scorolli and Claudia Mazzuca*
Chapter 19. Gesture in Reasoning: An Embodied Perspective *Martha Alibali, Rebecca Boncoddo, and Autumn Hostetter*
Chapter 22. Embodiment in Education *Virginia Flood*
Chapter 23. Embodied Learning: Translating Embodied Cognition Research *Sheila L. Macrine and Jennifer M.B. Fugate*
Chapter 25. Minds in the Matrix: Embodied Cognition and Virtual Reality *Paul Smart*
Chapter 26. Embodied Cognition and Movement-Driven Practices *Zuzanna Rucinska and Susanne Ravn*
Chapter 31. The Constitution of Group Cognition *Gerry Stahl*
Chapter 32. Varieties of Group Cognition *Georg Theiner*

Notes

The research reported here was supported by the Institute of Education Sciences, U.S. Department of Education, through Grant R305A200401 to Southern Methodist University and the University of Wisconsin – Madison. The opinions expressed are those of the authors and do not represent views of the Institute or the U.S. Department of Education.

References

3blue1brown (2018). www.3blue1brown.com/lessons/quaternions-and-3d-rotation
Abbott, E. A., (1884/1987). *Flatland: A Romance of Many Dimensions*. Penguin Books.
Abrahamson, D. (2009). Embodied Design: Constructing Means for Constructing Meaning. *Educational Studies in Mathematics*, 70(1), 27–47.
——— (2014). Building Educational Activities for Understanding: An Elaboration on the Embodied-Design Framework and its Epistemic Grounds. *International Journal of Child-Computer Interaction*, 2(1), 1–16.

Abrahamson, D., & Bakker, A. (2016). Making Sense of Movement in Embodied Design for Mathematics Learning. *Cognitive Research: Principles and Implications*, *1*(1), 1–13.

Abrahamson, D., Nathan, M. J., Williams-Pierce, C., Walkington, C., Ottmar, E. R., Soto, H. & Alibali, M. W. (2020). The Future of Embodied Design for Mathematics Teaching and Learning. *Frontiers in Education*, *5*(August), 1–29. doi: 10.3389/Feduc.2020.00147

Alcaraz-Carrión, D., Alibali, M. W., & Valenzuela, J. (2022). Adding and Subtracting by Hand: Metaphorical Representations of Arithmetic in Spontaneous Co-Speech Gestures. *Acta Psychologica*, *228*, 103624.

Alibali, M. W., & Nathan, M. J. (2012). Embodiment in Mathematics Teaching and Learning: Evidence from Learners' and Teachers' Gestures. *Journal of the Learning Sciences*, *21*(2), 247–286.

Alibali, M. W., Flevares, L. M., & Goldin-Meadow, S. (1997). Assessing Knowledge Conveyed in Gesture: Do Teachers Have the Upper Hand? *Journal of Educational Psychology*, *89*(1), 183.

Alibali, M. W., Nathan, M. J., Church, R. B., Wolfgram, M. S., Kim, S., & Knuth, E. J. (2013). Gesture and Speech In Mathematics Lessons: Forging Common Ground by Resolving Trouble Spots. *ZDM – International Journal on Mathematics Education*, *45*, 425–440. doi: 10.1007/S11858-012-0476-0

Arzarello, F., Bairral, M. A., & Danè, C. (2014). Moving from Dragging to Touchscreen: Geometrical Learning with Geometric Dynamic Software. *Teaching Mathematics and its Applications: International Journal of the IMA*, *33*(1), 39–51.

Baker, R.S., Nasiar, N., Ocumpaugh, J.L., Hutt, S., Andres, J.M.A.L., Slater, S., Schofield, M., Moore, A., Paquette, L., Munshi, A., Biswas, G. (2021) Affect-Targeted Interviews For Understanding Student Frustration. In I. Roll, D. McNamara, S. Sosnovsky, R. Luckin, V. Dimitrova (Eds), *Proceedings of the International Conference on Artificial Intelligence and Education*. Springer.

Barsalou, L. W. (2008). Grounded Cognition. *Annual Review of Psychology*, *59*(1), 617–645.

Beilock, S. L., & Goldin-Meadow, S. (2010). Gesture Changes Thought by Grounding it in Action. *Psychological Science*, *21*(11), 1605–1610.

Blikstein, P., & Worsley, M. (2016). Multimodal Learning Analytics and Education Data Mining: Using Computational Technologies to Measure Complex Learning Tasks. *Journal of Learning Analytics*, *3*(2), 220–238.

Bruner, J. (1966). *Toward a Theory of Instruction*. Cambridge, MA: Belknap Press

Carraher, T. N., Carraher, D. W., & Schliemann, A. D. (1985). Mathematics in the Streets and in Schools. *British Journal of Developmental Psychology*, *3*(1), 21–29.

Chemero, A. (2011). *Radical Embodied Cognitive Science*. MIT Press.

Clark, A. (2015). *Surfing Uncertainty: Prediction, Action, and the Embodied Mind*. Oxford University Press.

Clark, A., & Chalmers, D. (1998). The Extended Mind. *Analysis*, *58*(1), 7–19.

Damasio, A. R. (1999). *The Feeling of What Happens: Body and Emotion in the Making of Consciousness*. Houghton Mifflin Harcourt.

Danish, J. A. (2014). Applying An Activity Theory Lens To Designing Instruction For Learning About the Structure, Behavior, and Function of a Honeybee System. *Journal of the Learning Sciences*, *23*(2), 100–148.

Day, S. B., & Goldstone, R. L. (2011). Analogical Transfer from a Simulated Physical System. *Journal of Experimental Psychology: Learning, Memory, and Cognition*, *37*(3), 551–567. doi:10.1037/A0022333

de Freitas, E., & Sinclair, N. (2014). *Mathematics and the Body: Material Entanglements in the Classroom*. Cambridge University Press.

Dee, T.S. & Penner, E. (2019, October). *My Brother's Keeper? The Impact of Targeted Educational Supports* (CEPA Working Paper No. 19-07). Stanford, CA: Stanford Center for Education Policy Analysis.

Dimmel, J., Pandiscio, E., & Bock, C. (2021). The Geometry of Movement: Encounters with Spatial Inscriptions for Making and Exploring Mathematical Figures. *Digital Experiences in Mathematics Education*, *7*(1), 122–148.

Donovan, A. M., & Alibali, M. W. (2021). Action and Mathematics Learning. In Steven A. Stolz (Ed.), *The Body, Embodiment, and Education* (pp. 136–155). Routledge.

Flood, V. J. (2018). Multimodal Revoicing As An Interactional Mechanism for Connecting Scientific and Everyday Concepts. *Human Development, 61*(3), 145–173.

Flood, V. J., Shvarts, A., & Abrahamson, D. (2022). Responsive Teaching for Embodied Learning with Technology. In S. Macrine and J. Fugate (Eds), *Movement Matters: How Embodied Cognition Informs Teaching and Learning* (pp. 179–196). MIT Press.

Fogel, A., Swart, M., Grondin, M., & Nathan, M. J. (2022, November). Grounding Embodied Learning Using Online Motion-Detection in *The Hidden Village*. Iyer, S. et al. (Eds) Proceedings of the 30th International Conference on Computers in Education. Asia-Pacific Society for Computers in Education.

Fyfe, E. R., & Nathan, M. J. (2019). Making "Concreteness Fading" More Concrete as a Theory of Instruction for Promoting Transfer. *Educational Review, 71*(4), 403–422.

Gallagher, S. (2017). *Enactivist Interventions: Rethinking the Mind*. Oxford University Press.

Garcia, N., & Infante, N. E. (2012). Gestures As Facilitators to Proficient Mental Modelers. In L. R. Van Zoest, J.-J. Lo, & J. L. Kratky (Eds), *Proceedings of the 34th Annual Meeting of the North American Chapter of the International Group for the Psychology of Mathematics Education* (pp. 289–295). Kalamazoo, MI: Western Michigan University.

Gibson, J. J. (1977). *The Theory of Affordances*. Erlbaum Associates, Hillsdale, NJ.

Glenberg, A. M., & Robertson, D. A. (2000). Symbol Grounding and Meaning: A Comparison of High-Dimensional and Embodied Theories of Meaning. *Journal of Memory and Language, 43*(3), 379–401.

Glenberg, A. M., De Vega, M., & Graesser, A. C. (2008). Framing the Debate. Symbol, Embodiment, and Meaning. In M. De Vega, A. M. Glenberg, & A. C. Graesser (Eds), *Symbols and Embodiment: Debates on Meaning and Cognition*. Oxford, UK: Oxford University Press.

Goldstone, R. L., & Son, J. Y. (2005). The Transfer of Scientific Principles Using Concrete and Idealized Simulations. *Journal of the Learning Sciences, 14*(1), 69–110.

Goodwin, C. (2013). The Co-Operative, Transformative Organization of Human Action and Knowledge. *Journal of Pragmatics, 46*(1), 8–23.

Grondin, M. M., Swart, M. I., Xia, F., & Nathan, M. J. (2022, June). Assessing Engineering Students' Embodied Knowledge of Torsional Loading Through Gesture. In *2022 American Society of Engineering Education (ASEE) Annual Conference & Exposition*, Engineering Research Methods Division (ASEE Paper ID #2022-383, pp. 1–14). Minneapolis, MN: ASEE.

Hall, R., Ma, J. Y., & Nemirovsky, R. (2014). Rescaling Bodies in/as Representational Instruments in GPS Drawing. In *Learning Technologies and the Body* (pp. 124–143). Routledge.

Halliday, M. A. K. (1978). *Language As Social Semiotic: the Social Interpretation of Language and Meaning*. London: Edward Arnold.

Harnad, S. (1990). The Symbol Grounding Problem. *Physica D: Nonlinear Phenomena, 42*(1–3), 335–346.

Hohenwarter, M., Hohenwarter, J., Kreis, Y., & Lavicza, Z. (2008, July). Teaching and Learning Calculus with Free Dynamic Mathematics Software GeoGebra. In *Proceedings of the 11th International Congress on Mathematical Education* (ICME 11), Monterrey, Mexico. http://hdl.handle.net/10993/47219 Accessed on May 1, 2023.

Howison, M., Trninic, D., Reinholz, D., & Abrahamson, D. (2011, May). The Mathematical Imagery Trainer: From Embodied Interaction to Conceptual Learning. In *Proceedings of the SIGCHI Conference on Human Factors in Computing Systems* (pp. 1989–1998).

Huang, W., Walkington, C., & Nathan, M. J. (2023). Coordinating Modalities of Mathematical Collaboration in Shared VR Environments. *International Journal of Computer-Supported Collaborative Learning. 18*, 163–201. DOI: 10.1007/s11412-023-09397-x

Hutchins, E. (1995). *Cognition in the Wild*. Cambridge: MIT Press.

Hutt, S., Baker, R. S., Ocumpaugh, J., Munshi, A., Andres, J. M. A. L., Karumbaiah, S., Slater, S., Biswas, G., Paquette, L., Bosch, N., Van Velsen, M. (2022). Quick Red Fox: An App Supporting a New Paradigm in Qualitative Research on AIED for STEM. To appear in F. Ouyang, P. Jiao, B. M. McLaren, A. H. Alavi (Eds), *Artificial Intelligence in STEM Education: The Paradigmatic Shifts in Research, Education, and Technology*. (pp. 319–332). CRC Press.

Kang, K., Kushnarev, S., Pin, W. W., Ortiz, O., & Shihang, J. C. (2020). Impact of Virtual Reality on the Visualization of Partial Derivatives in a Multivariable Calculus Class. *IEEE Access, 8*, 58940–58947.

Kim, D. & Nathan, M. J. (2022). The Effect of Instructed Actions on Embodied Geometric Reasoning. Under review.

Koedinger, K. R., Alibali, M. W., & Nathan, M. J. (2008). Trade-Offs Between Grounded and Abstract Representations: Evidence from Algebra Problem Solving. *Cognitive Science*, 32(2), 366–397.

Lai, J. W., & Cheong, K. H. (2022). Adoption of Virtual and Augmented Reality For Mathematics Education: A Scoping Review. *IEEE Access*, 10, 13693–13703.

Lakoff, G. & Johnson, M. (1980). *Metaphors We Live By*. University of Chicago Press, Chicago.

Laukkonen, R. E., Ingledew, D. J., Grimmer, H. J., Schooler, J. W., & Tangen, J. M. (2021). Getting a Grip on Insight: Real-Time and Embodied Aha Experiences Predict Correct Solutions. *Cognition and Emotion*, 35(5), 918–935.

Lave, J. (1988). *Cognition in Practice: Mind, Mathematics and Culture in Everyday Life*. New York: Cambridge University Press.

Lee-Cultura, S., Sharma, K., & Giannakos, M. (2021). Children's Play and Problem-Solving in Motion-Based Learning Technologies Using a Multi-Modal Mixed Methods Approach. *International Journal of Child-Computer Interaction*, 100355. doi: 10.1016/J.Ijcci.2021.100355

Martin, T. & Schwartz, D. L. (2005). Physically Distributed Learning: Adapting and Reinterpreting Physical Environments in the Development of Fraction Concepts. *Cognitive Science*, 29(4), 587–625.

McKinney De Royston, M., Lee, C., Nasir, N. I. S., & Pea, R. (2020). Rethinking Schools, Rethinking Learning. *Phi Delta Kappan*, 102(3), 8–13. doi: 10.1177/0031721720970693

Menary, R. (2010). Introduction to the Special Issue on 4e Cognition. *Phenomenology and the Cognitive Sciences*, 9(4), 459–463.

Michaelis, J. & Nathan, M. J. (2014). The Role of Feedback in Interest Development in an Out-of-School Engineering Setting. In W. Penuel, S. A. Jurow, & K. O'Connor (Eds), *Learning and Becoming in Practice: Proceedings of the Eleventh International Conference of the Learning Sciences* (pp. 1525–1526). Boulder, CO: University of Colorado.

Miller, G. A. (1956). The Magical Number Seven, Plus or Minus Two: Some Limits on Our Capacity for Processing Information. *Psychological Review*, 63(2), 81.

Nasir, N., Givens, J. R., & Chatmon, C. (2018). *We Dare Say Love: Supporting Achievement in the Educational Life of Black Boys*. New York, NY: Teachers College Press.

Nathan, M. J. (2012). Rethinking formalisms in formal education. *Educational Psychologist*, 47(2), 125–148.

———— (2014). Grounded Mathematical Reasoning. In L. Shapiro (Ed.), *The Routledge Handbook of Embodied Cognition* (pp. 171–183). New York: Routledge.

———— (2021). *Foundations of Embodied Learning: A Paradigm for Education*. Routledge.

———— (2023). Disembodied AI and the Limits to Machine Understanding of Students' Embodied Interactions. *Frontiers in Artificial Intelligence–AI for Human Learning and Behavior Change*, 6, 1148227. doi: 10.3389/frai.2023.1148227

Nathan, M. J. & Alibali, M. W. (2021). An Embodied Theory of Transfer of Mathematical Learning. In Charles Hohensee and Joanne Lobato (Eds), *Transfer of Learning: Progressive Perspectives for Mathematics Education and Related Fields* (pp. 27–58). Springer.

Nathan, M. J., Baker, R. S., Hutt, S. & Swart, M. I. (2022a). Data-Driven Interviewing to Study the Embodied Cognitive Shifts that Occur During Geometry Learning. Proposal to National Science Foundation–Science of Learning and Augmented Intelligence. Unpublished grant proposal.

Nathan, M. J. & Martinez, C. V. (2015). Gesture As Model Enactment: The Role of Gesture in Mental Model Construction and Inference Making When Learning From Text. *Learning: Research and Practice*, 1(1), 4–37.

Nathan, M. J. & Sawyer, K. (2022). Foundations of Learning Sciences. In K. Sawyer (Ed.), *The Cambridge Handbook of the Learning Sciences* (3rd ed.; pp. 27–52). Cambridge, UK: Cambridge University Press. ISBN-13: 978-1108744669

Nathan, M. J., Schenck, K. E., Vinsonhaler, R., Michaelis, J. E., Swart, M. I., & Walkington, C. (2020). Embodied Geometric Reasoning: Dynamic Gestures During Intuition, Insight, and Proof. *Journal of Educational Psychology*, 113(5), 929.

Nathan, M. J. & Walkington, C. (2017). Grounded and Embodied Mathematical Cognition: Promoting Mathematical Insight and Proof Using Action and Language. *Cognitive Research: Principles and Implications*. doi: 10.1186/S41235-016-0040-5

Nathan, M. J., Walkington, C., & Swart, M. I. (2022b, June). Designs for Grounded and Embodied Mathematical Learning. In Chinn, C., Tan, E., Chan, C., & Kali, Y. (Eds), *Proceedings of the16th International Conference of the Learning Sciences-ICLS2022* (pp. 179–186). Hiroshima, Japan: International Society of the Learning Sciences.

Nemirovsky, Ricardo, and Ferrara, Francesca (2009). Mathematical imagination and embodied cognition. *Educational Studies in Mathematics*, 70, 159–174.

Newen, A., De Bruin, L., & Gallagher, S. (Eds). (2018). *The Oxford Handbook of 4e Cognition*. Oxford University Press.

Núñez, R. E., Edwards, L. D., & Filipe Matos, J. (1999). Embodied Cognition as Grounding for Situatedness and Context in Mathematics Education. *Educational Studies in Mathematics*, 39(1), 45–65.

Ochoa, X., Lang, A. C., & Siemens, G. (2017). Multimodal Learning Analytics. In C. Lang, G. Siemens, A. Wise, & D. Gašević (Eds), *Handbook of Learning Analytics* (pp. 129–141). Society for Learning Analytics Research. doi: 10.18608/Hla17

Ocumpaugh, J., Hutt, S., Andres, J. M. A. L., Baker, R. S., Biswas, G., Bosch, N., Paquette, L., & Munshi, A. (2021). Using Qualitative Data from Targeted Interviews to Inform Rapid AIED Development. In *Proceedings of the 29th International Conference on Computers in Education*.

O'Regan, J. K., & Noë, A. (2001). A Sensorimotor Account of Vision and Visual Consciousness. *Behavioral and Brain Sciences*, 24(5), 939–973.

Ottmar, E. R., Landy, D., Goldstone, R. L., and Weitnauer, E. (2015). "Getting From Here To There: Testing the Effectiveness of An Interactive Mathematics Intervention Embedding Perceptual Learning," In *Proceedings of the Thirty-Seventh Annual Conference of the Cognitive Science Society*, D. C. Noelle, R. Dale, A. S. Warlaumont, J. Yoshimi, T. Matlock, C. D. Jennings, et al. (Eds.), (pp. 1793–1798). Pasadena, CA: Cognitive Science Society.

Pier, E. L., Walkington, C., Clinton, V., Boncoddo, R., Williams-Pierce, C., Alibali, M. W., & Nathan, M. J. (2019). Embodied Truths: How Dynamic Gestures and Speech Contribute to Mathematical Proof Practices. *Contemporary Educational Psychology*, 58, 44–57.

Rau, M. A., Aleven, V., & Rummel, N. (2015). Successful Learning with Multiple Graphical Representations and Self-Explanation Prompts. *Journal of Educational Psychology*, 107(1), 30–46. doi: 10.1037/A0037211

Rubel, L. H., & Nicol, C. (2020). The Power of Place: Spatializing Critical Mathematics Education. *Mathematical Thinking and Learning*, 22(3), 173–194.

Saxe, G. B. (1982). Developing Forms of Arithmetical Thought Among the Oksapmin of Papua New Guinea. *Developmental Psychology*, 18(4), 583–594.

Schenck, K. & Nathan, M. J. (2021, June). Exploring Expanded Notions of Mathematical Reasoning: Spatial Systems, Anxiety, and Embodiment. In A. Wichmann, H. U. Hoppe, & N. Rummel (Eds.), *General Proceedings of the 1st Annual Meeting of the International Society of the Learning Sciences 2021* (pp. 113–114). Bochum, Germany: International Society of the Learning Sciences.

Schenck, K., Walkington, C., & Nathan, M. J. (2022). Groups that Move Together, Prove Together: Collaborative Gestures and Gesture Attitudes Among Teachers Performing Embodied Geometry. In S. Macrine and J. Fugate (Eds), *Movement Matters: How Embodied Cognition Informs Teaching and Learning* (pp. 131–145). MIT Press.

Schneider, B., Worsley, M., & Martinez-Maldonado, R. (2021). Gesture and Gaze: Multimodal Data in Dyadic Interactions. In *International Handbook of Computer-Supported Collaborative Learning* (pp. 625–641). Cham: Springer.

Schoenfeld, A. H. (1987/2013). *Cognitive Science and Mathematics Education*. Routledge.

—— (2016). Research in Mathematics Education. *Review of Research in Education*, 40(1), 497–528. doi: 10.3102/0091732X16658650

Searle, J. R. (1980). Minds, Brains, and Programs. *Behavioral and Brain Sciences*, 3(3), 417–424.

Shapiro, L. (2019). *Embodied Cognition* (2nd ed.). Routledge.

Sharma, K., & Giannakos, M. (2020). Multimodal Data Capabilities for Learning: What Can Multimodal Data Tell Us About Learning? *British Journal of Educational Technology*, 51(5), 1450–1484. doi: 10.1111/Bjet.12993

Shvarts, A., & Abrahamson, D. (2019). Dual-Eye-Tracking Vygotsky: A Microgenetic Account of a Teaching/Learning Collaboration in an Embodied-Interaction Technological Tutorial for Mathematics. *Learning, Culture and Social Interaction*, 22, 100316.

Simpson, A., Williams-Pierce, C., Shokeen, E., Katirci, N., Soto, H., Baker, J., DeLiema, D., Kapur, M., Ellis, A., Lockwood, E., Plaxco, D., Alibali, M. W., & Ramirez, D. (2022). ISLS. The Nature(S) of Embodied Mathematical Failure. In C. Chinn, E. Tan, C. Chan, & Y. Kali (Eds), *Proceedings of the 16th International Conference of the Learning Sciences – ICLS2022* (pp. 1787–1793). International Society of the Learning Sciences.

Sinclair, N., & Heyd-Metzuyanim, E. (2014). Learning Number with TouchCounts: The Role of Emotions and the Body in Mathematical Communication. *Technology, Knowledge and Learning*, 19(1), 81–99.

Sinclair, N., & Pimm, D. (2014). Number's Subtlet Touch: Expanding Finger Gnosis in the Era of Multitouch Technologies. *Proceeding of PME 38 and PME-NA 36*, 5, 209–216.

Stokes, D. E. (1997). *Pasteur's Quadrant: Basic Science and Technological Innovation*. Washington, DC: Brookings Institution Press.

Sung, H., Swart, M. I., & Nathan, M. J. (2021, October). Enhancing K-12 Pre-Service Teachers' Embodied Understanding of the Geometry Knowledge Through Online Collaborative Design. In Olanoff, D., Johnson, K., & Spitzer, S. M. (2021). *Proceedings of the Forty-Third Annual Meeting of the North American Chapter of the International Group for the Psychology of Mathematics Education* (pp. 909–917). Philadelphia, PA.

——— (2022, June). Methods for Analyzing Temporally Entangled Multimodal Data. In Weinberger, A. Chen, W., Hernández-Leo, D., & Chen, B. (Eds), *Proceedings of the 15th International Conference on Computer-Supported Collaborative Learning -CSCL 2022* (pp. 242–249). Hiroshima, Japan: International Society of the Learning Sciences.

Swart, M. I., Friedman, B., Kornkasem, S., Lee, A., Lyashevsky, I., Vitale, J. M., ... & Black, J. B. (2016). A Design-Based Approach to Situating Embodied Learning of Mathematical Fractions Using Narratives and Gestures in a Tablet-Based Game. In *2016 AERA National Conference, Washington, DC*.

Tancredi, S., Abdu, R., Abrahamson, D., & Balasubramaniam, R. (2021). Modeling Nonlinear Dynamics of Fluency Development in an Embodied-Design Mathematics Learning Environment With Recurrence Quantification Analysis. *International Journal of Child-Computer Interaction*, 29, 100297.

Tancredi, S., Chen, R. S. Y., Krause, C., & Siu, Y.-T. (2022). The Need for Speed: Rationale and Guiding Principles For Special-Education Embodied Design in Mathematics. In S. Macrine & J. Fugate (Eds), *Movement Matters: How Embodied Cognition Informs Teaching and Learning*. MIT Press.

Taylor, K. H. (2017). Learning Along Lines: Locative Literacies for Reading and Writing the City. *Journal of the Learning Sciences*, 26(4), 533–574.

——— (2020). Resuscitating (and Refusing) Cartesian Representations of Daily Life: when Mobile and Grid Epistemologies of the City Meet. *Cognition and Instruction*, 38(3), 407–426.

Thompson, E. (2010). *Mind in Life: Biology, Phenomenology, and the Sciences of Mind*. Harvard University Press.

Tomasello, M. (1999). The Human Adaptation for Culture. *Annual Review of Anthropology, 28*.

Valentine, K. D., & Kopcha, T. J. (2020). Manifestations of Middle School Learners' Problematization Activity as an Embodied Phenomenon. *Journal for Research in Mathematics Education*, 51(5), 541–573.

Vest, N. A., Fyfe, E. R., Nathan, M. J., & Alibali, M. W. (2020). Learning From an Avatar Video Instructor: The Role of Gesture Mimicry. *Gesture*, 19(1), 128–155.

Vieyra, R. & Vieyra, C. (2022). Immersive Learning Experiences in Augmented Reality (AR): Visualizing and Interacting with Magnetic Fields. In S. Macrine and J. Fugate (Eds.) *Movement Matters: How Embodied Cognition Informs Teaching and Learning* (pp. 217–236). MIT Press.

Walkington, C. & Nathan, M. J. (2020). *Exploring Collaborative Embodiment for Learning (EXCEL): Understanding Geometry Through Multiple Modalities*. Grant proposal to the U. S. Department of Education–Institute of Education Sciences. https://IES.Ed.Gov/Funding/Grantsearch/Details.Asp?ID=4484

Walkington, C., Chelule, G., Woods, D., & Nathan, M. J. (2019). Collaborative Gesture as a Case of Extended Mathematical Cognition. *Journal of Mathematical Behavior*. doi: 10.1016/J.Jmathb.2018.12.002

Walkington, C., Gravell, J., Velazque, J., He, T., Hickey, G., Nathan, M. J., & Cuevas, A. (2021, June). Collaborative Virtual Learning in the shAR Geometry Simulation Environment. In A. Wichmann, H. U. Hoppe, & N. Rummel (Eds), *General Proceedings of the 1st Annual Meeting of the International Society of the Learning Sciences 2021* (pp. 17–20). Bochum, Germany: International Society of the Learning Sciences.

Walkington, C., Nathan, M. J., Huang, W., Hunnicutt, J., & Washington, J. (2023a). Multimodal analysis of interaction data from embodied education technologies. *Educational Technology Research & Development*, 1–20. doi:10.1007/s11423-023-10254-9

Walkington, C., Nathan, M. J., Wang, M. & Schenck, K. (2022a). The Effect of Cognitive Relevance of Directed Actions On Mathematical Reasoning. *Cognitive Science*, 46(9), E13180. doi: 10.1111/Cogs.13180

Walkington, C., Nathan, M. J., Wang, M., Swart, M. I., Holcomb-Webb, K., Schenck, K., & Washington, J. (2023b). The development of gestural knowledge through collaborative problem posing of geometric movements. Manuscript under review.

Walkington, C., Nathan, M.J., Hunnicutt, J., Washington, J., & Holcomb-Webb, K. (2022b, June). Learning Geometry Through Collaborative, Embodied Explorations with Augmented Reality Holograms. In *Proceedings of the 16th International Conference of the Learning Sciences-ICLS2022* (pp. 1992–1993). Hiroshima, Japan: International Society of the Learning Sciences.

Walkington, C., Wang, M. & Nathan, M. J. (2020). Collaborative Gestures Among High School Students Conjointly Proving Geometric Conjectures. In *Proceedings of the 14th International Congress on Mathematics Education (ICME-14)*, Shanghai, China.

Wang, M., Walkington, C., & Dhingra, K. (2021). Facilitating Student-Created Math Walks. *Mathematics Teacher: Learning and Teaching PK-12, 114*(9), 670–676.

Wei, S. E., Ramakrishna, V., Kanade, T., & Sheikh, Y. (2016). Convolutional Pose Machines. In *Proceedings of the IEEE Conference on Computer Vision and Pattern Recognition* (pp. 4724–4732).

Williams-Pierce, C., & Thevenow-Harrison, J. T. (2021). Zones of Mathematical Play. *Journal of the Learning Sciences, 30*(3), 509–527.

Wilson, M. (2002). Six Views of Embodied Cognition. *Psychonomic Bulletin & Review, 9*(4), 625–636.

Xia, F., Schenck, K. E., Swart, M. I., & Nathan, M. J. (2022, June). The Role of Action-Prediction in Mathematical Reasoning. In *Proceedings of the 16th International Conference of the Learning Sciences-ICLS2022* (pp. 1469–1472). Hiroshima, Japan: International Society of the Learning Sciences.

Xia, F., Swart, M. I., Schenck, K. E., & Nathan, M. J. (2023). Gestural Replays Support Mathematical Reasoning by Simulating Geometric Transformations. Under review.

Zhao, Y. & Nathan, M. J. (2023, April). High School Students' Embodied Reasoning About Vectors. Paper Presented to the 2023 Annual Meeting of the American Educational Research Association, Chicago, IL: AERA.

Further Readings

Macrine, S. L., & Fugate, J. M. (Eds). (2022). *Movement Matters: How Embodied Cognition Informs Teaching and Learning*. MIT Press. Presents a broad range of contemporary research on mathematics education from an embodied perspective.

Nathan, M. J. (2021). *Foundations of embodied learning: A Paradigm for Education*. Routledge. ISBN-13: 9780367349769 (paperback); 9781000430073 (eBook) Reexamines views of learning, instruction, assessment, and the design of educational technologies by rethinking the learner as an integrated system of mind, body, and environment.

22

EMBODIMENT IN EDUCATION

Virginia J. Flood

Introduction

Embodiment in education is an interdisciplinary area with contributions from psychology, learning sciences, anthropology, and human computer interaction, among others. Like the embodied cognition program generally, theories of embodiment in education are far from unified and offer a variety of different perspectives to challenge information-processing theories of the learning mind (Shapiro and Stolz 2019). Interest in embodied perspectives has grown rapidly in the last 20 years: A Google Scholar query for "embodied learning" produces around 140 results between 1990 and 2000, 1,420 results from 2001 to 2010, and a whopping 8,890 results from 2011 to 2020. Since 2010, there has been a proliferation of volumes on embodiment in education.[1] In addition, many fruitful interdisciplinary collaborations of cognitive science philosophers and education researchers have sprung up (e.g., Gallagher and Lindgren 2015; Hutto et al. 2015).

Today's embodied turn is predated by a long history of interest in embodiment. Developmental psychologist Piaget (1953) recognized the indispensable role *sensorimotor experiences* play in shaping the developing human mind. Earlier, Vygotsky argued that the isolated brain is an unsuitable unit of analysis for studying learning and development: *Zones of proximal development* and the *mediational function* of cultural tools extend the mind to interactions with people, and practices and objects passed down through history by predecessors (Wertsch 1985). Long before Piaget and Vygotsky, Pestalozzi advocated for an *education of the head, heart, and hand* (Resnick et al. 1998). Later, Fröbel and Montessori argued for using specialized objects and designing environments to promote learning through embodied interaction and sensory exploration (Abrahamson 2014; Resnick et al. 1998). In the US, Dewey highlighted the importance of learning through transactional experiences with the environment and situated activity (Koschmann 2001).

During the cognitive revolution, as information-processing theories took hold of education, the body and its interactions with the environment were backgrounded. Information processing drew extensively on computational metaphors, treating the body as encasing hardware for a brain-bound software mind (Nathan 2021; Lee 2014). Education researchers even described patterns of mistakes in problem solving as "bugs," drawing parallels

DOI: 10.4324/9781003322511-29

with programming (Brown and Burton 1978). While information-processing models of learning are still common, they increasingly share the stage with embodiment's growing influence on education (e.g., Abrahamson et al. 2020). In this chapter, I provide an overview of how interdisciplinary scholars have taken up embodiment theories to understand learning, the design of educational environments, and teaching, and present implications of this recent work.

Conceptualization Hypotheses in Education: Embodied Metaphors

Conceptualization hypotheses posit that structural, biological features of the human body and its interactions with physical surroundings shape how humans conceptualize the world (Shapiro 2012). Lakoff and Johnson's (1999) embodied theory of conceptual metaphor (CMT) has had an especially large influence in education. They argue that all human concepts are based in perceptuomotor schemas built from perceiving and moving through the world with the particular bodies we have. Largely unconsciously, these perceptuomotor schemas provide inferential structures for mapping between familiar source domains (e.g., movement through space, object manipulation) and less familiar target domains (e.g., algebra or thermodynamics), allowing humans to imagine abstract ideas and possibilities that extend beyond everyday experience (Lakoff and Johnson 1999; Núñez et al. 1999).

Inspired by CMT, interdisciplinary scholars have documented how students, educators, and professionals alike draw on perceptuomotor schemes to understand abstract ideas that cannot be directly experienced by human senses. In mathematics, both students and mathematicians rely on perceptuomotor schemes for balance to solve algebraic equations, object manipulation for mathematical operations, and movement for functions and limits, among other examples (Nathan 2008; Núñez et al. 1999). Science students and scientists also use body-based metaphors to reason about heat, energy, electricity, and entropy (Amin 2015). For example, both scientists and students conceive of the concept of energy metaphorically as a substance that flows and is possessed by objects (Harrer 2017; Lancor 2012). There are abundant documented instances of teachers and textbook authors using body-based metaphors to introduce and explain new, abstract concepts by cueing students' body-based resources for understanding (Dreyfus et al. 2015; Núñez et al. 1999; Alibali and Nathan 2012). Professionals, instructors, and students also frequently evoke scientific and mathematical ideas through body-based metaphors in gesture (Alibali and Nathan 2012; Núñez et al. 1999).

While many educators raise concerns that metaphors can be misleading, there is robust evidence that students *need* to use and refine their body-based understandings to develop sophisticated expert-like concepts (diSessa 1993; Amin 2015). Although body-based intuitions and inferences do not always straightforwardly apply to scientific or mathematical phenomena (e.g., embodied metaphors from the macro-scale world often cannot hold in quantum mechanics; special relativity violates our everyday experiences with time and space), constructing expertise is a process of learning to differentiate into which contexts and circumstances body-based knowledge might be usefully extended (diSessa 1993). Educators can't ignore or eradicate embodied metaphors and try to replace them with formal concepts. Instead, teachers must be aware of students' initial ideas about abstract concepts in order to help them learn to draw on body-based understandings in the right contexts (Daane et al. 2018).

Constitution Hypotheses in Education: Embodied Simulation and Directed Action

Constitution theories of embodiment (Shapiro 2012) have proliferated in education and inspired numerous creative learning environments and tools. Constitution treats the body and its environmental interactions as playing a *constitutive* – and not a merely influential – role in cognitive processes (Shapiro 2012). For example, *embodied simulation* theories suggest that when thinking about an object like a chair or apple, we engage regions of the brain, nervous system, and body that are active when *actually* perceiving and interacting with these objects (e.g., sitting or biting) to *simulate* the experience, instead of using *amodal* or *symbolic* representations (Barsalou 2008). A robust collection of experimental work supports embodied simulation, including demonstrations that action words (like *lick*, *pick*, or *kick*) activate motor regions of the brain similarly to when people actually lick or kick (Pulvermüller et al. 2005).

Simulation theories have inspired the design of learning activities and tools that engage learners in choreographed movements intended to ground new ideas (Figure 22.1). Learners are instructed to perform specific actions thought to be meaningful for learning about particular situations or phenomena. Simulating body-based perceptuomotor states allows for recall and reasoning about target phenomena. These choreographed movements are described as "cued actions" (Lindgren 2014) or "directed actions" (Nathan 2021) and distinguished from *movement for the sake of movement itself* since they are *designed* to be *conceptually congruent* (Lindgren and Johnson-Glenberg 2013) or *conceptually relevant* (Walkington et al. 2022).[2] A diverse range of empirical studies across various age groups (kindergarten to adults) and learning domains (science, mathematics, foreign language, reading) have shown how directed actions can support learning.

Figure 22.1 Students can perform directed actions to ground understandings of abstract concepts.

In mathematics, for example, walking a number line increases understanding of number magnitudes and operations (Dackermann et al. 2017), grouping movements with the hands supports performance on mathematical equivalence problems (Goldin-Meadow et al. 2009), and embodying angles with arm movement improves angle understanding (Smith et al. 2014). Learners instructed to perform actions that spatio-dynamically embody aspects of geometric conjectures have more mathematical insights than those who performed *irrelevant* actions (Nathan et al. 2014). Nathan, Walkington, and colleagues have developed an immersive video game where students explore a remote village and perform conceptually relevant actions for making sense of geometric conjectures (Swart et al., 2020). In each case, these directed perceptuomotor experiences are thought to form the basis for embodied simulations that constitute new mathematical ideas.

Directed actions also support science, reading, and foreign language learning. Students instructed to act out a story with toys comprehended and remembered more (Glenberg et al. 2007), and students instructed to pantomime words in a new language have superior vocabulary learning outcomes (e.g., Mavilidi et al. 2015). Undergraduate students instructed to use gesture to represent molecular structures (Stieff et al. 2016) and middle-school science students who physically re-enacted the behavior of a meteor under the influence of a varying gravitational force (Lindgren 2014) outperform their peers. In addition, directed *haptic* experiences for learning are effective: Haptic experiences of angular momentum (Kontra et al., 2015), simulated molecular forces (Zohar and Levy 2021), and polar bear energy expenditure (Lyons et al. 2012) all promoted learning about the target phenomena. Directed forms of object manipulation also generally appear to be beneficial (for a review of manipulatives, see Donovan and Alibali 2022).

Despite common beliefs about "learning styles" or developmentally appropriate ages, intentionally involving the body in conceptually relevant action is likely beneficial to *all* learners, not just the very young, or those that consider themselves "kinesthetic" or "visual" (e.g., Lindgren and Johnson-Glenberg 2013). Engaging students in movements and physical experiences allows students to experience target concepts in multiple sensory modalities which may support embodied simulation. Diverse forms and scales of movement (e.g., hand motions to full-body walking) and proprioceptive experiences (e.g., traversing space, feeling pressure or resistance) all appear useful, so long as they are relevant to the target conceptual phenomena.

Introducing students to conceptually relevant choreographed movements and body positions can also inspire new insights for students about the phenomena they are learning about (e.g., molecular geometry, angular momentum). Nathan (2021) describes this phenomenon as *action-cognition transduction*. For example, chemistry students, unsure of the spatial arrangement of atoms in particular molecules, recalled and performed body movements from class for specific 3D molecular geometries and were able to extrapolate where each atom belongs in space (Flood et al. 2015). This bi-directional feedback from directed actions is an important justification for "making sense before symbol" (Abrahamson 2014) and against a "formalisms-first" (Nathan 2021) approach to learning.

Replacement Hypotheses in Education: Ecological Dynamics

Another family of embodied approaches – replacement theories – highlights cognitive processes that arise from the moving body's dynamic adaptations to everchanging environments, without the need to create or manipulate internal representations (Shapiro, 2012). By interacting with the world itself, it is unnecessary to represent the world internally; dynamic interaction *replaces* the need for representations. Suchman (1985) provides an example of a canoeist navigating rapids: Each paddle stroke is uniquely shaped "online" as an interactive adaptation to the particular swirl and resistance of different turbulent patches of water encountered with each new stroke. The canoeist has no need (or time) to mentally represent the water and then formulate a plan for the form and force of the stroke. Replacement theories are encountered in artificial intelligence (Brooks 1991), dynamic systems theory of development (Smith and Thelen 2003), and in sports psychology (Abrahamson and Sánchez-García 2016).

Abrahamson and Sánchez-García (2016) use *ecological dynamics* from sports psychology to study and explain the emergence of proportional reasoning from children's adaptive adjustments to solve a motor coordination problem. Drawing on the Gibsonian theory of affordances and dynamic systems, learning is seen as a property of complex, self-organizing, adaptive systems (Abrahamson and Sánchez-García 2016). In the Mathematical Imagery Trainer for Proportions, children are given two remotes to control cursors on a vertical screen. The screen changes from red to green, based on the positions of the cursors (Figure 22.2). Unknown to the children, a specific height ratio (e.g., 1:2, 2:3) has been programmed into the display. When children's hand heights fulfill this unknown ratio, the screen will be green, otherwise it is red.

After trial and error, coordinated ways of moving and perceiving arise that are not predetermined and do not require mental simulation or representation. They emerge from

Figure 22.2 The Mathematical Imagery Trainer for Proportions (developed by the Embodied Design Research Laboratory, directed by Dor Abrahamson); a child uses remotes to manipulate cursors on a screen.

exploratory probing as a way to stabilize performance within a dynamic system. As students become more consistent, a grid with numbers is introduced, which students spontaneously adopt to describe their ways of moving and attending to the display quantitatively: Through activity, an enactive proportional reasoning emerges (Abrahamson and Sánchez-García 2016). Another notable example of how mathematical objects emerge through perceptuomotor activity with specialized tools is the Math in Motion exhibit, a giant Etch-a-Sketch where participants operate two dials, controlling horizontal and vertical motion, as a line is drawn. Diagonal lines and circles – mathematical objects usually experienced as static entities – materialize through participants' adaptive, coordinated, dynamic perceptuomotor interactions with the dials, through what Nemirovsky et al. (2014) describe as *perceptuomotor integration.*

In these environments, mathematical ideas emerge as *learning to move in new ways* (Abrahamson and Sánchez-García 2016). Unlike directed action, where students are guided to perform particular choreographed movements to experience target learning phenomena, these environments provide non-deterministic opportunities for learners to coordinate and experience movement. Abrahamson and Sánchez-García (2016), drawing on developmental anthropology, advocate for creating "fields of promoted action" (Reed and Bril 1996) in educational environments: Learning environments should be designed with affordances that promote ways of perceiving and moving in the world (using specialized tools and tasks) that enact new ideas.

Extended Cognition, Distributed Cognition, and Collaborative Embodied Learning

Distributed and extended cognition are often seen as tackling a conceptual *unit of analysis* problem related to embodiment (Shapiro 2012). The boundaries of cognitive processes have important implications for characterizing teaching and learning processes, and arguments about how cognition is extended and distributed have been taken up in education research from surgery to mathematics. In studies of apprenticeship and complex technical work sites, cognitive anthropologists have shown how cognition is a distributed, embodied emergent property of human collaboration in socio-material environments (Goodwin 1997; Hutchins 1995; Lave 1988; Ingold 2000). Hutchins, for example, illustrated how complex forms of navigation emerge through divisions of labor, tools, and spatial layouts of specialized environments (developed and passed down by predecessors), and are irreducible to individual brains or bodies.

Distributed cognition is an inspiration for many collaborative, embodied learning environments (CELEs). CELEs feature interdependent coordination of large groups where participants intentionally use their bodies and tools to explore, create, solve problems, or complete challenges. Discoveries emerge based on ensemble configurations of movement that would not be possible for individual learners on their own. Consider a CELE where each student in a large group embodies a particle of matter. A Kinect system provides feedback about what state of matter the group is in based on students' speed and physical distance from each other. The discovery that particles coming together and ceasing movement will result in a solid is a collaborative achievement (DeLiema et al. 2019). Other examples of CELEs include large groups of learners exploring the complex system of an epidemic outbreak (Colella 2000), constructing enormous geometrical figures with ropes on a field (Ma 2016), modeling how energy changes in various systems (Scherr et al. 2013), or weaving and braiding large, complex patterns to explore their dynamic mathematical properties (Figure 22.3; Gerofsky forthcoming).

In CELEs, students can use their bodies to run through and explore scenarios together, even if they don't yet have a shared technical vocabulary to describe or explain proposals. Anyone can use their body to make embodied suggestions in the joint problem space, as opposed to a group working with a single computer or worksheet (Scherr et al. 2013). Bodily performances of ideas in a public arena become shared resources for reasoning, problem solving, and discovery. While working together to coordinate and negotiate each other's activities, participants often begin to progressively generalize and symbolize phenomena, and develop a shared language (Enyedy et al. 2012).

Participants in CELEs experience different scales, points of view, and forms of bodily engagement than during traditionally "seated" school learning (Gerofsky forthcoming). New tools, procedures, and criteria for approaching problems or creating models must be discovered and invented together (Ma, 2016). Students also navigate different perceptual vantage points and perspectives, fueling reflection and negotiation. For example, when constructing giant geometric figures at field scale with rope, no student has the same view of the figure under construction, requiring intense coordination among participants (Ma 2016). CELEs also encourage productive forms of *hybridity* because they often take place outside the classroom in spaces where students feel embodied knowledge from other contexts is relevant, useful, and valued (e.g., that Double Dutch jump ropes are a case of congruent, parallel lines; Ma 2016). This makes learning more inclusive, especially in mathematics and science, where narrow definitions of what counts as knowledge (e.g., often dictated by Western, White, and industrialized standards) prevail. Overall, embodied learning environments designed for collaboration, changes of scale, and interactions with novel objects/tools break learners out of habitual ways of approaching school subjects and encourage exploration, insight, and curiosity.

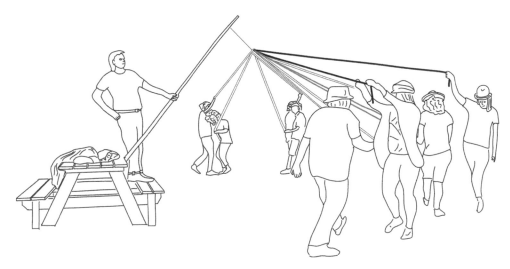

Figure 22.3 Gerofsky's participants move together as "bobbins," weaving a braided pattern in a collaborative embodied learning activity to explore algebraic and topological properties of braids.

Embodied Responsive Teaching

Embodied responsive teaching – how educators attend to, interpret, and respond to students' multimodally expressed, embodied ideas to shape instruction in the moment – is a critical part of facilitating embodied learning (Flood et al. 2020). Teachers do not merely listen to what students say (or write) but attend to the full range of multimodal, embodied resources students use to demonstrate and communicate discoveries and knowledge (e.g., gesture, bodily performances). Embodied responsive teaching creates important opportunities for educators to provide customized feedback and adjustments that help students connect embodied knowledge with more expert understandings (Flood et al. 2020; Flood 2021; Flood and Harrer 2022; Flood 2018).

Strategies for embodied responsive teaching include (a) *eliciting gestured elaborations* from students, especially when students have shared ambiguous or nonredundant information in speech and gesture or struggle to find the right words; (b) producing *multimodal candidate understandings* – gestured interpretations of what students have said for them to reject or ratify – which often encourages students to elaborate or specify their ideas; and (c) *co-constructing gestured explanations* with students by reaching into students' gestures to clarify what parts of a gesture mean and/or to build on students' gestures by adding new visuospatial imagery (Flood et al. 2020; Figure 22.4). Educators also repeat and subtly reformulate students' gestured and embodied contributions by *multimodally revoicing* (Shein 2012) or re-enacting students' embodied activity in ways that are less situated in the immediate circumstances and begin to highlight and generalize discoveries or patterns of interest (Flood 2018). Multimodal revoicing can provide an important bridge between students' initial embodied experiences and more formal, standardized concepts (Flood 2018; Flood 2021).

In traditional, whole-classroom environments, teachers are also responsive to the embodied ways students demonstrate and share their knowledge with the class: When students share ideas in whole-class discussions, teachers might repeat students' gestures and link them with refined verbal descriptions of phenomena, add new gestures to illustrate parts of an idea that were not expressed for the class, or elaborate students' existing gestures with

Figure 22.4 Instructors can interact with students' gestures to clarify and build on them.

more detail (Flood 2021). Sometimes students tentatively share embodied ideas through gesture without speaking or raising their hand. Teachers notice and selectively take up these silent *gestured candidate responses* and incorporate them into ongoing class discussions (Flood and Harrer 2022). Together, these forms of embodied responsive teaching allow educators to share and enhance individuals' embodied knowledge with the class as a whole, and endorse embodied knowledge as a valid way of knowing (Flood 2021; Flood and Harrer 2022).

Conclusions and Future Directions for Embodiment in Education

A variety of perspectives on embodiment have shaped research, design, and practice in education. Despite differences in these approaches, two overarching implications for teaching and learning emerge: (1) all students' body-based experiences should be attended to and drawn on as *resources* for learning, and not considered an impediment or intermediary stage to be grown out of; and (2) insisting that students first need to master abstract, decontextualized, and "rigorous" versions of concepts is misguided; instead, the strongest opportunities for learning are provided through early experiences that intentionally incorporate and foreground learners' bodies in meaningful ways in the discovery and exploration of new ideas.

Many rich new lines of research on embodiment in education are underway: Scholars are working to tease apart the effects of directed actions vs. forms of spontaneous gesturing (e.g., Walkington et al. 2022). Others are investigating how to make embodied learning environments – which typically require vision and hearing to participate – more inclusive for learners with sensory and learning differences (e.g., Abrahamson et al. 2019). Breakthroughs in artificial intelligence and machine learning have enabled new forms of *multimodal learning analytics* (Blikstein and Worsley 2016) that collect and analyze diverse data about embodied participation in learning environments. Multimodal learning analytics create new opportunities to understand embodiment in education and assess *learning as moving in new ways* (Tancredi et al. 2022). Finally, another active area of research is the design and refinement of professional development to support teachers in understanding embodied learning, developing embodied responsive teaching (Flood et al. 2020), and ways of incorporating embodied interaction technologies into their classrooms (e.g., Dimmel and Bock 2019).

Despite the growing impact of embodiment in education, many educational environments continue to be logocentric, and rely on static representations of knowledge and seated interaction with concepts. Deliberately designed embodied learning environments *position the body as a legitimate resource* for thinking, knowing, and learning. Together, embodied learning environments and embodied responsive teaching promote inclusivity and advance more expansive epistemologies for how human knowledge is discovered and advanced.

Related Topics

Grounded mathematical reasoning
Embodiment and language comprehension
Gesture in reasoning: An embodied perspective
Group cognition

Notes

1 Macrine, S.L. and Fugate, J.M. (2022) *Movement Matters: How Embodied Cognition Informs Teaching and Learning*, MIT Press; Nathan, M.J. (2021) *Foundations of Embodied Learning: A Paradigm for Education*, New York, NY, Routledge; and Stolz, S.A. (ed.) (2021) *The Body, Embodiment, and Education: An Interdisciplinary Approach*, Routledge. These follow several additional titles from the 2010s, including Lee, V.R. (ed.) (2014) *Learning technologies and the body: Integration and implementation in formal and informal learning environments*, Routledge; Edwards, L.D., Moore-Russo, D. and Ferrara, F. (eds.) (2014) *Emerging perspectives on gesture and embodiment in mathematics*, Information Age Publishing Inc.; and Amin, T.G., Jeppsson, F. and Haglund, J. (eds) (2018) *Conceptual metaphor and embodied cognition in science learning*, Routledge.
2 However, studies have found positive learning outcomes of incorporating exercise and general physical activity that is not related to learning concepts. This research is not reviewed here.

References

Abrahamson, D. (2014) "The monster in the machine, or why educational technology needs embodied design," in: Lee, V. (ed.) *Learning technologies and the body: Integration and implementation*.

Abrahamson, D., Flood, V.J., Miele, J.A., et al. (2019) "Enactivism and ethnomethodological conversation analysis as tools for expanding Universal Design for Learning: The case of visually impaired mathematics students," *ZDM Mathematics Education*, 51, 291–303.

Abrahamson, D., Nathan, M.J., Williams-Pierce, C., et al. (2020) "The Future of Embodied Design for Mathematics Teaching and Learning," *Frontiers in Education*, 5.

Abrahamson, D. and Sánchez-García, R. (2016) "Learning Is Moving in New Ways: The Ecological Dynamics of Mathematics Education," *Journal of the Learning Sciences*, 25, 203–239.

Alibali, M.W. and Nathan, M.J. (2012) "Embodiment in Mathematics Teaching and Learning: Evidence From Learners' and Teachers' Gestures," *Journal of the Learning Sciences*, 21, 247–286.

Amin, T.G. (2015) "Conceptual Metaphor and the Study of Conceptual Change: Research synthesis and future directions," *International Journal of Science Education*, 37, 966–991.

Barsalou, L.W. (2008) "Grounded Cognition," *Annual Review of Psychology*.

Blikstein, P. and Worsley, M. (2016) "Multimodal learning analytics and education data mining," *Journal of Learning Analytics*, 3, 220–238.

Brooks, R.A. (1991) "Intelligence without representation," *Artificial Intelligence*, 47, 139–159.

Brown, J.S. and Burton, R.R. (1978) "Diagnostic Models for Procedural Bugs in Basic Mathematical Skills," *Cognitive Science*, 2, 155–192.

Colella, V. (2000) "Participatory simulations: building collaborative understanding through immersive dynamic modeling," *Journal of the Learning Sciences*.

Daane, A.R., Haglund, J., Robertson, A.D., et al. (2018) "The pedagogical value of conceptual metaphor for secondary science teachers," *Science Education*, 102, 1051–1076.

Dackermann, T., Fischer, U., Nuerk, H.-C., et al. (2017) "Applying embodied cognition: from useful interventions and their theoretical underpinnings to practical applications," *Zdm*, 49, 545–557.

DeLiema, D., Enyedy, N. and Danish, J.A. (2019) "Roles, rules, and keys: How different play configurations shape collaborative science inquiry," *Journal of the Learning Sciences*, 28, 513–555.

Dimmel, J. and Bock, C. (2019) "Dynamic mathematical figures with immersive spatial displays: The case of Handwaver," *Technology in Mathematics Teaching*, Springer.

diSessa, A. (1993) "Toward an Epistemology of Physics," *Cognition and Instruction*, 10, 105–225.

Donovan, A.M. and Alibali, M.W. (2022) "Manipulatives and Mathematics Learning: The Roles of Perceptual and Interactive Features," in Macrine, S. L. and Fugate, J. M. B. (eds) "*Movement Matters*, Cambridge, MA: MIT Press.

Dreyfus, B.W., Gupta, A. and Redish, E.F. (2015) "Applying conceptual blending to model coordinated use of multiple ontological metaphors," *International Journal of Science Education*, 37, 812–838.

Enyedy, N., Danish, J.A., Delacruz, G., et al. (2012) "Learning physics through play in an augmented reality environment," *International Journal of Computer-Supported Collaborative Learning*.

Flood, V.J. (2018) "Multimodal revoicing as an interactional mechanism for connecting scientific and everyday concepts," *Human Development*, 61, 145–173.

——— (2021) "The secret multimodal life of IREs: Looking more closely at representational gestures in a familiar questioning sequence," *Linguistics and Education*, 63, 100913.

Flood, V.J., Amar, F.G., Nemirovsky, R., et al. (2015) "Paying attention to gesture when students talk chemistry: Interactional resources for responsive teaching," *Journal of Chemical Education*, 92, 11–22.

Flood, V.J. and Harrer, B.W. (2022) "Teachers' responsiveness to students' gestured candidate responses in whole-class STEM interactions," *Classroom Discourse*, 1–21.

Flood, V.J., Shvarts, A. and Abrahamson, D. (2020) "Teaching with embodied learning technologies for mathematics: Responsive teaching for embodied learning," *ZDM - Mathematics Education*, 52, 1307–1331.

Gallagher, S. and Lindgren, R. (2015) "Enactive Metaphors: Learning Through Full-Body Engagement," *Educational Psychology Review*, 27, 391–404.

Gerofsky, S. (forthcoming) "Experiencing mathematical relationships at a variety of scales through body movement, voice, and touch," in: Edwards, L. D. and Krause, C. M. (eds) *The body in mathematics: Theoretical and methodological lenses*, Brill.

Glenberg, A.M., Brown, M. and Levin, J.R. (2007) "Enhancing comprehension in small reading groups using a manipulation strategy," *Contemporary Educational Psychology*, 32, 389–399.

Goldin-Meadow, S., Cook, S.W. and Mitchell, Z.A. (2009) "Gesturing gives children new ideas about math," *Psychological Science*, 20, 267–272.

Goodwin, C. (1997) "The Blackness of Black: Color Categories as Situated Practice," in Resnick, L. B., Säljö, R., Pontecorvo, C. and Burge, B. (eds) *Discourse, Tools and Reasoning*.

Harrer, B.W. (2017) "On the origin of energy: Metaphors and manifestations as resources for conceptualizing and measuring the invisible, imponderable," *American Journal of Physics*, 85, 454–460.

Hutchins, E. (1995) *Cognition in the Wild*, Cambridge: MIT Press.

Hutto, D.D., Kirchhoff, M.D. and Abrahamson, D. (2015) "The Enactive Roots of STEM: Rethinking Educational Design in Mathematics," *Educational Psychology Review*, 27, 371–389.

Ingold, T. (2000) *The perception of the environment*, London, Routledge.

Kontra, C., Lyons, D.J., Fischer, S.M. and Beilock, S.L., (2015) "Physical experience enhances science learning," *Psychological Science*, 26(6), 737–749.

Koschmann, T. (2001) "A third metaphor for learning: Toward a Deweyan form of transactional inquiry," *in* Carver, S. M. and Klahr, D. (eds) *Cognition and instruction: Twenty-five years of progress*, Lawrence Erlbaum Associates, Inc.

Lakoff, G. and Johnson, M. (1999) *Philosophy in the Flesh: The Embodied Mind and Its Challenge to Western Thought*, New York: Basic Books.

Lancor, R. (2012) "Using Metaphor Theory to Examine Conceptions of Energy in Biology, Chemistry, and Physics," *Science and Education*, 23, 1245–1267.

Lave, J. (1988) *Cognition in practice: Mind, mathematics and culture in everyday life*, Cambridge University Press.

Lee, V.R. (ed.) (2014) *Learning technologies and the body: Integration and implementation in formal and informal learning environments*, Routledge.

Lindgren, R. (2014) "Getting into the cue: Embracing technology-facilitated body movements as a starting point for learning," in Lee, V. (ed.) *Learning Technologies and the Body*, Taylor and Francis Inc.

Lindgren, R. and Johnson-Glenberg, M. (2013) "Emboldened by embodiment: Six precepts for research on embodied learning and mixed reality," *Educational Researcher*.

Lyons, L., Slattery, B., Jimenez, P., et al. (2012) "Don't forget about the sweat: Effortful embodied interaction in support of learning," *Proc. of Tangible, Embodied, Embedded Interaction Conf.* New York: ACM.

Ma, J.Y. (2016) "Designing Disruptions for Productive Hybridity: The Case of Walking Scale Geometry," *Journal of the Learning Sciences*. Routledge.

Mavilidi, M.-F., Okely, A.D., Chandler, P., et al. (2015) "Effects of integrated physical exercises and gestures on preschool children's foreign language vocabulary learning," *Educational Psychology Review*, 27, 413–426.

Nathan, M. J. (2008) "An embodied cognition perspective on symbols, gesture, and grounding instruction," in Manuel de Vega, Arthur Glenburg, and Arthur Graesser (eds) *Symbols and Embodiment: Debates On Meaning and Cognition*, Oxford: Oxford University Press.

Nathan, M.J. (2021) *Foundations of Embodied Learning: A Paradigm for Education*, New York, NY: Routledge.

Nathan, M.J., Walkington, C., Boncoddo, R., et al. (2014) "Actions speak louder with words: The roles of action and pedagogical language for grounding mathematical proof," *Learning and Instruction*, 33, 182–193.

Nemirovsky, R., Kelton, M.L. and Rhodehamel, B. (2014) "Playing mathematical instruments: Emerging perceptuomotor integration with an interactive mathematics exhibit,"

Núñez, R.E., Edwards, L.D. and Matos, J.F. (1999) "Embodied cognition as grounding for situatedness and context in mathematics education," *Educational Studies in Mathematics*, 39, 45–65

Piaget, J. (1953) *Origin of Intelligence in the Child: Selected Works vol 3*, Routledge.

Pulvermüller, F., Shtyrov, Y. and Ilmoniemi, R. (2005) "Brain Signatures of Meaning Access in Action Word Recognition," *Journal of Cognitive Neuroscience*, 17, 884–892.

Reed, E.S. and Bril, B. (1996) "The primacy of action in developmennt," in Latash, M. L. and Turvey, M. T. (eds) *Dexterity and its development*, Mahwah: Lawrence Erlbaum Associates.

Resnick, M., Martin, F., Berg, R., et al. (1998) "Digital manipulatives: new toys to think with," Proceedings of the SIGCHI conference on Human factors in computing systems, 281–287.

Scherr, R.E., Close, H.G., Close, E.W., et al. (2013) "Negotiating energy dynamics through embodied action in a materially structured environment," *Physical Review Special Topics - Physics Education Research*, 9, 020105.

Shapiro, L. and Stolz, S.A. (2019) "Embodied cognition and its significance for education," *Theory and Research in Education*, 17, 19–39.

Shapiro, L.A. (2012) "Embodied Cognition," *in* Margolis, E., Samuels, R. and Stich, S. P. (eds) *The Oxford Handbook of Philosophy of Cognitive Science*, Oxford: Oxford University Press.

Shein, P.P. (2012) "Seeing with two eyes: A teacher's use of gestures in questioning and revoicing to engage English language learners in the repair of mathematical errors," *Journal for Research in Mathematics Education*, 43, 182–222.

Smith, C.P., King, B. and Hoyte, J. (2014) "Learning angles through movement: Critical actions for developing understanding in an embodied activity," *Journal of Mathematical Behavior*. Elsevier Inc.

Smith, L.B. and Thelen, E. (2003) "Development as a dynamic system," *Trends in Cognitive Sciences*, 7, 343–348.

Stieff, M., Lira, M.E. and Scopelitis, S.A. (2016) "Gesture Supports Spatial Thinking in STEM," *Cognition and Instruction*, 34, 80–99.

Suchman, L.A. (1985) "Plans and Situated Actions: The Problem of Human Machine Communication," *Contemporary Sociology*.

Swart, M., Schenck, K., Xia, F., Kwon, O. H., Nathan, M., Vinsonhaler, R., & Walkington, C. (2020) "Grounded and embodied mathematical cognition for intuition and proof playing a motion-capture video game," in Gresalfi, M. and Horn, I. S. (eds), *The Interdisciplinarity of the Learning Sciences, 14th International Conference of the Learning Sciences (ICLS) 2020*, 1, 175–182. Nashville, Tennessee: International Society of the Learning Sciences.

Tancredi, S., Abdu, R., Balasubramaniam, R., et al. (2022) "Intermodality in multimodal learning analytics for cognitive theory development: A case from embodied design for mathematics learning," *The Multimodal Learning Analytics Handbook*. Springer.

Walkington, C., Nathan, M.J., Wang, M., et al. (2022) "The Effect of Cognitive Relevance of Directed Actions on Mathematical Reasoning," *Cogn Sci*, 46, e13180.

Wertsch, J.V. (1985) *Vygotsky and the social formation of mind*, Cambridge: Harvard University Press.

Zohar, A.R. and Levy, S.T. (2021) "From feeling forces to understanding forces: The impact of bodily engagement on learning in science," *Journal of Research in Science Teaching*, 58, 1203–1237.

23

EMBODIED LEARNING

Translating Embodied Cognition Research

Sheila L. Macrine and Jennifer M.B. Fugate

Introduction

Cognitive psychology has undergone a paradigm shift in the understanding of how knowledge is acquired and represented. This shift represents a move away from brain-bound models of cognition towards embodied notions of thought, which hold that thinking occurs through mind–body–environment interactions grounded in sensory-motor processes (e.g., Barsalou 2008). A derivative of embodied cognition, embodied learning shifts the focus of teaching and learning from an exclusively mental effort toward an embodied, sensory-rich experience and offers new applications and strategies to maximize learning effectiveness.

Yet, the implications for how this shift in the science of learning impacts students' learning and teacher pedagogy (matching theoretical foundations or concepts with practical methods) has yet to be fully realized. In many instances, education systems often prioritize disembodied and decontextualized approaches in preparation for standardized tests. Here the teacher is seen as a 'talking head' transmitting the curriculum, and the students are treated as passive recipients (Fugate et al. 2019; Macrine 2002). Many of these disembodied and decontextualized, amodal approaches include rote memorization, and mindless drills and skills that are focused on test results. Schools, intentionally or not, still treat the mind and body as separate (Fugate et al. 2019).

Given our new understanding of cognition, we ask: Why hasn't the latest empirical evidence on the benefits of embodied learning had a greater impact on educational theory, pedagogy, and policy; and how might this gap be ameliorated?

In response, our goals have been to help get the latest research on embodied cognition and learning out to scholars/educators, to help bridge the research-to-practice gap, to validate early empirical studies, and to identify pedagogical principles and applications to explicate an embodied learning theory.

In this chapter, we briefly describe embodied cognition, and its derivative, embodied learning, and share some early content-specific applications. We address the confounding research-to-practice gap, and the resultant challenges of bridging embodied research with educational practice. We describe our translational framework (Macrine and Fugate 2021) for identifying principles and substantiating embodied learning theory and applications, as

DOI: 10.4324/9781003322511-30

well as advancing multidirectional collaborations among embodied research scientists, educators, and policy makers. We conclude by pointing toward the development of transdisciplinary embodied learning principles in an effort to articulate an overarching Embodied Learning Theory to help propagate applications of embodied learning throughout educational theory and teaching pedagogy.

Embodied Cognition: The Foundation of Embodied Learning

Embodied cognition (e.g., Abrahamson 2004; Barsalou 1999; Chemero 2009; Shapiro 2019; Varela et al. 1991; Wilson 2002) challenges the classical Cartesian mind–body separation (Merleau-Ponty 1962, 1974) that dominated the 20th century (Abrahamson et al. 2020; Nagataki and Hirose 2007; Zlatev 2007). Theories of embodied cognition argue that information is grounded in both perception and action, and that cognition is deeply dependent upon features of the physical body within an environment (e.g., Barsalou 1999, 2008; Golonka and Wilson 2012; Lakoff and Johnson 1999; Pfeifer and Bongard 2007; Shapiro 2011). According to embodied cognition theories: 1) cognition is dependent upon experiences that come from the body; and 2) experiences of the body are embedded in a more encompassing biological, psychological and cultural context (Varela et al. 1991: 173–199 for summary). In other words, the brain is not reactive but *predictive and actively involved in interpreting* sensory, bodily, and motoric information, and affordances within the context/environment. As a result, this information is shared, and the conceptual knowledge of the perceiver is built from the experience (see also Barrett 2017; Clark 2008).

Although there are a number of theories of embodied cognition, all are united in their emphasis on the body, and they converge (to varying degrees) on two points (Shapiro 2019; Weisberg and Newcombe 2017). *First*, cognition is *grounded* or *situated* between the individual and the environment (Barsalou 2003, 2008). Grounding may be direct through the body and sensory systems, or it may be mediated by mental representations. Embodied cognition theorists posit varying levels of abstraction for mental representations (from conservative views, e.g., Alsmith and Vignemont 2012; Gallese and Sinigaglia 2011; Goldman 2012, to more radical views, e.g., Di Paolo et al. 2017; Gallagher 2005; Hutto 2005; Hutto and Myin 2012, 2017; Thompson 2007). *Second*, cognition is *simulated* (Barsalou 1999, 2008; Gallese 2009). That is, thinking and recalling information involves re-experiencing the bodily states at the time of encoding. When information is later used (or retrieved), the body and/or brain simulate the details of the initial experience. Therefore, the richer and more nuanced the encoding of information (through multimodal, bodily-based approaches), the richer and more nuanced the simulation of that information is likely to be (see Fugate et al. 2019). Accordingly, moving or engaging the body and senses in ways that are congruent with both the actions of the object/domain of learning, and what the situation affords, enhances the learning and later use of that information.

Embodied cognition is associated with '4-E' cognition – where cognitive activity is also "extended, enacted, and embedded" in the perceptual and interactive richness of a person's environment (see Gallagher *in* Rowlands 2012: 98). For example, enactivism (Bruner 1966) is a philosophical framework that captures "thinking as situated doing" (Abrahamson et al. 2022; Thompson, 2007). It was later elaborated on by Maturana and Varela (1991: 173), who emphasized knowledge as arising out of "an active handling and coping with the world" (see also Petitmengin 2007).

While embodied cognition advocates active learning, embodied approaches go beyond traditional active learning by applying an empirical neuroscience basis for *why* body-based and experiential learning are effective. Embodied cognition also captures the unfolding of a person's own actions (and, in many cases, gestures and the observation of others' actions) as part of the environment and as shaped by environmental affordances that scaffold the process. So, what does this mean for teaching and learning?

Embodied Learning: What Isn't Translated in the Research-to-Practice Divide

Teachers are constantly searching for answers to improve their pedagogy and to maximize student learning. Yet, many of our current educational delivery systems (i.e., teacher education, pedagogy, curriculum, environmental design, technology, and educational psychology) perpetuate 'disembodied' views of human thinking and learning (Fugate et al. 2019; Macrine and Fugate 2020, 2021). Our education system often focuses on a narrow sliver of students' cognitive development with an emphasis on transmitting content knowledge, often to be memorized and repeated in the same form it was received (Flook 2019). Consequently, perceptual, sensory, and motor systems continue to be disregarded in learning processes (Shapiro 2011; Wilson 2002; Woodward et al. 2009). Moreover, teaching pedagogy and curriculum maintain the view of learning as brain-bound, both abstracted and separate from the body (Barsalou 1999; Fugate et al. 2019; Glenberg 2008, 2010; Macrine 2002). This fragmentation characterizes much of the confusion that teachers experience in learning to teach and then in negotiating ongoing professional development (PD) (Hammerness 2006). According to the Learning Policy Institute study of 2017, traditional PD rarely makes room for educators to connect the content to their individual contexts, to build understanding, and provides no opportunities for participants to learn skills or strategies by actively trying them out.[1]

In terms of education in general, although educators yearn to improve their pedagogy, few are privy to the research advances in the science of learning (Weinstein et al. 2018). Recently, Simmers (2020) conducted a Google search for online teaching tips and found over half a billion hits for teaching resources and guidance. We also conducted a Google search (2022) on 'brain-bound teaching approaches' and found over 53.5 million supportive articles, reinforcing age-old Cartesian separation. Thus, adding further confusion to the widespread acceptance of commonly held false "neuromyths" among educators (Macrine and Fugate 2021; Tokuhama-Espinosa 2019). These neuromyths remain remarkably prevalent (~50% endorsement or higher), regardless of exposure to education or neuroscience (Macdonald et al., 2017:13). For example, Kristin Simmers (2020: 2) writes that,

> the gap between what researchers know about learning and how classroom educators are applying this knowledge is still too large. Teachers don't need millions of tips to improve their practice. They need to know the ones that work.

Pointing to another example, Newton (2015) found an overwhelming majority (89%) of recent research papers on ERIC and PubMed that either directly or implicitly endorsed the use of the now discredited 'learning styles' approaches (Newton 2015). Clearly, educators need answers, yet the onus of responsibility to mend this divide cannot be placed only solely on K-12 educators and administrators. To mitigate and promote informed decision-making and research-based practice in education, the Every Student Succeeds Act (2015) called for *'evidence-based'* interventions that are proven to be effective leading to improved student outcomes. Yet how 'evidence-based' interventions are used to inform teaching and learning are problematic at best. One of the nation's foremost education researchers and policy analysts, Linda Darling-Hammond et al. (2020: 97), argue that "the rapid pace of our knowledge of human development and learning has impacted the emerging consensus about the science of learning and development and increased our opportunities to shape more effective educational practices." They conclude that we have not yet fulfilled those opportunities, and that doing so will require integrating insights across multiple fields and connecting them to successful approaches.

Confounding matters is the significant research-to-practice gap in education (Ulrich and McDaniels 2018; Wilcox et al. 2021), which contributes to confusion among teachers/educators. What's more, Roediger (2013:1) stated: "We cannot point to a well-developed translational educational science, in which research about learning and memory, thinking and reasoning, and related topics, is moved from the lab into controlled field trials (like clinical trials in medicine)."

Given this need and the paradigm shift in how cognition is now understood, both teaching and learning pedagogies need to be re-examined. While the latest psychological and neuroscientific evidence validates embodied cognition, current research in educational practice, teaching pedagogy, and curriculum continue to treat instruction as abstracted and separate from the body (Guerriero 2017; Macedonia 2019; Macrine 2002; Macrine and Fugate 2022). Even among teacher education and pedagogy that emphasize a constructivist approach, in practice much still devolves into *quantifiable, disembodied* knowledge, and skills and drills in preparation for standardized testing (see Klein et al. 2019; Macrine and Fugate 2020). Consequently, classroom teaching continues to rely on presenting the learner with disembodied concepts (Nathan 2012a), without the engagement of the sensori-motor systems, and without the understanding of how the body influences internalization of these concepts (see Macrine and Fugate 2020). For example, mathematics pedagogy continues to teach disembodied formalisms first (Nathan 2012b) – diagrams and symbols that are culturally designed to be abstract, amodal, and arbitrary (Glenberg et al. 2004) – that are regarded as objective and universal (Schenck et al. 2022).

Wilcox et al. (2021) argue that a major contributor to this divergence is the lack of concrete mechanisms for bridging neuroscience and education. While the promising field of educational neuroscience (Thomas et al. 2019) brings together researchers from neuroscience, psychology, and education to explore the neurocognitive processes underlying educational theory and practice, nevertheless, much of it is still brain-bound focused (Ansari and Coch, 2006; Goswami 2006; Macrine and Fugate 2020; Meltzoff et al. 2009; Wilcox et al. 2021). That said, if educational neuroscience is to move forward, "the traditional boundaries and methods must be bridged, and an infrastructure must be in place that allows for collaborative and productive exchanges" (Wilcox et al. 2021:1).

Translating Embodied Learning for the Classroom

Alternatively, the conceptualization of an overarching theory and set of principles for embodied learning that crosses disciplinary knowledge domains to inform pedagogy is not easy (Leung 2020). We (Macrine and Fugate 2021) believe that translating embodied cognitive theory into effective classroom applications will go a long way to support educators in applying embodied learning theory to their pedagogy. Nevertheless, there continue to be limited opportunities for crossing disciplinary knowledge domains and bidirectional sharing among cognitive scientists and educational practitioners (Henderson et al. 2017). For example, Nathan et al. (2013:1) posited that "the mechanisms for the integration of STEM's (science, technology, engineering, and mathematics) pedagogy remains largely underspecified in the research and policy literatures." This lacuna persists despite moves to build higher-level 'transdisciplinary STEM pedagogies' (NSTC 2022) that incorporate embodied learnings' emphasis "on action-to-abstraction through gesture, sketching, and analogical mapping" (Weisberg and Newcombe 2017:1). Still, existing efforts towards integration are lacking and need further theoretical and empirical development (ibid).

Recently a group of embodied mathematics design-based researchers (see Abrahamson et al. 2020) began working on synthesizing a set of principles for math educational design and pedagogy. They argue that embodied approaches demand new types of learning environments that "utilize interactive technologies to initially foster student enactment of conceptually oriented movement forms" (Abrahamson et al. 2020:1). They also concluded that,

> new research instruments, such as multimodal learning analytics, can enable researchers to aggregate, integrate, model, and represent students' physical movements, eye-gaze paths, and verbal–gestural utterance so as to track and evaluate emerging conceptual capacity.
>
> *(Abrahamson et al. 2020:147)*

They argue that only after employing such technologies to establish the groundwork for learning, can they be subsequently structured into disciplinary formats and language (Abrahamson et al. 2020).

Moreover, there is also a growing need for a cross-disciplinary consensus for a level-specific criterion of embodiment (Lux et al. 2021). Yet, psychology (and its related fields), along with education (and its related fields), have largely evolved in separate silos, with separate conferences resulting in very little cross-talk despite a great deal of overlap in research interests (e.g., improving learning by understanding how learning is accomplished). Therefore, a better understanding of the predictors of improved learning, research, and educational learning theory necessitates further cooperation and teamwork. While collaborations are vital to address increasingly complex challenges in the learning sciences and society, attention also needs to focus on a new understanding of cognition as embodied (Hall et al. 2018). Still, such collaborations continue to lack support from institutional structures and policies, scientific culture, and funding opportunities (Heitzmann et al. 2021).

So, for classroom teachers and teacher educators, it may not be so much a "not knowing," but "not having the right tools." This is where the cognitive science community, partnered with the educational community, can bring *new* thinking about embodied ways of knowing, approaches, and techniques. Unfortunately, as highlighted earlier, teachers want answers, but research takes a long time to trickle down to the classroom. And for the expertise of teachers to reach researchers, there needs to be an expedited process to make the necessary bidirectional connections. Although the research-to-practice gap has been widely publicized, few empirical data are available on how to ameliorate it. This means that the disconnect between educational research and pedagogical practice should be approached as a complex phenomenon.

From Lab to Classroom

We believe that an 'embodied learning' approach to teaching the whole person can make a significant impact on teacher pedagogy and improve student outcomes. Beginning in 2016, we began writing a series of reviews (Fugate et al. 2019; Macrine and Fugate 2020, 2021) on embodied learning in the fields of language comprehension, language acquisition, gesture, STEM, and SEL (social-emotional learning and embodied therapies) using simple manipulatives and complex virtual-reality methodologies. In our book, we curated the latest neuroscience and clinical research on embodiment translated for classroom applications (Macrine and Fugate 2022). The collection was the first to systematically gather, collate, translate, and disseminate the latest embodied research geared toward improved learning outcomes. It also shared some of the most significant breakthroughs and applications that recent embodied cognition research has made on the science of learning across specific content areas to improve content area learning outcomes for intersectionally diverse students.

Our nascent efforts have been to catalyze new collaborations across widely scattered fields, building an interdisciplinary web – a global network of international scholars keen on leveraging research to reshape education. As a result of this research, we found overlapping and quite similar principles in these discipline-specific approaches to embodied learning. We argued for an overarching embodied teaching and learning framework that elucidates the principles, commonalities, distinctions, and relationships among the cross-disciplinary learning sciences in education (Abrahamson et al. 2020; Burrows et al. 2006; Leung 2020; Macrine and Fugate 2021, 2022; Shapiro and Stolz 2019). Some of the work we featured included: early reading; vocabulary acquisition; language comprehension; letter identification; language writing and technology; early finger counting; geometry; mathematics, numerical processing, and probability; mathematic gesturing; geometry; physics; magnetic fields; special education; mindfulness and emotional granularity; imitative learning and mirror neurons; and autism spectrum disorder as a disorder of conceptual sensorimotor impairment (Macrine and Fugate 2022). As part of this edited volume, we began to outline a model of translational science for embodied learning, which we flesh out below.

Our Translational Model

Our work resulted in the identification of preliminary principles and steps to construct a framework (Macrine and Fugate 2020). We were influenced by NIH's (Daudelin et al. 2020) Translational Science Research model (based on Gilliland et al. 2017; Rubio et al. 2010), which emphasizes a need for appropriate professional development that fosters interdisciplinary approaches to quickly disseminate biomedical findings from the laboratory, clinic, and community into interventions to improve the health of individuals and the public. Our adapted model, the Translational Learning Sciences Research (Macrine and Fugate 2021), leverages empirical findings from embodied cognition research on why and how embodied learning works. The call for translational research for the benefit of education is not new, although the term 'translational' has only recently been applied in fields other than the natural sciences. We derived seven generalized goals in our model: 1) make sense of and disseminate clinical and empirical research findings; 2) close the gap between research and application; 3) combine cognitive science and pedagogy to share pertinent information; 4) improve teaching and learning through embodied applications; 5) confirm or debunk current trends, (i.e., neuromyths); 6) elucidate conceptual frameworks for sensorimotor and body-based learning; and 7) recommend curriculum, designs, taxonomies, technology, and development to inform policy. From these goals, we outlined the following four action steps: 1) promote the multidirectional and multidisciplinary integration of basic embodied research to trends in teaching and learning; 2) compile the embodied research to be analyzed and translated, and also to make connections to improve pedagogical approaches, with the long-term aim of improving teaching and learning; 3) develop and disseminate resources and tools to help individuals at all levels of expertise develop a better understanding of embodied learning; and 4) focus on the creation of appropriate embodied curriculum and the development of taxonomies to identify objectives, and track outcomes that will assess whether program objectives and competency requirements are being met. This framework provides an expeditious way to systematically collate, translate, and disseminate the latest embodied research for improved learning outcomes.

The model provides a space where multiple disciplinary fields meet to fundamentally shift how we understand and approach teaching the whole person, and how to inform the construction of embodied educational pedagogies, designs, and policies. The goal is to help educators better understand the current scholarship on embodied cognition and its applications to teaching and learning. While we know that research alone does not change practice, at issue is how to translate and disseminate embodied research to bridge the gap between research, educational psychology, and curriculum design and interventions. At the same time, our model works to eliminate the silos of knowledge in teaching and learning that impact student outcomes. "Meaningful educational change almost always involves coordinating and aligning related changes, e.g., in curriculum, technology use, pedagogy, assessment, and school leadership" (Roschelle et al., 2011: 33). We are advancing this translational model as a vehicle to continue to collate vetted examples of embodied learning as they relate to embodied cognition theory.

We believe that a translational framework can facilitate the development and dissemination of embodied multimodal learning principles that can be easily applied across content areas. Also, deriving embodied learning principles for transdisciplinary approaches can contribute to a contemporary pedagogical theory that emphasizes the use of the body in educational practice, as well as student–teacher interaction both in and outside the classroom (see also Georgiou and Ioannou, 2019; Kosmas and Zaphiris, 2019; Smyrnaiou et al. 2016). The educational importance of embodied learning and teaching lies in treating the learner as a complete entity, allowing them to experience themselves holistically, rather than as distinct physical and mental attributes unrelated to each other (Fugate et al., 2019; Macrine and Fugate 2021; Stolz 2015; Shapiro and Stolz 2019). Said another way, the cognitive structure of an individual – as defined by their own experiences and those supported by cultural norms and language – informs how information is first experienced by their body as well as later simulated (Fugate et al. 2019). To that extent, a person's current interactions with the world (including their movements and interpretations of those bodily sensations) will also be shaped by their past experiences (see Leung et al. 2011).

Conclusions

As cognitive science moves towards embodiment, it demands new theorizations in approaches that are grounded, or even constituted, in goal-oriented multimodal sensorimotor learning (Abrahamson et al. 2020). We believe that translating the latest research on embodied cognition, examining its implications for classroom learning, and uncovering what is working in teaching pedagogy, can effectively enhance embodied teaching and learning strategies, as well as lead to the development of taxonomies and assessments.

This chapter argues for the continued need to translate concepts from embodied cognition into a practice of embodied learning. We advance our translational framework to show how embodied research is based on the newer understanding of how the brain interacts with the body and sensorimotor systems in the context of the environment to understand the world around it. Given the burgeoning field of embodied cognition and learning, an inclusive learning sciences framework such as this is needed, especially for those involved in educational planning, design, and pedagogical approaches (Abrahamson et al. 2020), for those interested in developing an overarching embodied learning theory (Macrine and Fugate 2020, 2022), and for the development of embodied learning taxonomies (Johnson-Glenberg 2022; Skulmowski and Rey 2018). Clearly, embodied cognition provides the scientific validation for sensorimotor learning and offers potentially useful tools for educators' understanding of teaching and learning. Finally, translational learning sciences research can provide a useful road map and valuable resource for future explorers of embodied cognition as they make their own connections for embodied teaching and learning.

Note

1 https://learningpolicyinstitute.org/sites/default/files/product-files/Effective_Teacher_Professional_Development_REPORT.pdf

References

Abrahamson, D. (2004) "Embodied spatial articulation: A gesture perspective on student negotiation between kinesthetic schemas and epistemic forms in learning mathematics," in D. E. McDougall and J. A. Ross (Eds), *Proceedings of the Twenty Sixth Annual Meeting of the North American Chapter of the International Group for the Psychology of Mathematics Education* (Vol. 2, pp. 791–797) Toronto, Ontario: Preney.

Abrahamson, D., Dutton, E. and Bakker, A. (2022) "Towards an enactivist mathematics pedagogy," in S. A. Stolz (Ed.), *The body, embodiment, and education: An interdisciplinary approach* (pp. 156–182) Philadelphia, PA: Routledge.

Abrahamson, D., Nathan, M. J., Williams-Pierce, C., Walkington, C., Ottmar, E. R., Soto, H. and Alibali, M. W. (2020) "The future of embodied design for mathematics teaching and learning," in S. Ramanathan & I. A. C. Mok (Eds.), Futures of STEM education: Multiple perspectives from researchers (Special issue). *Frontiers of Education*, (Vol. 5, p.147). https://doi.org/10.3389/feduc.2020.00147

Alsmith, A. J. T. and Vignemont, F. (2012) "Embodying the mind and representing the body," *Review of Philosophy and Psychology* 3(1), 1–13.

Ansari, D. and Coch, D. (2006) "Bridges over troubled waters: Education and cognitive neuroscience," *Trends in Cognitive Sciences*, 10(4), 146–151. https://doi.org/10.1016/j.tics.2006.02.007

Barrett, L. F. (2017) *How Emotions are Made: The Secret Life of the Brain*, Houghton Mifflin Harcourt.

Barsalou, L. W. (1999) "Language comprehension: Archival memory or preparation for situated action," *Discourse Processes*, 28, 61–80.

—— (2003) "Situated simulation in the human conceptual system," *Language and Cognitive Processes*, 18(5–6), 513–562. https://doi.org/10.1080/01690960344000026

—— (2008) "Grounded cognition," *Annual Review Psychology*, 59, 617–645.

Bruner, J. (1966) *Toward a theory of instruction*. Belknap Press of Harvard University Press. ISBN 978-0674897007.

Burrows, V., Oehrtman, M., and Lawson, A. (2006) "Development of an integrated learning framework for STEM learning," *ASEE Annual Conference and Exposition, Conference Proceedings.*

Chemero, A. (2009) *Radical Embodied Cognitive Science*, MIT Press.

Clark, A. (2008) *Supersizing the mind: Embodiment, action, and cognitive extension*, OUP USA.

Darling-Hammond, L., Flook, L., Cook-Harvey, C., Barron, B. and Osher, D. (2020) "Implications for educational practice of the science of learning and development," *Applied Developmental Science*, 24(2), 97–140. https://doi.org/10.1080/10888691.2018.1537791

Daudelin, D.H., Peterson, L.E., Welch, L.C., et al. (2020) "Implementing Common Metrics across the NIH Clinical and Translational Science Awards (CTSA) consortium," *Journal of Clinical and Translational Science*, 4(1), 16–21. https://doi.org/10.1017/cts.2019.425

Di Paolo, E., Buhrmann, T., and Barandiaran, X. E. (2017) *Sensorimotor Life*, Oxford: Oxford University Press.

Flook, L. (2019) "Four ways schools can support the whole child," *The Greater Good*. 4-23-19. https://greatergood.berkeley.edu/article/item/four_ways_schools_can_support_the_whole_child

Fugate, J. M. B., Macrine, S. L., and Cipriano, C. (2019) "The role of embodied cognition for transforming learning," *International Journal of School and Educational Psychology*, 7(4), 274–288. https://doi.org/10.1080/21683603.2018.1443856

Gallagher, S. (2005) *How the Body Shapes the Mind*, Oxford, UK: Oxford University Press

Gallese, V. (2009) "Mirror neurons, embodied simulation, and the neural basis of social identification," *Psychoanalytic Dialogues*, 19(5), 519–536.

Gallese, V., & Sinigaglia, C. (2011). "What is so special about embodied simulation?" *Trends in Cognitive Sciences*, 15(11), 512–519. https://doi.org/10.1016/j.tics.2011.09.003

Georgiou, Y. and Ioannou, A. (2019) "Embodied learning in a digital world: A systematic review of empirical research in K-12 education," in Díaz, P., Ioannou, A., Bhagat, K., Spector, M. J. (eds), *Learning in a Digital World*, Singapore: Springer.

Gilliland, C. T., Sittampalam, G. S., Wang, P. Y., and Ryan, P. E. (2017) "The translational science training program at NIH: Introducing early career researchers to the science and operation of translation of basic research to medical interventions," *Biochemistry and Molecular Biology Education. Biology*, 45(1), 13–24. https://doi.org/10.1002/bmb.20978

Glenberg, A. M. (2008) "Embodiment for education," in Calvo, P. and Gomila, A. (eds), *Handbook of Cognitive Science: An Embodied Approach* (pp. 354–355). Amsterdam: Elsevier.

——— (2010) "Embodiment as a unifying perspective for psychology," *Wiley Interdisciplinary Reviews: Cognitive Science*, 1, 586–596.

Glenberg, A. M., Gutierrez, T., Levin, J. R., Japuntich, S., & Kaschak, M. P. (2004). "Activity and imagined activity can enhance young children's reading comprehension," *Journal of Educational Psychology*, 96(3), 424–436.

Goldman, A.I. (2012) "A Moderate Approach to Embodied Cognitive Science," *Review of Philosophy and Psychology*, 3, 71–88. https://doi.org/10.1007/s13164-012-0089-0

Golonka, S., and Wilson, A. D. (2012) "Gibson's ecological approach," *Avant: Trends in Interdisciplinary Studies*, 3(2), 40–53.

Goswami, U. (2006). "Neuroscience and education: from research to practice?" *Nat Rev Neurosci 7*, 406–413. https://doi.org/10.1038/nrn1907

Guerriero, S. (Ed.) (2017) *Pedagogical Knowledge and the Changing Nature of the Teaching Profession*, Paris: OECD Publishing.

Hall, K. L., Vogel, A. L., Huang, G. C., Serrano, K. J., Rice, E. L., Tsakraklides, S. P., and Fiore, S. M. (2018) "The science of team science: A review of the empirical evidence and research gaps on collaboration in science," *The American Psychologist*, 73(4), 532–548. https://doi.org/10.1037/amp0000319

Hammerness, K. (2006) "From Coherence in Theory to Coherence in Practice," *Teachers College Record*, 108(7), 1241–1265. https://ed.stanford.edu/sites/default/files/from_coherence_in_theory_to_coherence_in_practice.pdf

Heitzmann, N., Opitz, A., Stadler, M., Sommerhoff, D., Fink, M. C., Obersteiner, A., Schmidmaier, R., Neuhaus, B. J., Ufer, S., Seidel, T., Fischer, M. R., and Fischer, F. (2021) "Cross-disciplinary research on learning and instruction – Coming to terms," *Frontiers in Psychology*, 11. https://doi.org/10.3389/fpsyg.2021.562658

Henderson, M., Selwyn, N. and Aston, R. (2017) "What works and why? Student perceptions of 'useful' digital technology in university teaching and learning," *Studies in Higher Education*, 42(8), 1567–1579. https://doi.org10.1080/03075079.2015.1007946

Hutto, D., (2005) "Knowing what? Radical versus conservative enactivism," *Phenomenology and the Cognitive Sciences* 4(4), 389–405.

Hutto, D. & Myin, E. (2012). *Radicalizing Enactivism: Basic Minds without Content*. MIT Press, pp. 1–206. https://doi.org10.7551/mitpress/9780262018548.001.0001

Johnson-Glenberg M.C. (2022) "Evaluating Embodied Immersive STEM VR Using the Quality of Education in Virtual Reality Rubric (QUIVRR)," in S. L. Macrine and Fugate, J. M. B. (eds), *Movement Matters: How Embodied Cognition Informs Teaching and Learning*. Cambridge, MA: MIT Press.

Klein, E., Taylor, M., and Forgasz, R. (2019) "Using embodied practices with preservice teachers: Teaching and reflecting through the body to re-think teacher education," *Journal of Practitioner Research*, 4(2) https://doi.org/10.5038/2379-9951.4.2.1088

Kosmas, P., and Zaphiris, P. (2019) "Embodied interaction in language learning: Enhancing students' collaboration and emotional engagement," in D. Lamas, F. Loizides, L. Nacke, H. Petrie, M. Winckler, P. Zaphiris (eds), *Human interaction – INTERACT2019, Lecture notes in computer science*, Vol. 11747 (pp. 179–196) Springer. https://doi.org/10.1007/978-3-030-29384-0_11

Lakoff, G., and Johnson, M. (1999) *Philosophy in the Flesh: The Embodied Mind and Its Challenge to Western Thought*, New York: Basic Books.

Leung, A. (2020) "Boundary crossing pedagogy in STEM education," *International Journal of STEM Education*, 7(1), 1–11.

Leung, A.K., Qiu, L., Ong, L. and Tam, K.-P. (2011), "Embodied cultural cognition: Situating the study of embodied cognition in socio-cultural contexts," *Social and Personality Psychology Compass*, 5, 591–608. https://doi.org/10.1111/j.1751-9004.2011.00373.x

Lux, V., Non, A. L., Pexman, P. M., Stadler, W., Weber, L. A. E., and Krüger, M. (2021) "A developmental framework for embodiment research: The next step toward integrating concepts and methods," *Frontiers in Systems Neuroscience*, 15(July), 1–22. https://doi.org/10.3389/fnsys.2021.672740

Macdonald, K., Germine, L., Anderson, A., Christodoulou, J., and McGrath, L. M. (2017) "Dispelling the myth: Training in education or neuroscience decreases but does not eliminate beliefs in neuromyths," *Frontiers in Psychology*, 8(AUG). https://doi.org/10.3389/fpsyg.2017.01314

Macedonia, M. (2019) "Embodied learning: Why at school the mind needs the body," *Frontiers in Psychology*, 10, 2098. https://doi.org/10.3389/fpsyg.2019.02098

Macrine, S. L. (2002) "Pedagogical bondage: Body bound and gagged in a techno-rational world," in S. Shapiro (ed.), *Body Movements: Pedagogy, Politics and Social Change*. Cresskill, NJ: Hampton Press (pp. 133–145)

Macrine, S. L., and Fugate, J. M. B. (2020) "Embodied Cognition," in *Oxford Research Encyclopedia of Education*, Oxford, England: Oxford University Press. https://doi.org/10.1093/acrefore/9780190264093.013.885

——— (2021) "Translating Embodied Cognition for Embodied Learning in the Classroom," *Frontiers in Education*, 6. https://doi.org/10.3389/feduc.2021.712626

Macrine, S. L. and Fugate, J. M. B. (2022) *Movement Matters: How Embodied Cognition Informs Teaching and Learning*, Cambridge, MA: MIT Press.

Maturana, H. R., and Varela, F. J. (1991) *Autopoiesis and Cognition: The Realization of the Living* (Vol. 42) Reidel Publishing, Dordrecht, Holland.

Meltzoff, A.N., Kuhl, P. K., Movellan, J., and Seinowski, T.J. (2009). "Foundations for a new science of learning," *Science*, 325, 284–288. https://doi.org10.1126/science.1175626

Merleau-Ponty, M. (1962) *Phenomenology of Perception*, London: Routledge and Kegan Paul.

——— (1974) *Phenomenology, Language and Sociology: Selected Essays of Maurice Merleau-Ponty*, Heinemann Educational.

Nagataki, S. and Hirose, S. (2007) "Phenomenology and the third generation of cognitive science: Towards a cognitive phenomenology of the body," *Human Studies*, 30(3), 219–232.

Nathan, M.J. (2012a) *Foundations of Embodied Learning*, New York, NY: Routledge.

——— (2012b) "Rethinking formalisms in formal education," *Educational Psychologist*, 47(2), 125–148. https://doi.org/10.1080/00461520.2012.667063

Nathan, M.J., Srisurichan, R., Walkington, C., Wolfgram, M., Williams, C., and Alibali, M.W. (2013) "Building cohesion across representations: A mechanism for STEM integration," *Journal of Engineering Education*, 102, 77–116. https://doi.org/10.1002/jee.20000

National Science and Technology Council (NSTC), 2022-Public Report. P. 14 2022 https://www.whitehouse.gov/wp-content/uploads/2022/11/Convergence_Public-Report_Final.pdf

Newton, P. M. (2015) "The learning styles myth is thriving in higher education," *Frontiers in Psychology*, 6, 1908. https://doi.org/10.3389/fpsyg.2015.01908

Petitmengin, C. (2007) "Towards the source of thoughts: The gestural and transmodal dimension of lived experience," *Journal of Consciousness Studies* 14(3), 54–82.

Pfeifer, R., and Bongard, J. (2007) *How the Body Shapes the Way We Think: A New View of Intelligence*. Boston Review.

Roediger, H. L. (2013) "Applying cognitive psychology to education: Translational educational science," *Psychological Science in the Public Interest*, 14, 1–3.

Roschelle, J., Bakia, M., Toyama, Y., and Patton, C. (2011) "Eight issues for learning scientists about education and the economy," *Journal of the Learning Sciences*, 20(1), 3–49. https://doi.org/10.1080/10508406.2011.528318

Rowlands, M. (2012) "The Mind Embodied, Embedded, Enacted, and Extended," in *The New Science of the Mind: From Extended Mind to Embodied Phenomenology*. Cambridge, MA: MIT Press, p. 98. https://doi.org/10.7551/mitpress/9780262014557.003.0003

Rubio, D. M., Schoenbaum, E. E., Lee, L. S., Schteingart, D. E., Marantz, P. R., Anderson, K. E., Platt, L. D., Baez, A., and Esposito, K. (2010) "Defining translational research: Implications for training," *Academic Medicine: Journal of the Association of American Medical Colleges*, 85(3), 470–475. https://doi.org/10.1097/ACM.0b013e3181ccd618

Schenck, K.E., Walkington, C., & Nathan, M. J. (2022). "Groups that move together, prove together: Collaborative gestures and gesture attitudes among teachers performing embodied geometry," In Sheila Macrine and Jennifer Fugate (eds), *Movement Matters: How Embodied Cognition Informs Teaching and Learning* (pp. 131–145). Cambridge, MA: MIT Press.

Shapiro, L. (2011). *Embodied Cognition*, New York: Routledge Press.

——— (2019). *Embodied cognition* (2nd ed.). Routledge/Taylor & Francis Group. https://doi.org/10.4324/9781315180380

Shapiro, L., and Stolz, S. A. (2019) "Embodied cognition and its significance for education," *Theory and Research in Education*, 17(1), 19–39. https://doi.org/10.1177/1477878518822149

Simmers, K. (2020) "Education Research Is Still Too Dense. We Need More Teacher-Researcher Partnerships," | EdSurge News *EDSURGE*. https://doi.org/10.3389/frym.2020.00110

Skulmowski, A., and Rey, G.D. (2018) "Embodied learning: Introducing a taxonomy based on bodily engagement and task integration," *Cognitive Research*, 3(6). https://doi.org/10.1186/s41235-018-0092-9

Smyrnaiou, Z., Sotiriou, M., Georgakopoulou, E., and Papadopoulou, O. (2016) "Connecting embodied learning in educational practice to the realization of science educational scenarios through performing arts," Paper presented at the *Inspiring Science Education International Conference*, Athens, Greece (pp. 37–45)

Stolz, S. A. (2015) "Embodied Learning," *Educational Philosophy and Theory*, 47(5), 474–487.

Thomas, M.S.C., Ansari, D., and Knowland, V.C.P. (2019), "Annual Research Review: Educational neuroscience: Progress and prospects," *Journal of Child Psychology and Psychiatry*, 60, 477–492. https://doi.org/10.1111/jcpp.12973

Thompson, E. (2007) *Mind in Life*. Cambridge, MA: Harvard University Press.

Tokuhama-Espinosa, T. N. (2019) *Five Pillars of the Mind: Redesigning education to suit the brain*, New York, NY: W.W. Norton. ISBN: 978-0-393-71321-3

Ulrich, B., and McDaniels, A. (2018) *Addressing the Gap Between Education Research and Practice - Center for American Progress* The Center for American Progress. https://www.americanprogress.org/article/addressing-gap-education-research-practice/

Varela, F. J., Thompson, E. and Rosch, E. (1991) *The Embodied Mind: Cognitive Science and Human Experience*, MIT Press: Cambridge, MA.

Weinstein, Y., Madan, C.R. & Sumeracki, M.A. (2018). "Teaching the science of learning," *Cognitive Research*, 3, 2. https://doi.org/10.1186/s41235-017-0087-y

Weisberg, S.M., and Newcombe, N.S. (2017) "Embodied cognition and STEM learning: Overview of a topical collection in CR:PI," *Cognitive Research*, 2(1), 38. https://doi.org/10.1186/s41235-017-0071-6

Wilcox, G., Morett, L. M., Hawes, Z., and Dommett, E. J. (2021) "Why educational neuroscience needs educational and school psychology to effectively translate neuroscience to educational practice," *Frontiers in Psychology*, 11, 618449. https://doi.org/10.3389/fpsyg.2020.618449

Wilson, M. (2002) "Six views of embodied cognition," *Psychonomic Bulletin & Review*, 9, 625–636.

Woodward, A. L., Sommerville, JA., Gerson, S., Henderson, A. M. E., and Buresh, J. S. (2009) "The emergence of intention attribution in infancy," in B. Ross (Ed.), *The Psychology of Learning and Motivation*. Vol. 51. Academic Press. (pp. 187–222).

Zlatev, J. (2007) "Embodiment, Language, and Mimesis," in T. Ziemke, J. Zlatev and R. Frank, *Body, Language and Mind: Vol 1: Embodiment*. Berlin: Mouton.

PART 7

Virtual Reality

24

EMBODIED EXPERIENCES IN GAME PLAY

Tarja Susi and Niklas Torstensson

In this chapter we discuss games from an embodiment perspective and illustrate the importance of a particular category of embodied experience where perception, action, and socio-cultural context are closely interrelated. The embodied experiences we have in mind relate to young children's learning, in particular to understanding the abstract concept of risk awareness. We are interested in how young people can grasp this concept through embodied experiences mediated by a computer game. Online risk is inherently abstract for young children and as such is difficult to grasp due to their level of cognitive maturity. Since the abstract concept is not grounded in experience, it needs to be made concrete through their own hands-on experience. The overarching purpose is to enable young children to make sound decisions when faced with uncomfortable or even threatening situations during online interactions. The experiences we discuss include both game experiences and what we term *pre*-experiences which may be remembered at a later point in time when faced with real-world events.

There are a number of different perspectives on and approaches to research on embodied cognition. That versatility also entails that there is no uniform definition of embodied cognition, nor is it a well-defined theory (c.f., Gallagher 2014; Gibbs 2005; Shapiro 2011; Ziemke 2003). In fact, Shapiro (2011), writing that it is a challenge to find a unified theory, considers that embodied cognition is, rather, a research program with a number of central themes. The theorizing of embodied cognition is also complicated by the fact that embodied cognition is closely related to situated cognition, with each taking a different approach to cognition. The opposite is sometimes also true, with different approaches lumped together (Shapiro 2011). Hence, we find combinations of related (but different) concepts, with such terms as "embodied/embedded/situated cognition" implying they are inseparable. Definitions also vary depending on whether embodiment or situatedness, or some other aspect for that matter, is emphasized. Thus, embodiment is often described in terms of cognition. For instance, Gibbs (2005: 9) provides the following description: "cognition is what occurs when the body engages the physical, cultural world and must be studied in terms of the dynamical interactions between people and the environment. Human language and thought emerge from recurring patterns of embodied activity that constrain ongoing intelligent behavior." Barsalou (2010) prefers the term grounded cognition rather than

 DOI: 10.4324/9781003322511-32

embodied cognition, since embodied cognition "fails to capture the wide scope of grounding mechanisms, while simultaneously giving the mistaken impression that bodily states always determine the course of cognition. 'Grounded cognition' captures the broad scope of grounding mechanisms, while not placing undue emphasis on the body" (ibid.: 721). We do not attempt to define embodiment here. Instead, we attend to embodied experiences grounded in game play, from an embodied, situated cognitive perspective. The concepts of embodied and situated are not easily distinguished, since they are closely coupled. In this vein we consider cognition as emerging from the close coupling between brain, body, world, artifacts, and the socio-cultural environment (Clark 1997; Gibbs 2005; Rogoff 2003; Wilson 2002).

Embodied cognition has attracted interest within a number of different research areas, among them human–computer interaction (Dourish 2004; Pustejovsky & Krishnaswamy 2021), child–computer interaction (Antle & Hourcade 2021; Antle & Wise 2013), and game studies (Alton 2017; Klevjer 2022; Lankoski 2016). Arguably, the most prevalent discussions on embodiment in game studies concern the relation between players and their game avatars. Klevjer (2022), for instance, claims that it is a prosthetic relationship in which the avatar becomes an extension of the player's own body. Furthermore, he states that "The avatar is the embodied manifestation of the player' engagement with the game world; it is the player incarnated" (ibid.: 22). Avatars have also been related to virtual embodiment, in which players can inhabit avatars on a phenomenological level (Alton 2017). However, as in the case of defining embodiment in cognitive science, the use of embodiment in gaming literature is unclear and inconsistent, and it is defined or described in various ways (Farrow & Iacovides 2014).

What can be ascertained, however, is that games and gaming have become widespread in many people's everyday life. Similarly, the internet and the Web are ubiquitous parts of everyday life, readily at hand through the smartphone in every adult's or child's pocket. Nevertheless, as Smart (2014) points out, discussions regarding embodiment and the Web may seem out of place as research on embodied cognition tends to focus on interactions in the real world while interactions with the Web might seem to be something else. In our view the Web is a relevant area of research in relation to embodiment, especially with respect to social media and young people's online behavior. Social media is an arena for all kinds of positive experiences, but it also provides a channel for online predation where young people are targeted. Young people live parts of their lives online, but due to their cognitive maturity they are not aware of risks and do not always understand other people's potentially malicious intentions. Our approach to addressing online risk awareness is hands-on experience through a game that emulates real-world online events. The main point of our discussion is how embodied experiences can help in forming an understanding of the concept of online risk, and thereby increased risk awareness.

A tangible mixed-media game

It has been argued for quite some time that children's thinking skills do not develop in isolation from their environment, but instead are tied to physical hands-on actions and the environment, and that physical and social interactions are important for cognitive development and for learning to understand abstract ideas (e.g., Antle 2013; Gee 2003; Piaget 1972). To further the discussion on the game and embodied experiences, we first provide a short description of a game called Hidden in the Park[1] (translated from Swedish). It is an off-line adventure game with fun in-game events that can be accessed by accepting offers made available as part of the game mechanics. The game is a mixed-media multi-player game that includes a cardboard game board, game pieces, clue cards, and a tablet. The tablet has several functions. It contains, for instance, a virtual die and it shows the game board as a virtual 3D world where players hide treasures (Figure 24.1). When hiding a treasure, each player gets in return a set of clue cards placed face up on the table. The clue cards are connected to the tablet, and the technology can reveal a clue depending on what digital choices players make, for instance, whether they reply 'yes' or 'no' to a question. Hence, players need to take care of their clues so as not to have their hiding places revealed (and lose the game).

The tablet also contains a virtual smartphone that appears during game play and shows text messages sent to the players from unknown in-game characters. The in-game characters that send text messages use different strategies to make players take photos of their clue cards (with the tablet) and send them in return. Initial strategies to lure players to take photos are flattery ('you're doing really well'), bribes ('would you like some gold coins?'), and coercion ('pleeeease'). Players fall into these traps quite easily, but once a player has taken and sent a photo, they will be subjected to threats – a previously sent photo/clue card will be revealed to the other players, unless the player sends more photos.[2] Those game events and mechanics are designed to allow young players to experience choices and their consequences, and to evoke thoughts and reflections. Every time a message appears, the player has to make a choice, and reply with 'yes' or 'no' by tapping the virtual smartphone, just like using a real smartphone to send a message. While the game could be thought of as

Figure 24.1 Some of the tangible elements of the Hidden in the Park game. The tablet shows a 3D view of the gameboard (©Niklas Torstensson).

a metaphor, that is, a way to understand and experience one kind of thing in terms of another (Lakoff & Johnson 1980/2003), it is not a metaphor as such, but rather an emulation of real-world online interactions that allows young players to experience making decisions and then experience the consequences of their decisions. (For further description of the game see Susi & Torstensson 2019; Susi, Torstensson & Wilhelmsson 2019; Wilhelmsson, Susi & Torstensson 2021).

The game comprises two dimensions. One is the game as such, a fun adventure game where all players strive to reach fun in-game content and to finally win the game. The fun side of the game is in fact a disguise for the second dimension, which emulates real-world events where unknown people contact young children. Bridging these dimensions are the virtual smartphone and the clue cards.

The game's target group is children aged 8–10 years, which may seem very young when it comes to online risk awareness. However, in Sweden 93% of ten-year-olds use a smartphone daily, and seven out of ten use social media (The Swedish Media Council 2021). It is well known that children of that age, or even younger, are targeted by predators online and are at risk of being manipulated into falling for an offender's tricks. The cognitive maturity of young children in the target group poses a major challenge for coping with online risks. They need to grasp the relation between choices and potential consequences. Such cognitive reasoning skills, however, only mature at the age of 10 or 11 (Piaget 1972; Wadsworth 2004). Before that, children's reasoning and logic tends to be tied to available experience. Most children have difficulties applying logic to abstract or hypothetical problems, or reasoning about the future and possible consequences of their actions. A tangible object, like the game described here, serves as a tool allowing children to gain concrete first-hand experiences of choices and their consequences, and to relate the experience to online contacts. In other words, the game bridges the limited cognitive maturity of younger children and the abstract reasoning about potential online risks.

Game play as embodied activity

To illustrate how the game's different objectives are related and how it can help young children to learn an abstract concept, we use the Tangible Learning Design Framework (TLDF) discussed by Antle and Wise (2013). The framework is a structure for thinking about the tangible user interface (TUI) design for learning. The framework includes the following five design elements that should be integrated in a finished product: physical objects, digital objects, actions on objects, informational relations, and learning activities. Although the game was not intentionally designed according to the taxonomy, in hindsight we find that the different elements are integrated in the game system, that the game provides an opportunity for insights, and that the TLDF lends itself well to describing and discussing the game.

The *physical objects* are the materials through which players interact with the game. They have been designed with visual attributes like different colors; each player's game piece has a certain color, and the same color is used as a frame on that player's clue cards. This provides a cognitive scaffolding in that players can readily perceive which clue cards belong to whom. Children tend to move around and move objects, so the clue cards can become mixed up, but players only need to remember their own color. The *digital object* of the game is the tablet. The tablet's digital interface has visual attributes like symbols and colors, specifically designed to be easily perceived and understood by young players. The tablet also has auditory information that provides guidance, for instance, for whose turn it is to roll the die. The die is virtual and set in roll by dragging it with a finger. The auditory information is also a cognitive scaffolding that helps to keep game play on track. In sum, there is a lot of information readily perceivable and to be acted upon. Instead of keeping everything in mind or considering what mental information processing might take place, players experience the game as a perception-action cycle with a flow of information and action. As Gibson (1979: 223) phrased it, "we must perceive in order to move, but we must also move in order to perceive." We find this a good motivation for including analog parts in the game, since such physical objects are manipulated in a different way than in a digital game.

As further described by Antle and Wise (2013), the physical and digital objects need to be coupled through *actions on the objects*, and potential actions can be discovered and performed for intended purposes. The game play requires manipulation of both material and digital objects. When a player responds to a text message that requests a photo (of a clue card), the player manipulates tangible objects by selecting a clue card and placing it in a suitable position. The player also needs to manipulate the tablet to take the photo, and the input device in this case is the player's own finger when pressing a button to take the photo. A tablet was a deliberate choice of equipment due to what could be implemented technologically and also because it is well suited for grasping. Our investigations show that players do discover and perform actions for the purposes we intended.

Informal relations in this case are the couplings between physical and digital objects, and possible actions, with references to the real world. The virtual smartphone is a digital representation of a real one and is easily recognizable as such. The reference to a real-world object blurs the boundary between the fictional game world and the real world, and it does not take conscious reflection on what the virtual smartphone represents. The mapping between that particular graphical design element and a real-world object carries semantic aspects that are perceptual (the virtual smartphone represents a smartphone) and behavioral (press a button). The point here is that a digital object is digitally represented instead of being represented purely analogically.

The final design element of the framework is *learning activities*, which refers to "the context, instructions and guidance provided to learners to frame their interaction with the TUI System" (Antle & Wise 2013: 5). The game is intended to be played in elementary schools, in groups of 2–4 players, followed by discussion with a teacher (who observes the game play but does not take part). That sets the context of the game play. There are written and audible instructions to guide players through the game play. The game is intended to evoke insight and reflections on text messages, choices of how to respond, and potential negative consequences of the choices made. The game play and the choices and actions required translate the abstract concepts of online risk into a very concrete 'here-and-now' experience. To take a photo of a clue card and send it is very like sending actual private photos to unknown people, unaware of the negative consequences that may ensue.

According to Antle and Wise (2013) a TUI can be a standalone activity or a collaborative activity of learning, and a design can influence the way users take action and interact with each other. Even though the game discussed here may seem to be individual game play, it is in fact very much a collaborative activity. The game play is a process during which players discuss and find a common ground for what is actually unfolding. Our investigations have shown that there are clear relations between individual and collective reasoning, as it frequently happens that one of the players in the group gets the gist before the others, realizes that something strange is going on, and comments on that loudly. Common comments are, for instance, "No! Don't send a photo" or "You're being tricked!" Comments such as these lead to a great deal of discussion about the text messages and what they mean, and choices – to send a photo and gain an advantage in the game, without knowing who the receiver is, or just to say 'no.' During such discussions, it dawns on players unaware of the game plot what is really going on. They realize that sending photos to gain an advantage was not such a good idea after all given the consequences of having their photos revealed.

There is a lot of object manipulation and pointing, which guides joint attention and synchronization of actions. The players are seated around a table (even though they also tend to move around) and the focus is on the game board every time a player manipulates a tangible object. They collaborate by taking turns and in moving game pieces so that the player closest to a game piece that needs to be moved makes the move.

To summarize this discussion, we turn to Lakoff and Johnson (1980/2003) who claim that we, as humans, understand concepts through our experiences. They also describe what they term natural kinds of experience. Such experiences are said to be a product of embodiment (mental, perceptual, and motor capacities), and interaction with the physical environment (moving, object manipulation) and with other people within our culture (societal institutions). We consider game play to be a natural kind of experience that increases the understanding of a certain concept. This natural kind of experience includes the body and interactions with the physical and socio-cultural environment:

- *The players' bodies*. Perception and action are at the core of the game play, as are mental capacities like reasoning and decision-making.
- *The players' interactions with their physical environment*. The game play involves hands-on manipulation of tangible game objects such as when the tablet is picked up and used as a camera to take a photo of a clue card, and then the 'send' button is tapped.
- *The players' interactions with each other within their culture*. Players' interactions are guided by a shared culture that provides a frame of social norms, communication, and guidelines for how to act during game play as opposed to play in general.

The natural kinds of experience gained through the game play can be seen as a translation of an abstract concept into a concrete activity, with a distinct reference to real-world events. The tangible objects provide physicality and a means to gain concrete first-hand experience of what online risks may be. We also consider that experience as a *pre*-experience – an embodied experience of possible future events, something that can occur at some later point in time, in online interactions. As Gallagher (2014: 10) describes it (referring to Husserl's analysis of memory), "episodic memory involves a re-enactment of past perception." When the game has been played it becomes a past perceptual experience, and when encountering a situation that recalls the game, the pre-experience may evoke memories of past actions. To remember is to make something present again although in a modified sense, since two separate embodied, situated experiences are not likely to be identical even though they could be similar. Remembering past actions, then, like decisions made in game play that lead to negative consequences, may lead to more sound decisions in real-life situations. A relevant question here is whether different kinds of games can fulfill the same purpose. There are many different kinds of games, like table-top games, digital games, Virtual Reality (VR) games, and different forms of hybrid games. In theory, any form of game could potentially allow young children to learn about online risk, but in our view some kinds of games seem more suitable than others. In table-top games it can be hard to create realism. For instance, it would be hard to make realistically simulated text messages. Digital games focus on a screen and input tools, and so object manipulation becomes rather limited. Virtual reality games in turn can create an illusion of reality, but since players have to wear a VR helmet or glasses and use a virtual tool or virtual extension of a hand to manipulate virtual objects, they are shielded from true physical and social interaction. Social interaction is lost and instead replaced with avatar–avatar interactions if several players are within the same virtual setting.

The combination of a table-top game and digital tools creates an opportunity to emulate reality, with physical and social interaction, where the digital technology enables an easily recognizable relation to everyday life.

Summary

Game play is truly an embodied activity, with a close coupling between mind, brain, and body. The game play we have described provides an opportunity for a natural kind of experience within a here-and-now situation. At the same time, it is a hands-on pre-experience of possible future events. We cannot say with certainty that the pre-experience will safeguard children if they encounter people online with malicious intentions at some later point in time. But the game does provide a short-cut to grasping the abstract concept of online risk, which otherwise would be beyond their mental capacity to understand. The interaction between players demonstrates the interrelatedness of individual and social thinking and reasoning.

The game was designed as an external aid, a cognitive scaffold for grasping the concept of online risks, thereby increasing risk awareness. We believe that the hands-on object manipulation supports the young players' development of thinking skills as the game play provides a specific embodied, situated opportunity to practice decision-making and then see the outcome of their decisions. We also believe that most players come to understand why online risk awareness is a good thing. To quote Bekker and Antle (2011: 32), our job as designers of the game was "not to understand what a child can do and design to support that, but rather to understand what a child is able to practice doing or thinking about and to produce opportunities to practice those skills in a specific context with external aids." Different kinds of materials aimed at educating children regarding risk behavior, online as well as offline, of course exist. The bulk of such material consists of written instructions of do's and dont's in brochures and on websites. The approach described and discussed in this chapter adds the element of embodiment to the equation, a significant addition because learning involves more than mere internal mental processing. We hope to inspire others to consider embodied aspects of learning within games and gaming. This is clearly an important area for future research.

Notes

1 The game has been widely distributed free to elementary schools in Sweden.
2 The strategies used by the game characters are based on our research regarding offender strategies in real online grooming processes. Four of the most prevalent strategies found are flattery, bribes, coercion, and threats (Susi & Torstensson 2019).

References

Alton, C. (2017) "Experience, 60 Frames per Second: Virtual Embodiment and the Player/Avatar Relationship in Digital Games," *Loading ...*, 10(16), 214–227.

Antle, A.N. (2013) "Exploring How Children Use Their Hands to Think: An Embodied Interaction Analysis," *Behavior & Information Technology*, 32(9), 938–954.

Antle, A.N. and Hourcade, J.P. (2021) "Research in Child–Computer Interaction: Provocations and Envisioning Future Directions," *International Journal of Child-Computer Interaction*, 32, 100374.

Antle, A.N. and Wise, A.F. (2013) "Getting Down to Details: Using Theories of Cognition and Learning to Inform Tangible User Interface Design," *Interacting with Computers*, 25(1), 1–20.

Barsalou, L.W. (2010) "Grounded Cognition: Past, Present, and Future," *Topics in Cognitive Science*, 2(4), 716–724.

Bekker, M.M. and Antle, A.N. (2011) "Developmentally Situated Design (DSD): A Design Tool for Child–Computer Interaction," in *Proceedings of Conference on Human Factors in Computing Systems*, Vancouver, Canada, ACM Press, 2531–2540.

Clark, A. (1997) *Being There: Putting Brain, Body, and World Together Again*, Cambridge, MA: MIT Press.

Dourish, P. (2004) *Where the Action is: The Foundations of Embodied Interaction*, Cambridge, MA: MIT Press.

Farrow, R. and Iacovides, I. (2014) "Gaming and the Limits of Digital Embodiment," *Philosophy & Technology*, 27(2), 221–233.

Gallagher, S. (2014) "Phenomenology and Embodied Cognition," in L. Shapiro (ed.) *The Routledge Handbook of Embodied Cognition* (9–18). New York, NY: Routledge.

Gee, J.P. (2003) *What Video Games have to Teach us about Learning and Literacy*, New York: Palgrave MacMillan.

Gibbs, R. (2005) *Embodiment and Cognitive Science*, Cambridge: Cambridge University Press.

Gibson, J.J. (1979) *The Ecological Approach to Visual Perception*, Boston: Houghton Mifflin Company.

Klevjer, R. (2022) *What Is the Avatar?: Fiction and Embodiment in Avatar-based Singleplayer Computer Games* (Vol. 3), Bielefeld: Transcript Verlag.

Lakoff, G. and Johnson, M. (1980/2003) *Metaphors We Live By*, Chicago: The University of Chicago Press.

Lankoski, P. (2016) "Embodiment in Character-Based Videogames," in *Proceedings of the 20th International Academic Mindtrek Conference*, 358–365.

Piaget, J. (1972) "Intellectual Evolution from Adolescence to Adulthood," *Human Development*, 51(1), 40–47.

Pustejovsky, J. and Krishnaswamy, N. (2021) "Embodied Human Computer Interaction," *KI-Künstliche Intelligenz*, 35(3), 307–327.

Rogoff, B. (2003) *The Cultural Nature of Human Development*, Oxford: Oxford University Press.

Shapiro, L. (2011) *Embodied Cognition*, London: Routledge.

Smart, P.R. (2014) "Embodiment, Cognition and the World Wide Web," in L. Shapiro (ed.) *The Routledge Handbook of Embodied Cognition* (326–334). New York, NY: Routledge.

Susi, T. and Torstensson, N. (2019) "'Who's Texting?' – Playful Game Experiences for Learning to Cope with Online Risks," in *International Conference on Human-Computer Interaction* (427–441). Cham: Springer.

Susi, T., Torstensson, N. and Wilhelmsson, U. (2019) "'Can you send me a photo?' - A Game-based Approach for Increasing Young Children's Risk Awareness to Prevent Online Sexual Grooming," in *Proceedings of DiGRA 2019*, 1–16.

The Swedish Media Council (2021) *Ungar och medier 2021*. Statens medieråd.

Wadsworth, B.J. (2004) *Piaget's Theory of Cognitive and Affective Development*, Boston: Pearson Education Inc.

Wilhelmsson, U., Susi, T. and Torstensson, N. (2021) "Merging the Analogue and the Digital: Combining Opposite Activities in a Mixed Media Game," *Media and Communication*, 9(1), 17–27.

Wilson, M. (2002) "Six Views of Embodied Cognition," *Psychonomic Bulletin & Review*, 9(4), 625–636.

Ziemke, T. (2003) "What's that Thing Called Embodiment?," in *Proceedings of the Annual Meeting of the Cognitive Science Society* (Vol. 25, No. 25), 1305–1310.

25

MINDS IN THE MATRIX

Embodied Cognition and Virtual Reality

Paul Smart

Introduction

Recent years have seen an intensification of interest in virtual-reality technology. This interest is being fueled by advances in the development of virtual (or mixed) reality devices (e.g., virtual-reality headsets), as well as the increasing sophistication of computer graphics and game-engine technology. For the most part, the technological advances are being used for educational and entertainment purposes (e.g., immersive simulations and computer games); however, recent innovations such as the Metaverse suggest a somewhat broader role for virtual reality—one in which virtual reality experiences lie at the heart of a rich array of social, epistemic, and economic activities.

In the present chapter, I offer a brief introduction to some of the ways that virtual reality might affect the theory and practice of embodied cognitive science. The discussion will necessarily be selective, for there are many topics to explore here, and an exhaustive summary would require a much longer treatment than can be offered here (see Chapters 24, 26, and 27). As in earlier work, I will suggest that virtual reality can be used to support our understanding of the mechanisms that underlie various forms of embodied intelligence (Smart 2020a). This claim ought to be uncontroversial, at least when it comes to the design of mechanisms that drive a growing number of real-world autonomous systems. As noted by de Melo et al. (2022), virtual reality is a potent source of synthetic data, which can be used to train the control systems (or 'brains') of autonomous systems prior to their deployment in real-world environments. There have also been substantial advances in the development of industry-standard virtual worlds that can be used to support the development of autonomous systems, such as driverless cars and aerial drones (see Nikolenko 2021). Such innovations are, of course, directed to the synthesis of new embodied systems; they are seldom used to support the study of pre-existing or naturally occurring forms of embodied intelligence. In principle, however, there is no reason why virtual reality cannot be used for precisely this purpose. Indeed, I suspect the shift towards virtual reality may hold the key to resolving a number of issues that have long plagued research into the materially embodied and environmentally situated mind. The section "Virtual Worlds" attempts to provide one example of this, focusing on attempts to derive an integrated, mechanistically informed

 DOI: 10.4324/9781003322511-33

understanding of extended cognition via the construction of virtual creatures that inhabit virtual worlds. "The Virtues of the Virtual" highlights some of the virtues of virtual reality when it comes to both the analysis and synthesis of embodied cognitive systems. Finally, "Mind the Gap" addresses some of the problems that might be seen to undermine the appeal to virtual reality as part of work in embodied cognitive science. Such problems include the idea that virtual reality is a poor substitute for physical reality and that the interests of embodied cognitive science are best served by a focus on real-world systems. I challenge this view, arguing that virtual reality ought to be at the forefront of future (philosophical, scientific, and engineering) research into the embodied mind.

Virtual Worlds

What role does virtual reality play in our understanding of the materially embodied and environmentally situated mind? One answer to this question stems from the use of virtual reality to improve our understanding of the mechanisms that underlie various forms of embodied intelligence. In particular, one can use virtual reality to study the behavior of virtual creatures that are embedded in virtual worlds (see Terzopoulos et al. 1994, for a nice example). Such creatures can be equipped with virtual sensors that mimic the features of perceptual processes. They can also be equipped with virtual motors that enable the creature to, in effect, author its own sensory inputs by acting within the virtual world. In short, virtual reality provides us with a means of studying embodied cognition from a computational perspective. Using the same tools and techniques as those used to create contemporary computer games, we can build virtual worlds that enable us to better understand the way in which intelligent behavior emerges from the interaction of forces and factors that are spread across the brain, the body, and the world (see Chapters 24, 26, and 27).

In one sense, of course, there is nothing particularly new about this proposal—virtual environments have long been used in cognitive scientific research, especially in areas such as cognitive robotics and artificial life. The question, then, is whether there is anything new on the table: Does the use of virtual reality yield anything in the way of progress when it comes to our understanding of prominent issues in embodied cognitive science?

The answer to this question is, I think, a tentative "yes." There are a number of issues that could be explored here. In the interest of brevity, however, I will limit the discussion to one particular problem. This problem concerns the distinction between constitutive and causal relevance. According to proponents of extended cognition, extra-neural resources (such as a body part or technological artifact) can, on occasion, form part of the mechanisms that realize cognitive phenomena (e.g., the mechanism that realizes a particular cognitive process). In such cases, the extra-neural resource is deemed to be *constitutively relevant* to cognitive phenomena. Proponents of embedded cognition dispute this claim about the constitutive relevance of extra-neural resources. According to embedded theorists, extra-neural resources are merely *causally relevant* to cognition—they exert a causal influence on the operation of cognitive mechanisms, but they are not the constituents or components of such mechanisms.

This distinction between causal and constitutive relevance is one of the major points of disagreement between proponents of embedded and extended cognition (see Smart 2022a). To settle the ongoing dispute between these opposing philosophical camps, it would help to have a means of determining when a given resource is constitutively relevant to a phenomenon. That is to say, it would be useful to know when a given resource is a *bona fide* part of a given cognitive mechanism (i.e., a mechanism that realizes a cognitive phenomenon). This is sometimes known as the *problem of constitutive relevance* [CHAP_CROSS_REF]. The problem of constitutive relevance is not the only problem that needs to be resolved by the proponents of extended cognition, but it is, nevertheless, an important problem for those who wish to understand the role of bodily and worldly resources in the realization of intelligence (see Smart 2022a).

It might be thought that the study of virtual creatures embedded in virtual worlds is unlikely to yield much in the way of a solution to this particular problem. And yet, the attempt to create virtual versions of extended processes (or extended mechanisms) does, I think, produce a number of important insights. Consider, by way of example, the attempt to model the processes by which a spider spins a web. Drawing on prior ethological work, Krink and Vollrath (1998) implemented a virtual robot spider that constructed a virtual web. The precise details of this work need not concern us here. What matters is that a virtual world is being used to explore the mechanisms associated with a real-world form of intelligence, albeit one exhibited by an arthropod. Also important is the role of the spider's body in ensuring a successful outcome. As it turns out, spiders use their bodies as something akin to a representational device that helps them coordinate bodily responses with the demands of the web-weaving process. Initially, the spider produces a few strands of silk that attach themselves to surrounding environmental structures (e.g., an overhead branch). These strands then act as a constraint on the spatial positioning of the spider's legs. As each leg comes to rest on a given strand of silk, it yields a certain pattern of proprioceptive input regarding the angular displacement of the leg relative to the spider's body. As it turns out, this is all that is required for the spider to spin the web. In response to different patterns of sensory input (i.e., leg configurations), the spider produces further strands of silk, and each silk-producing action works to further constrain the bio-external problem space in which the spider operates.

To my mind, there ought to be little problem in recognizing this process as a candidate extended process. (Whether it counts as a specifically *cognitive* process is, I think, less clear, but let's park that.[1]) In considering spiders, it is natural for us to see them as the bearers of a particular sort of dispositional property. In particular, we deem them to be capable of producing a variety of silk-related artifacts, the canonical example being an orb web. Spiders, then, have a particular dispositional property, namely, a *capacity* to spin a web. Let us denote the spider as S and the relevant dispositional property as D. When the spider spins a web, it is engaged in a particular process. This is the process of spinning a web. Let us denote this process as P. P reflects the manifestation or exercise of D, which, recall, is ascribed to the spider S. P is realized by a mechanism (M), but this mechanism does not appear to be one that is confined to the biological borders of S. M is what we might call an *extended mechanism*. It is a mechanism that includes components (specifically, silk threads) that lie external to the thing to which a given dispositional property is ascribed.[2]

This gives us a rough and ready way of understanding the status of M as a specifically extended mechanism, and thus the status of P as an extended P (see Smart 2022b). But why should we regard the silk threads as constitutively relevant to P? What is it that makes these extra-organismic resources part of the mechanism (M) that realizes the relevant process (P)?

From a purely engineering perspective, this question is apt to sound a little odd. It is a bit like asking an automobile engineer how they know that a piston forms part of the propulsion mechanism for a conventional car. The reason the question sounds odd is because the problem of constitutive relevance is more a problem in the philosophy of science than it is the philosophy of engineering. From an engineering standpoint, there is no mystery as to how the web-spinning mechanism works or what the components of this mechanism are. This is because the engineer (the maker of mechanisms) is not in the same epistemic position as the scientist (the discoverer of mechanisms). The scientist needs to determine the causal structure of a mechanism, and this requires them to perform experiments that establish the precise causal role of each of the constituents within the mechanism. This is where we run into the problem of constitutive relevance (see Craver et al. 2021). For the engineer, however, there is no problem of constitutive relevance, for the causal structure of the mechanism is not something that needs to be determined: this causal structure has already been determined by the engineer as part of the mechanism design process. For the engineer, then, there is nothing to be gained by subjecting the mechanism to interventionist-style experimental manipulations, for such interventions will not tell the engineer anything that they do not already know, at least in regard to matters of constitutive relevance (see Smart 2022c). In the web-spinning case, we already know how the relevant mechanism works: the spider produces the silk, which constrains the spatial positioning of the spider's legs, which influences subsequent silk-producing actions, and round and round we go until the web is complete. This *is* the mechanism, and the mechanism is constituted by resources that correspond to the spider's 'brain' (the control system), the spider's body, and the silk threads that are produced as part of the web-spinning process. This may not be the actual mechanism that underlies real-world cases of spider-web weaving, but it is nevertheless a mechanism that is sufficient to realize a particular sort of functionality, and it is, moreover, a mechanism that has the hallmarks of an extended mechanism—a mechanism that features the inter-operation of forces and factors that are distributed across brain, body, and world.

My point here is not so much that virtual reality enables us to resolve the problem of constitutive relevance; it is more that a synthetically-oriented shift in our approach to the study of embodied systems alters the way we think about this problem. The problem of constitutive relevance arises whenever we confront a naturally occurring phenomenon, one whose mechanistic underpinnings are unknown to us. But this problem need not arise in the virtual world. In the Matrix, we know where the borders and boundaries of mechanisms lie. They lie precisely where the engineer (the maker of mechanisms) puts them.[3]

The Virtues of the Virtual

The construction of virtual worlds and virtual creatures is, of course, not the only means of prompting this synthetically-oriented shift in our approach to the problem of constitutive relevance. Instead of building a virtual creature, one could attempt to build a physical robot and study its performance in the real world. Perhaps, then, there is not much to be gained by the study of virtual mechanisms in virtual reality. Rather than rely on virtual reality, we should perhaps turn our attention to real-world implementations of embodied cognitive mechanisms.

The problem with this approach is that it overlooks many of the benefits of virtual reality. Consider the aforementioned web-spinning scenario. A real-world implementation of this scenario requires us to build a physical robot, but this effort, it should be clear, is not straightforward. Nor is the relevant implementation effort particularly 'cheap' in terms of the amount of time, effort, and often money that must be spent to achieve an accurate representation of the spider's morphological and biomechanical properties. The virtue of the virtual in this respect is that it often simplifies the effort to study the mechanisms that underlie various forms of embodied intelligence.

This is not to say that the engineering of virtual creatures is particularly easy or straight-forward. Such efforts often rely on a great deal of computational expertise, and not every-one will be in a position to design a 3D representation of a spider's body, replete with articulated joints, deformable materials, and a species-specific skeletal 'rig'. In general, however, this expertise is becoming increasingly available due to the growing interest in virtual reality, the widespread availability of game creation systems (such as Unity and Unreal), and the recent growth in so-called asset stores, which support the global sharing of virtual (reality) assets. This speaks to another benefit of virtual reality. Virtual assets are digital assets, and digital assets can be shared in a way that physical assets (e.g., a physical robot) cannot. Once designed, a virtual creature can be made available to a global commu-nity of researchers who can then incorporate the design into their own simulations. This is not something that can be readily achieved with a physical robot.

There are other virtues hereabouts. As noted by de Melo et al. (2022), virtual environ-ments permit a great deal of control over the structure of the environment in which a virtual creature is embedded. This can be important when it comes to establishing ground truth information, which is often important for machine learning.

Virtual environments also permit control over many of the forces and factors that govern intelligent behavior. If, for example, we want to know how maturational shifts in bodily parameters (e.g., changes in body morphology, sensor acuity, or motor function) affect the structure of intelligent behavior, then we can do this in the virtual world without the need to repeatedly disassemble and reassemble a physical robot.

There is a further virtue of virtual reality that is worth mentioning here. It concerns the way in which the recent interest in all things virtual provides us with an important oppor-tunity to expand the reach of embodied cognitive science, especially when it comes to the 'gamification' of research problems. Consider, by way of example, the attempt to design (or grow, or train, or evolve) a collection of robotic drones intended for off-world exploration (e.g., a fully autonomous Martian robot). Such design efforts could easily be rendered as a form of game, whereby candidate designs are both created and evaluated by a global com-munity of citizen scientists (or citizen engineers) (see Smart 2020a). Even if such efforts do not culminate in the development of an actual physical robot, they nevertheless provide an important opportunity for folks to learn about the various forces and factors that govern the shape of intelligent behavior, and this includes the role of the body (and body-world interactions) in determining both cognitive success and failure.

Mind the Gap

Notwithstanding the virtues of virtual reality, I suspect some will want to challenge the idea that the study of virtual creatures can yield much in the way of progress for our understand-ing of embodied cognition. High on the list of potential gripes is likely to be something called the *reality gap problem* (see Howard et al. 2021). This problem concerns the mis-match between the virtual and the 'real'—the fact that no matter how hard we try, there is always likely to be something missing from a virtual world. A virtual world, it seems, is no more than a mere approximation of the real world, and thus a reliance on the virtual could easily lead us to overlook some explanatorily crucial factor, one that is present in the real-world but absent from its virtual counterpart.

This is, to be sure, an important worry, and it is one that has led some scholars to eschew a commitment to virtual reality, as well as other forms of computer simulation. Brooks (1991: 140), for example, suggests that: "At each step we should build complete intelligent systems that we let loose in the real world with real sensing and real action. Anything less provides a candidate with which we can delude ourselves." Similarly, Pfeifer and Iida (2004: 18) argue that the "move into the real world" constitutes a grand challenge for work in embodied AI. "True intelligence," they suggest, "always requires the interaction with the real world."

Given these complaints, it seems that a preoccupation with virtual creatures and virtual worlds might be something of a mistake for the proponent of embodied cognition. Rather than direct our attention to virtual creatures and virtual worlds, it seems that we ought instead focus our attention on the realm of real-world embodied cognitive systems, mechanisms, and processes. To do otherwise is to risk an unwelcome form of computational abstraction, one that (historically speaking) much of the work in embodied cognitive science has sought to guard against.[4]

There is undoubtedly something important about the reality gap problem, but the problem is, I think, often overstated. Consider the aforementioned case of a virtual spider spinning a virtual web. The task of creating a lightweight miniature physical robot with the sensory and motoric competencies of a real-world spider is, at best, a difficult undertaking. Indeed, I doubt that is even possible with current technology. In what sense, then, does a focus on real-world systems enable us to close the purported reality gap when it comes to our understanding of a naturally-occurring case of embodied intelligence? Is it really possible, for example, to build a physical robotic spider with all the flexibility of its biological counterpart? Can we emulate the representational capacities engendered by the presence of eight articulated appendages? And what about the properties of the silk thread that play a crucial role in the overall problem-solving process? Can we really produce synthetic silk with all the material properties of biological silk, and, if not, how does the focus on real-world instantiations of the web weaving process help us understand the role of such properties in yielding the particular form of embodied intelligence that we are trying to emulate? Won't the exclusion of these properties exacerbate the risk of overlooking some explanatory crucial factor?

To be sure, there are clearly some situations where real-world analytic and synthetic efforts are indispensable for our understanding of embodied cognition. No one, I think, would want to question that. But to insist that a preoccupation with virtual reality risks the introduction of some sort of 'gap' is either to underestimate the sophistication of contemporary virtual reality technology or to overestimate our current abilities to recapitulate the features of bio-cognitive systems in a purely physical medium.

A further shortcoming of the reality gap problem is that it relies on a tacit assumption regarding the nature of reality itself. What proponents typically mean by the reality gap is that there is some sort of mismatch between the realm of the virtual and the 'real'—a difference between the realms of virtual and physical reality. But the notion of physical reality is not, I think, as clear-cut as the proponents of the reality gap problem seem to think. Physical reality is often understood as the sort of reality that exists here on planet Earth. It is, moreover, the sort of reality that human beings are familiar with, courtesy of our species-specific sensorimotor capabilities. Realities are, however, somewhat variable. Suppose, for the sake of example, that our aim is not merely to replicate the sorts of embodied intelligence that we find here on Earth, but to engineer embodied systems that are tasked with the exploration of extra-terrestrial environments, e.g., the oceans of Europa or the skies of Titan. In such cases, it should be clear that any robust commitment to the 'real' (or physical) is unlikely to pose much of a solution to the reality gap problem. The reason is that one cannot replicate the precise details of a remote alien environment within the comfort of one's terrestrial home. In order to deal with the vagaries of alien environmental conditions, one cannot merely study the performance of embodied robotic vehicles here on Earth, for to do this is to introduce a reality gap that is no less cavernous than that which motivates concerns about the ostensible shortcomings of virtual reality. Arguably, the best place to study the performance of robots intended for off-world exploration is within an environment that emulates the properties of the alien world that the robot will eventually inhabit. If, for example, one wants to understand the best bodily design for a Lunar robot, then it is arguably important to test candidate body designs in an environment that replicates the same gravitational forces as those encountered on the surface of the Moon. There is little point in trying to test such solutions in a terrestrial gravitational environment, for once the robot is dispatched to its Lunar destination, it will probably never encounter this sort of gravitational environment again. In such situations, the reality gap problem looms large, but this problem is not so much the mismatch between the virtual and the real; it is more the mismatch between our local terrestrial reality and the sort of reality that is to be found beyond the terrestrial frontier.

There are, then, some reasons to think that the reality gap problem is not necessarily narrowed by directing our attention to the realm of physical reality. But what about Pfeifer and Iida's (2004: 18) claim that "true intelligence *always* requires the interaction with the real world" (emphasis added)? Insofar as we can even make sense of the notion that there is a form of 'true' intelligence that ought to be distinguished from intelligence of the (one presumes) more ersatz variety, it is worth noting, I think, that advances in virtual reality are increasingly challenging the distinction between the virtual and the physical. In part this is due to technological advances in virtual reality; e.g., the development of increasingly sophisticated physics engines, the development of 3D models for biomimetic character animation, and the development of photorealistic graphics rendering pipelines. Beyond this, however, it is not clear that the search for genuine forms of intelligence ought to be limited to the world of the physical and the real—the sort of world to which we are accustomed.

Consider, by way of example, the fictional character of Joi in the movie *Blade Runner 2049* (Smart 2020b). Joi is a hologrammatic entity whose behavior is suggestive of a high degree of intelligence. Joi is, of course, a fictional character—a cinematic (hologrammatic) entity embedded within a cinematic (photonic) medium. But the fictional scenario speaks to the contemporary interest in using virtual reality as a means for instantiating new kinds of intelligent systems, including virtual humans (see Burden and Savin-Baden 2019). It is perhaps easy to assume that there is something 'unreal' about these virtual creatures, but the entire point of movies such as *Blade Runner 2049* is to challenge our intuitions on this front. In what sense would a Joi-like, hologrammatic entity fail to count as truly or genuinely intelligent? And what right do we have to insist that our reality (whatever that means) is the only place where *bona fide* forms of intelligence are to be found? Doesn't a consideration of virtual creatures open the door to the possibility that perfectly genuine forms of intelligence might emerge from the forms of photic flux that define the moving image? A virtual creature is, I suggest, not some sort of 'unreal' creature. Nor is it clear that such creatures ought to be seen as entirely virtual in nature. A virtual creature is a creature produced by computational processes, and there is nothing unreal or non-physical about computational processes. What is perhaps distinctive about virtual creatures is that they inhabit a photonic (or cinematic) medium. They are, perhaps, beings that are constituted (at least in part) by photonic elements. But is there any reason why the photonic medium should not be home to the next generation of intelligent (perhaps even conscious) beings? To my mind, this possibility sounds no less implausible than the idea that intelligence should emerge from the forms of electrochemical flux that characterize the whirrings and grindings of the biological brain.

At the end of the day, a virtual world is the product of a generative process that relies on one or more computationally-defined generative models (e.g., a model that describes the propagation of light or the operation of physical forces). But is this so very different to the idea that our own human forms of intelligence (including perhaps our conscious experiences) are tied to the operation of neurally-realized generative models (see Clark 2019)? Interestingly, one of the emerging areas of virtual reality research is what is called neural rendering, which relies on the use of deep generative models to produce photorealistic outputs (see de Melo et al. 2022). The resulting virtual realities might be seen as the real-world counterparts to the sorts of 'controlled hallucination' that define the shape of our own phenomenal experiences. In this sense, our human conscious experiences might be seen as a form of virtual reality—as a cinematic rendering of the real. Few, I suspect, would argue that human consciousness ought to lie beyond the realms of embodied cognitive science. But if that is so, then perhaps the proponent of embodied cognition ought not be so hasty in choosing between the proverbial red and blue pills. Rather than eschewing virtual reality, perhaps we are better off furrowing ever-deeper into the Matrix. At the very least, it will be interesting to see just how deep the rabbit hole goes.

Notes

1 This problem is not the same as the problem of constitutive relevance. It concerns the status of a phenomenon as a specifically cognitive phenomenon. This is what is known as the problem of cognitive status (Smart 2022a) or the mark of the cognitive problem (Adams and Garrison 2013).

2 Note that it would make no sense in this situation to say that D belongs to an 'extended' systemic organization comprising both the spider and the web (or the silk threads that comprise the web). The reason for this is that prior to the commencement of P, there is no web (nor are there any silk threads). The relevant extra-organismic resources are manufactured during the course of P, so it cannot be the case that such resources are the partial bearers of D, for prior to the initiation of P (which, recall, is the manifestation of D) there is no extended organization to which D could be ascribed.

3 This is, at least, the case for mechanisms that we ourselves design. In cases where a mechanism arises as the result of evolutionary processes (e.g., the use of genetic algorithms), then the causal structure of a mechanism may not be so clear-cut. In such cases, the engineer is placed in the same sort of epistemic position as the scientist. That is to say, the engineer needs to 'reverse engineer' the evolved mechanism, so as to understand how it works relative to the phenomenon (e.g., the process) that it realizes.

4 There is an associated issue here regarding the extent to which a virtual creature could be seen to possess a body. A virtual body, it might be thought, cannot count as a 'real' body, and therefore a virtual creature cannot count as a genuinely embodied system. This sort of problem—call it *the embodiment problem*—rejects the idea that there is any sort of virtual embodiment. Virtual creatures are little more than computational entities, and such entities are typically understood to be the opposite of embodied. Rather than being embodied creatures, they are more often understood to be disembodied. This sort of problem is discussed by Wheeler (2013). Wheeler suggests that a functionalist conception of the body allows for the possibility of virtual embodiment. According to this proposal, a virtual creature is no less embodied than is its physical (real-world) counterpart.

References

Adams, F., and Garrison, R. (2013) "The mark of the cognitive," *Minds and Machines*, 23(3), 339–352.

Brooks, R. A. (1991) "Intelligence without representation," *Artificial Intelligence*, 47, 139–160.

Burden, D., and Savin-Baden, M. (2019) *Virtual Humans: Today and Tomorrow*, CRC Press, London, UK.

Clark, A. (2019) "Consciousness as generative entanglement," *The Journal of Philosophy*, 116(12), 645–662.

Craver, C. F., Glennan, S., and Povich, M. (2021) "Constitutive relevance and mutual manipulability revisited," *Synthese*, 199(3), 8807–8828.

de Melo, C. M., Torralba, A., Guibas, L., DiCarlo, J., Chellappa, R., and Hodgins, J. (2022) "Next-generation deep learning based on simulators and synthetic data," *Trends in Cognitive Sciences*, 26(2), 174–187.

Howard, D., Collins, J., and Robinson, N. (2021) "Taking shape: A perspective on the future of embodied cognition and a new generation of evolutionary robotics," *IOP Conference Series: Materials Science and Engineering*, 1261, Article 012018.

Krink, T., and Vollrath, F. (1998) "Emergent properties in the behaviour of a virtual spider robot," *Proceedings of the Royal Society of London B: Biological Sciences*, 265(1410), 2051–2055.

Nikolenko, S. I. (2021) *Synthetic Data for Deep Learning*, Springer, Cham, Switzerland.

Pfeifer, R., and Iida, F. (2004) "Embodied Artificial Intelligence: Trends and Challenges," in F. Iida, R. Pfeifer, L. Steels and Y. Kuniyoshi (eds.), *Embodied Artificial Intelligence* (pp. 1–26). Springer-Verlag, Berlin, Germany.

Smart, P. R. (2020a) "Planet Braitenberg: Experiments in virtual psychology," *Cognitive Systems Research*, 64, 73–95.

——— (2020b) "The Joi of Holograms," in T. Shanahan and P. R. Smart (eds.), *Blade Runner 2049: A Philosophical Exploration* (pp. 127–148), Routledge, Abingdon, Oxon, UK.

——— (2022a) "Toward a mechanistic account of extended cognition," *Philosophical Psychology*, 35(8), 1107–1135.

——— (2022b) "Extended X: Extending the reach of active externalism," available at: http://doi.org/10.2139/ssrn.4106401

——— (2022c) "Minds in the metaverse: Extended cognition meets mixed reality," *Philosophy and Technology*, 35(Article 87), 1–29.

Terzopoulos, D., Tu, X., and Grzeszczuk, R. (1994) "Artificial fishes: Autonomous locomotion, perception, behavior, and learning in a simulated physical world," *Artificial Life*, 1(4), 327–351.

Wheeler, M. (2013) "What Matters: Real Bodies and Virtual Worlds," in I. Harvey, A. Cavoukian, G. Tomko, D. Borrett, H. Kwan and D. Hatzinakos (eds.), *SmartData: Privacy Meets Evolutionary Robotics* (pp. 69–80), Springer, New York, USA.

26

EMBODIED COGNITION AND MOVEMENT-DRIVEN PRACTICES

Zuzanna Rucińska and Susanne Ravn

In this chapter we focus on embodied engagement in movement-driven practices. In these practices, athletes strive to enhance their performance, and must, in different conditions, "think on the fly" while performing. Sport is a prototypical example of such embodied engagement; however movement-driven practices extend beyond traditional sports. Throughout the chapter, we provide examples of these different practices, such as boxing, climbing, aikido, dance and esports.[1] These activities present a specific kind of window for investigating and understanding the substantial role of the body in cognition. We argue for using a *strongly embodied cognitive* approach to provide a new perspective on how bodily and worldly aspects of practitioners' real-time engagement in an activity are part of such "thinking on the fly". We first describe and discuss the concept of Strong Embodied Cognition (EC). From a Strong EC approach to skillful action, we focus on how it is that thinking (including planning, reflecting and creativity) takes place as a strongly embodied process in different kinds of activities. We then consider the role of embodiment for incorporation of skills and interactive sense-making of expert athletes, and end with a discussion of the role of embodiment in esports and how esports constructively challenge the Strong EC approach.

Strong embodied cognition

Embodied Cognition (EC) is a research program in philosophy and cognitive science that conceives our cognitive capacities as dependent not just on what is happening in our brains, but also in substantial ways on our bodies and interactions with our environments. While many have embraced EC as a useful framework to reconceive the role of embodiment for cognition, especially in understanding cognitive capacities of athletes (Sutton 2007; Newen et al. 2018; Cappuccio 2019), some are skeptical of the reach of EC. Skeptics propose that embodiment primarily supports cognitive processing that is still essentially internal and representational (Adams and Aizawa 2008; Goldman and de Vignemont 2009). To clarify this, we propose to make a distinction between Strong and Weak EC (Alsmith and de Vignemont 2012; see also Gallagher and Rucińska 2021).

DOI: 10.4324/9781003322511-34

Strong EC proposes that cognition is rooted in motoric processes that operate in occurrent action, and that embodied cognition is *explicit*, in that bodily postures, proprioception, movement and body-environment coupling are active parts of cognitive processing. In short, the body features *in the process* of thinking.[2] In comparison, Weak EC endorses cognitivist assumptions by finding explanations in neuronal processing, "body-formatted representations", or internal representations of motor commands (Goldman 2006; Goldman and de Vignemont 2009; van Leeuwen 2011). According to Weak EC, the body informs the content of a representation but is not part of the process of thinking. This is a popular view amongst internalists, who acknowledge that embodiment plays some role in cognition but maintain that cognition is first and foremost representational, involving computations over information. In our view, Weak EC does not go far enough. Strong EC gives a "clear explanatory role to the body" (Alsmith and de Vignemont 2012: 3), referring to the role that the extra-neural body plays in cognition,[3] and recognizing that movement-driven performances involve the body in a way that cannot be uncoupled from the environment – not even in a virtual environment.

We propose that there is an added value in endorsing the Strong EC perspective in the context of sport psychology and movement-driven practices. The added value is that it can help us understand specific features of athletes' cognition and sporting practices that Weak EC cannot. Among these features is the role of bodily structures in constraining how an athlete performs a task, the role of environmental affordances in relation to action possibilities, and the role of interactions for developing cognitive, perceptual and even imaginative abilities of athletes. In response to Shapiro and Spaulding's question, "What new or novel connections between mind and body has embodied cognition discovered?" (2019: 4), we argue that Strong EC can further explicate central aspects of the integration between the athlete's mind and body. Strong EC (i) provides a new perspective on what constitutes *thinking* in sport, challenging, for instance, the distinction between *convergent* and *divergent* thinking found in sports psychology, (ii) facilitates a specific outlook on *skills* and on how they are central to "thinking on the fly", and (iii) brings forward the importance of *participatory sense-making* in sport, constructively adding to our understanding of how sense-making is *culturally embedded*. We will discuss these points in turn below.

Strongly embodied thinking

The Strong EC perspective rejects standard proposals on reflective thinking, planning and decision-making, treating them as slow and conscious internal processes. In these proposals, planning is typically seen as representing the action goal then selecting the means necessary to achieve it (Maldonato et al. 2019). Strong EC seeks to dismantle certain dichotomies created to account for decision-making processes, such as characterizing acts as mindful or mindless, being engaged in reflective thought vs. being in the "flow" (Dreyfus 2002), characterizing thinking as "fast or slow" (Kahneman 2011) or positing dual cognitive processes, such as rapid and autonomous (Type 1) vs. higher-order reasoning (Type 2) processes (Evans and Stanovich 2013). For instance, according to Evans and Stanovich, Type 1 processes "yield default responses unless intervened on by distinctive higher order reasoning [Type 2] processes" (*ibid.*: 223).[4] Thus, the latter – conscious, controlled and rule-based processes – are said to be involved in and responsible for planning and decision-making aspects in a performance.

The Strong EC alternative does not separate decision-making processes from action but situates them *in* the ongoing embodied activity of the performing agent. The idea of situated decision-making is in line with the hybrid understanding presented in the "Mesh" approach (Christensen et al. 2016), where control and decision-making are viewed as flexible ways of integrating information without explicit inferential reasoning processes. Strong EC proposes that skillful action involves dynamic processes that span brain, body and environment. On this view, cognitive processes should be identified with "bouts of extensive, embodied activity that take the form of more of less successful organism-environment couplings" (Hutto et al. 2019: 37). The dichotomy between acting deliberately and making plans *versus* being "absorbed" in the flow of the activity is challenged, because being absorbed can also be a *mindful* act (when one is paying attention to or monitoring what one is doing), just as planning can be done in the flow of the activity (cf. Christensen et al. 2015; Montero 2016).

Let us consider an example of how Strong EC can distance itself from a dualism between *convergent* and *divergent* thinking, popularized in sports psychological literature by Guilford (1967). As Memmert, Baker and Bertsch (2010: 4) claim, "[c]onvergent thinking refers to the ability to find the ideal solution to a given problem". It is seen as needed for planning the best move, where one is planning ahead of the activity and evaluating the best course of action that should follow. It reflects "rational" decision-making processes, such as that of an expert who has the ability to evaluate what is the best tactical solution to a given problem. Divergent thinking, in turn, is said to involve thinking of new or unusual solutions or engaging in flexible decision-making. It is "defined at the behavioral level as the unusualness, innovativeness, statistical rareness, or even uniqueness of solutions to a related task" (*ibid*). It is connected to a competence for generating many diverse ideas, which in sport is often associated with tactical creativity.

Strong EC does not oppose the idea that one can be engaged in more or less creative vs. targeted or goal-oriented activities (as seen in planning). However, it does find problematic the assumption that these activities must be driven by distinct "convergent and divergent" thought processes, which map onto specific, underlying, internal cognitive structures. Convergent thinking is, to date, explained through the *mental models* theory (Goodwin and Johnson-Laird 2005), according to which "humans construct internal representation of objects and relations in working memory" in order to perform relational inferences (Razumnikova 2013: 549). This assumes that planning is done in a complex internal cognitive architecture that allows one to represent the best outcome of an action, in advance of the action, by "selecting the single correct response" and "inhibit[ing] creative thought" (Razumnikova 2013: 549).[5] According to this approach, convergent thinking takes place when divergent thinking does not, which is problematic, as planning and being creative are not necessarily in opposition to one another.[6] Divergent thinking, in turn, is conceptualized as combining ideas in unexpected or new ways, "generating several possible solutions to an open-ended problem" (Beaty et al. 2016: 88) or "generating a large number of alternative responses" (Razumnikova 2013: 547). These are both computational metaphors that suggest that this type of thinking is done *in detachment* from embodiment.

Strong EC proposes a different way to construe planning and creativity that puts embodiment at the center. For one, it suggests that we conceive of planning as "an embodied and situated activity involving ongoing responsiveness to the environmental affordances, directed at optimal performance, without manipulation of mental representations of action goals" (Rucińska 2021: 11). In other words, planning is an ongoing calibration and re-calibration to the environmental affordances that become available when athletes engage in exploratory movements (Seifert et al. 2018). Moreover, according to Strong EC, practices attributed to "divergent thinking" can be achieved by acting flexibly on the affordances of the environment. Novel affordances, in turn, emerge *out of* practitioners' active embodied exploration and manipulation of the environment (Rucińska and Aggerholm 2019). For instance, Hristovski et al. (2011) reported that boxers created new movements that complemented their punching repertoire when they were asked to perform 60 punches at a static heavy-bag from ten different scaled distances, and when the heavy-bag was stochastically moved by an assistant to the left and right, which created new situations for hitting. By manipulating the environment to create a "divergent fist-target angle action configuration" (2011: 193), the boxers were able to create a novel move.

Thus, Strong EC's approach can recharacterize both convergent and divergent thinking through the notion of affordances. It also looks at the situation, not the disembodied thought processes alone: in the situation of planning, the agent is directed towards optimal performance, whereas in the situation of creating, the agent is responsive and open to a variety of affordances. In short, Strong EC holds that there is an active role for our bodies and environments to play in planning and creative thinking. Planning is not a process happening solely "in the head" prior to the acting in the world. And creativity is not necessarily a cognitive or computational trait of an agent. Instead, creativity could be thought of as an aptitude for being responsive to the available affordances of the situation and flexibly handling changes that are the result of the interaction between the agent and their environment.

Let us recapture the different facets of the Strong EC approach by looking at a concrete example: the expert rock climbing of Alex Honnold. Honnold prepares his *free solo* (climbing without a rope) by studying the route to be climbed, "reading" its surface, looking for the best holds, anticipating resting points, and "(v)isualizing every single move, everything that could possibly happen" (Honnold and Roberts 2016: 7; Rucińska 2021). While engaging in the climb, he adjusts his grip and the position of his body to the emerging demands of the climb, responding to the constraints of the rock. How can Strong EC explain Honnold's actions, without talking about mental plans representing the moves to come?

On the Strong EC model, an expert climber like Honnold can directly perceive (or otherwise engage with) the possibilities for action that the rock affords.[7] While on the rock, many climbers engage in exploratory movements that allow them to attune to the ecological information[8] and find the appropriate scaling between this information and their action capabilities (Hacques et al. 2021). The role of the body is clear: the dynamics between the perceptual information the climbers gain when facing the rock, the tactile, sensory and kinesthetic information they gain when touching the rock, the bodily sense of their own action capabilities (to grasp, reach or hold onto a grip), and their emotional and affective states *all come together* in the ongoing planning and re-planning of the climb. Honnold is not just spontaneously adapting to the environment, but mindfully attending to, tracking and selecting the newly discovered possibilities for action that become available in the midst of action and invite further actions.

What about the planning taking place ahead of the climb, before getting up on the rock? Strong EC can account for this, too. Considerations and reflections made before the climb *attune* the climber to the anticipated climbing performance. Those considerations are not necessarily themselves "disembodied": many climbers engage in explicit exploratory gestures (or "marking") when going through route preview (Sanchez-Garcia et al. 2019).

The explicit gesturing done right before the climb is part of the visualizing of how the climbing sequence should unfold – much like dancers who use marking when going over a new choreography. This is a process that is strongly embodied, one that does not need to rely on mental representations. But even without explicit gestures, the imagining of the upcoming climb is strongly embodied as well, as it involves actual motoric activations (Gallagher and Rucińska 2021). Honnold's visualizing of his every move is "densely textured in a cross-modal way: kinetic, tactile, kinesthetic, nociceptive, even olfactory and gustatory dynamics are pertinent" (Ilundáin-Agurruza 2017: 101). Such *corporeal imaginings* (ibid.) are closely tied to the environment, to the embodied expertise of the climber, and are still rooted in bodily processes, which is why they can be meaningfully thought of as explicitly embodied as well.

Incorporation of skills

We now move on to discuss how the Strong EC approach facilitates an outlook on incorporation of skills in movement-driven practices. Strong EC acknowledges that the process of *incorporation* of skills is open-ended and ongoing, and that flexible ways of acting on affordances are central to how athletes develop their way of "thinking on the fly".

In phenomenological descriptions, the incorporation of a skill is taken to be a process in which something that can be seen as extrinsic (e.g., a specified way of moving and acting) is actually grasped and brought forth within a body, so that it pervades the practitioner's way of being in the world by modifying their "very practical-perceptual relationship to the world, [their] '*I can*'" (Merleau-Ponty 2012; Leder 1990). Along with these descriptions it is emphasized that the process of incorporating a skill is also partly a matter of learning to perceive opportunities to exercise it. Having incorporated new skills entails that practitioners relate to environments and interact with others on novel conditions. For instance, after having practiced different kinds of jumps and moves in selected places in the city, skilled parkour runners start seeing the urban environment in new ways (Højbjerre Larsen 2016).

Skilled practitioners who are deliberately engaging in sports, dance, or martial arts also *strive for improvement* in different ways and degrees. Here it is important to make a distinction between the skilled engagements in movement-driven practices and everyday movement activities, like walking, running, or climbing the stairs, as the activities that demand striving for improvement differ from everyday activities of going about things (Breivik 2016; Ravn 2022a).[9] Everyday movement activities exemplify abilities that most people are able to do without having to engage in specific kinds of training. For example, running to catch a bus does not demand the specialized skills that are needed to perform in a 100-meter sprint, such as pushing off the ground and using the arms in active ways to gain extra momentum. Striving for improvement requires the athletes to engage in an ongoing process of developing their skills according to specific criteria of success and improvement as defined within the activity they are engaged in. In this process, sensing and adjusting to the environment are finetuned and expanded. This process is rarely immediately visible when the practice is observed from a third-person perspective. What might look like mere repetition of "automatized motor-actions" in fact involves ongoing deliberate engagement: trying things out or pushing things further, like attuning, nuancing and/or moderating the sensorial attention on micro-levels of the performance (Christensen et al. 2016).

Incorporating certain basic skills frees the athletes to attend to other aspects of their performances, whilst also giving shape to, and further informing, these kinds of attention.

For instance, a novice mountain biker focuses on getting their weight placed towards the back of the bike and adjusting their grip the right way for downhill riding on a given slope. But the skilled mountain biker, who has incorporated these kinds of adjustments on a body-schematic level, can engage in downhill riding on the same kind of slope while focusing on other aspects of their performance. The skilled rider will be able, for instance, to look at what lies ahead on the trail, and adjust to the grip, placement, gear and weight of the bike in order to cope with both the "here and now" demands of the race, and the challenges to come a few seconds later (Christensen et al. 2015). This allows them to adjust in optimal ways to the performative demands of the ride.

When skilled athletes become still more experienced, they move and use their attention in more sophisticated ways, guided directly by their perception and sensations. The skilled biker becomes more experienced in using the bike as a sophisticated tool, as they immediately adjust the way they distribute their weight while biking in unknown terrain. Skilled parkour runners are continuously responsive to the material surfaces of the wall as they intelligently handle stability and spatiality of their movement. Just as in the case of the skilled climber, these athletes have incorporated a sense of weight, grip and positioning that are central to the ways they engage with their environments, which allows them to develop still more specified ways of "seeing" the biking, running or climbing opportunities.

Interactive and culturally embedded sense-making

Until now, our descriptions of movement-driven practices have been focused on athletes as individual agents. But many movement-driven practices also involve direct and continuous *interactions* with other practitioners – while playing a ball game, dancing Argentinean tango, sparring with a partner in boxing or cycling in a competition. Take, for example, how Tour-de-France cyclists perform as part of a team. They must respond to the cyclists around them (competitors and teammates) and at the same time communicate with the manager of the team (heard through the earphones), all the while attending to the road. This demands close coordination and communication skills with their teammates, and re-planning of strategies in relation to the opponents. How does the Strong EC approach help us understand these practices better?

First, it facilitates our understanding of how perception–action dynamics can extend beyond the singularized body. According to De Jaegher and Di Paolo (2007), agents make sense of the world and their experiences in it through coordinated interaction. De Jaegher and Di Paolo have coined the term *participatory sense-making* to characterize the way meaning is generated and transformed in the unfolding interaction processes of agents. They specify that this interplay is displayed in co-regulated dynamics of coordination, which fluctuates between phases of synchronized, de-synchronized and in-between states. Such co-regulated dynamics can be recognized in analyses of actual practices, such as in Argentinean tango and elite sports dancing (Ravn 2016, 2019). The dancers report that they sense their movement *through* the movement of their partner, and in moments of synchronization, experience the interaction as having a life of its own – that they are being "danced by the dance". The actual steps taken and the way the dance is performed are shaped through the dyadic coordination between the dancers.[10]

Second, the Strong EC approach can capture specific aspects of how skilled performances are also socially mediated and *culturally embedded*. This might not be immediately apparent in sporting events taking place on global stages, orchestrated according to internationally defined rules and ideals. However, this aspect has been given specific attention in movement-driven practices that are closely linked to a specific cultural heritage. Consider the practice of the martial art form *aikido*, which is closely interwoven with Japanese apprenticeship and learning traditions. Japanese heritage both constrains and enables the aikido practice. There is a clear code of conduct, which includes a dress code (white *gi*, belt, *hakama* – traditional Japanese pants), ways of sitting on your knees (*seiza*), and ways of respectfully bowing to the opponent before and after an interaction. These codes of conduct facilitate a sense of interconnectedness to the other practitioners and constitute an "aikido ecology" (Ravn 2022b). Wearing the *gi* and *hakama* affects the practitioner's ways of carrying and sensing their body and influences how they engage in a specific technique with a partner. We can even speak of aikido-specific *sense-making*: processes of coordinating values and intentions, incorporating techniques and codes of conduct, harmonizing with the other, and the various sensations gained from the dress code, all of which interweave with the athlete's bodily style of performing aikido. In other words, mere "learning of correct moves" is not doing aikido. One could, in principle, selectively learn just some of the techniques, but as a martial art practice, aikido cannot be separated from its culture. The Strong EC approach makes it possible to emphasize the interconnectedness of embodiment and socio-cultural situations and can well account for how skilled movement can be part of a culturally embedded system (cf. Mingon and Sutton 2021). As the example indicates, the peculiarity of the clothes, respectful engagement, and continued use of Japanese words are part and parcel of the experience, shaping the embodied processes of what it is to do aikido.

Esports and strong EC

In this section we turn to esports as a paradigmatic case of a skillful practice that uses virtual tools. The appeal of looking at esports through Strong EC is that it takes the virtual phenomena seriously as bodily phenomena. In this section we will show how Strong EC can offer more depth and richness in the analysis of esports than disembodied approaches have historically managed to do.

Esports refers to an interconnection of multiple platforms: computing, gaming, media and a sporting event all wrapped up into one (cf. Jenny et al. 2017). It is seen as a "cybersport" with "athletes" that are electronically extended into digital worlds. Esports practitioners are competitive gamers who digitally compete and engage with virtual spaces in dynamic and highly complex ways. As in any sport, esports experts take control of the game, play the game strategically, and can surprise their opponent with an ability to predict their moves. They show technical dexterity and skillful coordination with a controller, manipulating buttons on a controller to effectively manage their on-screen avatars. Esport performance depends on rapid perception, decision-making, and motor response – in short, a "sporting intelligence" (Kretchmar 2005), allowing the practitioners to solve problems and perform creatively.

However, as esports performances take place in a virtual space aside the physical space, the role of the body is in question. Virtual spaces are seen as spaces where we are dealing with a fictional or a digital body (an avatar), which are "much more limited than nonvirtual bodies, and lack many of their functions" (Chalmers 2017: 341). Furthermore, the virtual movements central to esports performances have been accused of lacking "employment of developed physical skills and abilities within the context of gross physical activity" (Loy

1968: 6). Clearly, throwing virtual three-pointers does not require one to hold a real basketball in one's hands or really throw it. There is no direct contact with material objects (other than the physical gaming peripherals) and other players. Thus, there seems to be a tension between being embodied and being in a virtual space. Can we even understand performances in esports from a Strong EC perspective?

We believe that Strong EC can contribute in a significant way to understanding performances of esports athletes. While mindful of the many senses of the word "embodied" that can be at play here,[11] Strong EC's emphasis on perceptual-motor processes, utilization of motor skills and performance of explicit actions receives expression in esports.

First, the hypothesis of Strong EC is that perception of virtual affordances, or possibilities for action in the virtual world, is based on anticipating actions. That anticipation, in turn, involves bodily perceptual-motor processes that re-enact and rehearse the past, as well as synchronic motor activation of movement-related motor systems (Gallagher and Rucińska 2021). Strong EC therefore proposes that perception of virtual affordances is continuously affected (and constrained) by bodily possibilities – movements one can make and the kinesthetic sensations that accompany them – and by one's specific past bodily actions that have honed their existing skills (Ekdahl and Ravn 2019).

Second, the avatar moving and acting in a virtual world is physically initiated through the players' manipulation of specialized hardware. There are fine motor skills at play, including precise hand movements with increased accuracy and control.[12] One could say that there is genuine action taking place in virtual environments, as users "make real choices, [and] they really do things", in virtual spaces (Chalmers 2017: 339).[13]

Esports athletes are also part of a special environment where they engage with the affordances of the virtual world. Sophisticated users will learn to exploit these distinctive, virtual affordances, which help to train their perception–action loops in the game (Bideau et al. 2010). Thus, they also incorporate the use of virtual tools – tools that form extensions of their bodies. As we saw above, incorporation refers to integration of not just skills, but of equipment and tools as well – tools that can also be computer interfaces or virtual headsets. Such incorporation allows them to have a profound sense of bodily extension and presence in the virtual space (Ekdahl 2021).

Finally, there is an interactive complexity at play in esports. Esports athletes cooperate, communicate and form team dynamics (Ekdahl and Ravn 2022). They also interact as avatars with other avatars in the game, and interact with other teammates playing the game at the same time. Strong EC can propose describing this capacity of attending to both the virtual and the physical space as *double attunement*, an embodied skill whereby the esports practitioner is attuned to both the virtual affordances and the real word at the same time – much like an actor on a stage who is attuned to both what is happening in the play, and to what is happening on the stage in the theater (e.g., the lighting, the audience) (Gallagher and Gallagher 2019).

Thus, one prediction that Strong EC makes is that the embodiment at stake in esports is just typical sensorimotor embodiment, not a special kind of (dis)embodiment – the difference being that one is acting on unusual, *virtual* affordances. The virtual body (including the avatar, but also every ability or tool given to the player) becomes an extension of the biological body of the esports practitioner. One can consider this as "re-embodiment" in the virtual environment – the idea that technologies can become strongly integrated into our living bodies to the point of habituality or mastery (De Preester 2010; Ekdahl 2021).

Conclusion

Strongly embodied cognition offers a richer understanding of movement-driven practices, including sporting and esports performances. It gives a clear explanatory role to the body itself, highlighting the added value of sensorimotor processes and explicit bodily movements for understanding the practices of athletes, such as their capacities for strategic and creative thinking, planning or skillful engagement. Investigations of movement-driven practices indicate that incorporation of skill is open-ended and ongoing, and that skilled performances extend beyond the isolated body and are culturally embedded. By indicating specific body-and-world-involving aspects of "thinking on the fly", they further support a Strong EC approach. Esports are also not off-limits to a Strong EC perspective, which can account for e-athletes' engagement with virtual affordances and their skillful use of virtual tools that form extensions of their bodies. We believe that following a Strong EC approach to cognition presents a unique opportunity to further understand and investigate the cognitive skills of such practitioners and athletes. The ethical and practical consequences following from this perspective for learning environments and sports psychology in general is an important topic for future research.

Notes

1 We categorize these activities as movement-driven practices as they do not always represent a traditional sports discipline or involve sportive competition. Esports is even contested as a sport – but for views to the contrary, see Jenny et al. (2017).
2 Shapiro and Spaulding (2019) distinguish between three themes that the research on embodied cognition investigates: how to conceptualize embodiment, whether embodiment replaces computational processes, and whether embodiment is causal or constitutive to cognition. It is to this distinction that we clarify the position of Strong EC.
3 The explanatory power of Strong EC includes referring to, e.g., postures, movements, or "peripheral sensory organs and effectors in the channeling and structuring of information flow" to explain body schemas (Alsmith and de Vignemont 2012; Gallagher 2006). The added value of endorsing Strong EC explanations is that they are better equipped to account for and incorporate athletes' descriptions of their embodied engagements.
4 Notably, the dual process theory preserves the dichotomy between intelligent and non-intelligent action: the decision-making process has shifted from the personal to the sub-personal level, where it is still separate from the performance. For more on this, see Rucińska (2021).
5 "Convergent thinking narrows the available responses with the goal of selecting the single correct response ... and can inhibit creative though(t) as (it) stops on one most probable idea." (Razumnikova 2013: 549).
6 For instance, thinking of new, creative solutions "on the go" could, at times, involve evaluating what course of action to take. We'd like to thank our editors for this insight.
7 Whether one actually *perceives* affordances, "picks them out", or otherwise engages with them are contested points whose analysis is beyond the scope of this chapter. By speaking of perceiving affordances and treating them as non-representational posits, we follow mainstream ecological psychology, where this term was coined.
8 Ecological information is understood as the perceived patterns of stimulation contingent on the climbers' motion (Seifert et al. 2018). On the relationship between ecological information and affordances, see Heras-Escribano (2019).
9 Accordingly, we make a conceptual distinction between skills and mere abilities. Skills demand deliberate practice and can be evaluated or measured in degrees on the premises of the actual movement activity. In comparison, abilities are to be described according to the familiarity a subject has with the kind of everyday task to be accomplished.
10 The resulting interaction that is coordinated and shared does not, however, entail a loss of individual sense of autonomy. Elite and expert dancers strategically shift their sensorial attention and

know how to attune to the dancing partner *and* at the same time adjust their own bodily movements in dance.

11 When speaking of embodiment, one could refer to, e.g., body schemas, body images, having a continued sense of bodily agency or a sense of bodily ownership of a virtual body (Kilteni et al., 2012).

12 Even gross motor movements can be accounted for, such as with motion-based video games and virtual tools that enable players to move with their whole bodies while having a head-set on – should they be incorporated into esports one day.

13 Chalmers speaks of virtual reality spaces, not esports. However, we believe his point extends to the virtual space of esport as well.

References

Adams, F., and Aizawa, K. (2008) *The Bounds of Cognition*. Malden: Wiley-Blackwell.

Alsmith, A. J. T., and de Vignemont, F. (2012) "Embodying the mind and representing the body," *Review of Philosophy and Psychology, 3*, 1–13.

Beaty, R. E., Benedek, M., Silvia, P. J., and Schacter, D. L. (2016) "Creative cognition and brain network dynamics," *Trends in Cognitive Sciences, 20*(2), 87–95.

Bideau, B., Kulpa, R., Vignais, N., Brault, S., Multon, F., and Craig, C. (2010) "Using virtual reality to analyze sports performance," *IEEE Computer Graphics and Applications, 30*(2), 14–21.

Breivik, G. (2016) "The role of skill in sport," *Sport, Ethics and Philosophy, 10*, 222–236.

Cappuccio, M. L. (Ed.). (2019) *Handbook of Embodied Cognition and Sport Psychology*. Cambridge, MA: The MIT Press.

Chalmers, D. J. (2017) "The virtual and the real," *Disputatio, 9*(46), 309–352.

Christensen, W., Bicknell, K., McIlwain, D., and Sutton, J. (2015) "The sense of agency and its role in strategic control for expert mountain bikers," *Psychology of Consciousness: Theory, Research and Practice, 2*(3), 340–353.

Christensen, W., Sutton, J., and McIlwain, D. (2016) "Cognition in skilled action: Meshed control and the varieties of skill experience," *Mind & Language, 31*(1), 37–66.

De Jaegher, H. and Di Paolo, E. (2007) "Participatory sense-making: An enactive approach to social cognition," *Phenomenology and the Cognitive Sciences, 6*(4): 485–507.

De Preester, H. (2010) "Technology and the body: The (im)possibilitiesof re-embodiment," *Foundations of Science, 16*(2), 119–137.

Dreyfus, H. L. (2002) "Refocusing the question: Can there be skillful coping without propositional representations or brain representations?" *Phenomenology and the Cognitive Sciences, 1*(4), 413–425.

Ekdahl, D. (2021) "Mechanical keyboards and crystal arrows: Incorporation in Esports," *Journal of Consciousness Studies, 28*, 5(6), 30–57.

Ekdahl, D., and Ravn, S. (2019) "Embodied involvement in virtual worlds: The case of eSports practitioners," *Sport, Ethics and Philosophy, 13*(2), 132–144.

——— (2022) "Social bodies in virtual worlds," *Phenomenology and the Cognitive Sciences, 21*(2), 293–316.

Evans, J. S. B., and Stanovich, K. E. (2013) "Dual-process theories of higher cognition: Advancing the debate," *Perspectives on Psychological Science, 8*(3), 223–241.

Gallagher, S. (2006) *How the Body Shapes the Mind*. Oxford: Oxford University Press.

Gallagher, S., and Gallagher, J. (2019) "Acting oneself as another: An actor's empathy for her character," *Topoi, 39*(1), 1–12.

Gallagher, S., and Rucińska, Z. (2021) "Prospecting performance: Rehearsal and the nature of imagination," *Synthese, 199*(1–2), 4523–4541.

Goldman, A., and de Vignemont, F. (2009) "Is social cognition embodied?" *Trends in Cognitive Sciences, 13*(4), 154–159.

Goldman, A. I. (2006) *Simulating Minds: The Philosophy, Psychology, and Neuroscience of Mindreading*. Oxford: Oxford University Press.

Goodwin, G., and Johnson-Laird, P. (2005) "Reasoning about relations," *Psychological Review, 112*(2), 468–493.

Guilford, J. P. (1967) *The Nature of Human Intelligence*. New York: McGraw-Hill.

Hacques, G., Komar, J., Dicks, M., and Seifert, L. (2021) "Exploring to learn and learning to explore," *Psychological Research*, 85(4), 1367–1379.

Heras-Escribano, M. (2019) *The Philosophy of Affordances*. Cham: Palgrave Macmillan.

Højbjerre Larsen, S. (2016) "What can the parkour craftsmen tell us about bodily expertise and skilled movement?" *Sport, Ethics and Philosophy*, 10(3), 295–309.

Honnold, A., and Roberts, D. (2016) *Alone on the Wall*. New York, NY: W.W. Norton and Co.

Hristovski, R., Davids, K., Araujo, D., and Passos, P. (2011) "Constraints-induced emergence of functional novelty in complex neurobiological systems: A basis for creativity in sport," *Nonlinear Dynamics, Psychology, and Life Sciences*, 15(2), 175–206.

Hutto, D. D., Kirchhoff, M. D., and Renshaw, I. (2019) "Emotions on the playing field," in M. L. Cappuccio (Ed.), *Handbook of Embodied Cognition and Sport Psychology* (pp. 23–46). Cambridge, MA: MIT Press.

Ilundáin-Agurruza, J. (2017) "Muscular imaginings—A phenomenological and enactive model for imagination," *Sport, Ethics and Philosophy*, 11(1), 92–108.

Jenny, S. E., Manning, R. D., Keiper, M. C., and Olrich, T. W. (2017) "Virtual(ly) athletes: Where eSports fit within the definition of 'sport'," *Quest*, 69(1), 1–18.

Kahneman, D. (2011) *Thinking, Fast and Slow*. New York: Macmillan.

Kilteni, K., Groten, R., and Slater, M. (2012) "The sense of embodiment in virtual reality," *Presence Teleoperators and Virtual Environments*, 21(4), 373–387.

Kretchmar, R. S. (2005) *Practical Philosophy of Sport and Physical Activity*. Champaign, IL: Human Kinetics.

Leder, D. (1990) *The Absent Body*. Chicago: The University of Chicago Press.

Loy, J. W. (1968) "The nature of sport: A definitional effort," *Quest*, 10(1), 1–15.

Maldonato, N. M., Oliverio, A., and Esposito, A. (2019) "Prefiguration, anticipation, and improvisation: A neurocognitive and phenomenological perspective," in M. L. Cappuccio (Ed.), *Handbook of Embodied Cognition and Sport Psychology* (pp. 695–721). Cambridge, MA: MIT Press.

Memmert, D., Baker, J., and Bertsch, C. (2010) "Play and practice in the development of sport-specific creativity in team ball sports," *High Ability Studies*, 21(1), 3–18.

Merleau-Ponty, M. (2012) *The Phenomenology of Perception* (trans: D. A. Landes) London: Routledge.

Mingon, M., and Sutton, J. (2021) "Why robots can't haka: Skilled performance and embodied knowledge in the Māori haka," *Synthese*, 199(1), 4337–4365.

Montero, B. (2016) *Thought in Action: Expertise and the Conscious Mind*. Oxford, UK: Oxford University Press.

Newen, A., De Bruin, L., and Gallagher, S. (Eds.). (2018) *The Oxford Handbook of 4E Cognition*. Oxford, UK: Oxford University Press.

Ravn, S. (2016) "Embodying interaction in Argentinean tango and sports dance," in DeFrantz, T. F. and Rothfield, P. (Eds.), *RELAY: Theories in Motion*. London: Palgrave MacMillan.

——— (2019) "Improvisation and Argentinean tango – Playing with body memory," in Midgelow, V. (Ed.), *The Oxford Handbook of Improvisation in Dance* (pp. 297–310). New York: Oxford University Press.

——— (2022a) "Embodied learning in physical activity: Developing skills and attunement to interaction," *Frontiers in Sports and Active Living*, 4, 795733.

——— (2022b) "Cultivating one's skills through the experienced other in aikido," in K. Bicknell and J. Sutton (Eds.), *Embodied Performance: Ecologies of Skill*. London, New York, Oxford, New Delhi, Sydney: Bloomsbury Publishing Plc.

Razumnikova, O. M. (2013) "Divergent versus convergent thinking," in E. G. Carayannis (Ed.), *Encyclopedia of Creativity, Invention, Innovation and Entrepreneurship* (pp. 546–552). New York: Springer.

Rucińska, Z. (2021) "Enactive planning in rock climbing: Recalibration, visualization and nested affordances," *Synthese*, 199(1), 5285–5310.

Rucińska, Z., and Aggerholm, K. (2019) "Embodied and enacted creativity in sports," in M. Cappuccio (Ed.), *Handbook of Embodied Cognition and Sport Psychology* (pp. 669–694). Cambridge, MA: MIT Press.

Sanchez-Garcia, R., Fele, G., and Liberman, K. (2019) "Ethnomethodological respectifications of cognition in sport," in M. L. Cappuccio (Ed.), *Handbook of Embodied Cognition and Sport Psychology* (pp. 511–534). Cambridge, MA: The MIT Press.

Seifert, L., Orth, D., Mantel, B., Boulanger, J., Hérault, R., and Dicks, M. (2018) "Affordance realization in climbing: Learning and transfer," *Frontiers in Psychology*, 9, 820.

Shapiro, L., and Spaulding, S. (2019) "Embodied cognition and sport," in M. L. Cappuccio (Ed.), *Handbook of Embodied Cognition and Sport Psychology* (pp. 3–22). Cambridge, MA: The MIT Press.

Sutton, J. (2007) "Batting, habit and memory: The embodied mind and the nature of skill," *Sport in Society*, 10(5), 763–786.

Van Leeuwen, N. (2011) "Imagination is where the action is," *The Journal of Philosophy*, 108(2), 55–77.

27

HUMAN AUGMENTATION
Re-inventing embodiment

Frédérique de Vignemont

Introduction

Human augmentation technology enabling physical abilities via robotic systems is no longer a dream for a future age.[1] It is happening now and in many respects it appears promising. For instance, a number of exoskeletons are already on the market. They increase the strength of the person wearing them by a factor of 20 and reduce the effects of gravity and inertia. With an exoskeleton, it thus becomes possible to lift significant weights or to run for a long time without getting tired. Exoskeletons have only to become light enough for it to seem natural for everyone to put them on every morning like a coat. Extra robotic limbs are also under development, enabling several objects to be simultaneously held and manipulated. In the experimental domain, for instance, researchers have designed an extra finger (i.e., a third thumb) with two degrees of freedom, which allows its user to open a jar with only one hand by stabilizing the grip, among many other things (Kieliba et al. 2021). Some of these artificial devices are controlled by muscle activity (e.g., the two toes for the third thumb), while others can be directly interfaced with peripheral nerves, or even with the brain.

In the face of these technological advances, one might worry that they have wider implications than just acquiring the new skill of opening a water bottle with one hand only. What are the consequences if our body becomes partly biological, partly artificial? Andy Clark (2007: 263) claims that thanks to human augmentation, we will become "brand new integrated agents", both mind and body being extended. Within the framework of embodied cognition, it may indeed seem that by altering the body and its sensorimotor abilities, one alters the mind itself. However, in what sense is the augmented body *an intrinsically different body*? Can the artificial device become a proper part of the body? At stake is the ontological, but possibly also legal and moral, status of the artificial device. As Aas (2021) phrases it, if someone were to voluntarily damage it, would it be a situation of vandalism or of assault? I shall leave this fascinating question aside, and focus rather on the way the brain processes the device. The question then becomes whether information about the artificial system is processed in the same manner as information about one's own biological body part. Embodiment has often been suggested as the ideal for an amputee to achieve if she is to be satisfied with her prosthetic limb, and to regularly wear it (e.g., Scarry 1994;

DOI: 10.4324/9781003322511-35

Engdahl et al. 2020; Page et al. 2018; Graczyk et al. 2019). But is this ideal feasible in the case of augmentation technologies? And is it even desirable?

The difficulty here is that the term 'embodiment' may refer to different notions (Vignemont 2011). For the sake of this chapter, I shall simply distinguish between two interpretations. According to a strong interpretation, the question is whether an artificial system can be experienced as a proper part of the body. This phenomenological objective can be reached if the processing of the artificial system is sufficiently similar to the processing of biological body parts (*strong embodiment*). According to a weak interpretation, the question is whether an artificial system can be integrated within the body schema (*weak embodiment*). The body schema is defined here as the representation that carries information about the effector(s) in a format directly exploitable by the motor system to guide action planning and control (Vignemont et al. 2021). We shall see that this objective is easier to achieve, but possibly too easy, and that many objects may then qualify as weakly embodied without us becoming 'brand new agents'.

Rubber bodies

Cognitive research on human augmentation is still relatively recent (e.g., Di Pino et al. 2014; Dominijanni et al. 2021; Kieliba et al. 2021). It is thus sensible to look at domains in which the use of artificial limbs has been more extensively investigated, namely, the field of restorative technology in patients. There are actually some conditions in which the border between restoration and augmentation is unclear, as in the case of aging. Many devices used to enhance physical abilities in able-bodied individuals are often originally designed with a view to substituting a missing or impaired body function. One might then assume that restoration and augmentation are like two sides of the same coin. On this view, adding a sixth finger involves the same mechanisms as replacing a fifth finger. The principles governing the integration of artificial limbs are the same, whether it is to replace a missing limb after amputation or to add a supplementary one in addition to the healthy biological limbs. These principles, one may further argue, may be borrowed from the way one normally processes one's own body parts. One should then expect the artificial limb to be represented and experienced as a proper part of the body, to be *strongly embodied*. This seems to match amputees' own wishes. They often explicitly express satisfaction when their prosthesis subjectively appears to them exactly like their biological limbs:

> Well, to me it is as if, though I have not got my lower arm, it is as though I have got it and it is [the prosthesis] part of me now. It is as though I have got two hands, two arms.
>
> *(Murray 2010: 85)*

However, such an incorporation is rarely reported. Up to 45% of individuals missing a limb do not regularly wear their prosthesis, especially for upper limb replacements (Biddiss 2010). The issue may be partly technological, most prostheses still being relatively uncomfortable, but one may wonder about the existence of more fundamental obstacles to representing an artificial limb as a proper part of one's body.

The rubber hand illusion (RHI) is often taken as the proof of concept in this context (e.g., Bekrater-Bodmann 2020; Zbinden et al. 2022). In the classic set-up of the illusion, participants sit with their arm hidden behind a screen, while fixating on a rubber hand presented in their bodily alignment; both the rubber hand and the real hand are then stroked in synchrony or not (Botvinick and Cohen 1998). It has been found that after synchronous stimulations, some participants (a) feel tactile sensations to be located in the rubber hand, (b) experience the rubber hand as part of their body, (c) mislocalize their hand in the direction of the location of the rubber hand (i.e., proprioceptive drift) and (d) display an increase in arousal when the rubber hand is under threat. In brief, the rubber hand is strongly embodied. One might then hope that by analyzing the conditions under which one can elicit the RHI, one might be able to increase the amputees' satisfaction with their prosthesis.

The problem, however, is that the RHI cannot provide clear guidelines for strong embodiment of artificial limbs. To start with, one should note that it is far from being a systematic illusion, unlike classic visual illusions. It has been reported that at least 25% of the participants never experience it (Lush et al. 2020).[2] One may then investigate what explains this variability, and various options have been recently proposed, but the fact is that the RHI shows not only that it is possible to incorporate an external hand, but also that in many cases we do not incorporate it and we do not know why.

Notwithstanding intersubjective variability, one may also question the relevance of an illusion that is primarily *sensory* to understand the acquisition of new skills through human augmentation. The RHI is generally induced thanks to visuo-tactile congruency, and rarely involves motoric aspects. It has been found that subjects report no sense of control over the rubber hand and that action can remain immune to the effect of the proprioceptive drift (Longo et al. 2008; Kammers et al. 2009). This is at odds with the primary motor purpose of artificial limbs, which is to increase one's motor repertoire and to allow for fluid interactions with the world. On the basis of the RHI, it has been argued that multisensory integration is essential for bodily self-awareness (e.g., Blanke 2012). However, this cannot be the primary path for the appropriation of artificial limbs, given the general lack of somatosensory feedback in most current prostheses. Amputees generally do not feel from the inside the location of their prosthesis and what it touches. Their only access is visual. Hence, unlike the RHI, there cannot be any visuo-somatosensory congruence that could ground the appropriation of the artificial limb. As long as it lacks sensory feedback, it may seem that there is little hope for prosthesis strong embodiment.

Deafferented bodies

There is considerable research on the sensory dimension of artificial limbs (e.g., Bensmaia et al. 2020; Graczyk et al. 2019). So far, this has mainly involved providing information about contact between the device and objects, either by providing tactile stimulation on a displaced skin surface, or by directly activating the neural pathways originally supporting the sensory function. This research is motivated by the assumption that somatosensory feedback could improve motor control and the experience that users have of their prosthesis. For instance, two amputees described that their artificial limb felt as being more natural and their control more intuitive and less attention-demanding when their prosthesis was sensory enabled through neural interface than when it was not. Interestingly, when the phase trial of sensory restoration stopped, one patient noted that his prosthesis: "does not feel like me—went back to being an attachment" (Graczyk et al. 2019: 8). Evidence on the actual role of somatosensory feedback remains, however, anecdotal and its absence in most cases is not rated as the factor with the highest priority in survey studies inquiring about prosthesis abandonment (Zbinden et al. 2022). One may then ask how crucial somatosensory sensations are for embodiment by considering another case in which they lack such sensations, namely, after *peripheral deafferentation*.

After acute neuropathy, some patients can lose all proprioceptive and tactile signals from their damaged nerves. The most studied of these patients have almost their whole body (except the head) affected, though their motor nerves are spared. Hence, with their eyes closed, they do not know the location of their limbs and they may even report feeling as though they were "nothing but a head" (Gallagher and Cole 1995). At the beginning, they are unable to control their limbs, but with time, they learn how to guide their bodily movements on the only basis of visual information. Yet many have argued that the deafferented limbs are not fully re-embodied, even in the weak sense (Brewer 1995; Gallagher and Cole 1995; Paillard 1999; Wong 2015).

There are strong commonalities here with artificial limbs. Users have to control their devices in the absence of somatosensory feedback and on the sole basis of vision. The difference is that deafferented patients can still feel pain, heat and cold in their body, whereas prosthetic users have no sensations whatsoever. If the deafferented limbs remained disembodied despite those preserved sensations, how could fully insensitive rubber and metal devices claim to be embodied, even weakly?

However, one should not too hastily conclude that there could be no embodiment without somatosensory feedback. Let us first examine the reasons for which some deny weak embodiment in deafferentation. The patients have to rely exclusively on visual control, and, according to Gallagher and Cole (1995), this involves reflexive use of the visuo-spatial body image, instead of the body schema. It is not clear, however, why visual control could not be based on the body schema as well. The extensive use of vision in both deafferented and artificial cases does not fundamentally depart from what normally happens. Vision is the primary source of information about the world in which we act and it is pervasive in bodily control, no matter whether one is deafferented or not (Vignemont 2018). Furthermore, with training there is no longer the need to pay attention to what one is doing. Consider how good we become at driving, though it is mainly based on visual control. New skills, such as moving only on the basis of visual information, are cognitively demanding and effortful at the beginning but they become automatized with practice. After a learning phase, deafferented patients no longer need to reflexively think about what they are doing. The same is true for amputees with artificial limbs. Visual control requires less and less attention, until it becomes almost natural. For instance, patients with lower limb prostheses describe that they still need to consciously think about the position of their legs to start with but once in movement, they could "just walk" (Murray 2010: 85). Even after only five days of training with their third thumb, participants had no difficulty performing new actions with it, even with a simultaneous heavy cognitive load (Kieliba et al. 2021). Hence, contrary to what has been said, the body schema might not be missing in deafferentation, and, as a consequence, the current lack of somatosensory feedback might not be a fatal obstacle for prosthesis weak embodiment.

What about strong embodiment? Descartes famously said in his *Sixth Meditation*, "I am not only lodged in my body as a pilot in a vessel but that I am besides so intimately conjoined, and as it were intermixed with it, that my mind and body compose a certain unity". Even if the deafferented limbs are integrated in the body schema, it might seem that at the phenomenological level, the unity that Descartes describes is broken and that the deafferented patients experience their body as an external object that they pilot from the outside because they no longer feel it moving from the inside (Brewer 1995; Wong 2015).[3] Somatosensory feedback may thus be important for strong embodiment. However, it is time to determine whether strong embodiment should be an objective for human augmentation, because if augmentation technologies aim to truly expand the body, why should they try to merely replicate the way the body works?

Beyond what the body can afford

The type of plasticity that is required in human augmentation differs from what has been commonly described in the literature on restorative technology. At the neural level, the amputation leaves space in the primary somatosensory and motor cortex that can be co-opted by the new artificial limb. At the phenomenological level, amputees often feel the presence of the amputated limb, which can help the integration of the prosthesis, as if it were the material incarnation of their phantom (Murray 2010). By contrast, in the augmentation case, there is no body part missing, no phantom to materialize, no neural resources unused. Processing the artificial device as a body part will thus come at a price (Makin et al. 2020). In the domestic economy of the brain, developing one's abilities further can be associated with a decrease of other abilities. This is what has been called the 'neural resource allocation problem' (Dominijanni et al. 2021): how to channel motor commands and sensory information to and from the augmentative device without hindering the sensorimotor control of biological limbs. We may possibly gain a new body part, but we do not want to lose our own in the process.

One may then propose to apply a principle of time sharing. In this scenario, one would use one biological hand and one extra hand or the two biological hands together depending on the task. This solution is relatively parsimonious: it takes advantage of what already exists without requiring much adaptation. However, it closes the door to the possibility of simultaneously using all the biological and extra limbs together. Furthermore, it is not clear that it would work for artificial systems whose designs and functions can have little in common with the human body. Arguably, there are biological factors – and possibly also social ones – that shape the template of what counts as a body. We have priors, according to which the body has two arms, two legs and five fingers for each hand, for instance. Given these priors, it should be more difficult, if not impossible, to experience devices that do not follow a standard body template as proper parts of one's body. Hence, only augmentation technologies sufficiently consistent with body priors could be strongly embodied. Seeking strong embodiment thus reduces the scope of human augmentation. It almost seems paradoxical to expect new devices to be processed as proper parts of the body when their objective is to afford more than what the body affords.[4] On the other hand, if the goal is not to fit with a prior body template, one is not restricted to taking the human body as a model.

Human augmentation should not be reduced to the mere reproduction of artificial counterparts of body segments. It specifically aims to go beyond the standard body, to supplement it with abilities that it was not hard-wired for, and this cannot be achieved solely on the basis of an artificial ersatz of the body. For instance, a plausible example of human augmentation is the ability to fly. One must then look beyond human anatomy and enlarge the study to other animals' bodies and their abilities. Even then, one should not necessarily stick too closely to what biology teaches us. Consider Leonardo da Vinci's attempts to design a flying machine. He first analyzed birds and tried to reproduce their wings but adhering too closely to the original model led to failure. Later more successful attempts still involve wings but no longer directly in contact with the body. Now, if one considers SpaceX, the wings are reduced to their minima. At the individual level, jetpacks seem the most optimal solution. We are far from biological templates.

Just a new tool?

I have just argued that if human augmentation really aims at adding new abilities, and not at only expanding those we already have, it should not stick to the model of the body and it should give up on the ideal of strong embodiment. One may then reply that if the artificial device is not processed as a proper body part, then it is nothing more than a tool. For instance, Andy Clark (2007) imagines a critic challenging him to show that human augmentation does extend the agent:

> You are making quite a song and a dance out of this, what with talk of brand new systemic wholes and so on. But we all know we can use tools, and that we can sometimes learn to use them fluently and transparently. Why talk of new systemic wholes, of extended bodies and reconfigured users, rather than just the same old user in command of a new tool?
>
> *(Clark 2007: 271)*

Augmented devices and tools have many features in common. First, they enhance one's motor capabilities. Second, they do not need to bear any bodily resemblance. Third, they involve sensorimotor integration that allows for fluid interactions with the world. Could it be that an extra artificial arm is no different from a basic rake?

Clark replies that one should be careful not to confuse mere use with what he calls "true incorporation". Only true incorporation, on his view, extends the agent into a new systemic whole. Surprisingly maybe, his notion of true incorporation is relatively modest. It corresponds only to what I call weak embodiment. It involves the integration of the external device into the body schema. By contrast, Clark claims that mere use would involve some kind of inferences based on propositional knowledge about the physical and functional properties of the tool. One might say, for instance, that one merely uses an ATM, whereas one truly incorporates an exoskeleton. Though I agree with Clark's distinction, I fail to see how it shows that an extra artificial arm makes more difference to the agent than a rake. Indeed, there are numerous findings that show that tools can be integrated into the body schema. In one study by Cardinali et al. (2009), for instance, participants used a long mechanical grabber to grasp various objects. After their training session, they were subsequently re-tested with their hand alone without the grabber. The kinematics of their movements were then significantly modified, not only when performing movements that they trained with (reaching to grasp), but also when performing other movements that they had never done before with the grabber (pointing to the top of objects). In brief, they planned their movements as if their arm were longer than before using the grabber. Hence, tools can be truly incorporated in Clark's words, or weakly embodied in mine.

The question now is whether it would be problematic if artificial devices were processed in the same manner as tools. It is true that the tool model keeps the body and the external object distinct, instead of fusing the two into a new systemic whole agent, but there are advantages to the preserved boundary between the biological and the artificial. Indeed, we do not have the same kind of use for the two. Across the day, we keep switching from one tool to another. Unlike body parts, the dynamics are flexible, involving discontinuous use. The same could be true of human augmentation. It can involve many devices that we take and remove depending on the circumstances. To adjust to augmentations as we doff and don them, it is better to keep a representation of the body independently of them, a default body to come back to when we remove the device. This allows for increased malleability. Furthermore, as I defended elsewhere (Vignemont 2018), the body that one experiences as one's own is the body that has a unique affective significance, which grounds the primitive urge to protect it. If external devices were experienced as proper parts of one's own body, then one would tend to protect them in the same way as one protects one's body. However, part of the interest of human augmentation is to be able to do things in dangerous contexts in which one would not directly use one's body. In the same way one uses a spoon to stir one's burning coffee, one can wear one's exoskeleton to walk in an acid lake. In brief, human augmentation is more optimal if the biological and the artificial are not functionally identical. This proposal is in stark contrast to the standard conception of the extended mind. According to Clark and Chalmers (1998), for instance, Otto uses in the same way his memory and his notebook. Here I propose that the notebook can afford more to Otto if it is *not used* in the same way as his own memory.

At this stage, one may worry about the subjective experience that one might have if human augmentation involves only new tools. The phenomenology associated with smooth control over tools is mainly one of transparency and agency. We can almost forget the rake or the fork that we are holding in our hand, our attention being mainly focused on the leaves that we are picking or on the green peas that we are trying to skewer. We are only aware that the tool is under our control, but it remains at the background of consciousness. The same can actually be said with our biological limbs. When walking, we are barely aware of our legs, unless we are tired and it requires an effort. One can wish for a similar sense of agency associated with phenomenal transparency in successful human augmentation. The difference between legs and tools, however, is that there is normally a sense of bodily ownership associated with the former, but not with the latter. We are aware of our legs as being our own. By contrast, we typically do not experience ownership of the rake or the fork, even after spending hours using them. Is this absence of ownership feeling problematic for human augmentation?

One of the reasons that has been put forward to explain the amputees' limited used of their prostheses is that they often do not experience ownership of them. One might then generalize and argue that without ownership, one is less likely to use the augmented system. This conclusion, however, relies on the assumption that the same principles apply for restorative and augmentative technologies. The amputees have phenomenological expectations about the prosthesis. To successfully replace their missing limb, it should feel the same. Therefore, it should feel like a part of their body. They should feel sensations in it. They should also feel ownership towards it. By contrast, there are no such expectations for human augmentation. Since it is completely new, one has no anticipation on how it should feel, and thus, one does not reject it when it does not feel like a proper part of the body. The absence of ownership is then no more of a problem than for tools. Roughly speaking, we do not eat with our fingers just because we do not feel ownership of the fork. Hence, the fact that we experience no ownership of the augmented system does not entail that we shall use it less. Ownership is not compulsory for active use.[5]

The multiplicity of body schemata

Though human augmentation shares many common features with tool use, one might note that some of the augmentation technologies have an interesting specificity. Most tools involve a body part, generally the hand, to hold them and manipulate them. You cannot simultaneously use a rake and prune the trees, for instance. You need to drop one tool to be able to take the other. By contrast, wearing an exoskeleton does not impinge on your ability to do many other things. We saw earlier that one of the challenges for augmentation technologies is precisely to develop new systems to control the devices without interfering with normal bodily functioning. We might not have reached this stage but hopefully multitasking will be achievable in the near future. We may then summarize the difference with tools as follows: one does not 'use' a sixth finger or an exoskeleton; one 'wears' them. One then talks of *wearable robotics*. We wear our clothes, our watch, our ring, our glasses, and they are not strictly speaking tools. Still, we entertain a special relationship with them. Sometimes it is because they have a personal value and we never take them off, but even for clothes that we keep changing, they must somehow be processed in their continuity with the body so that we adjust our bodily movements. In Clark's terms, one might even say that they must be truly incorporated. Indeed, as Head and Holmes (1911: 188) famously noted when they first introduced the notion 'body schema':

> Anything which participates in the conscious movement of our bodies is added to the model of ourselves and becomes part of these schemata [body schemata]: a woman's power of localization may extend to the feather in her hat.

On this definition, many things can be integrated into the body schema, including many objects that do not look like a body part and that are not conceived as proper parts of the body: the feather at the top of the hat, a rake, a third thumb and so forth.[6] Hence, though it is called *body* schema, it does not entail that this type of internal sensorimotor model represents only *bodily* effectors. Is this definition too liberal? Since it is not constrained by bodily resemblance, does that mean that it can represent any objects under our control, however remote they are? This does not seem likely. One may propose that the body schema only encodes what is *in contiguity with the body*. Contiguity does not need to be direct because it can be conceived as a transitive relation. For instance, holding a rake with one's gardening gloves does not prevent incorporating the tool: the rake is in contact with the gloves, which are in contact with the hands. The notion of *wearable* robotics well captures the spatial feature of contiguity. By contrast, the cursor on the screen is not represented in the body schema. Though we plan and control our movements on the trackpad on the basis of the cursor location and we are aware that its motion is under our control, there is no contiguity with our body, not even indirect.

We can now refine our definition of the body schema. Its function is to carry information about effector(s) in bodily contiguity in a sensorimotor format to guide action planning and control. The schema qualifies as bodily, not because of bodily resemblance but only because of bodily contiguity. However, something still seems to be missing. It is too often assumed that all the effectors are represented within a unique bodily representation but, as noted by the neurologist Jacques Paillard, who reintroduced the term of body schema in the 1980s after Head and Holmes, there is more than one sensorimotor representation:

> It would thus seem that the 'body schema' could be fragmented into action subsystems corresponding to the motor instruments involved in the specification of the structure of the paths of considered visuomotor sub-spaces.
>
> *(Paillard 1982: 66, my translation)*

To claim that a tool or an augmentation technology is represented in the body schema thus does not entail that it is represented in the same inner model as the biological limbs. It only means that there is a specific representation whose function is to carry information about the artificial system in relation to the specific actions it can perform. One may further propose that this augmentation-specific body schema recycles the sensorimotor loops normally dedicated to the control of biological body parts (Makin et al. 2020). But at no point does it require that the biological and the artificial are fused together within the same internal model and that the boundaries between the two are erased.

In addition to these local body schemata that are effector specific, Paillard (1982: 67) further proposes that we have a higher-order representation (a "super-space") that serves to coordinate the subordinate effector-specific elements.[7] This super-space need not be conceived as a holistic body schema that depicts the whole body with all its extensions. It can simply index the various sub-spaces and encode their spatial and functional relationships. New skills enabled by augmentation devices thus require new local body schemata to be added that specifically encode the artificial systems. They also require us to update the higher-level representation that coordinates the various body schemata when the augmentation devices cooperate with the biological limbs (e.g., the third thumb with the other fingers).

Conclusion

The notion of embodiment is no more than an umbrella term that covers many different relations to the body. Here I distinguished between strong and weak embodiment, arguing that augmentation technologies should only claim for the weak version. Their successful use does not require that we represent them as proper parts of the body. On the contrary, strong embodiment can be detrimental. However, even within weak embodiment, we need to be able to account for differences among all the things that can be integrated into the body schema, including biological limbs, rubber hands, tools, hat feathers, restorative prostheses and augmentation technologies. Should we say that in every single case the agent is extended, as suggested by Clark? This would rely on an extremely weak notion of extension, which would be neither threatening nor exhilarating. The interest of human augmentation is not that it may give us a new body. It is that it gives us new skills. We should thus leave aside the notion of embodiment and focus instead on skill acquisition.

Notes

1 I shall focus here exclusively on the augmentation of physical abilities, leaving aside cognitive enhancement.
2 I myself have never succeeded.
3 One may still question whether the other sensations that they experience may not preserve this experiential unity (Vignemont, in press). What is clear, however, is that artificial limbs feel no pain, heat or cold, and that it is not even part of the research program to make these sensations possible.
4 One may reply that one can experience supernumerary limbs, as shown by some neurological syndromes and by versions of the RHI with two rubber hands simultaneously stroked (e.g., Ehrsson 2009; Folegatti et al. 2012). However, one may question whether all the hands, biological and artificial, are simultaneously embodied (de Vignemont and Farnè 2010). Furthermore, these extra limbs still look and function like biological limbs, whereas augmentation devices may work on completely different principles.

5 This is not to say that one can never experience ownership in human augmentation or in tools. One can induce what is known as the Toolish illusion, an equivalent of the RHI but for tools (Cardinali et al. 2021). It has also been shown that participants rated their sense of ownership significantly higher over the third thumb after using it for five days (Kieliba et al. 2021).

6 Though we do not act with the feather, we need to take it into account when moving, to avoid damaging it when getting into a car, for instance. In one sense, it is part of the head effector.

7 See Alsmith (2021) for a discussion of local and global body schema.

References

Aas, S. (2021) "Prosthetic embodiment," *Synthese*, 198(7), 6509–6532.

Alsmith, A. J. T. (2021) "Bodily structure and body representation," *Synthese*, 198(3), 2193–2222.

Bekrater-Bodmann, R. (2020) "Perceptual correlates of successful body–prosthesis interaction in lower limb amputees: Psychometric characterisation and development of the prosthesis embodiment scale," *Scientific Reports*, 10(1), 1–13.

Bensmaia, S. J., Tyler, D. J., Micera, S. (2020) "Restoration of sensory information via bionic hands," *Nature Biomedical Engineering*, 7, 443–455.

Biddiss, E. (2010) "Need-directed design of prostheses and enabling resources," in C. Murray (Ed.), *Amputation, prosthesis use, and phantom limb pain*. New York, NY: Springer, pp. 7–21.

Blanke, O. (2012) "Multisensory brain mechanisms of bodily self-consciousness," *Nature Reviews Neuroscience*, 13(8), 556–571.

Botvinick, M., Cohen, J. (1998) "Rubber hands 'feel' touch that eyes see," *Nature*, 391(6669), 756–756.

Brewer, B. (1995) "Bodily awareness and the self," in J. L. Bermúdez, T. Marcel, N. Eilan (Eds.), *The body and the self*. Cambridge, MA: MIT Press.

Cardinali, L., Frassinetti, F., Brozzoli, C., Urquizar, C., Roy, A. C., Farnè, A. (2009) "Tool-use induces morphological updating of the body schema," *Current Biology*, 19(12), R478–R479.

Cardinali, L., Zanini, A., Yanofsky, R., Roy, A. C., de Vignemont, F., Culham, J., Farne, A. (2021) "The toolish hand illusion: Embodiment of a tool based on similarity with the hand," *Scientific Reports*, 11(1), 1–9.

Clark, A. (2007) "Re-inventing ourselves: The plasticity of embodiment, sensing, and mind," *The Journal of Medicine and Philosophy*, 32(3), 263–282.

Clark, A., Chalmers, D. (1998) "The extended mind," *Analysis*, 58(1), 7–19.

Di Pino, G., Maravita, A., Zollo, L., Guglielmelli, E., Di Lazzaro, V. (2014) "Augmentation-related brain plasticity," *Frontiers in Systems Neuroscience*, 8, 109.

Dominijanni G., Shokur, S., Salvietta, G., Buehler, S., Palmerini, E., Rossi, S., de Vignemont, F., D'Avella, A., Makin, T., Prattichizzo, D., Micera, S. (2021) "The neural resource allocation problem when enhancing human bodies with extra robotic limbs," *Nature Machine Intelligence*, 3, 850–860

Ehrsson, H. H. (2009) "How many arms make a pair? Perceptual illusion of having an additional limb," *Perception*, 38, 310–312.

Engdahl, S. M., Meehan, S. K., Gates, D. H. (2020) "Differential experiences of embodiment between body-powered and myoelectric prosthesis users," *Scientific Reports*, 10(1), 1–10.

Folegatti, A., Farnè, A., de Vignemont, F. (2012) "The rubber hand illusion: Two's a company but three's a crowd," *Consciousness and Cognition*, 21, 799–812.

Gallagher, S., Cole, J. (1995) "Body image and body schema in a deafferented subject," *The Journal of Mind and Behavior*, 16, 369–389.

Graczyk, E. L., Gill, A., Tyler, D. J., Resnik, L. J. (2019) "The benefits of sensation on the experience of a hand: A qualitative case series," *PLoS One*, 14(1), e0211469.

Head, H., Holmes, G. (1911) "Sensory disturbances from cerebral lesions," *Brain*, 34(2–3), 102–254.

Kammers, M., de Vignemont, F., Verhagen, L., Dijkerman, H. C. (2009) "The rubber hand illusion in action," *Neuropsychologia*, 47(1), 204–211.

Kieliba, P., Clode, D., Maimon-Mor, R. O., Makin, T. R. (2021) "Robotic hand augmentation drives changes in neural body representation," *Science Robotics*, 6(54), eabd7935.

Longo, M. R., Schüür, F., Kammers, M. P., Tsakiris, M., Haggard, P. (2008) "What is embodiment? A psychometric approach," *Cognition*, 107(3), 978–998.

Lush, P., Botan, V., Scott, R. B., Seth, A. K., Ward, J., Dienes, Z. (2020) "Trait phenomenological control predicts experience of mirror synaesthesia and the rubber hand illusion," *Nature Communications*, 11(1), 1–10.

Makin, T., de Vignemont, F., Micera, S. (2020) "Soft embodiment for engineering artificial limbs," *Trends in Cognitive Science*, 4(12), 965–968.

Murray, C. (2010) "Understanding adjustment and coping to limb loss and absence through phenomenologies of prosthesis use," in C. Murray (Ed.), *Amputation, prosthesis use, and phantom limb pain*. New York, NY: Springer, pp. 81–99.

Page, D. M., George, J. A., Kluger, D. T., Duncan, C., Wendelken, S., Davis, T., Hutchinson, D. T., Clark, G. A. (2018) "Motor control and sensory feedback enhance prosthesis embodiment and reduce phantom pain after long-term hand amputation," *Frontiers in Human Neuroscience*, 12, 352.

Paillard, J. (1982) "Le corps: approche neuropsychologique et neurologique. Le corps et ses langages d'espace," in E. Jeddi (Ed.), *Le corps en Psychiatrie*, Paris: Masson, pp. 53–69.

——— (1999) "Body schema and body image: A double dissociation in deafferented patients," in G. N. Gantchev, S. Mori, J. Massion (Eds.), *Motor control, today and tomorrow*. Sofia: Academic Publishing House, pp. 197–214.

Scarry, E. (1994). "The merging of bodies and artifacts in the social contract," in Bender, G., Druckey, T. (Eds.), *Culture on the brink: Ideologies of technology*. 85–97 Toronto: Bay Press.

de Vignemont, F. (2011) "Embodiment, ownership and disownership," *Consciousness and Cognition*, 20(1), 82–93.

——— (2018) *Mind the body*, Oxford: Oxford University Press.

——— (in press) *Affective bodily awareness, Elements in philosophy of mind*. Cambridge University Press.

de Vignemont, F., Farnè, A. (2010) "Widening the body to rubber hands and tools: What's the difference?" *La revue de Neuropsychologie, Neurosciences Cognitives*, 2(3), 203–211.

de Vignemont, F., Pitron, V., Alsmith, A. J. T. (2021) "What is the body schema?" in Yochai Ataria, Shogo Tanaka, Shaun Gallagher (Eds.), *Body schema and body image: New directions*. Oxford: Oxford University Press.

Wong, H. Y. (2015) "On the significance of bodily awareness for action," *The Philosophical Quarterly*, 65(261), 790–812.

Zbinden, J., Lendaro, E., Ortiz-Catalan, M. (2022) "A multi-dimensional framework for prosthetic embodiment: A perspective for translational research," *Journal of NeuroEngineering and Rehabilitation*, 19(1), 1–11.

PART 8

Social and Moral Cognition and Emotion

28

EMBODIED COGNITION AND THEORY OF MIND

Shannon Spaulding

Introduction

Social cognition is the ability to understand and interact with other agents. Traditionally, philosophers and psychologists have assumed that in order to understand and successfully interact with other people, we must have a *theory of mind*, i.e., a theory about how mental states, such as beliefs, desires, and intentions, inform behavior and how behavior affects mental states. There are two main competing accounts of theory of mind: theory theory (TT) and simulation theory (ST).

TT holds that we explain and predict behavior by employing folk-psychological theories about how mental states inform behavior. With our folk-psychological theories, we infer from a target's behavior what his or her mental states probably are. From these inferences, plus the psychological principles in the theory connecting mental states to behavior, we predict the target's behavior.

ST, in contrast, holds that we explain and predict a target's behavior by using our own minds as a model. We imagine ourselves in the target's situation and figure out what our mental states would be and how we would behave if we were in the target's situation. We retrodictively simulate what the target's mental states could have been to cause the observed behavior, then we take the target's mental states in the form of pretend beliefs and pretend desires as input, run them through our own decision-making mechanism, take the resulting conclusion, and attribute it to the target.

TT and ST disagree about how theory of mind works. TT contends that it is an information-rich theoretical process, whereas ST maintains that it is an information-poor simulational process. Though TT and ST proponents disagree about how theory of mind operates, they agree that social cognition requires theory of mind. There is an extensive empirical literature on theory of mind that aims at testing whether our theory of mind is theoretical or simulational in nature, when children develop theory of mind, and whether our theory of mind concepts are innate or learned.

According to embodied cognition, the philosophical and empirical literature on theory of mind is misguided. Embodied cognition rejects the idea that social cognition requires theory of mind. It regards the intramural debate between TT and ST as irrelevant, and it

 DOI: 10.4324/9781003322511-37

dismisses the empirical studies on theory of mind as ill-conceived and misleading. Embodied cognition provides a novel deflationary account of social cognition that does not depend on theory of mind. In the next two sections, I shall describe embodied cognition's alternative to theory of mind and discuss three challenges it faces.

Embodied social cognition

Embodied cognition proponents reject the idea that social cognition is based on ascribing mental states to others. On their account, the capacity for more basic, non-mentalistic, interactive embodied practices underlies our ability to understand and interact with others. These interactive embodied practices consist in *primary intersubjectivity* and *secondary intersubjectivity*.

Primary intersubjectivity is the pre-theoretical, non-conceptual, embodied understanding of others that underlies and supports the higher-level cognitive skills posited in the theory of mind literature. It is

> the innate or early developing capacity to interact with others manifested at the level of perceptual experience – we see or more generally perceive in the other person's bodily movements, facial gestures, eye direction, and so on, what they intend and what they feel.
>
> *(Gallagher, 2005, p. 204)*

Primary intersubjectivity is manifested as the capacity for facial imitation and proprioceptive sense of one's body, the capacity to detect and track eye movement, to detect intentional behavior, and to read emotions from actions and expressive movements of others. Primary intersubjectivity consists in informational sensitivity and appropriate responsiveness to specific features of one's environment. It does not, embodied cognition theorists argue, involve representing those features. It simply requires certain practical abilities that have been shaped by selective pressures, e.g., being sensitive to certain bodily cues and facial expressions.

The development of secondary intersubjectivity occurs around age one, and it is marked by a move from one-on-one, immediate intersubjectivity to contexts of shared attention. In addition to tracking eye movement, detecting intentional behavior, and reading emotions, with the development of secondary intersubjectivity the child develops the capacity to communicate with others about objects and events in the environment. The child's interactions with caretakers begin to have reference to the things in their environment. At this stage, the child learns to follow gazes, point, and communicate with others about objects of shared attention. With secondary intersubjectivity, the child's capacity for social understanding is further developed, but according to embodied cognition this understanding is still non-mentalistic (Gallagher, 2005, p. 207).

Embodied cognition holds that these embodied intersubjective practices constitute our primary mode of social cognition (Gallagher, 2005; Hutto, 2008). Daniel Hutto claims, "Our primary worldly engagements are nonrepresentational and do not take the form of intellectual activity" (Hutto, 2008, p. 51). Theory of mind, it is argued, is a late-developing, rarely used, specialized skill. The embodied practices constituted by primary and secondary intersubjectivity are developmentally fundamental. That is, in order to develop the capacity to have beliefs about others' mental states, one must first have a grasp of these basic embodied practices. Moreover, embodied intersubjectivity continues to be our principal mode of social interaction even in adulthood. Even as adults, our ordinary social interactions consist primarily in being sensitive to others' embodied practices.[1]

Of course, as adults we do have a capacity for more sophisticated social cognition. This is undeniable. However, according to embodied cognition, this capacity for more sophisticated social cognition does not involve theory of mind. As adults, our everyday social cognition consists only in these embodied practices and our knowledge of the social norms and behavioral scripts distinctive of our social environments. Daniel Hutto's narrative practice hypothesis (NPH) is an embodied-cognition-inspired account of how children develop knowledge of social norms and behavioral practices. It is not the only possible embodied cognition account of sophisticated social cognition, but it is a particularly well-developed account.

NPH holds that the source of our capacity for sophisticated social cognition is direct encounters with folk-psychological narratives, stories that exemplify the forms and norms of social interactions. Stories like "Little Red Riding Hood" and "Goldilocks and the Three Bears" are paradigmatic folk-psychological narratives. The narratives provide exemplars of how agents act according to reasons in order to attain some goal. The child and her caretaker jointly attend to the narrative, and through guided interaction with a caretaker, the child becomes acquainted with forms and norms of acting for reasons. On this view, developing sophisticated social cognition consists in learning how to understand and provide reasons for actions. NPH is meant to be completely independent from theory of mind. Understanding the ways in which agents act for reasons does not consist in, nor does it depend on, attributing beliefs and desires to an agent in order to explain and predict the agent's behavior. Thus, our sophisticated capacity for social cognition does not consist in or depend on theory of mind (Gallagher and Hutto, 2008).

NPH holds that to be proficient in giving reasons for actions, children must first come to have and attribute propositional attitudes, they must learn how propositional attitudes – e.g., beliefs, desires, and emotions – combine to form reasons for action, and through exposure to folk-psychological narratives they learn the norms of acting for reasons. Only after we master natural language and become proficient in understanding and providing folk-psychological narratives can we learn what is now commonly referred to as *mind-reading*, i.e., explaining and predicting behavior on the basis of attributed mental states. But even then, mind-reading is a rarely used, specialized skill. We mind-read only when our primary modes of social cognition break down, i.e., only when embodied practices are ambiguous and we cannot understand an agent's behavior in terms of familiar social norms and behavioral scripts.

Because NPH holds that we develop our sophisticated social cognition skills by comprehending folk-psychological narratives, it implies that children could not even be candidate mind-readers until after they master natural language. Thus, there is a chasm between the preverbal social cognition of infants and that of older children and adults. On this view, only those who have mastered language and encountered folk-psychological narratives are capable of mind-reading. Non-linguistic and prelinguistic beings' understanding of others is limited to non-propositional, non-representational, and non-mental understanding (Hutto, 2008, ch. 3). Although NPH is not the only option for embodied cognition, many embodied cognition theorists accept the idea that children are not capable of mind-reading until after they master natural language (Gallagher and Zahavi, 2008; Ratcliffe, 2007).

This idea is allegedly bolstered by results in developmental psychology. For much of the last 30 years, the standard developmental picture of theory of mind has been that at around four years of age, children undergo a fundamental shift in their theory of mind abilities. As Heinz Wimmer and Josef Perner's experiments first revealed, and other experiments have since replicated, before the age of four children cannot pass standard false-belief tasks (Gopnik and Astington, 1988; Wimmer and Perner, 1983). In one task commonly referred to as the *Sally-Anne task*, children listen to a story as it is enacted with dolls named Sally and Anne. In the scene, Sally hides a toy in one place and then she leaves the scene. Anne moves the toy from the original hiding place to a new hiding place. When children younger than four years old are asked where Sally will look for the toy, they answer incorrectly. They say she will look in the new hiding place. Children four years and older, however, typically answer correctly. They say Sally will look in the original place, and give appropriate explanations for why she will look there. This evidence has been taken to show that there is a significant developmental shift in theory of mind abilities at around four years of age. At age four, children shift from lacking proficiency with the concept of belief to being able to appropriately apply the concept in a range of situations. That is, at age four children master the belief concept. Given that the concept of belief plays an important role in understanding others' mental states, the standard false-belief task has been taken to be the measuring stick of theory of mind abilities.

Embodied cognition theorists do not regard the standard false-belief task as evidence that theory of mind is *developmentally fundamental* or our *primary* mode of social cognition. They argue that the experimental set-up is not ecologically valid; it does not test our social cognition in ordinary interactions. Nevertheless, they do regard it as evidence for their developmental timeline because it explicitly requires the subject to attribute propositional attitudes to explain and predict the target's behavior. Embodied cognition theorists argue that children must first master language and become proficient in understanding and providing folk-psychological narratives. Only after these developments can children develop the ability to explain and predict behavior on the basis of propositional attitude ascriptions. Thus, despite the mistaken assumptions about the importance of the cognitive skills tested in the standard false-belief task, the fact that children first pass this task around the same age that they master the forms and norms of folk-psychological narratives is evidence for the developmental timeline suggested by embodied cognition.

Embodied cognition theorists take the results of the standard false-belief task as evidence for their claim that children are not even capable of mind-reading until fairly late in development, which suggests that theory of mind is not developmentally fundamental. What is developmentally fundamental is embodied intersubjectivity. Embodied intersubjectivity, along with knowledge of social norms and behavioral scripts, make up our ordinary social cognitive interactions even as adults.

Challenges for embodied cognition

In this section, I identify three challenges for embodied accounts of social cognition.[2] The first problem is that they rely on outdated empirical data. Second, they leave an unbridged gap between the kind of social cognitive capacities of preverbal children and the social cognitive capacities of older children and adults. Third, embodied theories of social cognition focus exclusively on "online" cognitive processes, thereby neglecting the legitimate and important role of "offline" cognitive processes. None of these challenges is insurmountable, but I do take them to be serious shortcomings that embodied cognition must address.

Outdated developmental timeline

As I pointed out above, embodied social cognition acquires evidence for its developmental timeline from the results of the standard false-belief task. However, the standard false-belief task is no longer regarded as a good test for theory of mind abilities. Paul Bloom and Tim German persuasively argue that passing the standard false-belief task is neither necessary nor sufficient for theory of mind. The standard false-belief task tests for a variety of general cognitive skills that are not specifically theory of mind skills, and explicit reasoning about false beliefs is not necessary for theory of mind (Bloom and German, 2000).

Kristine Onishi and Renée Baillargeon (2005) object to the standard false-belief tasks, arguing that these tasks are computationally and linguistically too taxing for children younger than four years old. The standard false-belief task requires children to remember the details of the story, who saw what and when, to interpret adults' questions, and give appropriate responses to these questions. Many of these task demands are unrelated to theory of mind per se. Rather, the demands of the standard false-belief task reveal performance of executive functions, e.g., memory and response inhibition. In lieu of the standard measuring stick, Onishi and Baillargeon opt for a simplified non-linguistic false-belief task to measure theory of mind abilities of younger children.

In their novel non-linguistic false-belief task, 15-month-old infants watch an actor put a toy watermelon slice in one of two adjacent boxes, a green box or yellow box. Next, the toy is moved. In half the trials the toy is moved halfway to the other box and then back to the original box, and in the other half of the trials the toy is moved to the other box. For both of these conditions the actor either does or does not see the movement of the toy. (In one variation she looks through an opening in the tops of the boxes, and in another variation she does not.) Using the violation-of-expectation method, Onishi and Baillargeon found that 15-month-old infants looked longer in two cases: first, when the actor does not see that the toy's location has changed, but searches in the correct box anyway, and second, when the actor does see the toy being relocated but the actor reaches into the incorrect box.

Onishi and Baillargeon interpret these results as showing that the 15-month-old infants expect the actor to search for the toy on the basis of her belief about the toy's location. When the actor does not search for the toy on the basis of her belief, the infants' expectations are violated and they thus looked longer at those events. Onishi and Baillargeon take this to be good evidence for the conclusion that 15-month-old infants already have mind-reading abilities and that the ability to mind-read, in at least a rudimentary form, is innate.

Onishi and Baillargeon were the first to use non-linguistic methods for testing false-belief understanding. Since the publication of their article, numerous studies employing a variety of non-verbal testing methods – anticipatory looking, violation of expectation, and active helping – have found evidence that preverbal infants are sensitive to others' intentions, perceptions, perspectives regarding objects, intentions in pretend scenarios, etc. (Gergely, Bekkering, and Kirly, 2002; Luo and Baillargeon, 2007; Onishi, Baillargeon, and Leslie, 2007; Song and Baillargeon, 2007). For example, Baillargeon and colleagues found that five-month-old infants expect agents to act according to their preferences, and they looked longer when agents act contrary to their exhibited preferences.

[A]fter watching familiarization events in which an agent repeatedly grasps object-A, infants look longer at test events if the agent now grasps object-B, but only if object-B is both present and visible to the agent during the familiarization events, so that infants have evidence that the agent prefers object-A over object-B. These different looking-patterns indicate that infants do not merely form associations but consider (at the very least) the motivational and reality-incongruent informational states that underlie agents' actions.

(Baillargeon, Scott, and He, 2010, p. 115)

This study, and dozens of others like it, purport to show that children are sensitive to others' mental states long before they can pass the standard false-belief task. The standard false-belief task, it is argued, tests for children's ability to express linguistically what they are capable of understanding long before age four.

Given that embodied cognition theorists are committed to the idea that children are not capable of mind-reading until after they master natural language and become proficient with folk-psychological narratives, they must reject these empirical findings. They must argue that we can explain the infants' behaviors without attributing to them precocious mind-reading abilities. Their task is to reinterpret the results in terms of non-mentalistic behavior-based explanations, e.g., infants learn the behavioral rule that "agents look for an object where they last saw it."

Currently, there is a vigorous debate about how to understand the results of these non-linguistic mind-reading tasks. Some argue that these studies show that infants understand false beliefs and perhaps already possess the belief concept. According to this interpretation, the reason children fail the standard false-belief task until age four is that up until age four the task is too demanding on younger children's executive system, e.g., short-term memory and response inhibition (Baillargeon *et al.*, 2010; Leslie, Friedman, and German, 2004; Onishi and Baillargeon, 2005). Others argue that these studies show that infants must be very clever behavior readers because it is not possible for infants to understand false beliefs or possess the belief concept. On this interpretation, children four years and younger fail the standard false-belief task because up until age four they do not fully grasp the belief concept (Perner and Ruffman, 2005).

Embodied cognition is committed to the latter interpretation of these studies, thus inevitably arguing for a reinterpretation of the results of the studies in terms of behavioral rules and associations. Unfortunately, however, embodied cognition theorists do not provide such a reinterpretation. They mostly ignore these findings because they regard them as tainted by the presupposition that mind-reading is a fundamental part of our ordinary social cognitive interactions. This is unfortunate for two reasons.

First, there is a growing body of evidence suggesting that infants really are capable of more than just non-mentalistic behavior-reading. This body of evidence is growing in terms of the diversity of experimental paradigms employed and the number of studies finding that infants are sensitive to others' mental states. As these findings become more robust, explaining away these results in terms of ad hoc behavioral associations and rules becomes less appealing. These experimental results make the developmental timeline of the standard false-belief task look much less plausible, which is bad news for embodied cognition's account of social cognition.

Second, although embodied cognition theorists may be right that these studies presuppose that mind-reading is a fundamental part of our ordinary social interactions, this does not mean they should simply ignore these findings. Embodied cognition theorists ought to explain what they think really is happening in these studies and how we should understand these results. Otherwise, embodied cognition is open to the obvious objection that it is in conflict with much of the contemporary data from developmental psychology. Thus, the first challenge that embodied cognition faces is to justify its reliance on a developmental timeline that appears to have been empirically falsified.

Cognitive gap

Suppose that embodied cognition's developmental timeline is correct, and we can explain adequately all the results of the new-wave, non-linguistic mind-reading tests in terms of non-mentalistic embodied cues and behavioral rules and associations. If this is the case, then infants and young children do not, indeed cannot, explain and predict behavior on the basis of mental state attributions. In other words, preverbal children cannot mind-read. Older children and adults, however, can mind-read. Thus, there is a cognitive gap between the social cognitive capacities of preverbal children and the social cognitive capacities of older children and adults. Even if mind-reading is rare for older children and adults, embodied cognition needs an account of *how* we develop the capacity for mind-reading from purely non-mentalistic embodied cues (Wilby, 2012).

A comprehensive account of social cognition must describe our social cognitive capacities as infants and young children, our social cognitive capacities as older children and adults, and how we develop the latter from the former. Embodied cognition theorists focus on denying that infants and young children can mind-read and denying that mind-reading is prevalent even in adults, the result of which is that they neglect to explain how we develop this capacity for mind-reading. This gap is problematic because it is not obvious how a capacity for mind-reading could develop from purely non-mentalistic embodied practices. Embodied cognition theorists often cite the mastery of natural language as the basis for developing the capacity for mind-reading. But this is not an explanation; it is a placeholder for an explanation. To have a comprehensive account, embodied cognition must explain how the mastery of natural language enables children to develop the capacity for mind-reading.[3]

NPH may offer the most promising account of how children develop the capacity for mind-reading. Once children master natural language and become proficient with the forms and norms of folk-psychological narratives, they can begin to understand how beliefs and desires interact to form reasons for actions. Once they understand reasons for actions, they learn to explain and predict behavior in terms of these reasons for actions. The problem with this account is that it seems to have the story backwards (Spaulding, 2011; Thompson, 2012). On the face of it, one could not understand folk-psychological narratives without already understanding how mental states cause behavior. Understanding the *folk-psychological* aspect of folk-psychological narratives seems to presuppose a capacity for mind-reading. To face this challenge, embodied cognition proponents must show that mastering folk-psychological narratives does not presuppose a capacity for mind-reading.

Neglect of offline processes

The final challenge for embodied cognition concerns the comprehensiveness of the account. Embodied cognition focuses exclusively on the role of *online* processes in social cognition (de Bruin and Kästner, 2012). Online processes are cognitive processes that involve responding directly to, rather than representing, features of the environment. Embodied cognition's notion of embodied intersubjectivity illustrates this well. Embodied intersubjectivity consists in primary and secondary intersubjectivity: facial imitation and proprioceptive sense of one's body, the capacity to detect and track eye movement, to detect intentional behavior, and to read emotions from actions and expressive movements of others, and joint attention. Embodied cognition regards these as online, non-representational cognitive processes, and aims to explain our social interactions in terms of these online processes.

Online processes are an important element of social cognition, of course. Embodied cognition is surely right that these online processes are developmentally fundamental. An account of social cognition would be inadequate if it failed to include a role for online processes such as facial imitation, tracking eye movement, and detecting intentional behavior. Embodied cognition theorists allege that theory of mind accounts are guilty of neglecting the role of online processes and focusing exclusively on *offline* processes.

In contrast to online processes, *offline* processes involve internal representations, which are not bound to the current features of the agent's body or her environment, e.g., propositional attitude ascriptions. Theory of mind accounts assume that the mind is an intracranial information-processing system. On this view, cognition is a computational process of manipulating symbolic representations. Theory of mind accounts focus on our ability to explain and predict others' behaviors in terms of mental state attributions. They explain these social cognitive capacities by adverting to computational processes, modular mechanisms, internal representations, and so on. Given the emphasis on these offline computational processes, these accounts tend to neglect the role of *online* processes in social cognition. Embodied cognition rejects the idea assumed in the philosophical and empirical literature on theory of mind that social cognition primarily involves offline processes. Embodied cognition theorists regard this assumption as false and aim to show that social cognition is best explicable in terms of online processes.

Of course, we employ both online and offline cognitive processes in our social interactions. Social cognition requires both responding directly to features of the environment and manipulating information that is absent from the environment and so has to be internally represented. Embodied cognition theorists do not deny this. They do not regard offline cognitive processes as impossible. They simply regard them as relatively unimportant. And this is a mistake. In many cases, it is beneficial to withdraw from the immediate surroundings so as not to automatically act upon particular affordances. Think of the enormous cognitive benefit the capacity to engage in counterfactual reasoning affords. Instead of simply engaging directly with the environment, the agent may consider other ways to respond to the environment, consider hypothetical action plans, evaluate various means of achieving one's goals, etc.

Moreover, the separation of online and offline processes is artificial. An agent's online and offline processes interact to yield cognitive flexibility and autonomy from environmental stimulation such that the agent becomes less dependent upon, and gains new ways of relating to, her environment and other agents in her environment. For example, when we perceive someone blushing, we may take into consideration what immediately happened that could have caused the blush, this person's recent history and personality, and social knowledge about what causes people to blush. Inferring that the person is blushing because she is angry gives rise to different interaction than inferring that she is embarrassed. And inferring that she is embarrassed about something *she* said yields a different sort of online interaction than inferring that she is embarrassed by something *you* said. When we perceive the blush, we automatically take into consideration background information, and the background information influences how we perceive the situation. In order to be a comprehensive account of social cognition, embodied cognition must recognize the legitimate and important role such offline processes play in social cognition.[4]

Conclusion

Embodied cognition's deflationary account is a welcome challenge to the theory of mind orthodoxy. It prompts traditional theory of mind accounts to justify the assumption that we must and often do attribute propositional attitudes to others in order to understand and interact with them. It spurs theory of mind advocates to consider the neglected role of embodied practices and online processes. Consideration of this deflationary account of social cognition brings to light assumptions of the theory of mind literature that need reconsideration. Embodied cognition encourages us to scrutinize the presuppositions and conclusions of the empirical literature on social cognition.

Embodied cognition provides a different paradigm for studying social cognition. To provide a comprehensive, adequate account of social cognition, embodied cognition needs to answer the challenges described above. This requires considering the new-wave false-belief tasks and other non-linguistic theory of mind tasks. Embodied cognition proponents need to respond to the objection that their account relies on an empirically disconfirmed developmental timeline and provide an alternative explanation of these empirical results. They must explain how exactly sophisticated social cognition develops from non-mentalistic embodied practices. And they must make room in their account for the legitimate and important role of offline processes in social cognition.

It is an open question whether embodied cognition or theory of mind offers a more compelling account of social cognition. My own view is that embodied cognition has some distance to go before we can declare it the superior account. It is clear, however, that the debate about social cognition has benefited greatly from this clash of paradigms. Embodied cognition highlights genuine shortcomings and questionable assumptions of theory of mind and provides a radically different alternative account of social cognition. The introduction of this radically different account has revived stagnant debates and spurred re-evaluation of old theory of mind dogmas. This clashing of paradigms is the best way forward for the debate about social cognition.

Notes

1 For a critical assessment of these ideas, see Spaulding, 2010.
2 See Spaulding, 2012, for a guide to discussions about embodied social cognition.
3 See Wilby, 2012, for an evaluation of various attempts to close this cognitive gap.
4 See de Bruin and Kästner, 2012, for an extended defense of this argument and a positive account of how online and offline social cognition processes dynamically interact.

References

Baillargeon, R., Scott, R., and He, Z. (2010). False-belief understanding in infants. *Trends in Cognitive Sciences, 14*(3), 110–118.

Bloom, P., and German, T. P. (2000). Two reasons to abandon the false belief task as a test of theory of mind. *Cognition, 77*(1), 25–31.

de Bruin, L. C., and Kästner, L. (2012). Dynamic embodied cognition. *Phenomenology and the Cognitive Sciences, 11*(4), 541–563.

Gallagher, S. (2005). *How the body shapes the mind.* New York: Oxford University Press.

Gallagher, S., and Hutto, D. D. (2008). Understanding others through primary interaction and narrative practice. In J. Zlatev, T. P. Racine, C. Sinha, and E. Itkonen (Eds.), *The shared mind: Perspectives on intersubjectivity*. Amsterdam: John Benjamins.

Gallagher, S., and Zahavi, D. (2008). *The phenomenological mind: An introduction to philosophy of mind and cognitive science*. New York: Routledge.

Gergely, G., Bekkering, H., and Kirly, I. (2002). Developmental psychology: Rational imitation in preverbal infants. *Nature, 415*(6873), 755–756.

Gopnik, A., and Astington, J. W. (1988). Children's understanding of representational change and its relation to the understanding of false belief and the appearance-reality distinction. *Child Development, 59*(1), 26–37.

Hutto, D. D. (2008). *Folk psychological narratives: The sociocultural basis of understanding reasons*. Cambridge, MA: MIT Press.

Leslie, A. M., Friedman, O., and German, T. P. (2004). Core mechanisms in "theory of mind". *Trends in Cognitive Sciences, 8*(12), 528–533.

Luo, Y., and Baillargeon, R. (2007). Do 12.5-month-old infants consider what objects others can see when interpreting their actions? *Cognition, 105*(3), 489–512.

Onishi, K. H., and Baillargeon, R. (2005). Do 15-month-old infants understand false beliefs? *Science, 308*(5719), 255–258.

Onishi, K. H., Baillargeon, R., and Leslie, A. M. (2007). 15-month-old infants detect violations in pretend scenarios. *Acta Psychologica, 124*(1), 106–128.

Perner, J., and Ruffman, T. (2005). Infants' insight into the mind: How deep? *Science, 308*(5719), 214.

Ratcliffe, M. (2007). *Rethinking commonsense psychology*. New York: Palgrave Macmillan.

Song, H., and Baillargeon, R. (2007). Can 9.5-month-old infants attribute to an agent a disposition to perform a particular action on objects? *Acta Psychologica, 124*(1), 79–105.

Spaulding, S. (2010). Embodied cognition and mindreading. *Mind & Language, 25*(1), 119–140.

——— (2011). A critique of embodied simulation. *Review of Philosophy and Psychology, 2*(3), 579–599.

——— (2012). Introduction to debates on embodied social cognition. *Phenomenology and the Cognitive Sciences, 11*(4), 431–448.

Thompson, J. (2012). Implicit mindreading and embodied cognition. *Phenomenology and the Cognitive Sciences, 11*(4), 449–466.

Wilby, M. (2012). Embodying the false-belief tasks. *Phenomenology and the Cognitive Sciences, 11*(4), 519–540.

Wimmer, H., and Perner, J. (1983). Beliefs about beliefs: Representation and constraining function of wrong beliefs in young children's understanding of deception. *Cognition, 13*(1), 103–128.

29

MINDSHAPING AND EMBODIED HABITS

Michelle Maiese

Introduction

During processes of enculturation, human agents are molded by their social surroundings. Existing practices are normatively structured, and partly by "internalizing" the rules and expectations associated with a particular sociocultural setting, agents augment their basic capacities and engage in coordinated activity with others. However, one of the dangers of enculturation is that individuals will be molded in pernicious ways, often without even being self-reflectively aware of it. This may lead them to participate readily in oppressive patterns of thought and action, even when doing so is in tension with their broader interests or desires. The fact that human agents sometimes participate so naturally in oppressive practices suggests that there is a "built-in normative stickiness" (McGeer 2019: 53) to established cultural routines. Resulting habits often become a matter of "common sense" for those inhabiting a particular social setting. Still, although individuals are *mindshaped* by their social environment, they remain active agents who are capable of resistance.

I argue that the enactivist notion of embodied habit offers a plausible conceptualization of the formative influence of social and cultural forces, one which emphasizes the fully embodied nature of mindshaping and the agency of individual participants. This account sheds light on the way in which social influences are internalized and anchored in the body, via the entrainment of brain and bodily dynamics, and why it is often difficult to change deeply engrained habits. In addition, it helps to reveal how mindshaping has the potential to be both empowering and destructive. To illustrate and support these ideas, I discuss the case of language use and consider how it can play a role in contributing to (a) racist habits, or (b) positive transformation.

An Enactivist Account of Embodied Habits

While standard approaches in cognitive science conceptualize cognition as individually realized and hold that explanation and prediction are our central modes of social cognition, enactivism (Weber and Varela 2002; Thompson 2007) emphasizes that cognition is fundamentally relational and environmentally situated. To regulate themselves and preserve their

 DOI: 10.4324/9781003322511-38

identity, living organisms need to exchange matter and energy with their environment and respond selectively to resources or dangers. To accomplish this, they do not passively form an internal representation of things in a pre-given world, but instead actively "bring forth" (i.e., enact) a unique cognitive domain. By way of "sense-making" (Thompson 2007), living agents gage what counts as a useful resource (or a threat), depending on their bodily structure, needs, and the way that they are coupled with their surroundings.

Among complex human animals with sophisticated nervous systems, engagement with the environment takes on an especially sophisticated form; objects of desire and need that are placed at a distance in space and time are conceptualized as "goals." Pursuit of these goals requires that agents execute coordinated movement sequences and be selectively attuned to relevant aspects of their surroundings. What counts as relevant and significant for human agents is not merely a matter of survival and self-maintenance, but also a matter of faring well in a specific sociocultural context. As perception and action continuously unfold in an interplay between their living body and their environment, agents develop a concerned point of view and begin to exhibit recurring patterns of bodily expressivity and response (Di Paolo et al. 2017).

Although a focus on computations and information processing has become central to much contemporary research in philosophy of mind and cognitive science, Egbert and Barandiaran (2014: 2) note that there is a long history of thought which emphasizes that the mind is "made out of *habits*, and by *habit*." Aristotle, Dewey, and Merleau-Ponty, for example, all characterize habit as a situation-sensitive, flexible ability to engage with the world that allows agents to act intelligently. Building on these ideas, enactivist theorists maintain that cognition involves "the adaptive preservation of a dynamical network of autonomous sensorimotor structures sustained by continuous interactions with the environment" (Froese and Di Paolo 2011: 18). Repeated enactments of a movement sequence reinforce a particular configuration of brain and bodily dynamics and result in engrained patterns that are self-sustaining and self-reinforcing: "the more frequently a pattern of behavior... is performed, the more likely it will be repeated in the future" (Egbert and Barandiaran 2014: 3). However, "engrained" does not mean completely inflexible. Enactivists have been careful to emphasize that habits should not be viewed as unconscious, mechanical, stimulus–response patterns. Although habits are stable in the sense that they involve built-up patterns of behavior and response, they are flexible in the sense that they are susceptible to ongoing adjustment and modification.

Different patterns of movement and response are often enacted together, so that they form "bundles of habits" (Barandiaran 2017) that help agents to navigate their surroundings. These include habitual ways of moving, of speaking, of handling artifacts, and of interacting with others. What Di Paolo et al. (2017: 144) term *"sensorimotor schemes"* are habit bundles (i.e., coordinated patterns of movement and response) that an agent reliably uses to perform a task and navigate a particular context. For example, there is one scheme for tying one's shoes, and another for brushing one's teeth. Over the course of behavioral development, behaviors are integrated into more complex sequences and "actions are linked into functionally coherent ensembles" (Di Paolo et al. 2017: 148). Once these structured behaviors become part of an agent's repertoire, are enacted repeatedly and explicitly for the sake of goals, and get refined on the basis of practice and feedback, we can begin to speak of *skills*. Everyday examples of highly coordinated activity include dancing, playing a sport, and using tools and technology.

These patterns of neurobiological and sensorimotor activity are self-sustaining and self-reinforcing: "the more frequently a pattern of behavior (i.e., sensorimotor coordination trajectory) is performed, the more likely it will be repeated in the future" (Egbert and Barandiaran 2014: 3). Sensorimotor schemes also are *precarious*: the muscular dispositions and neural connectivity patterns that support them become unstable if they are not exercised frequently enough. The exercise of a habit influences other sensorimotor schemes and subsequent behavior patterns such that they are similar to ones that have been executed in the past. A given scheme calls for, reinforces, or inhibits others, and the interdependence of schemes makes them richer in potentiality. What emerges is a self-sustaining behavioral "life form" that integrates brain, body, and sensorimotor dynamics and allows for new forms of coordinated activity that were not possible before.

While much theorizing about habits has focused on movement patterns, it is important to acknowledge that habits also are embodied in coordinated *patterns of attention*. Just as sensorimotor patterns are reinforced through repetition, what subjects focus on is modulated by what they have paid attention to in the past. Habits of mind encompass schemas for interacting with and interpreting one's surroundings, and include, for example, a tendency to notice some considerations while ignoring others, and to trust some sources of evidence while remaining suspicious of others. Habits of mind arise in conjunction with habitual movement patterns, via the development and self-maintenance of coherent neurobiological configurations and built-up patterns of bodily attunement. Their formation involves a dynamic network of brain and bodily processes, including the musculoskeletal system, metabolic systems, the endocrine system, and the cardiovascular system. These interdependent, self-stabilizing patterns of behavior and attention vary depending on context and what sort of activity is unfolding; "particular sets of habits will be regularly displayed by an agent depending on his current activities" and context (Ramírez-Vizcaya and Froese 2019). These recurring modes of engagement undergird what we commonly think of as people's enduring concerns and reflect *what they care about*. For example, if an agent has developed habits of biking to work, picking up trash on the beach, and paying attention to how much water they use, this indicates that they care about the environment.

Enactivists rightly emphasize that habit formation is socially embedded and fundamentally normative. Habits resemble autopoietic biological processes insofar as their self-maintenance is "contingent upon the existence of an appropriate environment" (Egbert and Barandiaran 2014: 10). However, what is distinctive about habit formation among human agents is the significant influence of social-relational factors. Just as biological processes of self-maintenance depend on energetic resources, the formation and maintenance of habits depends on social resources. Human agents develop habits over the course of their interaction with complex sociocultural environments. Because an agent's bodily habits and skills typically are deployed against the backdrop of some normative framework (e.g., considerations of efficiency), their "existing repertoire of sensorimotor schemes is modulated or transformed over time such as to address new behavioral challenges" (Buhrmann and Di Paolo 2015).

Shared cultural practices scaffold individual enactments of meaning by "prescribing and normalizing certain modes of experience and action while proscribing (and perhaps pathologizing) certain others" (Kirmayer and Ramstead 2017). These practices encompass customary ways of performing various tasks, dividing up resources, occupying space, using tools, speaking, thinking, and feeling. Rather than relying on explicit rules to tell them what to do, agents adapt continuously to the people around them and let the situation constrain their behavior so that they know, for example, how to adjust their bodily activity depending on whether they are at home or out in public. Related social norms and expectations modulate how they behave at parties, how they speak to their colleagues at work, and even how they walk down the street or sit on an airplane. As agents learn how to use tools, machinery, and other resources, neurobiological configurations and coordinated behavioral patterns form and take root.

The notion of habit allows us to make sense of the way in which sociocultural influences are internalized and anchored in patterns of bodily dynamics and engagement, so that agents' living bodies become "socially saturated" and socio-normatively laden. Insofar as these influences regulate and mold agents' habits of behavior and attention and coordinate their shared activity with others, they become part of their lives in a quite literal sense, by modifying their neurobiological dynamics and patterns of bodily attunement. Human agents are thereby *mindshaped*: their sense-making processes and embodied habits are *partially determined*, or *shaped*, by the social world.

How does this occur? Enactivists emphasize that bodily coordination is central to human sociality. De Jaegher and Di Paolo (2007) characterize "coordination" as the non-accidental correlation between two or more coupled systems, so that their behavior matches to a degree far beyond what is expected given what those systems are capable of doing. Once two or more interactors are part of a coupled system, their expressions, behaviors, and bodily dynamics modulate those of the other person(s). Habit, posture, and body alignment begin to resonate, so that other people exert a contagious pull—often without an agent being aware of it. Instances of mutual coordination in the realm of human activity include synchronization, mirroring, anticipation, and imitation (De Jaegher 2009). Such reciprocal bodily attunement begins in infancy and grows more complex over time as agents develop a range of projects that require them to communicate with others, exchange information, and selectively engage with action possibilities in a way that complements others' behavior. Partaking in coordinated activity requires that agents follow along with social norms associated with different settings.

Because humans are essentially social creatures who yearn for acceptance and connection, it's inevitable that the views and opinions of others will have significant impact on an individual's ongoing habit formation. Thus, mindshaping is unavoidable. However, as discussed further below, there are reciprocal feedback relations between agents and social influences. An individual agent is not simply *shaped*, but also is an active *shaper* of both other people and their social environment.

Mindshaping as Constructive v. Destructive

When someone is part of a social domain, they cannot but act in an ordered way, on the basis of impersonal norms that would apply to anyone who occupies the social role in question (Steiner and Stewart 2009); yet by belonging to this social domain, with its specific structures and norms, agents are able to augment their cognitive and agential powers and engage in a whole new range of activities.

Bodily habits and skills have an emancipatory aspect in part due to their dual stability and flexibility. First, the stability of habit helps to anchor an agent in the world, enabling a kind of poise that allows them to stay on course even when they encounter obstacles. Because habits integrate past experiences and dynamically guide action and perception, these stable patterns of organized behavior make possible "the achievement of infinitely diversified tasks" (Bourdieu 1977: 95). Once habits and skills become "fully embodied and embedded within the proper context" (Gallagher and Zahavi 2008), agents can control and manage their interactions with the environment without having to monitor what they are doing or rely on conscious reasoning. Second, the flexibility of habit allows agents to carry out fine-grained adjustments, change course in response to fluctuating environmental contingencies, or modify their response based on their own changing needs and concerns. For example, an agent might alter the manner in which they enact a habit, suppress a habit, or activate an entirely different habitual repertoire. This ability to shift between different modes of engagement as a situation unfolds, in accordance with various social demands, is central to effective agency.

Mindshaping often is constructive and enabling insofar as it helps agents to develop the habits and skills associated with various socially defined activities. Such habits are expressive of a practical form of understanding regarding what they can do with objects and what sorts of action possibilities are available and situationally appropriate. Because they can reliably expect that others will respond to, complement, or complete their own actions in particular ways, agents can coordinate their behavior and engage in various forms of joint activity. Social settings such as families and workplaces, for example, offer forms of social coordination that agents are highly motivated to engage in and which prove to be highly valuable (Haslanger 2019: 6); the fact that agents are mindshaped by various socionormative practices enables them to be part of a community and engage in cooperative activity. In some cases, this coordination of activity allows for the emergence of new insights and understandings that were not available to each individual on her own (De Jaegher and Di Paolo 2007: 497). To take just one example, consider how belonging to a feminist consciousness-raising group can scaffold someone's ability to reflect on social norms, develop skills for resistance, and collaborate with others to bring about social change.

However, mindshaping can also impose pernicious limitations. Precisely because the way in which agents are socially situated molds their behavior and interpretations, their habitual patterns of engagement can become *overdetermined* by social relations and structures, resulting in disruptions to cognition and agency. Ideally, habits are stable in the sense that they are "on tap" and readily available to guide and control agents' behavior, but flexible in the sense that they allow them to shift course as needed. However, habits can lose their "residue of dynamic criticality" and begin to operate more like "unchangeable automatisms" (Di Paolo et al. 2017: 102). "Bad habits" reflect a comportment or mode of behaving and responding that has become so rigidly sedimented in the body that it puts an end to plasticity. These inflexible behaviors and intransigent thinking patterns are difficult to modify; once they become 'second nature,' agents begin to enact them as a matter of common sense, even under circumstances that call for the activation of a different set of responses. Thus, what makes these habits "bad" is not simply that they are inflexible, but rather that they interfere with some of the agent's goals or "crowd out" the enactment of other habits that are important to them.

In cases of ideological oppression, for example, an agent's habits of behavior and attention are shaped by ideology (i.e., prevailing ideas and values) in such a way that that they are set up "to participate fluently in practices and structures of injustice" (Haslanger 2019: 6). The engrained habits associated with racism and sexism, for example, are often internalized at an early age and become rigidly embedded before agents are even capable of reflective self-awareness. Such habits often operate like automated frames of reference that make it difficult for agents to understand the world around them. Because agents over-identify with existing norms and lack the capacity to take up critical distance from them, they may not even be aware of the extent to which social influences pose moral, interactional, and existential problems for them. What is more, these overdetermined habits of mind may make it difficult for agents to attend to relevant considerations, integrate different kinds of information, and revise their beliefs about the world in response to available evidence. When embodied habits function as routine "scripts," there is little in the way of active contribution or experimentation on the part of the individual agent. In some cases, agents may even become "stuck" in specific patterns of behavior and attention, so that alternative ways of behaving and making sense of things effectively become closed off.

It is important to acknowledge that overly rigid habits become sedimented partly because they are sustained and reproduced at multiple levels: (i) larger-scale social institutions and structures, (ii) smaller-scale social groups and normative communities that operate alongside, and within, those larger-scale institutions, and (iii) the habits and enactments of individual agents.

First, the structures, practices, and ideas associated with large-scale social institutions are always already there when an individual agent is born (Steiner and Stewart 2009). From the beginning of life, their embodied habits are molded by political structures, dominant cultural practices, and norms communicated via popular media; this enculturation process begins before they even have the capacity to reflect upon how these social forces are influencing them. Second, these societal influences shape how members of smaller-scale communities and social groups relate to each other. Racist political practices and cultural ideas, for example, shape the relational dynamics of families, schools, and workplaces. By way of social conditioning, the shared practices, attitudes, and values of these social groups influence the habits of individuals and shape how individual agents interact and relate to one another. Along these lines, Slaby (2016) has discussed how "engaged, active collectives are capable of exerting a forceful affective pull on individuals" (10) in the context of workplace settings. He notes how colleagues often act as "mutual normative enforcers, keeping one another in line" (Slaby 2016: 25), and thereby reinforce, sanction, and influence one another's habits. This may make it especially difficult for individual agents to modify "bad habits" that are rewarded in these settings. Third, individuals repeatedly enact these habits, even when they are on their own or enter new social settings. As a result, these habitual enactments become more and more engrained, and also help to generate, reinforce, and sustain similar habits in other agents.

Nonetheless, although individual agents are mindshaped by their social environment, their behavior is not fully determined by social norms or practices. Rather than focusing simply on the way that the social environment modulates people's minds, the enactivist approach further emphasizes the importance of individual and collective agency. For one thing, this approach emphasizes that human agents "bring forth" what counts as meaningful and relevant, on the basis of their concerns and interests. Faced with a myriad of action possibilities, it is the agent themself who determines which of these possibilities will be actualized. This results in "systematic (non-random) patterns of behavior" that depend partly on the agent rather than being fully determined or dictated by the environment (Degenaar and O'Regan 2017: 399).

In addition, enactivism emphasizes that by way of reciprocal feedback loops between agent and environment, individual agents are not just shaped by the social world, but also mold (and thereby partially determine) their social environment via their active and reactive contributions and responses. While environmental settings do often funnel activities into a few constrained behavioral options, they don't undermine the real possibility of an agent breaking away from these activities (Di Paolo et al. 2017: 169). The way that an agent engages with social structures and norms, whether complying with or resisting them, makes an important difference to their ongoing habit formation, the habit formation of those around them, and the way that social dynamics unfold. Because they remain active and capable of resistance, human agents can resist, modify, or even transform existing social norms and dominant practices.

In many cases, agents engage in this reshaping together with others, in the context of smaller-scale social groups. Indeed, resistance to structures of domination often depends on communities of dominated people coming together to create alternative practices and bring about social change. These communities of resistance are comprised of individual agents who collectively create alternative "hidden" heterodox practices and values (Haslanger 2019: 15–20), ones which undercut prevailing social norms and cultural practices. These social groups accomplish things that a mere aggregate of individuals could not, by coordinating their actions and sense-making and creating opportunities to modulate participants' patterns of behavior and attention. Thus, mindshaping is complementarily and simultaneously both top-down *and* bottom-up; it occurs at multiple scales and in reciprocal feedback loops, whenever individual agents coordinate their actions and sense-making with other agents.

Mindshaping via Language

To see how mindshaping can be either constructive or destructive (or a mixture of the two), consider the case of language. Because the normative social structure of a shared language is always already there, human agents can speak and engage in various forms of dialog. During these collaborative processes of meaning-making, participants mutually regulate their coupling: the person taking a "dialogic turn" modulates the sense-making and orients the attention of the other participant(s) by way of verbal utterances, gestures, smiles, or intonations (Di Paolo et al. 2018). Language use thereby functions as a form of social coordination: "in conversational exchanges, emails, and elevator rides, we are constantly getting coordinated and constrained, and doing the same to others, whether or not we are aware of it" (Cuffari 2014: 4).

Such coordination generates various possibilities for behavioral alignment and joint activity, such as brainstorming, planning, and various forms of collaboration. Available evidence suggests that interlocutors who reciprocally adapt to each other's way of talking (i.e., with respect to speech rate, utterance length, and phonetic profile) tend to perform better on joint decision tasks; the more they mirror each other's ways of describing things, the better able they are to cooperate and the more they tend to like each other (Fusaroli and Tylen 2012: 117). Once task-specific shared vocabularies develop, stabilize, and become conventional, associated linguistic patterns "come to constitute a cognitive niche for the community of speakers, structuring, guiding, and constraining the very same coordinative dynamics from which they evolved" (Fusaroli and Tylen 2012: 119). These customary patterns can be easily adopted by new users, allowing members of a social group to share perspectives and understand one another. Established ways of speaking lay out what makes sense and what doesn't in an agent's language-speaking community: "if a person is to speak and make themselves understood, it will only be by acting in ways that fit with the patterns of doing things already mapped out in standing practices" (Kiverstein and Rietveld 2021: S186). Words *always already* have a meaning because of how they have been used and understood by other speakers in the past.

Because language "has a situating power that structures our interpretive interactions in meaningful milieus, or domains of significance" (Irwin 2017: 135), it contributes significantly to mindshaping. Commonly used distinctions, abstractions, and definitions shape an agent's sense of the meaning and significance of objects, events, states of affairs, and other people. Via the formation of linguistic habits and sensitivities, agents incarnate the attitudes, expectations, values, and concerns of those around them. However, they also play an active role in shaping others. The terms that an agent uses to construe a situation modulate the interpretations of those with whom they are communicating and thereby contribute to the mindshaping of others. For example, if an agent repeatedly refers to racial justice advocates as "rioters," this orients the attention of their dialog partners and modulates their sense-making in particular ways.

In some cases, conventional linguistic practices narrow agents' perspectives and contribute to overly rigid habits. Term and descriptive labels that refer to stereotypes (e.g., "the Black criminal") contribute to racist habits such as suspicious surveilling in shops, holding on tightly to one's handbag, and constricted breathing when confronted with the Black male body. Such habits reflect a comportment or mode of responding that has become sedimented in the body partly due to deeply embedded discourses (Ngo 2016) and language.

However, although customary linguistic practices can be understood as "invitations to speakers to continue patterns of activity set up in the past" (Kiverstein and Rietveld 2021: S189), agents retain the ability to adapt, reshape, and transform the expressive possibilities available to them, often in highly creative and innovative ways. Consider how the introduction of new terms or revamped ways of speaking often plays an important role in expanding, reshaping, or refining the existing habits of individual agents and collectives. Introduction of non-binary gender language and the use of the pronoun 'they,' for example, has helped to create new behavioral scripts and habits of mind, altering agents' sense of how they and others are expected to behave. Other examples of the power of language to contribute to constructive mindshaping and foster new understandings include the introduction of protest slogans such as "Black Lives Matter" and introduction of the term 'mansplaining' to draw attention to sexist conversational dynamics. Because language "unleashes inexhaustible potential ideas to give depth to the world through its incessant transfigurations" (Irwin 2017: 139), it has great potential to reshape the cultural world (Di Paolo et al. 2018) and contribute to constructive social change.

Conclusion

I have presented an enactivist account of mindshaping that emphasizes the importance of human embodiment, the normative dimension of cognition and agency, and the formative influence of social and cultural forces. However, it also acknowledges the agency of individual participants. Because there are reciprocal feedback relations between individuals and social activity, individuals are not simply shaped, but also operate as active shapers of other people and their broader social environment. Through their unique contributions, agents can influence the workings of social institutions (whether small-scale or large-scale) and comply with or resist dominant practices, to varying degrees. Likewise, smaller-scale social communities/collectives not only are shaped by dominant ideology, but also can play an important role in resisting, reshaping, or reinforcing that ideology. In short, it is true both (a) that social structures and institutions shape the actions and interactions of individual agents and collectives, and (b) that individual agents and collectives produce and reproduce structures. Given these complex, reciprocal dynamics, radical change needs to occur at multiple scales for constructive social change to occur. To address oppressive practices, we need to pay attention to larger-scale social structures, smaller-scale social groups, the embodied habits of individual agents, and the way in which they are entangled. Enactivism's emphasis on embodied habits helps to illuminate the way in which agents' living bodies are one key site of oppression, or alternatively, of liberation.

References

Barandiaran, X. (2017) "Autonomy and Enactivism: Towards a Theory of Sensorimotor Autonomous Agency," *Topoi* 36(3), pp. 409–430.

Bourdieu, P. (1977) *Outline of a Theory of Practice*, New York: Cambridge University Press.

Buhrmann, T. and Di Paolo, E. (2015) "The Sense of Agency—A Phenomenological Consequence of Enacting Sensorimotor Schemes," *Phenomenology and the Cognitive Sciences* 16, pp. 207–236.

Cuffari E. (2014) "Keep Meaning in Conversational Coordination," *Frontiers in Psychology* 5(1397), pp. 1–5.

De Jaegher, H. (2009) "Social Understanding Through Direct Perception? Yes, By Interacting," *Consciousness and Cognition* 18, pp. 535–542.

De Jaegher, H. and Di Paolo, E. (2007) "Participatory Sense-Making: An Enactive Approach to Social Cognition," *Phenomenology and the Cognitive Sciences* 6, pp. 485–507.

Degenaar, J. and O'Regan, J. (2017) "Sensorimotor Theory and Enactivism," *Topoi* 36(3), pp. 393–407.

Di Paolo, E., Buhrmann, T, and Barandiaran, X. (2017) *Sensorimotor Life: An Enactive Proposal*, Oxford, UK: Oxford University Press.

Di Paolo, E., Cuffari, E., and De Jaegher, H. (2018) *Linguistic Bodies: The Continuity Between Life and Language*, Cambridge: MIT Press.

Egbert, M. and Barandiaran, X. (2014) "Modeling Habits as Self-Sustaining Patterns of Sensorimotor Behavior," *Frontiers in Human Neuroscience* 8, p. 590.

Froese, T. and Di Paolo, E. (2011) "The Enactive Approach: Theoretical Sketches from Cell to Society," *Pragmatics and Cognition* 19, pp. 1–36.

Fusaroli, R. and Tylen, K. (2012) "Carving Language for Social Coordination: A Dynamical Approach," *Interaction Studies* 13(1), pp. 103–124.

Gallagher, S. and Zahavi, D. (2008) *The Phenomenological Mind: An Introduction to Philosophy of Mind and Cognitive Science*, New York: Routledge.

Haslanger, S. (2019) "Cognition as a Social Skill," *Australasian Philosophical Review* 3(1), pp. 5–25.

Irwin, B. (2017) "An Enactivist Account of Abstract Words: Lessons from Merleau-Ponty," *Phenomenology and the Cognitive Sciences* 16, pp. 133–153.

Kirmayer, L. and Ramstead, M. (2017) "Embodiment and Enactment in Cultural Psychiatry," in C. Durt, T. Fuchs, and C. Tewes (eds) *Embodiment, Enaction, and Culture: Investigating the Constitution of a Shared World*, Cambridge: MIT Press.

Kiverstein, J. and Rietveld, E. (2021) "Scaling-Up Skilled Intentionality to Linguistic Thought," *Synthese* 198(Suppl 1), pp. 175–194.

McGeer, V. (2019) "Mindshaping is Inescapable, Social Injustice is Not: Reflections on Haslanger's Critical Social Theory," *Australasian Philosophical Review* 3(1), pp. 48–59.

Ngo, H. (2016) "Racist Habits: A Phenomenological Analysis of Racism and the Habitual Body," *Philosophy and Social Criticism* 42(9), pp. 847–872.

Ramírez-Vizcaya, S. and Froese, T. (2019) "The Enactive Approach to Habits: New Concepts for the Cognitive Science of Bad Habits and Addiction," *Frontiers in Psychology* 10, p. 301.

Slaby, J. (2016) "Mind Invasion: Situated Affectivity and the Corporate Life Hack," *Frontiers in Psychology* 7, p. 266.

Steiner, P. and Stewart, J. (2009) "From Autonomy and Heteronomy (and Back): The Enaction of Social Life," *Phenomenology and the Cognitive Sciences* 8, pp. 527–550.

Thompson, E. (2007) *Mind in Life: Biology, Phenomenology, and the Sciences of the Mind*, Cambridge: Belknap Press.

Weber, A. and Varela, F. (2002) "Life After Kant: Natural Purposes and the Autopoietic Foundations of Biological Individuality," *Phenomenology and the Cognitive Sciences* 1, pp. 97–125.

30

THE EMBODIMENT OF CULTURE

Tamer Soliman and Arthur M. Glenberg

What is the nature of culture? Is it a form of human values that floats above individual experience? Or, does culture arise from the mundane interactions of individuals with their physical and social environments? We provide answers to these questions in the following four sections of this chapter. In the first, we describe problems with standard conceptions of culture, including how it is learned and transmitted and how culture interfaces with psychological experience. In the second, we develop an approach based on ideas of embodied cognition: at the level of the individual and the small group (e.g., family), culture is the tuning of sensorimotor systems for situated action. In the third and fourth sections, we sketch the results from two empirical investigations that demonstrate the promise of this approach. One of the investigations documents how culture can influence distance perception by taking into account expected effort of interaction (e.g., Proffitt, 2006) with in-group and out-group members. The second demonstrates how close physical interaction of the sort hypothesized to lead to sensorimotor tuning can literally change the body schema so that dyads become closely attuned to one another; that is, they form an in-group.

The problem: a dualistic conception of culture

Pinning down a commonly accepted psychological characterization of culture is difficult (cf. Atran, Medin, and Ross, 2005; Kitayama, 2002; Kroeber and Kluckhohn, 1963; Tripathi, 2001). Nonetheless, there are two common working assumptions. The first is that culture is a package of propositional constructs like values, beliefs, and world views (Markus and Kitayama, 1991; Oyserman, Coon, and Kemmelmeier, 2002; Triandis, 1995). These rule-like structures specify the normative or prescriptive social code prevailing in the local group. The second is that this cultural grammar provides frames for making sense of incoming information, and simultaneously functions as the motivational force that biases behavior in predictable directions (Hong and Chiu, 2001). Note that these working assumptions create a duality: culture is both a set of abstract norms and a set of sensorimotor behaviors.

This duality is found amongst researchers, with some arguing that culture proper should be exclusively identified with the abstract norms (Oyserman *et al.*, 2002), while others

DOI: 10.4324/9781003322511-39

advocate a broader conception of culture that encompasses both ideations and behaviors (Kitayama, 2002; Markus and Kitayama, 2010). The camps differ only as to whether genuine culture should be confined to one of the elements of this duality.

The duality raises questions such as, "What if stated values and observable behavior do not coincide?" and "Where should the label of 'genuine culture' be attached?" As an example, Cohen and colleagues (Cohen, Nisbett, Bowdle, and Schwarz, 1996) arranged for male participants from the southern and northern US to be bumped and then called "assholes." The researchers then collected biomarkers of stress and aggression and placed the participants once again in a potentially insulting situation. Relative to the northern participants, southerners showed an increase in cortisol (indexing stress) and testosterone (indexing potential aggression) levels, as well as a stronger behavioral face-off tendency during the second episode of potential insult. Thus, Cohen *et al.* produced strong behavioral and physiological evidence to claim that the South is dominated by a "culture of honor" that stresses masculine toughness and aggressive defense of reputation. Several years later, however, D'Andrade (2000) used verbal questionnaires to excavate the abstract normative value system that allegedly underlies those bodily manifestations of honor. But D'Andrade found no difference between southerners and northerners in value systems. Does honor exist apart from its bodily "manifestations?" Is the "value system" of honor psychologically real?

The discrepancy between the proposed genuine ideological foundations of culture and its behavioral manifestations is especially conspicuous in cognitive sociology. Swidler's (2001) informants endorsed the ideological belief that love is the basic motivation for marriage. But in contrast to this endorsed value, they did not actually bring their marriages to an end despite admitting that their marriages were no longer sentimentally fulfilling. Similarly, Vaisey (2008) interviewed teenage informants after they chose (on a survey) either to "do what makes me happy" or "do what God or scripture says." During the interview, both groups made similar decisions about acting in practical situations that implicitly required moral decisions. When asked to justify their behavioral choices, both converged on "gut instinct" and when pressed, they offered incoherent justifications. This finding is similar to those of Haidt and Hersh (2001) who report that participants rejected culturally degenerate acts (e.g., recreational drug use), but resorted to vague rationalizations for doing so.

The dual working assumptions also seem to produce a bias when interpreting observed effects of culture in regard to cause and effect. If in one and the same cultural population, a unique social characteristic is reliably established (e.g., how the individual relates to the in-group and out-groups) and a distinctive sensorimotor tendency is equally reliably marked as prevalent (e.g., the scope of visual attention, categorization biases, memory of inanimate scenes, or learning styles), only the former is characterized as defining for the cultural profile of the group, whereas the latter is typically conceived as the effect of culture on cognition (e.g., Nisbett and Miyamoto, 2005; Norenzayan, Smith, Kim, and Nisbett, 2002; Varnum, Grossman, Kitayama, and Nisbett, 2010). That is, the abstract norms are conceived as constitutive of the psychological fabric of culture and the sensorimotor behaviors as merely secondary or consequent.

Markus and Kitayama's (1991) seminal conception of the "self" is an exemplar of this bias in interpretation. The main postulate is that the "self" is an emergent, abstract set of norms reflecting the individual–group relationship dominant in the local setting. In individualistic societies (e.g., North America), the value system stresses freedom of choice and achievement, while collectivistic cultures (e.g., East Asians) stress group connectedness and social commitment. Individuals in the former setting typically develop "independent" self-construals with social orientations that center around self-direction, autonomy, and freedom of expression. In the collectivistic settings, "interdependent" self-construals are anchored in harmony and social commitment. Critically, Markus and Kitayama stressed that "these divergent views of the independent and interdependent selves can have a systematic influence on various aspects of cognition" (1991, p. 224), a view that is rephrased in their recent review of the theory as "Independence and interdependence have significant consequences for cognition" (Markus and Kitayama, 2010, p. 425).

An alternative: the sensorimotor account of culture and behavior

In our alternative, there is no self-contained, multilayered psychological structure that could be labeled "culture." We do not claim that culture does not exist, nor do we assert that culture is not a valuable construct at the sociological level of analysis. Instead the claim is that culture is not a psychological structure that exists apart from more mundane learning and behavior. Thus, our account aims to substitute for the dualistic value-behavior conception of culture a unifying postulate: the psychological underpinning of culture consists of an individual's sensorimotor tuning arising from and guiding social interactions.

An important point of departure for our account is a particular understanding of human knowledge. The embodied approach assumes that knowledge resides in the multimodal manner in which the agent interacts with the environment. On this account, the body is not a mere input and output device controlled by a cognitive machine. Instead, both the anatomical and physiological sensorimotor characteristics of the body define the knowledge profile of the agent.

Convincing examples come from developmental psychology. For example, Dahl *et al.* (2013) demonstrate how the maturation that enables crawling sets the stage for a new type of sensorimotor knowledge that then becomes the basis for understanding stability in the world and wariness of heights. When an infant is being carried, there is no consistent correlation between the infant's proprioception and visual stimulation. However, once the infant begins to crawl, she keeps her head steadily pointed toward the goal. In this way, the infant can experience the consistent and strong correlations between commands to the muscles, proprioceptive feedback, and importantly, optic flow. This correlation then becomes the basis for a stable world. That is, a particular type of movement produces a particular flow of optical information, and it is that correlation that indicates that the world is stable and it is the infant that is moving within it. When that correlation is disrupted, it is a signal that the world is changing and that caution is needed. For the infant in the laboratory, that disruption is caused by placing the infant near a visual cliff, which causes the infant distress, but only after it has learned to crawl and tune itself to the correlation of proprioception and optic flow. Adults experience this sort of distress when in a stopped car and another car in the periphery begins to move. The sensation is that the world is changing and that one's own car is moving, and it produces a fearful stomping on the brakes.

As another example, Sommerville, Woodward, and Needham (2005) show that three-month-old infants can attend to adult goals, such as grabbing an object, but only after the infant develops some skill in grabbing and holding objects herself. Similarly, with older children, categorization of objects depends on how they have interacted with them (Smith, 2005). These examples demonstrate how knowledge, both particular and abstract (e.g., knowledge defining a stable world, knowledge about goals, and knowledge about categories) arises from sensorimotor interaction with the world.

369

We propose, similarly, that culture enters the scene not as a self-contained layer on top of behavior, but as the sum of sensorimotor knowledge brought about by a bodily agent interacting in a social and physical context. As such, culture diffuses the web of sensorimotor knowledge, and can only be arbitrarily circumscribed from other knowledge.

In the next few paragraphs, and in the research we present later, we apply this sensorimotor account to the development of interdependent and independent selves. We do not see this as the only application of the account, but as an example of how it applies to questions regarding culture.

On our view, interdependent and independent selves are constituted primarily by two pervasive types of sensorimotor interactions that are acquired and maintained through immersion in environments with different patterns of interpersonal interactions. The interdependent self develops when there are close interactions with the family and in-group members. These interactions "tune" the sensorimotor system to promote efficient interactions within this group. By tuning, we mean a process of neuroplasticity, or learning. For example, on learning a new behavior (e.g., how to crawl, how to walk, or how to talk), the mirror neuron system (Gallese, Keysers, and Rizzolatti, 2004; Rizzolatti and Craighero, 2004) tunes itself so that these skills are used in recognizing the homologous actions taken by others. After tuning of this sort, recognizing those actions is faster and more efficient than before tuning.

Furthermore, we propose that after sufficient sensorimotor tuning, the familiarity and fluency of tuned actions confer on these routines a value-like normative status; they become the "natural" way of engaging the world. Thus, strong sensorimotor tuning creates an in-group: the people with whom interactions are literally easy, efficient, and thereby enjoyable. In contrast, when people look, dress, smell, or talk differently, it is, we propose, literally more difficult to interact with them. As an example, consider conversing with an unskilled speaker of English; it can be difficult and exhausting. The unskilled speaker will pronounce and use words in unusual ways, use new metaphors and gestures, and use a syntax that does not easily match our tuned system. Thus, there will be misunderstandings, ambiguities, and the need for restatement that literally takes time and effort, and may generate annoyance because the extended interaction interferes with other goals.

Again, the developmental literature provides a powerful example. Before an infant is strongly tuned to its native language, it can perceive phonetic distinctions that are not incorporated into the native language (e.g., Aslin, Jusczyk, and Pisoni, 1998; Kuhl, Williams, Lacerda, Stevens, and Lindblom, 1992). However, once the infant has had considerable experience with the native language, the ability to perceive non-native distinctions is lost (e.g., the inability of native Japanese speakers to perceive the /l/ versus /r/ distinction).

We propose furthermore that the frequency and familiarity of tuned interactions make them more accessible to reflective, discursive consciousness. Thus, these sorts of interactions can be communicated through language and endorsed to a lesser or greater degree when encountered on a survey.

In contrast with the interdependent self, we propose that the independent self arises from more varied interactions with a broader array of people, sights, sounds, and actions. Thus the independent sensorimotor system becomes less narrowly tuned to particular practices.

By way of analogy, consider the different tuning required for soccer and (American) football players. Their knowledge of the "natural" mode of conduct in their respective game cultures is fundamentally constituted by an implicit repertoire of how to engage the ball, team members (i.e., in-group), and opponents (out-groups). For example, the suppression of a reflexive motor command to handle a looming ball manually in the case of the soccer (but not football) player is a preverbal, non-ideological bodily tendency that establishes his belonging to the soccer culture.

Of course, becoming a coach necessitates acquiring some skill in communicating knowledge in the form of instructional rules. This, however, does not necessarily bring about a change in the representational format of the basic knowledge from sensorimotor to symbolic or abstract. That is, the coach may describe the rule verbally, but it requires physical practice to instantiate the rule in behavior.

Thus, contrary to the mainstream view, explicit, verbalizable value statements come secondarily to what makes up culture. From the enculturated layperson's view (when serving as a participant in a cross-cultural study), values are not the source for culture but are contingent attempts to find an abstract generalization that captures the relevant confluence of implicit bodily routines. As such, the verbal value statements conform to the underlying procedural dispositions to the extent that these are accessible to consciousness and can be verbalized.

For our account to have any force, it must be the case that social and physical environments that foster interdependent and independent selves differentially afford the sensorimotor tuning we propose. The following excerpt from Adams and Markus (2004, p. 343) suggests that is the case:

> Given an exclusive emphasis on "subjective culture", there is a tendency to interpret cultural patterns like independent and interdependent construals of self ... [citing Markus and Kitayama, 1991] as differences in subjective beliefs. Instead these concepts refer to different constructions: beliefs built into the physical patterns of everyday life. The independent constructions of self and relationship that are prominent in mainstream American settings are not merely beliefs about separation. Instead, they are linked to a reality of separation that is built into structures of everyday life like dating practices, residence in apartment units, and individual ownership. Similarly, the more relational or interdependent constructions of self and relationship that are prominent cultural patterns in many West African settings are not merely beliefs about connection. Instead, they are linked to a reality of connection that is built into structures of everyday life like arranged marriage, residence in lineage compounds and the practice of eating meals from a communal bowl.

Research on child attachment theory has also documented systematic differences in child-rearing practices between Western and Eastern settings. In Japan (Rothbaum, Weisz, Pott, Miyake, and Morelli, 2000), Cameroon (Keller, Voelker, and Yovsi, 2005), India (Saraswathi and Pai, 1997), and Mexico (Brazelton, Robey, and Collier, 1969), children are carried along in the daytime and sleep next to their mothers at night. Children are watched and even breastfed by neighbors and relatives. Mothers are keen to quickly or even anticipatorily respond to their children's distress signals, which "minimizes self-other distinction" (Greenfield, Keller, Fuligni, and Maynard, 2003, p. 470).

Thus, from birth onward, the child's sensory and motor systems are immersed in tangible socio-physical environments with a tacit predominance of either independence/individualistic or interdependence/collectivistic practices. Only (or predominantly) by virtue of their substantial incarnation in the palpable physical and interpersonal structures of the local environment do these practices gain their psychological force and appear to the researcher as an ideology. They carve a peculiar profile of sensorimotor tuning of the child's body as she strives to make sense and effectively participate in the daily behavioral "rituals" dictated by the local social and physical ecology.

In short, the account we advocate as an alternative does not stop at the assertion that culture is embodied. Rather, we understand culture, that is, sensorimotor tuning, to infuse virtually all knowledge. Culture does not have domain-specific mechanisms of its own, but works through biases in interactional sensorimotor mechanisms.

Clearly, this conception of culture raises enough empirical questions to fill several lifetimes of research. We begin by reporting on two projects that address some of those salient questions. In the first project, we ask if our conception of culture, based on tuning of sensorimotor mechanisms, can play out in a prototypical sensorimotor task: distance estimation. In the second, we ask if close sensorimotor interaction can result in the formation of an in-group.

Project 1: Culture and distance estimation

How do we estimate the distance to objects? Almost certainly, we are not born with built-in rulers that give us measures in feet or meters. Instead, we seem to use body-based rulers (Proffitt and Linkenauger, 2013): eye height provides the unit for measuring the height of an object (e.g., it's about as tall as I am), the hand is used for scaling graspable objects (I can easily grasp it), the length of the arm scales reachable objects in peripersonal space (I can reach it), and the amount of effort needed to traverse a distance is used as a measure of that distance. Thus, as reviewed in Proffitt (2006), participants reported inflated visual distance to targets that required more motor effort to reach. Similarly, participants who were wearing a backpack, exhausted, in poor fitness, elderly, or in ill health reported hills to appear steeper when compared with their fit, healthy, younger, or rested counterparts.

We combined Proffitt's insights with our speculations about culture to generate the cultural-effort hypothesis: because it is easier to interact with in-group members than out-group members, in-group members should be seen as literally closer than out-group members. However, because sensorimotor tuning to the in-group is stronger for those with interdependent self-construals than those with independent self-construals, we predicted that the difference in distance estimation would be greater for interdependents.

In the first experiment (for details, see Soliman, Gibson, and Glenberg, 2013), participants filled out the paper-and-pencil Singelis (1994) scales to get a measure of interdependence and independence. For example, agreeing that, "I feel good when I cooperate with others," is taken as evidence for an interdependent self-construal. We computed the ratio of the interdependence to independence scales, and we refer to this ratio as "measured interdependence." The participants practiced making distance judgments in terms of the number of seconds it would take to walk to a target, namely, an experimental confederate. Finally, the participants moved to a new location and judged distances to the confederate (literal distances were between 6.77 and 22.43 meters). Importantly, the participants were American students and the confederates were American students (in-group).

Of course, judged distance (seconds) increased as a function of literal distance; on average, each meter of literal distance increased the judged distance by 0.86 seconds (see Figure 30.1). More importantly for the cultural-effort hypothesis, there was a statistically significant interaction: the more interdependent the participant, the shorter the estimated distance to the in-group confederate, and this was particularly true for the longer distances.

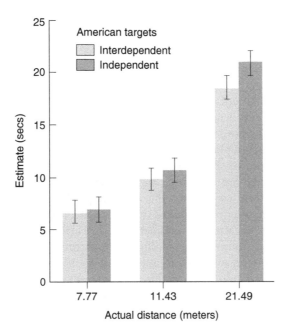

Figure 30.1 Mean estimated distance (in seconds, sec, to walk to the target) as a function of actual distance (in meters, m) for American participants judging distances to American (in-group) targets. The "interdependent" mean estimates are for one standard deviation above the mean measured interdependence; the "independent" mean estimates are for one standard deviation below the mean measured interdependence. Error bars indicate one standard error.

The fact that we observed an interaction (that the difference in judged distance between interdependents and independents increased with distance) and not simply an overall difference between interdependents and independents is important for demonstrating that the groups were using different measurement scales (Proffitt and Linkenauger, 2013). Note that when the unit of measurement differs, the difference becomes larger with increased distance (an interaction). For example, suppose that person A measures distance in feet, and person B measures distance in yards. At a distance of 1 yard, the two measurements, 3 (feet) and 1 (yard), differ by 2. But at a distance of 5 yards, the two measures, 15 (feet) and 5 (yards), differ by 10. Thus, the interaction is strong evidence that the interdependents and independents are measuring distance using different scales, namely different amounts of expected effort.

Although the data from Experiment 1 are consistent with the cultural-effort hypothesis, this novel finding needs to be replicated, it needs to be extended to other cultures, and we need to test additional predictions. For example, when judging distances to out-group members, we should find the reverse effect. That is, interdependents are strongly tuned to the in-group, and so interactions with out-group members should be seen as particularly effortful. For independents, who are not strongly tuned to the in-group, interactions with the out-group should not be particularly effortful. Thus, when interacting with the out-group, we predict that literal distances should appear farther for interdependents than for independents, the reverse of the data in Figure 30.1.

We tested these ideas in a new experiment that included both Arab and American participants. Our confederates were two dark-skinned women, one of whom wore a hijab (Arab head covering). The idea was to make it appear that the confederates were members of the in-group for the Arab participants and members of the out-group for the American participants.

The distance estimates are displayed in Figure 30.2. Again, there is a large increase in estimated distance with real distance (0.81 seconds/meter). In addition, there were two statistically significant interactions. The first interaction was between culture (Arab or American) and measured interdependence. For the Arabs, when judging distance to in-group members (the Arab-looking confederates), the interdependents produced smaller estimates than the independents, thus replicating the effects seen in Experiment 1, but with participants from a different culture. For the Americans, when judging distance to out-group members (the Arab-looking confederates), the interdependents produced larger estimates than the independents, thus confirming the reversal predicted from the cultural-effort hypothesis. The second interaction indicated that these effects of culture and self-construal increased with distance, replicating the interaction in Experiment 1, and strongly confirming the prediction that the groups are using different measurement scales.

These findings can be seen only as preliminary: it is still necessary to replicate using participants from additional cultures, and although Proffitt's mechanism of expected motor effort seems to be a plausible cause underlying these cultural differences in visual estimates, this mechanism still needs to be directly implicated. Nonetheless, the findings are clearly

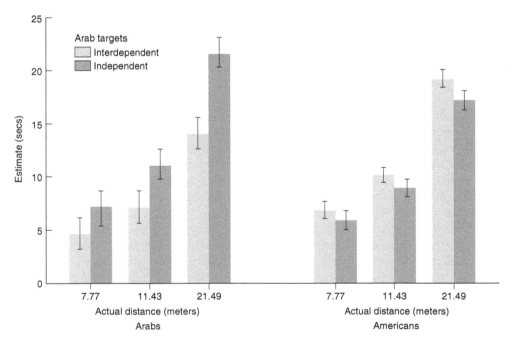

Figure 30.2 Mean estimated distance (in seconds, sec, to walk to the target) as a function of actual distance (in meters, m) for Arab participants (on the left) and for American participants (on the right). Both groups of participants judged distances to Arab-looking targets. The "interdependent" mean estimates are for one standard deviation above the mean measured interdependence (for Arab or American groups separately); the "independent" mean estimates are for one standard deviation below the mean measured interdependence. Error bars indicate one standard error.

consistent with the cultural-effort hypothesis in particular and with our claims about the sensorimotor nature of culture in general. They point to the possibility of redefining interdependence and independence by recourse, not to explicit values and beliefs, but to sensorimotor interpersonal repertoires that are either narrowly tuned to in-group interactional practices, or more broadly tuned, and appearing to be more culturally diverse.

Project 2: Tuning the sensorimotor system and the joint body schema

An important part of our approach to culture is the idea that frequent interaction and coordination tunes the sensorimotor system in the service of efficient interaction. The first project presumed greater tuning among same-culture participants and greater tuning for interdependents than independents. In the second project, we attempt to create sensorimotor tuning and measure some of its manifestations, namely, changes in the body schema.

Primates use a body schema to track the locations of their limbs. This schema is malleable (a) because it must change with development and growth, and (b) because it adapts with tool use (as reviewed below). Here we predict that adaptation of the body schema when coordinating with another person will be particularly strong among those with interdependent self-construals. That is, because interdependents have a developmental history of closely attending to (in-group) others, they should show a particularly robust adaptation of the body schema.

The experiments had two phases. In the first phase, the participant and the confederate coordinated for five minutes by moving a flexible wire back and forth to cut through candles (see Figure 30.3; for details, see Soliman, Ferguson, and Glenberg, n.d., submitted). The task required close coordination to keep the wire taut so that it would cut. In the basic experimental condition illustrated in Figure 30.3, the participant (on the right) uses her right hand to hold one end of the wire tool, and the confederate uses her left hand.

The second phase of the experiment was the flash/buzz paradigm as developed by Maravita, Spence, Kennett, and Driver (2002). Using this procedure, the participant has a cell phone buzzer attached to the index finger and another attached to the thumb. One of the buzzers is activated, and the task is to indicate (using a foot pedal) whether the thumb or index finger had been stimulated. The task is trivially easy. However, if the two fingers are held next to LEDs, and the LEDs flash in temporal synchrony with the buzzer but spatially incongruously (e.g., the thumb is stimulated by the buzzer but the LED next to the index finger is flashed), participants are slowed and make errors.

Maravita *et al.* (2002) demonstrated that tool use can modify the interference from incongruous trials in the flash/buzz procedure. Namely, before using a tool, the LEDs interfere with localization of the vibration only when they are near the fingers, that is, in peripersonal space. After using a tool (e.g., a rake), the LEDs can be located at the end of the tool, outside the usual peripersonal space, and still interfere with localization of the active buzzer.

Maravita and Iriki (2004) review the physiological basis for this effect. In brief, there are bimodal neurons in the parietal cortex that have both somatosensory and visual receptive fields focused on the hand. That is, touching or stimulating the hand increases the firing of these neurons on the basis of the somatosensory receptive field. The same neuron also has a visual receptive field so that looking near the hand increases the firing rate of the neuron. Thus, the neuron appears to be useful for coordinating between vision and touch. Furthermore, after tool use, the visual receptive field migrates to include the effector end of

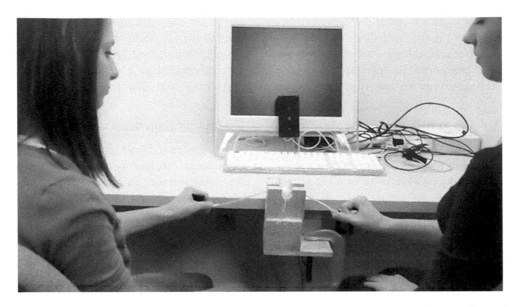

Figure 30.3 The arrangement for inducing and measuring the JBS (joint body schema) effect. The confederate, on the left, is using her left hand to help saw the candle. The participant, on the right, is using her right hand. Note that her left hand is in her lap. The candle is held horizontally in the wooden holder. The LEDs are mounted on the bottom of the screen. During the measurement phase, the confederate holds her left hand near the LEDs so that her index finger is near the top LED and her thumb is near the bottom LED.

the tool even if that end is outside peripersonal space. Now the neural firing serves to coordinate the sight of the end of the tool with the feel at the hand. Thus, tool use adapts the body schema so that it incorporates the tool in the service of effective wielding.

We had two questions. First, does close coordination with another person act to adapt the body schema as if the other person were a social tool? That is, would our participants adapt their own body schemas to incorporate aspects of the partner in the service of effective coordination? Second, would this adaptation of the body schema be more pronounced for those with interdependent self-construals? If so, then after coordination in the candle-cutting task, when the in-group confederate holds her hand near the LEDs, incongruous flashes should interfere with the interdependent participant's ability to localize the buzzing stimulus on her own fingers. We refer to this possibility as the development of a joint body schema (JBS).

The experiments also examined several other constraints on the development of the JBS. First, the interference produced by the confederate's fingers near the LEDs should only be found after the confederate and the participant jointly cooperate in cutting the candle. When the participant cuts the candle herself by using a wire with a plumb weight on one end (to replace the confederate), there should be little interference produced by the confederate's fingers near the LEDs. In fact, we will use as a measure of the JBS the following difference of differences. After the participant and the confederate have coordinated in cutting the candle, we measure the time for the participant to correctly localize the buzz on her fingers when the confederate has her fingers near the LEDs. The first difference is between the mean for incongruous trials compared with the mean for congruous trials (when the flashing LED is near the confederate's finger that is homologous to the participant's finger that is stimulated). This difference indicates the interference produced by incongruous trials. We also compute the same difference after the participant has cut the candle by herself, although the confederate holds her fingers near the LEDs. The difference of the differences is produced by subtracting from the first difference (the interference effect after coordination) the second difference (the interference effect after no coordination). This difference of differences tells us whether by coordinating with the confederate, the participant has adjusted her own body schema, that is, whether the confederate has become a social tool. This difference-of-differences score is depicted on the far left in Figure 30.4, and we will refer to it as the JBS effect.

Second, if the body schema of the participant is actually affected (rather than the participant simply learning to attend to the confederate's hand), then the JBS effect should be most pronounced when the participant is buzzed on her left hand, the hand homologous to that used by the confederate in jointly cutting the candle. The JBS effect should be reduced if the participant is buzzed on her right hand. The right-hand (non-significant) JBS effect is illustrated by the bar second from the left in Figure 30.4.

Third, if the confederate uses her right hand to cut the candle, then there should be a reduced JBS effect on the participant's left hand. This non-significant JBS effect is illustrated by the third bar.

Fourth, and most relevant to the current purposes, if the participant has an interdependent self-construal, that is, her developmental history has primed her to attend closely to

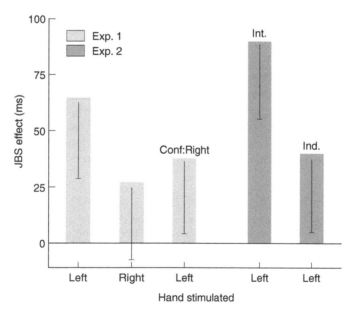

Figure 30.4 The mean JBS (joint body schema) effect (in milliseconds, ms, see text for explanation). In all conditions, the confederate held her left hand at the LED (see Figure 30.3). In all conditions except the one labeled "Conf:Right," the confederate had used her left hand to help cut the candle. For Experiment 2 (Exp 2), the "interdependent" (Int) mean estimate is for one standard deviation above the mean measured interdependence; the "independent" (Ind) mean estimate is for one standard deviation below the mean measured interdependence. Error bars are one standard error although only the lower error bars are illustrated.

others, then she should develop a large JBS effect compared to participants with independent self-construals. The statistically significant JBS effect for interdependent participants is illustrated in the fourth bar, and the non-significant effect for the participants with independent self-construals is illustrated in the fifth bar. (The data contributing to the first and fourth bars are from different participants. Thus the data provide a replication of the JBS effect across experiments; see Soliman, Ferguson *et al.*, n.d., submitted, for details.)

We think that the JBS effect is likely to be much more than a laboratory curiosity. Note that societies offer multiple opportunities for close coordination: dancing, singing, marching, praying, cooking, manufacturing. All of these opportunities can, we suspect, create multiple JBSs that become the basis for the in-group. Furthermore, we suspect that having a JBS is a precondition for a strong empathetic response. In fact, others have already demonstrated that synchronous behavior does enhance empathy. Finally, the notion of a JBS helps us to understand not just in-group favoritism, but also out-group derogation. That is, people with whom one has interacted feel close, perhaps even part of the self, because of the JBS. In contrast, people with whom one has not interacted appear distant, separate from the self, and perhaps even different in kind.

Conclusions

In this chapter, we presented the first pass of a unified sensorimotor account of culture. In place of dualistic conceptions that propose a distinction between values and behaviors, we conceive of culture as a repertoire of bodily modes of interaction. These modes develop through, and ultimately serve, effective participation in socio-physical ecologies. In support of this view, we empirically demonstrated two effects. First, part of having an interdependent self-construal is to experience more bodily effort when interactions with out-group members loom. Second, interdependents easily adapt their own body schemas to incorporate the kinematics of an in-group partner. Being an independent, on the other hand, partly means that one is likely to experience less differential effort when interacting with in- or out-group members, and after interacting, the independent will maintain a stronger distinction between self and other. These preverbal bodily ways of relating to others, we believe, constitute the foundations of the psychological fabric of culture.

References

Adams, G., and Markus, H. R. (2004). Toward a conception of culture suitable for a social psychology of culture. In M. Schaller and C. S. Crandall (Eds), *The psychological foundations of culture*. Hillsdale, NJ: Erlbaum.

Aslin, R. N., Jusczyk, P. W., and Pisoni, D. B. (1998). Speech and auditory processing during infancy. In D. Kuhn and R. Siegler (Eds), *Handbook of child psychology: Cognition, perception, and language* (5th ed.). New York: Wiley.

Atran, S., Medin, D., and Ross, N. (2005). The cultural mind: Environmental decision making and cultural modeling within and across populations. *Psychological Review*, 112(4), 744–776.

Brazelton, T. B., Robey, J. S., and Collier, G. (1969). Infant development in the Zinacanteco Indians of southern Mexico. *Pediatrics*, 44(2), 274–283.

Cohen, D., Nisbett, R. E., Bowdle, B. F., and Schwarz, N. (1996). Insult, aggression, and the southern culture of honor: An "experimental ethnography". *Journal of Personality and Social Psychology*, 70(5), 945–960.

D'Andrade, R. (2000). The action system hypothesis. Paper presented at a Colloquium Given by the Committee on Human Development at the University of Chicago, May.

Dahl, A., Campos, J. J., Anderson, D. I., Uchiyama, I., Witherington, D. C., Ueno, M., (2013). The epigenesis of wariness of heights. *Psychological Science, 24(7)*, 1361–1367.

Gallese, V., Keysers, C., and Rizzolatti, G. (2004). A unifying view of the basis of social cognition. *Trends in Cognitive Sciences, 8(9)*, 396–403.

Greenfield, P. M., Keller, H., Fuligni, A., and Maynard, A. (2003). Cultural pathways through universal development. *Annual Review of Psychology, 54*, 461–490.

Haidt, J., and Hersh, M. A. (2001). Sexual morality: The cultures and emotions of conservatives and liberals. *Journal of Applied Social Psychology, 31*, 191–221.

Hong, Y., and Chiu, C. (2001). Toward a paradigm shift: From cross-cultural differences in social cognition to social-cultural mediation of cultural differences. *Social Cognition, 19*, 181–196.

Keller, H., Voelker, S., and Yovsi, R. D. (2005). Conceptions of parenting in different cultural communities: The case of West African Nso and northern German women. *Social Development, 14(1)*, 158–180.

Kitayama, S. (2002). Culture and basic psychological processes–Toward a system view of culture: Comment on Oyserman (2002). *Psychological Bulletin, 128(1)*, 89–96.

Kroeber, A. L., and Kluckhohn, C. (1963). *Culture: A critical review of concepts and definitions.* Cambridge, MA: Harvard University Press. (Orig. publ. 1952.)

Kuhl, P. K., Williams, K. A., Lacerda, F., Stevens, K. N., and Lindblom, B. (1992). Linguistic experience alters phonetic perception in infants by 6 months of age. *Science, 255(5044)*, 606–608.

Maravita, A., and Iriki, A. (2004). Tools for the body (schema). *Trends in Cognitive Sciences, 8(2)*, 79–86.

Maravita, A., Spence, C., Kennett, S., and Driver, J. (2002). Tool-use changes multimodal spatial interactions between vision and touch in normal humans. *Cognition, 83(2)*, B25–34.

Markus, H. R., and Kitayama, S. (1991). Culture and the self: Implications for cognition, emotion, and motivation. *Psychological Review, 98(2)*, 224–253.

—— (2010). Culture and selves: A cycle of mutual constitution. *Perspectives on Psychological Science, 5(4)*, 420–430.

Nisbett, R. E., and Miyamoto, Y. (2005). The influence of culture: Holistic versus analytic perception. *Trends in Cognitive Sciences, 9(10)*, 467–473.

Norenzayan, A., Smith, E. E., Kim, B., and Nisbett, R. E. (2002). Cultural preferences for formal versus intuitive reasoning. *Cognitive Science, 26(5)*, 653–684.

Oyserman, D., Coon, H., and Kemmelmeier, M. (2002). Rethinking individualism and collectivism: Evaluation of theoretical assumptions and meta-analyses. *Psychological Bulletin, 128(1)*, 3–72.

Proffitt, D. R. (2006). Embodied perception and the economy of action. *Perspectives on Psychological Science, 1(2)*, 110–122.

Proffitt, D. R., and Linkenauger, S. A. (2013). Perception viewed as a phenotypic expression. In W. Prinz, M. Beisert, and A. Herwig (Eds), *Action science: Foundations of an emerging discipline.* Cambridge, MA: MIT Press.

Rizzolatti, G., and Craighero, L. (2004). The mirror neuron system. *Annual Review of Neuroscience, 27(1)*, 169–192.

Rothbaum, F., Weisz, J., Pott, M., Miyake, K., and Morelli, G. (2000). Attachment and culture: Security in the United States and Japan. *American Psychologist, 55(10)*, 1093–1104.

Saraswathi, T. S., and Pai, S. (1997). Socialization in the Indian context. In H. S. R. Kao and D. Sinha (Eds), *Asian perspectives on psychology.* Thousand Oaks, CA: Sage.

Singelis, T. (1994). The measurement of independent and interdependent self-construals. *Personality and Social Psychology Bulletin, 20(5)*, 580–591.

Smith, L. B. (2005). Action alters shape categories. *Cognitive Science, 29(4)*, 665–679.

Soliman, T., Ferguson, R., and Glenberg, A. M. (n.d. submitted). *Humans develop an interpersonal joint body schema.*

Soliman, T., Gibson, A., and Glenberg, A. M. (2013). Sensory motor mechanisms unify psychology: The embodiment of culture. *Frontiers in Psychology.* doi: 10.3389/fpsyg.2013.00885

Sommerville, J. A., Woodward, A. L., and Needham, A. (2005). Action experience alters 3-month-old infants' perception of others' actions. *Cognition, 96(1)*, B1–11.

Swidler, A. (2001). *Talk of love: How culture matters.* Chicago: University of Chicago Press.

Triandis, H. (1995). *Individualism and collectivism.* Boulder, CO: Westview Press.

Tripathi, L. (2001). Culture as a psychological construct. *Psychology and Developing Societies*, *13*(2), 129–140.

Vaisey, S. (2008). Socrates, Skinner, and Aristotle: Three ways of thinking about culture in action. *Sociological Forum*, *23*, 603–613.

Varnum, M., Grossman, I., Kitayama, S., and Nisbett, R. (2010). The origin of cultural differences in cognition: Evidence for the social orientation hypothesis. *Current Directions in Psychological Science*, *19*(1), 9–13.

31

THE CONSTITUTION OF GROUP COGNITION

Gerry Stahl

Cognition at multiple levels

There is a venerable tradition in philosophy that cognition is a mysterious faculty of individual human beings. Increasingly since the late nineteenth century, it has become clear that even when thoughts appear to be expressed by an individual they are the product of more complex factors. Cognitive abilities and perspectives develop over time through one's embeddedness in a physical, social, cultural and historical world. Thinking is closely related to speaking, a form of communication with others. Particularly in our technological world, thinking is mediated by a broad variety of artifacts and by other features of the context in which we are situated.

Rather than thinking about thinking, I try to explore cognition by generating data in which one can observe cognitive processes at work (Stahl, 2006, 2009, 2013). I do this by having small groups of students collaborate on mathematical problems in a setting where their whole interaction can be captured. The motivation for this approach is the theory of Vygotsky, the sociocultural psychologist who proposed that higher-level human mental abilities are acquired first in small-group interactions. In exploring such group cognition, I have found that there is a rich interplay of processes at individual, small-group and community levels of cognitive processing.

In the following, I will summarize three case studies in order to illustrate how cognitive processes at multiple levels can work together. In the first case, two students solve a high-school math problem that has stumped them for some time. The problem-solving steps the dyad go through as a team are typical for how proficient students solve problems individually. In the discourse captured in this case, one can see how the *group* integrates contributions from the two *individual* participants to accomplish a task in accordance with *community* standards of practice—illustrating the productive interplay of cognitive levels. The sequence of ten discourse moves by the group details their extended *sequential approach* to the problem. In the second study, three students develop techniques for helping each other to see what they are seeing in the diagram they have drawn for a math problem. This *persistent co-attention* to a shared object of analysis allows the team to solve their problem

DOI: 10.4324/9781003322511-40

as a group. Similarly in the third example, the students are able to work together because they effectively manage their *shared understanding* of the problem.

I propose that it is often fruitful to analyze cognition on multiple levels and that the processes at the different levels work together. A variety of *interactional resources* are typically at work bridging the levels. In the three illustrative case studies, topics in high-school mathematics centrally figure as resources that bring together individual, small-group and community cognitive processes.

Virtual math teams

The study of group cognition requires careful review and analysis of all the interaction within a group during the achievement of a cognitively significant task, such as solving a challenging problem. I have arranged for this by designing an online software environment in which several people can meet and interact effectively to solve math problems. This virtual math teams (VMT) environment supports synchronous text chat and a shared whiteboard for drawing figures (Stahl, 2009). Recently, it has been expanded to incorporate a multi-user version of dynamic geometry, in which geometric figures can be interactively constructed and dynamically dragged (Stahl, 2013). The software is instrumented to capture all interaction and to allow it to be displayed, replayed and analyzed. This avoids the many problems of audio and video recording in classrooms. Students communicate online, avoiding the interpretational issues of eye gaze, bodily gesture and vocal intonation. When possible, groups are composed of students who do not know each other outside the online setting, so that researchers reviewing a record of interaction can know everything about the participants and their background knowledge that the participants know about each other. Since group cognition is defined as consisting of those knowledge-building or problem-solving processes that take place in the group interaction (Stahl, 2006), the VMT environment can capture a complete history of group-cognitive events.

When a group enters the VMT environment, it is presented with a challenging math problem, designed to guide the group interaction in an academically productive direction. The problem acts as a resource for the group. The group must interpret the problem statement, elaborate the way in which it wants to conceive the problem and determine how to proceed. A math problem can serve as an effective interactional resource for bridging across cognitive levels. Typically, it introduces content—definitions, elements, procedures, principles, practices, proposals, theorems, questions—from the cultural traditions of mathematics and from school curriculum. In so doing, it recalls or stimulates individual cognitive responses—memories, skills, knowledge, calculations, deductions. It is then up to the group interaction to bring these together, to organize the individual contributions as they unfold in the ongoing interaction in order to achieve the goals called for by the community, institutional, disciplinary and historical sources. In this way, the group interaction may play a central role in the multilevel cognition, interpreting, enacting and integrating elements from the other levels, producing a unified cognitive result and thereby providing a model for future community practice or individual skill.

It may seem ironic that an online environment has been selected for the empirical study of how cognition is "embodied" in group interactions and community contexts. In the VMT environment, participants are not physically present to each other. They do not see interactional contributions being produced by individuals. Rather, text-chat postings suddenly appear as complete units on the screen and geometric elements are drawn or dragged without visible hands manipulating them. As we will see below, Aznx does not see how Bwang is gradually putting together and occasionally repairing a sentence to be posted. Jason cannot follow Qwertyuiop's gaze to see where his attention is focused. Yet, there are some elements of embodiment, at least virtually. Each participant is represented in the VMT interface with a login handle associated with their chat postings. There are awareness notices indicating who is typing a pending chat contribution or who is engaged in a geometric construction action. The software interface presents a complexly structured visual manifold. Students quickly develop online practices to adapt to the new environment, to overcome the limitations of the medium and to implement alternative means for missing abilities, as seen in the following case studies. Within this computer-mediated context, individual and group levels of cognition are focused on situated entities from specific perspectives; multilevel cognition is embodied in an intersubjective world.

Constructing diamonds

Cognition is neither a unitary phenomenon nor a temporally fixed one. Hegel described the logical stages involved in the development of cognition in his *Phenomenology of Mind* (1807/1967). Vygotsky explored the development of a person's cognition through psychological experiments reported in *Mind in Society* (1930/1978), emphasizing the priority of intersubjective group cognition:

> Every function in the child's cultural development appears twice: first, on the social level, and later, on the individual level; first, between people (*interpsychological*), and then *inside* the child (*intrapsychological*). This applies equally to voluntary attention, to logical memory, and to the formation of concepts. All the higher [human mental] functions originate as actual relations between human individuals.
>
> *(p. 57)*

Research on CSCL (computer-supported collaborative learning) (Stahl, Koschmann and Suthers, 2013) can make visible the development and the unfolding of cognitive functions in small groups, shedding light on the less visible processes that can subsequently be carried out by people individually or "internally." A research method for undertaking such analysis is suggested by the field of conversation analysis (CA) (Sacks, 1962/1995). CA was inspired by ethno-methodology, a sociological approach focused on describing the "work" that people typically do in interactions with others to establish social order and to construct meaning (Garfinkel, 1967). CA applies this approach to analyzing everyday conversation. A central finding of CA is that the work of conversation is accomplished through the sequential construction of "adjacency pairs," short sequences in which one person's utterance elicits a response in the form of a following utterance by an interlocutor—for instance a question-answer pair. In looking for examples of mathematical problem solving by groups, we are more interested in "longer sequences," in which a series of adjacency pairs are constructed to accomplish the larger cognitive goal.

Longer sequences have only been suggested in CA (Sacks, 1962/1995, Vol. 2, p. 354; Schegloff, 2007, pp. 12, 213), not extensively analyzed. In the final excerpt from a VMT interaction among three students, I analyzed their successful problem-solving effort as a longer sequence, consisting of ten discourse moves, each linguistically organized as an adjacency pair (Stahl, 2011). I treated their four-hour-long online interaction in terms of a

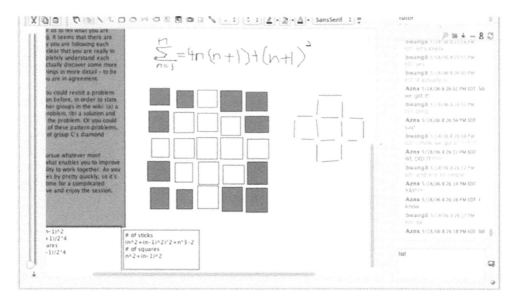

Figure 31.1 Discussion and drawings of diamond pattern.

temporal hierarchy of: a group event, four scheduled sessions, several conversational topics, many discourse moves, adjacency pairs, textual utterances and indexical references. In the first session, the students had been asked to work on a topic in mathematical combinatorics, determining the number of squares and composite sticks needed to build a stair-step pattern at different stages of growth. By the fourth session, the students had set themselves the topic of analyzing a diamond pattern, illustrated by them at stages n = 2 and n = 3 in the screen image of the VMT software interface in Figure 31.1.

In their final conversational topic, two students with login names of Bwang and Aznx decide to try again to solve this problem, despite not being able to do so for the past two hours and despite the fact that their scheduled online time is already over. In the course of ten minutes, 100 chat lines of text are posted. The analysis highlights ten adjacency pairs that were central to this discourse. Each adjacency pair is listed in Log 1, under an added descriptive heading. Although there is not space here to provide the full chat or a complete analysis, this selection from the interaction should give a sense of the problem-solving process.

Log 1 Ten moves of the problem-solving topic

Move 1. Open the topic
  Bwangi think we are very close to solving the problem here
  AznxWe can solve on that topic.
Move 2. Decide to start
  Bwangwell do you want to solve the problem
  AznxAlright.

Move 3. Pick an approach
    AznxHow do you want to approach it?
    Bwang1st level have 1*4 ... 4th level have (1+3+5+7)*4
Move 4. Identify the pattern
    AznxSo it's a pattern of +2s?
    Bwangyes
Move 5. Seek the equation
    Bwangwhat is it
    Aznxn^2 ... or (n/2)^2
Move 6. Negotiate the solution
    Aznxits n^2
    Bwangso that's wrong
Move 7. Check cases
    Aznxwould be 4n^2
    Bwangit actually is
Move 8. Celebrate the solution
    Bwangi think we got it!!!!!!!!!!!!
    AznxWE DID IT!!!!!!
Move 9. Present a formal solution
    AznxSo you're putting it in the wiki, right?
    Bwangyes
Move 10. Close
    Aznxwe should keep in touch
    Bwangyeah

There are several things to note here:

- Most importantly, the sequence of moves is strikingly similar to how an experienced math problem solver might approach the topic individually, as described at a particular granularity.
- The two students take turns contributing to the shared topic. The group direction is not set by either individual, but results from their interaction.
- Most opening utterances solicit a response, often in the explicit form of a question, and they always await a response.
- Each move is a situated response to the current state of the students' understanding of the topic as expressed in the discourse—rather than some kind of logical progression following a plan based on some kind of goal-subgoal hierarchy (Suchman, 2007).
- The focus of the group discourse moves is on the sharing, negotiation and agreement about their progress, rather than on details of mathematical facts or computations.
- The math content is handled by the individuals and contributed by them into the collaborative setting, for instance in move 3 or 5.
- The temporal structure of topics, moves and adjacency pairs is not imposed by the analyst, but is projected in the remarks of the participants as integral to how they make meaning for themselves about what they are doing.

If one follows the development of the students' understanding in their postings across the four sessions, one is struck by changing roles and confidence levels, as well as by their mastery of practices that one or the other introduced into the group. It is quite plausible that over time the lessons acquired in their collaborative interactions become manifested in their individual cognitive skills. The longer sequences of argumentation or problem solving become "internalized" (as Vygotsky called it) or adopted as cognitive practices of individuals. The power of collaborative learning is partially to bring together multiple perspectives, which can be debated, negotiated, synthesized, contextualized, structured and refined. However, another advantage is to extend the cognitive effort into *longer sequences* of argumentation through the stimulation and enjoyment of productive social interaction, increasing the time-on-task as needed to solve challenging problems. Thus, groups can achieve cognitive accomplishments that their members cannot—and the members can learn from these achievements.

Visualizing hexagons

Elsewhere, we have analyzed in some detail the intimate coordination of visual, narrative and symbolic activity involving the text chat and shared whiteboard in VMT sessions (Çakir and Stahl, 2013; Çakir, Zemel and Stahl, 2009). Here, we want to bring out the importance of literally looking at some mathematical object together in order to share the visual experience and to relate to—to intend or to "be at"—the entity together. People often use the expression "I do not see what you mean" in the metaphorical sense of not understanding what someone else is saying. In our second case study, we often encounter the expression used literally for not being able to visually perceive a graphical object, at least not being able to see it in the way that the speaker apparently sees it.

While empiricist philosophy refers to people taking in uninterpreted sense data much like arrays of computer pixels, post-cognitive philosophy emphasizes the phenomenon of "seeing as." Wittgenstein noted that one immediately sees a wire-frame drawing of a cube not as a set of lines, but as a cube oriented either one way or another (1953, §177). For Heidegger, seeing things as already meaningful is not the result of cognitive interpretation, but the precondition of being able to explicate that meaning further in understanding (1927/1996, pp. 139f.). For collaborative problem solving and mathematical deduction, it is clearly important that the participants see the visual mathematical objects as the same, in the same way. This seems to be an issue repeatedly in the online session excerpted in Log 2, involving three high-school students with login handles of Jason, Qwertyuiop and 137 (Stahl, Zhou, Çakir and Sarmiento-Klapper, 2011).

Student 137 proposes a mathematical task for the group in line 705 of Log 2. This is the first time that the term "hexagonal array" has been used. Coined in this posting, the term will become sedimented (Husserl, 1936/1989, p. 164) as a mathematical object for the group as the discourse continues. However, at this point it is problematic for both Qwertyuiop and Jason. In line 706, Qwertyuiop poses a question for clarification and receives an affirmative, but minimal, response. Jason, unsatisfied with the response, escalates the clarification request by asking for help in seeing the diagram in the whiteboard *as* a "hexagonal array," so he can see it *as* 137 sees it. Between Jason's request in line 709 and acceptance in line 710, Qwertyuiop and 137 work together to add lines outlining a large hexagon in the triangular array. Demonstrating his ability to now see the hexagons, Jason thereupon proceeds with the mathematical work, which he had halted in the beginning of

Log 2 Seeing a hexagonal array collaboratively

705	19:15:08	137	So do you want to first calculate the number of triangles in a hexagonal array?
706	19:15:45	qwertyuiop	What's the shape of the array? a hexagon?
707	19:16:02	137	Ya.
708	19:16:15	qwertyuiop	ok...
709	19:16:41	Jason	wait- can someone highlight the hexagonal array on the diagram? i don't really see what you mean...
710	19:17:30	Jason	hmm... okay
711	19:17:43	qwertyuiop	oops
712	19:17:44	Jason	so it has at least 6 triangles?
713	19:17:58	Jason	in this, for instance

line 709 in order to keep the group aligned. Jason tentatively proposes that every hexagon "has at least 6 triangles" and he makes this visible to everyone by pointing to an illustrative small hexagon from the chat posting, using the VMT graphical pointing tool. Later, the students take turns using these group-defined methods of supporting shared vision and attention: using colored lines and the pointing tool, as seen in Figure 31.2.

Jason dramatically halted group work with his "wait." For him, it was impossible to continue until everyone could see the same thing in the way that 137 saw it. During this session, the students taught each other how to change the color and thickness of lines they

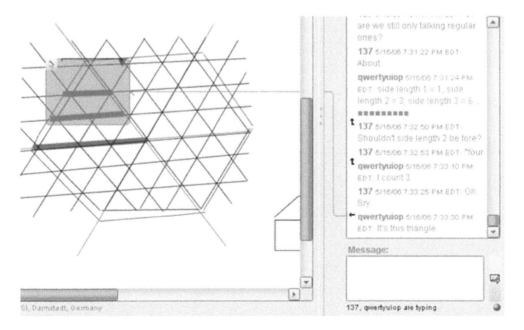

Figure 31.2 Discussion and drawing of hexagon grid.

constructed in the shared whiteboard. These were affordances of the VMT software, but the students had to learn how to use the features and they developed certain shared group practices of using colored lines to outline, highlight and draw attention to specific elements of the hexagonal grid. For instance, in Figure 31.2, blue lines outline a hexagon of side length 3; red lines divide that hexagon into six symmetric triangles; thick green lines pick out the three horizontal lines of length 1, 2 and 3 in one of the triangles; and the VMT pointing tool focuses attention on that triangle. There are many ways to count the number of unit sticks in the large hexagon. In order to count them as a group, everyone's attention must be focused on the same elements, such as the green horizontals. Then it is possible for each participant to count that subset visually: 1 + 2 + 3 = 6. Through similar shared attention to structural elements of the hexagon, all the group members know that there are three such arrays of lines like the green ones at different orientations in each of the six triangles. They can also see how this array of lines will increase as the hexagon itself progresses to successively longer side lengths. The achievement of the necessary *persistent co-attention* to construct and to follow this complicated analysis was the result of subtle interactions and the development of shared practices within the group.

Inscribing triangles

Our final case involves a group of three middle-school students given a topic in dynamic geometry (Stahl, 2013, §7.3). The students have not yet had a course in geometry, but have already spent four hours together in a version of VMT that incorporates interactive, multi-user support for dynamic geometry. In this topic, the students are given constructions of an equilateral triangle inscribed inside another equilateral triangle and a square inscribed inside another square (see Figure 31.3). In dynamic geometry, a student can drag one point of a figure like the inscribed squares and all the other points and lines will move accordingly, maintaining the geometric relationships or dependencies that have been built into the

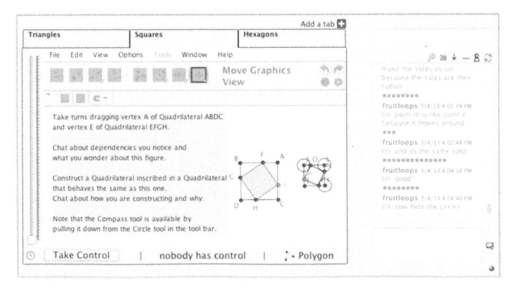

Figure 31.3 Discussion and constructions of inscribed squares.

construction of the figure. In previous sessions, the students had learned the dynamic-geometry equivalent of Euclid's first two propositions: the construction of an equilateral triangle (using software tools equivalent to a straight edge and compass) and the copying of a line-segment length.

In their fifth session, the three students took turns dragging points of the equilateral triangles and discussing the dependencies that were maintained. Then they tried to duplicate the given figure and to build in the relevant dependencies. For instance, the dependency defining the equilateral character of the outer triangle is that the lengths of the second and third sides must always be the same as the length of the base, even when the end points of the base segment are dragged, changing its length. Euclid's construction maintains this dependency because the lengths of all three sides are radii of circles of equal radius. Read today, Euclid's *Elements* (300 BCE/2002) in effect provides instructions for dynamic-geometry constructions. The "elements" of geometry are not so much the points, lines, circles, triangles and quadrilaterals, but the basic operations of constructing figures with important relationships, such as congruence or symmetry. Just as Euclidean geometry contributed significantly to the development of logical, deductive, apodictic cognition in Western thought and in the formative minds of many prospective mathematicians, so collaborative experiences with dynamic geometry may foster in students ways of thinking about dependencies in the world.

The students in the case study used Euclid's method to construct the outside triangle, but soon realized that the same procedure could not be used to construct the inscribed triangle, because of the additional constraint that its vertices all had to be on the sides of the inscribing triangle, which they had constructed. Considerable further dragging of points in the given figure and experimentation with various construction approaches were tried. Finally, the students noticed that when one point of the inner triangle was dragged along a side of the outer triangle, the other vertices of the inner triangle moved in a corresponding way, such that their positions along their sides of the outer triangle were the same as that of the dragged vertex on its side. Then they quickly decided to use the method they had learned for copying a line-segment length. They copied the length from one outer vertex of their new equilateral triangle to a point for an inner vertex. Then they placed this length along the other sides, starting at both of the other vertices. This determined the locations of the other inner vertices. When they connected the three points, they formed an inscribed triangle. When any point or line was dragged, both the inner and outer triangles remained equilateral and inscribed.

In their sixth session, the students tackled the topic of inscribed squares. All their previous work in dynamic geometry had involved triangles and they had not been exposed to a method of constructing a dynamic square. They spent most of the hour exploring possible construction methods, eventually inventing a method that was elegantly similar to that of the triangle construction. All three students then immediately saw how to construct the interior square by copying the length from a corner of the exterior square to a corner of the interior one along a side. In Figure 31.3, the circles used for copying the length are still visible. The clarity with which each of the students understood how to inscribe a square—once they were able to construct the exterior dynamic square—shows how well they had each individually mastered the technique from their prior collaborative experience involving the dynamic triangles.

Their collaborative solution of the inscribed-triangles topic is quite typical. We have observed a number of small groups working on this topic, including math teachers, researchers, graduate students and middle-school students. They all go through a similar process of dragging the original figure, experimenting with construction attempts, discovering the dependency of the distances between the interior and exterior vertices, then realizing how to copy that distance and finally checking that their construction has the same behavior as the given figure. While this topic poses a problem that is difficult for individuals, small groups tend to stick with it and solve it through collaborative effort within an hour or less. It takes a combination of many trials, observations and connections to accomplish the task. The collaborative approach allows individuals to contribute specific pieces of the puzzle, to build on each other's proposals and to discuss the implications.

The chat discourse is striking in how much the students make sure that everyone agrees with and understands each step that the group as a whole takes in constructing their figures. In addition to expressing agreement and affirming understanding, the students also demonstrate their *shared understanding* by fluidly building on each other's contributions. Successive steps are generally taken by different students, indicating that they are all following the logic of the collaborative effort.

Contributing to group cognition

"Cognition" in group cognition is not the same as individual cognition; it relies upon individual cognition to make essential contributions. However, one cannot say that all of the cognition should be analyzed at the individual unit, because the work of assembling the high-level argumentative structure occurs at the group unit of analysis. Surely, putting together problem-solving arguments must be considered a cognitive activity as much as the work that goes into making the detailed contributions to individual steps. In addition, the personal contributions are largely responses to what has gone before in the group interaction. Not only are these contributions expressions that would not have occurred without the preceding opening up for them and elicitation of them by the group process, but many of the contributions are largely reactions at the group level, which reference and interrelate resources available in the discourse context more than they introduce new elements from the personal perspective and individual background of the actor. The important cognitive achievement is emergent at the group level, rather than a simple collection of expressions of individual cognitive accomplishments.

Coherent and impressive examples of group cognition—such as solving a math problem that the group members would not have been able to solve on their own—do not occur whenever a number of people come together in conversation. In fact, the research field of computer-supported collaborative learning has documented that desirable forms of collaborative knowledge building are hard to find. The three studies summarized above indicate some reasons for this. First, it is difficult to set up a group interaction where everything relevant to the cognition at the group level of analysis is captured in a form adequate for detailed analysis. It took years of research to develop and deploy the VMT environment to successfully generate adequate data for the analysis of group cognition. Second, the group interaction must be directed and guided to focus on an appropriate cognitive task. Certain challenging math problems, carefully presented, seem to provide effective resources for stimulating interesting episodes of group cognition. Additionally—as the three studies summarized here have documented—the groups must work consistently to ensure the presence of certain preconditions of effective group cognition. They must persist in building *longer sequences* of responses to each other, they must maintain continuous *co-attention* to a shared focus of discussion and they must build and sustain a *shared understanding* of the topic of conversation.

The constitution of group cognition

The phenomenological tradition has always conceived of cognition as embodied in the world, rather than as a Cartesian mental process. Husserl (1929/1960, §14) emphasized that cognition is cognition *of* something; it is located at its object, not at some internal representation of that external object. Heidegger (1927/1996) therefore started from the experience of being-in-the-world instead of thinking-in-the-head. For him, cognition is a matter of being-with and caring-for things and people. The world is a shared world and the things we are there with are always already understood as meaningful. In Merleau-Ponty's (1945/2002) famous example of the blind man with the cane, the cane does not so much augment or extend the man's senses and awareness of external reality as it locates his cognition in the world at the tip of the cane.

If we look at the presented examples of group cognition, we see that the students are "there" in their group interaction with mathematical objects, seen in specific ways. Aznx and Bwang have drawn the horizontal sticks and the vertical sticks separately (not shown in the summary above). They have noticed a four-way symmetry, which allows them to reduce the problem of counting the sticks to a tractable pattern. They are focused together on the diamond as that symmetric pattern of sticks. Similarly, Jason, Qwertyuiop and 137 have worked hard to view their hexagonal array as a symmetrical pattern of sticks forming lines within triangles that make up a hexagon. As these groups work out their algebraic solutions to the topic, they are present together in a shared world at an object of interest, which they all see as structured in the same way. In the third case, after much work individually and collaboratively, and incorporating ideas from the ancient tradition of Euclidean geometry, the three students working on the inscribed squares all observe that when square EFGH is dragged within square ABCD the following segments along the outer square change but stay equal in length to each other: AE, CH, DG, BF. They then can all see that they have to construct square MONP within square IJKL so that segments, IP, JM, KO, LN, stay the same (see Figure 31.3). They collaborate in a shared world, manipulating a shared object physically, visually and imaginatively within a shared understanding of their problem, the geometric objects, the dynamic dependencies, the representational figure and the software affordances.

Following the phenomenologists, the ethnomethodologists showed that the shared social world is constituted continuously through group interaction (Garfinkel, 1967). In our VMT data, we can study precisely how that is accomplished. We see that it takes place over longer sequences of discourse moves, each centered on elicitation/response adjacency pairs. Carrying out these longer sequences requires maintaining persistent co-attention to a shared object; the being-there-together at the object provides a shared focus for the discourse. Accompanying this, there must be a shared understanding of the object and of the discourse context so that group members understand each other. If someone does not know what someone else means by a "hexagonal array" or by its "side length," does not see the same elements of a symmetrical pattern or the same set of line segments moving together, then the collaborative problem solving cannot continue productively.

Kant (1787/1999) argued that the human mind constitutes meaningful reality through a process of creative discovery, in which structure is imposed to create and discover objects in the world. In the preceding examples, we see how group interaction can constitute the character of objects in the shared world and we have suggested that the shared meaningful world is itself constituted through such interaction. The nature of reality—such as the symmetries of diamond patterns, hexagonal arrays and inscribed squares—is discovered through the creation of interpretive views of objects. Effective perspectives are constrained by reality, which is not knowable except through these views. The creation of perspectives at the level of group cognition shifts the constitutive role from Kant's individual cognition to group and social cognition. Like the students in the virtual math teams, we first learn to see things *as* others see them in group-cognitive processes (which generally incorporate culturally sanctioned approaches). Subsequently—due to the power of language (e.g., naming, verbal description)—we can be there with those objects (diamonds, hexagons, squares) when we are not physically (or virtually) present with them in a shared group setting. We can even "internalize" (to use Vygotsky's metaphor) our ability to be-there-with these meaningful objects in the internal speech of individual thought. However, the fact that introspection of adults discovers (and assumes) the existence of many individual mental objects does not mean that those objects were not at some point in our development internalized from group-cognitive experiences in community contexts. An adequate analysis of cognition should recognize the constitutive roles of group cognition and their integration with phenomena of individual and social cognition.

References

Çakir, M. P. and Stahl, G. (2013). The integration of mathematics discourse, graphical reasoning and symbolic expression by a virtual math team. In D. Martinovic, V. Freiman and Z. Karadag (Eds), *Visual mathematics and cyberlearning*. New York: Springer. Retrieved from http://GerryStahl.net/pub/visualmath.pdf

Çakir, M. P., Zemel, A. and Stahl, G. (2009). The joint organization of interaction within a multimodal CSCL medium. *International Journal of Computer-Supported Collaborative Learning*, 4(2), 115–149. Retrieved from http://GerryStahl.net/pub/ijCSCL_4_2_1.pdf

Euclid. (300 BCE/2002). *Euclid's elements* (T. L. Heath, Trans.). Santa Fe, NM: Green Lion Press.

Garfinkel, H. (1967). *Studies in ethnomethodology*. Englewood Cliffs, NJ: Prentice-Hall.

Hegel, G. W. F. (1807/1967). *Phenomenology of spirit* (J. B. Baillie, Trans.). New York: Harper & Row.

Heidegger, M. (1927/1996). *Being and time: A translation of Sein und Zeit* (J. Stambaugh, Trans.). Albany, NY: SUNY Press.

Husserl, E. (1929/1960). *Cartesian meditations: An introduction to phenomenology* (D. Cairns, Trans.). The Hague, Netherlands: Martinus Nijhoff.

——— (1936/1989). The origin of geometry (D. Carr, Trans.). In J. Derrida (Ed), *Edmund Husserl's origin of geometry: An introduction* (pp. 157–180). Lincoln, NE: University of Nebraska Press.

Kant, I. (1787/1999). *Critique of pure reason*. Cambridge: Cambridge University Press.

Merleau-Ponty, M. (1945/2002). *The phenomenology of perception* (C. Smith, Trans., 2nd ed.). New York: Routledge.

Sacks, H. (1962/1995). *Lectures on conversation*. Oxford: Blackwell.

Schegloff, E. A. (2007). *Sequence organization in interaction: A primer in conversation analysis*. Cambridge: Cambridge University Press.

Stahl, G. (2006). *Group cognition: Computer support for building collaborative knowledge*. Cambridge, MA: MIT Press. Retrieved from http://GerryStahl.net/elibrary/gc

——— (2009). *Studying virtual math teams*. New York: Springer. Retrieved from http://GerryStahl.net/elibrary/svmt

—— (2011). How a virtual math team structured its problem solving. In M. Spada, G. Stahl, N. Miyake and N. Law (Eds), *Connecting computer-supported collaborative learning to policy and practice: CSCL 2011 conference proceedings* (Vol. 1, pp. 256–263). Lulu: International Society of the Learning Sciences (ISLS). Retrieved from http://GerryStahl.net/pub/cscl2011stahl.pdf

—— (2013). *Translating Euclid: Creating a human-centered mathematics*. San Rafael, CA: Morgan & Claypool. Retrieved from http://GerryStahl.net/elibrary/euclid

Stahl, G., Koschmann, T. and Suthers, D. (2013). Computer-supported collaborative learning: An historical perspective. In R. K. Sawyer (Ed), *Cambridge handbook of the learning sciences* (Rev. ed.). Cambridge: Cambridge University Press. Retrieved from http://GerryStahl.net/pub/chls2.pdf

Stahl, G., Zhou, N., Çakir, M. P. and Sarmiento-Klapper, J. W. (2011). Seeing what we mean: Co-experiencing a shared virtual world. In M. Spada, G. Stahl, N. Miyake and N. Law (Eds), *Connecting computer-supported collaborative learning to policy and practice: CSCL 2011 conference proceedings* (Vol. 1, pp. 534–541). Lulu: International Society of the Learning Sciences (ISLS). Retrieved from http://GerryStahl.net/pub/cscl2011.pdf

Suchman, L. A. (2007). *Human-machine reconfigurations: Plans and situated actions* (2nd ed.). Cambridge: Cambridge University Press.

Vygotsky, L. (1930/1978). *Mind in society*. Cambridge, MA: Harvard University Press.

Wittgenstein, L. (1953). *Philosophical investigations*. New York: Macmillan.

32

VARIETIES OF GROUP COGNITION

Georg Theiner

Introduction

Benjamin Franklin famously wrote that "the good [that] men do separately is small compared with what they may do collectively" (Isaacson, 2004). The ability to join with others in groups to accomplish goals collectively that would hopelessly overwhelm the time, energy, and resources of individuals is indeed one of the greatest assets of our species. In the history of humankind, groups have been among the greatest workers, builders, producers, protectors, entertainers, explorers, discoverers, planners, problem solvers, and decision makers. During the late nineteenth and early twentieth century, many social scientists employed the notorious "group mind" idiom to express the sensible idea that groups can function as the seats of cognition, intelligence, and agency in their own right (Allport, 1968; Wilson, 2004). In their quest to stress (rightly) that group phenomena are something "over and above" the sum of individual contributions, a fondness for vitalist metaphors led them to believe (wrongly) that genuine group cognition must be the result of tapping into individualistically inaccessible, "holistic" forces. Today, inspired in part by historically unparalleled forms of mass collaboration enabled by the Internet, it has once again become popular to speak of collective intelligence, group agency, or even the emergence of a "global brain" (cf. the wiki-edited *MIT Handbook of Collective Intelligence* [MIT Center for Collective Intelligence, n.d.]).

In this chapter, I review some contemporary developments of the idea of group cognition, defined broadly as the collaborative performance of cognitive tasks such as remembering, problem solving, decision making, or verbal creativity for the purpose of producing a group-level outcome. My discussion serves a twofold purpose. First, by discussing how the idea of group cognition can be operationalized, I seek to show that we can retain some central theoretical insights of the "group mind" thesis without succumbing to its eccentric metaphysical overtones. Second, by providing a useful array of generalizable taxonomic resources, I hope to foster greater degrees of mutual awareness among insufficiently integrated areas of research on group performance.

DOI: 10.4324/9781003322511-41

From individual to group cognition

When people join together to solve a problem in groups, their performance depends on the knowledge, abilities, and resources of individual members, plus the interpersonal processes that determine how those are combined into a collective group activity or output. In his seminal work on group productivity, Steiner (1966, 1972) distinguished various types of combination processes in terms of the demands that are dictated by the task a group is trying to solve. He suggested that task demands vary depending on three main dimensions: the divisibility of a task, the desired type of output, and the combination scheme that is used to complete the task. Building on Steiner's taxonomy will help us to tighten our grip on the notoriously slippery notion of group cognition.

Steiner's first dimension concerns the question of whether a task can be broken down into different components. *Divisible* tasks have subcomponents that can be readily identified and assigned to different group members (e.g., running a football play), whereas *unitary* tasks cannot be performed in such piecemeal fashion (e.g., catching a football). The second dimension concerns a distinction between *maximization* tasks that call for a high rate of production, as opposed to *optimization* tasks in which the quality of a performance is measured by comparing it to some predetermined criterion. Running a 400-meter relay is an example of the former, whereas estimating the number of beans in a jar is an example of the latter. Laughlin (1980) similarly proposed a group task continuum that is flanked by *intellective* and *judgmental* tasks. Intellective tasks such as logic or math problems have demonstrably correct solutions within some agreed-upon conceptual framework, hence the proposed solutions can be objectively appraised as right or wrong. In contrast, judgmental tasks such as a jury deciding on a verdict, or a hiring committee deciding on a job candidate, involve evaluative judgments for which no single correct answer can be authoritatively determined.

Finally, group tasks can be distinguished in terms of how individual inputs are combined to yield a collective outcome. *Additive* tasks can be solved by summing up the contributions of co-acting individuals. An example would be a university admissions committee whose members independently process student applications without interacting with one another. In *compensatory* tasks, the group outcome is obtained by averaging the independently obtained judgments, estimates, or recommendations of its members. The surprising accuracy of compensatory decision making, which can be explained in terms of general information-theoretic properties of statistical sampling (Bettencourt, 2009), has been popularized lately as the "wisdom of crowds" (Surowiecki, 2004). Surowiecki's opening anecdote tells the story of legendary nineteenth-century polymath Francis Galton, well known for his elitist obsession with individual genius, who was flabbergasted when he discovered that the crowd at an English country fair had produced a more accurate estimate of an oxen's weight, when their guesses were averaged, than any of the recognized cattle experts. According to Surowiecki, the key to extracting wisdom from crowds is to foster a diversity of opinions, by allowing mutually independent individuals to draw on local, specialized sources of information, and to install a suitable mechanism for aggregating individual judgments (e.g., market pricing, as used in prediction markets). Importantly, the wisdom of crowds is not due to increased levels of collaboration, but results from a relative immunity to performance losses due to imitation, conformism, loafing, and other social phenomena that commonly occur in interacting, especially face-to-face groups.

In contrast, *conjunctive, disjunctive, discretionary*, and *complementary* tasks all depend more or less directly on interactions among group members. In *cooperative* interactions, all group members share the same goal or objective, and are equally affected by the consequences of a given outcome. This contrasts with *mixed-motive* interactions, such as social dilemmas, where different group members, or groups as opposed to individual members, have different preferences. Steiner's examples of interactive group tasks are of the cooperative variety, but differ in the respective degrees of cognitive interdependence they impose on its members. Conjunctive and disjunctive tasks are end points on a spectrum of how many members must succeed for the group to succeed. A disjunctive task, for example, would be a group of software engineers trying to identify a bug in a computer program. Here, the role of social interactions is mostly a matter of convincing the group to adopt the correct solution once it has been found by any one of its members. A conjunctive task would be a group of software engineers frantically typing up source code to meet an impending deadline, which requires that everybody works as fast and error-free as possible. In other words, a disjunctive task is one in which the quality of group performance depends on that of its most capable member, whereas a conjunctive task is one in which it is constrained by that of its least capable member. In addition, Steiner also identified a class of relatively unstructured tasks that can be completed by a variety of combination schemes, to be chosen at the discretion of the group. An example of a *discretionary* task would be the improvised performance of a jazz trio, or the corporate design of a new advertisement campaign.

The disjunctive–conjunctive continuum also corresponds to the spectrum of social combination models or decision schemes, which are formalized models of group processes that assign probabilities to each group response given all possible distributions of member preferences (Stasser, 1999). For example, a *minimal quorum* ("truth wins") assumes that a group response is correct if at least one member's response is correct (disjunctive), a *quorum of two* ("truth-supported wins") requires at least two correct responses, and *unanimity* requires that all members are correct (conjunctive). Other commonly used social decision schemes include *majority, proportionality*, or *delegation*. They provide an important class of baseline models which can be tested against actual group performance.

Based on his taxonomy, Steiner conceptualized the potential productivity of a group in terms of individual member resources and the demands of the group task. He recognized that groups often fail to achieve their full potential due to faulty group processes, and distinguished two main types of *process losses*. Motivation losses generally occur if members make a less than optimal contribution, either due to social loafing, free riding, or perhaps for selfish, competitive reasons. Coordination losses occur because of a less than optimal integration of individual members' contributions, such as when a group fails to acknowledge a correct solution proposed by one of its members. Even though process losses are very common, it is also possible for groups to exceed their potential, contrary to Steiner's pessimistic assessment. For example, since success in a conjunctive task is contingent on the performance of its weakest link, the proficiency of a group can often be improved by assigning different members to particular subtasks that fit best with their expertise, provided that the original task is divisible. This effectively turns a conjunctive task into what Steiner (1966) called a *complementary* task, in which group members collaboratively pool their diverse pieces of knowledge, skills, and resources into a single, collective outcome. Examples of complementary group performances with high levels of collaboration and cognitive interdependence include an orchestra performing a symphony, a football team running a play, or the police investigation of a crime scene.

The power of complementary problem solving is captured by the Gestalt maxim that "the whole is greater than the sum of its parts." It implies that a group may collectively achieve something that could not have been done by any single member – even the most capable – working alone, nor by the sum of members working individually towards the same outcome. Such an outcome is also known as an *assembly bonus effect* (Collins and Guetzkow, 1964; Larson, 2010). It exemplifies the broader concept of *synergy*, which occurs whenever the joint outcome of two or more interacting parts of a system differs from the aggregated outcome of the parts operating independently (Corning, 2003).

Based on these considerations, *group cognition* can be defined as the collaborative performance of cognitive tasks such as remembering, problem solving, decision making, or verbal creativity for the purpose of producing a group-level outcome. Importantly, our use of the term does not directly refer to any particular quality of the group-level outcome, such as the collective verdict of a jury, the co-authored publication of a scientific discovery, or the joint performance of an improvised dialog. Those outcomes may be the result of group cognition, but they are not intrinsically "group-cognitive." Instead, the defining feature of group cognition is the *collaborative interdependence* among cognizing group members – that is, it concerns emergent modes of organization by which the actions, ideas, and resources of individuals are coordinated, combined, and integrated into a group-level outcome (Theiner and O'Connor, 2010). The *emergent* character of group cognition can be understood as a failure of *aggregativity* in the sense of Wimsatt (1986). Wimsatt argued that properties of systems that are *aggregative* satisfy the following conditions: they (1) are invariant relative to the rearrangement of parts, (2) remain qualitatively similar under the addition or subtraction of parts, (3) are invariant relative to rearranging the parts into different subgroups, and (4) are not affected by any cooperative or inhibitory interactions among the parts. Many interesting phenomena that we would intuitively classify as instances of group cognition violate three or even all four of Wimsatt's diagnostic criteria (Theiner, Allen, and Goldstone, 2010; Theiner, 2013). In what follows, I discuss several research paradigms which have contributed to our understanding of group cognition in this sense.

Groups as decision-making units

There has been a growing trend in small-group research to consider collaborative groups as cognitive units in their own right (Wittenbaum *et al.*, 2004). This conception is based on a functional analysis of the steps or processes that groups generally follow in the course of producing a specified group-level cognitive outcome. For example, a standard functional model of group decision making involves a sequence of four main steps (Forsyth, 2006): (i) an *orientation* phase, during which a group has to define the problem, set its goals, and plan out its procedures, (ii) a *discussion* phase, during which a group needs to gather, exchange, analyze, and weigh information, (iii) a *decision* phase, during which a group has to map members' inputs into a collective solution based on one or more social decision schemes, and (iv) an *implementation* phase, in which the decision is put into action, and its impacts are being assessed. Based on this analysis, the main goal is then to describe in detail the cognitive, social, and communicative mechanisms by which these decision functions are carried out, and to identify the conditions under which groups tend to perform better than individuals. Taking a *collective information-processing* approach to group decision making implies that during the discussion stage, which is arguably the most critical part of the process, groups can benefit from improving their memory by increasing their information exchange and by processing information more thoroughly (Larson and Christensen, 1993; Hinsz, Tindale, and Vollrath, 1997; Propp, 1999). Each of these implications has been the subject of experimental research in social and organizational psychology.

Transactive memory

The ability of dyads and small groups to expand their collective memory capabilities through a division of mnemonic labor has been studied in the literature on *transactive memory* (Wegner, 1986; Ren and Argote, 2011). For example, one partner of a long-standing couple may remember how to procure their favorite food and pay their bills, while the other knows how to maintain their home security system and prepare their joint tax return. By cooperatively allocating the tasks of encoding, storing, modifying, and recalling task-relevant information among members with specialized abilities or knowledge, groups can build transactive memory systems (TMSs) that are greater than the sum of individual memory systems. The integrated functioning of a differentiated TMS requires that group members develop a shared set of higher-order ("transactive") memories for keeping track of who knows what, and for trusting each other's expertise. For example, transactive memories are used for determining how, and in what format incoming information ought to be stored in a group, and for cueing the recognized experts whenever an interactive information search is executed.

Research has shown that collaborating groups remember more than their average or even their best single member, but often remember less than same-sized collections of non-interacting individuals (Weldon and Bellinger, 1997; Harris, Barnier, and Sutton, 2013). The most common explanation for the occurrence of such *collaborative inhibition* is that hearing others recall disrupts individuals' idiosyncratic mnemonic strategies (Basden, Basden, Bryner, and Thomas, 1997). The detrimental effects of group recall can be reduced, or even reversed, by the choice of decision schemes such as consensus, which invite more collaborative forms of error checking, the skilful deployment of collaborative practices as found in teams of expert pilots remembering aviation-related scenarios, or when group members are actively encouraged to develop joint retrieval strategies during a period of shared encoding, especially when the material to be remembered is emotionally meaningful to the group (Harris *et al.*, 2013).

The search for assembly bonus effects is sometimes hampered by a one-sided understanding of the purposes which the activity of shared remembering fulfills for real-world groups. What is tested in many studies of transactive memory is the ability of groups to optimize the amount or accuracy of recall. This creates an incentive for members to remember different items, which rewards the development of differentiated transactive memory structures. However, an equally important function of collaborative remembering is to reinforce the social bonds among its members, by merging disparate memories into a stable rendering of shared past experiences (Hirst and Manier, 2008). This creates an incentive for members to remember the same information, which rewards the development of assimilated transactive memory structures. Viewed from this perspective, the relevant assembly bonus of group memory consists in the joint construction of collectively shared memories that more effectively support the enduring social identity of a group. Consistent with this more flexible interpretation of group memory is Hollingshead's (2001) proposal that the formation of a TMS is driven by the two fundamental processes of *cognitive interdependence*, which is a function of the extent to which each individual's contribution depends on those of others, and *convergent expectations*, which is a shared conception of what each member ought to do to achieve a positive group outcome (Harris, Keil, Sutton, Barnier, and McIlwain, 2011; Theiner, 2013).

Collective information sampling

The superiority of groups as decision makers is often justified with the idea that by pooling the resources of its members, groups can take into account far more information than any one of its members. However, research shows that groups are strongly biased towards discussing information that is already shared, and consistently underutilize information that is known only to a few (Wittenbaum *et al.*, 2004). Because of this bias, groups frequently fail to recognize superior decision alternatives that would require the integration of critical yet unshared information. This so-called *hidden profile* effect has been replicated under many experimental conditions, and is surprisingly robust (Stasser and Titus, 2003). It is stronger in groups that are working on judgmental rather than intellective tasks, and more pronounced when their members are under the impression that they lack sufficient information to make a fully informed decision.

The bias towards shared information reflects the double purposes of group discussions, which serves both informational and normative purposes. From a purely informational standpoint, one would expect that groups who are striving to make the best possible decision would primarily sample information that is unevenly distributed among its members. But concomitant desire for reaching a consensus, getting closure, or convincing others to adopt their own views counteracts that tendency. In addition, individual members may selectively withhold information to gain a competitive advantage over others, or to impress others by feigning agreement. The latter influence can be particularly hard to overcome, because people tend to rely on the exchange of shared information as a reliable social indicator of members' competence and task credibility. Consequently, since information that is unshared cannot be used to validate one another's expertise, group discussants will tend to rehash points that are already common knowledge, thus further diminishing the group's chance of discovering a hidden profile.

A variety of interventions have been shown to improve a group's attention to unshared information. For example, being designated an "expert" on some topic made it more likely for that person to contribute unique information in her designated area of expertise, and for her contribution to be acknowledged by the group. It is also known that senior group members, who usually enjoy a higher social status, are more likely to bring up, as well as repeat, information that is unshared. Other methods of avoiding the bias include increasing the diversity of opinions, emphasizing the importance of dissent, priming members with counterfactual thinking, introducing group discussion as a new order of business rather than a return to previously discussed material, and the use of computer-mediated decision support systems to display, access, and collaboratively modify the total stock of knowledge that is available to the group as a whole (Forsyth, 2006).

Collective induction

Groups have the potential not only to recall and exchange information more effectively than individuals, but to process information more deeply by evaluating the strengths and weaknesses of different options, correcting each other's errors, and integrating diverse viewpoints. *Collective induction* is the cooperative search for generalizations or rules which require groups such as scientific research teams, auditing teams, or air crash investigators to undergo a cycle of hypothesis generation and testing (Laughlin, 1999). Collective induction is a divisible and complementary task in which groups have the potential to collectively perceive patterns, propose and reject hypotheses, and arrive at interpretations that none of their members would have achieved individually.

Laughlin (1999) outlines a theory of collective induction which synthesizes a series of experiments in which groups had to induce a rule that partitions ordinary playing cards into examples and non-examples of the rule (e.g., "two diamonds alternate with two clubs") in as few trials as possible. Laughlin's rule-induction task has both intellective and judgmental components: non-plausible hypotheses may be demonstrated to be incorrect, but plausible hypotheses may not be demonstrated to be uniquely correct vis-à-vis other competitors. Given enough information and time, groups performed at the level of the best of an equivalent number of individuals. The best fit of social combination models with actual group performance indicates that: (1) if at least two members propose demonstrably correct and/or plausible hypotheses, the group selects among those only; otherwise, it selects among all; (2) if a majority of members proposes the same hypothesis, the group applies majority voting; otherwise, it takes turns among the proposed alternatives, and formulates an emergent hypothesis that was not proposed by any member with probability $1/(H + 1)$, where H is the number of group members. The experiments also revealed that collective induction improved more by increasing evidence than by increasing the number of hypotheses, and positive tests (examples) provide better evidence than negative tests (non-examples).

Subsequent work showed that groups of size three working on complex letter-to-numbers decoding problems were able to outperform even the *best* of a same-sized equivalent of independent individuals (Laughlin, Bonner, and Miner, 2002; Laughlin, Zander, Knievel, and Tan, 2003). Correct answers to these problems could be demonstrated by experimenter feedback, arithmetic, algebra, logical reasoning, or knowledge of certain number-theoretic properties. Because of the highly intellective nature of the task, there was a clear-cut way for members to recognize answers that were correct, and to reject erroneous responses. By combining different types of reasoning strategies to solve letter-to-numbers problems, groups were better at solving the task according to a complementary model, rather than by selecting the single best-member solution according to a disjunctive model (Laughlin, 2011).

Groups as distributed cognitive systems

The "distributed cognition" framework was pioneered in the mid-to-late 1980s by Edwin Hutchins as a new way of studying cognition (Perry, 2003). Contrary to traditional cognitive science, where cognition is equated with information processing at the level of the individual mind/brain, it analyzes collaborative work practices which are often heavily mediated by the use of technology and the physical layout of the workspace as distributed cognitive systems in their own right. The key to this outward extension is a functional conceptualization of cognitive processes in terms of the *propagation of representational states across different media* (Hutchins, 1995). The term *media* is understood broadly to encompass both covert representations formed inside a person's head, but also overt representations which are physically embodied in verbal exchanges, bodily gestures or movements, or artifacts such as maps, charts, tools, instruments, or computer displays. By focusing on the coordination mechanisms supporting the collaborative creation and transformation of representational states in the performance of various cognitive functions – rather than on any intrinsic substrate of cognition – the distributed cognition approach does not posit a deep gulf between mental/physical, individual/social, and cognitive/cultural resources. Instead, cognitive processes can be viewed as extending seamlessly across the traditional metaphysical boundaries between subjects and objects.

More specifically, cognitive processes can be distributed in at least three dimensions (Hollan, Hutchins, and Kirsh, 2000). First, cognitive processes may be distributed across the members of a social group. This means that the social organization of a group – together with the material structure of the environment in which it operates – can itself be seen as a form of cognitive architecture determining the patterns of information propagation. Conversely, it also means that the concepts and models used to describe socially distributed systems may also be fitting to describe the distributed organization of individual minds (Minsky, 1986). Second, cognitive processes can be distributed across neural, bodily, and environmental resources. In particular, work materials such as a blind man's cane, a cell biologist's microscope, or a mathematician's calculator can become so deeply integrated into one's cognitive processing, by scaffolding the structure of a task and even providing active sources of information processing, that they are more properly viewed as parts of an extended cognitive system, rather than as mere stimuli or passive external memory resources for a disembodied mind (Clark, 2008). Finally, cognitive processes may be distributed through time, such that the products of earlier events can greatly transform the task demands at subsequent stages of processing. From this perspective, culture can be seen as a potent, cumulative reservoir of resources for learning, problem solving, and reasoning, "ratcheting" up the collective insights of previous generations so individuals do not have to start from scratch. Taken together, the mediating effects of the social, technological, and cultural distribution of labor imply that the cognitive properties of groups may differ significantly from those of individuals.

The proper investigation of distributed cognitive systems requires an interdisciplinary kind of "cognitive ethnography" based heavily on participant observation, which brings together and refines many different techniques for capturing the richly embodied, socially embedded, and often surprisingly opportunistic nature of meaningful human activity in real-world settings. These observations provide naturalistic data that can be further tested by conducting more constrained experiments and developing formal models, but they also lead to concrete proposals for improving the design of cognitive artifacts and workplaces, which ultimately feed back into the process of theory construction. Detailed studies of distributed cognition "in the wild" include diverse collaborative activities performed by maritime navigation crews (Hutchins, 1995), emergency/rescue management operations (Garbis and Waern, 1999), theatrical practices in Elizabethan drama (Tribble, 2005), bioengineering labs (Nersessian, 2006), and crime scene investigation (Baber, Smith, Cross, Hunter, and McMaster, 2006).

Groups as complex adaptive systems

Many group-living species such as ants, fish, and humans display adaptive, remarkably robust forms of coordinated collective behavior that seem to arise spontaneously, in non-supervised fashion, in response to environmental changes. For example, to avoid a predator attack, a school of fish flees almost simultaneously, in near perfect synchrony, as if it was collectively sensing the imminent danger, even though there is no external blueprint or centralized controller who broadcasts instructions of how to respond. Instead, the adaptive group response results from the dynamic self-organization of large collections of partially connected agents, following relatively simple behavioral rules. Those agents interact either directly, through various sensory channels, or indirectly, by leaving stigmergic traces in the environment that can be sensed by others (Moussaid, Garnier, Theraulaz, and Helbing, 2009; Goldstone and Gureckis, 2009; Miller and Page, 2007).

A frequently cited example of self-organized collective information processing through indirect communication is the formation of foraging trails in ant colonies (Moussaid *et al.*, 2009). When a single ant randomly stumbles across a new food source, it drops phero-mones on its way back to the nest. The attractive influence of pheromones will cause nearby ants to modulate their random exploratory behavior towards the trail, which increases their chances of locating the same food source. This creates a positive feedback loop: as more ants are recruited to a given source, the concentration of pheromones increases, which in turn further increases the attractiveness of the trail. The resulting non-linear amplification of the incipient trail is held in check by negative feedback pro-cesses such as the evaporation of the pheromones, the depletion of the food source, but also the availability of nearby foragers, all of which help to stabilize the flow of ants. In addition, ants also modulate their trail-laying intensity in proportion to the quality of the food. Faced with a choice between two unequal food sites, what may initially be only a slightly higher pheromone concentration left on the trail towards the richer source will quickly become magnified, directing the colony to focus almost exclusively on the more profitable option. The same reinforcement mechanism also allows colonies to discover the shortest path to an existing food source.

The interplay between amplification and dampening of information underlies the syn-chronized responses of flocking birds or schooling fish (Couzin, 2009). The social interac-tions among the members of a flock, for example, are governed by a few rules such as near-range repulsion to maintain personal space, long-term attraction to ensure group cohesion, and a preference to align the direction of travel towards one's nearest neighbors. An external perturbation, such as the presence of a resource or a predator, may initially only be discovered by a small proportion of flockmates due to their limited sensory capabil-ities and crowded vision. However, the close behavioral coupling between nearest neigh-bors allows localized changes in movement to be amplified, and swiftly propagated through the flock. Hence, the flock as a whole forms a mobile, distributed perceptual system whose effective range exceeds that of any single member. Depending on the task demands, flocks can modify their interactions in context-sensitive ways. Under a threat of attack, individu-als tend to align more strongly with one another, thus increasing the collective vigilance of the flock, though at the expense of causing false alarms. Conversely, since long-term migra-tion requires that flocks are not too sensitive to local fluctuations in noisy, long-range resource gradients and to individual errors, birds adopt rules that favor social cohesion in order to facilitate a collective dampening of information.

Even though the self-organized dynamics of many forms of collective human behavior can often be modeled with surprisingly simple behavioral rules (Ball, 2004), the greater cognitive sophistication of humans introduces additional complexity that can interfere with collective dynamics. In particular, because people can quickly adopt new behavioral strate-gies in response to past experiences, novel behavioral conventions can emerge on much shorter timescales, for a larger variety of different settings, and in ways that are sensitive to cultural variations.

Group agency

In ordinary parlance, we often say that a government pursues ways to increase tax revenues, that a firm intends to release a new smartphone, or that a church opposes gay marriage. A literal attribution of agency to groups seems to imply that we consider groups as capable of having collective beliefs and desires, forming joint intentions, making evaluative judgments, managing their epistemic coherence through forms of collective reasoning that are robustly rational, and self-ascribing intentional attitudes from a first-person plural perspective (List and Pettit, 2011; Gilbert, 1989; Ludwig, 2007; Huebner, 2013). Drawing on a wide range of work on joint intentionality, social ontology, social choice theory, the sociology of collectives, and studies of collective responsibility and legal personhood, List and Pettit (2011) have forcefully argued that our concept of group agency cannot be reduced to that of individual agency, and indeed plays an indispensable causal-explanatory role in our ordinary as well as social-scientific discourse.

Their main argument against reduction is based on a logical paradox that arises when multi-member groups have to aggregate the distinct and possibly conflicting sets of intentional attitudes of its members into a single system of collective attitudes that is endorsed by the groups as a whole. In analogy to Arrow's (1951/1963) more widely known impossibility theorem about preference aggregation, List and Pettit (2002) have shown that there can be no judgment aggregation function that (i) accepts as input any possible profile of member attitudes (*universality*), (ii) produces a consistent and complete group output (*rationality*), (iii) gives all members equal weight in determining the outcome (*anonymity*), and (iv) is *systematic*, that is, the group attitude on each judgment depends only on members' attitudes towards that very judgment (*independence*), and that the same pattern of dependence between individual and collective attitudes is accepted for all judgments (*neutrality*). More constructively, this means that groups which seek to form collective attitudes must relax at least one of these four conditions.

List and Pettit suggest that the most promising organizational design in response to this dilemma is to lift systematicity, in particular independence, by prioritizing some judgments over others, and letting the group attitudes on the first set determine those of the second (without giving individuals any further say). This way of "collectivizing" reason most clearly reflects the purposes of a reason-driven collective agent, because it implies that coherent group outcomes can only be purchased at the expense of individual rationality. In addition, by further lifting anonymity, groups can implement distributed decision-making procedures in which different subgroups are assigned to "fix" the group's attitudes on specific judgments. Adopting the former procedure shows that a group's attitude cannot be derived in a strict, proposition-wise fashion from members' attitudes, and adopting the latter procedure also introduces heterogeneity because different members play different roles in determining the group outcome. Taken together, the fact that individual and group attitudes can come apart in surprising ways further underscores the theoretical autonomy of group agency.

References

Allport, G. W. (1968). The historical background of modern social psychology. In G. Lindzey and E. Aronson (Eds), *The handbook of social psychology* (2nd ed., Vol. *1*, pp. 1–80). Reading, MA: Addison-Wesley.

Arrow, K. J. (1951/1963). *Social choice and individual values*. New Haven, CT: Yale University Press.

Baber, C., Smith, P. A., Cross, J., Hunter, J., and McMaster, R. (2006). Crime scene investigation as distributed cognition. *Pragmatics and Cognition, 14*, 357–385.

Ball, P. (2004). *Critical mass: How one thing leads to another.* New York: Farrar, Straus & Giroux.

Basden, B. H., Basden, D. R., Bryner, S., and Thomas, R. L. (1997). A comparison of group and individual remembering: Does collaboration disrupt retrieval strategies? *Journal of Experimental Psychology: Learning, Memory and Cognition, 23*, 1176–1189.

Bettencourt, L. M. A. (2009). The rules of information aggregation and emergence of collective intelligent behavior. *Topics in Cognitive Science, 1*, 598–620.

Clark, A. (2008). *Supersizing the mind: Embodiment, action, and cognitive extension.* New York: Oxford University Press.

Collins, B. E., and Guetzkow, H. (1964). *A social psychology of group processes for decision-making.* New York: Wiley.

Corning, P. A. (2003). *Nature's magic: Synergy in evolution and the fate of humankind.* New York: Cambridge University Press.

Couzin, I. D. (2009). Collective cognition in animal groups. *Trends in Cognitive Sciences, 13*, 36–43.

Forsyth, D. (2006). *Group dynamics* (5th ed.). Belmont, CA: Wadsworth.

Garbis, C., and Waern, Y. (1999). Team co-ordination and communication in a rescue command staff: The role of public representations. *Le Travail Humain, 62*, 273–291.

Gilbert, M. (1989). *On social facts.* London: Routledge.

Goldstone, R., and Gureckis, T. (2009). Collective behavior. *Topics in Cognitive Science, 1*, 412–438.

Harris, C. B., Barnier, A. J., and Sutton, J. (2013). Shared encoding and the costs and benefits of collaborative recall. *Journal of Experimental Psychology. Learning, Memory, and Cognition, 39*, 183–195.

Harris, C. B., Keil, P. G., Sutton, J., Barnier, A., and McIlwain, D. (2011). We remember, we forget: Collaborative remembering in older couples. *Discourse Processes, 48*, 267–303.

Hinsz, V. B., Tindale, R. S., and Vollrath, D. A. (1997). The emerging conceptualization of groups as information processors. *Psychological Bulletin, 121*, 43–64.

Hirst, W., and Manier, D. (2008). Towards a psychology of collective memory. *Memory, 16*, 183–200.

Hollan, J., Hutchins, E., and Kirsh, D. (2000). Distributed cognition: Toward a new foundation for human-computer interaction research. *ACM Transactions on Computer-Human Interaction, 7*, 174–196.

Hollingshead, A. B. (2001). Cognitive interdependence and convergent expectations in transactive memory. *Journal of Personality and Social Psychology, 81*, 1080–1089.

Huebner, B. (2013) *Macrocognition: A theory of distributed minds and collective intentionality.* New York: Oxford University Press.

Hutchins, E. (1995). *Cognition in the wild.* Cambridge, MA: MIT Press.

Isaacson, W. (2004). *Benjamin Franklin: An American life.* New York: Simon & Schuster.

Larson, J. R. (2010). *In search of synergy in small group performance.* New York: Psychology Press.

Larson, J. R., and Christensen, C. (1993). Groups as problem-solving units: Toward a new meaning of social cognition. *British Journal of Social Psychology, 32*, 5–30.

Laughlin, P. R. (1980). Social combination processes of cooperative problem-solving groups on verbal intellective tasks. In M. Fishbein (Ed), *Progress in social psychology* (pp. 127–155). Hillsdale, NJ: Erlbaum.

———— (1999). Collective induction: Twelve postulates. *Organizational Behavior and Human Decision Processes, 80*, 50–69.

———— (2011). *Group problem solving.* Princeton: Princeton University Press.

Laughlin, P. R., Bonner, B. L., and Miner, A. G. (2002). Groups perform better than the best individuals on letters-to-numbers problems. *Organizational Behavior and Human Decision Processes, 88*(2), 605–620.

Laughlin, P. R., Zander, M. L., Knievel, E. M., and Tan, T. K. (2003). Groups perform better than the best individuals on letters-to-numbers problems: Informative equations and effective strategies. *Journal of Personality and Social Psychology, 85*(4), 684–694.

List, C., and Pettit, P. (2002). Aggregating sets of judgments: An impossibility result. *Economics and Philosophy*, *18*, 89–110.

———— (2011). *Group agency: The possibility, design, and status of corporate agents*. Oxford: Oxford University Press.

Ludwig, K. (2007). Collective intentional behavior from the standpoint of semantics. *Noûs*, *41*(3), 355–393.

Miller, J. H., and Page, S. E. (2007). *Complex adaptive systems: An introduction to computational models of social life*. Princeton: Princeton University Press.

Minsky, M. L. (1986). *The society of mind*. New York: Simon & Schuster.

MIT Center for Collective Intelligence (n.d.). *Handbook of collective intelligence*. MIT Center for Collective Intelligence website. Retrieved from http://scripts.mit.edu/‾cci/HCI/index.php

Moussaid, M., Garnier, S., Theraulaz, G., and Helbing, D. (2009). Collective information processing and pattern formation in swarms, flocks, and crowds. *Topics in Cognitive Science*, *1*, 469–497.

Nersessian, N. J. (2006). The cognitive-cultural systems of the research laboratory. *Organization Studies*, *27*(1), 125–145

Perry, M. (2003). Distributed cognition. In J. M. Carroll (Ed), *HCI models, theories, and frameworks: Toward an interdisciplinary science* (pp. 193–223). San Francisco: Morgan Kaufmann.

Propp, K. (1999). Collective information processing in groups. In L. Frey, D. S. Gouran, and M. S. Poole (Eds), *Handbook of group communication theory and research* (pp. 225–250). Thousand Oaks, CA: Sage.

Ren, Y., and Argote, L. (2011). Transactive memory systems 1985–2010: An integrative framework of key dimensions, antecedents, and consequences. *Academy of Management Annals*, *5*, 189–229.

Stasser, G. (1999). A primer of social decision scheme theory: Models of group influence, competitive model-testing, and prospective modeling. *Organizational Behavior and Human Decision Processes*, *80*(1), 3–20.

Stasser, G., and Titus, W. (2003). Hidden profiles: A brief history. *Psychological Inquiry*, *14*, 304–313.

Steiner, I. D. (1966). Models for inferring relationships between group size and potential group productivity. *Behavioral Science*, *11*, 273–283.

———— (1972). *Group process and productivity*. New York: Academic Press.

Surowiecki, J. (2004). *The wisdom of crowds: Why the many are smarter than the few and how collective wisdom shapes business, economies, societies and nations*. New York: Little, Brown.

Theiner, G. (2013). Transactive memory systems: A mechanistic analysis of emergent group memory. *Review of Philosophy and Psychology*, *4*, 65–89.

Theiner, G., Allen, C., and Goldstone, R. (2010). Recognizing group cognition. *Cognitive Systems Research*, *11*, 378–395.

Theiner, G., and O'Connor, T. (2010). The emergence of group cognition. In A. Corradini and T. O'Connor (Eds), *Emergence in science and philosophy* (pp. 78–117). New York: Routledge.

Tribble, E. B. (2005). Distributing cognition in the globe. *Shakespeare Quarterly*, *56*, 135–155.

Wegner, D. M. (1986). Transactive memory: A contemporary analysis of the group mind. In B. Mullen and G. R. Goethals (Eds), *Theories of group behavior* (pp. 185–208). New York: Springer.

Weldon, M. S., and Bellinger, K. D. (1997). Collective memory: Collaborative and individual processes in remembering. *Journal of Experimental Psychology: Learning, Memory, and Cognition*, *23*, 1160–1175.

Wilson, R. (2004). *Boundaries of the mind: The individual in the fragile sciences; Cognition*. Cambridge: Cambridge University Press.

Wimsatt, W. C. (1986). Forms of aggregativity. In M. G. Grene, A. Donagan, A. N. Perovich, and M. V. Wedin (Eds), *Human nature and natural knowledge* (pp. 259–291). Dordrecht: Reidel.

Wittenbaum, G. M., Hollingshead, A. B., Paulus, P. B., Hirokawa, R. Y., Ancona, D. G., Peterson, R. S., Jehn, K. A., and Yoon, K. (2004). The functional perspective as a lens for understanding groups. *Small Group Research*, *35*(1), 17–43.

33
MORALITY IN THE BODY

Brendan Strejcek and Chen-Bo Zhong

There is a long tradition of thought that conceives of morality as in opposition to the appetites and desires of the body. Such physical experiences have, at best, been seen as distractions from the expression of values guided by reason, and, at worst, as the direct cause of sin and immorality through temptation. However, this understanding is being called into question by recent theoretical and empirical work that supports the position that the body is not only an obstacle to morality and moral action, but also a contributor to moral reasoning. Moral concepts seem to be built using mental machinery that is also used for processing bodily experiences. Empirical work in social psychology has shown how intimately these two domains are intertwined, with both reason and bodily inputs feeding back into moral judgment and moral action.

This perspective is consistent with the emerging convergence in evolutionary biology, which claims that morality evolved through the body during the process of negotiating the various pressures of selection. Understanding this reciprocal relationship between morality and body may allow one to know when bodily input may result in maladaptation with regard to our current social environment. For example, the common derogation of the outsider, once perhaps adaptive to defend against invaders and the unknown, can now have many negative side effects, especially in a mass, diverse culture; this can include prejudice, fear, or discrimination when no real danger exists.

Philosophy, reason, and emotion

Historically, there have been two influential dualisms in philosophy: the ontological body/spirit duality (sometimes framed as body/mind) and the emotion/reason duality. These dualities have had numerous forebears, from the Platonic (which actually divided the soul into three parts: appetitive, rational, and spirited) to the Christian. Though several early influential philosophers, such as Democritus and Epicurus, did not separate the functioning of the mind from the functioning of the body, throughout the story of Western philosophy, dualism has mostly been ascendant. Descartes reaffirmed this tradition in the seventeenth century at the beginning of the scientific revolution by aligning dualist rationality with scientific progress in his *Discourse on Method* (1637). The dualism of Descartes was driven by

DOI: 10.4324/9781003322511-42

a desire to find a firm basis for a developing scientific epistemology, which was ultimately provided by the dictum "I think, therefore I am." Though many modern proponents of morality based on rationality do not subscribe to Cartesian substance dualism, the concept has framed the debate.

In all of these dualist conceptions, morality has been identified with reason, often in tension with the appetitive, emotional body. As such, morality has been investigated through the lens of reason. Bodily influence is even used as a mitigating factor in legal cases, as emotional influence is often seen as a loss of control or decrease in free will. For example, consider the "heat of passion" defenses. Emotional and bodily influence has thus been seen as a biasing factor in the proper expression of moral behavior. It is undeniable that sometimes emotions can motivate ethically problematic behavior, but modern cognitive science has been uncovering empirical evidence that the functioning of moral reasoning is expressed through the body using emotional cues. These cues manifest linguistically as metaphors, which have become the philosophical spur of modern embodiment research.

Metaphor

Many moral concepts are described and conceptualized through metaphors, which are often grounded in bodily experiences. Some of the key foundational physical metaphors that anchor moral reasoning include uprightness/height, balance, control/freedom of movement, health/strength, and purity (Lakoff and Johnson 1999, p. 333).

The "up" metaphor is particularly potent (associated with more, control, good, and rational). The emotion associated with being uplifted by the altruistic deeds of others is often referred to as elevation (it is almost impossible to even discuss this emotion without the assistance of metaphors). Ideas of value also have physical forebears, such as the concrete experience of ownership and quantity. Well-being is considered a form of wealth, and languages are rich with examples of accounting metaphors (cost, loss, gain) regarding happiness and the good life, and these metaphors extend to fairness, reciprocation, debt, revenge, and similar concepts. Finally, purity, corruption, contagion, health, and strength are all key terms in moral discourse and are almost synonymous with concepts of good and evil (consider the meaning of the sentences "he is corrupt," or "she is pure"). This collection of metaphors has provided a framework for social scientists to investigate the impact of bodily and physical experience on moral judgment.

It is thought that the evolutionary experience of survival has equipped the mind with a number of concrete concepts used for day-to-day survival (more nutrition is desirable, dirty things are sources of contagion, and so forth). These concepts were then available for repurposing in a pre-adaptive fashion (Rozin, 1999). This perspective is often discussed as a form of scaffolding, as the concrete experience being scaffolded into our conceptual development (Williams, Huang, and Bargh, 2009), which informs much of the rest of the analysis below. Though the structure of metaphors may be stable across cultures, specific expression can vary dramatically across time and space (thus, the unclean may be universally associated with the malevolent, but exactly what is considered to be unclean will likely vary by culture). That is, the concrete objects that satisfy specific metaphors are malleable, but the mental subsystem of, for example, disgust/dirtiness and avoidance seems to be available to people in general.

These associations are empirically observed in our use of language, but they do not in themselves lead to the conclusion that morality is shaped by bodily experience (as opposed to just being used descriptively). To make this link, both experimental psychology and neuroscience have found that experiences of these physical metaphors can affect moral judgment and moral action in measurable, significant ways.

Social intuitionism

Instead of seeing moral judgment as the process of rational analysis, numerous studies in experimental and social psychology have found that moral judgment tends to happen quickly and intuitively and is often influenced by bodily experiences. Haidt and Hersh (2001), for example, constructed hypothetical situations designed to be socially repugnant, but not harmful in any way, to question the idea that moral judgment was carefully and rationally constructed. They found that people's affective reactions to those vignettes were much stronger predictors of moral judgment than analysis of harm and moral principle. Participants in their studies typically express strong moral opposition to disgusting but harmless acts such as a consensual kiss between siblings; when pressed to explain their moral reasoning, however, a common reaction was moral dumbfounding – strong moral condemnation with an utter inability to rationally explain their position.

The social intuitionism model proposed by Jonathan Haidt to explain this phenomenon holds that moral reasoning is retroactive, with rational processing often happening after the fact to justify and explain decisions previously determined by non-rational means. Thus, the model questions the causal power of reasoning in moral judgment. This is congruent with the perspective of embodied morality, which sees morality arising through bodily experience often expressed as emotions. These means are primarily emotional, and involve revulsion and disgust. The emotions seem to be expressed through the medium of the body and understood using the language of metaphors (Haidt, 2001).

Social neuroscience

Historically, when confronted with different explanations for moral action, the tools for investigation were limited. Epicurus conceived of the functioning of the mind as physical movements in the chest, but this was almost more of a metaphysical position derived from the earlier Presocratic atomists. Now, with fMRI machines and the beginnings of brain maps, we begin to have a better picture of what goes on in the human body when thinking happens and decisions are made.

A number of prominent studies found that the brain regions that govern emotion regulation are intimately connected to moral reasoning and contemplation (Damasio, Tranel, and Damasio, 1990; Greene, Sommerville, Nystrom, Darley, and Cohen, 2001). Different parts of the brain are active when thinking about moral dilemmas that have rationally identical outcomes but different emotional engagement. For example, one intriguing thought experiment involves two structurally equivalent dilemmas in which a runaway trolley is headed toward five people and will kill them if not stopped. This dilemma is framed in two ways, a stand-in-distance "switch" version and an up-and-close "push" version. In the switch version, the only way to save the five is to hit a switch that will turn the trolley onto an alternate set of tracks where it will kill one person instead of five; in the push version of the dilemma, the only way to save the five is to push a stranger onto the tracks from a footbridge spanning the tracks. The stranger will die, but his body will stop the trolley from reaching the others. In both cases, people decide whether it is right to kill one person to save five others. Yet most people say that they would pull the switch but not push the person.

The former response represents utilitarian reasoning – people seem to suggest that sacrificing one person to save five is the right course of action because it produces greater good; the latter response represents Kantian reasoning that emphasizes the intrinsic value of a human life and the recognition that the rightness of an action is independent of its consequences (hence the outcome of saving five others cannot justify the killing of one). It is not hard to see that these two perspectives have irreconcilable principles: while utilitarian thinking puts the "good" before the "right," the Kantian perspective emphasizes that what is right precedes what is good. So how could rational thinking lead simultaneously to contradictory principles? A recent fMRI study found that this inconsistent moral aversion against pushing down a person to save others may stem from increased emotional engagement (Greene *et al.*, 2001) – the horrific thought of pushing someone to his or her death is much more emotionally arousing than pulling a switch. This again shows that emotional involvement is an important contributor to moral reasoning.

But some would go even further to suggest that emotional engagement may be necessary to moral choices. This is based on research showing that brain activities during contemplation of utilitarian dilemmas resembles non-moral dilemmas (Greene *et al.*, 2001) as well as the observation that individuals with antisocial traits tend to make more utilitarian choices in moral dilemmas (Bartels and Pizarro, 2011). Thus, Bloom (2011) questioned the moral nature of utilitarian reasoning altogether in that it is based on pure calculations that are largely devoid of context and meaning. This stronger view coincides with research based on patients with brain damage to their ventromedial prefrontal cortex (vmPFC), an important brain region that is involved in emotion regulation. These patients retain full capability of rational thought and reasoning, which are the type of processes required for utilitarian reasoning, but seem to have lost emotional connection and, more importantly, the ability to adapt to social and moral conventions. Over time, these patients tend to grow more antisocial (Damasio, Everitt, and Bishop, 1996).

One underlying theory is that emotional experience guides moral judgment and decision making through a series of bodily signals called somatic markers. Lacking proper somatic markers, as in the case of vmPFC-damaged patients, an otherwise functional brain is unable to attach moral weight or value to outcomes effectively (Damasio *et al.*, 1996). This proposition that emotional impairment leads to moral malfunction corroborates the position that moral reasoning can't only be the product of rationality (Lakoff and Johnson, 1999, p. 327).

Thus, research on linguistics, emotion, and neuroscience converge on the involvement of bodily experiences in moral development and reasoning. Not only do people appropriate physical concepts such as up vs. down and clean vs. dirty, and recast them in social and moral terms, but they also "recycle" emotions and associated brain circuitries developed for rudimental, physical tasks in early development and survival (e.g., disgust to avoid poisonous food) to help make sense of more abstract moral situations (e.g., disgust of betrayal and cheating). In the next section, we will discuss specific bodily experiences that may inform moral judgment and decision making to demonstrate how the physical and moral domains continue to overlap cognitively, emotionally, and neurologically.

Bodily experiences that influence morality

Several specific physical experiences that are related to the primary linguistic metaphors discussed above seem to contribute in various ways to moral judgment and moral decision making. The physical experiences most potent in influencing morality are those regarding disgust and purity, but many other embodied concepts such as position, color, and interior states have weight as well.

Emotion

The emotion of disgust was originally a gustatory emotion rooted in our evolutionary past as a motivational mechanism that avoids the consumption of contaminating substances. At the basic physical level, disgust serves as a guide for approach and avoidance, and it is obvious how to reason evolutionarily about how this function might have arisen, as it results in avoidance of external dangers (such as contamination from rotting organic matter) and enhancement of survival fitness. Disgust operates on many sensory levels, from visual to taste (which functions as a last line of defense against ingesting potentially harmful food). This low-level, physical aid to behavior, rooted deeply in bodily experience, has been co-opted for use by high-level, social functions, as a guide for avoiding potential social danger such as transgressions by others (Rozin, 1999).

Many studies have been done recently in social psychology that link moral transgression and physical contamination (Rozin, Haidt, and McCauley, 1993). Physical and moral disgust seem to use brain regions that overlap within the frontal and temporal lobes (Moll *et al.*, 2002; Borg, Lieberman, and Kiehl, 2008). Additionally, similar facial expressions have been found in response to both moral and physical disgust (Chapman, Kim, Susskind, and Anderson, 2009; Rozin, Lowery, and Ebert, 1994). These studies form a good foundation for the evolutionary concept of preadaptation and the reuse of cognitive capabilities shaped first for interacting with the physical environment but later conscripted for use by moral cognition.

This has particularly interesting implications for moral judgment being affected by indirect physical stimuli, such as when an emotion is not specifically elicited by a particular target of judgment. This has been shown in studies using hypnotism (Wheatley and Haidt, 2005), ambient smell (Schnall, Haidt, Clore, and Jordan, 2008; Jones and Fitness, 2008), and gustatory experiences such as bad taste (Eskine, Kacinik, and Prinz, 2011). All of these manipulations were found to impart negative qualities from the realm of the physical to the realm of the moral. These effects probably have differing magnitudes based in individual disgust sensitivity, as Jones and Fitness (2008) found that those who are more easily disgusted by physical contaminants are also more likely to engage in harsher moral judgment.

Sensory perception

Cleanliness

Cleanliness and purity have been an important part of religious ceremony for most major world religions throughout history. Given the importance of religion in our moral code, scholars such as Haidt argue that purity and sanctity constitute a fundamental moral foundation. It is not until recently, however, that empirical research in social psychology has started to demonstrate that the bodily perception of cleanliness can be both a consequence of moral status and a determinant of moral judgment and behavior.

This connection between physical purity and morality has been corroborated by several experimental findings. One set of results verifies this connection by observing that morally threatening situations prompt physical cleansing much like actual, physical dirtiness. For example, the following transgressions have all been found to induce a greater desire for cleansing products: reminding people of their own, past immoral acts (Zhong and Liljenquist, 2006); leaving false voicemail messages or lying through email (Lee and Schwarz, 2010); or playing violent video games (Gollwitzer and Melzer, 2012). Though these effects are similar, and presumably activate the same underlying cognitive machinery, the effects also have unique manifestations appropriate to a particular modality. Thus, mouthwash was most desired in Lee and Schwarz's voicemail experiment, whereas hand sanitizer was more strongly desired in the case of deception through email.

The most important aspect of these findings is how the physical and moral domains overlap and spill over into each other. Because of this relationship, the way that cleanliness signals the absence of contaminants and the way disgust alerts the body to the presence of contaminants can have moral ramifications as well. This sometimes irrational metaphorical link is nonetheless often quite potent in practice. One hypothesis based on this connection between the two domains is that not only does the immoral feel impure, but also the pure should feel moral. If that were true, then an increased sense of personal cleanliness might trigger feelings of moral superiority or moral righteousness. Cleanliness has been found in the lab to trigger feelings of moral purity (e.g., Helzer and Pizarro, 2011; Xu, Bègue, and Bushman, 2012; Yan, Ding, and Yan, 2011; Zhong, Strejcek, and Sivanathan, 2010b), and even proximity to symbols of cleanliness seems to affect moral standing. For example, Helzer and Pizarro measured harsher moral judgments arising from standing next to a hand sanitizer and Zhong, Strejcek *et al.* (2010b) found that feeling physically clean moralized various contested issues (such as littering and homosexuality) more harshly.

In addition to the influence of cleanliness on moral judgment, physical cleansing may also directly impact moral behavior because it alters people's moral self-image (Zhong, Strejcek *et al.*, 2010b). Thus, individuals who have transgressed are less likely to engage in compensatory and restitution behaviors if they have a chance to physically clean themselves, which serves as a symbolic means to restore moral balance. This was indeed what Zhong and Liljenquist (2006) found. In their study, participants who recalled past unethical behaviors who had a chance to wipe their hands using an antiseptic wipe were less likely to volunteer to help others compared to those who did not wash hands. Further, Reuven, Liberman, and Dar (2014) replicated this finding and found that this effect is more pronounced among patients with obsessive-compulsive disorder.

The moral appropriation of physical cleanliness can be seen dramatically throughout political and religious history. The untouchables in the Indian caste system and the Japanese Burakumin are clear examples of this tendency, and the book of Leviticus in the Old Testament, which is a guide to morality, is organized around differentiating the clean from the unclean. Purity of tradition is also central to nationalist discourse and has been used repeatedly to combat "foreign" influence or deflect anxiety onto convenient out-group scapegoats, which may be the basis of much anti-Semitism and other racial, cultural, or minority derogation (Strejcek and Zhong, 2012).

411

Color

Stain is another potent metaphor, connected in its physical manifestation to the experience of cleanliness at base, but also resulting in a complex visual metaphor system on its own. As any experience with mixing things of different colors will make clear, light colors are more easily besmirched than dark colors, and are thus more vulnerable to corruption or irreversible change. The structural concepts of pollution in food safety and other physical domains also map to this visual metaphor of whiteness as purity and blackness as dirt. If this visual color metaphor has moral relevance, it would be expected that various moral processing tasks would be affected by color, such as the degree to which things are judged to be good or bad.

The most basic form of this effect could be the speed of valence categorization, a type of moral Stroop effect, where incongruent visual presentation (i.e., combining white color and "bad" things) slows recognition time. In the classic Stroop effect, given the word "red" written in blue ink, it takes longer to state the actual color (blue) than if the word matches the color (such as the word "red" written in red ink). A similar effect was found based on the interaction between color and moral implication of words. In one experiment, Sherman and Clore (2009) found that hand-copying a story about an immoral action sped up reaction times for both words written in black and immoral words. Using a similar design to Zhong and Liljenquist (2006), the same experimenters found that cleaning products were also more desirable to those showing such a moral Stroop effect, which is another suggestion that the physical and moral domains overlap.

While perception of color as related to pollution and dirt has effects based on the experience of purity, the experience of darkness and light can have independent moral impact. This is based on research showing that people seem to feel more anonymous and uninhibited when they experience dim lighting (Hartley, 1974; Karnes, 1960; Page and Moss, 1976), which enables them to engage in more unethical behaviors. In one recent experiment, participants were assigned to rooms with either bright lighting or dim lighting and were asked to engage in some decision-making tasks where they could cheat. Even though it was made clear to them that all decisions were anonymous, those in the dim room tended to cheat more than those in the well-lit room. Another experiment had participants wear sunglasses (to create the experience of darkness) or regular glasses and found that those wearing sunglasses were more likely to cheat than those wearing regular glasses (Zhong, Lake, and Gino, 2010a). One might object that darkness does in fact increase anonymity. It is important to note, however, that in neither study did the lighting have anything to do with anonymity. Instead, these results seem to suggest that cues of reduced lighting create an illusionary sense of anonymity, which licensed unethical behavior. The observation that moral decision-making processes take cues from sensory perceptions of color and lighting provides further support to the somatic markers hypothesized by Damasio. If moral decisions were being made independently of physical and perceptual biases, the rational mind should easily be able to factor in the function of sunglasses, but empirically it does not seem to do so.

Taste

The experience of taste has been found to inform moral judgment in ways other than disgust. One might expect the opposite of disgust to also have effects, though in the other direction. As one test of this, researchers investigated the effect of sweetness. Specifically, in one experiment those described as liking sweet foods were judged to be more agreeable and in another experiment the preference for sweet foods was indeed associated with agreeableness. People who desired sweet foods more were also more likely to exhibit altruism in the form of intention to volunteer for clean-up efforts (Meier, Moeller, Riemer-Peltz, and Robinson, 2012). Related to taste, fishy smells have also been found to increase the sense of suspicion even to abstract things unrelated to physical or gustatory concerns, such as economic trust decisions (Lee and Schwarz, 2012). These results strengthen the case that bodily influence feeds into morality by showing associations with prosociality in addition to rejection and aversion.

Balance

Much of the Western philosophical foundations of moral codes rests upon the concept of reciprocity and justice. Both have to do with the idea of balance, whether it is in the "tit-for-tat" sense or the idea of fairness and equal rights before the law (Lakoff and Johnson, 1999). Even as early as the classical Greeks and Romans, justice was personified as a goddess bearing a scale. The dominant modern discourses about fairness also heavily make use of physical metaphors, such as the level playing field (which means that all participants operate under similar constraints), or the redistribution of benefits (so that different participants have balanced amounts of whatever resource is limited) (Leamer, 2007). The moral relevance of physical balance may manifest in two forms.

First, metaphors of balance of accounts are often used in moral conceptualizations. Well-being is seen as a form of wealth, something you can have more or less of, and thus something that can be compared (in quantity) with others. Justice, in this formulation, is the pursuit of fairness with regard to this quantitative well-being. This also holds with regard to the handling of debts; that is, one can have a moral debt to someone that must be "paid off," either in positive or negative senses, which is how retribution, revenge, and reciprocation play into this metaphorical scheme (Lakoff and Johnson, 1999).

Second, the experience of physical balance may tip moral judgment. The physical experience of balance seems to make abstract, conceptual metaphors such as parity and fairness implicitly more accessible. This bodily priming has been found to modify the judgment of political categories, which are often also labeled in a metaphorical (though arbitrary) way, such as the description of political philosophies as left or right. A study that shifted participants' physical balance slightly to the left or right demonstrated a tendency to judge an unrelated political position (note the metaphorical language that must be used even to discuss the concept) either as more left wing or right wing (congruent with the experimental manipulation). Thus, what one might expect to be a purely rational determination is shaped by the physical experience of the subject. The sense of balance has also been found to affect judgment, leading to an increase in the value placed on compromise choices. The mechanism behind this observed effect was hypothesized to be a metaphorical link between the concrete, physical sensation of balance and the abstract concept of parity, which is connected to moral ideas of fairness (Larson and Billeter, 2013). As categorization of political ideas tends to have moral weight (based on whether or not the person making the judgment has sympathy for those positions), the fact that physical balance can affect that judgment seems to offer at least further tangential evidence for the impact of the body on shaping moral judgment.

Interoception

Physical experiences are not limited to the perception of external reality; they also include interior states. Disgust, in addition to a response caused by external stimuli, can also be evoked by internal states such as nausea, and nausea is in fact the primary experience that results in permanent food dislike (Rozin, 1999). Not only can the real interoceptive experience influence decisions, the perceived experience can, too. This has been studied using sensory input masquerading as internal sensations, such as with false heartbeat. For example, images were judged more attractive when accompanied by false (recorded), fast heart-rate recordings that were presented as the subject's own heart rate (Valins, 1966). Thus, as Valins writes, "internal events facilitate emotional behavior," which is a sort of prelude to the more sophisticated somatic marker hypothesis. False feedback has also been used for behavioral therapy, to help alleviate irrational phobias. Specifically, avoidance behavior regarding snakes has been found to decrease when subjects were led to believe that their own internal reaction was lessened via false feedback (Valins and Ray, 1967).

A similar false-feedback paradigm has also been found to affect more directly moral behaviors, such as volunteering and deception. Specifically, increased heart rate was found to increase the incidence of volunteering for a charitable cause, reduce self-interested lying, and be less morally potent in the face of rational, deliberative framing (Gu, Zhong, and Page-Gould, 2012). Self-perception of heartbeat is hypothesized to be a somatic marker that signals situational stress and contributes to people's decisions regarding how much moral weight to give potential actions.

Thus, it seems like moral decision making in practice requires actual physical feedback as would be experienced at the time of action, not just an abstract formulation of the stakes and options. That is, if the perspective of embodied morality advanced in this chapter were true, it would be likely that people would potentially predict different actions than they might actually take. Experimentally, people have indeed been found to predict that they would take less moral action than they actually do, because moral forecasting does not sufficiently engage the emotions due to lack of somatic feedback (Teper, Inzlicht, and Page-Gould, 2011).

Discussion and conclusion

Though the effects discussed so far have important theoretical consequences, they may also have dramatic, real-world effects. For example, there is a cliché that justice is "what the judge ate for breakfast" (as stated by Judge Jerome Frank), meaning that the mood imparted by feelings of satiety or hunger affects judgment of guilt or innocence. More formally, the philosophy known as legal realism holds that legal decisions in practice depend on much more than just the letter or intent of the law, but rather are influenced by all manner of extraneous factors, some of which may be bodily factors. A study tested this by examining parole hearings where the default decision was to deny parole. The chance of parole being granted was highest at the beginning of the day or right after a food break, and decreased gradually as the session progressed, from over 60% on average to barely above 0% right before the next break. The subject judges (all of whom were experienced, with more than 20 years of practice on average) were thus found to become more severe in parole hearings the more depleted their resources became, whether that was due to hunger or exhaustion (Danziger, Levav, and Avnaim-Pesso, 2011). The exact connections of this sort of effect to metaphor-based embodied cognition remain to be elaborated, but the potential for significant impact in diverse areas of society is clear.

It might be asked whether these effects are merely biases, errors of judgment that should be overcome given sufficient cognitive effort. However, the neuroscience findings point in another direction. Though some of these bodily influences on morality do indeed result in biases, the elimination of emotional or bodily influence would likely not have the desired effect, due to the importance of somatic markers for identifying moral action. The patients that Damasio investigated in his fMRI studies were not deficient in any way regarding rational-processing power, but lacking appropriate bodily feedback, were unable to accurately weigh moral consequences in their decision making.

Taken together, these findings create a compelling case for a strong relationship between mental activities regarding low-level, physical tasks and high-level, abstract tasks, particularly socially potent abstractions such as morality. They also create a robust empirical basis for theoretical understanding in myriad fields, from psychology to philosophy and practical domains such as law.

References

Bartels, D., and Pizarro, D. A. (2011). The mismeasure of morals: Antisocial personality traits predict utilitarian responses to moral dilemmas. *Cognition, 121,* 154–161.

Bloom, P. (2011). Family, community, trolley problems, and the crisis in moral psychology. *Yale Review, 99,* 26–43.

Borg, J. S., Lieberman, D., and Kiehl, K. A. (2008). Infection, incest, and iniquity: Investigating the neural correlates of disgust and morality. *Journal of Cognitive Neuroscience, 20,* 1529–1546.

Chapman, H. A., Kim, D. A., Susskind, J. M., and Anderson, A. K. (2009). In bad taste: Evidence for the oral origins of moral disgust. *Science, 323,* 1222–1226.

Damasio, A. R., Everitt, B. J., and Bishop, D. (1996). The somatic marker hypothesis and the possible functions of the prefrontal cortex. *Philosophical Transactions of the Royal Society, B: Biological Sciences, 351*(1346), 1413–1420.

Damasio, A. R., Tranel, D., and Damasio, H. (1990). Individuals with sociopathic behavior caused by frontal damage fail to respond autonomically to social stimuli. *Behavioural Brain Research, 41,* 81–94.

Danziger, S., Levav, J., and Avnaim-Pesso, L. (2011). Extraneous factors in judicial decisions. *Proceedings of the National Academy of Sciences of the United States of America, 108,* 6889–6892.

Eskine, K. J., Kacinik, N. A., and Prinz, J. J. (2011). A bad taste in the mouth: Gustatory disgust influences moral judgment. *Psychological Science, 22,* 295–299.

Gollwitzer, M., and Melzer, A. (2012). Macbeth and the joystick: Evidence for moral cleansing after playing a violent video game. *Journal of Experimental Social Psychology, 48,* 1356–1360.

Greene, J. D., Sommerville, R. B., Nystrom, L. E., Darley, J. M., and Cohen, J. D. (2001). An fMRI investigation of emotional engagement in moral judgment. *Science, 293,* 2105–2108.

Gu, J., Zhong, C. B., and Page-Gould, E. (2012). Listen to your heart: False somatic feedback regulates deception. *Journal of Experimental Psychology: General, 142*(2), 307–312.

Haidt, J. (2001). The emotional dog and its rational tail: A social intuitionist approach to moral judgment. *Psychological Review, 108,* 814–834.

Haidt, J., and Hersh, M. A. (2001). Sexual morality: The cultures and emotions of conservatives and liberals. *Journal of Applied Social Psychology 31*(1), 191–221.

Hartley, J. E. (1974). *Lighting reinforces crime fight.* Pittsfield: Buttenheim Publishing Corporation.

Helzer, E. G., and Pizarro, D. A. (2011). Dirty liberals! Reminders of physical cleanliness influence moral and political attitudes. *Psychological Science, 22,* 517–522.

Jones, A., and Fitness, J. (2008). Moral hypervigilance: The influence of disgust sensitivity in the moral domain. *Emotion, 8,* 613–627.

Karnes, E. B. (1960). Well planned lighting is city progress. *American City Magazine, 75*(April), 104–105.

Lakoff, G., and Johnson, M. (1999). *Philosophy in the flesh.* Chicago: University of Chicago Press.

Larson, J., and Billeter, D. M. (2013). Consumer behavior in "equilibrium": How experiencing physical balance increases compromise choice. *Journal of Marketing Research*, *50*(4), 535–547.

Leamer, E. E. (2007). A flat world, a level playing field, a small world after all, or none of the above? A review of Thomas L Friedman's *The world is flat*. *Journal of Economic Literature*, *45*(1), 83–126.

Lee, S. W., and Schwarz, N. (2010). Dirty hands and dirty mouths: Embodiment of the moral-purity metaphor is specific to the motor modality involved in the moral transgression. *Psychological Science*, *21*, 1423–1425.

——— (2012). Bidirectionality, mediation, and moderation of metaphorical effects: The embodiment of social suspicion and fishy smells. *Journal of Personality and Social Psychology*, *103*(5), 737–749.

Meier, B. P., Moeller, S. K., Riemer-Peltz, M., and Robinson, M. D. (2012). Sweet taste preferences and experience predict prosocial inferences, personalities and behaviors. *Journal of Personality and Social Psychology*, *102*, 163–174.

Moll, J., de Oliveira-Souza, R., Eslinger, P. J., Bramati, I. E., Mourao-Miranda, J., Andreiuolo, P. A., and Pessoa, L. (2002). The neural correlates of moral sensitivity: A functional magnetic resonance imaging investigation of basic and moral emotions. *Journal of Neuroscience*, *22*, 2730–2736.

Page, R. A., and Moss, M. K. (1976). Environmental influences on aggression: The effects of darkness and proximity of victim. *Journal of Applied Social Psychology*, *6*, 126–133.

Reuven, O., Liberman, N., and Dar, R. (2014). The effect of physical cleaning on threatened morality in individuals with obsessive-compulsive disorder. *Clinical Psychological Science*, *2*, 224–229.

Rozin, P. (1999). Preadaptation and the puzzles and properties of pleasure. In D. Kahneman, E. Diener, and N. Schwarz (Eds), *Well-being: The foundations of hedonic psychology* (pp. 109–133). New York: Russell Sage.

Rozin, P., Haidt, J., and McCauley, C. R. (1993). Disgust. In M. Lewis and J. Haviland (Eds), *Handbook of emotions* (pp. 575–594). New York: Guilford.

Rozin, P., Lowery, L., and Ebert, R. (1994). Varieties of disgust faces and the structure of disgust. *Journal of Personality and Social Psychology*, *66*, 870–881.

Schnall, S., Haidt, J., Clore, G. L., and Jordan, A. H. (2008). Disgust as embodied moral judgment. *Personality and Social Psychology Bulletin*, *34*, 1096–1109.

Sherman, G. D., and Clore, G. L. (2009). The color of sin: White and black are perceptual symbols of moral purity and pollution. *Psychological Science*, *20*, 1019–1025.

Strejcek, B., and Zhong, C. B. (2012). The perils of cleanliness. In P. Rosch and U. Simon (Eds), *How purity is made* (pp. 57–67). Wiesbaden: Harrassowitz.

Teper, R., Inzlicht, M., and Page-Gould, E. (2011). Are we more moral than we think? Exploring the role of affect in moral behavior and moral forecasting. *Psychological Science*, *22*, 543–558.

Valins, S. (1966). Cognitive effects of false heart-rate feedback. *Journal of Personality and Social Psychology*, *4*, 400–408.

Valins, S., and Ray, A. (1967). Effects of cognitive desensitization on avoidance behavior. *Journal of Personality and Social Psychology*, *7*, 345–350.

Wheatley, T., and Haidt, J. (2005). Hypnotically induced disgust makes moral judgments more severe. *Psychological Science*, *16*, 780–784.

Williams, L. E., Huang, J. Y., and Bargh, J. A. (2009). The scaffolded mind: Higher mental processes are grounded in early experience of the physical world. *European Journal of Social Psychology*, *39*, 1257–1267.

Xu, H., Bègue, L., and Bushman, D. (2012). Too fatigued to care: Ego depletion, guilt, and prosocial behavior. *Journal of Experimental Social Psychology*, *48*, 1183–1186.

Yan, Z., Ding, D., and Yan, L. (2011). To wash your body, or purify your soul: Physical cleansing would strengthen the sense of high moral character. *Psychology*, *2*, 992–997.

Zhong, C. B., Lake, V. B., and Gino, F. (2010a). A good lamp is the best police: Darkness increases dishonesty and self-interested behavior. *Psychological Science*, *21*, 311–314

Zhong, C. B., and Liljenquist, K. A. (2006). Washing away your sins: Threatened morality and physical cleansing. *Science*, *313*, 1451–1452.

Zhong, C.-B., Strejcek, B., and Sivanathan, N. (2010b). A clean self can render harsh moral judgment. *Journal of Experimental Social Psychology*, *46*, 859–862.

34

EMBODIED EMOTION CONCEPTS

Paula M. Niedenthal, Adrienne Wood, Magdalena Rychlowska,
and Anna Orlowska

What are emotion concepts? The answer to this question is the topic of the present chapter. We begin with the observation that people possess the concepts of "joy", "sadness", and "fear", among others, as indicated by their language use and their behavior (e.g., Scarantino 2012; Barrett 2017). They also recognize perceptual input from other people, such as their faces and bodies, as meaning that those people feel "joy" and "sadness" and "fear". This chapter is about the representation of emotion concepts. What allows individuals to judge a face as expressing "disgust", and what happens when they identify the word "cruel" in a text?

The first section of the chapter reviews ways in which these kinds of everyday, non-scientific emotion concepts have been characterized in the psychological literature (Niedenthal 2008). After briefly describing dimensional, semantic primitives and prototype accounts, and the semantic network model, as well as the assumptions upon which these accounts are based, we present an alternative account – embodied emotion concepts. An embodiment account and supporting empirical evidence will be discussed in greater detail. We conclude that an embodied or seimulation account of emotion concepts provides solutions to a number of problems, or at least open questions, specific to the issue of how emotion concepts are represented, which prior accounts do not adequately address.

Semantics of emotions

Theories of emotion concepts have developed along two different lines. One line focuses on the conceptual structure of emotions as represented by words used to describe them (e.g., Ortony et al. 1987; Shaver et al. 1987). The questions that arise there include: What are the dimensions of similarity that bind emotion knowledge? What are the underlying factors? The best-known account of emotion concepts in this line is the dimensional approach, in which the underlying structure of emotion concepts is derived from people's judgments about their subjective feeling states. By analyzing such judgments with statistical scaling methods, researchers have hypothesized two bipolar dimensions (e.g., Bradley et al. 2022; Kuppens et al. 2013; Lang et al. 1990; Mayer and Gaschke 1988; Reisenzein 1994; Yik et al. 2022). The two dimensions are the degree to which an emotional state is pleasant

DOI: 10.4324/9781003322511-43

versus unpleasant (or positive versus negative) and the degree to which an emotional state is activated or deactivated (roughly, having high versus low arousal). Thus, the fundamental understanding that people have about emotions involves the degrees of pleasantness and activation that typically characterize them. For example, "anger" is conceptualized as highly unpleasant and moderately activated, and "fear" as moderately unpleasant and highly activated (e.g., Citron et al. 2014; Kuperman et al. 2014; Russell and Barrett 1999).

Importantly, analysis of judgments of emotions with methods of scaling does not reveal anything about representation. A passive assumption is that emotion knowledge is represented as lexical entries, or words that stand for experienced information. Two other approaches, the semantic primitives and the prototype analyses, attempt to explain difference, rather than similarity, in conceptual content between emotions. Rather than identifying the fundamental dimensions underlying the structure of emotion knowledge, these two additional accounts try to specify the conceptual content for a theoretically predetermined set of differentiated emotions.

The construction of lists of semantic primitives for emotions is a bootstrapping, bottom-up activity that involves the generation of possibilities and the attempt to define as many concepts as possible, independent of a specific language, and without adding more concepts. For instance, while the words "anger" and "sadness" are culture bound and language specific, semantic primitives such as "good" and "bad" and "want" and "happen" are not (Bromberek-Dyzman et al. 2021; Wierzbicka 1992). These primitives can describe some of the basic themes that characterize emotion (Johnson-Laird and Oatley 1989, 2021). For example, emotions involve good and bad things that happen to us and to other people, and that we and other people actively do. Emotions also comprise others' and our own evaluations of ourselves and our actions, and the relationships that can be constructed on the bases of these evaluations. Using semantic primitives to build emotion concepts seems to provide enough nuance to characterize many different emotions. But, despite its power, the semantic primitives approach also has some shortcomings. Although the definitions seem to contain something about the antecedents of and situations for emotions, the "hot" or bodily aspects of the emotion are not contained in the definition. This problem might be addressed by calling a set of basic emotions, such as fear, anger, happiness, sadness, and disgust, themselves, semantic primitives (Johnson-Laird and Oatley 1989, 2021). However, neither use of the semantic primitives approach addresses the way in which semantic primitives are represented and processed. While the assumption must be that the primitives are innate, it's still not clear what is being used when they are activated.

Although it focuses on conceptual structure and differences between emotions, the prototype approach to emotion concepts does not solve these problems either. In the prototype approach (Rosch 1973), emotion concepts are hierarchically organized and fuzzy, such that boundaries between related categories are not strict. Emotion concepts refer to events described in terms of temporally structured prototypes or scripts that comprise components of emotions, such as antecedents, situations, and bodily characteristics (Russell 1991, 2021). Such elements of the prototypes are probabilistic and not all-or-none in nature. One element, such as a facial expression or a behavior, can be classified as an instance of a particular emotion and these classifications reveal graded structure.

In the semantic network model of emotion (Bower 1981, 1991; Lang 1984), knowledge about emotion is represented in a network of units of representations called "nodes". Basic emotions are conceptualized as central organizing nodes. Units that represent beliefs, antecedents, and physiological patterns associated with a given emotion are linked to the central nodes by connecting pathways. When an emotion unit is activated above some threshold, activation spreads throughout the network to associated information. Autonomic reactions, expressive behaviors, emotion-related events, and personal memories are thereby excited and may enter consciousness. For instance, when one is feeling happy, the material in memory related to happiness becomes activated. As a consequence, one may experience an increase in heart rate and in blood pressure, an activation of the zygomaticus major muscle, and a heightened accessibility to the words and memories associated with happiness. The semantic network model generates hypotheses regarding the structure and content of emotion concepts (Niedenthal et al. 1994, for discussion); however, it fails as an explanatory account, which the following section will discuss.

All models described above are based on a general view of cognition that assumes that higher-order mental content is modal and abstract in format. Thus, it does not preserve analogical information about the low-level perceptual experience of objects, events, or states. The underlying assumption is that representation and initial sensory experience do not take place in the same system and that information taken from the initial experience needs to be described in mental symbols to represent emotion concepts (Bower 1981; Johnson-Laird and Oatley 1989; Ortony et al. 1987; Clore and Ortony 2013). Yet, an accumulating body of evidence is often more consistent with a view according to which the activation in the body's sensorimotor and affective systems in many cases constitutes the conceptual content itself.

Embodied simulation of emotion

Unlike amodal accounts of emotion concepts, theories of embodied or simulated concepts hold that perception and action are tightly coupled (Barsalou 1999; Damasio 1999; Ferrari and Coudé 2018; Gallese 2003; Glenberg 1997; Miellet et al. 2012; Niedenthal et al. 2005; Smith and Semin 2007; Wood et al. 2016). These basic principles are not new and have long roots in the philosophy of Merleau-Ponty and Heidegger, and the psychology of Vygotsky and Piaget (see also Prinz 2002). By these accounts, the modality-specific states that represent perception, action, and introspection when one experiences a particular object also serve to represent the object later, offline. Emotion concepts then would refer to bodily states situated in the causal context (Barrett 2006). For example, embodied emotions theorists suggest that the meanings of emotion words are grounded in their associated behaviors, such as facial expressions and gestures (Hietanen and Leppänen 2008; Niedenthal 2007; Winkielman et al. 2018; Wood et al. 2019). Because an emotional experience involves a complex interplay between the autonomic nervous system, behavior, facial expressions, cognition, and the limbic area of the brain, embodied representations of emotions themselves are distributed across modality-specific regions of the brain.

Behavioral and neuroimaging evidence supports an embodied emotion account of emotion concepts. In the next section we review findings of studies using language to probe emotion concepts. Then we review work on the face and the body. There are both experimental and correlational tests of the basic predictions of the embodiment of emotion concepts. The former rely on strategies for blocking or facilitating the involvement of the body's emotion systems in order to test their causal role in emotion concept use. Correlational studies use behavioral and neuroimaging methods to assess the occurrence of emotion simulation during emotion concept use. We review both types of evidence in order to evaluate the functional role of the sensorimotor and affect systems in executing tasks that rely on emotion concepts, such as the identification or use of emotion nouns, and the recognition or classification of facial or bodily expression of emotion.

Verbal probes to emotion concepts

A number of inventive methods have been used to block emotion processes during emotional language processing. Havas and colleagues (Havas et al. 2010) looked at the function of facial activity in the processing of emotion language by taking advantage of the beauty industry's response to aging: Botox. Botulinum toxin-A (BTX) is a neurotoxin that paralyzes muscles, reducing the appearance of wrinkles caused by preventing the underlying facial muscles from contracting. Havas et al. invited women who were about to receive BTX injections in the corrugator supercilii – which furrows the brows and can cause frown lines – to read happy, sad, and angry sentences, and answer comprehension questions. Two weeks later, the same women (now wrinkle-free) returned to read more sentences. Results showed that the BTX injections significantly slowed the women's reading speed for angry and sad, but not happy, sentences. Thus, the denervation of facial muscles blocks facial expressions and seems to hinder emotion-specific language processing. Recent findings also suggest that altering facial movements by holding chopsticks in one's mouth can interfere with emotion language processing indexed by brain event-related potentials (Davis et al. 2015, 2017).

Foroni and Semin (2009) also found that embodied simulation plays a role in non-conscious processing of emotion words. In this study Dutch students were exposed subliminally to either positive or negative verbs (e.g., "to smile", "to frown") and then were invited to rate the funniness of cartoons. During the cartoon-rating task, half of the participants held a pen between their lips in order to block facial responding. Subliminally presented positive verbs primed people to rate the cartoons as funnier when compared with exposure to negative verbs. This effect disappeared, however, for participants holding the pen between their lips. It appears that because these participants were unable to use the muscles involved in a smile while holding the pen, no motor resonance occurred in response to the positive subliminal emotion primes. Thus, in this condition the emotion words could not moderate later behavior, namely, the ratings of the funniness of cartoons.

In a neuroimaging study, Moseley et al. (2012) had 18 participants read emotion-related action words (such as "dread") while recording their brain activity in an fMRI scanner. The abstract emotion words activated not only limbic regions of the brain, which are involved in the experience of emotions, but also the motor cortex, suggesting that bodily and facial movements play a fundamental role in emotion concept comprehension. This suggests that we learn what it means to feel "angry" by connecting the gestures and facial expressions we see in others labeled as "angry" with how we feel when we are making those gestures and expressions. Thus, the meaning of "anger" is inevitably embedded in behaviors and internal states associated with the experience of anger.

Importantly, embodied simulation may not always be necessary, such as when emotion-knowledge tasks can be performed by recourse to lexical associations in memory of when emotional meaning is not central to task completion (Niedenthal et al. 2009). When reactivation of the modality-specific neural states associated with a given emotion is necessary for a task, such as emotion-expression recognition or deeper emotion concept processing, behavioral expressions of the somatic activation may occur. For instance, when activating an internal representation of the emotion "disgust", the facial muscles involved in the expression of disgust (picture yourself smelling a carton of sour milk) will become slightly active.

Niedenthal et al. (2009) took advantage of this feature of embodied simulation in order to examine when people do and do not rely on embodied representations of emotions. Specifically, they showed participants 60 concrete nouns, half of which were related to an emotion (e.g., "smile", "vomit", "torturer") and half of which were emotionally neutral (e.g., "chair", "pocket", "cube"). Participants were randomly assigned either to judge if the nouns were associated with an emotion, or to indicate whether they were written in capital or small letters, while facial muscle activity was assessed with EMG (electromyogram). Results showed that participants who judged association to emotion, but not the way the words were printed, demonstrated emotion-specific activation of facial muscles while processing the emotion nouns. When judging nouns associated with "joy", muscles that formed the smile were activated, and judging "anger"- and "disgust"-related nouns was accompanied by the activation of the emotion-specific muscles as well. Niedenthal and colleagues then replicated this study using nouns that refer to emotion states such as "delighted" and "repelled" and more abstract neutral words like "programmed" and found largely the same pattern of results. These two studies provide evidence for the importance of embodying emotion concepts when the meaning of the concepts is needed for the task. However, the findings are correlational in nature.

To test the causal role of embodiment in emotion concept processing, Niedenthal et al. (2009) conducted a third study using a task similar to the previous two studies, except all participants made the emotion-focused judgment and half of the participants held a pen between their lips throughout the experiment. Holding the pen alters the movement of the zygomaticus major, the muscle that pulls your mouth into a smile, as well as of the levator labii superioris, which allows you to curl your upper lip up in an expression of disgust. They predicted that, for emotion words that relate to joy or disgust, participants holding the pen between their lips would not be able to simulate the appropriate emotions. In fact, the pen significantly reduced accuracy in labeling joy- and disgust-related words as emotional or non-emotional, but had no effect on labeling of anger or neutral concepts. Similar findings have been reported in studies using other physiological indicators of emotion, such as skin conductance (e.g., Oosterwijk et al. 2010).

While associative network models of emotion concepts could be altered and, in a sense, made unconstrained in order to accommodate any component of emotion and the priming of the concept by each of these, the studies just presented seem more consistent with an account by which emotion concepts are the ability to simulate complex emotional experience as needed. A complete account of emotion concepts might indeed be the notion that the parts of an emotional experience that are relevant to a task are peripherally and centrally re-enacted and matched to or reasoned over, and this modality-specific activation is what emotion concept use actually is. This idea is further suggested by recent work on the processing of emotion from the face and body.

Face probes to emotion concepts

Theories of embodied simulation hold that the body's periphery – especially the face – as well as the brain's affective and motor areas are used in tasks of recognition and identification of facial expression of emotion (e.g., Ferrari and Coudé 2018; Niedenthal 2007; Niedenthal et al. 2010; Orlowska et al. 2020; Pitcher et al. 2008; Wood et al. 2016). In a behavioral study, Ponari et al. (2012, study 1) found that blocking mimicry on the lower half of perceivers' faces compromised the recognition of happiness and disgust expressions, while blocking mimicry on the upper half of perceivers' faces compromised the recognition of anger expressions. Both manipulations decreased the recognition of fear. Neither the recognition of surprise nor that of sadness was affected. These findings support the embodiment hypothesis because they link the use of muscles involved in a facial expression to its processing. Similar findings were reported by Maringer et al. (2011) in a study of the processing of different types of smiles. In that study, half of the experimental participants were able to freely mimic dynamically "true" and "false" smiles, whereas the remaining half held pencils in their mouths such that facial mimicry was functionally altered. The participants' task was to rate each smile on a scale of genuineness. Findings revealed that participants in the mimicry condition judged true smiles as more genuine than false smiles, consistent with previous validation studies. However, in the mimicry-blocked condition, participants' judgments of genuineness did not vary by smile type. Instead, all smiles were rated as equally genuine. Studies conducted by Rychlowska et al. (2014), where the participants also rated smile genuineness, revealed similar findings. Those whose facial expressions were altered with the use of a sports mouthguard perceived false and genuine smiles as more similar (but see also Orlowska et al. 2018). Moreover, research conducted by Orlowska et al. (2023) suggests that when smiles are presented with verbal vignettes, observers are less likely to be affected by the contextual information when they can freely mimic the smiles. Together, these results suggest that the ability to mimic smiles is important for understanding their subtle meanings.

A line of study inspired by research on mirror-touch synesthetes (MTS) also provides evidence in favor of an embodied account of the processing of facial expression. Individuals with MTS report the vicarious sensation of touch and show increased activation of sensorimotor cortex when they observe others being touched (Blakemore et al. 2005; Peled-Avron and Woolley 2022). Interestingly, MTS individuals also show better recognition of emotion in others than controls (Banissy et al. 2011). The extant research on MTS led Maister et al. (2013) to predict that when somatosensory resonance between the bodies of self and other is enhanced, emotional expression recognition is facilitated. They used a procedure for inducing resonance in which a participant sees the face of an unfamiliar other being stroked on the cheek with a cotton swab. If the participant experiences simultaneous strokes of a swab on their own cheek, they experience a type of self–other blurring called the "enfacement illusion". This simultaneous visuo-tactile experience causes individuals to perceive another's face as more similar to theirs, as indicated by several different tasks (Paladino et al. 2010; Panagiotopoulou et al. 2017). Thus, the enfacement illusion seems to lead individuals to incorporate features of the other into their self-concepts. To test the hypothesis that the enfacement illusion increases interpersonal somatosensory resonance, and thereby increases emotion recognition, Maister et al. (2013) measured emotion recognition before and after a period of synchronous (versus asynchronous versus control) visuo-tactile stimulation. On each trial of the emotion recognition task, an emotional expression (fear, happiness, or disgust) manifest at one of seven intensity levels was presented and participants categorized the expression as representing one of the three categories. Prior synchronous visuo-tactile stimulation significantly enhanced recognition of fear (although not the other expressions) at all levels of intensity.

Studies using methods of transcranial magnetic stimulation (TMS) have also supported an embodied account of emotion concepts. TMS can be used to temporarily inhibit the use of a targeted brain region in order to identify its role in a mental process. To the extent that a process is compromised when TMS has been directed at a particular region, that location can be inferred to support that process. The results of several studies implicate somatosensory cortices in the accurate identification of facial expressions (Balconi and Bortolotti 2012; Pitcher et al. 2008, 2011; Pourtois et al. 2004). Because the somatosensory system comprises the receptors and processing centers for the sense modalities, including proprioception from the face, this suggests that the body's perceptual experience, and not only visual input, contributes to processing emotion from the face.

Body probes to emotion concepts

The face can certainly communicate a large amount of complex emotion, but disembodied expressive heads are very unusual. Heads are attached to expressive bodies that gesticulate, cower in fear, stand proudly, and gloomily shuffle their feet. There is ample evidence for the role of bodily sensation in emotions (see Kreibig 2010), and any complete emotion-processing theory should take the role of body into account. Evidence suggests that facial expressions and body postures are processed holistically – that is, perceiving congruent emotion expressions of the face and body facilitates emotion recognition, while incongruence (such as a happy face on an angry body) hinders it (Aviezer et al. 2012a; Meeren et al. 2005).

A series of studies showed that emoting bodies influence the perceived emotions of ambiguous faces and voices (De Gelder 2016; Van den Stock et al. 2007; Witkower and Tracy 2019). Flack et al. (1999) manipulated people's facial and bodily emotion expressions by giving them precise directions without naming specific emotions: for instance, for a smile, they instructed participants to push the corners of their mouths up and back. After each position, participants completed mood measures. Both facial and bodily feedback influenced the participants' moods, and emotion ratings were most intense when the emotions of the face and body were congruent.

Bodily expressions may sometimes do more than simply supplement the information provided by the face. Aviezer et al. (2012b) showed that some expressions, such as anger and joy, become difficult to discriminate at their "peak intensities" because they all resemble a wide-mouthed scream. Thus, the body – slumped in sadness or standing triumphantly tall – provides perceivers with better information about the person's emotion. Other studies demonstrate that people can reliably infer emotion from others' gait patterns (Karg et al. 2010; Michalak et al. 2009), movement during dialog (Clarke et al. 2005), dynamic and static postures (Atkinson et al. 2004), and movement to music (Burger et al. 2012; Sievers et al. 2013). While it may be unsurprising that the body provides affective information, it is less clear how others process this information.

Insight into this question comes from human and non-human research into "mirror neurons", which become active both during the completion of a particular action and during the observation of somebody else performing that action (Rizzolatti et al. 2001; Ferrari and Coudé 2018; Heyes and Catmur 2022). If our brains simulate bodily actions of others, it is logical to assume that this applies to emotional bodily actions. Indeed, an fMRI study by Grèzes et al. (2007) showed that areas involved in action representation activated more when participants observed fearful, as opposed to neutral, dynamic bodies. This difference might be due to the unique importance of emotional movements: it is highly adaptive to quickly react to the fearful displays of others, so the brain may simulate such emotional actions more than neutral actions. Importantly, Oosterwijk et al. (2009) found that generating pride- or disappointment-related words alters how upright people sit in their chairs, suggesting that using emotion knowledge changes the bodily emotion expression. Such findings suggest that mirror neurons and action representations facilitate the processing of emotional information. Making that claim, however, requires experimental manipulation. To this end, Stepper and Strack (1993) administered a bogus achievement test to male participants positioned into slumped or upright postures. All participants were informed that they performed "far above the average" on the tests and then completed a mood questionnaire. The slumped participants reported feeling significantly less proud than the upright or control participants, but only if they were moved into the position directly before receiving feedback on their achievement tests. This provided preliminary evidence that bodily feedback while in a slumped posture reduces feelings of pride. Interestingly, an inverse relationship was observed for women (Roberts and Arefi-Afshar 2007). This finding may be due to gender differences in social dominance. Women, who typically experience less social dominance than men, may be less able to recognize the proprioceptive feedback involved in a proud, upright posture. While the moderation by gender complicates the story, it does not discount an embodied simulation explanation. Furthermore, a meta-analysis conducted by Coles et al. (2019), which included 138 studies, supported the hypothesis that facial feedback can modulate emotional experience. Nevertheless, the effects tend to be modest and inconsistent across various studies (e.g., Wagenmakers et al. 2016). These discrepancies can be attributed to the influence of various moderators (e.g., Coles et al. 2019; Plusquellec et al. 2023). Consequently, the full scope of how action representation of body movements aids in recognizing others' emotional states requires further investigation of the factors that can alter this effect. Overall, the theory and evidence summarized above suggest that mimicking another's gestures and postures may facilitate understanding of their emotional states. This indicates that embodied states are more than merely reflexive or associated responses. Rather, they may constitute the core of conceptual knowledge about emotion.

Conclusions

The present chapter reviewed evidence that when probed with language and facial and bodily expressions of emotion, emotion concepts seem to be embodied. Behavioral and neuroimaging results are consistent with the view that emotion concepts can be viewed as involving the capacity for emotional re-enactment. The findings are also consistent with a view of emotion as a complex, loosely coordinated experience involving the autonomic nervous system, behavior, facial expressions, cognition, and the limbic areas of the brain. As such, embodied representations of emotions are distributed across modality-specific regions of the brain. A probe to one of these systems may generate simulation in others, as needed for the task. It is important to note that embodied theories are evolving theories. There is strong evidence for the involvement of motor and somatosensory cortices and peripheral body parts in the processing of emotional information, but it is time to move from binary questions (such as whether embodiment is causal to information processing or not) to more precise statements about how and when the body's central sensorimotor, affective, and peripheral mechanisms are necessarily involved. In addition, important components of the theories require more precise definition. For instance, while facial mimicry seems to be important for identification of facial expression in some cases, both the definition of mimicry and its measurement in real time awaits substantial progress. A growing body of evidence suggests that the body's reproduction of parts of an emotional experience constitute conceptual content for emotion. The words "disgust" and "interest" are not mentally grounded by disembodied symbols but are grounded by parts of the bodily states that are re-enacted to support perception and thought.

References

Atkinson, A. P., Dittrich, W. H., Gemmell, A. J., and Young, A. W. (2004) "Emotion perception from dynamic and static body expressions in point-light and full-light displays." *Perception*, 33(6), 717–746. doi:10.1068/p5096

Aviezer, H., Trope, Y., and Todorov, A. (2012a) "Holistic person processing: Faces with bodies tell the whole story," *Journal of Personality and Social Psychology*, 103(1), 20–37.

—— (2012b) "Body cues, not facial expressions, discriminate between intense positive and negative emotions," *Science*, 338(6111), 1225–1229.

Balconi, M., and Bortolotti, A. (2012) "Detection of the facial expression of emotion and self-report measures in empathic situations are influenced by sensorimotor circuit inhibition by low-frequency rTMS," *Brain Stimulation*, 5(3), 330–336.

Banissy, M. J., Garrido, L., Kusnir, F., Duchaine, B., Walsh, V., and Ward, J. (2011) "Superior facial expression, but not identity recognition, in mirror-touch synesthesia," *The Journal of Neuroscience*, 31(5), 1820–1824.

Barrett, L. F. (2006) "Are emotions natural kinds?" *Perspectives on Psychological Science*, 1(1), 28–58.

—— (2017) "Categories and their role in the science of emotion," *Psychological Inquiry*, 28(1), 20–26.

Barsalou, L. W. (1999) "Perceptual symbol systems," *Behavioral and Brain Sciences*, 22(4), 577–660.

Blakemore, S. J., Bristow, D., Bird, G., Frith, C., and Ward, J. (2005) "Somatosensory activations during the observation of touch and a case of vision–touch synaesthesia," *Brain*, 128(7), 1571–1583. doi: 10.1093/brain/awh500

Bower, G. H. (1981) "Mood and memory," *American Psychologist*, 36(2), 129–148.

—— (1991) "Mood congruity of social judgments," *Emotion and Social Judgments*, 31–53.

Bradley, M. M., Sambuco, N., and Lang, P. J. (2022) "Affective perception: The power is in the picture," *Human Perception of Visual Information: Psychological and Computational Perspectives* (pp. 59–83). Cham: Springer.

Bromberek-Dyzman, K., Jończyk, R., Vasileanu, M., Niculescu-Gorpin, A. G., and Bąk, H. (2021) "Cross-linguistic differences affect emotion and emotion-laden word processing: Evidence from Polish-English and Romanian-English bilinguals," *International Journal of Bilingualism*, 25(5), 1161–1182.

Burger, B., Saarikallio, S., Luck, G., Thompson, M. R., and Toiviainen, P. (2012) "Emotions Move Us: Basic Emotions in Music Influence People's Movement to Music," *Proceedings of the 12th International Conference on Music Perception and Cognition*. Retrieved from http://icmpc-escom2012.web.auth.gr/sites/default/files/papers/177_Proc.pdf

Citron, F. M., Gray, M. A., Critchley, H. D., Weekes, B. S., and Ferstl, E. C. (2014) "Emotional valence and arousal affect reading in an interactive way: neuroimaging evidence for an approach-withdrawal framework," *Neuropsychologia*, 56, 79–89.

Clarke, T. J., Bradshaw, M. F., Field, D. T., Hampson, S. E., and Rose, D. (2005) "The perception of emotion from body movement in point-light displays of interpersonal dialogue," *Perception*, 34(10), 1171–1180. doi:10.1068/p5203

Clore, G. L., and Ortony, A. (2013) "Psychological construction in the OCC model of emotion," *Emotion Review*, 5(4), 335–343.

Coles, N. A., Larsen, J. T., and Lench, H. C. (2019) "A meta-analysis of the facial feedback literature: Effects of facial feedback on emotional experience are small and variable," *Psychological Bulletin*, 145(6), 610–651.

Damasio, A. R. (1999) *The feeling of what happens: Body and emotion in the making of consciousness*. New York: Harvest Books.

Davis, J. D., Winkielman, P., and Coulson, S. (2015) "Facial action and emotional language: ERP evidence that blocking facial feedback selectively impairs sentence comprehension," *Journal of Cognitive Neuroscience*, 27(11), 2269–2280.

—— (2017) "Sensorimotor simulation and emotion processing: Impairing facial action increases semantic retrieval demands," *Cognitive, Affective, and Behavioral Neuroscience*, 17, 652–664.

De Gelder B. (2016) *Emotions and the body*. New York, NY: Oxford University Press.

Ferrari, P. F., and Coudé, G. (2018) "Mirror neurons, embodied emotions, and empathy," in K. Z. Meyza and E. Knapska (eds), *Neuronal correlates of empathy: From rodent to human* (pp. 67–77). London: Elsevier Academic Press.

Flack, W. F., Laird, J. D., and Cavallaro, L. A. (1999) "Separate and combined effects of facial expressions and bodily postures on emotional feelings," *European Journal of Social Psychology*, 29, 203–217.

Foroni, F., and Semin, G. R. (2009) "Language that puts you in touch with your bodily feelings: The multimodal responsiveness of affective expressions," *Psychological Science*, 20(8), 974–980. doi:10.1111/j.1467-9280.2009.02400.x

Gallese, V. (2003) "The shared manifold nature of interpersonal relations: The quest for a common mechanism," *Philosophical Transactions of the Royal Society B: Biological Sciences*, 358(1431), 517–528.

Glenberg, A. M. (1997) "What memory is for: Creating meaning in the service of action," *Behavioral and brain sciences*, 20(01), 41–50.

Grèzes, J., Pichon, S., and de Gelder, B. (2007) "Perceiving fear in dynamic body expressions," *NeuroImage*, 35(2), 959–967. doi:10.1016/j.neuroimage.2006.11.030

Havas, D. A., Glenberg, A. M., Gutowski, K. A., Lucarelli, M. J., and Davidson, R. J. (2010) "Cosmetic use of botulinum toxin-A affects processing of emotional language," *Psychological Science*, 21(7), 895–900.

Heyes, C., and Catmur, C. (2022) "What happened to mirror neurons?" *Perspectives on Psychological Science*, 17(1), 153–168.

Hietanen, J. K., and Leppänen, J. M. (2008) "Judgment of other people's facial expressions of emotions is influenced by their concurrent affective hand movements," *Scandinavian Journal of Psychology*, 49(3), 221–230.

Johnson-Laird, P.N. and Oatley, K. (1989) "The meaning of emotions: Analysis of a semantic field," *Cognition and Emotion*, 3, 81–123.

Johnson-Laird, P. N., and Oatley, K. (2021) "Emotions, simulation, and abstract art," *Art and Perception*, 9(3), 260–292.

Karg, M., Kühnlenz, K., and Buss, M. (2010) "Recognition of affect based on gait patterns," *IEEE Transactions on Systems, Man, and Cybernetics, Part B: Cybernetics*, 40(4), 1050–1061.

Kreibig, S. D. (2010) "Autonomic nervous system activity in emotion: A review," *Biological Psychology*, 84(3), 394–421.

Kuperman, V., Estes, Z., Brysbaert, M., and Warriner, A. B. (2014) "Emotion and language: valence and arousal affect word recognition," *Journal of Experimental Psychology: General*, 143(3), 1065.

Kuppens, P., Tuerlinckx, F., Russell, J. A., and Barrett, L. F. (2013) "The relation between valence and arousal in subjective experience," *Psychological Bulletin*, 139(4), 917.

Lang, P.J. (1984) "Cognition in emotion: Cognition in action," in C.E. Izard, J. Kagan and R.B. Zajonc (eds), *Emotions, Cognition, and Behavior* (pp. 192–226). New York: Cambridge University Press.

Lang, P. J., Bradley, M. M., and Cuthbert, B. N. (1990) "Emotion, attention, and the startle reflex," *Psychological Review*, 97(3), 377–395.

Maister, L., Tsiakkas, E., and Tsakiris, M. (2013) "I feel your fear: Shared touch between faces facilitates recognition of fearful facial expressions," *Emotion*, 13(1), 7.

Maringer, M., Krumhuber, E. G., Fischer, A. H., and Niedenthal, P. M. (2011) "Beyond smile dynamics: mimicry and beliefs in judgments of smiles," *Emotion*, 11(1), 181.

Mayer, J.D. and Gaschke, Y.N. (1988) "The experience and meta-experience of mood," *Journal of Personality and Social Psychology*, 55, 102–111.

Meeren, H. K., van Heijnsbergen, C. C., and De Gelder, B. (2005) "Rapid perceptual integration of facial expression and emotional body language," *Proceedings of the National Academy of Sciences*, 102(45), 16518–16523.

Michalak, J., Troje, N. F., Fischer, J., Vollmar, P., Heidenreich, T., and Schulte, D. (2009) "Embodiment of Sadness and Depression--Gait Patterns Associated With Dysphoric Mood," *Psychosomatic Medicine*, 71(5), 580–587.

Miellet, S., Hoogenboom, N., and Kessler, K. (2012) "Visual and embodied perception of others: The neural correlates of the" Body Gestalt" effect," *Journal of Vision*, 12(9), 824–824.

Moseley, R., Carota, F., Hauk, O., Mohr, B., and Pulvermüller, F. (2012) "A role for the motor system in binding abstract emotional meaning," *Cerebral cortex*, 22(7), 1634–1647.

Niedenthal, P. M. (2007) "Embodying emotion," *Science*, 316(5827), 1002–1005.

Niedenthal, P.M. (2008) "Emotion concepts," in M. Lewis, J.M. Haviland-Jones, and L. F. Barrett (eds), *Handbook of emotion*, 3rd Edition. New York: Guilford.

Niedenthal, P. M., Barsalou, L. W., Winkielman, P., Krauth-Gruber, S., and Ric, F. (2005) "Embodiment in attitudes, social perception, and emotion," *Personality and Social Psychology Review*, 9(3), 184–211.

Niedenthal, P. M., Mermillod, M., Maringer, M., and Hess, U. (2010) "The simulation of smiles (SIMS) model: Embodied simulation and the meaning of facial expression," *Behavioral and Brain Sciences*, 33(6), 417–433.

Niedenthal, P. M., Setterlund, M. B., and Jones, D. E. (1994) "Emotional organization of perceptual memory," in P. M. Niedenthal and S. Kitayama (eds), *The heart's eye: Emotional influences in perception and attention* (pp. 87–113). San Diego: Academic Press.

Niedenthal, P. M., Winkielman, P., Mondillon, L., and Vermeulen, N. (2009) "Embodiment of emotion concepts," *Journal of Personality and Social Psychology*, 96(6), 1120.

Oosterwijk, S., Rotteveel, M., Fischer, A. H., and Hess, U. (2009) "Embodied emotion concepts: How generating words about pride and disappointment influences posture," *European Journal of Social Psychology*, 39(3), 457–466.

Oosterwijk, S., Topper, M., Rotteveel, M., and Fischer, A. H. (2010) "When the Mind Forms Fear: Embodied Fear Knowledge Potentiates Bodily Reactions to Fearful Stimuli," *Social Psychological and Personality Science*, 1(1), 65–72.

Orlowska, A. B., Krumhuber, E. G., Rychlowska, M., and Szarota, P. (2018) "Dynamics matter: Recognition of reward, affiliative, and dominance smiles from dynamic vs. static displays," *Frontiers in Psychology*, 9, 938.

Orlowska, A., Rychlowska, M., Szarota, P., and Krumhuber, E. G. (2023) "Facial mimicry and social context affect smile interpretation," *Journal of Nonverbal Behavior*, 47, 1–18.

Orlowska, A. B., Rychlowska, M., and Krumhuber, E. G. (2020) "The interplay between mimicry and social context in facial expression perception," in A. C. A. Freitas-Magalhães (ed.), *Handbook on Facial Expression of Emotion* (Vol. 3, pp. 121–153) Porto: Leya.

Ortony, A., Clore, G. L., and Foss, M. A. (1987) "The referential structure of the affective lexicon," *Cognitive Science*, 11(3), 341–364.

Paladino, M., Mazzurega, M., Pavani, F., and Schubert, T. W. (2010) "Synchronous multisensory stimulation blurs self-other boundaries," *Psychological Science*, 21(9), 1202–1207.

Panagiotopoulou, E., Filippetti, M. L., Tsakiris, M., and Fotopoulou, A. (2017) "Affective touch enhances self-face recognition during multisensory integration," *Scientific Reports*, 7(1), 12883.

Peled-Avron, L., and Woolley, J. D. (2022) "Understanding others through observed touch: neural correlates, developmental aspects, and psychopathology," *Current Opinion in Behavioral Sciences*, 43, 152–158.

Pitcher, D., Garrido, L., Walsh, V., and Duchaine, B. C. (2008) "Transcranial magnetic stimulation disrupts the perception and embodiment of facial expressions," *The Journal of Neuroscience*, 28(36), 8929–8933.

Pitcher, D., Walsh, V., and Duchaine, B. (2011) "Transcranial magnetic stimulation studies of face processing," in A. Calder, G. Rhodes, M. Johnson, and J. Haxby (eds), *Oxford Handbook of Face Perception* (pp. 362–378) Oxford: Oxford University Press.

Plusquellec, P., Smart, K., and Denault, V. (2023) "Facial reactivity to emotional stimuli is related to empathic concern, empathic distress, and depressive symptoms in social work students," *Psychological Reports*, 1–32. doi:10.1177/00332941231181027

Ponari, M., Conson, M., D'Amico, N. P., Grossi, D., and Trojano, L. (2012) *Mapping correspondence between facial mimicry and emotion recognition in healthy subjects*. American Psychological Association.

Pourtois, G., Sander, D., Andres, M., Grandjean, D., Reveret, L., Olivier, E., and Vuilleumier, P. (2004) "Dissociable roles of the human somatosensory and superior temporal cortices for processing social face signals," *The European Journal of Neuroscience*, 20(12), 3507–3515.

Prinz, J. J. (2002) "Consciousness, computation, and emotion," *Advances in Consciousness Research*, 44, 137–156.

Reisenzein, R. (1994) "Pleasure-arousal theory and the intensity of emotions," *Journal of Personality and Social Psychology*, 67, 525–525.

Rizzolatti, G., Fogassi, L., and Gallese, V. (2001) "Neurophysiological mechanisms underlying the understanding and imitation of action," *Nature Reviews Neuroscience*, 2(9), 661–670.

Roberts, T.-A., and Arefi-Afshar, Y. (2007) "Not all who stand tall are proud: Gender differences in the proprioceptive effects of upright posture," *Cognition and Emotion*, 21(4), 714–727.

Rosch, E.H. (1973) "Natural categories," *Cognitive Psychology*, 4, 328–350.

Russell, J.A. (1991) "In defense of a prototype approach to emotion concepts," *Journal of Personality and Social Psychology*, 60, 37–47.

Russell, J.A. and Barrett, L.F. (1999) "Core affect, prototypical emotional episodes, and other things called emotion: Dissecting the elephant," *Journal of Personality and Social Psychology*, 76, 805–819.

Russell, J. A. (2021) "Psychological construction of episodes called emotions," *History of Psychology*, 24(2), 116.

Rychlowska, M., Cañadas, E., Wood, A., Krumhuber, E. G., Fischer, A., and Niedenthal, P. M. (2014) "Blocking mimicry makes true and false smiles look the same," *PLoS One*, 9(3), e90876.

Scarantino, A. (2012) "How to define emotions scientifically," *Emotion Review*, 4(4), 358–368.

Shaver, P., Schwartz, J., Kirson, D., and O'Connor, C. (1987) "Emotion knowledge: Further exploration of a prototype approach," *Journal of Personality and Social Psychology*, 52, 1061–1086.

Sievers, B., Polansky, L., Casey, M., and Wheatley, T. (2013) "Music and movement share a dynamic structure that supports universal expressions of emotion," *Proceedings of the National Academy of Sciences*, 110(1), 70–75.

Smith, E. R., and Semin, G. R. (2007) "Situated social cognition," *Current Directions in Psychological Science*, 16(3), 132–135.

Stepper, S., and Strack, F. (1993) "Proprioceptive determinants of emotional and nonemotional feelings," *Journal of Personality and Social Psychology*, 64, 211–211.

Wagenmakers, E. J., Beek, T., Dijkhoff, L., Gronau, Q. F., Acosta, A., Adams Jr, R. B., ... and Zwaan, R. A. (2016) "Registered replication report: Strack, Martin, and Stepper (1988)," *Perspectives on Psychological Science*, 11(6), 917–928.

Wierzbicka, A. (1992) "Defining emotion concepts," *Cognitive Science*, 16, 539–581.

Winkielman, P., Coulson, S., and Niedenthal, P. (2018) "Dynamic grounding of emotion concepts," *Philosophical Transactions of the Royal Society B: Biological Sciences*, 373(1752), 20170127.

Witkower, Z., and Tracy, J. L. (2019) "Bodily communication of emotion: Evidence for extrafacial behavioral expressions and available coding systems," *Emotion Review*, 11(2), 184–193.

Wood, A., Rychlowska, M., Korb, S., and Niedenthal, P. (2016) "Fashioning the face: sensorimotor simulation contributes to facial expression recognition," *Trends in Cognitive Sciences*, 20(3), 227–240.

Wood, A., Martin, J. D., Alibali, M. W., and Niedenthal, P. M. (2019) "A sad thumbs up: incongruent gestures and disrupted sensorimotor activity both slow processing of facial expressions," *Cognition and Emotion*, 33(6), 1196–1209.

Van den Stock, J., Righart, R., and De Gelder, B. (2007) "Body expressions influence recognition of emotions in the face and voice," *Emotion*, 7(3), 487–494.

Yik, M., Mues, C., Sze, I. N. L., Kuppens, P., Tuerlinckx, F., De Roover, K., Kwok, F. H. C., Schwartz, S. H., Abu-Hilal, M., Adebayo, D. F., Aguilar, P., Al-Bahrani, M., Anderson, M. H., Andrade, L., Bratko, D., Bushina, E., Choi, J. W., Cieciuch, J., Dru, V., ...Russell, J. A. (2022) "On the relationship between valence and arousal in samples across the globe," *Emotion*. Advance online publication.

PART 9

Action and Memory

35

MEMORY AND ACTION

Katinka Dijkstra

Introduction

Memory has traditionally been regarded as the "great storehouse of information." Since the late 1960s, researchers have begun thinking of information as stored in the form of semantic networks. The general idea was that concepts were stored in nodes and that the links between nodes indicated an association between the concepts. Several decades later, it became clear that there is a fundamental problem with this view. The problem is that the concepts are merely labels in a network (i.e., "whale" or "tree"), and that the network is nothing more than a connection of linked labels. The labels have no meaning to the network, but they are meaningful to the user. As Harnad (1990) put it, the network is parasitic on us. Theories on how these networks operate cannot explain how they connect to the real world. Harnad dubbed this the *grounding problem.*

Since the publication of Harnad's influential paper, many scholars have tried to solve the grounding problem. Solutions to the grounding problem require rethinking the nature of mental representations. Mental representations need to be grounded in perception and action; they cannot be a free-floating system of symbols. A research tradition has emerged since then that aims to investigate how cognition is grounded in perception and action: embodied cognition.

Theoretical discussions on the groundedness of cognition were initially of a general nature. They dealt with the intricate relations between body and brain (Damasio 1994), perceptual symbol systems (Barsalou 1999; Barsalou et al. 2003), views on embodied cognition (Glenberg 1997; Wilson 2002) and simulation (Gallese 2003). What they had in common was a disagreement with the traditional view of cognition that is burdened with the grounding problem (Fodor 1975, 1983). These initial discussions also shared a focus on the central role of the body in shaping the mind (Wilson 2002) and the idea that perceptual and mental experiences imply neural activity in sensorimotor areas of the brain (Damasio 1989).

The first publications in this emerging field addressed the question of how language processing is grounded in action and perception (Glenberg and Kaschak 2002; Tucker and Ellis 1998; Zwaan, Stanfield, and Yaxley 2002). These studies suggested that there are

 DOI: 10.4324/9781003322511-45

interactions between language, and perception and action. Over the years, convergent evidence on these mutual interactions of action and perception with cognitive processes have given rise to an extensive line of research that explores ways in which different domains of cognition are grounded in various action and perception patterns (Barsalou, Simmons, Barbey, and Wilson 2003; Borghi and Cimatti 2010; Ianì and Bucciarelli 2018; Michalak, Rohde, and Troje 2015; Price, Peterson, and Harmon-Jones 2012; Veenstra, Schneider, and Koole 2017).

This chapter will focus on embodied cognition's perspective on memory and action. The chapter begins with a discussion of relevant insights on memory systems and the role of the body in cognitive processes. This is followed by a more in-depth discussion of empirical research that relates to the memory and action theme in different domains. The chapter continues with an exploration of new directions in memory and action research, specifically in clinical psychology (Michalak et al. 2014, 2015; Veenstra et al. 2017; Wilkes et al. 2017), and concludes with some purported limitations of the embodied cognition approach (Mahon and Caramazza 2008; Mahon 2015).

Theoretical perspectives on memory and action

Various perspectives on grounded and embodied cognition (Barsalou 1999; Glenberg 1997; Glenberg et al. 2013; Wilson 2002), episodic memory (Rubin 2006), and the neural architecture underlying recall and recognition (Damasio 1989, 1994) converge on the idea that memory processes have specific neural underpinnings. Rubin considers episodic memory to be a collection of interacting basic systems, including vision, emotion, language, search and retrieval, explicit memory, narrative, and motor systems in which each basic system has its own neural substrate (Rubin 2006). For example, the neural substrate of the search and retrieval system is in the frontal lobes, whereas the hippocampus and surrounding structures are relevant for binding aspects of a memory (Squire, Stark, and Clark 2004).

This notion of a neural basis of the basic systems is supported by research showing activation of specific brain areas while retrieving an autobiographical memory (Daselaar et al. 2005). At the start of the retrieval process, activation of areas associated with explicit memory, and search and retrieval (hippocampus and prefrontal cortex) increases, whereas activity in the visual cortex reflects the re-experience or maintenance of an event once it is retrieved. This corresponds to increases in amygdala activation and higher subjective ratings of reliving the event during the retrieval process. These interacting brain systems associated with memory-retrieval processes illustrate the grounding of cognition. In other words, the experience of an event and the reconstruction of an event when it is being retrieved occur in a similar way, and with the same brain activation and the same systems involved as during the original experience.

This description is consistent with Damasio's theory of the neural architecture underlying recall and recognition (1989), in which activity occurs in multiple brain areas near the sensory portals and motor output regions. Thus, instead of a single place for the integration of sensory and motor processes, multiple sites exist that are also recursive and iterative. The integration occurs in "convergence zones," zones that bind features of a sensory or motor activity into single entities and then bind entities into events or sets of events. This process of binding causes the integration of features and events at both perceptual and cognitive levels.

Components of Damasio's theory of a neural architecture underlying recall and recognition are also reflected in Barsalou's theory of grounded cognition (1999; Barsalou et al. 2003). On this view, cognition is grounded through the process of simulation. When retrieving an experience, neural states are re-enacted from action, perception, and introspective systems. Perception involves the sensory modalities, the motor modality includes movement and proprioception, and introspection is a modality that is comprised of affective states, mental models, and motivation. Together, these modalities are responsible for different aspects of experience. For example, when a stimulus (a horse) is perceived visually, neural feature detectors are active in the visual system. Conjunctive neurons located in an area nearby combine these active features to store them in memory for later retrieval. When there is no more visual input, these neurons can reactivate the original set of features to a certain extent to make a similar visual representation of the horse that was seen before. This is considered a simulation. Simulations are rich in detail because of their multimodal nature; they not only contain the visual (or other sensory) state when the stimulus was first perceived, or the event was first experienced, but also encompass the relevant motor and mental states that were part of the original experience. The result is an experience of reliving the situation during the re-enactment phase.

Apart from the idea that memory processes have neural underpinnings and involve simulation, another common element of embodied cognition perspectives is the central role that they attribute to the body in cognitive processes (Dijkstra and Post 2015). Cognitive processes support appropriate action for a certain situation by remembering the relevance of the action for that situation rather than by remembering what the situation entails (Wilson 2002). For example, verbal rehearsal and counting on one's fingers are action patterns to facilitate short-term memory. Episodic memory retrieval, such as describing yesterday's party, is related to the body when relevant sensorimotor aspects of the event are reconstructed along with details of what the party was about (Bietti 2012). Implicit memory is also based on action patterns of the body because motor skills that are difficult to learn initially (such as riding a bike) become automatized with practice and can bypass the representational bottleneck that is encountered when learning new things under time pressure.

Glenberg's seminal paper "What memory is for" (1997) also discusses the role of the body in cognitive domains. Specifically, memory can be defined in terms of integrated sets of action patterns that are constrained by our bodies. When a new instance of an action is undertaken, for example, cooking a meal on a stove, previous cooking experiences with certain foods that have been left on the stove for too long come into play. New action patterns (setting a timer while cooking) may be an adjustment of earlier ones and be incorporated into memory for these actions. Conscious recollection is therefore a form of action pattern completion that is reconstructive by nature. These action patterns are constrained by how individuals can move their bodies and manipulate objects in a particular environment. For example, reaching for a cup on the other side of the table requires a different kind of movement and grip than reaching for a pencil that is right in front of you.

Memory is especially important in offline tasks where actions do not take place in the "here and now" but involve remembering action patterns and experiences from the past, anticipating or planning things in the future, or imagining events that may never take place (Wilson 2002). The mutual relatedness between memory and action implies that manipulations of the body and movement may result in memory changes, and vice versa. The next section reviews the empirical support for these assumptions.

Empirical support for memory and action

Various studies across different domains demonstrate the effects of the body and action patterns on memory processes (e.g., Casasanto and Dijkstra 2010; Dijkstra, Kaschak, and Zwaan 2007; Dijkstra, MacMahon and Misirlisoy 2008; Ianì and Bucciarelli 2018; Seno, Kawabe, Ito, and Sunaga 2013; Van Dam, Rueschemeyer, Bekkering, and Lindemann 2013; Yang, Gallo, and Beilock 2009). These studies show how manipulations of the body result in changes in memory performance, and how manipulations of the task result in bodily changes. Together, these data suggest a reciprocal relationship between the body and memory processes.

The effect of body position on the ease of retrieval was examined in an autobiographical memory study (Dijkstra et al. 2007). Participants assumed a body position either congruent or incongruent with the original body position during a memory-retrieval event ("Tell me about a time you were at the dentist office?" – congruent: lying down on a recliner; incongruent: standing with feet wide and hands on the hips). Response times for the retrieval of the memories were calculated from the videorecording of the experimental session. Two weeks later, participants were asked which memories they remembered from the experimental session in a free recall task. The results indicated faster responses for memories that were retrieved during the experimental session in congruent compared with incongruent body positions. Moreover, participants demonstrated better free recall later of congruent than incongruent memories. Adopting a congruent body position apparently helped to reconstruct the earlier experience, which resulted in better memory access and a stronger memory trace over a long period of time. The findings suggest that memory retrieval involves an embodied simulation of the original experience that includes body position. Having relevant sensorimotor aspects from the original experience available for memory retrieval facilitates the ease and durability with which this happens.

Can body movements in contrast to position have an impact on autobiographical memory retrieval as well? A study by Casasanto and Dijkstra (2010) assessed the effect of motor actions on access to and content of autobiographical memories. This study examined how positive and negative emotions were expressed in the context of spatial metaphors of verticality, such as cheering with the arms in the air when our favorite soccer team wins or sitting slumped with our head in our hands when it loses. During the experiment, participants deposited marbles upward or downward from one box into another, creating a movement that was by itself unrelated to the task of retrieving memories to positive or negative prompts ("Tell me about a time you were proud/ashamed of yourself") but tapped into the association of the spatial metaphor and matching emotion: up = positive, and down = negative. In the first experiment, participants were faster at recounting memories during schema-congruent (up = positive, down = negative) than schema-incongruent movements. In the second experiment, participants retrieved memories to valence-neutral prompts while making the same upward or downward movements with the marbles. After recounting the memories, they evaluated the memories as either positive or negative, based on their emotional content. The results indicated that participants evaluated the memories more positively after they were initially retrieved during upward movements and more negatively after they were initially retrieved during downward movements with the marbles. Motor actions seem not only to facilitate access to one's memories when these actions are congruent with the valence of the memories, but they also affect the emotional content of the memory when a neutral retrieval cue is provided.

These findings underscore the effect of body movement in a memory task, influencing both access and content via schematic representations of up-down and positive-negative associations. A similar association between body position and emotion content was examined in a study that looked at the activation of emotion concepts on changes in posture (Oosterwijk, Rotteveel, Fischer, and Hess 2009). Participants generated words that were associated with positive and negative emotions, such as "pride" and "disappointment," based on the idea that this generation task should tap into the conceptual system in which associations of certain emotion concepts with action patterns are stored (pride = positive = upward position, disappointment = negative = downward position). At the same time, their posture height was measured with a hidden camera. This way, changes in posture due to the generation of pride or disappointment words could be measured. The results indicated that when participants generated disappointment words, their posture became more slumped, making their height lower than it was when they generated pride words. The results support the embodied cognition perspective that conceptual knowledge arises from action patterns and bodily states.

The link between the body and autobiographical memory retrieval has been examined in a motorically more indirect manner as well by manipulating the illusion of self-motion perception, or "vection" (Seno et al. 2013). Vection occurs when someone is observing upward- or downward-moving stimuli and having the illusion of self-motion in an opposite direction to the motion of the observed stimuli. Such a manipulation provides a way to disentangle possible visual effects of motion direction (watching up-down movements) from self-motion direction effects (making up-down movements) and to assess whether this illusion can affect the emotional valence of autobiographical memories. The results indicated that participants remembered positive episodes more often when perceiving upward vection, supporting the idea that illusory self-motion (Seno et al. 2013) can modulate the emotional valence of recollected memories.

These studies illustrate that the memory system can be influenced by body manipulations (Dijkstra and Post 2015; Ianì 2019). Action patterns in these studies were relevant for a certain situation, and activated existing mappings between abstract concepts and concrete experiences. Access to and retention of memories can be facilitated, and memory content can be affected, when appropriate action patterns are executed that facilitate the reconstruction process of a previously experienced event. Sensorimotor reactivation allows the memory system to retrieve information, and the studies discussed above show converging evidence of how this may work.

We discussed earlier that the mutual relatedness between memory and action implies that manipulations of the body and movement may result in memory changes, and vice versa. Previous experiences and built-up skills contribute to simulation ability (Körner, Topolinski, and Strack 2015), which implies that motor fluency and expertise in complex motor movements may facilitate and enhance memory performance (Dijkstra and Post 2015). For example, expert climbers remembered climbing routes better than less experienced climbers (Boschker, Bakker, and Michaels 2002). Such superior memory performance appears to be limited to expertise-related information, however. Experienced golfers remembered golf-related information better than participants who had never played golf before. Also, recall was better for golf-related and everyday items in both groups of participants when they were enacted than when read out loud (Dijkstra, MacMahon, and Misirlisoy 2008). Another effect of expertise in the context of embodiment can be that motor fluency for complex movements leads to memory errors when it overrules or interferes with decision-making processes (Dijkstra and Post 2015). Specifically, over-learned action patterns may hinder the ability to differentiate between patterns that were or were not observed previously. The next section discusses other effects of embodiment, such as interference.

Other effects of embodiment

Yang et al. (2009) examined the role of overlearned ability of motor movement, "motor fluency," and its negative effects on later recognition. Based on the evidence that an item's visual clarity can alter its perceptual fluency, the idea was that the same could happen with motor fluency. If observing the letter "p" leads to a covert simulation of the action of typing the letter "p" (with the little finger on your right hand if you are a typist), then this motor simulation should cause a feeling of familiarity. The activation of action plans associated with the stimuli would impact memory judgments, resulting in decision errors on a recognition task. In this study, skilled typists and novices examined a list of letter dyads that would normally be typed with the same finger (reflecting lower motor fluency because the same finger cannot be at more than one place at a time) or with different fingers (reflecting higher motor fluency). Skilled typists were expected to falsely recognize the letter that would be easier to type (have higher motor fluency). The results supported this assumption. Expert typists, who have more consistent mappings between specific letters and motor plans to type them, made more false recognition errors to different-finger letter dyads than non-fluent dyads. In contrast, novice typists did not show motor-fluency effects in recognition memory. Recognition memory thus seems to be affected by the covert simulation of actions associated with the dyads being evaluated. Motor fluency due to expertise development can therefore lead to a reconstruction bias and makes experts more vulnerable to false recognition.

The study discussed above showed evidence of a bias in reconstruction and motor fluency to create memory errors. Such errors may also occur in other situations, for example when the reconstruction process of a memory is biased due to selective attention and re-enactment of only a subset of represented features (Barsalou 1999), or when multiple tasks are executed during which interference may occur (Amico and Schaefer 2021; Ianì 2019). Interference is the counterpart of facilitation, which was discussed above. Interference can occur when the same neural circuits are engaged in action and memory processes (Dijkstra and Post 2015; Ianì 2019).

An example of this form of interference was demonstrated by Amico and Schaefer (2021) who assessed whether concurrent walking during the encoding and recall phase of a spatial information task led to better memory performance compared to incongruent encoding and recall conditions. Specifically, participants encoded the positions of target fields on the floor while standing still or walking towards them and recalled them while walking towards them or standing still. The hypothesis was that embodied context-dependent conditions (walking during encoding and recall) would yield better performance on the memory task compared to non-embodied conditions (i.e., walking during encoding and recall during standing). Unexpectedly, the results showed impaired performance on the spatial memory task under embodied conditions of walking. Walking had a negative effect on both encoding and recall. Apparently, motor information from the walking condition did not aid the memory process as an embodied cue to reinstate already encoded information. Instead, it required more attentional resources, suggesting interference of one's own motor information with encoding and recall of spatial information. This way, the spatial memory task turned into a more cognitively demanding dual task.

Research on the role of secondary actions in embodied memory tasks also reveals interference effects (Ianì and Bucciarelli, 2018). Participants listened to phrases by a speaker who in one condition used congruent gestures with the content, and in another condition did not move his body. During the recall phase, participants performed a motor task that involved either the same effectors used by the speaker (arms and hands) or different effectors (legs and feet). The results showed interference effects in the form of impaired memory performance when the same effectors were involved but not when different effectors were used in the recall task. Thus, the motor system is involved in both encoding and recall phases, taking up cognitive resources in the secondary motor task rather than offloading them to make the recall task easier.

The studies discussed above reveal situations in which interference occurs due to motor fluency, or dual engagement. There are also other examples of limitations of embodiment effects in memory and other domains (Dijkstra and Post 2015; Dutriaux and Gyselinck 2022; Pecher 2018; Zwaan 2014). It is important to be aware of these other effects, not only for greater insight into embodiment effects and for planning future studies, but also because they are relevant given the current debate on the tenability, specificity, and explanatory power of the embodied cognition approach (Goldinger, Papesh, Barnhart, Hansen, and Hout 2016; Körner, Topolinski, and Strack 2015; Mahon 2015; Mahon and Caramazza 2008; Willems and Francken 2012). It is beyond the scope of this chapter to tackle these issues in detail as the focus is on embodiment in memory and action, and not on the embodied cognition approach itself. In this chapter, the overview of empirical findings demonstrating embodiment in memory is relevant for a deeper insight into how exactly memory processes are grounded in action and perception, and under what conditions effects of embodiment may not occur. The last part of this review addresses other lines of research on embodied cognition, action, and memory that relate to the field of clinical psychology and legal psychology, and that may hold promise for application in the real world.

Embodiment in other domains

An emerging new line of research on embodiment and memory revolves around the role of the body in depression and emotion regulation. Several studies have employed the association of upward position and body movement with positive emotions, such as pride and feelings of power, and the association between a slumped body position or downward movement with negative emotions, such as feeling depressed, to assess whether depressive feelings could be alleviated or emotion regulation could be improved (Michalak, Mischnat, and Teismann 2014; Michalak, Rohde, and Troje 2015; Veenstra, Schneider, and Koole 2017; Wilkes, Kydd, Sagar, and Broadbent 2017). Specifically, Veenstra et al. (2017) examined how body posture could affect mood regulation. Participants were exposed to a negative or neutral mood induction with a mental imagery task before they were assigned to a stooped, straight, or self-chosen posture condition. Subsequently, they were instructed to list their thoughts while remaining in the assigned posture to support spontaneous mood regulation, then evaluated the valence of their thoughts after they rated their mood while assuming a natural posture. The results indicated that after a negative mood induction, participants in a stooped posture could not recover as well from their negative mood compared to participants in a straight posture condition. Moreover, participants in the stooped body condition had more negative thoughts than participants in the straight or self-chosen body condition. In other words, posture affected mood regulation.

Another study also looked at the role of a slumped and upright posture but this time in relation to individuals with depressive symptoms (Wilkes *et al.* 2017). The aim was to examine the effect of assuming an upright posture in mild to moderately depressed individuals while being engaged in a stressful task. This posture was expected to reduce negative feelings and fatigue, and to have an increase in positive feelings. The results indicated that participants in the upright condition reported higher positive affect and lower fatigue than participants in the usual posture condition. A manipulated upright posture may therefore improve positive affect in individuals with depressive symptoms, possibly breaking through a cycle of having negative thoughts in a slumped body position.

Several studies conducted by Michalak and colleagues (Michalak et al. 2014; Michalak et al. 2015) also examined the role of the body in relation to a population with depressive symptoms but the focus of these studies was on memory bias rather than affect. One study in particular (Michalak et al. 2014) examined patients who suffered from a major depression disorder. Participants were randomly assigned to a slumped or upright body position during which they created visual scenes by imagining themselves in connection with positive ("beauty") and depression-related ("dejection") words that were projected on a computer screen. After a distractor task, participants performed a surprise free recall task on these positive and depression-related words while remaining in the assigned posture. Memory bias was computed as the difference between the number of recalled positive and negative (depression-related) words. The results indicated that the patients in the slumped posture recalled more negative than positive words, thus displaying a negative memory bias to a greater extent than patients in the upright-sitting condition.

A follow-up study looked at the effect of gait modifications on affective memory bias among healthy participants (Michalak et al. 2015). Participants received biofeedback to change their existing gait pattern on a treadmill to make the gauge deflect in a certain way. What they did not know was that this deflection induced a happy or a depressed gait in which they continued to walk during the memory task. Participants first had to indicate how accurately positive and negative words described them during the encoding phase. In a surprise free recall test, they had to recall these words to the best of their ability. The difference between positive and negative words at recall was lower in the depressed gait pattern than in the happy gait pattern, again suggesting a memory bias due to a manipulation of the body, driven by recall of negative words in the depressed gait condition.

The findings of these studies not only provide insight about interactions between the body and memory processes, but also have implications for our understanding of depression, and may offer suggestions for behavior modification and treatment. Pathological cycles that sustain depression may be broken with body and gait manipulations (Michalak et al. 2014, 2015), whereas mood may be regulated with simple posture adaptions (Wilkes et al. 2017). More research is needed to establish whether these effects are robust, generalizable, and suitable for therapeutic applications.

Embodied cognition research shows a potential for practical application in other domains as well. In legal contexts, body manipulations may affect the outcome of judges' and jurors' decision making, morality judgments (Schnall, Benton, and Harvey 2008), or affect the tendency of suggestive gestures to potentially bias eyewitnesses (Broaders and Goldin-Meadow 2010). Life-span development is another area of research where embodiment effects could be relevant. The study discussed above on interference of embodiment effects in spatial memory also aimed to assess differential effects across the life span (Amico and Schaefer 2021). The authors predicted that older adults would be more impaired by walking conditions than younger participants because they need to invest more attentional resources into motor tasks as compensation for the age-related declines in their motor functioning. This assumption was supported by the evidence and strengthens the idea that embodiment effects could differ in older adults.

Studies on embodiment with application opportunities may be fruitful avenues for future research as they can be implemented relatively easily. Future research should also be mindful of the current debate regarding the explanatory power of the embodied cognition approach. In addition to empirical research, there is a need for models that allow for specific predictions regarding the underlying mechanisms of embodiment (Dijkstra and Post 2015; Willems and Francken 2012). Still uncertain is whether the construction of these models should come from an interdisciplinary framework of embodiment research (Lux, Non, Pexman, Stadler, Weber, and Krüger 2021), from an integration of existing knowledge of embodiment effects (Körner *et al.* 2015), or from an overview of conditions under which embodiment does or does not occur (Willems and Francken 2012). Already evident is that the body can facilitate memory processes under congruent body and memory task conditions and hinder them when similar motor and simulation systems draw from the same resources. The viability of the embodied cognition approach in the future will depend on efforts to differentiate it empirically from other views and to expand its explanatory power.

References

Amico, G., & Schaefer, S. (2021) "Negative effects of embodiment in a visuo-spatial working memory task in children, young adults, and older adults," *Frontiers in Psychology*, 12, 1–11.

Barsalou, L. (1999) "Perceptual symbol systems," *Behavioral and Brain Sciences*, 22, 577–660.

Barsalou, L. W., Simmons, W. K., Barbey, A. K., and Wilson, C. D. (2003) "Grounding conceptual knowledge in modality-specific systems," *Trends in Cognitive Sciences*, 7, 84–91.

Bietti, L. M. (2012) "Towards a cognitive pragmatics of collective remembering," *Pragmatics & Cognition* 20, 32–61.

Borghi, A. M., and Cimatti, F. (2010) "Embodied cognition and beyond: Acting and sensing the body," *Neuropsychologia*, 48, 763–773.

Boschker, M. S. J., Bakker, F. C., and Michaels, C. F. (2002) "Memory for the functional characteristics of climbing walls: Perceiving affordances," *Journal of Motor Behavior*, 34, 25–36.

Broaders, S., and Goldin-Meadow, S. (2010) "Truth is at hand: How gesture adds information during investigative interviews," *Psychological Science*, 21, 623–628.

Casasanto, D., and Dijkstra, K. (2010) "Motor action and emotional memory," *Cognition*, 115, 179–185.

Damasio, A. R. (1989) "Time-locked multiregional reactivation: A systems-level proposal for the neural substrates of recall and recognition," *Cognition*, 25–62.

——— (1994). *Descartes' error: Emotion, reason, and the human brain*, New York: Avon Books.

Daselaar, S. M., Rice, H. J., Greenberg, D. L., LaBar, K. S., Rubin, D. C., and Cabeza, R. (2005) "Time course of episodic retrieval activity: Brain regions involved in constructing and maintaining autobiographical memories," paper presented at Annual meeting of the Society of Neuroscience, Washington, DC.

Dijkstra, K., Kaschak, M. P., and Zwaan, R. A. (2007) "Body posture facilitates retrieval of autobiographical memories," *Cognition*, 102, 139–149.

Dijkstra, K., MacMahon, C., & Misirlisoy, M. (2008) "The effects of golf expertise and presentation modality on memory for golf and everyday items," *Acta Psychologica*, 128, 298–303.

Dijkstra, K., & Post, L. (2015) "Mechanisms of embodiment," *Frontiers in Psychology*, 6, 1–11.

Dutriaux, L., & Gyselinck, V. (2022) "The postural effect on the memory of manipulable objects," *Experimental Psychology*, 68, 333–339.

Fodor, J. A. (1975) *The language of thought*, Boston, MA: Harvard University Press.
———— (1983) *The modularity of mind: An essay on faculty psychology*, Cambridge, MA: MIT Press.
Gallese, V. (2003) "The manifold nature of interpersonal relations: The quest for a common mechanism," *Philosophical Transactions of the Royal Society of B: Biological Sciences, 358*, 517–528.
Glenberg, A. M. (1997) "What memory is for," *Behavior and Brain Sciences, 20*, 1–55.
Glenberg, A. M., and Kaschak, M. P. (2002) "Grounding language in action," *Psychonomic Bulletin & Review, 9*, 558–565.
Glenberg, A. M., Witt, J. K., & Metcalfe, J. (2013) "From the Revolution to Embodiment: 25 Years of Cognitive Psychology," *Perspectives on Psychological Science 8*, 573–585.
Goldinger, S. D., Papesh, M. H., Barnhart, A. S., Hansen, A., and Hout, M. C. (2016) "The poverty of embodied cognition," *Psychonomic Bulletin & Review 23*, 959–978.
Harnad, S. (1990) "The symbol grounding problem," *Physica D, 42*, 335–346.
Ianì, F. (2019) "Embodied memories: Reviewing the role of the body in memory processes," *Psychonomic Bulletin & Review, 26*, 1747–1766.
Ianì, F., & Bucciarelli, M. (2018) "Relevance of the listener's motor system in recalling phrases enacted by the speaker," *Memory, 26*, 1084–1092.
Körner, A., Topolinski, S., & Strack, F. (2015) "Routes to embodiment," *Frontiers in Psychology, 6*, 940.
Lux, V., Non, A. L., Pexman, P. M., Stadler, W., Weber, L. A., & Krüger, M. (2021) "A developmental framework for embodiment research: The next step toward integrating concepts and methods," *Frontiers in Systems Neuroscience, 70*, 1–22.
Mahon, B. Z., and Caramazza, A. (2008) "A critical look at the embodied cognition hypothesis and a new proposal for grounding conceptual content," *Journal of Physiology–Paris, 102*, 59–70.
Mahon, B. Z. (2015) "The burden of embodied cognition," *Canadian Journal of Experimental Psychology/Revue canadienne de psychologie expérimentale, 69*, 172178.
Michalak, J., Mischnat, J., & Teismann, T. (2014) "Sitting posture makes a difference – Embodiment effects on depressive memory bias," *Clinical Psychology and Psychotherapy, 21*, 519–524.
Michalak, J., Rohde, K., & Troje, N. F. (2015) "How we walk affects what we remember: Gait modifications through biofeedback change negative affective memory bias," *Journal of Behavior Therapy and Experimental Psychiatry, 46*, 121–125.
Oosterwijk, S., Rotteveel, M., Fischer, A. H., and Hess, U. (2009) "Embodied emotion concepts: How generating words about pride and disappointment influences posture," *European Journal of Social Psychology, 39*, 457–466.
Pecher, D. (2018) "Curb your embodiment," *Topics in Cognitive Science, 10*, 501–517.
Price, T. F., Peterson, C. K., and Harmon-Jones, E. (2012) "The emotive neuroscience of embodiment," *Motivation and Emotion, 36*, 27–37.
Rubin, D. C. (2006) "The basic-systems model of episodic memory," *Perspectives on Psychological Science, 1*, 277–311.
Schnall, S., Benton, J., and Harvey, S. (2008) "With a clean conscience: Cleanliness reduces the severity of moral judgments," *Psychological Science, 19*, 1219–1222.
Seno, T., Kawabe, T., Ito, H., and Sunaga, S. (2013) "Vection modulates emotional valence of autobiographical episodic memories," *Cognition, 126*, 115–120.
Squire, L. R., Stark, C. E., and Clark, R. E. (2004) "The medial temporal lobe," *Annual Review of Neuroscience, 27*, 279–306.
Tucker, M., and Ellis, R. (1998) "On the relations between seen objects and components of potential actions," *Journal of Experimental Psychology: Human Perception and Performance, 24*, 830–846.
Van Dam, W. O., Rueschemeyer, S. A., Bekkering, H., & Lindemann, O. (2013) "Embodied grounding of memory: Toward the effects of motor execution on memory consolidation," *The Quarterly Journal of Experimental Psychology, 66*, 2310–2328.
Veenstra, L., Schneider, I. K., & Koole, S. L. (2017) "Embodied mood regulation: the impact of body posture on mood recovery, negative thoughts, and mood-congruent recall," *Cognition and Emotion, 31*, 1361–1376.
Wilkes, C., Kydd, R., Sagar, M., & Broadbent, E. (2017) "Upright posture improves affect and fatigue in people with depressive symptoms," *Journal of Behavior Therapy and Experimental Psychiatry, 54*, 143–149.

Willems, R. M., & Francken, J. C. (2012) "Embodied cognition: taking the next step," *Frontiers in Psychology*, 3, 582.

Wilson, M. (2002) "Six views of embodied cognition," *Psychonomic Bulletin & Review*, 9, 625–636.

Yang, S., Gallo, D. A., and Beilock, S. L. (2009) "Embodied memory judgments: A case of motor fluency," *Journal of Experimental Psychology: Learning, Memory, and Cognition*, 35, 1359–1365.

Zwaan, R. A. (2014) "Embodiment and language comprehension: reframing the discussion," *Trends in Cognitive Science*, 18, 229–234.

Zwaan, R. A., Stanfield, R. A., and Yaxley, R. H. (2002) "Language comprehenders mentally represent the shapes of objects," *Psychological Science*, 13, 168–171.

36

MOTOR RESONANCE

Neurophysiological origin, functional role, and contribution of the motivational, moral, and social aspects of action

Laila Craighero

One of the most convincing results in support of embodied cognition is the evidence that when we observe another person performing an action, our sensorimotor system is activated up to the muscular level as if we were performing that same action (Fadiga et al. 1995). Taking its cue from physical acoustics, this phenomenon has been named *motor resonance*. In the case of acoustic resonance, a vibrating tuning-fork will cause a second identical tuning-fork to vibrate at the same frequency. Similarly, numerous studies have demonstrated that motor resonance follows somatotopic principles and happens in a muscle-specific manner (Alaerts et al. 2009; Borroni and Baldissera 2008; Brighina et al. 2000; Clark et al. 2004; Fadiga et al. 1995; Urgesi et al. 2006), and that it is coupled to the movement phases (Alaerts et al. 2012; Borroni et al. 2005; Gangitano et al. 2001; Montagna et al. 2005). Given that this automatically induced sensorimotor representation of the perceived action corresponds to what is spontaneously generated during actual action execution, the outcome of which would be known to the agent, embodied theories of cognition suggest that this motor replica may support action perception and understanding (Decety and Chaminade 2005; Gallese 2008, 2003; Keysers and Gazzola 2007). However, if the frequencies of the two tuning-forks differ, the acoustic resonance does not occur. It is sufficient to apply a clamp on the prongs of the second tuning-fork, thus changing the frequency of its oscillation, to interrupt the acoustic resonance phenomenon. Likewise, research described in this chapter shows how the clamp-like top-down influence of actor and observer intentions, values, and attitudes can affect motor resonance (Urgesi et al. 2020). The goal and, presumably, the final intention of the agent are cued by mapping other people's actions onto one's own sensorimotor representation, therefore motor resonance must necessarily encode additional information beyond the movement's kinematics. For example, although a butcher understands exactly how to use a knife to slaughter a cow, this is not enough for him/her to resonate with another person using the same knife to inflict a deadly wound on a human being.

The chapter will first describe the neurophysiological basis of motor resonance both in the monkey and in humans, then report evidence showing the role of sensorimotor activation in others' action perception and prediction. Finally, it will show research aimed at assessing which cognitive processes and neural mechanisms are involved in exerting a

DOI: 10.4324/9781003322511-46

top-down modulation of motor resonance according to stimulus features, task require-ments, and actors' and observers' motivational states.

Neurophysiological basis of motor resonance

Studies of single-neuron recordings in the monkey showed that each of the numerous archi-tectonically and functionally distinct areas that make up the posterior parietal cortex is engaged in the analysis of a different component of sensory data. Sensory information is subsequently translated into action thanks to the parietal regions' strong and precise connec-tions to the motor cortex (sensorimotor transformation). The parietal and premotor areas, which are strongly connected, may share common functional characteristics and form pari-etofrontal circuits that are generally independent of one another (Colby and Goldberg 1999; Craighero 2014; Rizzolatti et al. 1997a, 1997b). The most famous parietofrontal circuit involved in sensorimotor transformations for action links the ventral premotor area F5 to the anterior intraparietal area. Its fame is likely a result of some of the neurons it contains, whose behavior suggests that cognitive processes may be rooted in perception and action. These so-called mirror neurons activate both when the monkey acts and when the monkey observes another animal performing the same action (di Pellegrino et al. 1992; Gallese et al. 1996). Thus, the neuron "mirrors" the actions of the other or, like a tuning-fork, it resonates with them. The requirement for mirror neurons to resonate in the monkey is that the observed action be part of the monkey's motor repertoire, i.e., that it represents an action that the monkey usually knows and performs. Mirror neurons require an interaction between a biological effector (hand or mouth) and an object in order to be activated by visual stimuli. The mere sight of an object, the observation of someone imitating an action in the absence of the object, or using a tool to perform an action, or performing intransitive gestures, are all ineffective in activating mirror neurons. In fact, a monkey in the jungle would never pretend to hold a missing fruit or use pliers to peel a banana. Those are behaviors without a purpose for the monkey; the monkey has no motivation to carry them out. Since an *action* is defined as a movement performed with a certain goal (Rizzolatti and Fogassi 2014), for the monkey these do not represent actions and, consequently, do not represent effective stimuli to activate mirror neurons. On the other hand, a detailed portrayal of the action is not necessary to activate the mirror neurons. In fact, any stimulus that can call to mind the action is effective. No matter what the grasped object is, the response is the same whether it is a piece of food or a geometric solid. Likewise, it does not matter whether the hand of a monkey or a human performs the action, or whether the action is performed close to or far from the monkey (Caggiano et al. 2009). Finally, complete visual information is not neces-sary. Some neurons fire in response to actions the final parts of which are hidden from view (Umiltà et al. 2001), and some respond not only to the sight of an action but also to the sound of an action (audiovisual mirror neurons, see Kohler et al. 2002). Therefore, in the monkey, mirror neurons work as a modality to encode object-directed actions (Shapiro 2009). Movements outside a monkey's motor repertoire are not encoded by the mirror neu-rons, in the same way that the auditory system does not encode a light.

Neuroscience studies have indicated that an action–observation matching system also exists in humans (Fabbri-Destro and Rizzolatti 2008; Giorello and Sinigaglia 2007; Molenberghs et al. 2012; Rizzolatti and Craighero 2004). For ethical reasons, it is not possible to record single-neuron activity in humans for use in research; however, many functional magnetic resonance imaging (fMRI) studies have shown that the two main nodes of the human mirror system are the inferior parietal lobule (IPL) and the ventral premotor cortex (PMv), plus the caudal part of the inferior frontal gyrus (IFG) (Rizzolatti et al. 2014). These are cortical areas activated both when the individual performs an action and when he/she merely observes someone else performing it. The localization of the human parietofrontal mirror system closely corresponds to that of the homologous mirror neuron system of the monkey. However, a substantial difference is present, not determined by the functional characteristics of the system (i.e., motor involvement during action observation), but by the different definition of action. It appears that humans need not face a physical item in order to recall the motor knowledge necessary for interaction with it. This primitive form of abstraction reveals itself in the activation of the mirror neuron system even in cases of intransitive actions (Brass et al. 2000; Buccino et al. 2001; Fadiga et al. 1995) and pantomimes (Fadiga et al. 2009, 2006). People frequently employ these types of movements to express or clarify ideas, sentiments, and experiences; they use instruments, they dance, they play sports, and they teach these skills by showing others how to do so. Thus, people tend to think that every movement made by another person has a purpose and, therefore, is perceived as an action. As a consequence, motor resonance is present whenever the individual observes another person moving.

Functional MRI is not the best technique to describe the effects of action observation on the activity of the motor system. In fact, fMRI can determine if the blood-oxygen-level-dependent (BOLD) signal within a certain voxel is augmented during both action observation and execution. However, the signal may be determined by the presence of two distinct populations of neurons, one responding only during motor execution and one only during action observation. For this reason, the term *shared voxels* has been proposed to describe voxels active during both action perception and execution (Gazzola & Keysers 2009). Consequently, the presence of shared voxels is not proof that a perceptual task such as action observation automatically recruits the motor system. Transcranial magnetic stimulation (TMS) studies provide more direct evidence of motor resonance. When TMS is applied to the motor cortex (M1), motor-evoked potentials (MEPs) can be recorded from contralateral extremity muscles. The modulation of MEPs' amplitude can be used to assess changes in corticospinal (CS) excitability induced by the activity of various brain regions connected with M1 and involved in the concomitant task. Many experiments have shown that perception of others' actions is constantly accompanied by motor facilitation of the observer's CS system (Buccino et al. 2004a; Fadiga et al. 1995, 2005; Fadiga & Craighero 2004). As already mentioned, this motor activation occurs in a muscle-specific fashion according to somatotopic rules (Alaerts et al. 2009; Fadiga et al. 1995; Urgesi et al. 2006). This means that only the muscles involved in the actual execution of the observed action are activated (i.e., presence of MEPs). Moreover, the activation is time-locked to the movement phases (Alaerts et al. 2012; Gangitano et al. 2001). For example, during observation of a sinusoidal flexion-extension of the wrist, a parallel cyclic excitability modulation of the observer's MEP responses with identical period as the observed movement is present (Borroni et al. 2005).

The role of sensorimotor activation in others' action perception and prediction

One might wonder why it is necessary to have a dedicated sensorimotor system to encode goal-directed actions. The visual system might be sufficient, as it provides information about moving objects, like a car or a bending tree on a windy day. However, the visual system is sensitive only to the displacement of the image on the retina, indicating that an object is changing position relative to the fixation point. In contrast, motor resonance, the inner replica of the observed action, gives the opportunity to reuse the knowledge accumulated as the consequences of one's actions. Thanks to this knowledge, individuals have the ability to anticipate and predict the outcome of others' actions. For instance, we have long known that the distal goal of an action influences movement execution (Marteniuk et al. 1987). When grasping a bottle, the positioning of the fingers depends on the intention to pour, move, throw (Ansuini et al., 2008, 2006), show it (Sartori et al. 2009a), or pass it to somebody (Sartori et al. 2009b). Sensorimotor representations are formed with the repeated experience of interacting with the world and are shared among those with identical goals (Rizzolatti and Craighero 2004). This sharing allows observers to be sensitive to early differences in visual kinematics and to use them to discriminate between movements performed with different intentions (Sartori et al. 2011; Stapel et al. 2012). This ability is mediated by motor resonance and increases as the motor ability to replicate the observed movement increases, as suggested by consistent results found in children (Falck-Ytter et al. 2006), professional athletes (Aglioti et al. 2008), dancers (Calvo-Merino et al. 2005), and musicians (Furukawa et al. 2017). Furthermore, motor knowledge may help in discriminating intentions by comparing congruency between kinematics and environmental context (Amoruso et al. 2016).

In humans, the opportunity to learn new motor abilities may be another potential use of a dedicated system for coding actions based on accumulated motor knowledge. Likely, this function belongs exclusively to the human mirror system since it requires the possibility of interpreting as goal directed even strange movements performed by a dance teacher. This involves the activation of the human mirror system and the consequent retrieval of the sensorimotor representation of the most similar movement or posture (e.g., the first position in ballet may just be translated into: "stand with heels almost touching and feet turned outwards"). As a result, and with additional training, new motor skills are gradually developed, and new sensorimotor representations are created, enabling not only better execution of the movement but also more accurate perception of the observed movement. This interpretation is supported by many experimental results showing that mirror activation is greater for familiar actions but that even unfamiliar actions can cause it (Buccino et al. 2004b; Calvo-Merino et al. 2005), and that the greater the motor competence in the observed action, the greater the activation of the human mirror system, even when familiarity is controlled (Calvo-Merino et al. 2006; Candidi et al. 2014; Cross et al. 2009, 2006). It should be noted that the goal in intransitive actions like dancing is the exact execution of the movement. Therefore, the greater the coincidence of motor skills with the actor, the greater the resonance capacity for the observer.

Top-down modulation of motor resonance

In summary, evidence indicates that the mirror system resonates like a tuning-fork when the observed movement is interpreted as "action", a movement performed with a certain goal (Rizzolatti and Fogassi 2014). It is precisely sharing a goal with an agent that activates the resonance mechanism in the observer (Rizzolatti and Craighero 2004). The goal is shared when the action belongs to the motor repertoire of the observer. We know that only when two tuning-forks vibrate at the same frequency do they enter into resonance. The vibration frequency metaphor therefore suggests that when goals are not shared there should be no resonance. Motor resonance has historically been thought of as an internal, automatic simulation of any observed action (Naish et al. 2014), independently of related contextual cues, past experience, and social and motivational states. It should be noted, however, that research emphasizing these characteristics has often relied on movement stimuli that appear in isolation. Thus, the video of a hand grasping something on a white background evokes only the idea of a hand grasping something, i.e., a neutral goal shared by everyone. Therefore, the results cannot be generalized to real situations where the context is present. Some recent research overcame this limitation and demonstrated that motor resonance is not entirely impervious to top-down modulations (for a review see Amoruso and Finisguerra 2019). However, experimental paradigms used to investigate this issue are the subject of much methodological criticism. For example, according to the new idea, it is plausible that the information on the weight of the to-be-grasped object modulates CS excitability in the observer who is a priori aware of the different muscular involvement required. But, this modulation may be easily induced by the observed different kinematic profile or by the degree of hand contraction (Alaerts et al. 2012, 2010; Senot et al. 2011). Therefore, to show that motor resonance is influenced by top-down processing, it is necessary to compare the effects of the same stimuli moving with the same kinematics in different experimental conditions. Furthermore, experimental paradigms should individuate actions whose goal is not shared with the agent; this is a challenging option to test in humans who perceive every voluntary movement as goal directed. One possibility is to consider an action that the observer has never engaged in because it would endanger him or violate his moral convictions.

Grasping a sharp object is an example of a painful action that is not part of an individual's motor repertoire, as it has never been performed and would never be performed spontaneously. On these considerations a combined TMS and behavioral study was performed (Craighero et al. 2014). As a stimulus, a video of an agent grasping a parallelepiped-shaped object was employed. This was considered an action whose goal was shared between the agent and the observer. Using video-editing software, the parallelepiped was replaced with a similar object of the same size but with very sharp tips at the finger opposition space, creating a movie in which the hand's kinematics remained the same but the action was perceived as painful. Prior to the experiment participants were also encouraged to try to hold the sharp object with the same grip used by the agent, without success. Consequently, this was considered an action whose goal was not shared. Consistent with the hypothesis, the results indicated that motor resonance was only present when watching the video with the parallelepiped-shaped object. The same experimental paradigm has been used in other studies obtaining the same results (Craighero et al. 2015; Gentile et al. 2022). Even performing an action that harms another person may not be part of the motor repertoire of an individual who shares the moral principles derived from social norms and regard for others. This possibility was verified by a TMS study in which participants observed a video showing a hand reaching and squeezing a bulb horn (Craighero and Mele 2018). Thanks to the complicity of some actors, the participant was led to believe that, depending on the experimental session, the squeezing of the bulb horn would have had negative (i.e., a constant and increasing inflation of a cuff placed around the upper arm) or positive (i.e., a constant and progressive deflation of the cuff) effects on the person present in the adjacent room. Before each experimental session, participants experienced these effects by means of a sphygmomanometer applied to their arm and either inflated (to its maximum) or deflated with the same timing used during the experiment. The results showed a decrease in motor resonance when the observer was led to believe that the action shown in the video was causing negative effects to the other person. Similar results were obtained showing static pictures of a hand stealing a wallet *vs.* picking up a notepaper, but only in individuals with an increased level of harm-avoidance personality trait (Liuzza et al. 2015).

These findings agree with the hypothesis that the absence of a shared goal prevents motor resonance. Failure to share is determined by the fact that the action seen is not considered "feasible".

Finally, probably the best example of top-down processing comes from evidence that the degree of motor resonance changes according to the observer's idea of his or her social position. Using our analogy again, when a tuning-fork is placed on an elastic body, the intensity of the sound is lower than when it is placed on a sounding board. Similarly, high-power and high-socioeconomic-level individuals have been reported to display less motor system activity during action observation than individuals from lower socioeconomic levels. The first evidence came from a TMS study in which the different level of power was induced by a priming procedure (i.e., participants had to write an essay about an experience where someone had power over them, or they had power over someone) (Hogeveen et al. 2014). The second study used Instagram "follower to following" ratio as an index for online sense of status and power. Leaders were defined as individuals who have more followers than they are following, and the opposite for Followers. Results showed that Followers exhibited increased motor resonance compared to Leaders (Farwaha and Obhi 2019). These findings agree with the psychological literature on power indicating that the powerful, because they already control resources, tend not to process individuating information about the less powerful. In contrast, the powerless, because they do not control resources, are motivated to process individuating information about the powerful (Fiske and Dépret 1996; Goodwin et al. 2000). Remembering our analogy, the power is represented by the base on which the tuning-forks are positioned. Individuals in such different positions perceive action events differently.

This chapter has attempted to explain the neurophysiological roots of motor resonance, and to present evidence that its function in understanding and anticipating the actions of others requires sharing goals with them. Without this sharing, the motor resonance and, perhaps, a true understanding of the intentions behind others' behaviors are absent. Furthermore, there is evidence that sharing the immediate goal of an action is insufficient to produce motor resonance, and that it is also necessary to share the motivational, moral, and social aspects that lead to its performance.

References

Aglioti, S. M., Cesari, P., Romani, M., & Urgesi, C. (2008) "Action anticipation and motor resonance in elite basketball players," *Nature Neuroscience*, 11(9), 1109–1116. https://doi.org/10.1038/nn.2182

Alaerts, K., de Beukelaar, T. T., Swinnen, S. P., & Wenderoth, N. (2012) "Observing how others lift light or heavy objects: Time-dependent encoding of grip force in the primary motor cortex," *Psychological Research*, 76(4), 503–513. https://doi.org/10.1007/s00426-011-0380-1

Alaerts, K., Heremans, E., Swinnen, S. P., & Wenderoth, N. (2009) "How are observed actions mapped to the observer's motor system? Influence of posture and perspective," *Neuropsychologia*, 47(2). https://doi.org/10.1016/j.neuropsychologia.2008.09.012

Alaerts, K., Senot, P., Swinnen, S. P., Craighero, L., Wenderoth, N., & Fadiga, L. (2010) "Force requirements of observed object lifting are encoded by the observer's motor system: A TMS study,"

European Journal of Neuroscience, 31(6), 1144–1153. https://doi.org/10.1111/j.1460-9568. 2010.07124.x

Amoruso, L., & Finisguerra, A. (2019) "Low or High-Level Motor Coding? The Role of Stimulus Complexity," *Frontiers in Human Neuroscience, 13*. https://doi.org/10.3389/fnhum.2019.00332

Amoruso, L., Finisguerra, A., & Urgesi, C. (2016) "Tracking the time course of top-down contextual effects on motor responses during action comprehension," *Journal of Neuroscience, 36*(46). https://doi.org/10.1523/JNEUROSCI.4340-15.2016

Ansuini, C., Giosa, L., Turella, L., Altoè, G., & Castiello, U. (2008) "An object for an action, the same object for other actions: Effects on hand shaping," *Experimental Brain Research, 185*(1), 111–119. https://doi.org/10.1007/s00221-007-1136-4

Ansuini, C., Santello, M., Massaccesi, S., & Castiello, U. (2006) "Effects of end-goal on hand shaping," *Journal of Neurophysiology, 95*(4). https://doi.org/10.1152/jn.01107.2005

Borroni, P., & Baldissera, F. (2008) "Activation of motor pathways during observation and execution of hand movements," *Social Neuroscience, 3*(3–4), 276–288. https://doi.org/10.1080/17470910701515269

Borroni, P., Montagna, M., Cerri, G., & Baldissera, F. (2005) "Cyclic time course of motor excitability modulation during the observation of a cyclic hand movement," *Brain Research, 1065*(1–2). https://doi.org/10.1016/j.brainres.2005.10.034

Brass, M., Bekkering, H., Wohlschläger, A., & Prinz, W. (2000) "Compatibility between observed and executed finger movements: Comparing symbolic, spatial, and imitative cues," *Brain and Cognition, 44*(2), 124–143. https://doi.org/10.1006/brcg.2000.1225

Brighina, F., La Bua, A., Oliveri, M., Piazza, A., & Fierro, B. (2000) "Magnetic stimulation study during observation of motor tasks," *Journal of the Neurological Sciences, 174*(2), 122–126. https://doi.org/10.1016/S0022-510X(00)00271-9

Buccino, G., Binkofski, F., Fink, G. R., Fadiga, L., Fogassi, L., Gallese, V., Seitz, R. J., Zilles, K., Rizzolatti, G., & Freund, H. J. (2001) "Action observation activates premotor and parietal areas in a somatotopic manner: An fMRI study," *European Journal of Neuroscience, 13*(2), 400–404. https://doi.org/10.1046/j.1460-9568.2001.01385.x

Buccino, G., Binkofski, F., & Riggio, L. (2004a) "The mirror neuron system and action recognition," in *Brain and Language* 89 (2), 370–376. https://doi.org/10.1016/S0093-934X(03)00356-0

Buccino, G., Lui, F., Canessa, N., Patteri, I., Lagravinese, G., Benuzzi, F., Porro, C. A., & Rizzolatti, G. (2004b) "Neural Circuits Involved in the Recognition of Actions Performed by Nonconspecifics: An fMRI Study," *Journal of Cognitive Neuroscience, 16*(1), 114–126. https://doi.org/10.1162/089892904322755601

Caggiano, V., Fogassi, L., Rizzolatti, G., Thier, P., & Casile, A. (2009) "Mirror neurons differentially encode the peripersonal and extrapersonal space of monkeys," *Science, 324*(5925). https://doi.org/10.1126/science.1166818

Calvo-Merino, B., Glaser, D. E., Grèzes, J., Passingham, R. E., & Haggard, P. (2005) "Action observation and acquired motor skills: An fMRI study with expert dancers," *Cerebral Cortex, 15*(8), 1243–1249. https://doi.org/10.1093/cercor/bhi007

Calvo-Merino, Beatriz, Grèzes, J., Glaser, D. E., Passingham, R. E., & Haggard, P. (2006) "Seeing or doing? Influence of visual and motor familiarity in action observation," *Current Biology, 16*(19). https://doi.org/10.1016/j.cub.2006.07.065

Candidi, M., Sacheli, L. M., Mega, I., & Aglioti, S. M. (2014) "Somatotopic mapping of piano fingering errors in sensorimotor experts: TMS studies in pianists and visually trained musically naïves," *Cerebral Cortex, 24*(2). https://doi.org/10.1093/cercor/bhs325

Clark, S., Tremblay, F., & Ste-Marie, D. (2004) "Differential modulation of corticospinal excitability during observation, mental imagery and imitation of hand actions," *Neuropsychologia, 42*(1), 105–112. https://doi.org/10.1016/S0028-3932(03)00144-1

Colby, C. L., & Goldberg, M. E. (1999) "Space and attention in parietal cortex," *Annual Review of Neuroscience, 22*. https://doi.org/10.1146/annurev.neuro.22.1.319

Craighero, L. (2014) "The role of the motor system in cognitive functions," in *The Routledge Handbook of Embodied Cognition* (pp. 51–58). https://doi.org/10.4324/9781315775845

Craighero, L., & Mele, S. (2018) "Equal kinematics and visual context but different purposes: Observer's moral rules modulate motor resonance," *Cortex, 104*, 1–11. https://doi.org/10.1016/j.cortex.2018.03.032

Craighero, L., Mele, S., & Zorzi, V. (2015) "An object-identity probability cueing paradigm during grasping observation: The facilitating effect is present only when the observed kinematics is suitable for the cued object," *Frontiers in Psychology*, 6. https://doi.org/10.3389/fpsyg.2015.01479

Craighero, L., Zorzi, V., Canto, R., & Franca, M. (2014) "Same kinematics but different objects during action observation: Detection times and motor evoked potentials," *Visual Cognition*, 22(5), 653–671. https://doi.org/10.1080/13506285.2014.904460

Cross, E. S., Hamilton, A. F. d. C, & Grafton, S. T. (2006) "Building a motor simulation de novo: Observation of dance by dancers," *NeuroImage*, 31(3), 1257–1267. https://doi.org/10.1016/j.neuroimage.2006.01.033

Cross, E. S., Kraemer, D. J. M., Hamilton, A. F. D. C., Kelley, W. M., & Grafton, S. T. (2009) "Sensitivity of the action observation network to physical and observational learning," *Cerebral Cortex*, 19(2). https://doi.org/10.1093/cercor/bhn083

Decety, J., & Chaminade, T. (2005) "The Neurophysiology of Imitation and Intersubjectivity," in S. Hurley & N. Chater (Eds), *Perspectives on Imitation* (pp. 119–140), The MIT Press. https://doi.org/10.7551/mitpress/5330.003.0005

di Pellegrino, G., Fadiga, L., Fogassi, L., Gallese, V., & Rizzolatti, G. (1992) "Understanding motor events: A neurophysiological study," *Experimental Brain Research*, 91(1), 176–180. https://doi.org/10.1007/BF00230027

Fabbri-Destro, M., & Rizzolatti, G. (2008) "Mirror neurons and mirror systems in monkeys and humans," *Physiology*, 23(3), 171–179. https://doi.org/10.1152/physiol.00004.2008

Fadiga, L., Craighero, L., Destro, M. F., Finos, L., Cotillon-Williams, N., Smith, A. T., & Castiello, U. (2006) "Language in shadow," *Social Neuroscience*, 1(2).

Fadiga, L., Fogassi, L., Pavesi, G., & Rizzolatti, G. (1995) "Motor facilitation during action observation: a magnetic stimulation study," *Journal of Neurophysiology*, 73(6), 2608–2611. https://doi.org/10.1152/jn.1995.73.6.2608

Fadiga, L., & Craighero, L. (2004) "Electrophysiology of action representation," *Journal of Clinical Neurophysiology*, 21(3), 157–169. https://doi.org/10.1097/00004691-200405000-00004

Fadiga, L., Craighero, L., & D'Ausilio, A. (2009) "Broca's area in language, action, and music," *Annals of the New York Academy of Sciences*, 1169, 448–458. https://doi.org/10.1111/j.1749-6632.2009.04582.x

Fadiga, L., Craighero, L., & Olivier, E. (2005) "Human motor cortex excitability during the perception of others' action," *Current Opinion in Neurobiology*, 15(2), 213–218. https://doi.org/10.1016/j.conb.2005.03.013

Falck-Ytter, T., Gredebäck, G., & Von Hofsten, C. (2006) "Infants predict other people's action goals," *Nature Neuroscience*, 9(7), 878–879. https://doi.org/10.1038/nn1729

Farwaha, S., & Obhi, S. S. (2019) "Differential motor facilitation during action observation in followers and leaders on instagram," *Frontiers in Human Neuroscience*, 13. https://doi.org/10.3389/fnhum.2019.00067

Fiske, S. T., & Dépret, E. (1996) "Control, Interdependence and Power: Understanding Social Cognition in Its Social Context," *European Review of Social Psychology*, 7(1). https://doi.org/10.1080/14792779443000094

Furukawa, Y., Uehara, K., & Furuya, S. (2017) "Expertise-dependent motor somatotopy of music perception," *Neuroscience Letters*, 650. https://doi.org/10.1016/j.neulet.2017.04.033

Gallese, V. (2003) "The roots of empathy: The shared manifold hypothesis and the neural basis of intersubjectivity," *Psychopathology*, 36(4), 171–180. https://doi.org/10.1159/000072786

——— (2008) "Embodied Simulation: From Mirror Neuron Systems to Interpersonal Relations," in *Empathy and Fairness* (pp. 3–12), Wiley. https://doi.org/10.1002/9780470030585.ch2

Gallese, V., Fadiga, L., Fogassi, L., & Rizzolatti, G. (1996) "Action recognition in the premotor cortex," *Brain*, 119(2), 593–609. https://doi.org/10.1093/brain/119.2.593

Gangitano, M., Mottaghy, F. M., & Pascual-Leone, A. (2001) "Phase-specific modulation of cortical motor output during movement observation," *NeuroReport*, 12(7), 1489–1492. https://doi.org/10.1097/00001756-200105250-00038

Gazzola, V., & Keysers, C. (2009) "The observation and execution of actions share motor and somatosensory voxels in all tested subjects: Single-subject analyses of unsmoothed fMRI data," *Cerebral Cortex*, 19(6). https://doi.org/10.1093/cercor/bhn181

Gentile, E., Brunetti, A., Ricci, K., Bevilacqua, V., Craighero, L., & de Tommaso, M. (2022) "Movement observation activates motor cortex in fibromyalgia patients: a fNIRS study," *Scientific Reports, 12*(1). https://doi.org/10.1038/s41598-022-08578-2

Giorello, G., & Sinigaglia, C. (2007) "Perception in action," *Acta Biomedica, 78*(SUPPL. 1), 49–57. https://doi.org/10.5040/9781492595625.ch-005

Goodwin, S. A., Gubin, A., Fiske, S. T., & Yzerbyt, V. Y. (2000) "Power Can Bias Impression Processes: Stereotyping Subordinates by Default and by Design," *Group Processes & Intergroup Relations, 3*(3). https://doi.org/10.1177/1368430200003003001

Hogeveen, J., Inzlicht, M., & Obhi, S. S. (2014) "Power changes how the brain responds to others," *Journal of Experimental Psychology: General, 143*(2). https://doi.org/10.1037/a0033477

Keysers, C., & Gazzola, V. (2007) "Integrating simulation and theory of mind: from self to social cognition," *Trends in Cognitive Sciences, 11*(5), 194–196. https://doi.org/10.1016/j.tics.2007.02.002

Kohler, E., Keysers, C., Umilta, M. A., Fogassi, L., Gallese, V., & Rizzolatti, G. (2002) "Hearing sounds, understanding actions: Action representation in mirror neurons," *Science, 297*(5582). https://doi.org/10.1126/science.1070311

Liuzza, M. T., Candidi, M., Sforza, A. L., & Aglioti, S. M. (2015) "Harm avoiders suppress motor resonance to observed immoral actions," *Social Cognitive and Affective Neuroscience, 10*(1), 1–6. https://doi.org/10.1093/scan/nsu025

Marteniuk, R. G., MacKenzie, C. L., Jeannerod, M., Athenes, S., & Dugas, C. (1987) "Constraints on human arm movement trajectories," *Canadian Journal of Psychology, 41*(3), 365–378. https://doi.org/10.1037/h0084157

Molenberghs, P., Cunnington, R., & Mattingley, J. B. (2012) "Brain regions with mirror properties: A meta-analysis of 125 human fMRI studies," *Neuroscience and Biobehavioral Reviews, 36*(1), 341–349). https://doi.org/10.1016/j.neubiorev.2011.07.004

Montagna, M., Cerri, G., Borroni, P., & Baldissera, F. (2005) "Excitability changes in human corticospinal projections to muscles moving hand and fingers while viewing a reaching and grasping action," *European Journal of Neuroscience, 22*(6), 1513–1520. https://doi.org/10.1111/j.1460-9568.2005.04336.x

Naish, K. R., Houston-Price, C., Bremner, A. J., & Holmes, N. P. (2014) "Effects of action observation on corticospinal excitability: Muscle specificity, direction, and timing of the mirror response," *Neuropsychologia, 64*, 331–348. https://doi.org/10.1016/j.neuropsychologia.2014.09.034

Rizzolatti, G., Cattaneo, L., Fabbri-Destro, M., & Rozzi, S. (2014) "Cortical mechanisms underlying the organization of goal-directed actions and mirror neuron-based action understanding," *Physiological Reviews, 94*(2), 655–706. https://doi.org/10.1152/physrev.00009.2013

Rizzolatti, G., & Craighero, L. (2004) "The mirror-neuron system," *Annual Review of Neuroscience, 27*. https://doi.org/10.1146/annurev.neuro.27.070203.144230

Rizzolatti, G., Fadiga, L., Fogassi, L., & Gallese, V. (1997a) "The space around us," *Science, 277*(5323). https://doi.org/10.1126/science.277.5323.190

Rizzolatti, G., & Fogassi, L. (2014) "The mirror mechanism: Recent findings and perspectives," *Philosophical Transactions of the Royal Society B: Biological Sciences, 369*(1644), 20130420. https://doi.org/10.1098/rstb.2013.0420

Rizzolatti, G., Fogassi, L., & Gallese, V. (1997b) "Parietal cortex: From sight to action," *Current Opinion in Neurobiology, 7*(4). https://doi.org/10.1016/S0959-4388(97)80037-2

Sartori, L., Becchio, C., Bara, B. G., & Castiello, U. (2009a) "Does the intention to communicate affect action kinematics?" *Consciousness and Cognition, 18*(3), 766–772. https://doi.org/10.1016/j.concog.2009.06.004

Sartori, L., Becchio, C., Bulgheroni, M., & Castiello, U. (2009b) "Modulation of the Action Control System by Social Intention: Unexpected Social Requests Override Preplanned Action," *Journal of Experimental Psychology: Human Perception and Performance, 35*(5). https://doi.org/10.1037/a0015777

Sartori, L., Becchio, C., & Castiello, U. (2011) "Cues to intention: The role of movement information," *Cognition, 119*(2), 242–252. https://doi.org/10.1016/j.cognition.2011.01.014

Senot, P., D'Ausilio, A., Franca, M., Caselli, L., Craighero, L., & Fadiga, L. (2011) "Effect of weight-related labels on corticospinal excitability during observation of grasping: A TMS study," *Experimental Brain Research, 211*(1), 161–167. https://doi.org/10.1007/s00221-011-2635-x

Shapiro, L. (2009) "Making sense of mirror neurons," *Synthese, 167*(3). https://doi.org/10.1007/s11229-008-9385-8

Stapel, J. C., Hunnius, S., & Bekkering, H. (2012) "Online prediction of others' actions: The contribution of the target object, action context and movement kinematics," *Psychological Research, 76*(4). https://doi.org/10.1007/s00426-012-0423-2

Umiltà, M. A., Kohler, E., Gallese, V., Fogassi, L., Fadiga, L., Keysers, C., & Rizzolatti, G. (2001) "I know what you are doing: A neurophysiological study," *Neuron, 31*(1), 155–165. https://doi.org/10.1016/S0896-6273(01)00337-3

Urgesi, C., Alaerts, K., & Craighero, L. (2020) "Editorial: How Do Motivational States Influence Motor Resonance?" *Frontiers in Human Neuroscience, 14.* https://doi.org/10.3389/fnhum.2020.00027

Urgesi, C., Candidi, M., Fabbro, F., Romani, M., & Aglioti, S. M. (2006) "Motor facilitation during action observation: Topographic mapping of the target muscle and influence of the onlooker's posture," *European Journal of Neuroscience, 23*(9). https://doi.org/10.1111/j.1460-9568.2006.04772.x

37

THE EMBODIMENT OF ATTENTION IN THE PERCEPTION-ACTION LOOP

Michael J. Spivey and Stephanie Huette

Introduction

Decades ago, the sciences of mind were busy drawing insights from computer engineering. Cognitive scientists reasoned that if a computer can process information in an intelligent fashion, perhaps humans are exhibiting their intelligence via similar mechanisms. It was thought that we could "reverse engineer" the human mind by drawing an analogy to how a computer is engineered. Of course, this was not the first time that a new and exciting piece of technology had been used as a metaphor for the mind. The Greeks likened to the mind to a water pump, eighteenth-century Western philosophers likened the mind to a clock, and then theories of cognition were inspired by the steam engine, then by the telegraph, then by relay circuits, and now the computer (see Daugman, 1993). After using the computer metaphor for several decades now, is it possible that the insights it can provide have all been plumbed?

This chapter describes a series of examples of where the computer metaphor of the mind breaks down, with a special emphasis on attention, and points to an embodied and situated account of mind that can naturally accommodate those problematic phenomena that undermine the computer metaphor. Rather than proposing the next new metaphor for the mind, we instead encourage drawing eclectic inspiration from embodied cognition (to appreciate how the body itself performs some cognitive operations), ecological psychology (to appreciate how the relation between organism and environment produces cognition), dynamical systems theory (to carry out analog information-processing simulations), and cognitive neuroscience (to stay grounded with the real physical material that lies at the hub of cognitive phenomena).

Stage-based models of attention

Early models of attention were based on the assumption that the vast onslaught of raw uninterpreted sensory input that barrages our sensors must be filtered down to a small subset of processed cognitive items that would be analyzed by a central executive with limited capacity. This perspective inspired "filter" models of attention that immediately

DOI: 10.4324/9781003322511-47

drew a distinction between "pre-attentive" filters, which processed a full sensory array of information in parallel, and "attentive" filters, which processed a condensed set of information serially, one item at a time (Broadbent, 1958; Treisman, 1969; see also Lachter, Forster, and Ruthruff, 2004). An example of a pre-attentive filter could be a topographically arranged collection of color-sensitive neurons in visual cortex, functioning like a feature map that detects, say, the color red anywhere in the visual field. Due to its parallel processing, this feature map will locate a solitary red target in the visual field essentially immediately, no matter how many non-red distractor objects are there. Therefore, reaction times do not increase as one adds non-red distractor objects. By contrast, if the target can only be identified by a conjunction of two features, say red and vertical (because there are some red non-vertical distractors and also some non-red vertical distractors), then the "redness" feature map and the "verticalness" feature map will each have multiple regions of activation on them – making pre-attentive identification of the lone target impossible. In this circumstance, the feature integration theory (Treisman and Gelade, 1980) of visual search proposed that attention must combine those feature maps into a "master map," and this master map is searched serially, as though by a spotlight that focuses on each object one at a time until the target is found. The feature integration theory of visual search was a powerfully influential filter-based account of attention for more than a decade.

However, a number of findings posed problems for the model. For example, some conjunctions of certain types of features appear to elicit parallel search processing, rather than serial (Nakayama and Silverman, 1986). Continuous gradations in similarity between a target and its distractors account for reaction time patterns better than treating visual features as discretely belonging to one feature map or another (Duncan and Humphreys, 1989). Analysis of a million trials across dozens of visual search experiments reveals no evidence for one population of serial search phenomena and a separate population of parallel search phenomena (Wolfe, 1998). And when the visual display spends its first 100 milliseconds configured with a single feature distinguishing the target, before then converting to a conjunction of features, one sees neither a parallel search nor a serial search, but something clearly in between (Olds, Cowan, and Jolicoeur, 2000). These types of findings all led to treating visual search as belonging on a continuum of efficiency, rather than being implemented by either a pre-attentive parallel filtering mechanism or an attentive serial filtering mechanism. As the passive feedforward filter approach to visual attention failed to account for new findings, it made room for a more proactive goal-oriented approach to attention (Allport, 1989). Rather than the emphasis being on how perceptual systems convert stimuli into interpretations, a new emphasis was building on how attention results from motor systems making real-time demands on what sensory input is needed or expected next (Hommel, Müsseler, Aschersleben, and Prinz, 2001; Jordan, 1999; Kawato, 1999; van der Heijden, 1996; see also Gibson, 1979).

Interactive models of attention

This more proactive approach to attention raises the question: Where in this goal-oriented account of attention do the goals come from? Desimone and Duncan (1995) proposed a neurally inspired account of visual attention in which neural representations of objects (i.e., Hebbian cell assemblies, or population codes) compete against one another in parallel for the privilege of eliciting their associated motor output, such as an eye movement or a reaching movement. Neural feedback projections from frontal brain regions to visual brain regions can then bias this competition process based on goals and other information from other sensory sources. This "biased competition" account of attention has been extremely influential, and naturally makes a number of empirical predictions that have indeed been reported in the experimental literature.

For example, when a visual stimulus is especially relevant for the goals of a visuomotor task, single-cell recording in monkeys shows that neurons responsive to that stimulus exhibit a higher firing rate than when that same visual stimulus is presented to that receptive field but is irrelevant to the task (Moran and Desimone, 1985; Motter, 1993). Moreover, fMRI results with humans show that when a tactile pre-cue is spatially congruent with a visual stimulus, activation in visual cortex for that visual stimulus is greater than when the tactile pre-cue is spatially incongruent (Macaluso, Frith, and Driver, 2000). Visual input of a face can trick the process of speech recognition into perceiving a spoken syllable one way or another (McGurk and MacDonald, 1976). Auditory input can trick the visual system into perceiving a visual event one way or another (Sekuler, Sekuler, and Lau, 1997; Shams, Kamitani, and Shimojo, 2000). And spoken linguistic input can make a conjunction search process function as though it were a parallel process, uninfluenced by the number of distractors (Chiu and Spivey, 2011; Spivey, Tyler, Eberhard, and Tanenhaus, 2001). In sharp contrast to Fodor's (1983) proposal of sensory systems as informationally encapsulated modules, these kinds of findings support a radically interactive and distributed account of attention, where even purportedly "unimodal" perceptual systems are being biased by other modalities (Driver and Spence, 2000; Lupyan and Spivey, 2008; O'Reilly, Wyatte, Herd, Mingus, and Jilk, 2013).

Cascaded models of attention

Even if every subsystem is influencing practically every other subsystem, this leaves open the question of how immediately those influences are transmitted. Traditional stage-based accounts of processing function by having each stage complete its operations before then passing an output to the next stage. This is quite different from a type of system that functions on partial, fuzzy, incomplete, and distributed information that is constantly in flux. It may feel counter-intuitive to think of attention as something this diffuse and partial – rather than it being narrow and directed – but many studies have shown that we operate as best we can with a constant flow of partial bits and pieces of information (Coles, Gratton, Bashore, Eriksen, and Donchin, 1985; for review, see Spivey, 2007).

The cascade model put forward by McClelland (1979) posits a few components to this kind of account, namely that the inputs to a particular level of processing are based on the outputs from the neighboring level(s), and that at each level of processing, the output is continuously available to the neighboring level(s). That is to say, the output is not a singular symbol or conclusion, but rather an unfolding of activation that is continuously being streamed to the neighboring level(s). Thus, the activation at any given level is determined by the connections between levels, as well as the pattern of activation in the neighboring level(s).

A cascaded flow of information from perceptual systems to motor systems is particularly well demonstrated by the work of Gold and Shadlen (2000). While briefly presenting a somewhat ambiguous visual stimulus to a monkey, to which it was trained to respond with an eye movement to one or another response location, they microstimulated cells in its frontal eye fields (FEF) to elicit a neutral direction of eye movement. With more and more time to process the visual stimulus, this electrically evoked saccadic eye movement showed more and more partial influence of the monkey's voluntary response eye movement, averaged into the angle of the neutral evoked saccade. Thus, over the course of a few hundred milliseconds, the continuous accrual of perceptual information in visual brain areas was constantly cascading into oculomotor brain areas to contribute to the gradual development of an eye-movement command. When microstimulation then triggered the evoked saccade in a neutral direction, some portion of that still developing voluntary response was also active in FEF. The resulting movement was a weighted average of the evoked neutral saccade and the partially accrued command for the voluntary response saccade. Clearly, the motor system is not patiently waiting to be delivered a completed command from the cognitive system, but is instead continuously participating in the development of the understanding of what a stimulus means for the organism – thus blurring the line between what is "motor" and what is "cognitive."

This kind of partial processing can be found in many decision-making tasks, where information can cascade through the system even without subjective awareness. Van Rullen and Thorpe (2001) trained participants to rapidly identify whether an animal or means of transportation was present in a picture displayed for a mere 20 milliseconds on the screen and then masked. Animal and transportation trials occurred in separate blocks, and responses were made via a go, no-go paradigm. Participants were extremely accurate in this task (94% correct on average) in identifying whether these objects were present or not. An initial interpretation of this result might be that in a mere 20 milliseconds of input, the feedforward sweep of sensory information appears to be enough to carry out visual object identification in a seemingly context-free manner (before frontal brain regions would have time to respond and send feedback to visual areas). However, this neglects the fact that the task of identifying a pre-specified object's presence or absence is itself a goal-oriented task. Goals are driven by frontal and prefrontal cortex, which has feedback connections to visual cortex. What is likely happening in this scenario then is not a context-free feedforward sweep whereby some particular category is rapidly identified, but rather the goal of looking for this target, even before a stimulus is presented, involves feedback signals from frontal regions tuning those visual receptive fields to temporarily become "car detectors" or "animal detectors," focusing processing on features that are associated with those categories.

What then directs where attention goes, if it works in this radically distributed interactive fashion? If we have a system that cascades its information from subsystem to subsystem so promiscuously that we lose track of which signals are feedforward and which are feedback, can we still have something coherent enough to be called "attention"? Rather than conceiving of attention as a "spotlight" directed by a central executive, a more scientifically sound approach may be to conceive of attention as the emergent result of biased competition among multiple partially active representations (Desimone and Duncan, 1995). Rather than assuming that the focus of mental activity at any one point in time somehow derives from one source, like the central processing unit of a computer, perhaps it instead derives from myriad sources. Some of these sources are goals and biases from neighboring neural subsystems. Some of them are biases from immediately perceivable environmental constraints. Some of them are biases from signals delivered by other people in the environment. At longer timescales, some of these biases are social norms and cultural constraints. At even longer timescales, some of these sources are evolutionary influences. The density of perceptual acuity at a particular moment in time – the sense of "who we are" and "what we're about" at that moment – is something that emerges nonlinearly out of the complex interactions among innumerable informational biases competing and cooperating in real time (Spivey, 2013).

Cascaded interaction spreads

With different sensory, cognitive, and motor systems continuously biasing one another in real time, there is no point in time during which a given subsystem is processing its input in a context-free manner. There will always have been some form of contextual bias that was busy influencing the given subsystem immediately before some new afferent sensory input enters it. If continuous distributed interactions between sensory systems make vision no longer an encapsulated module, and audition no longer an encapsulated module, then continuous distributed interactions among cognitive processes and motor processes make cognition no longer a module that is separate from action – hence, embodied cognition. In fact, given the millisecond timescale at which various motor movements continuously update the sensory input, which continuously updates cognitive processes, which continuously update the ongoing motor commands, perhaps those external actions themselves may not even be informationally encapsulated from cognition. As Sue Hurley (1998, p. 3) put it: "if internal relations can qualify as [representational] vehicles, why not external relations? Given a continuous complex dynamic system of reciprocal causal relations between organism and environment, what in principle stops the spread? The idea that [representational] vehicles might go external takes the notion of distributed processing to its logical extreme."

A famous example of cognitive processes "going external" comes from Kirsh and Maglio's (1994) Tetris experiments. They found that novice Tetris players tended to perform something equivalent to "mental rotation" (à la Shepard and Metzler, 1971) of the shapes in the game to determine where to place them. By contrast, expert Tetris players offloaded that cognitive operation onto their environment by frequently using the fast-rotate button. This allowed the computer interface in front of a participant to perform the cognitive operation of image rotation and the neural system in their skull to perform the cognitive operation of perceptual matching. The result was that these experts were significantly faster and more accurate than the novices.

Skeletal motor movements are a useful way to perform cognitive operations, such as pressing keys on an interactive computer interface. But there is a far more ubiquitous motor movement, happening about three times per second, that performs cognitive operations during your entire waking life, no matter where you are, or what you are doing: eye movements. Ballard, Hayhoe, Pook, and Rao (1997) demonstrated that a given eye fixation can function like a "pointer" (in a content-addressable computer memory). Rather than forming neural representations of complex visual objects in memory while viewing a scene, people often simply maintain spatial locations in memory, and send the eyes to those locations to access the "content" in those "addresses." Essentially, people exhibit a strong tendency to use one's environment as an external memory store (see also O'Regan, 1992).

Thus, on the timescale of a few hundred milliseconds, eye movements are changing how the environment impacts your sensors, which changes how you cognize your environment, which changes the next eye movement, which changes the next sensory input, and so on. This is a recurrent causal loop that cannot be unraveled to find the chicken versus the egg. Half of the data transformations that constitute an organism's attention are actually happening outside the body, in how the body's movements have altered how light projects onto the retinas. So much so that one could be tempted to suggest that much of your "visual experience" is itself happening in the space around you, rather than solely inside your brain (O'Regan and Noë, 2001; see also Clark and Chalmers, 1998).

Eye movements and the perception–action loop

It has long been understood that a there is a close link between visual attention and eye movements. Even when an experimental participant fixates a central dot on a computer screen and covertly directs attention to the periphery for several hundred milliseconds – as is often done in cognitive psychology experiments (Posner, Snyder, and Davidson, 1980) – oculomotor systems of the brain are essentially programming an eye movement and then holding back from executing it, and this process is part and parcel of visual attention (Corbetta, 1998; Deubel and Schneider, 1996). In fact, neurons in parietal cortex receive feedback from oculomotor regions signaling an upcoming saccade, such that they are able to shift their receptive fields to the new upcoming region in the visual field and begin responding to a visual stimulus that is not yet in their classical receptive field (Colby, Duhamel, and Goldberg, 1996). This prospective responsiveness to visual input, in anticipation of a saccade, clearly blurs the line between the motor programming of a saccade planning and the process of covert visual attention. As a result of this close link between these two processes, the vast majority of covert shifts of attention are immediately followed by an eye movement to that same location. Thus, eye movements are quite literally a physical embodiment of visual attention. They allow even a subtle cognitive bias about what is goal-relevant in the environment to be converted – in just a couple of hundred milliseconds – into a powerful perceptual bias for what is dominating visual processing, via the high-resolution fovea.

In this way, not only are eye movements highly useful for the experimenter, as a record of what is drawing attention at any moment, but they are also highly useful for the organism itself. A different pattern of eye movements on the same scene will not only *reveal* a different thought process about that environment (Yarbus, 1967), it can *cause* a different thought process about that environment. For example, just as recording eye movements during mechanical problem-solving has provided a deeper understanding of mechanical reasoning (Hegarty and Just, 1993; Rozenblit, Spivey, and Wojslawowicz, 2002), it has also provided inspiration for improvement of training with technical devices (Hegarty, 2005).

Even high-level conceptual insights can be jump-started, or missed entirely, by different eye-movement patterns on a diagram associated with an insight problem. People who are 30 seconds away from solving a diagram-based version of Karl Duncker's famous tumor-and-lasers radiation problem tend to make a characteristic pattern of eye movements on the diagram (Grant and Spivey, 2003). Those who are 30 seconds away from *giving up* on the problem exhibit less of that eye-movement pattern. Interestingly, this pattern of eye movements was not merely an indicator to the experimenters that a person was about to solve the problem, but that pattern of eye movements was actually assisting the person in arriving at the solution. In their second experiment, Grant and Spivey subtly animated the diagram in a way that unconsciously induced that pattern of eye movements, and it doubled the proportion of people solving the problem. Thomas and Lleras (2007) followed up this work with a version of the task where participants were explicitly instructed to move their eyes in a pattern across the diagram. Participants who moved their eyes in the pattern that produced converging lines on the tumor exhibited a higher rate of finding the solution. As one might expect, based on the overlap between attentional mechanisms and eye-movement mechanisms, even when participants don't move their eyes at all, but instead move their attention covertly in this converging-lines pattern, performance on this insight problem is improved (Thomas and Lleras, 2009). Based on results like these, it may be useful to treat the relation between organism and environment as not only the place where perception and action take place (e.g., Gibson, 1979), but also the place where cognition takes place.

The embodiment of attention

Cognitive science has a long history of drawing inspiration from the computer metaphor of the mind and placing the bulk of its emphasis on how external stimuli influence mental processing, but this is only one half of the story. The other half, of equal importance, is how mental processing influences external stimuli. When attention gets physically embodied in motor movements (even subtle and brief ones like eye movements and other muscle twitches), those movements change the way the environment impacts our sensors in ways that abide by continuous physical laws (Gibson, 1979; Turvey, 1992; Chemero, 2009). The result is that while the environment is catalyzing events in the brain, the brain is simultaneously catalyzing events (i.e., motor movements) in the environment. This autocatalytic loop, whereby the brain and the environment produce an emergent phenomenon called cognition, steers our understanding of the mind away from the formal logical computer metaphor, where genuine autocatalysis is not logically possible. And it is radically changing how we conceptualize joint action when two people are sharing an environment, and intermingling their perception–action loops (Dale, Fusaroli, Duran, and Richardson, 2013; Spivey, 2012). If we acknowledge that attention in particular, and the mind in general, is an emergent property of an embodied brain interacting with its environment, then the future of cognitive science will require a complex dynamical systems approach to cognition (Spivey, 2007), drawing insights from embodied cognition (Barsalou, 1999), ecological psychology (Turvey and Carello, 1995), complexity theory (Van Orden, Holden, and Turvey, 2003), computational neuroscience (Kello, 2013), and robotics (Pezzulo *et al.*, 2011).

References

Allport, A. (1989). Visual attention. In M. I. Posner (Ed.), *Foundations of cognitive science* (pp. 631–682). Cambridge, MA: MIT Press.

Ballard, D. H., Hayhoe, M. M., Pook, P. K., and Rao, R. P. (1997). Deictic codes for the embodiment of cognition. *Behavioral and Brain Sciences*, 20(4), 723–742.

Barsalou, L. W. (1999). Perceptual symbol systems. *Behavioral and Brain Sciences*, 22(4), 577–660.

Broadbent, D. E. (1958). *Perception and communication*. New York: Oxford University Press.

Chemero, A. (2009). *Radical embodied cognitive science*. Cambridge, MA: MIT Press.

Chiu, E. M., and Spivey, M. J. (2011). Linguistic mediation of visual search: effects of speech timing and display. In B. Kokinov, A. Karmiloff-Smith, and N. J. Nersessian (Eds), *European perspectives on cognitive science*. Sofia: New Bulgarian University Press.

Clark, A., and Chalmers, D. (1998). The extended mind. *Analysis*, 58(1), 7–19.

Colby, C. L., Duhamel, J. R., and Goldberg, M. E. (1996). Visual, presaccadic, and cognitive activation of single neurons in monkey lateral intraparietal area. *Journal of Neurophysiology*, 76(5), 2841–2852.

Coles, M., Gratton, G., Bashore, T., Eriksen, C., and Donchin, E. (1985). A psychophysiological investigation of the continuous flow model of human information processing. *Journal of Experimental Psychology: Human Perception and Performance*, 11, 529–553.

Corbetta, M. (1998). Frontoparietal cortical networks for directing attention and the eye to visual locations: Identical, independent, or overlapping neural systems? *Proceedings of the National Academy of Sciences of the United States of America*, 95(3), 831–838.

Dale, R., Fusaroli, R., Duran, N., and Richardson, D. C. (2013). The self-organization of human interaction. *Psychology of Learning and Motivation, 59*, 43–95.

Daugman, J. G. (1993). Brain metaphor and brain theory. In E. L. Schwartz (Ed.), *Computational neuroscience* (pp. 9–18). Cambridge, MA: MIT Press.

Desimone, R., and Duncan, J. (1995). Neural mechanisms of selective visual attention. *Annual Review of Neuroscience, 18(1)*, 193–222.

Deubel, H., and Schneider, W. X. (1996). Saccade target selection and object recognition: Evidence for a common attentional mechanism. *Vision Research, 36(12)*, 1827–1837.

Driver, J., and Spence, C. (2000). Multisensory perception: Beyond modularity and convergence. *Current Biology, 10(20)*, R731–35.

Duncan, J., and Humphreys, G. W. (1989). Visual search and stimulus similarity. *Psychological Review, 96(3)*, 433–458.

Fodor, J. (1983). *The modularity of mind.* Cambridge, MA: MIT Press.

Gibson, J. J. (1979). *The ecological approach to visual perception.* Boston: Houghton Mifflin.

Gold, J., and Shadlen, M. (2000). Representation of a perceptual decision in developing oculomotor commands. *Nature, 404*, 390–394.

Grant, E. R., and Spivey, M. J. (2003). Eye movements and problem solving guiding attention guides thought. *Psychological Science, 14(5)*, 462–466.

Hegarty, M. (2005). Multimedia learning about physical systems. In R. Mayer (Ed.), *The Cambridge handbook of multimedia learning* (pp. 447–465). New York: Cambridge University Press.

Hegarty, M., and Just, M. A. (1993). Constructing mental models of machines from text and diagrams. *Journal of Memory and Language, 32(6)*, 717–742.

Hommel, B., Müsseler, J., Aschersleben, G., and Prinz, W. (2001). The theory of event coding (TEC): A framework for perception and action planning. *Behavioral and Brain Sciences, 24(5)*, 849–878.

Hurley, S. (1998). Vehicles, contents, conceptual structures, and externalism. *Analysis, 58*, 1–6.

Jordan, J. S. (1999). Cognition and spatial perception: Production of output or control of input? *Advances in Psychology, 129*, 69–90.

Kawato, M. (1999). Internal models for motor control and trajectory planning. *Current Opinion in Neurobiology, 9(6)*, 718–727.

Kello, C. T. (2013). Critical branching neural networks. *Psychological Review, 120(1)*, 230–254.

Kirsh, D., and Maglio, P. (1994). On distinguishing epistemic from pragmatic action. *Cognitive Science, 18(4)*, 513–549.

Lachter, J., Forster, K. I., and Ruthruff, E. (2004). Forty-five years after Broadbent (1958): Still no identification without attention. *Psychological Review, 111(4)*, 880–913.

Lupyan, G., and Spivey, M. J. (2008). Perceptual processing is facilitated by ascribing meaning to novel stimuli. *Current Biology, 18(10)*, R410–12.

Macaluso, E., Frith, C. D., and Driver, J. (2000). Modulation of human visual cortex by crossmodal spatial attention. *Science, 289(5482)*, 1206–1208.

McClelland, J. (1979). On the time relations of mental processes: An examination of systems of processes in cascade. *Psychological Review, 86*, 287–330.

McGurk, H., and MacDonald, J. (1976). Hearing lips and seeing voices. *Nature, 264(5588)*, 746–748.

Moran, J., and Desimone, R. (1985). Selective attention gates visual processing in the extrastriate cortex. *Science, 229(4715)*, 782–784.

Motter, B. C. (1993). Focal attention produces spatially selective processing in visual cortical areas V1, V2, and V4 in the presence of competing stimuli. *Journal of Neurophysiology, 70(3)*, 909–919.

Nakayama, K., and Silverman, G. H. (1986). Serial and parallel processing of visual feature conjunctions. *Nature, 320(6059)*, 264–265.

Olds, E. S., Cowan, W. B., and Jolicoeur, P. (2000). The time-course of pop-out search. *Vision Research, 40(8)*, 891–912.

O'Regan, J. K. (1992). Solving the "real" mysteries of visual perception: The world as an outside memory. *Canadian Journal of Psychology, 46(3)*, 461–488.

O'Regan, J. K., and Noë, A. (2001). A sensorimotor account of vision and visual consciousness. *Behavioral and Brain Sciences, 24(5)*, 939–972.

459

O'Reilly, R. C., Wyatte, D., Herd, S., Mingus, B., and Jilk, D. J. (2013). Recurrent processing during object recognition. *Frontiers in Psychology, 4(124)*, 1–14.

Pezzulo, G., Barsalou, L. W., Cangelosi, A., Fischer, M. H., McRae, K., and Spivey, M. J. (2011). The mechanics of embodiment: A dialog on embodiment and computational modeling. *Frontiers in Psychology, 2(5)*, 1–21.

Posner, M. I., Snyder, C. R., and Davidson, B. J. (1980). Attention and the detection of signals. *Journal of Experimental Psychology: General, 109(2)*, 160–174.

Rozenblit, L., Spivey, M., and Wojslawowicz, J. (2002). Mechanical reasoning about gear-and-belt systems: Do eye movements predict performance? In M. Anderson, B. Meyer, and P. Olivier (Eds), *Diagrammatic representation and reasoning*. Berlin: Springer.

Sekuler, R., Sekuler, A. B., and Lau, R. (1997). Sound alters visual motion perception. *Nature, 385(6614)*, 308.

Shams, L., Kamitani, Y., and Shimojo, S. (2000). What you see is what you hear. *Nature, 408(6814)*, 788.

Shepard, R., and Metzler, J. (1971). Mental rotation of three-dimensional objects. *Science, 171(3972)*, 701–703.

Spivey, M. J. (2007). *The continuity of mind*. New York: Oxford University Press.

———— (2012). The spatial intersection of minds. *Cognitive Processing, 13*, 343–346.

———— (2013). The emergence of intentionality. *Ecological Psychology, 25(3)*, 233–239.

Spivey, M. J., Tyler, M. J., Eberhard, K. M., and Tanenhaus, M. K. (2001). Linguistically mediated visual search. *Psychological Science, 12(4)*, 282–286.

Thomas, L. E., and Lleras, A. (2007). Moving eyes and moving thought: On the spatial compatibility between eye movements and cognition. *Psychonomic Bulletin & Review, 14(4)*, 663–668.

———— (2009). Covert shifts of attention function as an implicit aid to insight. *Cognition, 111(2)*, 168–174.

Treisman, A. M. (1969). Strategies and models of selective attention. *Psychological Review, 76(3)*, 282–299.

Treisman, A. M., and Gelade, G. (1980). A feature-integration theory of attention. *Cognitive Psychology, 12(1)*, 97–136.

Turvey, M. T. (1992). Affordances and prospective control: An outline of the ontology. *Ecological Psychology, 4(3)*, 173–187.

Turvey, M. T., and Carello, C. (1995). Some dynamical themes in perception and action. In R. F. Port and T. Van Gelder (Eds), *Mind as motion: Explorations in the dynamics of cognition*. Cambridge, MA: MIT Press.

van der Heijden, A. H. C. (1996). Perception for selection, selection for action, and action for perception. *Visual Cognition, 3*, 357–361.

Van Orden, G. C., Holden, J. G., and Turvey, M. T. (2003). Self-organization of cognitive performance. *Journal of Experimental Psychology: General, 132(3)*, 331–350.

Van Rullen, R., and Thorpe, S. (2001). Is it a bird? Is it a plane? Ultra-rapid categorization of natural and artificial objects. *Perception, 30*, 655–668.

Wolfe, J. M. (1998). What can 1 million trials tell us about visual search? *Psychological Science, 9(1)*, 33–39.

Yarbus, A. L. (1967). *Eye movements and vision*. New York: Plenum Press.

38

EMBODIED REMEMBERING

John Sutton and Kellie Williamson

Introduction: the diversity of embodied remembering

Experiences of embodied remembering are familiar and diverse. We settle bodily into familiar chairs or find our way easily round familiar rooms. We inhabit our own kitchens or cars or workspaces effectively and comfortably, and feel disrupted when our habitual and accustomed objects or technologies change or break or are not available. Hearing a particular song can viscerally bring back either one conversation long ago, or just the urge to dance. Some people explicitly use their bodies to record, store, or cue memories. Others can move skilfully, without stopping to think, in complex and changing environments thanks to the cumulative expertise accrued in their history of fighting fires, or dancing, or playing hockey. The forms of memory involved in these cases may be distinct, operating at different timescales and levels, and by way of different mechanisms and media, but they often cooperate in the many contexts of our practices of remembering.

We share Maxine Sheets-Johnstone's suspicion that labels like "embodied" and "embodiment" sometimes function as "lexical band-aids" to cover residual theoretical gaps or wounds (2009a: 375) – after all, what else could cognition and remembering be, if not embodied? But we use the terms to mark the mundane but fascinating range of everyday experiences which the terms naturally cover. Though it is true that writers use "embodied memory" in very different ways, this is not necessarily a sign of endemic confusion. Given the dramatic variety of the relevant phenomena, embodied memory is appropriately of interest in both basic and applied studies of many distinctive topics – dance and sport, trauma and therapy, emotion and expertise, to mention just a few. It is a topic which rightly spans not only the range of the cognitive sciences, but also social science and the humanities. Two-way benefits could flow between theory and practice: academic discussions of "embodied cognition," which can sometimes be curiously abstract or anecdotal, could fruitfully engage with and in turn contribute to rich bodies of lore and expertise among practitioners of bodily skills and well-developed research traditions in fields like sports science, music psychology, and dance cognition.

Human beings are unusual in the variety of ways we relate to our history. Past events can be explicitly and consciously recollected, or can have more implicit influences on body,

 DOI: 10.4324/9781003322511-48

mind, and action. As well as the many respects in which the cumulative effects of the past drive our biology and our behavior, we also have the peculiar capacity to think *about* our histories. We can remember cooking a particular dish on a specific occasion for just that group of friends, though of course such memories are fallible. I remember cooking that meal *because* I did so, and this past experience is itself also the *object* of my thought. But we can also remember *how* to cook, as we show simply by doing so. In the latter case, accumulated experiences are actively embodied in actions. I need not explicitly recollect any specific past events, or even recognize that I am remembering, unless my smooth coping is disrupted. As Edward Casey puts it, such memory is intrinsic to the body: "because it re-enacts the past, it need not represent it" (1987: 147, 178).

Across different theoretical traditions, more implicit or habitual forms of body memory are thus distinguished from "personal" or "episodic" or "autobiographical" remembering (Sutton, Harris, and Barnier 2010). Below we explore the differences between these forms of memory: without committing to any view on whether they are parts of distinct memory "systems," we suggest that by initially distinguishing them we can address intriguing questions about the many ways in which they interact. Any discussion of our topic has to be able to deal with the variety of these phenomena. It would be misleading to restrict an account of embodied remembering either to the realm of meaning and conceptualization, or in contrast to embodied skills and habits alone.

The idea that explicit personal recall, when I remember particular past events, is a close ally of remembering how to perform bodily actions, was stated powerfully by Bartlett (1932: 201–2).

> Suppose I am making a stroke in a quick game, such as tennis or cricket ... When I make the stroke I do not, as a matter of fact, produce something absolutely new, and I never merely repeat something old. The stroke is literally manufactured out of the living visual and postural "schemata" of the moment and their interrelations. I may say, I may think that I reproduce exactly a series of text-book movements, but demonstrably I do not; just as, under other circumstances, I may say and think that I reproduce exactly some isolated event which I want to remember, and again demonstrably I do not.

In his radical constructivism, Bartlett suggests that the unique contextual processes of retrieval sculpt, not just the form or expression of a memory, but its very content. Just as the dynamic, on-the-fly embodied production of another successful backhand in tennis brings about a shot that may be familiar in type but is "absolutely new" in detail, so in remembering events my changing beliefs, interests, and motivations select and filter out materials to construct versions of the past (Saito 2000; Middleton and Brown 2005; Winter 2012). Like Bartlett, we treat remembering as itself an embodied skill. In dynamic self-organizing psychobiological systems like us, embodiment brings transformation.

A fuller treatment of our topic would include a section on the history of embodied remembering, showing that embodiment is a surprisingly pervasive theme, from the longer time frames studied in cognitive archaeology (Donald 1991; Jones 2007; Sutton 2008), through the intense attention offered to bodily aspects of memory and self by Descartes and Locke (Reiss 1996; Sutton 1998), to the key theoretical works of Nietzsche, Freud, the pragmatists James and Dewey, and the major phenomenologists Bergson (1991) and Merleau-Ponty (1962). But we can pick up one historical thread here by noting that some of Locke's remarks on memory, place, and embodied context were cited by Godden and Baddeley (1975) in one of the most striking experimental studies of embodied memory in modern cognitive psychology: divers who learned material underwater (in open-water sites near Oban in Scotland) had better memory when tested underwater, while material learned on dry land was recalled better on dry land. If the context dependence of memory, as they argued, is "robust enough to affect normal behaviour and performance away from the laboratory," then the location, state, and nature of our bodies both at the time of the original experience and at the time of later retrieval drive what and how we remember. Mainstream psychologists have long been systematically studying the context dependence of memory (Tulving and Thomson 1971; Smith and Vela 2001). This paved the way for a concerted movement, arising in the 1980s and 1990s from within the cognitive sciences, to study practical aspects of everyday memory in the wild (Neisser 1978, 1997). Updating both Bartlett's constructivism and his vision of a social and cultural psychology of memory, cognitive theorists drew on connectionism and on Vygotskian developmental psychology, and at the same time found experimental and institutional space for the rapid expansion of work on autobiographical memory and self in real-world contexts (Conway 2005; Sutton 2009; Fivush 2011). These strands of the recent history of the sciences of memory are perhaps sometimes neglected by writers on embodied cognition in general, in their urgency to paint the new paradigm as a radical break from the bad old days of rigid cognitivist individualism (Glenberg 1997; Brockmeier 2010; Glenberg, Witt, and Metcalfe 2013). Some areas of memory science do certainly retain neurocentric tendencies, treating body and world either as merely external influences on the true internal memory processes, or as just the objects of memory: but pluralist alternatives have long been available by which to thematize the multiple resources of everyday ecologies of memory (Engel 1999; Conway and Pleydell-Pearce 2000; Siegel 2001; Welzer and Markowitsch 2005). We illustrate this by examining autobiographical memory and habitual or skill memory in turn: in each case, we suggest not only that the forms of remembering involved are in various respects "embodied," but also that there are intricate relationships between them.

Embodied autobiographical memory

Recent psychological studies of autobiographical remembering emphasize that tracking the past is not necessarily its key function. Remembering also plays important and heavily context-sensitive roles in maintaining and renegotiating self-narratives, in promoting social relations, and in directing future action (Bluck, Alea, Habermas, and Rubin 2005); recent work especially stresses the future-oriented role of memory in guiding simulations of possible future events (Schacter and Addis 2007; Boyer 2009). Personal narratives, social interactions, and future planning are often expressed and embodied in rich social and material settings. So autobiographical recall is embodied in that it is often *for* action and communication (Glenberg 1997; Middleton and Brown 2005), even though the specific past experiences I now remember may be long gone and may have left little or no trace on my current environment.

As well as being a conduit for sharing and renegotiating experience, the body can also be a cue or trigger for personal memory experiences, which can occur either deliberately or unintentionally. The involuntary activation of a particular memory by way of sensory triggers is most commonly associated with smells and tastes, as classically in Proust (Berntsen 2009). But even Proust's narrator is just as powerfully drawn back into explicit recollection by way of the body's familiarity with certain places – rooms, the location of furniture, the angle of the sunlight, the orientation of the body on the bed (see Casey 1987: 169–78). The mnemonic significance of objects, places, and environments operates by way of temperature or inter-oceptive bodily sensations such as hunger, as well as through encounters with specific remembered landmarks and locations. There can be different relations between familiarity and recollection. The pre-reflective sense of embodied intimacy with a setting may coexist or merge both with culturally anchored schemata that suggest what usually happens here according to the social frameworks of memory, and with the more precise evocation of particular located personal experiences (Halbwachs 1925/1992; de Certeau 1984; Habermas and Paha 2002; Hill 2011). More deliberate bodily anchors for personal memory include using the body to store information or evocative cues temporarily, as in writing a phone number on one's palm, or indelibly, as in the "system" of tattoos and other traces laboriously and fallibly constructed by Leonard in *Memento* (Sutton 2009). For those without Leonard's amnesic difficulties, bodily movements such as gestures can be an effective complement to other forms of thinking, remembering, and communicating, often stabilizing or anchoring complex concepts so as to facilitate communication or reconsideration (Hutchins 2005, 2010; Streeck, Goodwin, and LeBaron 2012; Bietti and Galiana Castello 2013).

Further claims about the body's influence on autobiographical recall come from cognitive psychological research on the importance of sensory and motor functions in memory. One tradition examines enhanced memory for actions performed by the subject herself, compared with observing actions being performed by others (Zimmer *et al.* 2001). Other experimental research addresses embodiment in the form of facial expression and body posture, as discussed in the chapter by Dijkstra (Chapter 35, this volume). Future work might extend these methods to examine the mnemonic significance of those culturally specific postures by which social norms and distinctions are incorporated (Connerton 1989: 73–74).

In addition to these ways in which bodily processes influence autobiographical memory, we can also make sense of the stronger idea that the body just is, or perhaps is the vehicle of, such explicit recall. In developing their systematic causal theory of declarative memory, C. B. Martin and Max Deutscher (1966) began by outlining a striking case in which remembering a particular event is actually constituted by certain bodily movements. Consider, they asked us,

> the case where some swimming is an example of remembering and not, as is usual, an example of remembering how. Suppose that someone has never dog-paddled. He is not good at visualization and has never learned any words which would describe swimming. His method of representing the one time at which he saw a man dog-paddle is his actually doing the dog-paddle stroke. We can imagine him trying to remember the curious action that the man went through in the water. He cannot describe it, and cannot form any picture of it. He cannot bring it back. He gets into the water, experimenting a little until suddenly he gets it right and exclaims, "Aha, that's it!".
>
> *(Martin and Deutscher 1966: 161–62)*

Here the body is the very vehicle of episodic memory. Indeed, the recall of personally experienced events even in more typical contexts often has a kinesthetic component. As I am telling you about a difficult conversation at work, or recollecting my pleasurable walk in the park the other day, specific movement tendencies may arise, in addition to other sensory-perceptual, spatial, and emotional detail (Rubin 2006). I may actually move my head and eyes, or partly reinstate a pattern of gestures in remembering the embodied alignment of that earlier conversation; or I may merely retouch or alight briefly again on the specific combination of physical warmth and affective comfort I felt during that summer stroll. When those who play music or sport pick up a household tool and quietly enact a momentary shadow performance, or simply run a fragment of air guitar or a backhand down the line, they are sometimes just remembering how to play. But on other occasions, perhaps especially in joyous re-enactment of pleasurable performance, or when something hasn't been quite right, they are also remembering a particular incident or episode: in the latter case, merging that embodied autobiographical memory with an equally specific form of operative motor imagination, they can work in a more or less goal-directed fashion towards a refashioning of embodied style.

These phenomena are returning us to consideration of more habitual forms of embodied remembering. We suggest that both when remembering our past alone, and when talking together about shared experiences, there can be an iterative, mutually reinforcing play between personal memory and embodied habits or skills. The familiar actions involved in cooking or dancing, or in enjoying a conversation with old friends are, as Bartlett noted, neither precise and mechanical repetitions, nor wholly unprecedented novelties. Cooking utensils which embody collective family memories, for example, also often elicit, more or less explicitly, specific personal and interpersonal memories: not just about what we used to do or would always do, but sometimes about particular family stories (Sutton and Hernandez 2007; Shore 2009).

Before scoring his second goal in the 1986 World Cup quarter-final against England, Diego Maradona ran through the defense, with his center forward Jorge Valdano keeping pace alongside. As Valdano later told it, after the game Maradona apologized for not passing, even though at first he intended to: "Maradona explained that, as he neared the England goal, he remembered being in a similar situation against Peter Shilton seven years earlier at Wembley. In 1979 he had missed but, thinking about it now, he realised where he'd made his mistake. Maradona concluded that he didn't need Valdano after all and could score by himself" (Winner 2011: 23). Obviously Maradona's success here relies on exquisitely honed bodily and technical skills. But he was also set apart from other players by effective decision making at unimaginable speed: here his choice draws directly on a specific past experience. Such precise use of episodic memory to dictate or sculpt present action is striking because it demonstrates the openness of our motor processes to fast, effortless top-down influence, and the conversion of personal memory into usable online form to feed bodily skill in real time. Such interanimation of skill or habit memory with personal memory is not always easy to notice: but, we suggest, it is a widespread feature of the practice of everyday life.

Embodied skill memory

In textbooks on memory in psychology and cognitive neuroscience, the topics discussed under the term "procedural memory" (memory for the performance of particular actions) sometimes focus primarily on lower-level phenomena of conditioning and associative learning (Eichenbaum and Cohen 2001). This allows for coverage of the neuroanatomy of habit learning, and of the rapidly developing study of molecular mechanisms. Though dynamic, network-oriented neuroscience is increasingly devoted to examining interactions between distinct brain systems, it can sometimes be hard to see how these phenomena of procedural memory scale up to the kinds of habits and skills involved in embodied, culturally embedded human routines, performances, and rituals. Yet on initial description at least, embodied habits and skills do seem to share certain features with basic bodily responses to repeated experience. Consequently they too can appear to differ dramatically from other more explicit forms of memory: this is underlined by the apparent neural dissociation, such that some people with dense amnesia for specific events in their own history seem nonetheless to be able to learn new skills (Squire 2004; but compare Stanley and Krakauer 2013). Because the forms of memory seem so different, some have suggested that procedural memory is not a form of "memory" at all (Moyal-Sharrock 2009), and others have argued that "memory" does not qualify as a coherent natural kind for scientific investigation (Michaelian 2011). While we take the more ecumenical view that the various ways in which history animates body and mind are interconnected, more embodied forms of memory do have features that sharply mark them as distinctive.

If I remember how to cook, ride a bike, or play a cover drive in cricket, I have engaged in practice and training: these embodied memories derive from many repeated experiences rather than one. There is no single, specific past event which causes my current activity, as there is in episodic memory, nor do I need be aware at all of any previous performances or of the historical source of my know-how (indeed, it is often crucial that I am not aware of anything beyond the present context) (Sutton 2007). In his phenomenological study, Edward Casey offers a working definition of "habitual body memory": it is "an active immanence of the past in the body that informs present bodily actions in an efficacious, orienting, and regular manner" (1987: 149; see also Casey 2000; Connerton 1989: 72; Summa, Koch, Fuchs, and Müller 2012). These are not rote mechanical processes which simply reproduce past performances; rather, such body memory operates flexibly, as the practitioner adapts and adjusts to changing circumstances, subtly modifying her responses to fit the needs of the moment. Some theorists have sought to downgrade "habits" to more reflex-like status. For Ryle, "mere habits" are single-track dispositions implemented automatically, unlike the flexible exercise of practical intelligence (1963:. 41–50, 126–30). Others place habits within the realm of intentional action, noting the role of care and attention; no matter how effectively we have grooved our expertise as drivers, Brett points out, "the habit of paying attention to the road is one of the necessary ingredients in being a good driver" (1981: 365–66; see also Pollard 2006). But it is hard to pin down just what kinds of attention or awareness are in play here.

Although skills, habits, and embodied movement capacities are often easy to initiate spontaneously in the right context, they are difficult to think through consciously, and to articulate verbally. Some coaches and teachers are better than others at finding instructions, metaphors, or nudges to help novice and expert practitioners, and some critics and commentators can describe flowing performance with more striking explicit descriptions. Learning by apprenticeship is a central part of human socialization, and does sometimes involve explicit description and some decomposition of tasks (Sterelny 2012; Sutton 2013). But talking well about embodied skills is, in most contexts, an entirely different skill from the first-order capacities themselves, which rely more on complex pattern recognition and on other coordinated perceptual-motor-memory processes which no-one really understands (Sutton 2007). For this reason, practitioners and theorists alike often draw sharp lines between embodied skill memory, on the one hand, and more "cognitive" or "mindful" processes: Hubert Dreyfus, for example, argues that "mindedness is the enemy of embodied coping" (Dreyfus 2007: 353; see also Ennen 2003). Performers are all too aware that certain forms of reflection and thought can disrupt their skilful action, and often talk of relying on their body memory alone, and allowing automated responses to flow intuitively. But this does not mean that one is unconscious when actively remembering how to do something: in different contexts, various forms of kinetic or kinesthetic awareness or circumspection allow for the ongoing monitoring of skilful performance (Sheets-Johnstone 2003; Wheeler 2005: 131–43). Talk about embodied skills can be analogical and indirect, with groups of experts often evolving local responses to the challenges of languaging experience, often "beyond the easy flow of everyday speech" (Sheets-Johnstone 2009b: 336; see Candau 2010 for the case of finding words for olfactory experience and thus sharing memory for smells). It is a mistake to treat embodied memory as so entirely intuitive as to be outside the psychological realm, for this is to reinforce dichotomies between acting and thinking, and between body and mind, which need to be thoroughly dismantled to achieve better understanding of these complex phenomena (Montero 2010; Sutton, McIlwain, Christensen, and Geeves 2011).

Accounts of body memory can, further, address the bodily systems of interoception and affect which partly ground our deep feelings of familiarity in our world, and our awareness of self and time (Damasio 2003). They can extend the taxonomy to include situational and intercorporeal memory, covering our spatial awareness and our implicit sense of a history of embodied experiences with other people (Fuchs 2012: 13–15), and the way the body carries cultural norms and tastes, by way of incorporated techniques, practices, or ceremonies (Bourdieu 1977: 72–87; Connerton 1989: 79–88; Strathern 1996). Questions about the bodily nature of memory are under intense investigation in the cognitive anthropology of religion and ritual behavior, where varying levels of emotional arousal are seen, on different theories, as grounding different kinds of memory and thus dictating the required frequency of religious ritual performance (Whitehouse 2005; Czachesz 2010). Other writers focus on memory for pain and trauma, and cases in which the usual pre-reflective nature of embodied memory breaks down (Casey 1987: 154–57; Haaken 1998; Fuchs 2012: 16–18). We now briefly mention two further lines of research about the body and memory.

In a phenomenological investigation of certain kinds of "bodily micromovements" which she calls "ghost gestures," Elizabeth Behnke (1997) analyzes a range of "tendencies to movement" such as "persisting patterns of trying, bracing, freezing" which persist as "the effective presence of the past," the inadvertent residues of embodied activities (such as digging in the garden) or specific historical patterns of comportment (such as hugging the computer). Signature patterns of movement, posture, and gesture are often coupled with particular modes of affective experience and expression: as Behnke argues, they can sometimes be opened up to kinesthetic awareness, as we counter our easy sensorimotor amnesia, and find ways of noticing and perhaps shifting our more rigid or fused bodily habits (Behnke 1997, 2008; see also Samudra 2008; Shusterman 2011; McIlwain and Sutton 2014).

More dramatic pathologies of memory arise in the amnesias and dementias: in some cases, embodied remembering can here act as a partial counter to a gradual or sudden loss of explicit memory. As explicit access to particular past experiences comes under threat, and with it the possibility of incorporating distinct episodes into roughly coherent life narratives, other ways of stabilizing or inhabiting a familiar world become more salient. The fictional case of Leonard in *Memento*, as we noted, dramatizes a reliance on both habits and procedures and on systems of embodied or externalized traces (Sutton 2009). In real cases of dementia, the relation between explicit knowledge of one's own past and the forms of bodily familiarity with one's world can be complicated, though remembering how to do various tasks does often persist longer. The anthropologist Janelle Taylor argues that interpersonal care and mutual recognition can rest on broader patterns of shared activities than simply talking about particular past events and experiences: conversation, for example, involves tone, voice pattern, and turn-taking corporeal sequencing as much as the exchange of information (2008: 326–28). As well as deploying compensatory social or material scaffolding to externalize access to lost information (Drayson and Clark, in press), people experiencing the early stages of dementia may still rely on practical, situational familiarity with environments, objects, and sequences of bodily actions in buffering themselves from the immediate effects of decline in explicit memory.

But some of the most powerful empirical and ethnographic studies of embodied skill memory have been undertaken in the context not of deficit and struggle but of extraordinary or expert capacities. In music, concert pianist Gabriela Imreh collaborated with cognitive psychologist Roger Chaffin and colleagues in long-term experimental studies of the precise stages by which she memorized Bach's *Italian Concerto* (Chaffin, Imreh, and Crawford 2002; Geeves, Christensen, Sutton, and McIlwain 2008). In a quite distinctive musical and theoretical register, David Sudnow documented the often agonizing process of learning improvisational jazz piano: in gradually remembering how to find ways round the keyboard and the ongoing musical piece in a flowing rather than disjointed way, Sudnow has to incorporate an open-ended but constrained repertoire of possible muscular and affective patterns of musical action (Sudnow 2001). In studying embodied remembering in contemporary dance, Catherine Stevens and colleagues have investigated the interplay of verbal and movement phrases during rehearsal and in the process of choreographic creativity (Stevens, Malloch, McKechnie, and Steven 2003; see also Sheets-Johnstone 2012), while David Kirsh's team implemented mixed-method research on the memory functions of dancers' "marking" practices, when they re-embody or rehearse various fragmentary or partial movement forms (Kirsh 2013).

Embodied memory in these contexts is firmly embedded in complex and idiosyncratic cultural settings, with unique social and historical backgrounds and norms. These cases remind us that by examining activities and practices of remembering, and in giving consideration to the role of bodily as well as neural resources, we also open up memory's public dimensions. Embodied remembering occurs in a social and material world in which objects and other people may support or transform the processes, form, and content of memory. If memory is embodied, it is also arguably situated and distributed.

In this chapter we have selectively introduced key themes from contemporary studies of the diverse forms of embodied remembering. We need to draw on philosophy of mind and action, phenomenology, psychology, cognitive neuroscience, anthropology, and performance studies if we are effectively to mesh conceptual, experimental, and ethnographic approaches to these diverse and complex phenomena. For this reason, in this short chapter we have sought to provide points of entry into these rich multidisciplinary literatures, hoping to encourage others to engage with these fascinating topics.

Embodied Remembering update

Across the disciplines of memory research, studies of embodied remembering have flourished since the first edition of this handbook. We leave our chapter as it stands as an advanced introduction, and we encourage readers to explore the current state of the field using the following entry points.

For recent reviews of experimental work on embodied remembering in psychology and cognitive neuroscience respectively, see Francesco Iani, 'Embodied memories: reviewing the role of the body in memory processes,' *Psychonomic Bulletin & Review 26* (2019), 747–1766; Giuseppe Riva, 'The neuroscience of body memory: from the self through the space to the others,' *Cortex 104* (2018), 241–260. Such evidence is put to original philosophical use by Denis Perrin, 'Embodied episodic memory: a new case for causalism?,' *Intellectica 74* (2021), 229–252, while important new concepts are introduced by Mark Rowlands, 'Rilkean memory,' *Southern Journal of Philosophy 53* (2015), 141–154, and Marina Trakas, 'Kinetic memories: an embodied form of remembering the personal past,' *Journal of Mind and Behavior 42* (2021), 139–174. Interesting links with dynamical systems theory, robotics, and virtual reality are made respectively in Tom Froese & Eduardo J. Izquierdo, 'A dynamical approach to the phenomenology of body memory,' *Journal of Consciousness Studies 25* (2018), 20–46; Antonio Chella, 'Rilkean memories and the self of a robot,' *Philosophies 4* (2019), 20; Anco Peeters & Miguel Segundo-Ortin, 'Misplacing memories? An enactive approach to the virtual memory palace,' *Consciousness & Cognition 76* (2019), 102834.

A number of papers have defended enhanced accounts of procedural or embodied memory as rich and open to other cognitive processes, sometimes challenging the sharpness of the dichotomy between declarative and procedural memory on conceptual, empirical, and phenomenological grounds: see Wayne Christensen, John Sutton, & Kath Bicknell, 'Memory systems and the control of skilled action,' *Philosophical Psychology 32* (2019), 693–719; Felipe de Brigard, 'Know-how, intellectualism, and memory systems,' *Philosophical Psychology 32* (2019), 720–759; and Jonathan Najenson, 'Mnemic systems and the mnemic character of procedural memory,' *British Journal for the Philosophy of Science* (in press).

Embodied remembering plays a central part in recent work on situated and distributed emotions: see Giovanna Colombetti & Joel Krueger, 'Scaffoldings of the affective mind,' *Philosophical Psychology 28* (2015), 1157–1176, and McArthur Mingon & John Sutton, 'Why robots can't haka: skilled performance and embodied knowledge in the Māori haka,' *Synthese 199* (2021), 4337–4365.

Phenomenological and ethnographic work in social and clinical psychology and in cultural memory studies applies theories of embodied remembering to complex social phenomena: see Rafael F. Narváez, *Embodied Collective Memory* (University Press of America, 2013); Maria Tumarkin, 'Crumbs of memory: tracing the more-than-representational in family memory,' *Memory Studies 6,* (2013), 310–320; Steven D. Brown & Paula Reavey, *Vital Memory and Affect: living with a difficult past* (Routledge, 2015); Christian Tewes, 'Embodied habitual memory formation: enacted or extended?', in G. Etzelmüller & C. Tewes (eds), *Embodiment in Evolution and Culture* (Mohr Siebeck, 2016), 31–56; Emily Keightley & Michael Pickering, *Memory and the Management of Change: repossessing the past* (Palgrave, 2017); Lars-Christer Hydén, 'Dementia, embodied memories, and the self,' *Journal of Consciousness Studies 25* (2018), 225–241; Allan Køster, 'Longing for concreteness: how body memory matters for continuing bonds,' *Mortality 25* (2020), 389–401; Charishma Ratnam & Danielle Drozdzewski, 'Detour: bodies, memories, and mobilities in and around the home,' *Mobilities 15* (2020), 757–775; Carla Carmona, 'Practices of remembering a movement in the dance studio,' *Synthese 199* (2021), 3611–3643; and Julia Giese & Emily Keightley, 'Dancing through time: a methodological exploration of embodied memories,' *Memory Studies* (in press).

References

Bartlett, F. (1932) *Remembering: A study in experimental and social psychology*, Cambridge: Cambridge University Press.

Behnke, E. A. (1997) "Ghost gestures: Phenomenological investigations of bodily micromovements and their intercorporeal implications," *Human Studies*, 20(2), 181–201.

———— (2008) "Interkinaesthetic affectivity: A phenomenological approach," *Continental Philosophy Review*, 41, 143–161.

Bergson, H. (1991) *Matter and memory* (5th ed.; N. M. Paul and W. S. Palmer, Trans.), New York: Zone Books. (Orig. publ. 1896.)

Berntsen, D. (2009) *Involuntary autobiographical memories: An introduction to the unbidden past*, Cambridge: Cambridge University Press.

Bietti, L. M., and Galiana Castello, F. (2013) "Embodied reminders in family interactions: Multimodal collaboration in remembering activities," *Discourse Studies*, 15(6).

Bluck, S., Alea, N., Habermas, T., and Rubin, D. C. (2005) "A tale of three functions: The self-reported uses of autobiographical memory," *Social Cognition*, 23(1), 91–117.

Bourdieu, P. (1977) *Outline of a theory of practice*, Cambridge: Cambridge University Press.

Boyer, P. (2009) "What are memories for? Functions of recall in cognition and culture," in P. Boyer and J. Wertsch (eds), *Memory in mind and culture* (pp. 3–28). Cambridge: Cambridge University Press.

Brett, N. (1981) "Human habits," *Canadian Journal of Philosophy*, 11, 357–376.

Brockmeier, J. (2010) "After the archive: Remapping memory," *Culture & Psychology*, 16(1), 5–35.

Candau, J. (2010) "Shared memory, odours and sociotransmitters, or "Save the interaction!" *Outlines: Critical Practice Studies*, 2, 29–42.

Casey, E. (1987) *Remembering: A Phenomenological Study*, Bloomington, IN: Indiana University Press.

———— (2000) "The ghost of embodiment: On bodily habitudes and schemata," in D. Welton (ed.), *Body and flesh* (pp. 207–225), Oxford: Blackwell.

Chaffin, R., Imreh, G., and Crawford, M. (2002) *Practicing perfection: Memory and piano performance*, Mahwah, NJ: Erlbaum.

Connerton, P. (1989) *How societies remember*, Cambridge: Cambridge University Press.

Conway, M. A. (2005) "Memory and the self," *Journal of Memory and Language*, 53(4), 594–628.

Conway, M. A., and Pleydell-Pearce, C. W. (2000) "The construction of autobiographical memories in the self-memory system," *Psychological Review*, 107(2), 261.

Czachesz, I. (2010) "Long-term, explicit memory in rituals," *Journal of Cognition and Culture*, 10, 327–339.

Damasio, A. (2003) "Feelings of emotion and the self," *Annals of the New York Academy of Sciences*, 1001, 253–261.

de Certeau, M. (1984) *The practice of everyday life*, Berkeley: University of California Press.

Donald, M. (1991) *Origins of the modern mind: Three stages in the evolution of culture and cognition*, Cambridge, MA: Harvard University Press.

Drayson, Z., and Clark, A. (in press) "Augmentation, agency, and the spreading of the mental state," *Consciousness and Cognition*.

Dreyfus, H. L. (2007) "The return of the myth of the mental," *Inquiry*, 50, 352–365.

Eichenbaum, H., and Cohen, N. J. (2001) *From conditioning to conscious recollection: Memory systems of the brain*, New York: Oxford University Press.

Engel, S. (1999) *Context is everything: The nature of memory*, New York: Freeman.

Ennen, E. (2003) "Phenomenological coping skills and the striatal memory system," *Phenomenology and the Cognitive Sciences*, 2, 299–325.

Fivush, R. (2011) "The development of autobiographical memory," *Annual Review of Psychology*, 62, 559–582.

Fuchs, T. (2012) "The phenomenology of body memory," in S. C. Koch, T. Fuchs, M. Summa, and C. Müller (eds), *Body memory, metaphor and movement* (pp. 9–22). Amsterdam: John Benjamins.

Geeves, A., Christensen, W., Sutton, J., and McIlwain, D. J. F. (2008) Critical review of the book *Practicing perfection: Memory and piano performance*, by R. Chaffin, G. Imreh, and M. Crawford. *Empirical Musicology Review*, 3(3), 163–172.

Glenberg, A. M. (1997) "What memory is for," *Behavioral and Brain Sciences*, 20, 1–55.

Glenberg, A. M., Witt, J. K., and Metcalfe, J. (2013) "From the revolution to embodiment: 25 years of cognitive psychology," *Perspectives on Psychological Science*, 8, 573–585.

Godden, D. R., and Baddeley, A. D. (1975) "Context-dependent memory in two natural environments: On land and underwater," *British Journal of Psychology*, 66(3), 325–331.

Haaken, J. (1998) *Pillar of salt: Gender, memory, and the perils of looking back*, New Brunswick, NJ: Rutgers University Press.

Habermas, T., and Paha, C. (2002) "Souvenirs and other personal objects: Reminding of past events and significant others in the transition to university," in J. D. Webster and B. K. Haight (eds), *Critical advances in reminiscence work* (pp. 123–138). New York: Springer.

Halbwachs, M. (1925/1992) "The social frameworks of memory," in L. Coser (ed.), *On collective memory*. Chicago: Chicago University Press.

Hill, S. (2011) "Memory in place," *New Zealand Geographer*, 67, 16–20.

Hutchins, E. (2005) "Material anchors for conceptual blends," *Journal of Pragmatics*, 37, 1555–1577.

——— (2010) "Imagining the cognitive life of things," in L. Malafouris and C. Renfrew (eds), *The cognitive life of things: Recasting the boundaries of the mind* (pp. 91–101). Cambridge: McDonald Archaeological Institute.

Jones, A. (2007) *Memory and material culture*, Cambridge: Cambridge University Press.

Kirsh, D. (2013) "Embodied cognition and the magical future of interaction design," *ACM Transactions on Computer-Human Interaction*, 20(1), 30.

Martin, C. B., and Deutscher, M. (1966) "Remembering," *Philosophical Review*, 75(2), 161–196.

McIlwain, D. J. F., and Sutton, J. (2014) "Yoga from the mat up: How words alight on bodies," *Educational Philosophy and Theory*. doi:10.1080/00131857.2013.779216

Merleau-Ponty, M. (1962) *Phenomenology of perception* (C. Smith, Trans.), London: Routledge. (Orig. publ. 1945.)

Michaelian, K. (2011) "Is memory a natural kind?" *Memory Studies*, 4, 170–189.

Middleton, D., and Brown, S. D. (2005) *The social psychology of experience: Studies in remembering and forgetting*, London: Sage.

Montero, B. (2010) "Does bodily awareness interfere with highly skilled movement?" *Inquiry*, 53, 105–122.

Moyal-Sharrock, D. (2009) "Wittgenstein and the memory debate," *New Ideas in Psychology*, 27, 213–227.

Neisser, U. (Ed.) (1978) *Memory observed: Remembering in natural contexts*, New York: W. H. Freeman.

Neisser, U. (1997) "The ecological study of memory," *Philosophical Transactions of the Royal Society B: Biological Sciences*, 352(1362), 1697–1701.

Pollard, B. (2006) "Explaining actions with habits," *American Philosophical Quarterly*, 43, 57–68.

Reiss, T. J. (1996) "Denying the body? Memory and the dilemmas of history in Descartes," *Journal of the History of Ideas*, 57, 587–607.

Rubin, D. C. (2006) "The basic-systems model of episodic memory," *Perspectives on Psychological Science*, 1(4), 277–311.

Ryle, G. (1963) *The concept of mind*, Harmondsworth: Penguin. (Orig. publ. 1949.)

Saito, A. (Ed.) (2000) *Bartlett, culture and cognition*, Hove, East Sussex: Psychology Press.

Samudra, J. K. (2008) "Memory in our body: Thick participation and the translation of kinesthetic experience," *American Ethnologist*, 35, 665–681.

Schacter, D. L., and Addis, D. R. (2007) "On the constructive episodic simulation of past and future events," *Behavioral and Brain Sciences*, 30, 299–351.

Sheets-Johnstone, M. (2003) "Kinesthetic memory," *Theoria et Historia Scientiarum*, 7, 69–92.

——— (2009a) "Animation: The fundamental, essential, and properly descriptive concept," *Continental Philosophy Review*, 42, 375–400.

——— (2009b) *The corporeal turn*, Exeter: Imprint Academic.

——— (2012) "From movement to dance," *Phenomenology and the Cognitive Sciences*, 11, 39–57.

Shore, B. (2009) "Making time for family: Schemas for long-term family memory," *Social Indicators Research*, 93, 95–103.

Shusterman, R. (2011) "Muscle memory and the somaesthetic pathologies of everyday life," *Human Movement*, 12, 4–15.

Siegel, D. J. (2001) "Memory: An overview, with emphasis on developmental, interpersonal, and neuro-biological aspects," *Journal of the American Academy of Child & Adolescent Psychiatry,* 40(9), 997–1011.

Smith, S. M., and Vela, E. (2001) "Environmental context-dependent memory: A review and meta-analysis," *Psychonomic Bulletin & Review,* 8(2), 203–220.

Squire, L. (2004) "Memory systems of the brain: A brief history and current perspective," *Neurobiology of Learning and Memory,* 82, 171–177.

Stanley, J., and Krakauer, J. W. (2013) "Motor skill depends on knowledge of facts," *Frontiers in Human Neuroscience,* 7(503).

Sterelny, K. (2012) *The evolved apprentice,* Cambridge, MA: MIT Press.

Stevens, C., Malloch, S., McKechnie, S., and Steven, N. (2003) "Choreographic cognition: The time-course and phenomenology of creating a dance," *Pragmatics and Cognition,* 11, 299–329.

Strathern, A. (1996) *Body thoughts,* Ann Arbor: University of Michigan Press.

Streeck, J., Goodwin, C., and LeBaron, C. (eds) (2012) *Embodied interaction: Language and body in the material world,* Cambridge: Cambridge University Press.

Sudnow, D. (2001) *Ways of the hand: A rewritten account,* Cambridge, MA: MIT Press (Orig. publ. 1978.)

Summa, M., Koch, S. C., Fuchs, T., and Müller, C. (2012) "Body memory: An integration," in S. C. Koch, T. Fuchs, M. Summa, and C. Müller (eds), *Body memory, metaphor and movement* (pp. 417–444). Amsterdam: John Benjamins.

Sutton, D., and Hernandez, M. (2007) "Voices in the kitchen: Cooking tools as inalienable possessions," *Oral History,* 35, 67–76.

Sutton, J. (1998) *Philosophy and memory traces: Descartes to connectionism,* Cambridge: Cambridge University Press.

———— (2007) "Batting, habit, and memory: The embodied mind and the nature of skill," *Sport in Society,* 10, 763–786.

———— (2008). Material agency, skills, and history: Distributed cognition and the archaeology of memory. In L. Malafouris and C. Knappett (eds), *Material agency: Towards a non-anthropocentric approach* (pp. 37–55). Berlin: Springer.

———— (2009) "The feel of the world: Exograms, habits, and the confusion of types of memory," in A. Kania (ed.), *Memento* (pp. 65–86) (Philosophers on Film), London: Routledge.

———— (2013) "Skill and collaboration in the evolution of human cognition," *Biological Theory,* 8(1), 28–36.

Sutton, J., Harris, C. B., and Barnier, A. J. (2010) "Memory and cognition," in S. Radstone and B. Schwarz (eds), *Memory: Histories, theories, debates* (pp. 209–226), New York: Fordham University Press.

Sutton, J., McIlwain, D. J. F., Christensen, W., and Geeves, A. (2011) "Applying intelligence to the reflexes: Embodied skills and habits between Dreyfus and Descartes." *Journal of the British Society for Phenomenology,* 42(1), 78–103.

Taylor, J. S. (2008) "On recognition, caring, and dementia," *Medical Anthropology Quarterly,* 22, 313–335.

Tewes, Christian. (2016) "Embodied habitual memory formation: enacted or extended?," in G. Etzelmüller, and C. Tewes (eds), *Embodiment in evolution and culture* (pp. 31–56). Tübingen: Mohr Siebeck.

Tulving, E., and Thomson, D. M. (1971) "Retrieval Processes in recognition memory: Effects of associative context," *Journal of Experimental Psychology,* 87(1), 116–124.

Welzer, H., and Markowitsch, H. (2005) "Towards a bio-psycho-social model of autobiographical memory," *Memory,* 13(1), 63–78.

Wheeler, M. (2005) *Reconstructing the cognitive world: The next step,* Cambridge, MA: MIT Press.

Whitehouse, H. (2005) "Emotion, memory, and religious rituals: An assessment of two theories," in K. Milton and M. Svasek (eds), *Mixed emotions: Anthropological studies of feeling* (pp. 91–108), Oxford: Berg.

Winner, D. (2011) "Dennis Bergkamp," *Blizzard: The Football Quarterly,* 1, 22–30.

Winter, A. (2012) *Memory: Fragments of a modern history,* Chicago: University of Chicago Press.

Zimmer, H. D., Cohen, R. L., Guynn, M. J., Engelkamp, J., Kormi-Nouri, R., and Foley, M. A. (2001) *Memory for action: A distinct form of episodic memory?* Oxford: Oxford University Press.

PART 10

Reflections on Embodied Cognition

39

THE REPLICATION CRISIS IN EMBODIED COGNITION RESEARCH

Edouard Machery

During the 2010s, psychology has witnessed an unexpected number of failed replications, some of which have cast doubt on whole research programs such as social priming or ego depletion.[1] Some prominent replication failures have implicated findings in embodied cognition research, including foundational ones. This chapter reviews these replication failures and assesses their impact for the prospects of embodied cognition research. I argue that these failures suggest treating the empirical literature with caution.

Embodied cognition research is diverse (Shapiro 2019): it ranges from claims about the role of the body in cognition to claims about the re-enactment of perceptual experiences in thought, about language understanding, and about the constitutive (in contrast to merely causal) role of bodily representations in cognition. Its boundaries are also vague, and embodied cognition research often blends into other research programs such as situated cognition. The diversity of evidence brought to bear on embodied cognition research is thus, unsurprisingly, diverse, ranging from behavioral data to neuroimaging data to neuropsychological data. Because of this diversity, assessing the significance of replication failures for the whole research program is difficult: Even if some important studies fail to replicate, others, perhaps many others, do, or at least might. As a result, the present assessment of embodied research programs in light of replication failures should be viewed as tentative.

In the section "Replication," I discuss the nature and interpretation of replications in order to provide a framework for interpreting the replication failures discussed in the remainder of this chapter. In "Mind-Body Coupling," I review replication failures bearing on the coupling between the mind and the body. The section "Perceptual and Motor Representations in Cognition and Language Comprehension" discusses replication failures bearing on the relation between concepts and percepts as well as language comprehension. I discuss the general significance of replication failures for embodied cognition research in the conclusion.

Replication

The nature and typology of replication has been extensively debated in recent years (e.g., Schmidt 2009; Machery 2020; Nosek and Errington 2020). Generally, to replicate an experiment is to redo it while changing some of its features. Different types of replications

 DOI: 10.4324/9781003322511-50

change different aspects of the original experiments (i.e., the experiments that are replicated). An important type of replication, often called "exact" or "direct replication" (or "experimental-units replication" in Machery 2020), involves redoing an original experiment with new participants (or, more broadly, new experimental units if participants aren't individuals, but, e.g., classrooms or companies).

The success of a replication can be assessed in different ways, all of which have strengths and weaknesses. The most commonly used method is statistical significance: The replication succeeds if it is significant. Confidence intervals have also been used: The replication succeeds if the statistic of interest in the replication is within the confidence interval of the corresponding statistic in the original study, or, inversely, the statistic of interest in the original study is within the confidence interval of the corresponding statistic in the replication. Others prefer aggregating the results of the original study and the replication, and assessing whether there is an effect by examining the pooled data. In this chapter, I will embrace a pluralist approach: Success or failure depends on the convergence of criteria.

One should exert caution in interpreting failed replications because a replication can fail even if the original result is a true positive. A failed replication can simply be a false negative due to random sampling or measurement error; it can also result from insufficient power, when the original effect size was overestimated and when the replication's sample size was set so as to detect this original effect size. Replications can also fail because of sometimes subtle differences between the original study and its replication; particularly noteworthy is the possibility that the participants in the original study and its replication differ (because of cultural differences or because an effect that was real then no longer exists years later).

Of course, a replication can also fail because the original result was a false positive. False positives too happen for many reasons, including random sampling. Much discussed however is the role of questionable research practices, scientific practices that increase the proportion of false positives among significant results. Publication bias happens when only a subset of the research conducted, primarily the research that results in significant results, is published (Rosenthal 1979); p-hacking occurs when scientists engage in practices (dropping outliers, adding or removing covariates, etc.) that increase the probability of obtaining a significant result (Simmons et al. 2011). While questionable research practices are not instances of scientific misconduct, they nonetheless reduce the reliability of scientific literatures. Surveys have shown that questionable research practices are common in psychology (for a review, see Lakens 2022).

Mind–Body Coupling

Embodied cognition researchers have often emphasized that the body and the mind are tightly coupled, and that this coupling should be central to psychological theories (about cognition, perception, emotion): Their dynamics are inseparable. The idea of a coupling between the mind and the body has received apparent support from influential research programs, but these programs have been undermined by a decade of replication failures.

Power pose is the idea that more or less assertive displays (e.g., the Wonder Woman pose) impact one's attitude toward risk, allegedly by influencing hormones such as testosterone and cortisol (Carney et al. 2010). Carney and colleagues also took their findings to be evidence for the significance of embodiment for the mind (2010: 1363):

> [P]osing in displays of power caused advantaged and adaptive psychological, physiological, and behavioral changes, and these findings suggest that embodiment extends beyond mere thinking and feeling, to physiology and subsequent behavioral choices.

Carney et al.'s groundbreaking paper was followed by a flurry of apparently converging papers (Carney et al. 2015 refer to 24 experiments supporting the original results)—a phenomenon I call "ghost literatures" (previously "zombie literatures" in Machery 2021).[2]

Power pose research has been largely discredited. A first replication failure by Ranehill et al. (2015) was followed by an analysis of the power pose literature (Simmons and Simonsohn 2017). A p-curve[3] showed that this literature contains no evidence for a detectable effect. In line with this p-curve, further replications failed to find evidence for power pose (see the second issue of the 2017 volume of *Comprehensive Results in Social Psychology*).

Why did the original article and the following publications appear to provide evidence for the hypothesis that body posture influences risk aversion and decision making? Of all the possible analyses of Carney et al.'s data (Credé and Phillips 2017), only a few produce significant results, suggesting that Carney et al.'s results were p-hacked. In a remarkable online letter, Carney herself recognized that the results were tainted by practices that were common before 2010 but that we now recognize as questionable research practices.

Power pose research was in part inspired by the idea that physical postures influence emotions. The facial feedback effect, first proposed by Darwin (1872), is a textbook illustration of this mind–body coupling (e.g., Laird 1974; Tourangeau and Ellsworth 1979): in substance, someone's facial expressions influence their emotions. This general hypothesis has been specified in various ways, depending on which aspect of facial expression is taken to influence emotions, on whether facial expressions are taken to be necessary for having emotions, on whether facial expressions are assumed to merely modulate emotions or to be able to elicit emotions *de novo*, and on how facial expressions are thought to influence emotions.

An important, influential empirical contribution to the facial feedback literature was the demonstration by Strack et al. (1988) that causing people to smile or pout unintentionally impacts their experience of "funniness." In Study 1, participants rated how funny some cartoons are while holding a pen between their lips (eliciting a pout) or their teeth (eliciting a smile). The results appeared to support the facial feedback hypothesis: In brief, smiling makes you happy, pouting sad! Just like power pose, follow-up studies apparently provided convergent support to the original report (e.g., Kraft and Pressman 2012; Larsen et al. 1992; Soussignan 2002). Strack et al.'s result was significant for two reasons: Because participants were not asked to mimic a particular facial expression, in contrast to the previous studies supporting the facial feedback hypothesis, the results cannot be explained by experimenter demands. It was also debated whether people had to be aware of their facial expression for this expression to influence emotions; Strack and colleagues' experiments suggest a negative answer since participants were plausibly unaware of their facial expressions.

However, in a study involving 17 labs in eight countries, Wagenmakers et al. (2016) failed to replicate the pen-in-the-mouth study: For each lab and across the 17 labs, the effect was indistinguishable from zero (despite a very large sample size for the pooled data).

Wagenmakers and colleagues caution readers not to generalize from this replication failure to the lack of support for the facial feedback hypothesis in general. However, Wagenmakers and colleagues' replication differed from Strack et al.'s Study 1 in an important respect: Participants were video recorded, which might have interfered with the influence of facial expressions on emotions (Strack 2016). Indeed, Strack and colleagues' study replicated successfully when participants were not recorded, but not when they were (Noah et al. 2018). On the other hand, the interaction between recording and the impact of facial expression in Noah et al. (2018) was not significant; furthermore, the experimenter remained present during Strack et al.'s original experiment, and it is unclear why being video recorded would matter, while being observed by a psychologist wouldn't; finally, Coles et al.'s (2019) meta-analysis showed that video monitoring did not moderate the evidence for the facial feedback hypothesis.

A multi-lab, international study showed that facial feedback is probably a real but small effect, while casting further doubts on the pen-in-the-mouth phenomenon (Coles et al. 2022). Online participants (who were not video recorded) either imitated a facial expression presented in a picture, moved some muscles associated with a prototypical facial expression of happiness, or put a pen in their mouth. They then reported their happiness, either while watching positive images or not. Aggregating across the three ways of manipulating facial expression, people who smiled reported more happiness, although the effect varied across manipulations: The pen-in-the-mouth effect was not observed in this study, consistent with the results of Wagenmakers and colleagues. The effect size of the aggregated manipulations was small, suggesting that facial expression is only one of the many components contributing to felt happiness. Furthermore, the effect size depended on participants' awareness of the hypothesis tested in the experiment: It is smaller when participants are not aware of the hypothesis, suggesting that the effect is in part due to experimenter demands (see also Coles et al. 2023). Unfortunately, Coles and colleagues do not report how small the effect is when controlling for participants' awareness of the hypothesis.

All in all, then, emotional experience seems to be influenced, to a small degree, by facial expression, but the pen-in-the-mouth study appears to be inappropriate to show this. In my opinion, concerns about experimenter demands still remain.

Social psychologists have paid great attention to the role of bodily states such as gaze direction (up vs. down), warmth, weight, smells, body posture, and cleanliness on social judgment, including moral judgments, and social decision (e.g., prosocial decision). This literature is unfortunately filled with unreplicable empirical reports, so much so that it has become a paradigmatically unreplicable literature in psychology. It shares various features with other unreplicable literatures, notably a focus on subtle cues that are prima facie unrelated with the content of judgments and that are said to bypass the impact of awareness (for previous discussion, see Lakens 2014); much of the literature is also underpowered, with small sample sizes.

The literature on moral judgment and embodiment illustrates the problem. The Macbeth effect is the idea that cleaning one's hands "alleviates the upsetting consequences of unethical behavior and reduces threats to one's moral self-image" (Zhong and Liljenquist 2006: 1451), a surprising effect that does not replicate well (e.g., Favard et al. 2009; Earp et al. 2014; Siev et al. 2018). Disgust, understood as an "especially embodied emotion because of its strong connection to nausea and the physical process of expelling contaminants" (Schnall et al. 2008: 1220), has also been said to influence moral judgment, but there too empirical reports appear to be often unreplicable (Johnson et al., 2014; see also Ghelfi et al. 2020 vs.

Eskine et al. 2011).[4] Similar challenges have been found for the influence of warmth on generosity (Williams and Bargh 2008; Lynott et al. 2014) and the impact of having one's hand on the heart on lying (Cantarero et al. 2017).[5]

In sum, it is possible that bodily cues influence social judgment and decision making, but the existing literature overall fails to show it convincingly. It also fails to show how widespread and substantial the influence of bodily information on social judgment and decision making is.

Finally, embodied cognition researchers have claimed that perceptual processes are influenced by bodily information or, more radically, constituted by bodily representations (for discussion, see Firestone 2016): The world looks different depending on bodily feedback. For instance, wearing a backpack makes hills look steeper (Bhalla and Proffitt 1999), and holding one's arms out makes doors look narrower (Stefanucci and Geuss 2009).

The empirical literature on embodied effect in perception, often associated with the New New Look (Machery 2015), suffers from replicability challenges. In the first experiment of Proffitt et al. (2003), participants estimated the distance of objects from an egocentric point of view, with or without wearing a heavy backpack. Estimates were larger in the former than the latter condition (see a similar effect about the slant of a hill in Bhalla and Proffitt 1999). However, Hutchison and Loomis (2006) and Woods et al. (2009) were unable to replicate this result. Similarly, in Study 1 of Witt et al. (2004), participants estimated distances after throwing either a light or a heavy ball: Estimates were higher in the latter than in the former condition. Woods et al. (2009) failed to replicate this and other results by Witt and colleagues.

The poor replicability of this literature is probably due, at least in part, to publication bias. Balcetis and Dunning (2006) reported five studies suggesting that desirable objects were viewed as being closer than undesirable objects, but as Francis (2012) noted, their studies had a low power, and it was consequently unlikely that Balcetis and Dunning had only obtained positive effects. Rather, their article was likely to suffer from publication bias: Experiments resulting in positive findings had been selectively reported.

Perceptual and Motor Representations in Cognition and Language Comprehension

An important thread in embodied cognition research is the claim that entertaining a concept and understanding a word involves re-enacting perceptual and motor representations (e.g., Barsalou 1999, 2020; Prinz 2004). A rich and diverse empirical literature supports this research program, but it is not without problems (Mahon and Caramazza 2008; Lakens 2014; Machery 2007, 2016, 2023). This section focuses on replication failures affecting this literature.

Embodied cognition researchers have proposed that concepts of actions are, or involve, motor representations, i.e., those representations of the bodily motions involved in these actions. Glenberg and Kaschak (2002: 558) drew the following prediction from this simple idea, which they call the "action–sentence compatibility effect": "When a sentence implied action in one direction (e.g., "Close the drawer" implies action away from the body), the participants had difficulty making a sensibility judgment requiring a response in the opposite direction." They then presented three studies supporting the reality of the action–sentence compatibility effect. Subsequently, this effect appeared to receive support from follow-up studies (e.g., Borreggine and Kaschak 2006).

In a multi-lab study, Morey et al. (2022) replicated an experiment from Borreggine and Kaschak (2006). Participants judged whether a sentence describing a motion makes sense by making a motion toward or away from their body. None of the 18 labs involved observed an effect (see also the replication failures in nine studies in Papesh 2015). Why did several studies observe an action–sentence compatibility effect if the effect does not replicate well? The literature on this effect appears to suffer from publication bias (Winter et al. 2022), which might explain the apparent support found in the literature.

Other effects bearing on the role of motor representations in cognition and language comprehension fail to replicate. Shebani and Pulvermüller (2018) reported a fascinating double dissociation: Asking people to tap a complex pattern with their hands impaired memorizing the order of arm-related words (e.g., "clap"), while asking people to tap with the feet affected leg-related words (e.g., "kick"). Not only were Montero-Melis et al. (2022) unable to replicate this finding, they provided strong evidence against its reality with a much larger sample size and a more careful data analysis. Relatedly, the literature examining the impact of stimulating the premotor cortex on comprehending action sentences suffers from publication bias, is underpowered, and does not provide clear evidence for the role of the premotor cortex in language comprehension (Solana and Santiago 2022).

Beyond language comprehension, embodied cognition research on mathematical cognition also suffers from replication failures. A large study involving 17 labs failed to replicate the attentional spatial-numerical association of response codes effect (Fischer et al. 2003): Targets in the left visual field are allegedly primed by small numbers, targets in the right visual field by large numbers (Colling et al. 2020). Similarly, starting to count with the left or the right hand does not appear to affect arithmetic problem solving (Morrissey et al. 2020).

Finally, some studies do appear to replicate successfully. Mathôt et al. (2017) presented evidence that pupil size decreases when words refer to brighter objects (e.g., "sun"), and Mathôt et al. (2019) replicated this effect. Zwaan and Pecher (2012) replicated findings that a sentence suggesting the orientation or shape of an object facilitated the recognition of a picture when the represented object had this orientation or shape, but not the finding that a sentence suggesting the color of an object inhibited the recognition of a picture when the represented object had this color.[6]

Conclusion

There is little doubt that surprisingly many findings in embodied cognition research do not replicate, and unreplicability affects research on decision making, emotion, perception, language comprehension, and mathematical cognition. Furthermore, evidence of publication bias has been found in several areas of research, perhaps explaining the replication failures. It is of course unknown how many studies (a third, a majority?) fail to replicate: Some appear to replicate successfully, and embodied cognition research in any case appeals to a diverse body of evidence. However, the frequency of failed replications, particularly among paradigmatic studies, and the frequency of ghost literatures should lead us to view with caution, if not outright skepticism, the alleged findings in embodied cognition research until their replicability has been demonstrated. Cognitive scientists, including philosophers, should be more careful when relying on the embodied cognition literature (Machery and Doris 2017).

Notes

1 I do not use "replication" and "replicate" as success terms: Replications can fail or succeed. To refer to the outcomes of replications, I use "replication failure" or "replication success."
2 A ghost literature is made up of articles apparently providing converging evidence for a phenomenon that is not real.
3 P-curves plot the significant statistics in a literature (Simonsohn et al. 2014). The resulting curve can be used to assess whether this literature contains evidence for a phenomenon and whether p-hacking has taken place.
4 Once publication bias is taken into account, no effect of incidental disgust is found in the literature on disgust and morality (Landy and Goodwin 2015).
5 The influence of bodily cues on other evaluative judgments has also run into replicability problems: see Goltzsche et al. (2012) on weight and judgment of importance (vs. Chandler et al. 2012).
6 Replications by independent labs would have been preferable.

References

Balcetis, E., and Dunning, D. (2006) "See What You Want to See: Motivational Influences on Visual Perception," *Journal of Personality and Social Psychology* 91: 612–25.

Barsalou, L. W. (1999) "Perceptual Symbol Systems," *Behavioral and brain sciences* 22: 577–660.

——— (2020) "Challenges and Opportunities for Grounding Cognition," *Journal of Cognition* 3: 1–24

Borreggine, K. L., and Kaschak, M. P. (2006) "The Action–Sentence Compatibility Effect: It's All in the Timing," *Cognitive Science* 30: 1097–112.

Bhalla, M., and Proffitt, D. R. (1999) "Visual–Motor Recalibration in Geographical Slant Perception," *Journal of Experimental Psychology: Human Perception and Performance* 25: 1076–96.

Cantarero, K., Parzuchowski, M., and Dukala, K. (2017) "White Lies in Hand: Are Other-Oriented Lies Modified by Hand gestures? Possibly Not," *Frontiers in Psychology* 8: 814.

Carney, D. R., Cuddy, A. J. C., and Yap, A. J. (2010) "Power Posing: Brief Nonverbal Displays Affect Neuroendocrine Levels and Risk Tolerance," *Psychological Science* 21: 1363–8.

——— (2015) "Review and Summary of Research on the Embodied Effects of Expansive (vs. Contractive) Nonverbal Displays," *Psychological Science* 26: 657–63.

Chandler, J. J., Reinhard, D., and Schwarz, N. (2012) "To Judge a Book by its Weight You Need to Know its Content: Knowledge Moderates the Use of Embodied Cues," *Journal of Experimental Social Psychology* 48: 948–52.

Coles, N. A., Larsen, J. T., and Lench, H. C. (2019) "A Meta-Analysis of the Facial Feedback Literature: Effects of Facial Feedback on Emotional Experience Are Small and Variable," *Psychological Bulletin* 145: 610–51.

Coles, N. A., et al. (2022) "A Multi-Lab Test of the Facial Feedback Hypothesis by the Many Smiles Collaboration," *Nature Human Behaviour* 6: 1731–42.

Coles, N. A., Gaertner, L., Frohlich, B., Larsen, J. T., and Basnight-Brown, D. M. (2023) "Fact or Artifact? Demand Characteristics and Participants' Beliefs Can Moderate, But Do Not Fully Account for, the Effects of Facial Feedback on Emotional Experience," *Journal of Personality and Social Psychology* 124: 287–310.

Colling, L. J., et al. (2020) "Registered Replication Report on Fischer, Castel, Dodd, and Pratt (2003)," *Advances in Methods and Practices in Psychological Science* 3: 143–62.

Credé, M., and Phillips, L. A. (2017) "Revisiting the Power Pose Effect: How Robust Are the Results Reported by Carney, Cuddy, and Yap (2010) to Data Analytic Decisions?," *Social Psychological and Personality Science* 8: 493–9.

Darwin, C. (1872) *The Expression of the Emotions in Man and Animals*, London: John Murray.

Earp, B. D., Everett, J. A., Madva, E. N., and Hamlin, J. K. (2014) "Out, Damned Spot: Can the "Macbeth Effect" be Replicated?," *Basic and Applied Social Psychology* 36: 91–8.

Eskine, K. J., Kacinik, N. A., and Prinz, J. J. (2011) "A Bad Taste in the Mouth: Gustatory Disgust Influences Moral Judgment," *Psychological Science* 22: 295–9.

Fayard, J. V., Bassi, A. K., Bernstein, D. M., and Roberts, B. W. (2009). "Is cleanliness next to godliness? Dispelling old wives' tales: Failure to replicate Zhong and Liljenquist (2006)," *Journal of Articles in Support of the Null Hypothesis*, 6: 1539–8714.

Firestone, C. (2016) "Embodiment in Perception: Will We Know it When We See It?," in B. P. McLaughlin and H. Kornblith (eds), *Goldman and his Critics* (pp. 318–334), Malden, MA: John Wiley & Sons, Inc.

Fischer, M. H., Castel, A. D., Dodd, M. D., and Pratt, J. (2003) "Perceiving Numbers Causes Spatial Shifts of Attention," *Nature Neuroscience* 6: 555–6.

Francis, G. (2012) "The Same Old New Look: Publication Bias in a Study of Wishful Seeing," *i-Perception* 3: 176–8.

Glenberg, A. M., and Kaschak, M. P. (2002) "Grounding Language in Action," *Psychonomic Bulletin & Review* 9: 558–65.

Goltzsche, H., Levy, G., Uhlmann, A., and Lutz, J. (2012) "The effect of Weight on Judgments of Importance: Replication Attempt of Chandler et al. (2012, Study 1)," https://osf.io/549eq/

Ghelfi, E., et al. (2020) "Reexamining the Effect of Gustatory Disgust on Moral Judgment: A Multilab Direct Replication of Eskine, Kacinik, and Prinz (2011)," *Advances in Methods and Practices in Psychological Science* 3: 3–23.

Hutchison, J. J., and Loomis, J. M. (2006) "Does Energy Expenditure Affect the Perception of Egocentric Distance? A Failure to Replicate Experiment 1 of Proffitt, Stefanucci, Banton, and Epstein (2003)," *Spanish Journal of Psychology* 9: 332–9.

Johnson, D. J., Cheung, F., and Donnellan, M. B. (2014) "Does Cleanliness Influence Moral Judgments?," *Social Psychology* 45: 209–15.

Kraft, T. L., and Pressman, S. D. (2012) "Grin and Bear It: The Influence of Manipulated Facial Expression on the Stress Response," *Psychological Science* 23: 1372–8.

Laird, J. D. (1974) "Self-Attribution of Emotion: The Effects of Expressive Behavior on the Quality of Emotional Experience," *Journal of Personality and Social Psychology* 29: 475–86.

Lakens, D. (2014) "Grounding Social Embodiment," *Social Cognition* 32: 168–83.

———— (2022) *Improving Your Statistical Inferences*. Retrieved from https://lakens.github.io/statistical_inferences/. https://doi.org/10.5281/zenodo.6409077

Landy, J. F., and Goodwin, G. P. (2015) "Does Incidental Disgust Amplify Moral Judgment? A Meta-Analytic Review of Experimental Evidence," *Perspectives on Psychological Science* 10: 518–36.

Larsen, R. J., Kasimatis, M., and Frey, K. (1992) "Facilitating the Furrowed Brow: An unobtrusive tTst of the Facial Feedback Hypothesis Applied to Unpleasant Affect," *Cognition and Emotion* 6: 321–38.

Lynott, D., Corker, K. S., Wortman, J., Connell, L., Donnellan, M. B., Lucas, R. E., and O'Brien, K. (2014) "Replication of "Experiencing Physical Warmth Promotes Interpersonal Warmth" by Williams and Bargh (2008)," *Social Psychology* 45: 216–222.

Machery, E. (2007) "Concept Empiricism: A Methodological Critique," *Cognition* 104: 19–46.

———— (2015) "Cognitive Penetrability: A No-Progress Report," in J. Zeimbekis and A. Raftapoulos (eds) *The Cognitive Penetrability of Perception* (pp. 59–74), Oxford: Oxford University Press.

———— (2016) "The Amodal Brain and the Offloading Hypothesis," *Psychonomic Bulletin & Review* 23: 1090–5.

———— (2020) "What is a Replication?," *Philosophy of Science* 87: 545–67.

———— (2021) "A Mistaken Confidence in Data," *European Journal for Philosophy of Science* 11: 34.

———— (2023) "The Significance of Supramodality for Embodied Cognition: Commentary on Calzavarini (2023)," *Language, Cognition and Neuroscience*, 1-3.

Machery, E., and Doris, J. M. (2017) "An Open Letter to Our Students: Doing Interdisciplinary Moral Psychology," in B. G. Voyer and T. Tarantola (eds) *Moral Psychology: A Multidisciplinary Guide* (pp. 119–43), Berlin: Springer.

Mahon, B. Z., and Caramazza, A. (2008) "A Critical Look at the Embodied Cognition Hypothesis and a New Proposal for Grounding Conceptual Content," *Journal of Physiology-Paris* 102: 59–70.

Mathôt, S., Grainger, J., and Strijkers, K. (2017) "Pupillary Responses to Words that Convey a Sense of Brightness or Darkness," *Psychological Science* 28: 1116–24.

Mathôt, S., Sundermann, L., and van Rijn, H. (2019) "The Effect of Semantic Brightness on Pupil Size: A Replication With Dutch Words," *bioRxiv* 689265.

Montero-Melis, G., Van Paridon, J., Ostarek, M., and Bylund, E. (2022) "No Evidence for Embodiment: The Motor System is Not Needed to Keep Action Verbs in Working Memory," *Cortex* 150: 108–25.

Morey, R. D., et al. (2022) "A Pre-Registered, Multi-Lab Non-Replication of the Action-Sentence Compatibility Effect (ACE)," *Psychonomic Bulletin & Review* 29: 613–26.

Morrissey, K., Hallett, D., Wynes, R., Kang, J., and Han, M. (2020). "Finger-counting Habits, Not Finger Movements, Predict Simple Arithmetic Problem Solving," *Psychological Research* 84, 140–151.

Noah, T., Schul, Y., and Mayo, R. (2018) "When Both the Original Study and Its Failed Replication are Correct: Feeling Observed Eliminates the Facial-Feedback Effect," *Journal of Personality and Social Psychology* 114: 657–64.

Nosek, B. A., and Errington, T. M. (2020) "What is replication?", *PLoS Biology* 18: e3000691.

Prinz, J. J. (2004) *Furnishing the Mind: Concepts and Their Perceptual Basis*, Cambridge, MA: MIT Press.

Papesh, M. H. (2015) "Just out of Reach: On the Reliability of the Action-Sentence Compatibility Effect," *Journal of Experimental Psychology: General* 144: e116.

Proffitt, D. R., Stefanucci, J., Banton, T., and Epstein, W. (2003) "The Role of Effort in Perceiving Distance," *Psychological Science* 14: 106–12.

Ranehill, E., Dreber, A., Johannesson, M., Leiberg, S., Sul, S., and Weber, R. A. (2015) "Assessing the Robustness of Power Posing: No Effect on Hormones and Risk Tolerance in a Large Sample of Men and Women," *Psychological Science* 26: 653–6.

Rosenthal, R. (1979) "The "File Drawer Problem" and Tolerance for Null Results," *Psychological Bulletin* 86: 638–41.

Schnall, S., Haidt, J., Clore, G. L., and Jordan, A. H. (2008) "Disgust as Embodied Moral Judgment," *Personality and Social Psychology Bulletin* 34: 1096–109.

Schmidt, S. (2009) "Shall We Really Do It Again? The Powerful Concept of Replication is Neglected in the Social Sciences," *Review of General Psychology* 13: 90–100.

Shapiro, L. (2019) *Embodied Cognition*, New York: Routledge.

Shebani, Z., and Pulvermüller, F. (2018) "Flexibility in Language Action Interaction: The Influence of Movement Type," *Frontiers in Human Neuroscience* 12: 252.

Siev, J., Zuckerman, S. E., and Siev, J. J. (2018) "The Relationship Between Immorality and Cleansing," *Social Psychology* 49: 303–9.

Simmons, J. and Simonsohn, U. (2017) "Power Posing: P-Curving the Evidence," *Psychological Science* 28, 687–693.

Simonsohn, U., Nelson, L. D., and Simmons, J. P. (2014) "P-Curve: A Key to the File Drawer," *Journal of Experimental Psychology: General* 143: 534–47.

Simmons, J. P., Nelson, L. D., and Simonsohn, U. (2011) "False Positive Psychology: Undisclosed Flexibility in Data Collection and Analysis Allows Presenting Anything as Significant," *Psychological Science* 22: 1359–66.

Solana, P., and Santiago, J. (2022) "Does the Involvement of Motor Cortex in Embodied Language Comprehension Stand on Solid Ground? A P-Curve Analysis and Test for Excess Significance of the TMS and tDCS Evidence," *Neuroscience & Biobehavioral Reviews* 141: 104834.

Soussignan, R. (2002) "Duchenne Smile, Emotional Experience, and Autonomic Reactivity: A Test of the Facial Feedback Hypothesis," *Emotion* 2: 52–74.

Stefanucci, J. K., and Geuss, M. N. (2009) "Big People, Little World: The Body Influences Size Perception," *Perception* 38: 1782–95.

Strack, F. (2016) "Reflection on the Smiling Registered Replication Report," *Perspectives on Psychological Science* 11: 929–30.

Strack, F., Martin, L.L., and Stepper, S. (1988) "Inhibiting and Facilitating Conditions of The Human Smile: A Nonobtrusive Test of the Facial Feedback Hypothesis," *Journal of Personality and Social Psychology* 54: 768–77.

Tourangeau, R., and Ellsworth, P. C. (1979) "The Role of Facial Response in the Experience of Emotion," *Journal of Personality and Social Psychology* 37: 1519–31.

Wagenmakers, E. J., et al. (2016) "Registered Replication Report: Strack, Martin, and Stepper (1988)," *Perspectives on Psychological Science* 11: 917–28.

Williams, L. E., and Bargh, J. A. (2008) "Experiencing Physical Warmth Promotes Interpersonal Warmth," *Science* 322: 606–7.

Winter, A., Dudschig, C., Miller, J., Ulrich, R. and Kaup, B. (2022), "The Action-Sentence Compatibility Effect (ACE): Meta-Analysis of a Benchmark Finding for Embodiment," *Acta Psychologica* 230: 103712.

Witt, J. K., Proffitt, D. R., and Epstein, W. (2004) "Perceiving Distance: A Role of effort and Intent," *Perception* 33: 570–90.

Woods, A. J., Philbeck, J. W., and Danoff, J. V. (2009) "The Various Perceptions of Distance: An Alternative View of How Effort affects Distance judgments," *Journal of Experimental Psychology: Human Perception & Performance* 35: 1104–17.

Zhong, C. B., and Liljenquist, K. (2006) "Washing Away Your Sins: Threatened Morality and Physical Cleansing," *Science* 313: 1451–2.

Zwaan, R. A., and Pecher, D. (2012) "Revisiting Mental Simulation in Language Comprehension: Six Replication Attempts," *PloS one* 7: e51382.

40

EMBODIED COGNITION NEEDS AN UPGRADE

Guy Dove

Although there have been a few well-publicized replication failures (Morey *et al.* 2022; Zwaan 2021) and some close shaves (Coles *et al.* 2022), embodied cognition has been a remarkably productive research program. The conjecture that many psychological processes are influenced by body morphology and intimately linked to bodily experience has transformed and shaped many areas of research in the psychological and brain sciences (Anderson 2003; Shapiro 2019). With this productivity in mind, my aim in this chapter is not to question the importance of embodiment to cognition. Instead, I intend to critically assess one of the central ways that this idea is put into practice. In particular, I am going to examine the way that embodiment is commonly understood in the context of explaining how our concepts are encoded in the brain.

Prior to the emergence of embodied cognition, it was common to view the neuromechanisms responsible for cognition as functionally separate from those responsible for perception and action. Hurley (2001) colorfully refers to this orthodoxy as the classical sandwich view—a theoretical approach in which cognition acts as the meat and sensorimotor systems act as the slices of bread. On this view, cognition relies on amodal neural representations (i.e., representations not located in perception and action systems; Anderson 1983; Fodor 1975; Pylyshyn 1984). In contrast to this view, a robust and growing body of evidence suggests cognition relies, at least in part, on the activation of representations contained within cortical regions typically employed during perception and action (Barsalou 2016; Borghesani and Piazza 2017; Conca and Tettamanti 2018; Kemmerer 2015; Martin 2016; Meteyard *et al.* 2012; Pulvermüller 2018). This evidence has led researchers to propose that our concepts are grounded in experiential systems. In other words, we appear to think about the world by means of the same neural mechanisms that we use to perceive and act upon it (Casasanto 2024; Craighero 2024; Kaschak *et al.* 2024; Scorolli and Mazzuca, 2024).

Following Kemmerer (2022), I am going to refer to this as the grounded cognition model (GCM). This model presupposes that cognition depends on neurally realized representations (Piccinini 2020; Shea 2018) and is thus incompatible with radical forms of embodied cognition that deny the importance of the concept of representation for understanding how the mind works (Chemero 2011).[1] The GCM embraces two important conjectures. The first

DOI: 10.4324/9781003322511-51

concerns what sort of representations are causally relevant to conceptual processing. This model holds that concepts primarily depend on the redeployment of representations located in primary or lower-level sensorimotor cortical areas.[2] The second conjecture concerns which kinds of representations are causally irrelevant to conceptual processing. This model excludes representations located in amodal or even multimodal regions.[3] In what follows, I argue that the GCM is flawed and needs to be revised. I provide reasons to think that, while semantic memory may rely in part on lower-level, modality-specific representations, it also relies on higher-level sensorimotor representations as well as those located in multimodal areas of the cortex.

Beyond Primary Areas

The GCM appeals to representations located in lower-level perception and action areas. This is driven in large part by behavioral and neuroimaging studies implicating such representations in cognitive tasks, but it also fits with the hypothesis that our concepts are grounded in our bodily engagement with physical referents (Glenberg 2010).

As critics of embodied cognition have noted (Machery 2007, 2016; Mahon 2015; Mahon and Caramazza 2008), many of the relevant studies implicate higher-level sensorimotor areas rather than lower-level ones. A few specific examples may help make the issues clear. Some of the most compelling evidence for the GCM implicate the motor system in the processing of action words associated with specific parts of the body (e.g., Hauk, Johnsrude and Pulvermüller 2004; Willems, Hagoort and Casasanto 2010). The motor cortex is organized in a somatotopic fashion; areas involved with the movement of specific body parts are organized in an inverted body map (often referred to as a homunculus) that extends in a roughly vertical strip from the top of the brain downward. Kemmerer et al. (2012) reviewed several fMRI studies that examined the activations elicited by verbs involving leg/foot, arm/hand, and face/mouth actions. They found that *both* premotor and motor areas were implicated.

These findings align with the broad generalization that action-related words elicit effector-specific activation, but the contribution of premotor regions suggests that a degree of abstraction might be at play in the representation of action concepts. Perhaps the connection between body parts and conceptual content is more complicated than the traditional interpretation of the GCM would lead us to believe. For example, building on a series of neurostimulation experiments on monkeys, Graziano and Aflalo (2007) propose that the motor system is not organized around a map of the body but a map of actions. Others have suggested that the motor system might involve both somatotopy and actotopy (Fernandino and Iacoboni 2010; Kemmerer and Gonzalez-Castillo 2010).

Relatively high-level perception areas have also been implicated in the processing of action concepts. For example, a body of evidence suggests that a portion of the visual system known as the lateral occipitotemporal cortex (LOTC) contributes to their processing (Kemmerer 2019). This region includes—but is not limited to—the human middle temporal cortex (hMT+), which responds selectively to motion (Lingnau and Downing 2015), and the extrastriate body area (EBA), which responds selectively to images of our own body parts and those of others (Myers and Snoweden 2008).[4]

A compelling argument can be made that the collective focus on lower-level areas was mistaken and—more importantly—not driven by the central theoretical claims of the GCM. In fact, Kemmerer (2022: 4) suggests that, properly construed, the GCM involves "relatively high-level sectors of the pertinent modality-specific cortical systems." Although it does not fit with the orthodox conception of embodiment, the GCM is compatible with modality-specific representations at higher levels.

Modal Specificity Reconsidered

The move toward a more inclusive approach to the grounding of our concepts can be seen as a welcome development for the GCM. Unfortunately, this is not enough to ensure its viability. A new problem has recently entered the discussion that goes to the heart of the model: people have begun to challenge the relevance and tractability of the orthodox commitment to modal specificity. This problem is significant because the notion of modal specificity is thought to define sensorimotor grounding. According to the GCM, such grounding is realized by means of the reactivation of modality-specific representations. Without a workable definition of modal specificity, though, the model cannot adequately explain conceptual embodiment.

The critical reappraisal of modal specificity has taken three main forms. The first points to the fact that there is no agreed-upon characterization of sensory modalities (Haimovici 2018; Michel 2020). Individuating the senses turns out to be a deceptively complicated task. For instance, Keeley (2002) finds that three distinct methods for individuating are employed by neuroscientists in general: one that relies on characteristic experiences; another that relies on the physical qualities of the perceived objects; and a third that relies on sense organs. Unfortunately, each method individuates the senses differently. Reacting to this disagreement, Fulkerson (2014) defends a robust sensory pluralism in which there in no single correct way to individuate the senses. If Fulkerson is correct, it is going to be difficult to determine just what the requirement of modal specificity entails. What might count as a single modality on one method might not count as one on another. Do we limit the GCM to those sensory modalities identified by all methods? Or should we leave room for those sensory modalities that are identified by any of the methods? Some of the methods? The problem threatens GCM because embodiment is often explained in terms of modality-specific grounding. If the individuation of sensory modalities is a context-dependent enterprise, the concept of modality specificity is unlikely to support robust generalizations about conceptual grounding and, by extension, embodiment.

The second critical reappraisal raises the stakes. Even if it is possible to find a workable method of individuating sensory modalities, some of the evidence supporting the GCM involves regions that are clearly multimodal (Dove 2022). Consider for example regions associated with taste. Reading flavor-related words has been found to activate primary gustatory cortices more than words that are not flavor-related (Barrós-Loscertales *et al.* 2012). Echoing the discussion in the previous section, some studies have found that flavor-related words activate secondary rather than primary gustatory areas (Goldberg *et al.* 2006). The problem for the GCM is that flavor is a robustly multisensory phenomenon (Auvray and Spence 2008). The apparent contribution of gustatory areas to semantic processing fits with the hypothesis that our concepts depend on the reuse of experiential areas but runs contrary to the notion that these areas are modal specific.[5]

The third critical reappraisal goes even further and proposes that multisensory processing is the rule rather than the exception. Much of our phenomenal experience depends on multisensory processing. For example, early visual areas can be modulated by auditory stimuli (Iurilli *et al.* 2012). It is even possible to induce visual illusions by means of the presence of sounds (Shams, Kamitani and Shimojo 2000). Portions of the early auditory cortex can similarly be modulated by somatosensory stimuli (Foxe *et al.* 2002). These kinds of interactions are so widespread that Ghazanfar and Schroeder (2006) conjecture that the entire neocortex is multisensory. Calzavarini (2021) argues that the apparent ubiquity of multisensory processing undermines the central commitment to modal specificity that characterizes many approaches to embodied cognition.

Modal specificity has become part of the origin story of embodied cognition in general and the GCM in specific. Even supporters of so-called *Weak Embodiment* (Meteyard *et al.* 2012)—which explicitly leaves room for multimodal areas to play a role in semantic memory—often appeal to modal specificity when elaborating the notion of experiential grounding. Modal specificity has become something of a shorthand to distinguish embodied cognition from traditional amodal views. The considerations outlined in this section show that this terminology may have outlived its usefulness.

The emphasis on modal specificity is—and frankly always was—questionable. The GCM presupposes that these regions are distinctive in their anatomy and function. As we have seen, it is often difficult to distinguish these regions from those that are multimodal. The answer may depend in part on the phenomena one is studying and the research questions that one is seeking to answer (Fulkerson 2014). Furthermore, when one examines sensory regions, one finds the same sort of functional organization that one finds in clearly multimodal regions. They contain the same sort of complicated feedforward, lateral, and top-down connections. In both, higher-level representations are used to encode physical properties that exhibit a degree of abstraction. For example, the ventral stream of the visual system contains an anatomical hierarchy in which higher-level regions contain populations of neurons that selectively respond to complex object properties while remaining unresponsive to various context-specific properties (Rust and DiCarlo 2010). Similarly, bi-modal neurons that respond to both visual and tactile stimuli have been associated with the representation of extra-personal space (Graziano 2018).

The Importance of Transmodal Regions

Abstraction is an important design feature of our conceptual system. Concepts enable us to identify categories and draw inferences by generalizing and abstracting away from experiential particulars. While there has been a great deal of discussion of the challenges posed by abstract concepts for embodied cognition (Borghi *et al.* 2017; Dove 2021), abstraction remains an important feature of all concepts.[6] It thus represents a deep and broad problem for the GCM—one that extends to both concrete and abstract concepts.

Several researchers have suggested that representations located within cortical regions not directly associated with immediate experience contribute to the conceptual system's capacity for abstraction (e.g., Binder and Desai 2011; Dove 2022; Kuhnke *et al.* 2023). Assessing these proposals has been complicated somewhat by the lack of an agreed-upon terminology. High-level multimodal regions have been variously characterized as amodal, cross-modal, heteromodal or supramodal. For the sake of clarity, I am going to use the term *transmodal* to identify multimodal regions that exhibit a degree of insensitivity to features of immediate experience. Because such insensitivity is a graded property, transmodal applies to high-level multimodal regions that retain some links to modality-specific input (as is often thought to be the case with convergence zones) as well as those that are completely insensitive to such features (as is often thought to be the case with purely amodal regions).

A growing body of research suggests that transmodal regions play an important role in conceptual processing (Kemmerer 2015; Lambon Ralph 2014). While a complete review of this literature is beyond the reach of this chapter, some examples may prove instructive. One of the clearest cases for the causal relevance of transmodal regions emerges from research on patients with semantic dementia (SD). SD typically involves a progressive bilateral atrophy of the anterior temporal lobes (ATL) that leads to an increasing loss of conceptual knowledge (Patterson, Nestor and Rogers 2007). In keeping with this, brain imaging experiments with neurotypical participants have implicated the ATL in the representation of semantic knowledge (Coutanche and Thompson-Schill 2015; Visser *et al.* 2012). The application of repetitive transcranial magnetic stimulation (rTMS) to the ATL also leads to a generalized slowing of conceptual processing (Pobric, Jefferies and Lambon Ralph 2010). A striking feature of SD is that concepts are typically impaired in a cross-modal fashion: that is, patients lose the ability to access the meanings of words in way that is insensitive to testing modality (Bozeat *et al.* 2000; Garrard and Carroll 2006). For example, a patient might not be able to access the meaning of the word *eagle* in response to either a picture-naming task or a verbal task (Patterson, Nestor and Rogers 2007). Several researchers have noted that the nature of the deficit experienced by SD patients fits better with an amodal model of concepts than it does with a grounded one in which conceptual knowledge is linked to modality-specific representations (Mahon 2015; McCaffrey 2015).

Research involving congenitally or early blind individuals provides another strong case for the importance of transmodal regions. This evidence is important because early blind individuals have been shown to perform remarkably well on several semantic tasks involving color terms (Bedny *et al.* 2019; Bottini *et al.* 2022). Two recent studies comparing the brain responses of these individuals with sighted participants (Bottini *et al.* 2020; Wang *et al.* 2020) found evidence of the involvement of both sensory-based and transmodal representations in the processing of color concepts. In the sighted participants, but not the early blind ones, color similarity appeared to be encoded in posterior regions in the V4 complex. This is consistent with the proposal that perceptual simulation plays a role in these concepts. In both groups, though, color similarity also appeared to be encoded in the left dorsal region of the ATL. This suggests that the left dorsal ATL houses non-sensory representations that contribute to conceptual processing (Bi 2021).

The left dorsal ATL is not the only transmodal region implicated in conceptual processing. Indeed, a widely distributed collection of transmodal "hubs" (Sporns, Honey and Kotter 2007) have been implicated in the conceptual system (Binder *et al.* 2016). A recent meta-analysis of 212 neuroimaging experiments, for instance, finds that concepts elicit activation in both regions associated with sensorimotor experience and multimodal convergence zones (Kuhnke *et al.* 2023).

Evidence of such hierarchical organization has inspired new theories of the neuromechanisms responsible for semantic memory. One prominent example is the embodied abstraction theory (Binder and Desai 2011), which holds that concepts are made up of experiential representations at multiple levels of abstraction. On this theory, concepts depend on an interactive continuum of hierarchically organized representations. The highest levels contain highly schematic representations, and the conceptual system can employ progressively richer experiential representations when deeper processing is required. Another prominent example is the dynamic multilevel framework (Reilly *et al.* 2016), which holds that our concepts are handled by a system of low- and high-order hubs. Conceptual knowledge is gradually abstracted through a series of processing stages that extend from sensory regions to heteromodal regions to, ultimately, amodal regions.

Despite the general similarity of these theories, they diverge in important ways—particularly with respect to the location and character of higher-level hubs. A particular point of contention concerns the function of hubs located within anterior gyrus and the temporal pole. Another issue that remains unresolved is whether or not the conceptual system contains fully amodal regions (Michel 2020). We can bracket such disagreements for the moment, though, because what is important for our purposes is that these theories signal the emergence of a research program that is inspired by grounded cognition but embraces the need for transmodal regions and hierarchical organization.

A New Approach

In this chapter, I have defended three conclusions: (1) that relatively high-level sensorimotor regions contribute to conceptual processing; (2) that at least some of these regions are multimodal; and (3) that higher-level transmodal regions also play an important role. These conclusions suggest that the GCM, with its focus on modality-specific regions, needs an upgrade. To be clear, I am not suggesting that we abandon the hypothesis that conceptual understanding relies on the reuse of experiential systems. Instead, I am suggesting that this hypothesis, with its implicit commitment to a flat cognitive architecture, needs to be rethought in light of the available evidence. More broadly, embodied cognition needs to confront the apparent fact that the conceptual system is multimodal and multilevel. The hierarchical nature of semantic memory contributes to an important design feature of our concepts: their capacity for abstraction.[7]

Kompa (2019) identifies several weaknesses in the case for embodied cognition: the inconsistency of the activation in experiential areas during conceptual tasks, the lack of a precise overlap in the activations associated with experience and cognition, the absence of expected cognitive deficits in patients with damage to experiential modalities, the cross-modal nature of the conceptual deficits exhibited in patients with SD, and the existence of similar activation patterns in the processing of visual action words by early blind and sighted individuals.[8] The addition of multimodal and transmodal regions to the embodied cognition toolkit provides the theoretical resources to address these challenges, but a clear explanation of their role is needed. Unfortunately, the GCM is simply not up this task. It is incompatible with the observed flexibility of conceptual system. Supporters of embodiment need to recognize the dynamic and multimodal nature of experience and move beyond the modal/amodal dichotomy. The complex organization of semantic memory fits poorly with the GCM. A new hierarchical model is needed (Kemmerer 2015; Kuhnke *et al.* 2023). The conceptual system may well be deeply intertwined with the systems involved in perception and action, but this interaction appears to be elastic and dependent on multimodal and transmodal regions.

Notes

1 Given that much of the evidence supporting embodied cognition concerns which cortical regions are responsible for conceptual reasoning, a non-representational version of the GCM— perhaps one tied to the notion of neural reuse (Anderson 2014)—remains possible.

2 It is worth noting that Kemmerer associates the GCM with the reuse of *relatively high-level* sensorimotor representations. While this fits with the evidence discussed in this paper, it is not the standard position among researchers. Supporters and critics of embodied cognition alike

overwhelmingly view the GCM in terms of a commitment to lower-level (if not primary) modali-ty-specific representations (Mahon 2015; Speed and Majid 2020).

3 Some might wonder why I did not reduce these two claims to a single universally quantified claim asserting that all conceptual representations are contained within lower-level modality-specific areas. If I did, then all I would have to falsify this claim would be to provide evidence that some conceptual processing involves higher-level or truly multimodal representations. My aim, though, is not to simply to show that this universalized claim is false. Instead, I want to show that the model fails in substantial and systematic ways.

4 In keeping with the argument laid out in the subsequent section that many purportedly modali-ty-specific areas are in fact multimodal, the EBA has been found to respond to the performance of motor actions in the absence of visual stimulus (Astiev *et al.* 2004).

5 Speed and Majid (2020) argue that the evidence for conceptual grounding in olfactory and gusta-tory systems is weak. Part of their reasoning depends on the inconsistent evidence of activation in primary sensorimotor regions.

6 No part of my argument rests on the viability of the abstract/concrete distinction. I am even happy to concede that individual concepts may be used in relatively more abstract or more concrete ways in given contexts (Barsalou 2020). My focus on concrete concepts in this section is simply meant to show that the problem of abstraction is not limited to abstract concepts.

7 Some might argue that a dramatic theoretical overhaul is not needed. After all, there has been a general shift in the literature away from what has been called strong embodiment towards weak embodiment (Meteyard *et al.* 2012). In addition, some supporters of grounded cognition have long emphasized the situatedness of concepts (e.g., Barsalou 1999, 2010, 2020), which would seem to require resources that extend beyond low-level sensorimotor regions. I acknowledge that these developments are important—indeed, they are part of the impetus for this chapter. I suggest, though, that the theoretical difficulties faced by the GCM are too great to be explained away by such a deflationary defense.

8 There is a temptation to conclude from these difficulties that an entirely amodal account of con-cepts is needed. Amodalism, though, faces its own empirical difficulties. For example, it struggles to explain the abundant evidence that experiential regions are causally relevant to semantic pro-cessing (Dove 2022).

References

Anderson, J. R. (1983) *The Architecture of Cognition*. Cambridge, MA: Harvard University Press.

Anderson, M. L. (2003) "Embodied cognition: A field guide," *Artificial Intelligence*, 149(1), 91–130.

——— (2014) *After Phrenology: Neural Reuse and the Interactive Brain*, Cambridge, MA: MIT Press.

Astiev, S. V., Stanley, C. M., and Corbetta, M. (2004) "Extrastriate body area in human occipital cortex responds to the performance of motor actions," *Nature Neuroscience*, 7, 542–548.

Auvray, M., & Spence, C. (2008) "The multisensory perception of flavor," *Consciousness and Cognition*, 17(3), 1016–1031.

Barrós-Loscertales, A., González, J., Pulvermüller, F. Ventura-Campos, N., Bustamante, J., Costumero, V., Parcet, M., and Ávila, C. (2012) "Reading salt activates gustatory brain regions: fMRI evidence for semantic grounding in a novel sensory modality," *Cerebral Cortex*, 22(11), 2554–2563.

Barsalou, L. W. (1999) "Perceptual symbol systems," *Behavioral and Brain Sciences*, 22, 577–609.

——— (2010) "Grounded cognition: Past, present, and future," *Topics in Cognitive Science*, 2, 716–724.

——— (2016) "On staying grounded and avoiding Quixotic dead ends," *Psychonomic Bulletin & Review*, 23, 1122–1142.

——— (2020) "Challenges and Opportunities for Grounding Cognition," *Journal of Cognition*, 3(1), 1–24.

Bedny, M., Koster-Hale, J., Elli, G., Yazzolino, L., and Saxe, R. (2019) "There's more to sparkle than meets the eye: Knowledge of vision and light verbs among congenitally blind and sighted individuals," *Cognition*, 189, 105–115.

Bi, Y. (2021) "Dual coding of knowledge in the human brain," *Trends in Cognitive Science*, 25(10), 883–895.

Binder, J. R., Conant, L. L., Humphries, C. J., Fernandino, L., Simons, S. B., Aguilar, M., and Desai, R. H. (2016) "Toward a brain-based componential semantic representation," *Cognitive Neuropsychology*, 33(3–4), 130–174.

Binder, J. R., and Desai, R. H. (2011) "The neurobiology of semantic memory," *Trends in Cognitive Sciences*, 15, 527–536.

Borghesani, V., and Piazza, M. (2017) "The neurocognitive representation of symbols: The case of concrete words," *Neuropsychologia*, 105, 4–17.

Borghi, A. M., *et al.*, (2017). "The challenge of abstract concepts," *Psychological Bulletin*, 143(3), 263–292.

Bottini, R., Ferraro, S., Nigri, A., Cuccarini, V., Bruzzone, M. G. and Collignon, O. (2020). "Brain regions involved in conceptual retrieval in sighted and blind people," *Journal of Cognitive Neuroscience*, 32(6), 1009–1025.

Bottini, R., Morucci, P., D'Urso, A., Collignon, O., and Crepaldi, D. (2022) "The concreteness advantage in lexical decision does not depend on perceptual simulations," *Journal of Experimental Psychology: General*, 151(3), 731–738.

Bozeat, S., Lambon Ralph, M. A., Patterson, K., Garrard, P., and Hodges, J. R. (2000) "Non-verbal semantic impairment in semantic dementia," *Neuropsychologia*, 38, 1207–1215.

Calzavarini, F. (2021) "The conceptual format debate and the challenge from (global) supramodality," *British Journal for the Philosophy of Science*, 1–31.

Casasanto, D. (2024) "Bodily Relativity," in L. Shapiro & S. Spaulding (Eds), *The Routledge Handbook of Embodied Cognition*, Second Edition. London, UK: Routledge.

Chemero, A. (2011) *Radical Embodied Cognitive Science*, Cambridge, MA: MIT Press.

Coles, N. A., *et al.* (2022) "A multi-lab test of the facial feedback hypothesis by the Many Smiles Collaboration," *Nature Human Behavior*, 1–15.

Conca, F., and Tettamanti, M. (2018) "Conceptual semantics as grounded in personal experience," *Phenomenology and Mind*, 14, 98–116.

Coutanche, M. N., Thompson-Schill, S. L. (2015) "Creating concepts from converging features in human cortex," *Cerebral Cortex*, 25(9), 2584–2593.

Craighero, L. (2024) "Motor Resonance: Neurophysiological Origin, Functional Role, and Contribution of the Moral and Social Aspects of Action," in L. Shapiro & S. Spaulding (Eds), *The Routledge Handbook of Embodied Cognition*, Second Edition. London, UK: Routledge.

Dove, G. (2021). "The Challenges of Abstract Concepts," in M. Robinson & L. E. Thomas (Eds), *Handbook of Embodied Psychology: Thinking, Feeling, and Acting* (pp. 171–195). Cham, Switzerland: Springer.

——— (2022) *Abstract Concepts and the Embodied Mind: Rethinking Grounded Cognition*, Oxford, UK: Oxford University Press.

Fernandino, L., and Iacoboni, M. (2010) "Are cortical maps based on body parts or coordinated action? Implications for embodied semantics," *Brain and Language*, 112, 44–53.

Fodor, J. A. (1975) *The Language of Thought*, Cambridge, MA: MIT Press.

Foxe, J. J., Wylie, G. R., Martinez, A., Schroeder, C. E., Javitt, D. C., Guilfoyle, D., Ritter, W., and Murray, M. M. (2002) "Auditory somatosensory multisensory processing in auditory association cortex: An fMRI study," *Journal of Neurophysiology*, 88(1), 540–543.

Fulkerson, M. (2014) "Rethinking the senses and their interactions: The case for sensory pluralism," *Frontiers in Psychology*, 5, 1–14.

Garrard, P., and Carroll, E. (2006) "Lost in semantic space: A multi-modal, non-verbal assessment of feature knowledge in semantic dementia," *Brain*, 129, 1152–1163.

Ghazanfar, A. A., and Schroeder, C. E. (2006) "Is neocortex essentially multisensory?" *Trends in Cognitive Science*, 10(6), 278–285.

Glenberg, A. M. (2010) "Embodiment as a unifying perspective for psychology," *WIREs Cognitive Science*, 1(4), 586–596.

Goldberg, R. F., Perfetti, C. A., and Schneider, W. (2006) "Distinct and common cortical activations for multimodal semantic categories," *Cognitive, Affective & Behavioral Neuroscience*, 6(3), 214–222.

Graziano, M. S. A., (2018) *The Space between Us: A Story of Neuroscience, Evolution, and Human Nature*, Oxford, UK: Oxford University Press.

Graziano, M. S. A., and Aflalo, T. N. (2007) "Mapping the behavioral repertoire onto the cortex," *Neuron*, 56(2), 239–251.

Haimovici, S. (2018) "The Modal-Amodal distinction in the debate on conceptual format," *Philosophies*, 3(2), 1–13.

Hauk, O., Johnsrude, I., and Pulvermüller, F. (2004) "Somatopic representation of action words in human motor and premotor cortex," *Neuron*, 41, 301–307.

Hurley, S. (2001) "Perception and action: Alternative views," *Synthese*, 129(1), 3–40.

Iurilli, G., Ghezzi, D. Olcese, U., Lassi, G., Nazzaro, C., Tonini, R. Tucci, V., Benfenati, F. and Medini, P. (2012) "Sound-driven synaptic inhibition in primary visual cortex," *Neuron*, 73(4–2), 814–828.

Kaschak, M., Long, M., and Madden, J. (2024) "Embodied Approaches to Language Comprehension," in L. Shapiro & S. Spaulding (Eds), *The Routledge Handbook of Embodied Cognition*, Second Edition. London, UK: Routledge.

Keeley, B. (2002) "Making sense of the senses: Individuating modalities in humans and other animals," *Journal of Philosophy*, 99(1), 5–28.

Kemmerer, D. (2015) "Are the motor features of verb meanings represented in the precentral motor cortices? Yes, but within the context of a flexible, multilevel architecture for conceptual knowledge," *Psychological Bulletin and Review*, 22, 1068–1075.

——— (2019) *Concepts in the Brain: The View from Cross-Linguistic Diversity*, Oxford, UK: Oxford University Press.

——— (2022) "Grounded Cognition Entails Linguistic Relativity: A neglected Implication of a Major Semantic Theory," *Topics in Cognitive Science*, 15(4), 615–647.

Kemmerer, D., and Gonzalez-Castillo, J. (2010) "The two-level theory of verb meaning: An approach to integrating the semantics of action with the mirror neuron system," *Brain and Language*, 112, 54–76.

Kemmerer, D., Rudrauf, D., Manzel, K., and Tranel, D. (2012) "Behavioral patterns and lesion sites associated with impaired processing of lexical and conceptual knowledge of actions," *Cortex*, 48, 826–848.

Kompa, N. A. (2019) "Language and embodiment: On the cognitive benefits of abstract representations," *Mind and Language*, 36, 27–47.

Kuhnke, P., Beaupain, M. C., Arola, J., Kiefer, M. and Hartwigen, G. (2023) "Meta-analytic evidence for a novel hierarchical model of conceptual processing," *Neuroscience and Biobehavioral Reviews*, 144, 1–17.

Lambon Ralph, M. A. (2014) "Neurocognitive insights on conceptual knowledge and its breakdown," *Philosophical Transactions of the Royal Society, B*, 369(1634), 1–11.

Lingnau, A., and Downing, P. E. (2015) "The lateral occipitotemporal cortex in action," *Trends in Cognitive Science*, 19, 268–277.

Machery, E. (2007) "Concept empiricism: A methodological critique," *Cognition*, 104, 19–46.

——— (2016) "The amodal brain and the offloading hypothesis," *Psychonomic Bulletin & Review*, 23, 1090–1095.

Mahon, B. Z. (2015) "What is embodied about cognition?" *Language, Cognition and Neuroscience*, 30(4), 420–429.

Mahon, B. Z., and Caramazza, A. (2008) "A critical look at the embodied cognition hypothesis and a new proposal for grounding conceptual content," *Journal of Physiology of Paris*, 102, 59–70.

Martin, A. (2016) "GRAPES—Grounding representations in action, perception, and emotion systems: How object properties and categories are represented in the human brain," *Psychonomic Bulletin & Review*, 23, 979–990.

McCaffrey, J. (2015) "Reconceiving conceptual vehicles: Lessons from semantic dementia," *Philosophical Psychology*, 28, 337–354.

Meteyard, L., Cuadrado, S. R., Bahrami, B., and Viglocco, G. (2012) "Coming of age: A review of embodiment and the neuroscience of semantics," *Cortex*, 48, 788–804.

Michel, C. (2020) "Overcoming the modal/amodal dichotomy of concepts," *Phenomenology and the Cognitive Sciences*, 20, 655–677.

Morey, R. D., *et al.* (2022) "A pre-registered, multi-lab non-replication of the action-sentence compatibility effect (ACE)," *Psychonomic Bulletin & Review*, 29, 613–626.

Myers, A., and Snoweden, P. (2008) "Your hand or mine? The extrastriate body area," *Neuroimage*, 42(4), 1669–1677.

Patterson, K., Nestor, P. J., and Rogers, T. T. (2007) "Where do you know what you know? The representation of semantic knowledge in the human brain," *Nature Reviews Neuroscience*, 8, 976–987.

Piccinini, G. (2020) *Neurocognitive Mechanisms: Explaining Biological Cognition*, Oxford, UK: Oxford University Press.

Pobric, G., Jefferies, E., and Lambon Ralph, M. A. (2010) "Amodal semantic representations depend on both left and right anterior temporal lobes: New rTMS evidence," *Neuropsychologia*, 48, 1336–1342.

Pulvermüller, F. (2018) "Neural reuse of action perception circuits for language, concepts and communication," *Progress in Neurobiology*, 160, 1–44.

Pylyshyn, Z. W. (1984) *Computation and Cognition: Toward a Foundation for Cognitive Science*, Cambridge, MA: MIT Press.

Reilly, J., Peele, J. E., Garcia, A., and Crutch, S. J. (2016) "Linking somatic and symbolic representation in the semantic memory: The dynamic multilevel representation framework," *Psychonomic Bulletin & Review*, 23, 1002–1014.

Rust, N. C., and DiCarlo, J. J. (2010) "Selectivity and tolerance ("invariance") both increase as visual information propogates from cortical area V4 to IT," *Journal of Neuroscience*, 30(39), 12978–12995.

Scorolli, C., and Mazzuca, C. (2024) "The Grounding of Concrete and Abstract Knowledge: Consolidated Evidence, New Issues, and New Challenges," in L. Shapiro & S. Spaulding (Eds), *The Routledge Handbook of Embodied Cognition*, Second Edition. London, UK: Routledge.

Shams, L., Kamitani, Y., and Shimojo, S. (2000) "What you see is what you hear," *Nature*, 408, 788.

Shapiro, L. (2019). *Embodied Cognition* (2nd Ed.) New York: Routledge.

Shea, N. (2018) *Representation in Cognitive Science*, Oxford, UK: Oxford University Press.

Speed, L., & Majid, A. (2020) "Grounding language in the neglected senses of touch, taste, and smell," *Cognitive Neuropsycholgy*, 37(5–6), 363–392.

Sporns, O., Honey, C. J., and Kotter, R. (2007) "Identification and classification of hubs in brain networks," *PlOs One*, 10, 1–14.

Visser, M., Jefferies, E., Embleton, K. V., and Lambon Ralph, M. A. (2012) "Both the middle temporal gyrus and the ventral temporal area are crucial for multimodal semantic processing: Distortion-corrected fMRI evidence for a double gradient of information convergence in the temporal lobes," *Journal of Cognitive Neuroscience*, 24, 1766–1778.

Wang, X., Men, W., Gao, J., Caramazza, A., and Bi, Y. (2020) "Two Forms of Knowledge Representations in the Human Brain," *Neuron*, 107(2), 383–393.e5.

Willems, I. E., Hagoort, P., and Casasanto, D. (2010) "Body-specific representation of action words: Neural evidence from right- and left-handers," *Psychological Science*, 21, 67–74.

Zwaan, R. (2021) "Two challenges to 'Embodied Cognition' research and how to overcome them," 4(1), 1–9.

41

COGNITION

Gary Hatfield

Introduction

The study of cognition was widespread in experimental psychology after behaviorism's decline and was a reason for the decline. A specific notion of cognition was central to the rise of the interdisciplinary program of cognitive science. The perceptual psychologist James J. Gibson thought that postulation of cognitive processes should be avoided. Cognition, as knowledge, has long been studied in philosophy. Nowadays, cognitive psychology and cognitive science come in various flavors, including classical, connectionist, dynamic, ecological, embodied, embedded, enactive, and extended. These flavors differ in their conceptions of cognition and on the roles of the body and the environment in cognitive processes.

But what is cognition? What makes a process cognitive? These questions have been answered differently by various investigators and theoretical traditions. Even so, there are some commonalities, allowing us to specify a few contrasting answers to these questions. The main commonalities involve the notion that cognition is information processing that explains intelligent behavior. The differences concern whether early perceptual processes are cognitive, whether representations are needed to explain cognition, what makes something a representation, and whether cognitive processes are limited to the nervous system and brain, or include other bodily structures or the environment itself.

After unearthing some root notions of cognition in the development of cognitive psychology and cognitive science, this chapter considers the commonalities and differences just scouted, examines Wheeler's (2005) reference to Descartes' works in describing "Cartesian" cognitive theory, finds the real target of situated approaches in classical symbolic cognitive science, and suggests that, instead of revisiting that target, attention should turn to characterizing the varieties of intelligent (adaptive, appropriate, flexible) behavior.

Some root notions of cognition

Bernard Baars (1985), in his excellent study of the "cognitive revolution," describes cognitive psychology as a metatheory that supplanted the previous behavioristic metatheory.

 DOI: 10.4324/9781003322511-52

Behaviorism was many-splendored. It came in Watsonian, Hullian, Tolmanian, and Skinnerian varieties. All agreed that behavior provides the evidence and object of explanation for psychology, and all but Tolman excluded mentalistic terms in describing and explaining that behavior. Tolman allowed intentionality, Gestalt principles of perceptual organization, and representational cognitive maps (Hatfield 2003).

By the 1950s, Hullian learning theory, which was deeply theoretical (positing non-mentalistic inner states), was in retreat, while Skinner's "hollow organism" behaviorism, which shunned internal states in psychological explanation, was ascendant. Against both Hull and Skinner, some psychologists – sometimes in league with computer scientists and linguists, and sometimes extending ongoing work (from earlier in the century, including that of Gestalt psychology) in perception, attention, and memory – began to posit internal states described in terms of information processing or information flow. In Baars's (1985) account, these psychologists used behavioral data to infer unobservable internal constructs, such as "purposes," "ideas," "memory," "attention," and "meaning" (pp. 7, 144). Psychologists came to speak of "representations" that organisms have of themselves and their world, and they construed the transformation of such representations as "information processing" (p. 7). Such internal representations were only reluctantly described as "conscious" or as subject to introspection (pp. 169, 414).[1] Starting from Baars's portrayal, we can distinguish several conceptions of cognition in the literature.

Cognitive mechanisms and information processing

In 1967, Ulric Neisser published a signal work entitled *Cognitive Psychology*. It included two major parts, on visual and auditory cognition, and a brief part on higher mental processes. Neisser offered two glosses on the term "cognitive psychology," indicating a broader and a narrower conception of cognition. In a broad sense, cognitive psychology studies the "cognitive mechanisms," which include perception, pattern recognition, imagery, retention, recall, problem solving, concept formation, and thinking (Neisser 1967, p. 4, 10, 11). In a narrow sense, Neisser promoted a conception of cognition as "the flow of information in the organism," including many transformations and reconstructions of that information (pp. vii, 208). In his view, "Whatever we know about reality is mediated, not only by the organs of sense but by complex systems which interpret and reinterpret sensory information" (p. 3). His cognitive psychology largely focused on visual and auditory information processing. He described such processing as yielding not only behavior but also "those private experiences of seeing, hearing, imagining, and thinking to which verbal descriptions never do full justice" (p. 3). His book refers to behavioral data but also describes perceptual experiences. Although not labeling these as "conscious," he clearly included conscious experience among the discussables.

By contrast with theories to come, I should note that Neisser was aware of comparisons between human cognition and digital computers, and found comparing human processes with computer programs to be useful but limited; he expressed deep skepticism of AI (artificial intelligence) models, such as that of Newell, Shaw, and Simon (1958), and, by his own account, largely put them aside (Neisser 1967: p. 9). Neisser's cognitive psychology invoked psychological processes of construction and synthesis, which were characterized in task-specific terms. His heroes included especially Bartlett (1932, 1958), who worked on memory, but also Broadbent (1958), who worked on attentional constraints in auditory perception, and Bruner, who worked on concept formation (Bruner, Goodnow, and Austin 1956).

Neisser's approach (1967, 304–5) did not focus on explaining the behavior of human beings freely acting "in the wild" (i.e., outside the laboratory). Rather, he aimed to discover information-processing mechanisms by inferring their characteristics from the available data. This information-processing approach to psychology, which sees its subject matter as the information-processing mechanisms underlying perception, attention, recognition, categorization, memory, learning, problem solving, thinking, and speech, became entrenched. Often, information processing was itself the root notion (Lindsay and Norman 1972; Massaro 1989), and "cognition" (a term these authors used sparingly) was distinguished from perception as pertaining to the processes in recognition, problem solving, and memory. This runs counter to Neisser's conception of cognitive psychology as concerned with all information processing, including perception. Neisser's conception lives on, as seen in Dawson (1998) and Eysenck and Keane (2020), but with a difference: the conception of information processing is now allied to computation.

Cognition as symbol processing

Comparisons with computers as information handling devices were not uncommon in the 1950s and 1960s. With the formulation of Fodor's (1975) language-of-thought hypothesis, the computer analogy became the foundation of a new, interdisciplinary enterprise soon to be called "cognitive science" (e.g., Collins 1977). Fodor's approach was to extract a common set of computational assumptions from recent work in cognitive psychology and psycholinguistics. His main examples were rational choice, concept learning, perceptual belief, and language learning. In his terms, such theories involved computations defined over symbolic representations. (Actually, he would have considered "symbolic representation" to be redundant, since he unceremoniously treated the terms as interchangeable; Fodor, 1975, p. 55.)

Fodor grounded his notion of symbol in a comparison with the machine language in a standard digital computer. Humans are "built to use" their native language of thought (Fodor, 1975, p. 66). Empirically, we know we have the right computational theories when symbolically characterized inputs, internal processes, and outputs line up with stimuli and with responses as described in subjects' propositional attitudes (pp. 74–75). The posited internal formulae should line up with a subject's beliefs or other intentional states. A cognitive theory "tries to characterize the ways in which the propositional attitudes of an organism are contingent upon its data processes, where 'data processes' are sequences of operations upon formulae of the internal language" (p. 77). Standard or "classical" cognitive science was born.

John Haugeland soon clarified the object and the structure of explanation of "cognitivism" (1978) or "cognitive science" (1981). As he put it: "The basic idea of cognitive science is that *intelligent beings are semantic engines* – in other words, automatic formal systems with interpretations under which they consistently make sense" (Haugeland 1981, p. 31). Haugeland here endorses symbolic computationalism, imputing a formal system under an interpretation to cognitive systems. The formal system, like that in a computer, can be characterized wholly in syntactic terms. In a theory of cognition, the theorist assigns an interpretation to the computational states that "makes sense of" the organism's behavior in relation to its situation (pp. 28–33). That is, the theorist proposes that states of the system intrinsically have certain meanings or contents.[2] Haugeland also expresses a conception of cognition that has become widespread: cognition is what supports intelligent behavior.

Computation and representation without symbol systems

In the early days of classicism, David Marr (1982) proposed a useful way of thinking about perceptual and cognitive processes. He distinguished three levels of analysis: computational, algorithmic, and implementational. The computational level essentially was a task analysis: it specifies what task the given perceptual or cognitive system is supposed to fulfill in the organism. The algorithmic level proposes concrete processing operations that, in models of vision (Marr's target), would operate on optical inputs and transform them into a representation of the distal scene. Finally, the implementational level is the hardware realization of the processing operations. His approach also charted the employment in the visual system of environmental regularities, such as that surfaces are comparatively smooth.

Marr (1982, p. 343) thought of the algorithms and their implementation in classical, symbolist terms. But he need not have done so. His three-level analysis allowed others to propose alternative schemes for thinking about algorithms and implementation. Theories of vision had long postulated operations to combine information. While some theorists, such as Irvin Rock (1975), conceived of these operations as inferential (and carried out in a language-like, albeit insulated, system of representations; Rock 1983, p. 13), other theorists recognized that such operations might combine perceptual information, conceived in analog terms (e.g., as continuously varying magnitudes), without the benefit of cognitive and conceptual processes such as inference (Hatfield 1988; see also Hatfield and Epstein 1985; Epstein 1973). Processes that combine optical information for visual angle with a registered value for distance to yield size perception fit this bill, but so might mechanisms for recovering Gibsonian higher-order stimulus variables.

In 1984, Kosslyn and Hatfield proposed a connectionist interpretation as especially suited to perceptual processing, explicitly reinterpreting Marr's algorithms as non-symbolic but representational, with a neural-net or connectionist implementation. Such processing models might invoke rules of information combination and notions of representations of proximal and distal states, without thinking of the rules as explicitly represented (as in symbolic models) or of the representations as syntactic (they might be analog). In a later terminology, the processing rules might be *instantiated* without being explicitly represented (Hatfield 1991a, 1991b). Kosslyn and Hatfield also observed that Marr's "assumptions" about environmental regularities could be construed not as explicitly stated rules but as "engineering assumptions," by which they meant that "it is as if the system were engineered in such a way that it will work in environments where certain conditions are met" (Kosslyn and Hatfield 1984, p. 1040).[3]

Connectionist models come in a variety of forms, associated with sometimes opposing conceptions of representation, such as local versus distributed representations (for an overview, see Bechtel and Abrahamsen 1991). In models of early perceptual achievements, such as the creation of visual representations of shaped surfaces at a distance, connectionist networks can provide a happy medium for modeling rule-instantiating analog perceptual processes. The connectionist approach has also been applied to complex cognitive tasks such as language processing, using dynamical models that allow continuously varying magnitudes to serve as (sub-symbolic) representations (Smolensky 1988).[4] Connectionism is not a specific approach but offers a family of model types that enable various ways of thinking about perception and cognition without going symbolic from the start. Although such models are not essentially situated, it makes sense in thinking about connectionist processes to see them as adjusted to environmental regularities (Hatfield 1988, 1990). Not having the symbolic metaphor to fall back on, such models may (or should) appeal to environmentally conditioned task analyses in grounding their notions of what is computed and what representations are needed.

Cognition as what supports intelligent behavior

The cognitive revolution entrenched the notion that cognitive processes are responsible for effective behavior. This idea is expressed by Bechtel and colleagues: "Cognitive science is the multidisciplinary scientific study of cognition and its role in intelligent agency. It examines what cognition is, what it does, and how it works" (Bechtel, Abrahamsen, and Graham 1998, p. 3). As they make clear, this definition is broad enough to cover various conceptions of how cognition works: classical, connectionist, and situated (pp. 91–92). Some of these approaches, under the umbrella of situated cognition, challenge the notion of cognition as information processing in the head. But such challengers retain a steady conception of what cognition does, which is "to enable agents to interact intelligently with their environments" (p. 92).

Recourse to the notion of "intelligent agency" (or the earlier "intelligent beings") invites reflection on the notion of intelligence. The term plays a prominent role in discussion but is not found in the index or table of contents (except as "Artificial Intelligence" and "Unconscious Intelligence," Bechtel and Graham 1998, p. vi). The chapter on "Unconscious Intelligence" characterizes unconscious processes as "smart" or "intelligent" if they are "sophisticated, flexible, and adaptive" (Allen and Reber 1998, p. 314). This description may exclude reflexes and also instincts (on many conceptions). Otherwise, it is open-ended, presumably including early visual processes that underlie the perceptual constancies and other sensory processes that are world directed, as well as action guidance, concept formation, emotion (at least cognitive theories of the emotions), problem solving, and reasoning.

When Haugeland (1981) spoke of cognitive processes as providing an account of intelligence, these processes were conceived as occurring between stimulus and response. Cognitive theories replaced behavioristic intervening variables with mentalistic ones. Those were at first symbolically conceived, but connectionism soon provided an alternative that also accommodated notions of representation and information processing. In the usual paradigms, cognition occurs between stimulus and response and does not consider the effects of responses on stimulation or take account of bodily organization, and only in some cases (including Marr) is it put in relation to environmental regularities. As it happens, the push toward embodiment and environmental embeddedness originally came from a theorist who was anti-cognitivist.

Gibson and his impact: the importance of the environment

While the information-processing psychologists of the 1950s, 1960s, and 1970s were filling in between the sense organs and behavior (focusing on internal processes), Gibson was arguing that organisms are active in perceiving (1950), that sensory systems evolved to respond to environmental regularities (1966), and in favor of an ecological psychology in which the environment is described in organism-relative terms, yielding an "ecological physics" (1979). Gibson held that traditional theories of visual perception overlooked significant aspects of sensory information, including adequate information in the light to specify the distal environment. Consequently, he found no need to posit cognitive operations to supplement sensory information. He held that physiological mechanisms pick up information by "resonating" to it (Gibson 1966, pp. 4–5), but he did not fill out the resonance analogy. Even if his view is not completely right (about either rich information or the elision of psychological processes to recover it; Hatfield 1988, 1990; Neisser 1976), Gibson's work directed attention to the tie between perception and action and the fact that an organism's own activity in relation to the environment generates stimulus information (e.g., bodily motion in a direction creates optic flow that specifies that direction).

Gibson's outlook spurred a substantial research tradition, including many who shared his anti-cognitivist outlook. Within this tradition, Turvey and his colleagues developed a dynamical systems approach to picking up Gibsonian information, which rejects any appeal to representations or traditional information processing. Nonetheless, they did offer a view of cognition. According to Turvey and Carello, "The term 'cognition' is taken, very generally, to refer to the coordination of any organism (as an epistemic agent) and its environment (as the support for its acts). The task of cognitive theory is to explain this epistemic, intentional coordination of organism and environment" (1981, p. 313). Rejecting internal representations and unsecured attributions of intelligence, they emphasized Gibsonian realism, his commitment to organism–environment informational relations, an ecological scale of analysis, and appeal to dynamic physical systems to portray internal processes (thereby elaborating the resonance analogy). "Intentional" relations to the environment are reduced to informational relations between environment and organism. In a more recent overview, these authors conclude: "Consistent with a strategic approach to perception and action that minimizes (and, for all practical purposes, precludes) mental representations and computations, we have identified some dynamical themes that have been exploited in ecological research in haptic perception and coordinated movement" (Turvey and Carello 1995, p. 396). The specific examples include visual-tactual coordination in learning to juggle and to use control levers. In this more recent survey, they avoid the term "cognition" altogether.

Gibson incited even mainstream cognitivists to alter their conceptions so as to take account of embodiment, environmental embeddedness, and organismic action. In 1976, Neisser published a second book sounding these themes. He conceived perception as a cycle that incorporates action and in which cognitive schemata direct exploration of the environment and the sampling of present objects, acquiring information that in turn alters the schemata (Neisser 1976, pp. 20–24). He considered the processes by which the schemata direct exploration and incorporate information to be cognitive. His definition of cognition was quite abstract: "Cognition is the activity of knowing: the acquisition, organization, and use of knowledge" (p. 1). But his intent was clear: he wished to join a Gibsonian outlook with mentalistic notions from the information-processing tradition (p. 24). Marr, with his emphasis on ecologically valid environmental assumptions, was also deeply indebted to Gibson's approach (Marr 1982, pp. 29–31).

Fast-forwarding, theoretical outlooks that fall under the umbrella of situated cognition (dynamic, ecological, embodied, embedded, enactive, and extended) have proliferated. Among these, Gibsonian inspiration is often but not everywhere acknowledged. The notion of cognition remains that of the new mainstream: cognition supports intelligent behavior (Clark 2010, p. 92). Michael Wheeler (2005), from the extended cognition camp, has been especially explicit on the breadth that he desires in interpreting the notion of intelligence. He sees cognitive processing as yielding "displays of intelligence" that involve "behaving appropriately (e.g., adaptively, in a context-sensitive fashion) with respect to some (usually) external target state of affairs" (p. 3). The notions of "intelligence" and "cognition" are here used in a "deliberately broad and nonanthropocentric manner," to include not only human capacities for reflective thought and conceptualization but also "cases in which an agent coordinates sensing and movement, in real time, so as to generate fluid and flexible responses to incoming stimuli" (ibid.). Animal cognition is included (e.g., tracking mates, avoiding predators). Action is intelligent, including navigating the terrain as an animal moves along. Cognition includes both "knowing that" and "knowing how" (p. 4). The processes that support intelligent behavior are conceived as dynamical systems, and only sometimes involve internal representations (see also van Gelder and Port 1995, pp. 11–12).[5]

The core notion of cognition started as information processing and was then modified by differing models of how information is processed, including classical and connectionist visions. As work proceeded, the notion of cognition as supporting intelligent behavior gained currency.[6] How it does so has been variously conceived. The past two decades have seen rapid growth in conceptions of situated cognition.

Commonalities and differences in the notion of cognition

If one wanted a notion of the cognitive that could cover all the above usages, including Turvey and Carello (1981) and other non-representational dynamical systems approaches (e.g., Kelso 1995; Chemero 2009), it would have to be defined at the *molar* level, as a type of behavior of the whole organism. Cognitive behavior would be adaptive, appropriate, and flexible in relation to environmental and organismic circumstances.

There is something to be said for seeking to identify the forms of behavior that are cognitive at the molar level. However, it is more idiomatic to call such behavior "intelligent" than "cognitive." This aspect of linguistic usage favors the notion that cognition is mental and that the mind is more than its behavioral expression. Still, molar-level analyses of what makes behaviors intelligent or flexibly adaptive would be useful. This might have something of the feel of Ryle's (1949) analysis of clever behavior, but without the added rider that there can be no intraorganismic explanation of the cleverness. With such a molar description in place, one might choose to use the term "cognitive" to describe the processes that explain intelligent behavior. It might then be best to restrict that term to those processes that involve mentalistic notions such as representation or mental content and that have a place in "cognitive mechanisms" such as those listed earlier (pp. 000–00).[7] Accordingly, all the above usages would be included, except that of Turvey and Carello (1981) and other non-representational dynamicists.

Within this still quite large group, there are differences in what counts as cognition. Especially in the decades from the 1960s through the 1980s, a significant number of theorists distinguished perception from cognition. This occurred at two different levels of analysis. First, at the molar level, the perceptual theorist Rock distinguished "sensory processes" that constitute perception from "cognitive processes" (1975, p. 24). He assigned to the first group the formation of a perceptual object through the perception of shape, size, distance, direction, orientation, and rest or motion. The second category begins "where perception ends," with "the perceived object," and includes "recognition, recall, association, attention, abstraction, concept formation, understanding and meaningful learning, problem solving, and thinking" (ibid.). In this scheme, the cognitive and the conceptual go together. This sort of usage matches that of Lindsay and Norman (1972) and Massaro (1989).

Among those distinguishing perception from cognition, the second level of analysis concerns the character of the underlying processes that yield molar perception and cognition. Rock (1983), while maintaining a distinction between perceptual (in vision, picture-like) and cognitive (recognitional) achievements, proposed that perception is mediated internally by inferential operations that might easily be labeled "cognitive." For instance, he suggested that perceptual processes involve language-like, propositional descriptions that enter into deductive inferences (pp. 13, 240). Elizabeth Spelke (1988) argued the other way, that the processes underlying perception are essentially non-conceptual. For that reason, she assigns molar-level object perception to cognitive or conceptual processes, as when she says that "the apprehension of objects is a cognitive act, brought about by a mechanism that begins to operate at the point where perception ends" and brings concepts to bear (p. 199). I made the same alignment of "cognitive" with "conceptual" in Hatfield (1988), so that by "non-cognitive" processes I meant non-conceptual algorithms involving non-conceptual perceptual representations. This more restricted usage has faded, and the term "cognition" is now frequently applied even to early vision.[8]

Other theoretical differences arise in considering situated cognition. As amply illustrated in this volume, the embodied cognition camp assigns the body a significant role in cognitive achievements. They sometimes claim to replace the machinery of representations with non-representational dynamic processing. That the structure of the body is important in the cycle of perception and action would not be denied by a theorist such as Neisser (1976). But he weds the outlook with information-processing accounts. Those who do otherwise (non-representationalists) cannot be arguing simply from the fact of embodiment; rather, they must give other reasons for rejecting representations. The extended cognition thesis also comes in representationalist (e.g., Clark and Chalmers 1998) and non-representationalist forms (discussed in Wheeler 2005; see Chemero 2009). Again, the extended cognition hypothesis, according to which the world itself can enter into cognitive processes that guide effective behavior, is not intrinsically non-representational. The need for representations surely hinges on whether, in order to explain intelligent (adaptive, appropriate, flexible) behavior in its many manifestations, representations bring explanatory advantages some or all of the time (see Shapiro 2019: chs. 7, 10).[9]

Anti-Cartesian cognitive science

In the cognitive science literature, there is much talk of rejecting a Cartesian picture of the mind in favor of some other view, representationalist or not. This can mean many things, including rejecting Cartesian dualism (Bechtel *et al.* 1998, p. 62), or rejecting the view that rational manipulation of internal representations, ignoring body and environment, suffices for effective behavior (Rowlands 1999, pp. 4–5; van Gelder 1995, pp. 380–81). For the most part, anti-Cartesians avoid engaging Descartes' own writings. Wheeler (2005) is an exception. He engages Descartes directly. Because this proponent of extended cognition considered it important to show that Descartes held the to-be-rejected views, correcting this mistaken impression is worthwhile. Leaving substance dualism aside and focusing on intelligent or situationally appropriate behavior, I present Descartes as an advocate of embodied behavioral effectiveness and extended memory.

Wheeler (2005: chs. 2–3) seeks to establish that Descartes subscribed to five theses that form part of a contemporary "Cartesian psychology." They are: (1) mind is representational, (2) intelligent action occurs through sense-represent-plan-move cycles, (3) perception is essentially inferential, (4) most intelligent human action comes from general-purpose reasoning mechanisms, and (5) the environment provides only problems, sensory inputs, and a stage for pre-planned actions (Wheeler 2005: ch. 3). Here, I challenge (2)–(5).

There is no doubt that Descartes held that mind is representational. Further, he would contend that true intelligence is mental. But he denied that all situationally appropriate behavior arises from the mind and that the mind simply uses the body to carry out actions. On the contrary, he held that many behaviors result from physiological processes: "a very large number of the motions occurring in us do not depend on mind," including "actions such as walking, singing, and the like, when these occur without the mind attending to them" (Descartes 1984, p. 161). Bodily mechanisms are attuned to environmental circumstances: "When people take a fall, and stick out their hands so as to protect their head, it is not reason that instructs them to do this; it is simply that the sight of the impending fall reaches the brain and sends the animal spirits into the nerves in the manner necessary to produce this movement even without any volition" (ibid.).[10] Descartes advanced a theory of the passions or emotions according to which, at the sight of a frightful animal, brain processes alone cause the body to turn and flee. These same processes simultaneously cause the feeling of fear. The function of this feeling is "to encourage the soul to want to flee"; the passions more generally have the function of "disposing the soul to want the things" that the body is already engaged in (Descartes 1985, p. 343). Note that there is no "sense-represent-plan-move cycle" here. Rather, there is: bodily process, which causes movement and an emotion that inclines the soul or mind (without rational deliberation or "general reasoning") to want to carry on the movement (see Hatfield 2007). In these cases, the behavioral agent (i.e., the human subject) is not the mind alone, but the body plus mind, and the mind's function need not be deliberative.

Descartes did not regard all perception as inferential; he developed a sophisticated physiological model of distance perception, according to which an experience of distance is directly caused in the mind by brain mechanisms (see Hatfield 2015, pp. 123–39).[11] Perhaps the most surprising passage to cite here concerns embodied and extended memory. In a letter explaining his views on memory, Descartes of course affirms that the brain is involved in memory. But so is the body: "I think that all the nerves and muscles can be so utilized [for memory], so that a lute player, for instance, has a part of his memory in his hands" (Descartes 1991, p. 146). And there is "extended" memory: "what people call 'local memory' is outside us: for instance, when we have read a book, not all the impressions which can remind us of its contents are in our brain. Many of them are on the paper of the copy which we have read" (ibid.). Presumably, some of the book's content enters brain memory; the printed pages constitute a more extensive memory record. Descartes does not hold that the page is part of the mind, but it is part of the phenomenon of memory.

One could pile on examples to show how Cartesian psychology and theory of mind has been caricatured in recent times, abetting a deep postmodern animosity toward Descartes.[12] That is not the present point. Rather, we should believe that this version of Cartesian psychology as targeted by adherents of situated cognition was invented for a reason, to portray an opponent. But, leaving substance dualism aside, the real opponent is not Descartes. So, what is it?

Conclusion: the real target? And whence now?

The real target of many of those who emphasize situatedness and environmental embedding is the classical symbolist conception, or that together with those connectionist models that eschew environmental relations. The static "rules and representations" that are usually the target of rebellion are explicitly represented rules conjoined with symbolic representations.[13] A fine target. But there have been alternatives to that paradigm all along. An attack that merely shows that some behaviors are successfully modeled without invoking symbolic computation is not news. Effort should instead be spent on articulating what the alternative frameworks are actually saying.

Concerning representation, we have met two alternative frameworks. One allows representations to vary continuously and one seeks to avoid representations altogether. A third variant uses representations sometimes but not others (e.g., Wheeler 2005). All three seek to include the body and the environment.

The non-representationalist frameworks may explain behaviors such as toddler walking and perseverative reaching behavior in infants (Smith and Thelen 2003). Dyed-in-the-wool symbolists would model these behaviors symbolically. But others, including Descartes, might explain them through non-mentalistic physiological processes. Other behaviors, such as tracking and catching prey, or using a mass transit system, may invite other sorts of modeling, perhaps requiring or at least inviting internal representations.

Let us accept Wheeler's (2005) plea that cognitive psychology and cognitive science, construed broadly, should aim to explain a wide range of intelligent (adaptive, appropriate, flexible) behaviors. If intelligent behavior, broadly construed, is the object of explanation – perhaps augmented by human perceptual and other types of experience[14] – then there needs to be consideration of the varieties of behavior (and experiences). This may lead to the notion of a variety of intelligences.

Evolution is frequently omitted from situated discussion (but see Gibson 1966: ch. 9; Rowlands 1999: chs. 4, 11; Wilson 2004).[15] The literature on the evolution of mind might help in thinking about the varieties of behavior and intelligence. In the evolution of the hominid line, group hunting, tool making, and habitat improvement arose at various points. What cognitive mechanisms allowed for these behaviors to arise? Some theorists posit the evolution of several different types of modular intelligence (e.g., Mithen 1996, 2013). Others emphasize a smaller set of adaptations, perhaps starting from auto-cued motor sequences used for making tools and then for dancing (e.g., Donald 1991, 2013). Even if not all actions are planned, skilled action may involve representational routines to guide its manifestation. Engaging in helping behavior may require intention-reading (Warneken 2013). Other animals show other ranges of skills, requiring specific types of competencies (e.g., Seyfarth and Cheney 2013).

There is no such thing as intelligent behavior in general. What may be needed now is a survey of behavioral and cognitive skills and other tendencies, with an eye toward the explanatory resources that can account for them. Representations, including non-conceptual and conceptual, action-guiding and recognitional, individual and intention-sharing or cooperation-affording, are sure to be in the mix. They need not be symbolic or come formulated in explicit rules. Connectionist and dynamical systems may use them. They may vary continuously or be discrete. But they are here to stay.

Notes

1 On the renewal of cognitive approaches, including other portrayals, see Hatfield, 2002. See also Bechtel, Abrahamsen, and Graham, 1998. On the history of psychology and the cognitive revolution, Greenwood, 2015, chs. 10–12.

2 The "assignment" of intentional content is not merely instrumental but imputes "original intentionality" to the system (Haugeland, 1981, p. 33). Such assignments must make sense of the agent's behavior "relative to the environment." While the conditions on an adding machine are simple formal truth, in assigning content to behaving organisms "other conditions" are important, including context, that is, considering outputs "in relation to one another and in relation to the situation in which they are produced" (pp. 32–33). Fodor (1975, ch. 2, esp. pp. 71–73) also recognizes environmental constraints in interpreting propositional attitudes (hence internal formulae), but less clearly or forcefully. Subsequently, Fodor (1980) proposed that cognitive science should be concerned only with the formal operations mediating between input and output and not with relations to the environment. Methodological solipsism (or so-called "narrow content") was not a founding or essential feature of symbolic computationalism. Shapiro (1994) contrasts behavior narrowly construed with the objects of investigation in mainstream cognitive psychology of the 1970s and 1980s. He shows that many discussions in philosophy of psychology treated behavior as mere physically described movement, by contrast with environmentally related descriptions of behavior by ethologists, behaviorists, and cognitive psychologists.

3 On Marr's theory and debates over wide and narrow content, see Shapiro, 1993.

4 On affinities between connectionism with a dynamical systems approach and the field theories of Gestalt psychology, see Hatfield and Epstein, 1985, pp. 179–83, and Epstein and Hatfield, 1994, pp. 175–77.

5 Some adherents of dynamical systems approach acknowledge affinity with Gestalt field theories (e.g., Kelso, 1995).

6 Other, broader specifications of cognitive science, which define it as "a cross-disciplinary enterprise devoted to exploring and understanding the nature of the mind" (Frankish and Ramsey, 2012, p. 1), apparently equate *mind* with *cognition*, either unacceptably narrowing the former term or expanding the latter.

7 There have been attempts to specify a "mark of the cognitive." Adams and Aizawa (2008) propose that part of the mark is underived content, belonging to a system intrinsically. This accords with my notion of mentalistic representation and mental content. Perceptual and cognitive psychologists normally assume underived content. To this, Adams and Aizawa (2008, ch. 4) add that, for a system to be cognitive, certain sorts of processes must take place, which they indicate through example. In a different spirit, some (see Thompson 2007, pp. 122–27) extend the "cognitive" to include all effective activities for self-maintenance in relation to the environment (so that every living thing on Earth is cognitive).

8 It may still be useful to distinguish non-conceptual cognitive-perceptual processes from conceptual ones. One might even consider non-conceptual perceptual content, of which size and shape at a distance are typical instances (Dretske, 1981, ch. 6), to be "cognitive" in that they stably represent the spatial environment (the latter is not Dretske's usage). Such usage would prize apart the conceptual and the cognitive. (Thanks to Louise Daoust for this suggestion.)

9 Wilson (2004) renders individuals as the bearers of *psychological* states but regards *cognitive* states as locationally wide (extending into the environment) and treats Gibsonian optical arrays as parts of locationally wide computational systems (Wilson, 2004, ch. 7, esp. p. 171). His distinction between psychological and cognitive states needs fuller articulation, as does the sense in which the optic array is cognitive (as opposed to being an environmental condition that sensory systems exploit, including those deemed to engage in information processing).

10 In Descartes' scheme, "animal spirits" are purely material processes that serve neural functions.

11 Descartes also described mechanisms for size and distance perception involving inference (Hatfield, 2015, pp. 140–43).

12 The caricatures often arise from reading Descartes' *Meditations* as if every statement, including those made under radical doubt, should be taken at face value (see Fodor, 1980, pp. 64–65). When Descartes speaks of being only a mind, he is taken literally, despite his subsequent conclusion that

the human being consists of mind and body (1984, pp. 24, 61). His skepticism toward the senses is allowed to stand, despite his reconception of sensory function as embodied and embedded; the primary function of the senses is bodily preservation in environmental circumstances (Descartes, 1984, pp. 56–61).

13 An even smaller target, frequently invoked, is the subclass of classical (symbolist) models espousing methodological solipsism or narrow content. Fodor (1980) advanced methodological solipsism in despair of fixing representational content by environmental relations: accordingly, cognitive science should study only internal symbolic computations. Stich (1983) embraced the despair; under renewed Gibsonian inspiration, few would now.

14 Human perceptual experience and other forms of consciousness are included in contemporary research, both as objects of explanation and sources of data. Phenomenal experience certainly is included in vision science (Palmer, 1999). The situated cognition literature is mixed anent its interest in such data.

15 Among environmentally attuned representationalist views, evolutionary considerations have been invoked in teleosemantics, e.g., Dretske, 1986, Neander, 2017.

References

Adams, F., and Aizawa, K. (2008) *The bounds of cognition*, Malden, MA: Blackwell.

Allen, R., and Reber, A. S. (1998) "Unconscious intelligence," in W. Bechtel and G. Graham (Eds), *A Companion to cognitive science* (pp. 314–323). Malden, MA: Blackwell.

Baars, B. J. (1985) *The cognitive revolution in psychology*, New York: Guilford.

Bartlett, F. C. (1932) *Remembering: A study in experimental and social psychology*, Cambridge: Cambridge University Press.

——— (1958) *Thinking: An experimental and social study*, New York: Basic Books.

Bechtel, W., and Abrahamsen, A. (1991) *Connectionism and the mind: An introduction to parallel processing in networks*, Oxford: Basil Blackwell.

Bechtel, W., Abrahamsen, A., and Graham, G. (1998) "The life of cognitive science," in W. Bechtel and G. Graham (Eds), *A companion to cognitive science* (pp. 1–104). Malden, MA: Blackwell.

Bechtel, W., and Graham, G. (Eds) (1998) *A companion to cognitive science*, Malden, MA: Blackwell.

Broadbent, D. E. (1958) *Perception and communication*, New York: Pergamon Press.

Bruner, J. S., Goodnow, J. J., and Austin, G. A. (1956) *A study of thinking*, New York: Wiley.

Chemero, A. (2009) *Radical embodied cognitive science*, Cambridge, MA: MIT Press.

Clark, A. (2010) "Coupling, constitution, and the cognitive kind: A reply to Adams and Aizawa," in Richard Menary (ed.), *The extended mind* (pp. 81–99). Cambridge, MA: MIT Press.

Clark, A., and Chalmers, D. (1998) "The extended mind," *Analysis, 58*, 7–19.

Collins, A. (1977) "Why cognitive science," *Cognitive Science, 1*, 1–2.

Dawson, M. R. W. (1998) *Understanding cognitive science*, Malden, MA: Blackwell.

Descartes, R. (1984) *Philosophical writings of Descartes*: Vol. 2 (J. Cottingham, R. Stoothoff, and D. Murdoch, Trans.), Cambridge: Cambridge University Press.

——— (1985) *Philosophical writings of Descartes*: Vol. 1 (J. Cottingham, R. Stoothoff, and D. Murdoch, Trans.), Cambridge: Cambridge University Press.

——— (1991) *Philosophical writings of Descartes*: Vol. 3. *Correspondence* (J. Cottingham, R. Stoothoff, D. Murdoch, and A. Kenny, Trans.), Cambridge: Cambridge University Press.

Donald, M. (1991) *Origins of the modern mind*, Cambridge, MA: Harvard University Press.

——— (2013) "Mimesis theory re-examined, twenty years after the fact," in G. Hatfield and H. Pittman (Eds), *Evolution of mind, brain, and culture* (pp. 169–192), Philadelphia, PA: University of Pennsylvania Museum of Anthropology and Archaeology.

Dretske, F. (1981) *Knowledge and the flow of information*, Cambridge, MA: MIT Press.

——— (1986) "Misrepresentation," in R. J. Bogdan (ed.), *Belief: Form, content, and function* (pp. 17–36), Oxford: Oxford University Press.

Epstein, W. (1973) "The process of "taking into account" in visual perception," *Perception, 11*, 75–83.

Epstein, W., and Hatfield, G. (1994) "Gestalt psychology and the philosophy of mind," *Philosophical Psychology, 7*, 163–181.

Eysenck, M. W., and Keane, M. T. (2020) *Cognitive psychology: A student's handbook* (8th ed.), Abingdon: Routledge.

Fodor, J. A. (1975) *Language of thought*, New York: Crowell.

———— (1980) "Methodological solipsism considered as a research strategy in cognitive psychology," *Behavioral and Brain Sciences*, 3, 63–109.

Frankish, K., and Ramsey, W. M. (2012) "Introduction," in K. Frankish and W. M. Ramsey (Eds), *The Cambridge handbook of cognitive science* (pp. 1–6), Cambridge: Cambridge University Press.

Gibson, J. J. (1950) *The perception of the visual world*, Boston: Houghton Mifflin.

———— (1966) *The senses considered as perceptual systems*, Boston: Houghton Mifflin.

———— (1979) *The ecological approach to visual perception*, Boston: Houghton Mifflin.

Greenwood, J. D. (2015) *A conceptual history of psychology: Exploring the tangled web* (2nd ed.), Cambridge: Cambridge University Press.

Hatfield, G. (1988) "Representation and content in some (actual) theories of perception," *Studies in History and Philosophy of Science*, 19, 175–214.

———— (1990) "Gibsonian representations and connectionist symbol-processing: Prospects for unification," *Psychological Research*, 52, 243–252.

———— (1991a) "Representation and rule-instantiation in connectionist systems," in T. Horgan and J. Tienson (Eds), *Connectionism and the philosophy of mind* (pp. 90–112), Boston: Kluwer.

———— (1991b) "Representation in perception and cognition: Connectionist affordances," in W. Ramsey, D. E. Rumelhart, and S. P. Stich (Eds), *Philosophy and connectionist theory* (pp. 163–195), Hillsdale, NJ: Erlbaum.

———— (2002) "Psychology, philosophy, and cognitive science: Reflections on the history and philosophy of experimental psychology," *Mind and Language*, 17, 207–232.

———— (2003) "Behaviourism and psychology," in *Cambridge history of philosophy, 1870–1945*, T. Baldwin (ed.), (pp. 640–648), Cambridge: Cambridge University Press.

———— (2007) "The *Passions of the Soul* and Descartes's machine psychology," *Studies in History and Philosophy of Science*, 38, 1–35.

———— (2015) "Natural geometry in Descartes and Kepler," *Res Philosophica*, 92, 117–148.

Hatfield, G., and Epstein, W. (1985) "The status of the minimum principle in the theoretical analysis of vision," *Psychological Bulletin*, 97, 155–186.

Haugeland, J. (1978) "The nature and plausibility of cognitivism," *Behaviorial and Brain Sciences*, 1, 215–226.

———— (1981) "Semantic engines: An introduction to mind design," in J. Haugeland (ed.), *Mind design* (pp. 1–34). Cambridge, MA: MIT Press.

Kelso, J. A. S. (1995) *Dynamic patterns: The self-organization of brain and behavior*, Cambridge, MA: MIT Press.

Kosslyn, S. M., and Hatfield, G. (1984) "Representation without symbol systems," *Social Research*, 51, 1019–1045.

Lindsay, P. H., and Norman, D. A. (1972) *Human information processing: An introduction to psychology*, New York: Academic Press.

Marr, D. (1982) *Vision: Computational investigation into the human representation and processing of visual information*, San Francisco: Freeman.

Massaro, D. W. (1989) *Experimental psychology: An information processing approach*, San Diego: Harcourt Brace Jovanovich.

Mithen, S. (1996) *The prehistory of the mind: A search for the origin of art, science and religion*, London: Thames & Hudson.

———— (2013) "The cathedral model for the evolution of human cognition," in G. Hatfield and H. Pittman (Eds), *Evolution of mind, brain, and culture* (pp. 217–233,. Philadelphia, PA: University of Pennsylvania Museum of Anthropology and Archaeology.

Neander, K. (2017) *A mark of the mental: In defense of informational teleosemantics*, Cambridge, MA: MIT Press.

Neisser, U. (1967) *Cognitive psychology*, New York: Appleton-Century-Crofts.

———— (1976) *Cognition and reality: Principles and implications of cognitive psychology*, San Francisco: Freeman.

Newell, A., Shaw, J. C., and Simon, H. A. (1958) "Elements of a theory of human problem solving," *Psychological Review*, 65, 151–166.

Palmer, S. E. (1999) *Vision science: Photons to phenomenology*, Cambridge, MA: MIT Press.

Rock, I. (1975) *Introduction to perception*, New York: Macmillan.

—— (1983) *The logic of perception*, Cambridge, MA: MIT Press.

Rowlands, M. (1999) *The body in mind: Understanding cognitive processes*, Cambridge: Cambridge University Press.

Ryle, G. (1949) *The concept of mind*, London: Hutchinson.

Seyfarth, R. M., and Cheney, D. L. (2013) "The primate mind before tools, language, and culture," in G. Hatfield and H. Pittman (Eds), *Evolution of mind, brain, and culture* (pp. 105–121). Philadelphia, PA: University of Pennsylvania Museum of Anthropology and Archaeology.

Shapiro, L. (1993) "Content, kinds, and individualism in Marr's theory of vision," *Philosophical Review*, 102, 489–513.

—— (1994) "Behavior, ISO functionalism, and psychology," *Studies in History and Philosophy of Science*, 25, 191–209.

—— (2019) *Embodied cognition* (2nd ed.), London: Routledge.

Smith, L. B., and Thelen, E. (2003) "Development as a dynamic system," *Trends in Cognitive Sciences*, 7, 343–348.

Smolensky, P. (1988) "On the proper treatment of connectionism," *Behavioral and Brain Sciences*, 11, 1–74.

Spelke, E. S. (1988) "Where perceiving ends and thinking begins: The apprehension of objects in infancy," in A. Yonas (ed.), *Perceptual development in infancy* (pp. 197–234). Hillsdale: Erlbaum.

Stich, S. (1983) *From folk psychology to cognitive science: The case against belief*, Cambridge, MA: MIT Press.

Thompson, E. (2007) *Mind in life: Biology, phenomenology, and the sciences of mind*, Cambridge, MA: Harvard University Press.

Turvey, M. T., and Carello, C. (1981) "Cognition: The view from ecological realism," *Cognition*, 10, 313–321.

—— (1995) "Some dynamical themes in perception and action," in R. F. Port and T. Van Gelder (Eds), *Mind as motion: Explorations in the dynamics of cognition* (pp. 373–401), Cambridge, MA: MIT Press.

van Gelder, T. (1995) "What might cognition be, if not computation?" *Journal of Philosophy*, 92, 345–381.

van Gelder, T., and Port, R. F. (1995) "It's about time: An overview of the dynamical approach to cognition," in R. F. Port and T. Van Gelder (Eds), *Mind as motion: Explorations in the dynamics of cognition* (pp. 1–43), Cambridge, MA: MIT Press.

Warneken, F. (2013) "The origins of human cooperation from a developmental and comparative perspective," in G. Hatfield and H. Pittman (Eds), *Evolution of mind, brain, and culture* (pp. 149–168), Philadelphia, PA: University of Pennsylvania Museum of Anthropology and Archaeology.

Wheeler, M. (2005) *Reconstructing the cognitive world: The next step*, Cambridge, MA: MIT Press.

Wilson, R. (2004) *Boundaries of the Mind: The Individual in the Fragile Sciences –Cognition*, New York: Cambridge University Press.

42

REVOLUTION, REFORM OR BUSINESS AS USUAL?

The future prospects for embodied cognition

Michael Wheeler

A pre-revolutionary situation?

When all the data and arguments are in, will the recent flurry of work in embodied cognition deliver a revolutionary paradigm shift in the sciences and philosophy of mind? Or will it be a case of business as usual in the mind-targeting laboratories and armchairs around the globe? Or is the most likely outcome a reformist tweak in which embodied cognition research is recognized as making genuine and important methodological or orienting contributions to cognitive science, while leaving the most fundamental conceptual foundations of the field intact – as Rupert nicely puts it in his sobering set of conclusions regarding the revolutionary implications of embodied approaches in general, "more of a nudging than a coup" (Rupert, 2009, p. 242)?

Reaching a judgment on this issue is trickier than it may at first appear, since it is not simply a matter of working out whether or not some homogeneous and well-delineated new research program in cognitive science has succeeded, or will succeed, in substantively reforming, or even deposing, the orthodox view in the field. (For present purposes, the orthodox view may be located by its adherence to the principle that intelligent thought and action are standardly to be explained in terms of the building and manipulation of inner representational states by inner computational processes.) Indeed, if we consider the assortment of thinkers who congregate under the banner of embodied cognition, and we reflect on the range of theoretical approaches on offer, it turns out that they constitute a far from univocal crowd. Because of this, my goal in this chapter is not to pronounce on the future prospects for embodied cognition research *in general* – that would require at least one book – but rather to evaluate the prospects for a limited number of specific but prominent views that march under that banner. In each case I shall endeavor to get clear about the fundamental theoretical commitments of the view in relation to a specific diagnostic issue, namely what its advocates mean by the presumably foundational notion of being "embodied."

DOI: 10.4324/9781003322511-53

The implementational body

According to the hypothesis of *extended cognition* (ExC), there are actual (in this world) cases of intelligent thought and action in which the thinking and thoughts (more precisely, the material vehicles that realize the thinking and thoughts) are spatially distributed over brain, body, and world, in such a way that the external (beyond-the-skull-and-skin) factors concerned are rightly accorded cognitive status.[1] To bring ExC into proper view, it is useful to compare it with an adjacent position in intellectual space, namely the hypothesis of *embedded cognition*. According to this second and arguably less radical position, intelligent thought and action are regularly, and perhaps sometimes necessarily, causally dependent on the bodily exploitation of certain external props or scaffolds.[2] So, consider the example of a mathematical calculation achieved, in part, through the bodily manipulation of pen and paper. For both the embedded view and ExC, what we have here is a brain-body-pen-and-paper system involving a beyond-the-skin element that, perhaps among other things, helps to transform a difficult cognitive problem into a set of simpler ones (e.g., by acting as storage for intermediate calculations). For the embedded theorist, however, even if it is true that the overall mathematical problem could not have been solved, at least by some particular mathematician, without the use of pen and paper, nevertheless the external resource in play retains the status of a non-cognitive aid to some internally located thinking system. It certainly does not qualify as a proper part of the cognitive architecture itself. In other words, the thinking in evidence remains a resolutely inner, paradigmatically neural, phenomenon, although one that has been given a performance boost by its local technological ecology. By contrast, for the advocate of ExC, the coupled system of pen-and-paper resource, appropriate bodily manipulations and in-the-head processing *may* itself count as a cognitive architecture, even though it is a dynamically assembled (rather than hard-wired) and essentially temporary (rather than persisting) coalition of elements. In other words, each of the differently located components of this distributed (over brain, body and world) multifactor system enjoys cognitive status, where the term "cognitive status" should be understood as indicating whatever status it is that we ordinarily grant the brain in mainstream cognitive science. Another way to put this is to say that, according to the embedded view, the dependence of cognition on environmental factors is "merely" causal, whereas, according to ExC, that dependence is constitutive (Adams and Aizawa, 2008).

ExC naturally qualifies as a species of embodied cognition, because it takes non-neural bodily factors (e.g., manipulative movements of the body) to be parts of the realizing substrate of cognitive phenomena. Given our present remit, however, it is instructive to bring out the precise nature of the style of embodiment that is on offer. Here is an orienting thought. Surprisingly, perhaps, the possibility of extended cognition is a straightforward consequence of what still deserves to be labeled the house philosophy of mind in cognitive science, namely *functionalism*. The cognitive-scientific functionalist holds that what makes a state or process cognitive is not its material composition, but the functional role it plays in generating psychological phenomena, by intervening causally between systemic inputs, systemic outputs and other functionally identified, intrasystemic states and processes. Computational explanations, as pursued in, say, cognitive psychology and artificial intelligence (AI), are functionalist in this sense. Of course, historically, the assumption in cognitive science has been that the organized collection of states and processes that the functionalist takes to be the machinery of mind will be realized by the nervous system (or, in hypothetical cases of minded robots or aliens, whatever the counterpart of the nervous system inside the bodily boundaries of those cognitive agents turns out to be). In truth, however, there isn't anything in the letter of functionalism that mandates this internalism (Wheeler, 2010a, 2010b). After all, what functionalism demands is that we specify the causal relations that exist between some target element and a certain set of systemic inputs, systemic outputs and other functionally identified, intrasystemic elements. Nothing here demands internalism, since the boundaries of the functionally identified system of interest – i.e., the cognitive system – may in principle fall beyond boundaries of the organic sensorimotor interface.

Clark (2008a, 2008b, followed by Wheeler 2010a, 2010b, 2011a) uses the term *extended functionalism* to describe the combination of functionalism and ExC. This moniker is useful, as long as one remembers that the qualification "extended" attaches to the nature of cognition and not to the thesis of functionalism. Nothing about that venerable philosophical thesis has changed, since the claim that cognition might be extended merely unpacks one implication of the functionalist picture that had been there all along. As one might put it, ExC, if true, is simply a footnote to functionalism. If we look at things from the other direction, however, the alliance with functionalism gives the ExC theorist something she needs – assuming, that is, that she wants to hold onto the presumably attractive thought that the very same type-identified cognitive process may, on some occasions, take place wholly inside the head, while on others it may take place in an extended brain-body-environment system. To explain: even if some mathematical calculations are simply too difficult for me to complete entirely in my brain, there are others for which it seems plausible to say that, although on Monday I may carry them out using pen and paper, on Thursday I may call only on my organic resources. Now, if we are to describe these alternative problem-solving routines as two realizations of the very same mathematical cognition, it must be possible for the very same psychological reasoning process to enjoy (at least) two different material instantiations. In other words, the target cognitive phenomenon must be *multiply realizable*. And while functionalism may not be necessary for multiple realizability, it is standardly thought to be sufficient, since a function is something that enjoys a particular kind of independence from its implementing material substrate. Indeed, it seems plausible that anything worthy of being a function must, in principle, be multiply realizable.[3]

Functionalism makes extended cognition a conceptual possibility, but it doesn't make ExC true. What is needed, additionally, is an account of which functional contributions count as cognitive contributions and which don't. After all, as the critics of ExC have often observed, there undoubtedly will be functional differences between a distributed system and a purely inner system that allegedly realize the same cognitive process. For example, our brain-body-pen-and-paper mathematical system involves visual access to, and the bodily manipulation of, the material symbols on the page. *At some level of functional description*, there will be aspects of these processes that have no counterparts in the purely inner case (e.g., the functions involved in controlling visual gaze). So we will need to know which, if any, of the functional differences in evidence are relevant to determining the cognitive (or otherwise) status of the external elements. In other words, we need to provide a *mark of the cognitive* (Adams and Aizawa, 2008), a scientifically informed account of what it is to be a proper part of a cognitive system that, so as not to beg any questions, is independent of where any candidate element happens to be spatially located (Wheeler, 2010a, 2010b, 2011a, 2011b). The idea is that once a mark of the cognitive is specified, further philosophical and empirical legwork will be required to find out where cognition (so conceived) falls – in the brain, in the non-neural body, in the environment, or, as ExC predicts will sometimes be the case, in a system that extends across all of these aspects of the world.

To see how this might work, let's consider a candidate for a functionalist-friendly mark of the cognitive (Wheeler, 2011a). Newell and Simon famously claimed that a suitably organized "physical symbol system has the necessary and sufficient means for general intelligent action" (Newell and Simon, 1976, p. 116). A physical symbol system (henceforth PSS) is (roughly) a classical computational system instantiated in the physical world, where a classical computational system is (roughly) a system in which atomic symbols are combined and manipulated by structure-sensitive processes in accordance with a language-like combinatorial syntax and semantics. Although Newell and Simon adopted what we might call an unrestricted form of the claim that cognition (which I am taking to be equivalent to "the necessary and sufficient means for general intelligent action") is a matter of classical symbol manipulation, one might reasonably restrict the claim to a narrower range of phenomena, perhaps most obviously to "high-end" achievements such as linguistic behavior, natural deduction and mathematical reasoning. And although classical cognitive scientists in general thought of the symbol systems in question here as being realized inside the head, there is nothing in the basic concept of a PSS that rules out the possibility of extended material implementations (cf. the traditional move of bolting internalism onto functionalism). What this line of reasoning gives us, then, is the claim that "being a suitably organized PSS" is one mark of the cognitive.

So what? Bechtel (1996) defends the view that cognitive achievements such as mathematical reasoning, natural-language processing and natural deduction are (at least sometimes) the result of sensorimotor-mediated interactions between internal connectionist networks and external symbol systems, where the latter (but not the former) feature various forms of combinatorial syntax and semantics. So in these cases the combinatorial structure that, if our mark of the cognitive is correct, is indicative of cognition, resides not in our internal processing engine, but rather in public systems of external representations (e.g., written or spoken language, mathematical notations). The capacity of connectionist networks to recognize and generalize from patterns in bodies of training data (e.g., large numbers of correct derivations in sentential arguments), plus the temporal constraints that characterize real embodied engagements with stretches of external symbol structures (e.g., different parts of the input will be available to the network at different times, due to the restrictions imposed by temporal processing windows) are then harnessed to allow those networks to be appropriately sensitive to the constraints of an external compositional syntax. One might be tempted to conclude from this that a Bechtel-style network-plus-symbol-system architecture is an extended PSS. Of course, more would need to be said before we should give in wholeheartedly to this temptation (Wheeler, 2011a). However, let's assume that any concerns can be addressed. If the further thought that I have flirted with is correct, and being a suitably organized PSS is a mark of the cognitive, then, by virtue of being an extended PSS, the Bechtel architecture is also an extended cognitive system.

There are, then, reasons to think that extended functionalism may deliver ExC. And if extended functionalism is a form of embodied cognition, then the future prospects for embodied cognition are correspondingly rosy. But however revolutionary a result extended functionalism may mandate in relation to where cognition is to be found, the fact is that that outcome neither signals a fundamental change in our understanding of the relationship between cognition and material embodiment, nor (relatedly, as we shall see in a moment) forces us in the direction of a radically new theoretical language in which to carry out cognitive science.

On the first point, consider that, for the functionalist, *and thus for the extended functionalist*, the physical body is relevant "only" as an explanation of how cognitive states and processes are implemented in the material world. Indeed, since multiple realizability, as established by functionalism, requires that a single type of cognitive state or process may enjoy a range of different material instantiations, there is no conceptual room for the specific material embodiment of a particular instantiation to be an essential feature of mind. (Although it may be true that some functions can, as a matter of empirical fact, be implemented only in certain kinds of extant material system, that would be no more than a practical constraint.) So, despite the fact that, along one dimension (see above), extended functionalism is a fully paid-up member of the embodied cognition fraternity, there is another, arguably more fundamental, dimension along which the view emerges as having a peculiarly disembodied character. (Here one is reminded of Searle's observation that functionalism, although standardly depicted as a materialist theory of mind, is fully consistent with substance dualism [Searle, 1980].) This leads us to our second point. In observing that functionalism is the house philosophy of mind in orthodox cognitive science, one thereby highlights the close theoretical connection that obtains between functionalism and representational-computational models of mind. Indeed, the traditional account of the relation between a computational virtual machine and the range of physical machines in which that virtual machine may be instantiated is a particular version of the implementation relation that characterizes functionalist multiple realizability, while the notion of a computational system, via research in AI and computational cognitive psychology, provides a concrete and scientifically productive technological realization of the functionalist schema. It is unsurprising, then, that extended functionalism is routinely pursued in a computational register. Indeed, arguably the most common proposal for an extended cognitive system involves external representational elements that are taken to be constitutive components of the cognitive architecture in question precisely because of the way in which they are poised to contribute to the (distributed) implementation of an information-processing solution to some cognitive problem. Here one might mention the canonical example of the linguistic inscriptions in Otto's notebook that allegedly realize the content of his extended dispositional beliefs (Clark and Chalmers, 1998), but the case above of an extended PSS is an example of the very same signature.

If all this is right, then although extended functionalism, through its rejection of neurocentric internalism, may in some ways advance the embodied cause, it nonetheless leaves the conventional explanatory language of cognitive science fully intact. By analogy with Russian history, this is 1905, not 1917.

The vital body

Alan Turing once remarked that, "[i]n the nervous system chemical phenomena are at least as important as electrical" (Turing, 1950, p. 46). This is a striking comment, especially when one recognizes that, even in the connectionist regions of cognitive science, where the abstract physical organization of the brain, depicted as a distributed network of simple processing units, inspires the abstract structure of the cognitive architecture on offer, neural processes are treated as essentially a matter of electrical signals transmitted along wires. Connectionist networks are, of course, standardly interpreted as computational (and thus as representational) systems, even though they often need to be analyzed in terms of cognitive functions specified at a finer level of grain than those performed by classical computational systems (e.g., using mathematical relations between units that do not respect the boundaries of linguistic or conceptual thought). In the present context, the importance of this interpretation of connectionism is captured by Clark's (1989) philosophical gloss on the field as advocating a "microfunctionalist" account of cognition. As we have seen, functionalism demands an implementational notion of embodiment, a fact that surely remains unaffected by the "micro" nature of the functional grain appropriate to connectionist theorizing. Tying these thoughts together, one might speculate that the conceptualization of the brain as an electrical signaling system – a conceptualization that depends, in part, on abstracting away from the chemical dynamics of the brain – plausibly contributes positively to whatever cogency the computationalist-microfunctionalist picture has. So what happens when the chemical dynamics of brains are brought into view? Does this herald the arrival of a radical notion of embodiment, and thus of embodied cognition, one that brings revolution to the door?

To focus on a concrete example, consider reaction-diffusion (RD) systems. These are distributed chemical mechanisms involving constituents that are (a) transformed into each other by local chemical reactions and (b) spread out in space by diffusion. RD systems plausibly explain the kind of behavior in some unicellular organisms (e.g., slime molds) that researchers in the field of artificial life describe as minimally cognitive, behavior such as distinguishing between different relevant environmental factors, adapting to environmental change and organizing collective behavior. Many of the molecular pathways present in unicellular organisms have been conserved by evolution to play important roles in animal brains, so an understanding of the ways in which RD systems may generate minimally cognitive behavior will plausibly help us to explain the mechanisms underlying higher-level natural cognition. Against this background, Dale and Husbands (2010) show that a simulated RD system (conceived as a one-dimensional ring of cells within which the concentration of two coupled chemicals changes according to differential equations governing within-cell reactions and between-cell diffusion) is capable of intervening between sensory input (from whiskers) and motor output (wheeled locomotion) to enable a situated robot to achieve the following minimally cognitive behaviors: (i) tracking a falling circle (thus demonstrating orientation); (ii) fixating on a circle as opposed to a diamond (thus demonstrating discrimination); and (iii) switching from circle fixation behavior to circle avoidance behavior on the presentation of a particular stimulus (thus demonstrating memory).

To see why this result might be thought to have insurrectionary implications, let's introduce Collins's notion of *embrained knowledge*. According to Collins, knowledge is embrained just when "cognitive abilities have to do with the physical setup of the brain," where the term "physical setup" signals not merely the "way neurons are interconnected," but also factors to do with "the brain as a piece of chemistry or a collection of solid shapes" (Collins, 2000, p. 182). When deployed to generate minimally cognitive behavior, RD systems, characterized as they are by the exploitation of spatio-temporal chemical dynamics, plausibly instantiate such embrained knowledge. But what does this tell us? At first sight it might seem that embrained knowledge must fail to reward any functionalist (or microfunctionalist) gloss. Indeed, given the critical role played by low-level spatio-temporal dynamics in the chemistry of the brain, the notion seems to import a radical understanding of the relation between cognition and physical embodiment, one that Clark (2008a) calls *total implementation sensitivity* and that Wheeler (2010b, 2011a, 2013) calls *vital materiality*. According to this understanding, bodily factors make a special, non-substitutable contribution to cognition, meaning that the multiple realizability of the cognitive, and thus functionalism, must fail.[4]

The preceding line of thought is tempting, but ultimately undermotivated. Indeed, we need to take care not to allow the phrase "have to do with the physical setup of the brain" in Collins's specification of embrained knowledge to run away with us. Multiple realizability does not entail that cognition has *nothing* to do with the physical set-up of the brain. How a function is implemented in a physical system may have all kinds of interesting implications for cognitive science, especially (but not only) in areas such as speed, timing and breakdown profile. For example, let's consider some function that is specified in terms of multiple effects. It may be crucial to understanding the precise temporal structure of those effects that we understand them to be achieved via a form of volume signaling in the brain, in which tiny neuromodulators travel not via neural wiring, but freely diffuse through the brain in clouds, pretty much regardless of the surrounding cellular and membrane structures. (For further information on such chemical signaling, see, e.g., Husbands, Smith, Jakobi, and O'Shea, 1998) All this is consistent with the multiple realizability of the cognitive function in question, even if, in certain circumstances, a different implementation would result in explanatorily significant differences in the temporal structure of thought or behavior. But if "having to do with the physical setup of the brain" does not undermine multiple realizability, then it doesn't necessarily establish the more radical relation between cognition and embodiment that was attracting our revolution-hunting attention.

The sense-making body

Perhaps the seeds of revolution are to be found in a different view of embodiment, one that hails ultimately from contemporary European phenomenology (especially Merleau-Ponty, 1945/1962), but which has had an important influence in some regions of embodied cognition research (e.g., Gallagher, 2005). From this alternative perspective, the body is conceived as the pre-reflective medium by which the world is opened up in lived experience as a domain of value and significance. Crucially, advocates of this style of embodiment (e.g., Dreyfus, 1996) standardly hold that its role in our sense-making practices cannot be understood in representational terms. Given the plausibility of the general thought that representation is necessary for computation, if the sense-making body cannot be understood in representational terms, then neither can it be understood in computational terms. So an embodied cognitive science built on this notion of embodiment would be a revolutionary threat to the received explanatory framework. But how does the challenge to representation get off the ground? Exhibit one in this debate is the so-called *problem of relevance*.

Arguably one of the most remarkable capacities that human beings possess is our fluid and flexible sensitivity to what is, and what is not, contextually relevant in some situation, a capacity which is typically operative, even in the sort of dynamically shifting and open-ended scenarios in which we often find ourselves. Cognitive science ought to explain this capacity, and to do so in a wholly scientific manner (i.e., without appeal to some magical, naturalistically undischarged relevance detector). This is the problem of relevance, also known (in AI) as the frame problem (see, e.g., Shanahan, 2009).

If one approaches the problem of relevance from the perspective of orthodox cognitive science, and thus of any view such as extended functionalism that buys into the same fundamental principles, the difficulty manifests itself as the dual problem of how to retrieve just those behavior-guiding internal representations that are contextually appropriate, and how to update those representations in contextually appropriate ways. But how is the computational agent able to locate the relevant, and only the relevant, representations? The natural representationalist thought is that context itself should be modeled. In other words, the agent should deploy context-specifying representations to determine which of her other stored representations are currently relevant. What is wrong with this strategy? According to Dreyfus (1990, with more than a nod to Heidegger), the root problem is this: any attempt to determine the relevance of representational structures using other representational structures is an invitation to an infinite regress, since those latter representational structures will need to have their own contextual relevance specified by further representations. But these new representations will need to have their contextual relevance specified by yet further representations, and so on.

Dreyfus's conclusion is that the problem of relevance is an artifact of representationalism (Dreyfus, 2008, p. 358). So whatever neutralizes that problem must be non-representational in character. One way to unpack this idea is through Merleau-Ponty's (1945/1962) notion of the *intentional arc*, according to which skills are not represented, but are realized as contextually situated solicitations by one's environment (Dreyfus, 2008, p. 340). To borrow an example from Gallagher (2008), when poised to engage in the action of climbing a mountain, the skilled climber does not build a cognitive representation of the mountain and infer from that plus additionally represented knowledge of her own abilities that it is climbable by her. Rather, from a certain distance, in particular visual conditions, the mountain "simply" looks climbable to her. Her climbing know-how is "sedimented" in how the mountain looks to her. The mountain solicits climbing from her.

Rietveld (2012) puts some flesh on this skeleton, by drawing a distinction between different kinds of *affordance* (Gibson's term for the possibilities for action presented by the environment; Gibson, 1979). It is here that the connection with our more radical species of embodiment is finally exposed. Given a specific situation, some affordances are mere possibilities for action, where "mere" signals the fact that although the agent *could* respond to them, such a response would be contextually inappropriate. For example, the table at which I am working affords "dancing on top of," but that possibility is not a feature of my current paper-writing context, so right now I am not primed to respond to it. Some affordances, however, precisely because they are either directly contextually relevant to the task at hand, or have proved to be relevant in similar situations in the past, prime us for action by being what Rietveld calls *bodily potentiating*. It is affordances of the latter sort that are identified by Rietveld as different kinds of Merleau-Pontian solicitation. Figure solicitations are those with which we are actively concerned. For example, in my current paper-writing context, my keyboard summons typing from me. Ground solicitations are those with which we are not currently concerned, but for which we are currently bodily potentiated, and which are thus poised to summon us to act. For example, the teacup on my table that is peripheral with respect to my current focus of activity is nevertheless a feature of my paper-writing context and so is poised to summon me to act in appropriate ways. Human relevance-sensitivity is thus explained by shifting affordance landscapes, by varying patterns of active and body-potentiating solicitations.

Conceived on the Rietveld model, affordances depend constitutively, at least in part, on the kinds of bodies that we have, bodies that can dance, type, grip and lift. So if Dreyfus is right that the skills that explain relevance-sensitivity are realized by our non-representational ability to respond to contextually situated solicitations, and if that non-representational capacity is essentially embodied in the way suggested by Rietveld's affordance-based analysis, then the notion of embodiment that will explain a central feature of cognition is one that will fuel the fires of revolution in cognitive science.

So far so good, but if the present conception of embodiment is to have any traction in cognitive science, its advocates will need to say rather more about the naturalistically acceptable processes that causally explain solicitation and summoning. The most developed story here hails from Dreyfus (2008), who suggests that the solution lies with something like Freeman's neurodynamical framework (Freeman, 2000). According to Freeman, the brain is a non-representational dynamical system primed by past experience to actively pick up and enrich significance, a system whose constantly shifting attractor landscape causally explains how newly encountered significances may interact with existing patterns of inner organization to create new global structures for interpreting and responding to stimuli. Now, it may well be plausible that a Freeman-esque capacity for bottom-up, large-scale, adaptive reconfiguration, avoiding debilitating context-specifying representations, will be part of a naturalistic solution to the problem of relevance. But the fact remains that the all-important holistic reconfigurations of the attractor landscape that are at the heart of things here need to be explained in a way that doesn't smuggle in a magic relevance detector. In relation to this demand, Dreyfus appeals to shifts in attention that are correlated with the pivotal reconfigurations (Dreyfus, 2008, p. 360), but this doesn't seem to do enough work (Wheeler, 2010c). For if the attentional shift is the *cause* of a reconfiguration, then the relevance-sensitivity itself remains unexplained, since shifts in attention are at least sometimes presumably governed by, and so presuppose, sensitivity to what is relevant. But if the attentional shift is an *effect* of the reconfiguration, then we are still owed an explanation of how it is that the relevant attractor is the one that is selected. In sum, the account of relevance-sensitivity on offer from the perspective of Merleau-Pontian, sense-making embodiment may well be revolutionary (non-representational, non-computational) in its implications, but it is dangerously incomplete, because it fails to deliver a compelling causal explanation of the phenomenon at issue. Indeed, the shortfall here is serious enough that one might wonder whether it constitutes a genuine advance over the representationalist alternative.

Breaking the tie

At first sight, the result of our deliberations is an honorable draw between the reformist embodiment of extended functionalism and the revolutionary embodiment of the sense-making view. After all, neither has a cast-iron solution to the problem of relevance. At this point, however, what ought to kick in is a perfectly healthy methodological principle regarding theory change in science, namely that we should give our support to the competitor theory that requires the less extensive revision of our established explanatory principles, unless we have good reason not to; and that means that, on the strength of the evidence and arguments considered here, the deciding vote goes to extended functionalism, which rejects internalism, while maintaining a conception of the body as an implementational substrate for functionally specified cognitive states and processes that is comfortingly familiar from orthodox representational-computational cognitive science. The right conclusion, then, is that the most plausible of the embodied views that we have canvassed today is, in a theoretically important sense, the least embodied of them all.

Acknowledgments

Some passages in this chapter have been adapted with revision from Wheeler, 2011a, 2011c, 2013; Wheeler and Di Paolo, 2011.

Notes

1 The still-canonical presentation of ExC is by Clark and Chalmers (1998). Clark's own more recent treatment may be found in Clark, 2008b. For a field-defining collection that places the original Clark and Chalmers paper alongside a range of developments, criticisms and defenses of the notion of extended cognition, see Menary, 2010.

2 The case for embedded cognition has been made repeatedly. For just two of the available philosophical treatments, see Clark, 1997, and Wheeler, 2005.

3 In this chapter I assume that the notion of multiple realizability is clear and in good order, but I note that not everyone shares my confidence (see, e.g., Shapiro, 2000; Milcowski, 2013).

4 Here I explore only one way in which vital materiality might be motivated. For critical discussion of certain other routes to that position, see Wheeler, 2010b, 2011a, 2013.

References

Adams, F., and Aizawa, K. (2008). *The bounds of cognition*. Malden, MA: Blackwell.

Bechtel, W. (1996). What knowledge must be in the head in order to acquire language. In B. Velichkovsky and D. M. Rumbaugh (Eds), *Communicating meaning: The evolution and development of language*. Hillsdale, NJ: Lawrence Erlbaum Associates.

Clark, A. (1989). *Microcognition: Philosophy, cognitive science, and parallel distributed processing*. Cambridge, MA: MIT Press.

——— (1997). *Being there: Putting brain, body, and world together again*. Cambridge, MA: MIT Press.

——— (2008a). Pressing the flesh: A tension in the study of the embodied, embedded mind? *Philosophy and Phenomenological Research, 76(1)*, 37–59.

——— (2008b). *Supersizing the mind: Embodiment, action, and cognitive extension*. New York: Oxford University Press.

Clark, A., and Chalmers, D. (1998). The extended mind. *Analysis, 58(1)*, 7–19.

Collins, H. (2000). Four kinds of knowledge, two (or maybe three) kinds of embodiment, and the question of artificial intelligence. In M. Wrathall and J. Malpas (Eds), *Heidegger, coping and cognitive science: Essays in honor of Hubert L. Dreyfus* (Vol. 2, pp. 179–195). Cambridge, MA: MIT Press.

Dale, K., and Husbands, P. (2010). The evolution of reaction-diffusion controllers for minimally cognitive agents. *Artificial Life, 16(1)*, 1–19.

Dreyfus, H. L. (1990). *Being-in-the-world: A commentary on Heidegger's being and time, Division I*. Cambridge, MA: MIT Press.

——— (1996). The current relevance of Merleau-Ponty's phenomenology of embodiment. *Electronic Journal of Analytic Philosophy, 4(3)*. Retrieved from http://ejap.louisiana.edu/EJAP/1996.spring/dreyfus.1996.spring.html

——— (2008). Why Heideggerian AI failed and how fixing it would require making it more Heideggerian. In P. Husbands, O. Holland, and M. Wheeler (Eds), *The mechanical mind in history* (pp. 331–371). Cambridge, MA: MIT Press.

Freeman, W. (2000). *How brains make up their minds*. New York: Columbia University Press.

Gallagher, S. (2005). *How the body shapes the mind*. Oxford: Oxford University Press.

——— (2008). Are minimal representations still representations? *International Journal of Philosophical Studies, 16(3)*, 351–369.

Gibson, J. J. (1979). *The ecological approach to visual perception*. Boston: Houghton Mifflin.

Husbands, P., Smith, T., Jakobi, N., and O'Shea, M. (1998). Better living through chemistry: Evolving GasNets for robot control. *Connection Science, 10*, 185–210.

Menary, R. (Ed.) (2010). *The extended mind*. Cambridge, MA: MIT Press.

Merleau-Ponty, M. (1945/1962). *Phenomenology of perception*, London: Routledge.

Milcowski, M. (2013). *Explaining the computational mind*. Cambridge, MA: MIT Press.

Newell, A., and Simon, H. A. (1976). Computer science as empirical inquiry: Symbols and search. *Communications of the Association for Computing Machinery, 19*(3), 113–126.

Rietveld, E. (2012). Context-switching and responsiveness to real relevance. In J. Kiverstein and M. Wheeler (Eds), *Heidegger and cognitive science* (pp. 105–134). Basingstoke: Palgrave Macmillan.

Rupert, R. (2009). *Cognitive systems and the extended mind*. Oxford: Oxford University Press.

Searle, J. R. (1980). Minds, brains, and programs. *Behavioral and Brain Sciences, 3*(3), 417–457.

Shanahan, M. (2009). The frame problem. In E. N. Zalta (Ed.), *The Stanford Encyclopedia of Philosophy* (Winter 2009 ed.). Retrieved 25 October 2013, from http://plato.stanford.edu/archives/win2009/entries/frame-problem/

Shapiro, L. A. (2000). Multiple realizations. *Journal of Philosophy, 97*(12), 635–654.

Turing, A. M. (1950). Computing machinery and intelligence. *Mind, 59*, 433–460. Repr. in M. A. Boden (Ed.), *The philosophy of artificial intelligence* (pp. 40–66). Oxford: Oxford University Press, 1990. (Page references to the repr. ed.)

Wheeler, M. (2005). *Reconstructing the cognitive world: The next step*. Cambridge, MA: MIT Press.

———— (2010a). In defense of extended functionalism. In R. Menary (Ed.), *The extended mind* (pp. 245–270). Cambridge, MA: MIT Press.

———— (2010b). Minds, things, and materiality. In L. Malafouris and C. Renfrew (Eds), *The cognitive life of things: Recasting the boundaries of the mind* (pp. 29–37). Cambridge: McDonald Archaeological Institute.

———— (2010c). Plastic machines: Behavioural diversity and the Turing test. *Kybernetes, 39*(3), 466–480.

———— (2011a). Embodied cognition and the extended mind. In J. Garvey (Ed.), *The Continuum companion to philosophy of mind* (pp. 220–238). London: Continuum.

———— (2011b). In search of clarity about parity. *Philosophical Studies, 152*(3), 417–425.

———— (2011c). Thinking beyond the brain: Educating and building from the standpoint of extended cognition. *Computational Culture, 1*. Retrieved from http://computationalculture.net/article/beyond-the-brain

———— (2013). What matters: Real bodies and virtual worlds. In I. Harvey, A. Cavoukian, G. Tomko, D. Borrett, H. Kwan, and D. Hatzinakos (Eds), *SmartData: Privacy meets evolutionary robotics* (pp. 69–80). Berlin: Springer.

Wheeler, M., and Di Paolo, E. (2011). Existentialism and cognitive science. In F. Joseph, J. Reynolds, and A. Woodward (Eds), *Continuum companion to existentialism* (pp. 241–259). London: Continuum.

INDEX

Pages in *italics* refer to figures, pages in **bold** refer to tables, and pages followed by 'n' refer to notes.

1E: systems 37; *see also* first-order embodiment
1/f scaling 69–70; and fractal nature of social
    behavior 71; in human neural activity 70
1PP *see* first-person perspective
2E: systems 37; *see also* second-order
    embodiment
3E: systems 37; *see also* third-order embodiment
4e cognition 292; and GEL framework 264; and
    mathematical reasoning 262–264, 269

Abbott, E. A., *Flatland* 269
abductive inference 246
Abrahamson, D. 283, 284, 295
abstract concepts: of action 122; category of
    208; and representational gestures 236
abstract norms 367–368
abstract thoughts 185
abstract units 116
abstract–concrete distinction 207
abstraction 125, 488, 490, 491n6; computa-
    tional 318; primitive form of 444; in
    representation of action concepts 486
abstractness 204–208; evidence on concepts and
    words **205**
ACE *see* action–sentence compatibility effect
Acharya, U. R. 70
action concepts, processing of 486
action goal, and effectors 202
action language, body specificity of 182–183
action modes 29
action patterns 433; and conceptual knowledge
    435; overlearned 436
action planning 24

action possibilities 361, 362
action readiness 104
action simulation, in language comprehension
    192–193
action verb understanding 181, 182–183, 202
action–cognition transduction 262, 263, 266,
    271, 282
action–environment coupling 145
action-observation matching system 443–444
action–perception cycles 113, 116
action–perception processes 143, 145, 147; and
    XR technologies 153–154
action-readiness 14
action-relevant language, and motor activity
    193
action(s) 13; abstract 122; and boredom 20;
    brain's preparation for 120, 123; and
    conceptual knowledge 201; cued 281; and
    decision-making processes 324; definition
    443; directed 281–282; embodied 105, 106,
    108; and emotional states 187–188; experi-
    ences of 17; exploratory 162; and gesture(s)
    234–235, 242; goal-directed 246; imagined
    182; intelligent and non-intelligent 330n4;
    intentional 17, 18, 466; joint 71; and
    language 196; and memory 432–436;
    observed movement interpreted as 445; and
    past experience 120–121; and perception 27,
    103, 104, 105, 107, 169–170, 175, 235,
    236, 358, 419, 431, 500; perception as
    173–175; perception for 170–171; percep-
    tion with 171–173; phenomenological
    analysis of 16; in problem solving 233, 237;

in reasoning 233; reflective consciousness of 19; remembering how to perform 462; skillful 324, 504; valid 147; and visual attention 227; and visual perception 130–131; *see also* motor action

action–sentence compatibility effect (ACE) 192, 193, 202; replicability challenges 479–480

active externalism 58

active externalization 80–81

active sensing, in bats 77–79

activity: of brain 135; coordinated 358–359, 360; embodied 308–311, 324; everyday movement 326; exploratory 156, 159; joint 361, 363; mental 106; minded 90; peripheral physiological 124; situated 279; stream of 220; and temporal scale 254

actotopy 486

ad hoc categories 121, 124

Adams, G. 371, 505n7

adaptation 161

adaptivity 86; and autonomy 90–91

additive tasks 395

adjacency pairs 383; elicitation/response 391

affect: bodily 20; and body memory 467

affective motivation 181, 187, 189

affective processes 124

affective valence 183

affectivity 19–20; role in erotic perception 21n4

affordances 20, 23, 25, 79, 104, 516–517; of artifacts 81; in education 283, 284; environmental 293, 323, 324–325; flexible ways of acting on 326; modifying 80; notion of 14, 27, 172–173, 325; perception of 330n7; perceptual 270; virtual 329, 330

Aflalo, T. N. 486

agency 86, 340; attentional, visual 40–42, 43, 47; effective 361; individual and collective 362; intelligent 499; phenomenology of 17–18; shared 151; *see also* group agency

agent–environment coupling 78, 79, 81, 93

agent–object interactions 200

agent(s) 103; and use of language 364

aggregation 403

aggregativity 397

Aglioti, S. 170

AI *see* artificial intelligence

aikido 328

AIS *see* augmented intelligence systems

Aizawa, Ken 131, 505n7

Akins, Kathleen 137n7

algebraic operations 262

algorithms 498

Alibali, M. W. 234–235, 237–238, 240

alien hand syndrome 45

alignment, behavioral studies 363

allocentric stimulation 183

alternation 239

Amico, G. 436

amnesia 466, 467

amodalism 491n8

amplification, and dampening of information 402

amygdala activation 432

analogical mapping 246

analysis: auto-recurrence 69; conversation 383; cross-recurrence 67, 69, 70–71; dynamical 65–68; fractal 67–69; levels of 498; multi-modal 267–268; non-linear 65; recurrence 65–67, 66, 69, 70; time-series 65, 67, 68

anarchic hand syndrome 16

anger 120, 122–123, 124, 418, 420

animal cognition 501

anososognosia 45

ant colonies 402; Simon's parable of 78

anterior insula 18

anterior intraparietal area 443

anterior temporal lobes (ATL) 489

anticipation 326, 329, 360

anti-Semitism 411

Antle, A. N. 308, 309, 311

Anwesenheit 40

apprenticeship, learning by 466

approach motivation, and handedness 188

AR *see* augmented reality

archives, living 150, 152–153

Arieli, Amos 135

Aristotle 358

arithmetic 267

Arrow, K. J. 403

art and science case studies, XR-based 150–153

artifacts, affordances of 81

artificial devices 334; and tools 339–342

artificial intelligence (AI): bottom-up approaches to 37; embodied 318; and human multi-modal activity monitoring 268; models 496; and replacement theories 283

artificial limbs 335, 338, 342n3; sensory dimension of 336–337

Aschersleben, G. 175

asomatognosia 45

assembly bonus effect 397, 398

assessment methods 271

association 246

associationism 30

associative learning mechanisms 185, 189, 465

associative network models 421

athletes 322, 325, 326; practices of 330; use of attention 326–327

ATL *see* anterior temporal lobes

attention 26, 221, 228, 466; biased competition account of 454, 455–456; cascaded models of 454–456; conscious and intentional

aspects of 16; early control of 227–229; education of 23, 30; embodiment of 458; and feature weighting 174; filter models of 452–453; and gesture(s) 234; interactive models of 453–454; introspective 39; joint 310; patterns of 359, 362–363; selective 436; self-directed 40; shifts in 517; stage-based models of 452–453; top-down 46; as used by athletes 326–327
attentional agency 40–42, 43, 47
attentional shift 517
attunement 172, 325; to changing conditions 19; double 329; patterns of 359, 360; and sensorimotor account 162–163, 166
auditory cortex 488
auditory input 454
auditory motion, perception of 195
auditory processing, in bat brain 78
auditory stimulation 161–162
augmentation technologies 334–343
augmented intelligence systems (AIS) 268–269
augmented reality (AR), and mathematical reasoning 265
autobiographical memory 432, 434; embodied 463–465; retrieval 435
autonomous systems 313
autonomy 3, 48, 92, 163; and adaptivity 90–91; concept of 86, 94; and coordinated interaction 330–331n10; enactive notion of 85, 90; modeling 91–92; and operational closure 89–90, 94n3; and precariousness 89–90, 91; and sense-making 90–91, 92
autopoiesis 86
auto-recurrence analysis 69
avatars 147, 328, 329; in game studies 306; *see also* embodied virtual avatars (EVAs)
Aviezer, H. 423
avoidance motivation, and handedness 188

Baars, Bernard 495, 496
bacterial chemotaxis 91–92
bad habits 361, 362
Baddeley, A. D. 115, 463
Baillargeon, Renée 351–352
Baker, J. 324
balance 107; moral 411; and moral judgment 413; sense of 46
Balance Number Line 265
Balcetis, E. 479
Ballard, Dana 137n1, 173, 221, 456
Banks, B. 207–208
Barandiaran, X. 166, 358
Baron-Cohen, S. 219
Barsalou, L. W. 43, 191, 207, 305–306, 433
Bartlett, F. 462, 465, 496
bats, and echolocation 77–79

Bayesian learning 28
Bayesian predictive coding models, of neural processing 136
beat gestures 234
Bechtel, W. 499, 512
Beer, R. D. 221
behavior: biological 252; clever 501; coordinated collective 401–402; goal-directed 247; intelligent 247, 314, 317, 495, 499, 504; and metabolism 92; moral 407; online 306, 311; patterns of 358–359, 362–363; predicting 347, 350, 353; problem-solving 256; ritual 467; sensorimotor account of 369–378; synchronous 378; of virtual creatures 314–315
behavioral studies 16
behaviorism 25, 496; and cognitivism 81, 114
Behnke, Elizabeth 467
Bekker, M. M. 311
belief, concept of 350, 352
Bergen, B. 204, 209, 211n7, 236
Bergson, Henri 462
Bertsch, C. 324
Bhalla, M. 479
bias(es) 415; judgment 186; memory 438; publication 476, 479, 480; *see also* attention: biased competition account of
Bicknell, Kath 469
bimodal neurons 488; in parietal cortex 375–376
Binkofski, F. 207
biofeedback 152
biological behavior, understanding 252
biological processes, autopoietic 359
bio-robotics 37; evolutionary 38
birds, flocking 402
Blade Runner 319
blinking 158–159
blood-oxygen-level-dependent (BOLD) signal 444
Bloom, Paul 351, 409
bodily affect 20
bodily chauvinism 104
bodily control 337
bodily coordination 360
bodily effectors 341
bodily experience 19; in dreams 41–42; and moral judgment 408, 409–415; role in constructing mind 183
bodily extension 329
bodily influence, on morality 407
bodily information, influence on social judgment 479
bodily interfaces 147; in human–computer interaction 145
bodily movement, and sensory stimulation 161

bodily perception illusions 149
bodily potentiating 516
bodily processes 326; and autobiographical memory 464; effects on cognition 16
bodily relativity 181–189
bodily representations 102–103
bodily sensations, interoceptive 464
bodily states 135; and emotion concepts 419; and moral judgment 478; as peripheral physiological activity 124
bodily structures 323
body: as autonomous 85–91; and cognition 112; critical phenomenology of 14–15; enactive approach 94; implementational 510–513; and language 182; and morality 406–415; as pre-reflective medium 515; sense-making 515–517; spatiality of 14; template of what counts as 338; vital 513–515
body awareness, prereflective 19
body identification: passive 46; phenomenology of 40
body integrity identity disorder 45
body islands 44
body memory 462; and affect 467; habitual 466; and interoception 467
body model(s) 38–40; conscious 47; integrated 44, 48; unconscious 43
body ownership, sense of 17–18, 340
body position: and emotion content 435; and retrieval process 434
body schema 14–15, 20n1, 375; in deafferentation 337; definition 335; integration of external device into 339; joint 376–378; multiplicity of 340–342; notion of 38, 341; unconscious 44
body size 173
body units 171
body-as-object 13
body-as-subject 13, 14
body-based learning 293, 297
body-based metaphors, in education 280
body–environment coupling 323
body-for-others 14
body-specificity hypothesis 181–189
body/spirit duality 406
body–world interaction 181
BOLD signal *see* blood-oxygen-level-dependent signal
Boncoddo, R. 239
boredom, and action 20
Borghi, A. M. 201, 202, 206–207
Borreggine, K. L. 192, 480
Botox 420
boxers 325
brain: 1/f scaling in 69–70; activity 135; artificially tuned 165; interaction-dominant dynamics in 72; as non-representational dynamical system 517; as prediction machine 102, 114; predictive functional architecture of 123–124; preparation for action 120, 123; role of 136
brain connectivity 70
brain function, predictive processing account of 120–121
brain networks 123–124
brain–body–world interactions 103
Brett, N. 466
Brigard, Felipe de 469
Broadbent, D. E. 496
Brooks, R. A. 318
Brookshire, Geoffrey 188
Brown, Steven D. 469
Bruineberg, J. 103, 104
Bruner, J. S. 496
Bub, D. N. 192
Buhrmann, T. 166
bundles of habits 358
Byrne, David, *How Music Works* 147

CA *see* conversation analysis
Cabri Geometry 269
Calzavarini, F. 488
Caramazza, A. 196
card sorting tasks 252; rule induction in 252–256
Cardinali, L. 339
Carello, C. 30, 500, 501
Carmona, Carla 469
Carney, D. R. 477
Cartesian psychology 503
Cartesian theater 132
Casasanto, D. 434
cascades 252; *see also* attention: cascaded models of; interaction(s): cascaded
Casey, Edward 462, 466
categories 121–122, 124
causal relevance, and constitutive relevance 314–315
causation, reciprocal 105
Cavagna, A. 64
CELEs *see* collaborative embodied learning environments
Chaffin, Roger 468
Chalmers, David 54–55, 57, 58, 59–60, 331n13, 340, 518n1
Chan, Lau T. T. 209
Chapman strategy 24
Chella, Antonio 469
Chemero, A. 61n13, 70
child attachment theory 371
child development 349–350; outdated timeline 351–353

child-rearing practices, systematic differences in 371

children: interest, learning, and sensorimotor behavior 228; word acquisition by 219–220, 222–229

Christensen, Wayne 469

Chrysikou, Evangelia 185

Chu, M. 237–238, 240

Clark, Andy 54–55, 56, 57, 58, 59–60, 103, 104, 110, 111, 112, 113, 114, 137, 154, 165–166, 334, 339, 340, 341, 511, 514, 518n1

classical computational system 512

classical sandwich view 77, 78, 485

classical symbolist conception 504

cleanliness, and moral judgment 410–411, 478

clever behavior 501

Clore, G. L. 412

closure, topological property of 87–88

CMT *see* conceptual metaphor theory

co-attention, persistent 381–382, 388, 391

cognition: and body 112; commonalities and differences in notion of 501–502; concept of 156; definitions 305, 500; distributed 284–285; effects of bodily processes on 16; embedded 314; embodied 101, 221, 248–249, 292–293, 305–306, 313–320, 322–323, 328–329, 330; enactive account of 263; extended 54–60, 72–73, 284, 314; grounded 306, 431, 433; and intelligent behavior 499, 500; involvement of body and action 103; at multiple levels 381–382; off-line 261; online 261; and predictions 124; root notions of 495–501; rooted in perception and action 236; and sense-making 94; simulated 292; situated 78–79; social 124; study of 495; as symbol processing 497

cognitive, mark of 511–512

cognitive archaeology 462

cognitive equivalence 54–58, 60

cognitive gap, between preverbal and older children 353

cognitive interdependence 398–399

cognitive mechanisms, and information processing 496–497

cognitive neuroscience: embodied remembering in 469; predictive processing approach to 135

cognitive processing 323

cognitive psychology 291, 495, 496; and substantial resistance 56–58

cognitive research, on human augmentation 335

cognitive robotics 314

cognitive scaffolding 81, 113, 114

cognitive science 497; anti-Cartesian 502–503; embodied 78, 81; and role of environment 80–81

cognitive sociology 368

cognitive status, problem of 320n1

cognitivism, and behaviorism 81, 114

Cohen, D. 368

Cole, J. 337

Coles, N. A. 424, 478

collaborative embodied learning environments (CELEs) 284–285, 287

collaborative gestures 263

collaborative inhibition 398

collaborative interdependence 397

collaborative learning 386; computer-supported 383, 390

collective behavior 402; coordinated 401–402

collective group activity 395

collective induction 399–400

collective information sampling 399

collective intelligence 394

collectivistic cultures 368–369

Collins, H. 514, 515

Colombetti, Giovanna 469

color(s): and moral judgment 412; perception of 159–160; similarity 489

commitment problem 114

common coding approach *see* theory of event coding (TEC)

communication, social theory of 266

communities of resistance 363

compatibility 114; PP–EC 110–111, 113, 115–117

compensatory tasks 395

complementary problem solving 397

complementary tasks 396

complex dynamical systems 63–65; cognitive 69–73

complex social phenomena, and embodied remembering 469

complexity, interactive 329

computation 497; disembodied 26; without symbol systems 498–499

computational abstraction 318

computational explanations 510

computationalism, symbolic 497, 505n2

computationalism–representationalism (CR) 247–248, 256–257

computer games, embodied experience in 305–311

computer-supported collaborative learning (CSCL) 383, 390

conceivability, argument from 166

concepts 488; abstract 122, 208, 236; situatedness of 491n7; *see also* emotion concepts

conceptual knowledge, and action 201

conceptual metaphor theory (CMT) 280

conceptual processing 489, 490

conceptualization 76; hypotheses 280

concert halls of future 149, 152
concrete words 200–204; representation(s) 207–208; and specificity of simulations 203
concreteness fading 270–271
conditioning 465
confidence intervals 476
conjunctive neurons 433
conjunctive tasks 396
connectionism 463, 498, 513–514
connectivity, feedback 135
Connell, L. 194, 207–208
conscious experience 39
consciousness, visual 136
constitution 76, 281; hypotheses 281–282
constitutive relevance: and causal relevance 314–315; problem of 315–316
constructed emotion: and predictive processing 120–121; theory of 120
context, role of 124
context sensitivity 135
control: of attention 227–229; bodily 337; delusions of 16; experimental 148; global 47–48
convergence zones 432, 488
convergent thinking 324, 325, 330n5
conversation analysis (CA) 383
Cook, S. W. 235
cooperative interactions 396
coordinated activity 358–359, 360
coordinated collective behavior 401–402
coordinated social behavior 64
coordinating behavior 112
coordination: bodily 360; social 361, 363
coordination losses 396
coping, minded 21n3
co-presence 147
corporeal imaginings 326
Correll, J. 72
Cosmelli, D. 165
counterfactual reasoning 354
coupling 61n13, 360; action–environment 145; between agents and environments 78, 79, 81, 93; arguments for 58–60; body–environment 323; mind–body 476–479; sensorimotor–cognition 221
coupling–constitution fallacy 59, 60
CR *see* computationalism–representationalism
Craver, Carl 134
creativity 325
Creem-Regehr, S. H. 169
cross-modal integration 267–268
cross-recurrence analysis 67, 69, 70–71
Cruse, Holk 38
CSCL *see* computer-supported collaborative learning
cued action(s) 281

cultural differences, and prediction(s) 126
cultural heritage, preservation of 150
cultural practices, shared 359–360
cultural tools, mediational function of 279
culture: and distance estimation 372–375; dualistic conception of 367–369; as repertoire of bodily modes of interaction 378; sensorimotor account of 369–378
cyber-sport 328–329

Dahl, A. 369
dAI *see* disembodied AI
Dale, K. 514
Dale, R. 71
Damasio, A. R. 412, 415, 432–433
dampening, and amplification of information 402
dance 468
D'Andrade, R. 368
Daoust, Louise 505n8
darkness, and moral judgment 412
Darling-Hammond, Linda 294
Darwin, Charles 477
data, synthetic 313
data collection, and mathematical reasoning 265–266
Dawson, M. R. W. 497
de Beauvoir, Simone 15
De Jaegher, H. 92, 93, 327
de Melo, C. M. 313, 317
deafferented bodies 336–338
decision schemes 396, 398
decision-making processes 323, 330n4; and action 324; by groups 397–400; situated 324
declarative memory: and procedural memory 469; systematic causal theory of 464
default mode network (DMN) 123, 124, 125, 135
Delignières, D. 71
delusions of control 16
dementia 467, 468
Democritus 406
Dennett, Daniel 28, 55–56, 132, 134
depression, role of body in 437, 438
Descartes, René 462, 495, 502–503, 504, 505n11; animal spirits 503, 505n10; *Discourse on Method* 406–407; *Meditations* 505–506n12; *Sixth Meditation* 337
design: embodied 269; modern approaches to 81
Desimone, R. 453–454
DeSouza, J. F. 170
detectors 268
Deutscher, Max 464
developmental psychology 349–350, 369, 463

developmental timeline 351–353
Dewey, John 279, 358, 462
Di Paolo, E. A. 92, 93, 166, 327, 358
dialog 363–364
dialogic gestures 263
differentiation 30
digital tools 150
digitalization 150
Dijkstra, K. 434
dimensionality, understanding of 269
direct learning 31, 32
directed action(s): in education 281–282, *281*;
  vs. spontaneous gesturing 287
discretionary tasks 396
disembodied AI (dAI) 268–269
disembodied computation 26
disgust 414, 478; and moral judgment 410
disjunctive tasks 396
dissipative structures 249–251
distal events 174
distance estimation, and culture 372–375
distortion, brought about by glasses 161
distributed cognition 400–401; in education
  284–285
Ditton, T. 146
divergent thinking 324, 325
divisible tasks 395
Dixon, J. A. 69–70, 239
DMN *see* default mode network
dorsal processing 131, 170–171
Dotov, D. 70
double attunement 329
dreams and dreaming 41–42, 47; visual
  experience in 164–165
Dreyfus, Hubert 14, 19, 94n1, 466, 516, 517
Drozdzewski, Danielle 469
dual engagement 437
dual process theory 330n4
dualism 406–407; organism–environment (O–E)
  24
Dudschig, C. 195
Duncan, J. 453–454
Duncker, Karl 246, 457
Duncker's radiation problem 237
Dunning, D. 479
dyadic entrainment 152
dynamic depictive gestures 263, 266
dynamic geometry 388–389
dynamic interaction 172
dynamic multilevel framework 489
dynamical analysis 65–68
dynamical systems 63; complex 63–65; complex
  cognitive 69–73; models of mind 136;
  non-representational 517; and replacement
  theories 283; temporally extended 116; and
  vision 134

dynamical systems theory, and embodied
  remembering 469
dynamics, intentional 28–29

early word learning 219–220
EBA *see* extrastriate body area
Ebbinghaus illusion 170
EC *see* embodied cognition
echolocation 77–79
ecological approach 171–172, 175; to perception and action 23
ecological dynamics, in education 282–284
ecological information 330n8
ecological psychology 23–32
ecological validity: and experimental control
  148; simulated 148–149
EDS *see* electrical dissipative structure
education, embodiment in 279–288
educational neuroscience 294
effectors: and action goal 202; bodily 341
effector-specific activity 183, 486
efficacy and efficiency 113
efficient neural coding 116
Egbert, Matthew 92, 358
egocentric stimulation 183
Ehrsson, Henrik 46
Eiler, B. A. 71–72
electrical dissipative structure (EDS) 250–251,
  250
electromagnetism 115
elite sports dancing 327, 330–331n10
embedded cognition 78–79, 314, 510, 518n2;
  and mathematical reasoning 263–264
embedded learning 267
embedded vision 130–131
embodied abstraction theory 489
embodied activity 324; game play as 308–311
embodied approaches to visual experience,
  future directions for 136–137
embodied categories 124
embodied cognition (EC) 101, 221, 248–249,
  292–293; future prospects for 509–518; and
  mathematical reasoning 263; and predictive
  processing 103, 113–115, *115*, 117; strong
  322–323, 328–329, 330n2, 330n3, 330;
  theorizing of 305–306; and theory of mind
  347–355; and virtual reality 313–320; weak
  323
embodied cognition research: practical application potential 438–439; replication crisis in
  475–481
embodied design 269
embodied habits 466; enactivist account of
  357–360
embodied interventions, technology-based 270
embodied learning 279

embodied memory 503; as term 461
embodied metaphors, in education 280
embodied morality 408
embodied music cognition theory 145
embodied music interaction 148
embodied neuroscience, of vision 134–136
embodied predictions 122; and imagery 125
embodied predictive processing (EPP) 104–107; new directions in 115–117
embodied remembering: diversity of 461–463; habitual forms of 465; update 468–469
embodied responsive teaching 286–287
embodied semantics 116
embodied simulation 201; in education 281–282; theories 125
embodied thinking 323–326
embodied virtual avatars (EVAs) 149; and musicians 150–151
embodiment: constitution theories of 281; degrees of 79–80; in emotion perception 124–126; future directions in education 287; incomplete version of 196; intrinsic 250–251; notion of 342; sense-making 517; as term 335; and underdetermination 78–79; virtual 144, 145, 146–147, *146*, 148, 149, 154, 306, 320n4; and Web 306
embodiment theory, developments in 262–264
embodiment thesis 85, 94n2
embrained knowledge 514, 515
emergent behavior 63–64
emotion concepts 417, 424; and bodily states 419; body probes to 423–424, 435; dimensional approach 417–418; face probes to 421–423; prototype approach to 418; verbal probes to 420–421
emotional engagement, and moral choices 409
emotional valence 181; and left–right space 183–187
emotion/reason duality 406
emotion(s) 124; and action 187–188; body specificity of 183–187; constructed 120–121; embodied simulation of 419–420; hemispheric organization of 186; as mental event 122; and morality 407, 410; perception 124–126; predictive model of 120–124; role of bodily sensation in 423; semantics of 417–419; situated and distributed 469; *see also* emotion concepts
empathy, and synchronous behavior 378
enactive cognition, and mathematical reasoning 263
enactive ideas, application of 91–93
enactive vision 133–134, 156–166
enactivism 292; autopoietic 86; and embodied habits 357–360, 362–363; and sensorimotor account 156–157; as term 137n5

enculturation 357, 362
engagement, recurring modes of 359
entanglement, between perception, action, and language 204
entrainment, dyadic 152
environment: in cognitive science 80–81; engagement with 358; *see also* agent–environment coupling; organism–environment (O–E) mutuality
environmental affordances 293, 323, 324–325
Epicurus 406, 408
episodic memory 310, 432; retrieval 433
epistemology, materialist 261
EPP *see* embodied predictive processing
ergodicity 249
esports 330n1, 330; and strong embodied cognition 328–329
ethics 49n2
ethno-methodology 383, 391
Etzelmüller, G. 469
Euclid, *Elements* 389
Evans, J. S. B. 323
EVAs *see* embodied virtual avatars
event coding *see* theory of event coding (TEC)
Every Student Succeeds Act (2015) 294
everyday conversation, analyzing 383
everyday movement activities 326
evidentiary boundary 107, 108n4, 111
evolution 504
evolutionary biology 406
EVPS *see* externalism about the vehicles of perceptual states
ExC *see* extended cognition
exoskeletons 334, 340, 341
expanded vision 158–159
experience: conscious 39; homogeneity of 158; natural kinds of 310; *see also* bodily experience; perceptual experience; visual experience
experiential learning 293
experimental control, and ecological validity 148
expertise 19; in context of embodiment 435–436
exploitative representations 116
exploratory activity 156, 159, 162
extended cognition (ExC) 54–60, 72–73, 314, 500–501, 502, 510, 518n1; in education 284; and functionalism 511–512; and mathematical reasoning 263
extended functionalism 511, 512–513, 515, 517
extended mind 210, 340
extended reality (XR) 143–144; and action–perception processes 153–154; human embodied perspective 145–147; immersive 269; and mathematical reasoning 265;

and music 150–152; new spaces for music and science 147–150, *148*, 152–153, 154; technological perspective 144–145
extended vision 131–132
external context, impact of 124
externalism 58
externalism about the vehicles of perceptual states (EVPS) 131–132, 134
externalization 80–81
extra-neural resources 314
extrastriate body area (EBA) 486, 491n4
extrinsic events *see* distal events
eye movements 456; blinking 158–159; dream and real 41; involuntary 130; and perception–action loop 457–458
eye tracking devices 266
Eysenck, M. W. 497

face processing, emotional 124
facial expression(s) 419, 477, 478; processing of 422; in processing of emotion language 420; understanding 241
facial feedback hypothesis 477–478
fading 270–271
failure events 268
fairness, and physical metaphors 413
Fajen, B. R. 172, 173
false feedback 414
false-belief tasks 350, 351–352, 355
Fanon, Franz 14–15
Farrer, C. 18
Fath, A. J. 173
FBIs *see* full-body illusions
fear 122, 124, 418
feature weighting 174
feedback 78, 79; connectivity 135; facial 477–478; false 414; somatosensory 336–337
feelSpace belt 106
figure solicitations 516
filters, attentive and pre-attentive 452–453
first-order embodiment (1E) 37–38
first-person perspective (1PP) 46, 47, 145
Fisher, J. 55, 56
Fitness, J. 410
Flack, W. F. 423
FLE *see* foreign language effect
flocking 402
Flood, V. J. 263
Flores, F. 94n1
Fodor, J. A. 497, 505n2, 506n13
Foglia, L. 94n2
folk psychology 57
folk-psychological narratives 349, 353
foreign language effect (FLE) 209–210
foreign language learning, and directed actions 282

formalisms first 271, 294
Foroni, F. 420
fractal analysis 67–69
fractal patterns *68*
frame problem 515
framework, as term 115, 116
Francis, G. 479
Franklin, Benjamin 394
free energy principle 94n4, 103; and prediction error 108n3
Freeman, Walter 137n6, 517
Freud, Sigmund 462
Friston, K. 107
Frith, C. D. 18
Fröbel, Friedrich 279
Froese, Tom 61n13, 469
frontal lobes 432
frontoparietal control network 123
Fulkerson, M. 487
full-body illusions (FBIs) 37, 39; and minimal phenomenal selfhood (MPS) 45–48
functional connectivity, of brain at rest 124
functionalism 510–513, 514–515; in cognitive science 86
fundamental problem for visual theory 106

gait modifications, effect on affective memory bias 438
Gallagher, S. 93, 310, 337, 348, 516
Galton, Francis 395
game play: embodied experience in 305–311; and strong embodied cognition 328–329
game studies 306
Garrod, S. 196
gaze(s) 15
GCM *see* grounded cognition model
GEL framework *see* grounded and embodied learning framework
gender difference(s), in social dominance 424
gender salience, and social stereotypes 71–72
generation effect 56–57
generative model 103, 107, 116
GeoGebra 269
geo-spatial methods, and mathematical reasoning 267
German, Tim 351
Gershenson, C. 61n13
Gestalt: field theories 505n5; psychology 496
gestural replays 266
gesture as simulated action (GSA) framework 233, 234–235, 237
gesture(s) 233, 261, 419; beat 234; body-based metaphors in 280; collaborative 263; dialogic 263; as distinct from action(s) 234–235; dynamic depictive 263, 266; in education 286, 287; as form of action 242; and

information packaging 239; interactive 234; and listeners' reasoning 240–241; in mathematical proof 239; measuring production of 266; pointing 234, 236, 240, 242; in preparation for activity 326; and reasoning 235–242; representational 234, 236, 240, 242
Geuss, M. N. 171, 173
Ghazanfar, A. A. 488
ghost gestures 467
ghost literatures 477, 481n2
Gianelli, C. 209
Gibbs, R. 305
Gibson, E. J. 30–31
Gibson, James 14, 30–31, 79, 115, 136, 171–172, 173, 175, 309, 495, 516; importance of environment 499–501
Giese, Julia 469
Ginns, P. 237
Glenberg, A. M. 191, 201, 433, 479
global availability 40, 49n5
global brain 394
global control 47–48
goal-directed action 246, 247, 445–446
goals 358, 453–454, 455; shared 445–447
Godden, D. R. 463
Gold, J. 454–455
Goldman, S. R. 235
Goodale, M. A. 170
grammatical features 202, 204
Grant, E. R. 457
Graspable Math 269, 270
Grassé, P. P. 80
Grau, O. 144
Graziano, M. S. A. 486
Grèzes, J. 423
gross motor movements 331n12
ground solicitations 516
grounded and embodied learning (GEL) framework 261, 269–270; and 4e cognition *264*; applied to mathematical reasoning **261**
grounded cognition 306
grounded cognition model (GCM) 485–487, 488, 490
grounding 43, 262, 292; experiential 488
grounding problem 431
grounding relations, connecting 1E, 2E, and 3E 42–44
group agency 394, 403
group cognition 395–397; constitution of 391–392; contributing to 390–391; study of 382–383; varieties of 394–403
group facilitation 246
group mind 394
group productivity 395

groups 394; as complex adaptive systems 401–402; as decision-making units 397–400; as distributed cognitive systems 400–401
GSA framework *see* gesture as simulated action framework
Guilford, J. P. 324
gustatory areas, and semantic processing 487
gymnasts 107

habit(s) 358; bundles of 358; flexibility of 361; formation of 19, 359; and ideology 361–362; notion of 360; stability of 360–361; *see also* embodied habits
habitual body memory 466
Haidt, Jonathan 368, 408, 410–411
handedness *see* right- and left-handedness
hands 187–188; *see also* right- and left-handedness
haptic experiences, for learning 282
Harnad, S. 191, 431
Harrison, S. J. 71–72
Hatano, G. 238–239
Hatfield, G. 498, 502
Haugeland, John 497, 499
Havas, D. A. 420
Hayhoe, M. M. 456
He, Z. 351–352
Head, Henry 20n1, 341
head-mounted displays (HMDs) 147
heartbeat, self-perception of 414
heautoscopy 49n3
Hegel, G. W. F., *Phenomenology of Mind* 383
Heidegger, Martin 13, 14, 386, 391, 419, 516
Heilig, Morton 144
Helzer, E. G. 411
hemispheric specialization, motivation model of 188
Hempel, C. G. 111
heritage preservation 150
Hersh, M. A. 368, 408
Hidden in the Park game 306–308, *307*
hidden profile effect 399
hierarchical systems, multiscale nesting across 251–252
hippocampus 432
historico-racial schema 15
HMDs *see* head-mounted displays
hMT+ *see* human middle temporal cortex
Hohwy, Jakob 104, 107, 110, 111, 112, 114
Holler, J. 241
Hollingshead, A. B. 398–399
Holmes, G. 341
homeostatic property clusters 55
Hommel, B. 173–174
homogeneity, of experience 158
homunculus 486

Honnold, Alex 325–326
honor, bodily manifestations of 368
Hostetter, A. B. 234–235, 241
Huang, W. 268
Hubel, David 135
Huettig, F. 211
Hull, Clark 496
human augmentation 334–343
human becoming, enactive account of 93
human behavior: collective 402; ordered
    regularity of 65; problem-solving 256
human knowledge, understanding of 369
human middle temporal cortex (hMT+) 486
human mirror system 445
human musical coordination 152
human neural activity, 1/f scaling in 70
human relevance-sensitivity 516
human vision 130–131, 132
human–computer interaction, bodily interfaces
    145
hunger 21n5
Hurley, Susan 132, 134, 456, 485
Husbands, P. 514
Husserl, Edmund 13–14, 391
Hutchins, Edwin 81, 284, 400
Hutchison, J. J. 479
Hutto, Daniel 348, 349
Hutton, James 115
hybridity, in CELEs 285
Hydén, Lars-Christer 469

I can, concept of 14
Iani, Francesco 469
Ibanez, A. 192
Iberall, A. S. 27, 29
identification, and grounding 43
ideology 365; and habits 361–362
IFG *see* inferior frontal gyrus
Iida, F. 318, 319
illusions: visual 170; *see also* bodily perception
    illusions; full-body illusions (FBIs); rubber
    hand illusion (RHI)
imagery, and embodied predictions 125
imaginary environments, multisensory 149
imagination, and predictions 124
imitation 360
immanent purposiveness 89, 90
immersive displays 147; multisensory 144–145
implementational body 510–513
implicit memory 433
Imreh, Gabriela 468
inclusive learning sciences framework 298
incoming sensory signals 121, 122
incorporation 326–327, 329, 330, 335; true
    339, 341
individualistic societies 368–369

individuation, of bodies 85–86, 90
induction, collective 399–400
inertia 31
inference 172; abductive 246; notion of 106;
    perceptual v. active 104; probabilistic 116; as
    reconstructive process 112; sensorimotor
    104, 105, 107–108; unconscious 76–77
inferential processing, knowledge-driven 76–77
inferior frontal gyrus (IFG) 444
inferior parietal lobule (IPL) 444
information: concept of 31; ecological 330n8;
    packaging 239; and perception 26; as term 25
information processing 495; and cognitive
    mechanisms 496–497; and mathematical
    reasoning 262; models of learning 279–280;
    self-organized collective 402
information sampling, collective 399
information space 31
information-for-learning 31
Inga-Otto thought experiment 54–55, 56–57, 60
inhibition, collaborative 398
inhibition effects 246
instantiation, of processing rules 498
Institute of Psychoacoustics and Electronic
    Music (IPEM) 152–153
integration 101; multisensory 336
intellective tasks 395
intelligence: collective 394; loans of 28; notion
    of 501; varieties of 504
intelligent agency 499
intelligent behavior 38, 247, 314, 317, 495,
    504; and cognition 499, 500
intention, origins of 29
intentional action(s) 17, 466
intentional arc 516
intentional aspect, of SA 18
intentional content, assignment of 505n2
intentional dynamics 28–29
intentionality, affective 21n4
interaction dominance 64–65; in brain 72–73
interaction(s): body–world 181; cascaded
    456–457; cooperative 396; dynamic 172;
    with environment 103; human–computer
    145; mixed-motive 396; music 148; object–
    agent 200; organism–environment (O–E)
    165; parent–child 222–227, *223*; scientific
    study of 93; social 92–93, *221*
interactive gestures 234
interactive XR spaces 150
intercorporeity 21n2
interdependence: cognitive 398–399; collabora-
    tive 397
interest, as macro-level concept 227–228
interference effects 436, 437
interleaving 267–268
internal context 124

internal mentation 124
internalism 163–166, 511; rejection of 517
internet, and embodiment 306
internet of things (IoT), musical 149
interoception 120, 122; and body memory 467; and moral judgment 414
intersubjective existence 15
intersubjectivity 21n2; embodied 348–349, 350, 353–354; enactive account of 92
intrinsic embodiment, and non-equilibrium stability 250–251
intrinsic teleology 89, 90
introspection 433
introspective attention 39
inversion studies 161
inverted body map 486
involuntary movement 18
IPL *see* inferior parietal lobule
ipseity 17
Iriki, A. 375
Isenhower, R. 69–70
Izquierdo, Eduardo J. 469

Jacobs, D. M. 31
James, William 462
Johnson, M. 94n1, 236, 280, 310
joint action 71
joint activity 361, 363
joint body schema (JBS), development of 376–378, 376, 377
joint synchronization 151–152
Jonas, Hans 133
Jones, A. 410
judgment bias, body-specific 186
judgmental tasks 395

Kallen, R. W. 71–72
Kamermans, K. 235
Kant, Immanuel 90, 392
Kantian reasoning 409
Kaschak, M. P. 192, 193, 195, 201, 479, 480
Keane, M. T. 497
Keeley, B. 487
Keightley, Emily 469
Kelley, E. 239
Kemmerer, D. 485, 486–487, 490–491n2
kinesthesia 19; role in perception 13
Kirsh, David 60n1, 456, 468
Kismet 80
Kita, S. 237–238, 240
Kitayama, S. 368–369
Kiverstein, J. 103
Klevjer, R. 306
knowledge: conceptual 201; embrained 514, 515; of sensorimotor contingencies 162–163; stereotypical 209; *see also* human knowledge

knowledge expression, multimodal forms of 271
Köhler, W. 246
Kosslyn, S. M. 498
Køster, Allan 469
Krink, T. 315
Krueger, Joel 469
Kunz, B. R. 169

Ladyman, James 132
Lakoff, G. 94n1, 236, 280, 310
Land, Michael 137n1
language: and action 196; and the body 182; cultural and social features of 208–210; embodied approaches to 196–197, 200; in mindshaping 363–364; and predictions 124–125
language and situated simulation (LASS) theory 207
language comprehension: action simulation in 192–193; perceptual simulation in 194–196
language processing: emotional 420; grounded in action and perception 431–432
language-of-thought hypothesis 497
languaging, enactive account of 93
lateral occipitotemporal cortex (LOTC) 486
Laughlin, P. R. 395, 400
learner(s), as complete entity 297
learning 31; embedded 267; embodied 291–298; and memory 30; process of 370; view as brain-bound 293; *see also* education; grounded and embodied learning (GEL) framework
learning environments, collaborative, embodied 284–285, 287
learning styles 293
Lee, David 172
Lee, S. W. 411
left-handedness *see* right- and left-handedness
left–right space, and emotional valence 183–187
legal realism 414
Leonardo da Vinci, flying machine 338
liberal functionalism 57–58
light, and moral judgment 412
Liljenquist, K. A. 411, 412
Lindsay, P. H. 502
linguistic behavior 512
linguistic practices, customary 364
linguistic stimuli, and stereotypical knowledge 209
Linkenauger, S. A. 171
List, C. 403
listening, and gesture(s) 240–241
lived body 13, 14
living archive 150, 152–153
Lleras, A. 237, 457–458
loans of intelligence 28

locative literacies 267
Locke, John 462–463
Lombard, M. 146
Loomis, J. M. 479
lopsidedness 184
LOTC *see* lateral occipitotemporal cortex

MA *see* multimodal analysis
Macbeth effect 478
Machado, Antonio 156
Machery, E. 476
machine learning 268
MacKay, Donald 159
Maglio, P. 60n1, 456
Mahon, B. Z. 196
Maier's two-string problem 237
Maister, L. 422
Majid, A. 491n5
Malone, M. 71
mapping, analogical 246
Maradona, Diego 465
Maravita, A. 375
Marghetis, T. 236
Maringer, M. 422
Mark, L. S. 173
mark of the cognitive 511–512
Markus, H. R. 368–369, 371
Marr, David 26, 130, 498, 500
Martin, C. B. 464
Massaro, D. W. 502
Masson, M. E. J. 192
materialist epistemology 261
math walks 267
mathematical knowledge, collaborative
    construction of 265
mathematical proof, and gesture(s) 239
mathematical reasoning (MR) 260–262, 512;
    areas for future development 271–272; and
    embodiment theory developments 262–264,
    269–271; and GEL framework **261**; and
    perceptuomotor schemas 280; and research
    methods developments 266–269, 270–271; and
    technological developments 264–266, 268–270
mathematics 260; virtual teams 382–390
mathematics education 269; and directed
    actions 282
Mathematics Imagery Trainer for Proportion
    270, *283*
Mathôt, S. 480
Maturana, Humberto 86, 137n5, 292
maximization tasks 395
Maxwell, James Clerk 115
Mazzuca, C. 208
McClelland, J. 454
meaning-making, collaborative processes of
    363–364

media, as term 400
MediaPipe Holistic 265
Memmert, D. 324
memory 431; and action 432–436; autobio-
    graphical 432, 434, 435, 463–465; context
    dependence of 463; declarative 469;
    embodied and extended 503; episodic 310,
    432, 433; errors 436; future-oriented role of
    463; and learning 30; and predictions 124;
    procedural 465, 466, 469; processing 57;
    transactive 398–399; working 115; *see also*
    remembering
memory bias, affective 438
memory search 246
Menary, R. 55
mental activity 106
mental models theory 324
mental representations 431
Merleau-Ponty, Maurice 13, 14, 21n2, 21n3,
    21n4, 90, 133, 173, 358, 391, 419, 462, 516
metabolism, and behavior 92
metaphor(s): embodied 280; and morality
    407–408, 412, 413
metaverse 313; musical 149
Meteyard, L. 195
methodological solipsism 505n2, 506n13
Meyer, A. S. 211
Michaels, C. F. 30, 31, 32, 174–175
Michalak, J. 438
Michel, C. 114
micromovements 467
Miłkowski, M. 114
MIM *see* Musical Instruments Museum
mimicry 422; gestural 241
mind–body coupling, replicability challenges
    476–479
minded activity 90
mind-reading 219; development of 349, 352, 353
mind(s): in action 81; extended 210, 340;
    understanding other people's 124
mindshaping 360–363; enactivist account of
    364–365; via language 363–364
mineness, sense of 17
Mingon, Mcarthur 469
minimal phenomenal selfhood (MPS) 37; and
    full-body illusions (FBIs) 45–48
mirror neurons 423, 443, 444
mirror system 445
mirroring 360
mirror-touch synesthetes (MTS) 422
mixed-motive interactions 396
MMC-body model 38
MMLA *see* multimodal learning analytics
modal specificity, reappraisal of 487–488
mode of acquisition (MOA) construct 206,
    211n10

model(s) 91
modularity 72
molar perception 502
monkeys 443
Montero-Melis, G. 480
Montessori, Maria 279
mood regulation, and postural activity 437–438
Moog, Robert 143
moral choices, and emotional engagement 409
moral dumbfounding 408
moral judgment: and bodily experience 409–415; and emotion(s) 410; and sensory perception 410–414; and social intuitionism 408
moral reasoning: and the body 406; and social neuroscience 408–409
morality 406; and the body 406–415; and reason 407
Moreno, A. 94n3
Morey, R. D. 193, 211, 480
Moseley, R. 420
Mossio, M. 94n3
moths, and echolocation 77
motion capture 269
motivation 183; affective 181, 187, 189; and motor action 187–188
motivation losses 396
motivation model, of hemispheric specialization 188
motor action 102; and motivation 187–188; and verb meaning 182–183
motor activity, and action-relevant language 193
motor compatibility effects 193
motor control, body-schematic 16
motor control aspect, of SA 18
motor cortex 486
motor experience, and abstract thoughts 185
motor fluency 436; and interference effects 437
motor imagery 181; body specificity of 182–183
motor information, role in sentence comprehension 192
motor representations, replicability challenges 479–480
motor resonance 442; neurophysiological basis of 443–444; top-down modulation of 445–447
motor-informational weave 113
movement 433; everyday 326; involuntary 18; and memory tasks 434–435; observed 445; and sensory stimulation 161; *see also* eye movements; micromovements
movement-driven practices 330n1; and embodied cognition 322–331
MPS *see* minimal phenomenal selfhood
MR *see* mathematical reasoning

MRTs *see* multiple representation theories
MTS *see* mirror-touch synesthetes
Müller, Johannes 160
Müller-Lyer illusion 170
multimodal analysis (MA) 267–268
multimodal data, analytic methods for 265, 266
multimodal incongruencies 149
multimodal learning analytics (MMLA) 267, 268, 287
multimodal regions, high-level 488
multimodal revoicing 286
multimodal systems, in brain and body 125
multimodal word learning, case study 222–227
multimodality, methodological commitment to 266
multiple realizability 513, 515, 518n3
multiple representation theories (MRTs) 207–208
multiscale nesting 251–252
multisensory imaginary environments 149
multisensory integration 336
multisensory processing 487–488
murmurations 63–65
museums, of future 150
music 143, 468; concert halls of future 149, 152; and extended reality 150–152; new spaces *148*; research spaces of future 148–149; as shaped by space and environment 147
music cognition theory 145
music interaction 148
musical instruments 143
Musical Instruments Museum (MIM) 152–153
musicians, and EVAs 150–151
mutuality, organism–environment (O–E) 24–25

Najenson, Jonathan 469
narrative practice hypothesis (NPH) 349, 353
Narváez, Rafael F. 469
Nathan, M. J. 237, 260, 261, 264, 282, 295
nationalist discourse 411
natural deduction 512
nausea 414
near distances, studies of 171
Needham, A. 369
negative transfer effect 56, 57
Neisser, Ulric 500, 502; *Cognitive Psychology* 496–497
Nemirovsky, R. 284
neocortex 488
neural activity: and generation of perceptual experience 164–165; patterns of 191; in premotor area 183; in sensorimotor areas of brain 431
neural coding 116
neural context 124

neural overlap 125
neural processing, Bayesian predictive coding
    models 136
neural representations, amodal 485
neural resource allocation problem 338
neuroimaging 125
neuromechanisms 485
neuromyths 293
neuronal processing 323
neurons: bimodal 375–376, 488; conjunctive
    433; mirror 423, 443, 444; visual 135
neuropathy 337
neuroplasticity, process of 370
neuroscience 16, 17–18, 18; educational 294;
    embodied 134–136; social 408–409; and
    vision 136
New New Look 479
Newell, A. 496, 512
Newton, P. M. 293
NHP *see* narrative practice hypothesis
Nie, L. 70
Niedenthal, P. M. 421
Nietzsche, Friedrich 462
Noë, Alva 105, 106, 116, 131, 132, 156,
    157–158, 160, 161, 162, 173
non-binary gender language 364
non-derived content, and resistance 55–56
non-equilibrium sensitivity 251
non-equilibrium stability, and intrinsic embodi-
    ment 250–251
non-homogeneity, and homogeneity 158
non-linear analysis 65
non-linearity 65
non-linguistic theory of mind tasks 351–352,
    355
non-representationalist frameworks 504
nonverbal ways of knowing 271
Norman, D. A. 502
normativity 91
norms, self-generation of 89
Núñez, R. 236

OBEs *see* out-of-body experiences
object manipulation, directed forms of 282
object properties 201
object–agent interactions 200
objective body 13
object-seeing 159, 166
O'Brien, G. 164
Odin Teatret 153
O–E *see* organism–environment
off-line cognition 261
off-line processes, neglect of 353–355
offloading 262
Olmstead, A. J. 193
Onishi, Kristine 351

online behavior, of young people 306, 311
online cognition 261
online processes 353, 354
online risk 305, 306, 311
Oosterwijk, S. 423
operational closure 87–88, *88*; and autonomy
    89–90, 94n3
operational thought, mathematically valid 266
Opie, J. 164
optical arrays 172, 505n9
optimization tasks 395
O'Regan, Kevin 131, 156, 157–158, 160, 161,
    162, 173
organism–environment (O–E), interactions 165
organism–environment (O–E) dualism 24
organism–environment (O–E) mutuality 24–25
Ostarek, M. 195–196
other-agency 18
outfielder problem 24, 112
out-of-body experiences (OBEs) 39; asomatic
    47, 49n6
overdetermination, and habits 361–362
ownership, of body 17–18

Pacherie, E. 19
Paillard, Jacques 341, 342
Papesh, M. H. 193
paradigm, as term 115, 116
parent–child interaction, word learning through
    222–227, *223*
parietal cortex, bimodal neurons in 375–376
Parkinson's disease 192
parkour runners 326
partial adaptation 161
partial processing 455
participation 262
participatory sense-making 92–93, 323, 327
passive body identification 46
patterns: of attention 359, 362–363; of behavior
    358–359, 362–363; fractal 67, *68*; of neural
    activity 191; origins of 28; self-similar 67, *68*
PD *see* professional development
Pecher, D. 194, 211, 480
pedagogy 293; teaching and learning 294–295
Peeters, Anco 469
PEM *see* prediction error: minimization
penetrative thinking 238
pen-in-the-mouth phenomenon 478
perception 433; and action 27, 103, 104, 105,
    107, 169–170; for action 170–171; with
    action 171–173; as action 173–175; and
    action 175, 235, 236, 358, 419, 431, 500;
    vs. cognition 501–502; conscious and
    intentional aspects of 16; as detection of
    information 26; ecological theory of 79; of
    emotion 124–126; erotic 21n4; indirect

theories of 172; intentional structure of 14; philosophy of 136; role of kinesthesia in 13; as skillful activity 158; underdetermination in 76–77; visual 130–131; *see also* sensory perception

perception and vision, sensorimotor account of 166

perception–action cycles 112, 502; computer game as 309

perception–action dynamics 327

perception–action loop, and eye movements 457–458

perception–action system 29

perception-as-phenotype approach 171, 175

perceptual experience: and bodily interactions 165; and neural activity 164–165; qualitative character of 159–160, 166

perceptual simulation, in language comprehension 194–196

perceptuomotor integration 284

perceptuormotor schemas 280

performance, phenomenology of 18–19

peripheral deafferentation 337

Perner, Josef 350

Perrin, Denis 469

personal memory, bodily anchors for 464

personhood, enactive account of 93

Pesciarelli, F. 209

Pestalozzi, Johann Heinrich 279

Pettit, P. 403

Pfeifer, R. 318, 319

p-hacking 476

phantom limbs 45; study of 16

phase transitions 256

phenomenal self, as subject 47

phenomenal self-model (PSM) 37; bodily partition of 39

phenomenology 13, 20, 515; of agency 17–18; of body 14–15; of body identification 40; of performance 18–19; in science 15–17

philosophy: dualisms in 406–407; post-cognitive 386

philosophy of perception, orthodox view 136

physical presence 146–147

physical psychology 23, 27, 29

physical purity, and morality 411

physical symbol system (PSS) 512

Piaget, J. 279, 419

Pickering, M. J. 196

Pickering, Michael 469

Pier, E. 239, 266

Pinocchio effect 16

Pizarro, D. A. 411

planning 323, 324–325

plasticity, in human augmentation 338

PMv *see* ventral premotor cortex

pointing gestures 234, 236, 240, 242

Ponari, M. 421–422

Ponzo illusion 170

Pook, P. K. 456

portable devices, eye tracking 266

post-cognitive philosophy 386

postural activity 71, 323; and emotions 423–424, 435, 477; and mood regulation 437–438

Pouw, W. 241

poverty of stimulus 76

power pose 476–477

PP *see* predictive processing

practical cognition, research on 81

Practicing Odin Teatret Archive (POTA) 153

preadaptation 410

precariousness 163, 359; and autonomy 89–90, 91

precision signals 121

precision weighting 115–116, 117n5

prediction error 105, 121; and free energy 108n3; minimization 106–107; minimization (PEM) 110, 111, 112, 115, 116

prediction(s): affective 124; of behavior 347, 350, 353; as concepts 121–123; and cultural differences 126; development across lifespan 126; embodied 122, 125; in emotion perception 124–126; proprioceptive 102

predictive processing (PP) 101, 102, 110, 136; approach to cognitive neuroscience 135; as central to social cognitive processes 125; embodied 103, 104–107, 115–117; and embodied cognition 103, 113–115, 115, 117; and inference 106; and mathematical reasoning 264; and theory of constructed emotion 120–121

pre-experience 310, 311

prefrontal cortex 432

presence 149; concept of 146–147, 148, 154

preverbal infants 351–352; cognitive gap 353

primary intersubjectivity 348, 354

Prinz, J. 162

Prinz, W. 173–174, 175

probabilistic inference 116

problem of cognitive status 320n1

problem of constitutive relevance 315–316

problem of relevance 515–516, 517

problem of underdetermination 76

problem solving: collaborative 383, 386; complementary 397; embodied dynamics of 246–257; facilitated by actions 237

problem-solving behavior, human 256

procedural memory 465, 466; and declarative memory 469

process losses 396

productive laziness 113, 114

professional development (PD) 293
Proffitt, D. R. 171, 372, 479
propositional attitudes, acquisition by children 349
proprioception 19, 102, 323, 433
prostheses 335, 336, 337, 338, 340
Proust, Marcel 463
PSM *see* phenomenal self-model
PSS *see* physical symbol system
psychiatry 93
psychology 295; ecological 23–32; embodied remembering in 469; physical 27, 29
publication bias 476, 479, 480
Pulvermüller, F. 183, 480
purposiveness, immanent 89, 90

Quine, W. 134, 219

racism 361, 362
Radinsky, J. 235
Ramenzoni, V. C. 71
Ranehill, E. 477
Rao, R. P. 456
Ratnam, Charisma 469
reaction–diffusion (RD) systems 514
reading learning, and directed actions 282
reality, nature of 318
reality gap problem 317–319
reason, and morality 407
reasoning 233, 246; counterfactual 354; and gesture(s) 235–242; *see also* mathematical reasoning (MR); moral reasoning
Reavey, Paula 469
recall and recognition: explicit personal 462; neural architecture underlying 432–433
reciprocal causation, between brain, body, and world 105
recurrence analysis 65–67, 69, 70; categorical and continuous 66
recurrent behavior, complex patterns of 69–70
re-embodiment, in virtual environment 329
referential uncertainty, problem of 227
regularities, detecting 252
relational properties 201–202
relativity: bodily 181–189; linguistic 209
relevance, problem of 515–516, 517
relevance-sensitivity 516–517
reliability condition 59
religion, and morality 410–411
remembering, embodied 461–463, 465, 468–469
replacement 76; hypotheses 282–284
replication 475–476; and action–sentence compatibility effect 479–480; and mind–body coupling 476–479; and motor representations 479–480

replication crisis 210
representational gestures 234, 240, 242; and abstract ideas 236
representational structures 516
representationalism 161
representationality, as graded property 43
representation(s) 496, 504; abstract 270; amodal neural 485; bodily 102–103; and computation 247–248; conceptual 208; exploitative 116; higher-level 488; under linguistic meaning 192; in lower-level perception and action areas 486; mental 431; multiple types of 207–208; as necessary for computation 515; need for 502; objectivist view 133, 135; relevant 516; and self-consciousness 44; visual 136; without symbol systems 498–499
reproducibility crisis 210–211
research methods, developments in 266–268
research practices, questionable 476
research program, as term 115, 116
research-to-practice gap 291, 293–294, 295
resistance, communities of 363
restorative technology 335, 338
retrieval process 432, 462; and body position 434
Revonsuo, Antti 164
RHI *see* rubber hand illusion
Richardson, D. C. 71
Richardson, M. J. 71–72
Rietveld, E. 103, 516–517
right- and left-handedness 480; and action language 182–183; and emotional valence 183–187; and motivation 187–189
Riley, M. A. 172
RISE principles 264
risk, online 305, 306, 311
ritual behavior 467
Riva, Giuseppe 469
Roberts, T. 61n13
robotic limbs 334
robotics: cognitive 314; and embodied remembering 469; wearable 341
Rock, Irvin 498, 501, 502
rock climbing 325–326
Roediger, H. L. 294
Rommers, J. 196, 211
Rosch, E. 156
Rosenblueth, D. A. 61n13
Ross, Don 32
Rosso, M. 151
Rowlands, Mark 57–58, 60n2, 61n9, 469
rubber bodies 335–336
rubber hand illusion (RHI) 16, 17, 335–336, 342n4
Rubin, D. C. 432

Runeson, S. 27
Rupert, R. 56, 57, 509
Rychlowska, M. 422
Ryle, G. 466, 501

SA *see* sense of agency
sadness 418
salience network 123, 124
Sally–Anne task 350
Sánchez-García, R. 283, 284
Sartre, Jean-Paul 13, 14, 21n2
scaffolding 361, 468; cognitive 81, 113, 114
Schaefer, S. 436
Schilling, Malte 38
schizophrenia, loss of SA in 17
Schoenfeld, A. H. 263
Schroeder, C. E. 488
Schwarz, N. 411
science learning, and directed actions 282
science of design, and embodied cognitive
    science 81
Scorolli, C. 202, 204, 209
Scott, R. 351–352
Scribner, S. 81
scripts 362
SD *see* semantic dementia
Searle, J. 136, 513
secondary actions, in embodied memory tasks 437
secondary intersubjectivity 348, 354
second-order embodiment (2E) 37, 38–39
seeing as 386
Segundo-Ortin, Miguel 469
self: conception of 368–369; independent 378;
    interdependent 370, 378
self grounding problem 37
self-agency 18
self-awareness 19; bodily 45, 336
self-consciousness: bodily 40; and representation
    44
self-directed attention 40
self-generation, of norms 89
selfhood 39–40; bodily 45; and grounding 43
self-individuation 85–86, 163
self-movement, experiences of 17
self-organization 64
self-presence 147
self-relevant thought 124
self-similar patterns 67, *68*
Sell, A. J. 193
Sellars, Wilfrid 134
semantic dementia (SD) 489
semantic knowledge, representation of 489
semantic memory 486, 489; hierarchical nature
    of 490
semantic network model 431; of emotion
    418–419

semantic primitives, for emotions 418
semantic processing, and gustatory areas 487
semantics, embodied 116
Semin, G. R. 420
sense of agency (SA) 17–18
sense of ownership (SO) 17–18, 343n5; bodily
    340
sense-making 86, 358; as adaptive self-
    regulation 94; and autonomy 90–91, 92; and
    cognition 94; culturally embedded 327–328;
    enactivist concept of 133–134, 137; interac-
    tive 327; participatory 92–93, 323, 327
sense-making body 515–517
senses, individuating 487
sense–think–act cycle 77
sensorimotor activation, in action perception
    and prediction 444–445
sensorimotor approach 157, 173; to culture and
    behavior 369–378; enactive 166; supporting
    evidence for 160–162
sensorimotor behavior, and attention 227
sensorimotor contingency theory 157–160
sensorimotor contingencies 116, 131, 135–136,
    156, 161, 166; in visual behavior and
    attunement 162–163
sensorimotor embodiment 329
sensorimotor experiences, in human develop-
    ment 279
sensorimotor grounding 487
sensorimotor inference 104, 105, 107–108
sensorimotor regions, high-level 490
sensorimotor schemes 358–359
sensorimotor theory 145
sensorimotor tuning 370, 371–372; and joint
    body schema 375–378
sensorimotor–cognition couplings 221
sensors, wearable 266
sensory augmentation devices 106
sensory modalities 487
sensory perception, and moral judgment
    410–414
sensory qualities 159–160
sensory signals, incoming 121, 122
sensory simulations 122
sensory stimulation, and bodily movement 161
sensory substitution devices 161–162
sensory triggers 463
sentence comprehension, role of motor informa-
    tion in 192
sentence–picture paradigm 194
sexism 361
Shadlen, M. 454–455
Shapiro, L. A. 76, 115, 305, 323, 330n2, 505n2
shared agency 151
shared voxels 444
Shaw, J. C. 496

Shaw, R. 28
Shebani, Z. 480
Sheets-Johnstone, Maxine 461
Sherman, G. D. 412
Shockley, K. 70–71
Simmers, Kristin 293
Simon, H. A. 496, 512; *The Sciences of the Artificial* 81
simulated cognition 292
simulation theory (ST) 347–348
simulation(s) 261, 433; embodied 125, 281–282; sensory 122; specificity of 200–204, 203; *see also* action simulation; gesture as simulated action (GSA) framework; perceptual simulation
Singer, M. A. 235
situated activity, in learning 279
situated categories 124
situated cognition 78–79, 499, 500, 501, 502
situated decision-making 324
situated vision 130–131
size perception 170
skill memory, embodied 465–468
skillful action 324
skills 358, 504; vs. abilities 330n9; incorporation of 330, 326–327; and intentional arc 516
Skinner, B. F. 496
Slaby, J. 362
Slater, M. 147
Smart, P. R. 306
smart perceptual device(s) 27
smiles 422
SNARC effects *see* spatial-numerical association of response codes effects
SO *see* sense of ownership
social behavior: and 1/f scaling 71; coordinated 64; dynamics of 70–71
social cognition 124, 347–348, 350, 354; embodied 348–355
social combination models 396
social conditioning 362
social coordination 363
social cues, in word learning 219–220
social distortions 15
social groups, smaller-scale 363
social institutions 364–365; large-scale 362
social interaction 92–93; embodied *221*
social intuitionism, and moral judgment 408
social media 306
social neuroscience, and moral reasoning 408–409
social perspective, two forms of 209–210
social presence 147, 151
social robots 80
social stereotypes, and gender salience 71–72
social theory of communication 266

societal influences 362
sociocultural influences, internalization of 360
soft assembly 64
solicitations 516–517
somatic markers 409, 412, 414
somatoparaphrenia 16, 45
somatosensory feedback 336–337
somatotopy 486
Sommerville, J. A. 369
Soodak, H. 29
space–valence associations, body-specific 183–187
spatiality, of body 14
spatial-numerical association of response codes (SNARC) effects 208
spatio-temporal self-location 46
Spaulding, S. 323, 330n2
specific nerve energies, historical doctrine of 160
specificity 25
Speed, L. J. 195, 491n5
Spelke, Elizabeth 502
spiders, web-spinning 315–316, 316–317, 318
Spivey, M. J. 457
spontaneity 89; of living bodies 90
sport 322
sporting intelligence 328
sports psychology 323, 324; and replacement theories 283
Sprevak, M. 114, 115
S–R compatibility *see* stimulus–response compatibility
ST *see* simulation theory
stability, non-equilibrium 250–251
standardized tests 291
Stanfield, R. A. 194
Stanovich, K. E. 323
statistical significance 476
Stefanucci, J. K. 171, 173
Steiner, I. D. 395–396
Stephen, D. 69–70
Stepper, S. 424
Stevens, Catherine 468
Stich, S. 506n13
stigmergy 80
stimulation, auditory 161–162
stimuli: auditory 487–488; linguistic 209; and moral judgment 410; somatosensory 488
stimulus, poverty of 76
stimulus–response (S–R) compatibility 174–175
Strack, F. 424, 477, 478
Stratton, G. M. 161
Straus, Erwin 15
Strejcek, B. 411
strong embodiment 335, 342; and human augmentation 337–338, 339
structures: bodily 323; dissipative 249–251; representational 516

Sturmer, B. 175
substance dualism 513
substantial resistance: and cognitive psychology 56–58; and non-derived content 55–56
Suchman, L. A. 283
Sudnow, David 468
summoning 517
superior anterior temporal lobes 208
supervenience theory 43, 49n7
Surowiecki, J. 395
survival, evolutionary experience of 407
Sutherland, Ivan 144
Sutton, John 464, 467, 469
sweetness, and moral judgment 412–413
Swidler, A. 368
sword and shield hypothesis 188
symbol grounding problem 191–192
symbol processing 497
synapses 248–249
synchronization 360; joint 151–152
synchronous behavior, and empathy 378
synchrony, between gestures, speech, and mathematical inscription 266
synergy 64, 71, 397
synthetic data 313
system behavior 64–65, 66, 72
systems, autonomous 313

tactile qualities, experience of 159
Tanenhaus, M. K. 235
tangible learning design framework (TLDF) 308
tangible user interface (TUI) 308, 309
taste: and moral judgment 412–413; regions associated with 487
Taylor, Janelle 467–468
Taylor, L. J. 192
TCC *see* time to contact
teaching: embodied learning approach to 294–297; embodied responsive 286–287; *see also* education
TEC *see* theory of event coding
technology-based embodied interventions 270
TECs *see* transient extended cognitive systems
teleology, intrinsic 89, 90
teleosemantics 506n15
telepresence 147
temporal atomism 132
temporal scale, and activity 254
termites 80
Tetris thought experiment 60n1
Tewes, Christian 469
theory of event coding (TEC) 173–174, 175
theory of mind 219; and embodied cognition 347–355
theory theory (TT) 347–348
Theremin, Leon 143

thinking 381; penetrative 238; strongly embodied 323–326
thinking on the fly 322, 323, 326
third-order embodiment (3E) 37, 39–40, 48; global aspects of 45–46
Thomas, L. E. 237, 457–458
Thompson, Evan 133, 134, 137n5, 156, 165
Thorpe, S. 455
thought, operational 266
time, and space 193
time to contact (TCC) 172
time-series analysis 65, 68; fractal 67
TLDF *see* tangible learning design framework
TMS *see* transcranial magnetic stimulation
TMSs *see* transactive memory systems
Tolman, Edward C. 496
toolish illusion 343n5
tools, and artificial devices 339–342
top-down attention 46
top-down effects 116
total implementation sensitivity 514
TouchCounts 269, 270
trade-offs 113
Trakas, Marina 469
transactive memory systems (TMSs) 398–399
transcranial magnetic stimulation (TMS) 422, 444; repetitive 489
transduction 262, 263, 266
transfer, embodied theories of 271
transient extended cognitive systems (TECs) 113
translational science, model for embodied learning 296–298
transmodal regions: higher-level 490; importance of 488–490
transparency 340; phenomenal 39
triangulation 267
trouble spots 268
TT *see* theory theory
TUI *see* tangible user interface
Tumarkin, Maria 469
tuning 370
Turing, Alan 513
Turvey, Michael 27, 172, 500, 501
two-visual-systems hypothesis 131

Umwelt 79, 80
unconscious inference 76–77
underdetermination: and embodiment 78–79; in perception 76–77; problem of 76
unitary tasks 395
"up" metaphor 407
utilitarian reasoning 409

Vaisey, S. 368
Valins, S. 414
value, ideas of 407

Van Kerrebroeck, B. 151
Van Rullen, R. 455
Varela, Francisco 86, 89, 137n5, 156, 292
vection 435
Veenstra, L. 437–438
ventral premotor area F5 443
ventral premotor cortex (PMv) 444
ventral processing 131, 170–171
ventromedial prefrontal cortex (vmPFC) 409
verbalizations, during reasoning and problem-
    solving 235
VHF emotion studies 185–186, 187
Vigliocco, G. 195
virtual, virtues of 316–317
virtual affordances 330; perception of 329
virtual creatures 319–320, 320n4; study of
    314–315
virtual embodiment 144, 145, 146–147, 148,
    149, 154, 306, 320n4; overview of concept
    146
virtual environments 317, 328–329
virtual reality (VR): and embodied cognition
    313–320; and embodied remembering 469;
    and mathematical reasoning 265
virtual spaces 328
virtual teams, mathematics example 382–390
virtual worlds 314–316, 320; affordances of 329
vision: dynamical systems approach to 134;
    embedded and situated 130–131; embodied
    neuroscience of 134–136; enactive 133–134,
    156–166; extended 131–132; and neurosci-
    ence 136; as primary source of information
    337; theories of 116, 498, 499
visual attention: and eye movements 457; joint
    266; stabilized 225–226
visual attentional agency 40–42, 43, 47, 136–137
visual consciousness, nature of 136
visual experience 130–137
visual illusions 170
visual neurons 135
visual perspective, changes of 149
visual processing, human 76, 131
visual theory, fundamental problem for 106
visuo-spatial body image 337
vital body 513–515
vital materiality 514, 518n4
vmPFC *see* ventromedial prefrontal cortex
Vollrath, F. 315
von Sobbe, L. 193
von Uexküll, Jakob 79
voxels, shared 444
VR *see* virtual reality
Vygotsky, L. 279, 381, 419; *Mind in Society* 383

Wagenmakers, E. J. 477–478
Wakefield, E. M. 240, 241
Walkington, C. A. 239, 263, 266
Warren, W. H. 173
WAT *see* words: as tools
ways of speaking 363–364
WCST *see* Wisconsin Card Sort Test
weak embodiment 335, 339, 342, 488
weak ergodicity breaking 249
wearable robotics 341
wearable sensors 266
well-being, and moral conceptualizations 413
Whang, S. 173
Wheeler, K. 204
Wheeler, Michael 320n4, 495, 500–501,
    502–503, 504, 514
whole-body displacement 16
Wiesel, Torsten 135
Wilcox, G. 294
Wilkin, K. 241
Wilson, R. 505n9
Wilson, R. A. 94n2
Wilson-Mendenhall, C. D. 124
Wimmer, Heinz 350
Wimsatt, W. C. 397
Winograd, T. 94n1
Winter, B. 211n7
Wisconsin Card Sort Test (WCST) 252
wisdom of crowds 395
Wise, A. F. 308, 309
Witt, J. K. 171, 479
Wittgenstein, L. 386
woman as Other 15
Woods, A. J. 479
Woodward, A. L. 369
words 364; abstract **205**; acquisition 206–207;
    acquisition by children 219–220, 222–229;
    concrete 200–204; as surrogates for
    interactions 200; as tools (WAT) 207,
    208–209
working memory, model of 115
workplace settings 362

Xia, F. 266
XR *see* extended reality

Yarbus, Alfred 137n1
Young, Iris Marion 14, 15

Zhong, C. B. 411, 412
zombie literatures 477
zones of proximal development 279
Zwaan, R. A. 192, 194, 211, 480

Milton Keynes UK
Ingram Content Group UK Ltd.
UKHW020843141024
449569UK00009B/596

9 781032 345123